Lecture Notes in Computer Science 11232

More information about this series at http://www.springer.com/series/7408

Jing Sun · Meng Sun (Eds.)

Formal Methods and Software Engineering

20th International Conference on Formal Engineering Methods, ICFEM 2018 Gold Coast, QLD, Australia, November 12–16, 2018 Proceedings

Editors
Jing Sun
University of Auckland
Auckland, New Zealand

Meng Sun
Peking University
Beijing, China

ISSN 0302-9743 ISSN 1611-3349 (electronic)
Lecture Notes in Computer Science
ISBN 978-3-030-02449-9 ISBN 978-3-030-02450-5 (eBook)
https://doi.org/10.1007/978-3-030-02450-5

Library of Congress Control Number: 2018957483

LNCS Sublibrary: SL2 – Programming and Software Engineering

This Springer imprint is published by the registered company Springer Nature Switzerland AG
The registered company address is: Gewerbestrasse 11, 6330 Cham, Switzerland

Preface

This volume contains the papers presented at the 20th International Conference on Formal Engineering Methods (ICFEM 2018) held during November 12–16, 2018, in Gold Coast, Australia.

Since 1997, ICFEM has served as an international forum for researchers and practitioners who have been dedicated to developing practical formal methods for software engineering or applying existing formal techniques to improve software development process in practical systems. We are celebrating its 20-year series in 2018.

This year, we received 66 valid submissions from 25 different countries. Each paper went through a thorough review process by at least three members of the Program Committee. After extensive discussions, the committee decided to accept 22 regular papers, giving an acceptance rate of 33.3%. The proceedings also include three extended abstracts from the keynote speakers, 12 short papers from the doctoral symposium, and four invited abstracts from the special session.

ICFEM 2018 was organized and sponsored by the Institute for Integrated and Intelligent Systems (IIIS) at Griffith University, Australia. We owe our thanks to the Organizing Committee for their wonderful work in making ICFEM 2018 a successful event. We would like to thank our sponsor from the Destination Gold Coast for their generous donation. We are grateful to the Program Committee members and additional reviewers for their support and professionalism in completing high-quality reviews on time, and most importantly, to all the authors for their valuable contributions to the conference.

We would like to express our gratitude to the doctoral symposium co-chairs, Zhe Hou and Yamine Ait-Ameur, for their hard work in organizing the PhD symposium session. Finally, we would like to thank the EasyChair conference system, which indeed made the whole process much easier to manage.

August 2018

Jing Sun
Meng Sun

Organization

Program Committee

Bernhard K. Aichernig	TU Graz, Austria
Cyrille Valentin Artho	KTH Royal Institute of Technology, Sweden
Christian Attiogbe	University of Nantes, France
Christel Baier	TU Dresden, Germany
Richard Banach	The University of Manchester, UK
Luis Barbosa	University of Minho, Portugal
Michael Butler	University of Southampton, UK
Franck Cassez	Macquarie University, Australia
Ana Cavalcanti	University of York, UK
Zhenbang Chen	National University of Defense Technology, China
Sylvain Conchon	Université Paris-Sud, France
Frank De Boer	Centrum Wiskunde & Informatica (CWI), The Netherlands
Yuxin Deng	East China Normal University, China
Jin Song Dong	National University of Singapore, Singapore
Zhenhua Duan	Xidian University, China
Marc Frappier	Université de Sherbrooke, Canada
Stefania Gnesi	ISTI-CNR, Italy
Lindsay Groves	Victoria University of Wellington, New Zealand
Ichiro Hasuo	National Institute of Informatics, Japan
Xudong He	Florida International University, USA
Zhenjiang Hu	National Institute of Informatics
Jie-Hong Roland Jiang	National Taiwan University, Taiwan
Gerwin Klein	The University of New South Wales, Australia
Fabrice Kordon	LIP6/Sorbonne Université and CNRS, France
Michael Leuschel	University of Düsseldorf, Germany
Yuan-Fang Li	Monash University, Australia
Shaoying Liu	Hosei University, Japan
Shuang Liu	Tianjin University, China
Yang Liu	Nanyang Technological University, Singapore
Zhiming Liu	Southwest University
Brendan Mahony	Defence Science and Technology
Jim McCarthy	Defence Science and Technology
Stephan Merz	Inria Nancy, France
Mohammadreza Mousavi	University of Leicester, UK
Shin Nakajima	National Institute of Informatics, Japan
Jun Pang	University of Luxembourg, Luxembourg
Yu Pei	The Hong Kong Polytechnic University, China

Geguang Pu	East China Normal University, China
Shengchao Qin	Teesside University, UK
Silvio Ranise	FBK-Irst, Italy
Adrian Riesco	Universidad Complutense de Madrid, Spain
Graeme Smith	The University of Queensland, Australia
Harald Sondergaard	The University of Melbourne, Australia
Jing Sun	The University of Auckland, New Zealand
Jun Sun	Singapore University of Technology and Design, Singapore
Meng Sun	Peking University, China
Cong Tian	Xidian University, China
Jaco van de Pol	University of Twente, The Netherlands
Hai H. Wang	University of Aston, UK
Zijiang Yang	Western Michigan University, USA
Wang Yi	Uppsala University, Sweden
Jian Zhang	Chinese Academy of Sciences, China
Peter Ölveczky	University of Oslo, Norway

Additional Reviewers

Basile, Davide
Boulton, Graham
Bride, Hadrien
Carbone, Roberto
Colange, Maximilien
Craciun, Florin
Dalvandi, Mohammadsadegh
Dghaym, Dana
Fantechi, Alessandro
Foster, Simon
Gardy, Patrick
He, Mengda
Hou, Zhe
Hussain, Nazmul
Ishikawa, Fuyuki
Kafle, Bishoksan
Khoo, Teck Ping
Lai, Hong
Li, Jiaying
Li, Xin
Li, Yi
Liyun, Dai
Ma, Feifei
Miyazawa, Alvaro
Murray, Toby
Poppleton, Michael
Ribeiro, Pedro
Robert, Thomas
Schachte, Peter
Shi, Ling
Spagnolo, Giorgio Oronzo
Ting, Su
Tomasi, Alessandro
Tueno Fotso, Steve Jeffrey
Wang, Jingyi
Weikai, Miao
Wu, Peng
Xu, Zhiwu
Yan, Rongjie
Zhang, Min
Zhang, Xiyue

Abstracts from Keynotes and Invited Talks

Algebra, Logic, Geometry at the Foundation of Computer Science

Tony Hoare[1,2,3]

[1] Computing Laboratory, Cambridge University, UK
[2] Microsoft Research, Cambridge, UK
[3] Institute for Integrated and Intelligent Systems, Griffith University, Australia

I predict that one day a Unified Theory of Programming will be generally taught throughout a Degree Course in Computing. It will tell students a simple method for planning, developing and testing their practical exercises and assignments. The initial level of mathematical presentation of the Theory is that of High School lessons in Algebra, Logic and Geometry. The Theory will be put to immediate practical use by a Software Development Environment for students, providing guidance and immediate checking for the programs which they write.

I start with a review of Boolean Algebra, illustrated by familiar laws and theorems for disjunction. A deductive logic with implication and proof rules is derived from the algebra in the standard way. The algebra is extended by operators for sequential and concurrent composition. They share a unit, they are associative and distribute through disjunction. An Interchange axiom formalises a basic principle of concurrency, in that it shows how an arbitrarily concurrent program can be executed directly by interleaving on a single sequential computer, without the overhead of interpretation. Proof rules are derived for a modal logic of time and space. Its rules are definitionally equivalent to two historic logics due to Hoare and Milner, which are now used widely for mechanical reasoning about correctness of programs and of implementations of programming languages. These two rival theories have at last been unified.

The lecture ends with an account of the applications of algebra to programs, and a discussion of its limitations as the foundation of Computer Science.

Security Protocols: Model Checking Standards

David Basin

Department of Computer Science, ETH Zurich, Switzerland

The design of security protocols is typically approached more as an art than a science, and often with disastrous consequences. But this needs not be so! I have been working for about 20 years on foundations, methods, and tools, both for developing protocols that are correct by construction and for the post-hoc verification of existing designs. In this talk, I will introduce my work in this area and describe my experience analyzing, improving, and contributing to different industry standards, both existing and upcoming.

Scaling Up Formal Engineering

Brendan Mahony, Jim McCarthy, and Kylie Williams

Defence Science and Technology Group, Department of Defence, Australia
{brendan.mahony, jim.mccathy, kylie.williams}
@dst.defence.gov.au

Abstract. The desirability of formal verification of cyber critical systems has long been acknowledged, particularly in Defence evaluation standards such as TCSEC, ITSEC, Common Criteria, DefStan 00-55 and Def(AUST) 5679. However, the technology options available for formal verification have proved challenging to adopt and the will to break through the associated usability barriers has largely proved lacking for many reasons. Formal verification success stories largely addressed highly abstracted algorithms, such as abstract credential exchange protocols, or static analysis for program quality assurance. In consequence, little of the world's existing cyber infrastructure has been subjected to formal analysis and evaluation, so that little can be confidently said regarding technical correctness or suitability for service.

Recent successes in the formal verification of low level cyber system infrastructure (such as seL4) have demonstrated the feasibility of formal evaluation for medium scale systems. They have also shown that the level of effort and the quality of personnel required remains a challenge to all but the most committed agents.

In this paper we consider the prospect of formal analysis applied to very large scale systems so as to provide assured and appropriate cyber infrastructure in the era of ubiquitous computing and the internet of things.

Security Assurance for Cyber Systems

Australia's Cyber Security Strategy [1] notes the rising prevalence and cost of cybercrime activity.

> *Figures vary, but ... the real impact of cybercrime to Australia could be around* $17 *billion annually. These costs are expected to rise.*

The emerging cyber threat is also a major theme of the 2016 *Defence White Paper* [5].

> *Cyber attacks are a direct threat to the ADF's warfighting ability given its reliance on information networks.*

Perhaps a little surprisingly, the potential dangers of designing computers, information systems and infrastructure with cyber attack surfaces have been well recognised since before the advent of the internet age.

Beginning in the late 1960's, efforts throughout the world led to the release of evaluation criteria documents such as the US TCSEC [7], Europe's ITSEC [8],

Canada's CTCPEC and, finally, an international consolidation effort under the banner of the Common Criteria [4].

Apart from recognising the need to minimise the cyber attack surface of sensitive systems, all of these evaluation criteria also recognised the need for careful systems analysis efforts aimed at supporting a strength of assurance argument appropriate to the sensitivity of the application. The TCSEC observes [7, p. 67] that testing is of little use in the absence of a clear theoretical model of system behaviour.

> *no test procedure for something as complex as a computer can be truly exhaustive*

Instead, assurance arguments for complex system must be synthesised from the empirical properties of their smaller, therefore testable, components. At the highest level of sensitivity, these analysis efforts were to be based on machine checkable mathematical modelling or *formal methods*. Nevertheless, fielded products with formally verified security properties remain extremely rare.

The Situation in Formal Methods

It should be noted that the analysis activities prescribed by the various criteria are highly targeted and limited with a view to what was considered tractable, given the state of the art current at the time. Generally, the requirement is for a formal statement of a security policy and a high level design, together with a proof of conformance. This, of course, gives only modest assurance that specific components of a system have not been deliberately designed to provide an extensive cyber attack surface. In practice the roll out of Common Criteria based evaluation programmes lead to a focus on low assurance applications and a de-emphasis of analytic assurance in favour of empirical approaches such as penetration testing with hard to justify epistemological foundations.

At least in part, this under-utilisation of analytic techniques stemmed from the intractability of applying them across the application stack at medium to large scales of system complexity. The ideal of fully verified systems, "from silicon up", was a dream shared both by accreditation authorities and the research community that has remained tantalisingly out of reach.

Much of the scalability issue in formal modelling has stemmed from a lack of the required computational power. Over the last few years, both the computational power available to formal modelling efforts and the sophistication of tools making use of the power has reached a point that has emboldened a number of research groups to make a concerted attempt at applying formal techniques to the most critical parts of the application stack. The most prominent examples are probably the separate research efforts that have produced the seL4 system kernel [9] and the CompCert verified C compiler [2].

Of equal significance to this narrative has been a growing appreciation in Mathematics that many modern proofs are at an order of complexity that fundamentally challenges the traditional peer review approach. A growing community of mathematicians and computer scientists are devoting effort to realising significant bodies of mathematical knowledge in machine checkable formalisms [10]. This is, of course, fortunate for the formal assurance program, as fully addressing the correctness of cyber systems will require the formalisation of all of the mathematics underpinning the design and construction of their hardware as well as their function logic.

Scaling Formal Reasoning Tools

While there exist several dedicated verification tools, such as the B Tool and the Key tool [3], it is logical framework tools such as Isabelle/HOL [11] and Coq [6] that are most associated with the current uptick in formal verification effort and particularly with formal mathematical modelling.

In discussing the scaling features of these tools, we can distinguish between the scaling or modularity (outer) features afforded to theory development and (inner) features afforded to modelling efforts within the theories. Generally, the outer modularity features are based around the theory: a collection of named data types, functions and associated theorems comparable in power to module features available in familiar programming languages, effectively a record. Inner modularity features are generally based around function abstraction and associated type theoretic structures. For example, aside from function types and product types, Isabelle/HOL offers *type classes* which collect related functions through a shared type parameter and *locales* which collect related functions through a multi-parameter curried predicate. In neither case is the modular structure embodied in the associated type theory so that it can become a general purpose building block for large scale development. Equally importantly, the power of function abstraction and type theory cannot be brought to bear on the problem of structuring large scale theory development; the potential power of which is hinted at by the development of category theory and homotopy type theory.

In order to progress formal development efforts to significantly larger scales of model complexity, the authors believe that both the outer and inner modularity features of logical frameworks need to become significantly more flexible and importantly they need to be properly integrated. To this end, we propose that first class record types, record merging and record sub-typing be introduced to serve as the primary inner-level structuring tools. The feature naming aspect together with sub-typing make records a significantly more tractable approach to system composition than product spaces; precious few programming or logical (outer) languages restrict themselves to using only sequential numbers as identifiers. Properly integrated with higher order type theory, records will provide a highly flexible approach to constructing, decomposing and abstracting over large system models. In order that outer-level modelling activity should also benefit from and properly serve inner structuring, we also propose that theories be *reflected* into the inner language as record types and that record based structures be *evaluated* into the outer language as (complex) theories.

References

1. ACSC.: Australia's Cyber Security Strategy. Commonwealth of Australia (2016)
2. Appel, A.W., Beringer, L., Chlipala, A., Pierce, B.C., Zhong, S., Weirich, S., Zdancewic, S.: Position paper: the science of deep specification. Philos. Trans. R. Soc. Lond. A: Math. Phys. Eng. Sci. **375**(2104) (2017)

3. Beckert, B., Hähnle, R.: Reasoning and verification: state of the art and current trends. IEEE Intell. Syst. **29**(1), 20–29 (2014)
4. CCRA.: Common Criteria for Information Technology Security Evaluation Version 3.1. Number CCMB-2017-04-003. Common Criteria Recognition Arrangement, April 2017
5. Department of Defence.: 2016 Defence White Paper. Commonwealth of Australia (2016)
6. The Coq development team.: The coq proof assistant reference manual: Version 8.8.1, March 2018. https://coq.inria.fr/distrib/current/refman/
7. DOD.: Trusted Computer System Evaluation Criteria. Number 5200.28-STD. United States Government, Department of Defence (1985)
8. EEC.: Information Technology Security Evaluation Criteria (ITSEC). Office for Official Publications of the European Communities (1991)
9. Klein, G., Andronick, J., Keller, G., Matichuk, D., Murray, T.: Provably trustworthy systems. Philos. Trans. R. Soc. Lond. A: Math. Phys. Eng. Sci. **375**(2104) (2017)
10. Paulson, L.: Proof assistants: from symbolic logic to real mathematics? In: Avigad, J., Gonthier, G., Martin, U., Moore, J.S.: Paulson, L., Pitts, A., Shankar, N. (eds.) Big Proof Programme, June 2017
11. Wenzel, M.: The Isabelle/Isar reference manual, October 2017. https://isabelle.in.tum.de/documentation.html

Security Analysis in the Real World

Cristina Cifuentes

Oracle Labs, Brisbane, Australia

Over the past year we have seen an increase in security vulnerabilities in software used in a variety of domains, from classical enterprise software to mobile platforms. The impact of any exploit of such a vulnerability can be tremendous. The recent emergence of new technologies such as Blockchain, Cloud and Machine Learning/Artificial Intelligence, promises many digital advances that can help us all into the digital future, but, who is looking into the security of such systems?

In this talk I will give a brief overview of the Parfait static program analysis tool we developed at Oracle Labs that detects thousands of bugs and vulnerabilities in systems-level code and enterprise-level software. With the advent of the above mentioned technologies, I will talk to new challenges in analysing and verifying code developed for these technologies including analysis of programs written in languages such as JavaScript and Python. With the emergence of speculative execution side channel attacks in 2018, the analysis and verification communities need to develop hardware related abstractions. I will conclude by challenging the programming languages community to develop secure languages; languages that can assist developers write code that is guaranteed to be secure.

Contents

Invited Keynote Paper

Formal Models

Verification

Network Systems

Refinement and Transition Systems

Emerging Applications of Formal Methods

Doctoral Symposium

Invited Keynote Paper

Engineering a Theory of Concurrent Programming

Ian J. Hayes(✉)

The University of Queensland, Brisbane, QLD, Australia
Ian.Hayes@uq.edu.au

Abstract. Our original goal was to develop a refinement calculus for shared-memory concurrent programs to support Jones-style rely/guarantee developments. Our semantics was based on Aczel traces, which explicitly include environment steps as well as program steps, and were originally proposed as a basis for showing the rely/guarantee rules are sound. Where we have ended up is with a hierarchy of algebraic theories that provide a foundation for concurrent program refinement, which allows us to prove Jones-style rely/guarantee laws, as well as new laws. Our algebraic theory is based on a lattice of commands that includes a sub-lattice of test commands (similar to Kozen's Kleene Algebra with Tests) and a sub-algebra of atomic step commands (similar to Milner's SCCS) but with a structure that supports Aczel's program and environment steps as atomic step commands. The latter allows us to directly encode rely and guarantee commands to represent rely/guarantee specifications, and to encode fair execution of a command.

1 Introduction

Our recent research has been to develop a refinement calculus for concurrent programs based on the rely/guarantee approach of Jones [20–22]. The theory underlying the calculus is based on a set of algebras starting from a lattice of commands and building theories to support sequential composition, parallel composition, tests, atomicity, etc. [8,12–14,16]. The objective of this paper is to look back over the development of the main ideas that form the basis of the algebraic theories. Our choice of references relates to the work that influenced our approach and hence may not refer to the historically earliest originator of the idea.

2 Nondeterminism

2.1 Verification

The seminal works on program verification are those of Floyd [11] and Hoare [17]. Floyd's work examines paths in a control flow graph and uses assertions at the beginning and end of the paths, which act as preconditions and postconditions,

J. Sun and M. Sun (Eds.): ICFEM 2018, LNCS 11232, pp. 3–18, 2018.
https://doi.org/10.1007/978-3-030-02450-5_1

respectively. Provided each path satisfies its pre/post specification, the whole graph satisfies its pre/post specification. Loops in the graph are considered specially and such cyclic paths are required to decrease a well-founded loop variant to show termination.

Hoare's work has the advantage that it is applied to structured programming language constructs with a single entry point and a single exit point. Hoare triples of the form $\{p\}\ c\ \{q\}$ assert that if p holds initially then execution of c will establish the postcondition q provided c terminates. Hoare's original paper only considered partial correctness (hence the termination proviso in the previous sentence) but his approach has been extended to handle total correctness (termination) and we assume the total correctness version in our discussion below. Each kind of language construct (assignment, sequential composition, conditional, loop, etc.) has a rule for verifying it satisfies a Hoare triple, where the premises for structured statements include Hoare triples for their component statements.

There are two aspects of the work of Floyd and Hoare that distinguish their specifications from algorithmic programming language descriptions:

- their specifications are implicitly *nondeterministic* in that they allow any final state that satisfies a postcondition and there may be multiple such states, and
- preconditions explicitly record *assumptions* about the initial state.

Both these aspects are essential in a specification language.

2.2 Nondeterminism in Programming Languages

Dijkstra observed that while parallelism implicitly introduces nondeterminism into the behaviour of programs, it is also advantageous to allow the semantics of sequential programming constructs to be nondeterministic [9,10]. Dijkstra's guarded command language generalised conditional and iterative program control structures to allow multiple guarded branches and allowed a nondeterministic choice of which branch to execute if more than one branch had a true guard. Rather than provide a default behaviour of doing nothing if none of the guards of a conditional is true, Dijkstra defined its behaviour in this case to be the same as **abort**, the worse possible command that gives no guarantees about its behaviour at all. The intent being that the programmer must ensure the guards cover all states that satisfy the precondition of the conditional. There are three observations that can be made about his work:

- the design of his programming language focused on supporting reasoning about programs,
- he emphasised developing an algorithm along with its proof of correctness, and
- he gave a weakest precondition semantics for his language: $wp(c, q)$ is the weakest condition that on execution of c from a state in which $wp(c, q)$ holds, is guaranteed to terminate in a state satisfying q. Hence the Hoare triple $\{p\}c\{q\}$ holds if and only if $p \Rrightarrow wp(c, q)$.

Nondeterminism in a construct corresponds to logical conjunction in its weakest precondition definition which allows one to define the weakest precondition semantics of a nondeterministic choice operator $\sqcap$ as

$$wp(c \sqcap d, p) = wp(c, p) \wedge wp(d, p). \tag{1}$$

Because $c \sqcap d$ allows any behaviour of either c or d, both must guarantee to achieve p.

A basic requirement of weakest preconditions is that they are *monotonic* in their postconditions, i.e. if $q \Rrightarrow r$ then $wp(c, q) \Rrightarrow wp(c, r)$. From that, one can deduce that $wp(c, q \wedge r) \Rrightarrow wp(c, q) \wedge wp(c, r)$. Dijkstra also required his commands to be conjunctive, i.e. $wp(c, q \wedge r) \equiv wp(c, q) \wedge wp(c, r)$. That restriction means his commands also have a relational model.

2.3 Lattice Theory and Fixed Points

In terms of lattice theory the nondeterministic choice $c \sqcap d$ is the greatest lower bound of c and d, also known as their meet. The lattice of commands induces a *refinement* ordering, "$c \sqsubseteq d$", meaning that c is refined (or implemented) by d and defined by[1]

$$c \sqsubseteq d \mathrel{\widehat{=}} c \sqcap d = c.$$

The least element of the lattice is Dijkstra's **abort** command, which is refined (i.e. implemented) by any other command: **abort** $\sqsubseteq c$. A lattice also has a least upper bound (or join) operator, $c \sqcup d$, which is the least command that refines both c and d. For a relational model the least upper bound corresponds to the intersection of relations.

Fixed Points. To handle recursion and iteration one can utilise the fixed point calculus [1] to define least and greatest fixed points of monotonic functions over a complete lattice. Axioms (2) and (3) characterise the least fixed point, μf, of a function f, and axioms (4) and (5) characterise its greatest fixed point, νf.

$$\mu f = f(\mu f) \tag{2}$$

$$f(x) \sqsubseteq x \Rightarrow \mu f \sqsubseteq x \tag{3}$$

$$\nu f = f(\nu f) \tag{4}$$

$$x \sqsubseteq f(x) \Rightarrow x \sqsubseteq \nu f \tag{5}$$

One may then define a **while** loop as a least fixed point:

$$\mathbf{while}\ b\ \mathbf{do}\ c \mathrel{\widehat{=}} (\mu x \bullet \mathbf{if}\ b\ \mathbf{then}\ c;\ x\ \mathbf{else}\ \mathbf{nil}).$$

Sequential composition is the highest precedence binary operator and nondeterministic choice the lowest; we make no assumptions about the relative precedence of other operators. Greatest fixed points may be used to define

[1] Note that some authors, e.g. Kozen [24], make use of the dual lattice with a reversed ordering $d \leq c$ that mean d refines c, and hence their nondeterministic choice operator is the lattice join (rather than meet).

finite iteration of a command zero or more times (the Kleene star operator)[2]

$$c^\star \mathrel{\widehat=} (\nu x \bullet c;\ x \sqcap \mathbf{nil})$$

and least fixed points to define iteration of a command zero or more times where infinite iteration is allowed.

$$c^\omega \mathrel{\widehat=} (\mu x \bullet c;\ x \sqcap \mathbf{nil})$$

Note that the number of iterations of both these iteration operators is nondeterministic. From these definitions and the axioms of fixed points (2–5), one obtains the usual unfolding and induction properties of the iteration operators:

$$c^\star = c;\ c^\star \sqcap \mathbf{nil} \quad (6) \qquad\qquad x \sqsubseteq c;\ x \sqcap \mathbf{nil} \Rightarrow x \sqsubseteq c^\star \quad (8)$$

$$c^\omega = c;\ c^\omega \sqcap \mathbf{nil} \quad (7) \qquad\qquad c;\ x \sqcap \mathbf{nil} \sqsubseteq x \Rightarrow c^\omega \sqsubseteq x \quad (9)$$

3 Specification Languages

VDM [23] and Z [2,3,15] make extensive use of logic and set theory to specify operations more abstractly. Postconditions are expressed as predicates on two states, for example, Z uses an unprimed variable x for its value in the initial state and a primed x' for its value in the final state. Semantically such postconditions can be viewed as binary relations on states.

Both VDM and Z make extensive use of set theoretical constructs such as relations, functions (maps) and sequences, as well as inductively defined data types that allow one to define recursive structures, such as trees. Both VDM and Z provide record-like structures (composite objects in VDM and schemas in Z) but unlike programming language record structures, they allow an invariant to constrain the valid objects of the type. Schemas are used extensively in Z to represent record types, program state and state-to-state relations.

To provide a succinct and readable specification of operations, VDM and Z make use of abstract models of the state defined in terms of set theory. Data refinement is then used to map the abstract operation specifications to implementation data structures, such as arrays, records, trees, etc., while refining the observable semantics of the operation.

4 Refinement Calculus

An important development was to combine specification and programming languages to give a wide-spectrum language [5]. That allows components of a program to be specifications rather than code and thus allows stepwise refinement from a specification to code via intermediate stages that are a combination of the two. A crucial idea behind the refinement calculus is to provide commands that represent pre/post specifications. Perhaps an indication of its importance is that many authors have invented (or reinvented) essentially the same idea.

[2] Authors using the dual lattice make use of the dual of greatest fixed point, i.e. least fixed point.

- Schwarz added generic (specification) commands [30] with the syntax "$\{p \Rightarrow q\}$", with the meaning that if it is executed in a state satisfying the precondition p it terminates in a state satisfying the postcondition q.
- Back developed a refinement calculus with a similar specification construct that also handles adding and removing variables from the state space [4].
- Morris defined a *prescription* with the syntax $(p \parallel q)$, not to be confused with parallel composition, that if executed in a state satisfying the precondition p terminates in a state satisfying the postcondition q [29]. Its semantics may be given in terms of Dijkstra's weakest preconditions: $wp((p \parallel q), r) = p \wedge (\forall \overline{v} \bullet q \Rightarrow r)$, where $\overline{v}$ is the list of all the program variables.
- Morgan defined a pre/post specification statement with the syntax $[p, q]$, with a two-state (relational) postcondition q (similar to Z) [26]. It has a weakest precondition semantics similar to Morris' prescription but adapted to handle its two-state postcondition. Morgan also introduced a specification statement with a frame, $w : [p, q]$, representing that only variables in w can be modified [27].

Such specifications are quite expressive and include infeasible specifications, such as $[\mathit{true}, \mathit{false}]$, which is referred to as **magic** because it breaks Dijkstra's law of the excluded miracle.

The refinement calculus allows specification commands to be used anywhere other commands are allowed, thus providing a rich specification language. A further refinement was to split a specification command into two primitives: a precondition or assert command $\{p\}$ and a postcondition command $[q]$. A pre/post specification is then written $\{p\}; [q]$. The primitive commands each have simpler definitions and properties compared to the combined command, whose properties can be derived from those of the primitives.

Another interesting construct from the refinement calculus is the "invariant" command, $(\mathbf{inv}\, I \cdot c)$, of Morgan and Vickers [28] that imposes and invariant I on a command c, that is, its behaviours are those of c but restricted to those behaviours that maintain the invariant I. For example, $(\mathbf{inv}\, x \in \mathbb{N} \cdot c)$ imposes a type restriction on x that it is a natural number, and $(\mathbf{inv}\, x \leq y \cdot c)$ restricts all states of the execution of c to satisfy $x \leq y$.

5 Program Algebra

Another way of representing programs is via approaches such as relational and Kleene algebra.

- Blikle represented programming constructs as binary relations with nondeterministic choice represented by relational union and sequential composition as relational composition [6].
- Hoare et al. developed an algebraic theory of programming based on a set of laws of programming [18].
- Hoare and He's unifying theories of programming (UTP) made extensive use of a relational semantics in which the relations could be on pairs of states for sequential programs (similar to Blikle), or on traces for concurrent programs [19].

- Kozen made use of a more abstract algebraic approach that added tests (or guards) to Kleene Algebra in order to represent programs abstractly [24].
- Kleene algebra only supports finite iteration and hence does not allow one to represent nonterminating behaviour of loops. To address this Cohen made use of an omega algebra that supports infinite iterations as well [7].
- Von Wright developed a demonic refinement algebra that provided an abstract algebraic representation of the refinement calculus [31].

Some correspondences between the different approaches are shown in Fig. 1.

Kleene algebra	Relational algebra	Program algebra
$e \mid f$	$r \cup s$	$c \sqcap d$
$\varnothing$	$\varnothing$	**magic**
$e \cdot f$	$r \mathbin{⨾} s$	$c;\, d$
ϵ	id	**nil**
$e^\star$	$r^\star$	$c^\star$

Fig. 1. Relationship between Kleene algebra, relational algebra and program algebra, in which e and f are regular expressions, r and s are binary relations, c and d are commands, ⨾ is relational composition, and id is the identity relation.

6 Tests (Guards)

A simple but important advance was the recognition that tests (or guards) can be treated as a separate primitive, rather than only being considered as part of a larger construct. This separation has been recognised in multiple approaches to program semantics which we overview below.

6.1 Relational Algebra

Subsets of the identity relation can be used to represent tests [6,19] for example, an **if** statement can be defined as follows,

$$\textbf{if } b \textbf{ then } c \textbf{ else } d = (b \lhd \mathrm{id}) \mathbin{⨾} c \cup (\overline{b} \lhd \mathrm{id}) \mathbin{⨾} d$$

where $b \lhd \mathrm{id}$ restricts to domain of the identity relation id to the set b and $\overline{b}$ is the complement of the set b.

6.2 Refinement Calculus

A specification command that does not allow any variables to be modified acts as a null command if its postcondition holds but is infeasible otherwise and hence it provides a suitable representation of a guard (or test). This observation allows a conditional to be defined in terms of nondeterministic choice and guards, where an empty frame is represented by $\varnothing$.

$$\textbf{if } b \textbf{ then } c \textbf{ else } d = \varnothing\!:\![b];\ c \sqcap \varnothing\!:\![\neg\, b];\ d$$

This approach allows Dijkstra's conditional to be defined in a similar manner.

$$\begin{array}{lcl} \textbf{if } b_0 \rightarrow c_0 & = & \varnothing{:}[b_0]\,;\,c_0 \\ \square\ b_1 \rightarrow c_1 & & \sqcap\ \varnothing{:}[b_1]\,;\,c_1 \\ \vdots & & \vdots \\ \square\ b_n \rightarrow c_n & & \sqcap\ \varnothing{:}[b_n]\,;\,c_n \\ \textbf{od} & & \sqcap\ \varnothing{:}[\neg\,(b_0 \vee b_1 \vee \cdots \vee b_n)]\,;\,\textbf{abort} \end{array}$$

The fact that both forms of conditional can be defined in terms of more primitive constructs is important for building a theoretical basis for the refinement calculus, as rules for reasoning about them can be derived from the properties of the primitive constructs in their definitions. Furthermore the primitives, such as nondeterministic choice and guards, have simpler algebra properties.

6.3 Kleene Algebra with Tests

Kozen extended Kleene algebra with tests (or in Dijkstra's terminology, guards) [24]. He did so in an abstract manner: tests are identified as a subset of commands that form a boolean sub-algebra. His work can be seen as an abstraction of both the relational algebra and refinement calculus approaches to tests. A conditional (**if**) statement with a test t can be represented by $t;\ c \sqcap \neg\ t;\ d$.

7 Well-Founded Relations

To handle termination of recursive programs and loops one can make use of a well-founded relation. Proofs of such laws make use of well-founded induction, which for a set T and a property $P(k)$ defined on elements of T, can be stated as follows: $\prec$ is well founded on T if and only if

$$(\forall\, k \in T \bullet (\forall\, j \in T \bullet j \prec k \Rightarrow P(j)) \Rightarrow P(k)) \quad \Rightarrow \quad (\forall\, k \in T \bullet P(k)). \qquad (10)$$

Using a variant over a well-founded relation gives a more general approach than using a natural-number valued variant.

8 Shared Memory Concurrency

Jones [20–22] introduced a compositional approach to reasoning about concurrent processes based on a rely condition, a binary relation on states that represents an assumption about the allowable interference from the environment. Complementing this, if a process has a rely condition of r, all the processes in its environment need to guarantee that each step they make satisfies a guarantee condition g that implies r.

Jones extended Hoare triples to quintuples of the form $\{p, r\}c\{g, q\}$, in which p is a precondition, r is a rely condition, g is a guarantee condition and q a postcondition, and p characterises a set of states while r, g and q characterise binary relations on states. Provided c starts in a start satisfying p and all steps made by the environment satisfy r, all program steps of c will satisfy g and c will terminate in a state that satisfies q. Note that program steps of c are only required to satisfy the guarantee g as long as its environment steps satisfy r, i.e. once an environment step does not satisfy r, c no longer needs to maintain the guarantee or the postcondition. For example, the following is a rule for verifying a parallel composition in terms of its components.

$$\frac{\begin{array}{c}\{p, r \vee r_0\} c_0 \{g_0, q_0\} \\ \{p, r \vee r_1\} c_1 \{g_1, q_1\} \\ g_0 \Rrightarrow r_1 \\ g_1 \Rrightarrow r_0\end{array}}{\{p, r\} c_0 \parallel c_1 \{g_0 \vee g_1, q_0 \wedge q_1\}} \tag{11}$$

For this rule, r represents the interference from the environment on the whole parallel composition, r_0 is the additional interference on c_0, which must be ensured by the guarantee g_1 of c_1, and symmetrically, r_1 is the additional interference on c_1, which must be ensured by the guarantee g_0 of c_0. Because c_0 guarantees g_0 and c_1 guarantees g_1, their parallel composition $c_0 \parallel c_1$ only guarantees $g_0 \vee g_1$.

9 Concurrent Program Algebras

Milner defined a synchronous version of CCS, SCCS [25]. In SCCS an atomic step a synchronises $(\times)$ with atomic step b to give $a \times b$. For parallel composition of commands, each atomic step of the composition is a synchronisation of the first step of the two processes followed by the parallel composition of their remainders. This is encapsulated in the following property, in which a and b are atomic steps and c and d are arbitrary commands.

$$a.c \parallel b.d = (a \times b).(c \parallel d) \tag{12}$$

To allow for an interleaving interpretation $\times$ has an identity element 1, such that for any atomic step a, $a \times 1 = a$. For example,

$$a.c \parallel 1.d = (a \times 1).(c \parallel d) = a.(c \parallel d).$$

10 Concurrent Refinement Calculus

Basis. Our own work on a concurrent refinement algebra builds on the ideas presented above. At its base is a complete lattice of commands with nondeterministic choice as the lattice meet. To this we add sequential composition (with identity **nil**) and parallel composition (with identity **skip**). A novel additional operator is weak conjunction $(\Cap)$ – see below.

Tests. Following Kozen, we identify a subset of commands that form the boolean sub-algebra of tests. In addition, we need to define how tests interact with other commands. The algebra abstracts from the details of tests: they are just a subset of commands that forms a boolean algebra.

The algebra can be instantiated for a state-based model by introducing a set Σ representing the program's state. A test command $\tau(p)$ is then associated with a set of states p; its execution succeeds if the initial state is in p, otherwise it is infeasible. Special cases are when p is empty, $\tau(\varnothing)$, which corresponds to the everywhere infeasible command $\top$, also called **magic**, and when p is the complete state space Σ, $\tau(\Sigma)$, which always succeeds and corresponds to the identity of sequential composition, **nil**.

Atomic Steps. We also identify another subset of commands that form a boolean sub-algebra of atomic steps and, as for tests, define how they interact with other commands, including tests [13]. Our atomic steps are a subset of commands and are composed using the same operators as general commands; that differs from Milner who uses a disjoint carrier set with a separate composition operator [25].

Program and Environment Steps. As for Milner's SCCS we identify an atomic command, $\boldsymbol{\epsilon}$, that is a atomic step identity of parallel that allows the environment of a process to make a step, i.e. $a \parallel \boldsymbol{\epsilon} = a$. Because atomic steps form a boolean algebra, the complement of $\boldsymbol{\epsilon}$, written $!\boldsymbol{\epsilon}$, is well defined and corresponds to the atomic command, $\boldsymbol{\pi}$, that can perform any program step.

The abstract atomic program and environment commands may be instantiated over relations on the state space Σ. For a binary relation r between states, we define a program step command $\pi(r)$ as the command that allows a single program step from state σ to σ' if and only if $(\sigma, \sigma') \in r$, and an environment step command $\epsilon(r)$ similarly. Both $\pi(\varnothing)$ and $\epsilon(\varnothing)$ correspond to the infeasible command $\top$. The command $\pi(\Sigma \times \Sigma)$, abbreviated $\boldsymbol{\pi}$, allows any program step at all, and likewise $\epsilon(\Sigma \times \Sigma)$, abbreviated $\boldsymbol{\epsilon}$, allows any environment step. Each atomic step command is then a nondeterministic choice between some program step command and some environment step command.

Introducing the primitive atomic step commands, $\pi(r)$ and $\epsilon(r)$, allows one to define commands to represent relies, guarantees, postcondition specifications, termination, fairness, etc., for our concurrent refinement algebra. It continues the theme of building the theory from primitives with simple properties, rather than defining more complex commands directly in the semantics.

Guarantee Command. In the rely/guarantee approach of Jones [20–22] a command satisfies a guarantee condition g, a binary relation on states, if every program step it makes satisfies g. A guarantee command, **guar** g, can be defined that only allows program steps that satisfy g but allows any environment step. A single step of **guar** g allows $\pi(g) \sqcap \boldsymbol{\epsilon}$, and the guarantee command allows any number of these steps:

$$\mathbf{guar}\ g \mathrel{\widehat{=}} (\pi(g) \sqcap \boldsymbol{\epsilon})^{\omega} \tag{13}$$

Weak Conjunction. If c is a non-aborting command, a guarantee of g can be imposed on c by using the conjunction (lattice join) operator: $(\mathbf{guar}\ g) \sqcup c$, however, if c can abort this is too strong because $(\mathbf{guar}\ g)$ is non-aborting and hence when it is conjoined with c any aborting behaviour of c is eliminated. To address this issue, the weak conjunction operator, $\Cap$, can be used instead. It behaves like conjunction for non-aborting commands but is abort strict, that is $c \Cap \mathbf{abort} = \mathbf{abort}$, for any command c. Hence one can use $(\mathbf{guar}\ g) \Cap c$ to represent the command c constrained by the guarantee g unless c aborts. This faithfully represents Jones' guarantee condition. The command $\boldsymbol{\pi} \sqcap \boldsymbol{\epsilon}$ allows any atomic step; it is the atomic step identity of weak conjunction.

The representation of a guarantee by a command was originally inspired by the invariant command of Morgan and Vickers [28], in fact the initial syntax was $(\mathbf{guar}\ g \cdot c)$. However, it was later realised that it was simpler to just define a guarantee command, $(\mathbf{guar}\ g)$, and use weak conjunction to combine it with other commands. This continues the theme of focusing on primitives that can be combined to give more complex constructs. For example, the law for strengthening a guarantee, $(\mathbf{guar}\ g_0 \cdot c) \sqsubseteq (\mathbf{guar}\ g_1 \cdot c)$ if $g_1 \subseteq g_0$, using the old syntax, can be replaced in the new syntax by the simpler law $\mathbf{guar}\ g_0 \sqsubseteq \mathbf{guar}\ g_1$ if $g_1 \subseteq g_0$, that focuses solely on the guarantee. This law can be proven by expanding the definition of the guarantee command (13).

The weak conjunction operator ($\Cap$) was invented while trying to give the semantics of the (old syntax) guarantee command. It was only after inventing it for use in the semantics, that we realised it was a useful operator in its own right. By promoting weak conjunction to an operator in our wide-spectrum language we were able to define more complex constructs in terms of more primitive commands, such as the (new syntax) guarantee command, which has a simpler set refinement laws.

Rely Command. A rely condition is an assumption about the behaviour of the environment of a process that every atomic step the environment makes satisfies r. It is similar to a precondition, in that if the environment breaks the rely condition, the process is free to do any behaviour whatsoever from that point on, i.e. it is free to abort. The environment making a step that does not satisfy r is represented by $\epsilon(\overline{r})$; the occurrence of such a step allows the process to abort. Any other step, i.e. an environment step satisfying r, $\epsilon(r)$, or any program step, $\boldsymbol{\pi}$, is allowed (without abort). The rely command is then the iteration of this behaviour any number of times, including infinitely many times.

$$\mathbf{rely}\ r \mathrel{\widehat{=}} (\boldsymbol{\pi} \sqcap \epsilon(r) \sqcap \epsilon(\overline{r});\ \mathbf{abort})^{\omega}$$

A rely command may be combined with a command c using the weak conjunction operator: $(\mathbf{rely}\ r) \Cap c$. This combination behaves as c unless the environment makes a step that does not satisfy r, in which case the combination aborts. Recall that the main difference between conjunction ($\sqcup$) and weak conjunction ($\Cap$) is that weak conjunction is abort strict, i.e. $c \Cap \mathbf{abort} = \mathbf{abort}$. This difference is crucial here.

Parallel Introduction Law. The commands developed so far allow one to present a refinement law equivalent to the parallel law of Jones above (11) as follows. If $g_0 \Rrightarrow r_1$ and $g_1 \Rrightarrow r_0$,

$$(\textbf{rely}\ r) \Cap (\textbf{guar}\ g_0 \vee g_1) \Cap \{p\};\ [q_0 \wedge q_1]$$
$$\sqsubseteq (\textbf{rely}\ r \vee r_0) \Cap (\textbf{guar}\ g_0) \Cap \{p\};\ [q_0] \parallel (\textbf{rely}\ r \vee r_1) \Cap (\textbf{guar}\ g_1) \Cap \{p\};\ [q_1]$$

Termination. For a sequential program, termination requires that it only performs a finite number of program steps. The same applies for a concurrent program, however, there is a subtlety with environment steps. We take the approach that single process has no direct control over whether it may be preempted by its environment and hence from some point on may perform only environment steps, forever. Hence while a terminating process may only ever perform a finite number of program steps, the number of environments steps its allows may be infinite. Of course, if the process is executed fairly, it will not be interrupted forever, and hence will only perform a finite number of steps overall. Fairness is addressed below. The most general terminating program is characterised by the command **term**.

$$\textbf{term} \mathrel{\widehat{=}} (\boldsymbol{\pi} \sqcap \boldsymbol{\epsilon})^\star;\ \boldsymbol{\epsilon}^\omega$$

We say c terminates if $\textbf{term} \sqsubseteq c$.

Fairness. A process is executed fairly if it is not preempted by its environment forever. Fair execution can be characterised by the program **fair** that does not allow any contiguous subsequence of environment steps to be infinite.

$$\textbf{fair} \mathrel{\widehat{=}} (\boldsymbol{\epsilon}^\star;\ \boldsymbol{\pi})^\omega;\ \boldsymbol{\epsilon}^\star$$

Fair execution of a process c can be imposed on it via weak conjunction with **fair**, i.e. $c \Cap \textbf{fair}$ represents fair execution of c. Note that

$$\textbf{term} \Cap \textbf{fair} = (\boldsymbol{\epsilon}^\star;\ \boldsymbol{\pi})^\star;\ \boldsymbol{\epsilon}^\omega \Cap (\boldsymbol{\epsilon}^\star;\ \boldsymbol{\pi})^\omega;\ \boldsymbol{\epsilon}^\star = (\boldsymbol{\epsilon}^\star;\ \boldsymbol{\pi})^\star;\ \boldsymbol{\epsilon}^\star = (\boldsymbol{\pi} \sqcap \boldsymbol{\epsilon})^\star$$

and hence only admits a finite number of steps, both program and environment. If a command c is terminating, i.e. $\textbf{term} \sqsubseteq c$, then fair execution of c only performs a finite number of steps overall because

$$(\boldsymbol{\pi} \sqcap \boldsymbol{\epsilon})^\star = \textbf{term} \Cap \textbf{fair} \sqsubseteq c \Cap \textbf{fair}.$$

The command **fair** allows one to consider fair execution of a process in isolation. This contrasts to the common approach to fairness in which the parallel composition operator is defined to be fair. In our theory no fairness assumptions are made of the primitive parallel operator ($\parallel$) but a fair parallel operator can be defined in terms of **fair** and the primitive parallel operator.

Synchronisation Operators. The three operators parallel ($\|$), weak conjunction ($\Cap$) and the lattice join or conjunction ($\sqcup$), all act as *synchronisation* operators; the main difference between them is how they synchronise individual atomic steps. We recognise their similarities by providing a theory of an abstract synchronisation operator ($\otimes$) which is then instantiated for each of the three operators. The synchronisation operator satisfies the following axioms.

$$a;\ c \otimes b;\ d = (a \otimes b);\ (c \otimes d) \tag{14}$$

$$\mathbf{nil} \otimes \mathbf{nil} = \mathbf{nil} \tag{15}$$

$$a;\ c \otimes \mathbf{nil} = \top \tag{16}$$

Axiom (14) corresponds to Milner's (12) although we assume atomic steps are a subset of commands and hence use $\otimes$ to combine both atomic steps a and b as well a more general commands c and d. Axiom (15) represents that the synchronisation of two null commands is null. If one process insists on performing at least one step before terminating and the other can only terminate immediately, their synchronisation is infeasible (16). From these properties one can deduce laws such as the following.

$$a^\star;\ c \otimes b^\star;\ d = (a \otimes b)^\star;\ ((c \otimes b^\star;\ d) \sqcap (a^\star;\ c \sqcap d))$$

A corollary of which is $a^\star \otimes b^\star = (a \otimes b)^\star$.

The instantiations of $\otimes$ for parallel and weak conjunction differ in the way they synchronise atomic steps.

$$\epsilon(r_0) \| \epsilon(r_1) = \epsilon(r_0 \cap r_1) \tag{17}$$

$$\pi(r_0) \| \epsilon(r_1) = \pi(r_0 \cap r_1) \tag{18}$$

$$\pi(r_0) \parallel \pi(r_1) = \top \tag{19}$$

$$\epsilon(r_0) \Cap \epsilon(r_1) = \epsilon(r_0 \cap r_1) \tag{20}$$

$$\pi(r_0) \Cap \pi(r_1) = \pi(r_0 \cap r_1) \tag{21}$$

$$\pi(r_0) \Cap \epsilon(r_1) = \top \tag{22}$$

Both combine two environment steps to give an environment step: (17) and (20). Parallel synchronises a program step only with an environment step (18) and weak conjunction synchronises a program step only with a program step (21). Conjunction ($\sqcup$) is also an instantiation of the synchronisation operator. It behaves the same as weak conjunction on atomic steps (i.e. $a \sqcup b = a \Cap b$) but differs in that weak conjunction is abort strict, i.e. $c \Cap \mathbf{abort} = \mathbf{abort}$.

By using the synchronisation operator as an abstraction of all three operators, $\|$, $\Cap$ and $\sqcup$, a large part of the theory of these operators can be developed just once and instantiated three times.

Representing Non-atomic Expressions. If an expression e refers to shared variables that are being modified by its environment, its evaluation is not atomic. Even if the expression only contains a single reference to a single shared variable, its evaluation may result in a value that is the value of e in some intermediate state and may not correspond to e's value in either the initial or final state of its evaluation. Handling expression evaluation in the context of interference requires care. Often it is prudent to limit the forms of expressions allowed. Common special cases that may be treated more simply are expressions containing only variables not subject to change by the environment or more generally expressions containing only a single reference to a single variable that may be modified by the environment. The above assume reading a single variable is atomic; if this is not the case stronger assumptions are needed about whether/how its value may change.

Assignment commands also need careful treatment because (i) the expression in an assignment may be subject to interference during its evaluation, and (ii) the variable being assigned to may be shared. A further complication arises if writing to the variable being assigned is not atomic.

Handling Conditionals. The test in a conditional is subject to the issues of expression evaluation discussed above. Just because a boolean expression b evaluates to true, does not mean it is still true after its evaluation because the environment may modify variables on which it depends. However, if the rely condition r of the process maintains b, i.e. $b \wedge r \Rrightarrow b'$, it will remain true under interference satisfying r, e.g. the rely condition $x \leq x'$ maintains the condition $0 \leq x$. Note that if r maintains b, it may not necessarily maintain its complement $\neg\, b$, e.g. $x \leq x'$ does not maintain $x < 0$.

Recursion. Recursive programs can be built on top of the fixed point calculus. Showing termination of a recursive program can be handled via well founded induction (10). To show a terminating specification s is refined by a recursive program μf, one can use well founded relation $\prec$ on a variant expression v of type T.

$$(\forall k \in T \bullet (\forall j \in T \bullet j \prec k \Rightarrow (\{v = j\};\, s \sqsubseteq \mu f)) \Rightarrow (\{v = k\};\, s \sqsubseteq \mu f))$$
$$\Rightarrow (\forall k \in T \bullet (\{v = k\};\, s \sqsubseteq \mu f)).$$

This may be simplified to the following.

$$(\forall k \in T \bullet (\{v \prec k\};\, s \sqsubseteq \mu f) \Rightarrow (\{v = k\};\, s \sqsubseteq \mu f)) \quad \Rightarrow \quad (s \sqsubseteq \mu f).$$

This approach can be adapted to concurrent processes in a straightforward manner.

Because a **while** loop is defined as a least fixed point of a conditional, the rule for a **while** loop can be derived from the rules for recursion and conditionals.

Local Variables. A local variable block (**local** $x \cdot c$) introduces a new local variable x for the duration of c. In the context of concurrency a local variable is not subject to any interference. To model this we make use of the command (**demand** r) that allows any program steps but only environment steps satisfying r.

$$\mathbf{demand}\ r \mathrel{\widehat{=}} (\boldsymbol{\pi} \sqcap \epsilon(r))^{\omega}$$

The command ($\mathbf{demand}\ x' = x$) only allows environment steps that do not modify x. If the variable x is fresh then a local block could be modelled by ($\mathbf{demand}\ x' = x$) $\Cap$ c but that does not cope with the case where there is a (non-local) variable x in the outer scope already. To handle that one needs to take the behaviour of ($\mathbf{demand}\ x' = x$) $\Cap$ c but liberate x, where the liberation operator $c \backslash x$ for any variable x and command c behaves exactly like c except the value of x in every state is liberated, i.e. x can take on any value. Note that we take each trace of c and then liberate x in every state of the trace to get a set of liberated traces. Finally the local variable block does not modify a non-local occurrence of x. That can be modelled by a guarantee ($\mathbf{guar}\, x' = x$) and completes our definition of a local variable block.

$$\mathbf{local}\ x \cdot c \mathrel{\widehat{=}} (c \Cap (\mathbf{demand}\ x' = x)) \backslash x \Cap (\mathbf{guar}\, x' = x)$$

Note that in the definition, x is liberated before the guarantee is enforced on any outer x. The definition of a local variable block requires a new primitive liberation operator ($\backslash$) but the other constructs used in its definition are already part of our theory.

11 Conclusions

A common theme throughout this paper is that developing a theory of (concurrent) programming is greatly facilitated if one can build the theory from a set of primitive operators and primitive commands, which have simple algebraic properties.

Our theory has a basis of lattice theory in which the lattice order ($\sqsubseteq$) is refinement, its meet ($\sqcap$) is nondeterministic choice ans its join ($\sqcup$) is conjunction. To this we add sequential composition (;), parallel composition ($\parallel$), weak conjunction ($\Cap$), and the liberation operator ($\backslash$). We identify two subsets of commands that correspond to tests and atomic steps, respectively; both these subsets form boolean algebras. We also identify two subsets of atomic steps that represent program and environment steps, respectively; both these subsets also form boolean algebras. An advantage of this approach is that it allows reuse of the rich theory of boolean algebra many times over, which saves one proving many straightforward properties of tests and atomic commands that are available from boolean algebra.

Another theory that we make use of multiple times is the theory of synchronising operators ($\otimes$), which is instantiated three times for parallel ($\parallel$), weak conjunction ($\Cap$) and conjunction ($\sqcup$). That allows the properties common to these operators, of which there are many relevant to our concurrent refinement algebra, to be proven once and reused multiple times.

The theory we have developed is rich enough to develop a fully fledged concurrent refinement calculus that supports the rely/guarantee approach of Jones. But if we instantiate our atomic steps with sets of events rather than relations, we also have a foundation for a process algebra such as Milner's SCCS. The theories have been encoded in Isabelle/HOL making significant use of its class and locale constructs to structure the theory, and a trace-based semantics has been developed to show our axiomatisations are consistent.

Acknowledgements. This research was supported Australian Research Council Discovery Grant DP130102901. Thanks are due to Joakim von Wright for introducing us to program algebra and Robert Colvin, Cliff Jones, Larissa Meinicke, Patrick Meiring, Kim Solin, Andrius Velykis, and Kirsten Winter, for their input on ideas presented here.

References

1. Aarts, C., et al.: Fixed-point calculus. Inf. Process. Lett. **53**, 131–136 (1995). Mathematics of Program Construction Group
2. Abrial, J.R.: The specification language Z: basic library. Internal report, Programming Research Group, Oxford University (1982)
3. Abrial, J.R., Schuman, S.A., Meyer, B.: Specification language and on the construction of programs: an advanced course. In: McKeag, R.M., Macnaghten, A.M. (eds.) On the Construction of Programs: An Advanced Course, pp. 343–410. Cambridge University Press, Cambridge (1980)
4. Back, R.-J.R., von Wright, J.: Refinement Calculus: A Systematic Introduction. Springer, New York (1998). https://doi.org/10.1007/978-1-4612-1674-2
5. Bauer, F.L., Broy, M., Gnatz, R., Hesse, W., Krieg-Brückner, B.: A wide spectrum language for program development. In: 3rd International Symposium Programming, Paris, pp. 1–15 (1978)
6. Blikle, A.: Specified programming. In: Blum, E.K., Paul, M., Takasu, S. (eds.) Mathematical Studies of Information Processing. LNCS, vol. 75, pp. 228–251. Springer, Heidelberg (1979). https://doi.org/10.1007/3-540-09541-1_29
7. Cohen, E.: Separation and reduction. In: Backhouse, R., Oliveira, J.N. (eds.) MPC 2000. LNCS, vol. 1837, pp. 45–59. Springer, Heidelberg (2000). https://doi.org/10.1007/10722010_4
8. Colvin, R.J., Hayes, I.J., Meinicke, L.A.: Designing a semantic model for a wide-spectrum language with concurrency. Formal Aspects Comput. **29**, 853–875 (2016)
9. Dijkstra, E.W.: Guarded commands, nondeterminacy, and a formal derivation of programs. CACM **18**, 453–458 (1975)
10. Dijkstra, E.W.: A Discipline of Programming. Prentice-Hall, Upper Saddle River (1976)
11. Floyd, R.W.: Assigning meanings to programs. In: Proceedings of Symposia in Applied Mathematics: Mathematical Aspects of Computer Science, vol. 19, pp. 19–32 (1967)
12. Hayes, I.J.: Generalised rely-guarantee concurrency: an algebraic foundation. Formal Aspects Comput. **28**(6), 1057–1078 (2016)
13. Hayes, I.J., Colvin, R.J., Meinicke, L.A., Winter, K., Velykis, A.: An algebra of synchronous atomic steps. In: Fitzgerald, J., Heitmeyer, C., Gnesi, S., Philippou, A. (eds.) FM 2016. LNCS, vol. 9995, pp. 352–369. Springer, Cham (2016). https://doi.org/10.1007/978-3-319-48989-6_22
14. Hayes, I.J., Jones, C.B., Colvin, R.J.: Laws and semantics for rely-guarantee refinement. Technical report CS-TR-1425, Newcastle University, July 2014
15. Hayes, I. (ed.): Specification Case Studies. Second edn. Prentice Hall International, Upper Saddle River (1993)

16. Hayes, I.J., Meinicke, L.A., Winter, K., Colvin, R.J.: A synchronous program algebra: a basis for reasoning about shared-memory and event-based concurrency. Formal Aspects Comput. (2018). https://doi.org/10.1007/s00165-018-0464-4
17. Hoare, C.A.R.: An axiomatic basis for computer programming. Commun. ACM **12**(10), 576–580 (1969). 583
18. Hoare, C.A.R., et al.: Laws of programming. Commun. ACM, **30**(8), 672–686 (1987). Corrigenda: CACM 30(9):770
19. Hoare, C.A.R., He, J.: Unifying Theories of Programming. Prentice Hall, Upper Saddle River (1998)
20. Jones, C.B.: Development Methods for Computer Programs including a Notion of Interference. Ph.D. thesis, Oxford University, June 1981. Available as: Oxford University Computing Laboratory (now Computer Science) Technical Monograph PRG-25
21. Jones, C.B.: Specification and design of (parallel) programs. In: Proceedings of IFIP 1983, pp. 321–332. North-Holland (1983)
22. Jones, C.B.: Tentative steps toward a development method for interfering programs. ACM ToPLaS **5**(4), 596–619 (1983)
23. Jones, C.B.: Systematic Software Development Using VDM, Second edn. Prentice Hall International, Upper Saddle River (1990)
24. Kozen, D.: Kleene algebra with tests. ACM Trans. Program. Lang. Syst. **19**(3), 427–443 (1997)
25. Milner, R.: Calculi for synchrony and asynchrony. Theoret. Comput. Sci. **25**(3), 267–310 (1983)
26. Morgan, C.C.: The specification statement. ACM Trans. Program. Lang. Syst. **10**(3), 403–419 (1988)
27. Morgan, C.C.: Programming from Specifications, Second edn. Prentice Hall, Upper Saddle River (1994)
28. Morgan, C.C., Vickers, T.N.: Types and invariants in the refinement calculus. Sci. Comput. Program. **14**, 281–304 (1990)
29. Morris, J.M.: A theoretical basis for stepwise refinement and the programming calculus. Sci. Comput. Program. **9**(3), 287–306 (1987)
30. Schwarz, J.: Generic commands–a tool for partial correctness formalisms. Comput. J. **20**(2), 151–155 (1977)
31. von Wright, J.: Towards a refinement algebra. Sci. Comput. Program. **51**, 23–45 (2004)

Formal Models

Behaviour-Driven Formal Model Development

Colin Snook[1(✉)], Thai Son Hoang[1], Dana Dghyam[1], Michael Butler[1], Tomas Fischer[2], Rupert Schlick[3], and Keming Wang[4]

[1] ECS, University of Southampton, Southampton, UK
{cfs,t.s.hoang,D.Dghaym,mjb}@ecs.soton.ac.uk
[2] Thales Austria GmbH, Vienna, Austria
tomas.fischer@thalesgroup.com
[3] AIT Austrian Institute of Technology GmbH, Vienna, Austria
Rupert.Schlick@ait.ac.at
[4] Southwest Jiaotong University, Chengdu, China
kmwang@swjtu.edu.cn

Abstract. Formal systems modelling offers a rigorous system-level analysis resulting in a precise and reliable specification. However, some issues remain: Modellers need to understand the requirements in order to formulate the models, formal verification may focus on safety properties rather than temporal behaviour, domain experts need to validate the final models to ensure they fit the needs of stakeholders. In this paper we discuss how the principles of Behaviour-Driven Development (BDD) can be applied to formal systems modelling and validation. We propose a process where manually authored scenarios are used initially to support the requirements and help the modeller. The same scenarios are used to verify behavioural properties of the model. The model is then mutated to automatically generate scenarios that have a more complete coverage than the manual ones. These automatically generated scenarios are used to animate the model in a final acceptance stage. For this acceptance stage, it is important that a domain expert decides whether or not the behaviour is useful.

Keywords: Formal modelling · Scenarios · Mutation testing Acceptance testing

1 Introduction

For highly dependable systems, formal modelling offers a rigorous system-level analysis to ensure that the specification is consistent with important properties such as safety and security. Using theorem provers, such properties can be proven to hold generically without instantiation and testing. However, modellers need

All data supporting this study are openly available from the University of Southampton repository at https://doi.org/10.5258/SOTON/D0604.

J. Sun and M. Sun (Eds.): ICFEM 2018, LNCS 11232, pp. 21–36, 2018.
https://doi.org/10.1007/978-3-030-02450-5_2

to understand the requirements in order to formulate correct and useful models. The human centric processes of understanding a natural language or semi-formal requirements document and representing it in mathematical abstraction is subjective and intellectual, leading to misinterpretation. Formal verification may then focus on safety properties rather than desired behaviour which is more difficult to verify as a proof obligation. Even if these difficulties are averted, the requirements may not represent the customer's needs. Domain experts need to validate the final models to show that they capture the informally specified customer requirements and ensure they fit the needs of stakeholders.

A widely-used and reliable validation method is acceptance testing, which with adequate coverage, provides assurance that a system, in our case embodied by a formal model, represents the informal customer requirements. Acceptance tests describe a sequence of simulation steps involving concrete data examples to exhibit the functional responses of the system. However, acceptance tests can also be viewed as a collection of scenarios providing a useful and definitive specification of the behavioural requirements of the system. The high level nature of acceptance tests, which are both human-readable and executable, guarantees that they reflect the current state of the product and do not become outdated. They are also necessarily precise and concise to ensure that the acceptance tests are repeatable. As such, the acceptance test may be seen as the single reference or *source of truth*.

Behaviour-Driven Development (BDD) [15] is a software development process based on writing precise semi-formal scenarios as a behavioural specification and using them as acceptance tests. In this paper we discuss how the principles of BDD can be applied to formal systems modelling and validation. We propose a process where manually authored scenarios are used initially to support the requirements and help the modeller. The same scenarios are used to verify behavioural properties of the model. However, the manually written tests may have limited coverage. To address this, the model is mutated to automatically generate further scenarios that have a more complete coverage than the manual ones. The additional scenarios should be accepted or rejected by domain experts to ensure they, and hence the model, represent the desired behaviour. These automatically generated scenarios are used to animate the model in a final acceptance stage. For this acceptance stage, it is important that a domain expert decides whether or not the behaviour is desirable.

Customer requirements are typically based on a domain model, which is often expressed in terms of entities with attributes and relationships. State-machines and activity diagrams can be used to describe the behaviour. On the other hand, a formal model (such as Event-B) is based on set theory and predicate logic [1]. In a creative process, the modelling engineer uses ingenuity to translate the domain model into appropriate formal structures. The mismatch between the semi-formal models understood by the domain experts and the mathematical notations used for formal modelling leads to a conflict. The acceptance tests need to be expressed in terms of the formal model, but they also need to be understood by the domain experts who are not familiar with the formal notations. It would be more desirable to express the acceptance tests in terms of the domain model so that domain experts can easily create and validate them.

iUML-B [13,16] provides a UML-like diagrammatic modelling notation, including class diagrams and state-machines, with automatic generation of Event-B formal models. Hence, iUML-B is a formal notation which is intuitive to write and understand and is much closer to the domain model.

Gherkin [18, Chap. 3] is a structured language for describing scenarios and expected behaviour in a readable but executable form. In this paper we show how Gherkin supported by the *Cucumber* tool, can be used to encode and execute acceptance tests for validating Event-B and iUML-B formal models. This helps domain experts by allowing them to define acceptance tests without requiring expertise in formal modelling. It also helps the formal experts by providing means to systematically validate formal models via input from domain experts.

The remainder of the paper is structured as follows. In Sect. 2 we introduce the "Lift" examples used throughout the paper. In Sect. 3 we provide an overview of the Cucumber framework and Gherkin notation for executing scenarios, the formal methods Event-B and iUML-B that we use and MoMuT which we use as a scenario generation tool. In Sect. 4 we introduce our approach to behaviour-driven formal model development and then, in Sect. 5, demonstrate how to use Gherkin and Cucumber for testing formal models written in Event-B and iUML-B. Section 6 describes related work and Sect. 7 concludes.

2 Running Examples

This section gives a brief overview of our running examples. The main running example in this paper is a single-shaft lift controller. In Sect. 5.2, we extend this example to a multi-shaft lift controller to illustrate our contribution on linking Gherkin/Cucumber with iUML-B.

A Single-Shaft Lift. First we consider a single shaft lift operating between several floors, Fig. 1. The cabin has request buttons for each floor and each floor has an up and down request button. The cabin is moved up and down by winding, resp. unwinding, a motor. The cabin door may only open when the lift is not moving. The full requirements of the single-shaft lift are given in [4]. The cabin should only move to respond to requests and should only change direction when there are no requests ahead in its direction of travel. Any requests associated with the current floor are cleared when the door begins to open.

A Multi-Shaft Lift. This system manages multiple lifts with a single cabin in each shaft. The behaviour of the cabin motor and door is similar to the single-shaft lift. Similarly, the cabin floor requests are dealt with internally by each lift. The main difference is in the up/down requests at the floor levels. The up/down floor requests are assigned by a central controller to the nearest serving cabin. The nearest cabin is determined by calculating the 'figure of suitability' of each lift, which depends on the direction of the lift, the direction of the call and the distance to the calling floor. Once a request is assigned to a lift, the cabin will serve the request similar to the single shaft example. The full requirements of the multi-shaft lift are given in [4].

3 Background and Technologies

In this section, we first review the Gherkin/Cucumber approach to BDD, followed by a short description of the Event-B method and its iUML-B diagrammatic notation.

3.1 Behaviour-Driven Development with Gherkin/Cucumber

The BDD principle aims for pure domain oriented feature description without any technical knowledge. In particular, BDD aims for understandable tests which can be executed on the specifications of a system. BDD is important for communication between the business stakeholders and the software developers. Gherkin/Cucumber [18] is one of the various frameworks supporting BDD [17].

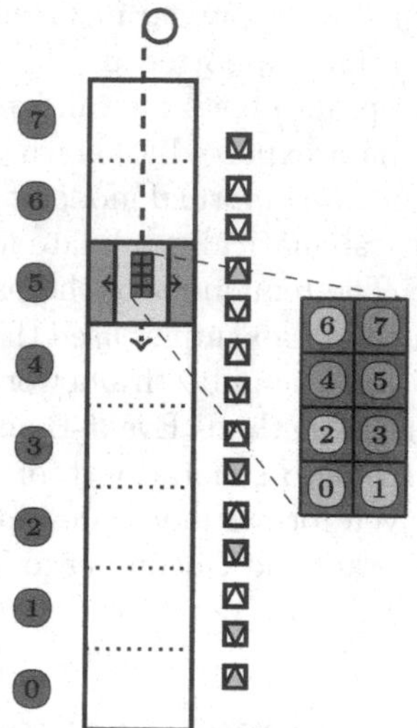

Fig. 1. A lift system

Gherkin. Gherkin [18, Chap. 3] is a language that defines lightweight structures for describing the expected behaviour in a plain text, readable by both stakeholders and developers, which is still automatically executable. Each Gherkin feature starts with some description, followed by a list of scenarios. The feature is often written as a story, e.g.,

"*As a* «role» *I want* «feature» *so that* «business value»".

Scenario. Each scenario represents one use case. There are no technical restrictions about the number of scenarios in a feature; yet they all should be related to the feature being described.

In the simplest case the scenario also contains the test data and thus represents an individual test case. It is however advantageous to separate the general requirement description from the concrete test cases and to describe a group of similar use cases at once. For this purpose, a scenario outline with a placeholder for the particular test data specified separately as a list of examples can be used. In the following, we focus on different scenario steps.

Steps. Every scenario consists of steps starting with one of the keywords: Given, When, Then, And or But.

- Keyword Given is used for writing test preconditions that describe how to put the system under test in a known state. This should happen without any user interaction. It is good practice to check whether the system reached the specified state.
- Keyword When is used to describe the tested interaction including the provided input. This is the stimulus triggering the execution.
- Keyword Then is used to test postconditions that describe the expected output. Only the observable outcome should be compared, not the internal system state. The test fails if the real observation differs from the expected results.
- Keywords And and But can be used for additional test constructs.

Cucumber. Cucumber is a framework for executing acceptance tests written in Gherkin language and provides Gherkin language parser, test automation as well as report generation. In order to make such test cases automatically executable, the user must supply the actual step definitions providing the gluing code, which implements the interaction with the System Under Test (SUT). The steps shall be written in a generic way, i.e. serving multiple features. This keeps the number of step definitions much smaller than the number of tests. It is an antipattern to supply feature-coupled step definitions which cannot be re-used across features or scenarios.

Compound steps may encapsulate complex interaction with a system caused by a single domain activity, thus decoupling the features from the technical interfaces of the SUT. This defines a new domain-related testing language, which may simplify the feature description. The description of the business functionality is, however, still contained in the features.

An example of a scenario for the single-shaft lift system is shown in Listing 1.

3.2 Event-B

Event-B [1] is a formal method for system development. An Event-B model contains two parts: *contexts* and *machines*. Contexts contain *carrier sets* s, *constants* c, and *axioms* $\mathsf{A(c)}$ that constrain the carrier sets and constants. Note that the model may be underspecified, e.g., the value of the sets and constants can be any value satisfying the axioms. Machines contain *variables* v, *invariants* $\mathsf{I(v)}$ that constrain the variables, and *events*. An event comprises a guard denoting its enabling-condition and an action describing how the variables are modified when the event is executed. In general, an event e has the following form, where t are the event parameters, $\mathsf{G(t,v)}$ is the guard of the event, and $\mathsf{v := E(t,v)}$ is the action of the event.

$$\textbf{any}\ \mathsf{t}\ \textbf{where}\ \mathsf{G(t,v)}\ \textbf{then}\ \mathsf{v := E(t,v)}\ \textbf{end}$$

```
Scenario: Press a DOWN button

Given can press DOWN button at floor "2"
When press DOWN button at floor "2"
Then DOWN button at floor "2" is lit
And can wind the lift motor
And cannot open door

When motor starts winding
Then lift can move up
And cannot open door

When lift moves up
Then floor is "1"
And lift can move up
```

Listing 1. A test scenario for single-shaft lift

Actions in Event-B are, in the most general cases, non-deterministic [7], e.g., of the form v : E(v) (v is assigned any element from the set E(v)) or v : P(v,v') (v is assigned any value satisfying the before-after predicate P(v,v')). A special event called INITIALISATION without parameters and guards is used to put the system into the initial state.

A machine in Event-B corresponds to a transition system where *variables* represent the state and *events* specify the transitions. Event-B uses a mathematical language that is based on set theory and predicate logic.

Contexts can be *extended* by adding new carrier sets, constants, axioms, and theorems. Machines can be *refined* by adding and modifying variables, invariants, events. In this paper, we do not focus on context extension and machine refinement.

Event-B is supported by the Rodin Platform (Rodin) [2], an extensible open source toolkit which includes facilities for modelling, verifying the consistency of models using theorem proving and model checking techniques, and validating models with simulation-based approaches.

3.3 MoMuT

MoMuT is a test case generation tool able to derive tests from behaviour models. The behaviour model represents a system specification, the generated tests can be used as black box tests on an implementation. They help to ensure that every behaviour that is specified, is also implemented correctly.

In contrast to other model based testing tools, the generated test cases do not target structural coverage of the model, but target exposing artificial faults systematically injected into the model. These faults are representatives of potential faults in the implementation; a test finding them in the model can be assumed to find its direct counterpart as well as similar, not only identical problems in the implementation [6].

As input models, MoMuT accepts Object Oriented Action Systems (OOAS) [9], an object oriented extension of Back's Action systems [3]. The underlying concepts of Action systems and Event-B are both closely related to Dijkstra's guarded command language [5]. For a subset of UML, for some Domain Specific Languages (DSLs) and for a subset of Event-B, transformations into OOAS are available.

MoMuT strives to produce effective tests, i.e. tests exposing faults, as well as efficient tests i.e. keeping the test suite's size close to the necessary minimum. Thereby, the tests are also suitable as manually reviewed acceptance tests.

3.4 iUML-B

iUML-B [13,16], an extension of the Rodin Platform, provides a 'UML like' diagrammatic modelling notation for Event-B in the form of class-diagrams and state-machines. The diagrammatic elements are contained within an Event-B model and generate or contribute to parts of it. The iUML-B makes the formal models more visual and thus easier to comprehend. We omit the description of state-machines and focus on class-diagrams, which are used in the example in Sect. 5.2.

Class diagrams provide a way to visually model data relationships. Classes, attributes and associations are linked to Event-B data elements (carrier sets, constants, or variables) and generate constraints on those elements. Methods elaborate Event-B events and contribute additional parameter representing the class instance.

4 Behaviour-Driven Formal Model Development

In this section, we present our approach for behaviour-driven formal model development. We assume that a natural language description of the requirements is available and this is supported by a number of manually written scenarios. The process, shown in Fig. 2, consists of the following steps.

1. In the *modelling* step, the model is produced from the *requirements* and the *manually written scenarios*. The output of the modelling step is a *safe model*, in the sense that it is fully proven to be consistent with respect to its invariants. (We use 'safe' in a wide sense to include any important properties). In this paper, we use Event-B/iUML-B as our modelling method.
2. The safe model is *behaviourally verified* against the manually written scenarios. The purpose is to verify that the safe model exhibits the behaviour specified in the requirements which cannot be expressed via invariants. The output of this step is a (safe and) *behaviourally verified model*. In this paper, we use Cucumber for Event-B/iUML-B (see Sect. 5) for verifying the behaviour of our model written in Event-B/iUMLB.

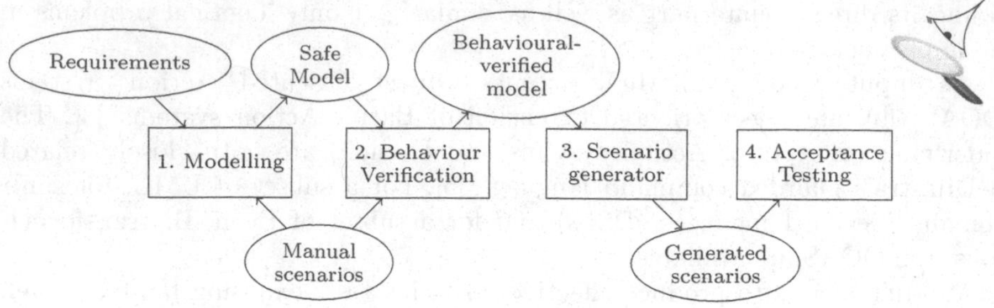

Fig. 2. A behaviour-driven formal model development method

3. The behaviourally-verified model is used as the input for a *scenario generator*, which automatically produces a collection of *generated scenarios*. In this paper, we use an Event-B-enabled version of MoMuT (see Sect. 3) as the scenario generator. The generated scenarios should be reviewed to ensure they represent desired behaviour. If the model still contains undesirable behaviour, that was not detected in the previous step, this will be reflected in the generated scenarios.
4. The generated scenarios are used for acceptance testing of the behaviourally verified model. Acceptance testing allows stakeholders to assess the usefulness of the model by watching its behaviour. We again use Cucumber for Event-B/iUML-B to automatically illustrate the generated scenarios to different stakeholders. The scenarios are in "natural language" and it is easy to see the correspondence between the scenarios and the requirements.

Our hypotheses about our approach are as follows.

H1 In the modelling step, scenarios help to improve the validity of the model.
H2 Scenarios are useful for verifying temporal properties.
H3 Generated scenarios are more complete than manually written scenarios.

In the following sections, we analyse the steps of the process in more detail with experiments to verify the above hypotheses.

4.1 Modelling

To validate Hypothesis **H1**, we perform an experiment using the single-shaft lift controller introduced in Sect. 2. The requirements of the system are given to two developers who are expert in Event-B modelling. To one developer, we also gave a set of desirable scenarios of the system. The full scenarios can be seen in [4]. The summary of the scenarios is as follows.

Scenario 1 User 1 enters the lift from Floor 0 and presses the button for Floor 2. User 2 presses the *up* button on Floor 1. The lift will go from Floor 0 to Floor 2, in between stop at Floor 1 to serve User 2's request.

Scenario 2 User 1 enters the lift from Floor 0 and presses the button for Floor 2. User 2 presses the *down* button on Floor 1. The lift will first go from Floor 0 to Floor 2, before changing the direction to go down to Floor 1 to serve User 2's request.

Scenario 3 User 1 enters the lift from Floor 0 and presses the button for Floor 2. User 2 presses the *down* button on Floor 1. The lift will first go from Floor 0 to Floor 2, before changing the direction to go down (still at Floor 2) to serve User 2's request.

Afterwards, we compare the models produced by the two developers in terms of their validity with respect to the requirements and the scenarios. The comparison is done by executing the scenarios on the models and reviewing their behaviour.

We did not find much difference in terms of valid behaviour between the two models. This may be due to tacit knowledge of the lift example. However, we found that the scenarios have some effect on the form of the models. The model developed with scenarios aligns more closely with the details presented in the scenario: The lift responses directly to the buttons pressed by the users. In the model developed without scenarios, an abstract notion of "requests" is introduced, which are eventually linked with the buttons. Having such a strong example of actual behaviour seems to *reduce the inclination to make abstractions*. On the one hand, the model without abstraction has less refinement steps and is more obviously valid since it directly correlates with the acceptance criteria. On the other hand, the model with abstraction has principles that can be adapted to different concrete implementations and hence may be more reusable. Scenarios help with validation of the models but may reduce their reusability. A possible mitigation is to develop "abstract" scenarios from the original concrete scenarios. We consider this as a direction for our future work.

4.2 Behaviour Verification

In this section, we describe our experiment to validate Hypothesis **H2**. The purpose of the behaviour verification step is to ensure that our safe model also satisfies behaviours which are specified using the scenarios. We use versions of the single-shaft lift model that has been seeded with several faults as follows.

1. (**Fault 1**) The lift is prevented from moving to the top floor. Event MovesUp's guard is changed from $\mathsf{floor} < \mathsf{TOP\_FLOOR}$ to $\mathsf{floor} < \mathsf{TOP\_FLOOR} - 1$.
2. (**Fault 2**) The up requests are not cleared after the door is open. Here the action to clear the up button for floor f, i.e., $\mathsf{up\_buttons} := \mathsf{up\_buttons} \setminus \{\mathsf{floor}\}$, is omitted in the faulty version of event UpButtonCleared.
3. (**Fault 3**) The down requests are ignored by the door, i.e., the door will not open if there is only a down request at a floor. Here, a guard of event DoorClosed2Half is changed from

$$\mathsf{direction} = \mathsf{DOWN} \Rightarrow \mathsf{floor} \in \mathsf{floor\_buttons} \cup \mathsf{down\_buttons}$$

to

$$\text{direction} = \text{DOWN} \Rightarrow \text{floor} \in \text{floor\_buttons}$$

These type of faults are typical in developing system models using Event-B and are *not detected* by verification using invariant proofs. In other words, the models with temporal faults are still fully proved to be consistent with their safety invariants.

In these experiments the manual scenarios found two of the seeded faults. Fault 2 is found by all scenarios, while Fault 3 is found by **Scenario 2** and **Scenario 3**. Since none of the manual scenarios get the lift cabin to the top floor, Fault 1 is not discovered. Nevertheless, our experiment confirms that the scenarios are useful for verifying behaviours of the system, which cannot be directly expressed and verified using invariants. In general, scenarios must also be verified and validated to ensure that they represent desirable behaviours of the system.

4.3 Scenario Generator

In this section, we verify Hypothesis **H3** by comparing the scenarios generated automatically by MoMuT with the manually written scenarios. We use MoMuT as our scenario generator on the model of the lift example. The generator explores a subset of the model's state space and checks where mutations, like exchanged operators or conditions set to a fixed value, cause the externally visible behaviour to differ from the original model. This information is used to build test scenarios that succeed on the original model, but fail on a model containing the mutation.

For the exploration, we tried three strategies: (a) random exploration, (b) exploration using rapidly expanding random trees (RRT) and (c) full exploration up to depth 12 (BFS12). The exploration depth for BFS12 was limited by the memory of the computer we used.

Table 1. Comparison of scenario sets

Scenario set	Fault 1	Fault 2	Fault 3	Coverage	Steps
Manual	No	Yes	Yes	72%	87
Random	Yes	Yes	Yes	63%	305
RRT	Yes	Yes	Yes	67%	204
BFS12	No	Yes	Yes	79%	82

Table 1 shows, for each generation strategy, which of the manually seeded faults was detected, what percentage of the automatically generated model mutation faults were detected and the length in steps of the generated scenarios. A mutant is found when, during the exploration of the model, the modelling element (here the Event-B event) containing the mutant is executed. As a result, the (mutant) coverage criteria is a property of the scenario sets with respect to the formal model.

As can be seen in Table 1, the manual set already achieves a high mutation coverage of 72% of the 616 inserted mutations, and is only outperformed by the BFS12 scenarios, achieving higher coverage (79%) with even fewer steps. Nonetheless, both the manual set and BFS12 fail to catch our first seeded fault, because both do not try to go to the third floor. The scenarios from the two other strategies catch the first seeded fault, but perform less well regarding overall coverage number and coverage achieved in relation to steps needed.

Analysis of the generated scenarios shows that the different groups of scenarios do not subsume each other. Thus, putting all automatically generated scenarios together, an even higher mutation coverage score of 83% can be reached. Although the gap is smaller than expected, the experimental results support Hypothesis **H3**.

Since the overall size of the scenario sets is not too much bigger than the manual scenarios, manual review of the generated scenarios is feasible. Automated reduction of the tests or more optimised generation techniques would improve that even more. Longer random scenarios could increase the fault-finding capacity, but at the cost of review feasibility. The problem with random tests is not only the length of the scenarios. The more random a generated scenario is, the more tiresome it is to work through during acceptance testing, because there is no intention recognisable.

5 Scenario Automation for Event-B/iUML-B

In this section, we present our Cucumber step definitions for Event-B and iUML-B. Cucumber for Event-B/iUML-B allows us to execute the Gherkin scenario directly on the Event-B/iUML-B models.

5.1 Automation: Cucumber for Event-B

'Cucumber for Event-B' allows Cucumber to execute Gherkin scenarios on an Event-B model. It is a collection of step definitions which defines a traversal of the Event-B state space. Below we intersperse the Gherkin step definitions with comments to explain how to interpret them.

Given *machine with* "≪formula≫"

// Setup constants with the given constraints and initialize the machine.

When *fire event* "≪name≫" *with* "≪formula≫"

// Fire the given event with the given parameter constraints.

Then *event* "≪name≫" *with* "≪formula≫" *is enabled*

// Check if the given event with the given parameter constraints is enabled.

Then *event* "≪name≫" *with* "≪formula≫" *is disabled*

// Check if the given event with the given parameter constraints is disabled.

Then *formula* "≪formula≫" *is TRUE*

// Check if the given formula evaluates to TRUE.

Then *formula* "≪formula≫" *is FALSE*

// Check if the given formula evaluates to FALSE.

An essential property of acceptance tests is reproducibility. Therefore all step definitions check whether the specified event can be unambiguously chosen (using given parameters constraints). The user should make sure that the tested machine is deterministic and, if not, refine it further. Also abstract constants may lead to non-reproducible tests; however, they do not need to be specified by the model refinement, but can also be provided by the test case as test data.

The scenario to test the functionality of a single-shaft lift system in Listing 1 can be rewritten for the Event-B model as shown in Listing 2.

```
Scenario: Press the DOWN button

Given machine with "TopFloor = 3"
When fire event "DownButtonPresses" with "f = 2"
Then formula "2 : down_buttons" is TRUE
And event "MotorWinds" is enabled
And event "DoorClosed2Half" is disabled

When fire event "MotorWinds"
Then formula "motor = WINDING" is TRUE
And event "MovesUp" is enabled
And event "DoorClosed2Half" is disabled

When fire event "MovesUp"
Then formula "floor = 1" is TRUE
And event "MovesUp" is enabled
```

Listing 2. Test scenario using plain step definitions

Such an acceptance test is fairly straightforward in terms of syntax but is couched in terms of the relatively low-level formalism of Event-B. Domain engineers are often more used to higher-level modelling representations such as UML. In Sect. 5.2 we go further towards meeting the BDD approach which advocates minimising the language barriers between domain and system engineers.

5.2 Cucumber for iUML-B

Cucumber for iUML-B provides a Gherkin syntax based on the iUML-B diagrammatic modelling notation. iUML-B class diagrams and state-machines resemble the equivalent notations of UML and should feel more familiar for domain engineers. For the multi-shaft lift example, we have used iUML-B class diagrams to illustrate scenario testing of behaviour 'lifted' to a set of instances (i.e. a class). Although not shown here, Cucumber for iUML-B also supports scenario testing of state-machines including state-machines that are owned (i.e. contained) by a class in a class diagram.

Cucumber for iUML-B consists of iUML-B based step definitions which are translated into the corresponding underlying Event-B model elements for execution. Clearly, the translation of Cucumber for iUML-B scenarios must match the corresponding translation of the actual target model under test. Therefore Cucumber for iUML-B must access attributes of the iUML-B model in order to infer the proper Event-B events and variables and to derive implicit event parameters (e.g. 'self name' representing the class instance).

Cucumber for Class Diagrams. The following Gherkin syntax is be defined for validating class diagrams.

Given *class* "≪name≫:≪inst≫"
  // Preset the given class with the given instance.
When *call method* "≪name≫" *with* "≪formula≫"
  // Call the given class instance method.
Then *method* "≪name≫" *with* "≪formula≫" *is enabled*
  // Check if the given class instance method is enabled.
Then *method* "≪name≫" *with* "≪formula≫" *is disabled*
  // Check if the given class instance method is disabled.
Then *attribute* "≪attr≫" *is* "≪value≫"
  // Check if the given class instance attribute is equal to the given value.
Then *association* "≪assoc≫" *is* "≪value≫"
  // Check if the given class instance association is equal to the given value.

In general, class attributes and associations can be any binary relation (i.e., not necessarily functional), hence further checks can be defined accordingly.

Multi-shaft Lift System in iUML-B Class Diagrams. Figure 3 represents the class diagram of the lift requests, before introducing the motor and door behaviour. Class Bldg_Lift is a constant representing the lift cabins in a building. Each lift has two attributes lift_status and lift_direction to indicate whether the lift is moving or not and the lift direction (up/down). Floors is a constant representing the different floors in a building.

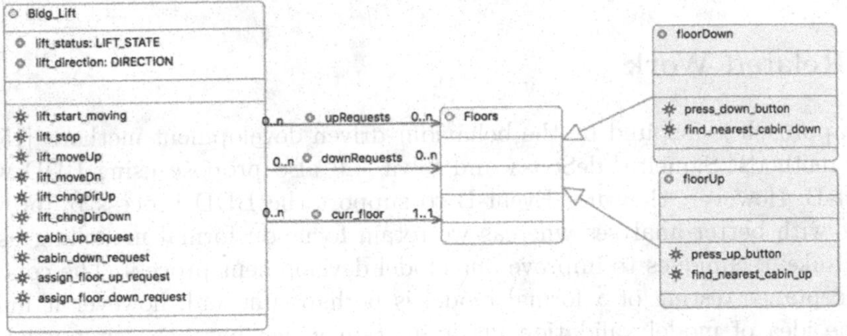

Fig. 3. iUML-B class diagram of the multi shaft lift: requests

The associations upRequests and downRequests between the Bldg_Lift and Floors are variables that represent the floors to be served by the lift, and whether they are above or below the current position of the lift, while curr_floor represents the current floor position of the lift. floorUp and floorDown are variable sets of type Floors, that respectively represent floor up and down requests, these requests are generated by the events press_up_button and press_down_button. At this stage the floor requests are not assigned to a specific lift, once the controller finds the nearest serving lift (find_nearest_cabin_up, find_nearest_cabin_down), these requests will be assigned to the nearest lift in the Bldg_Lift events assign_floor_up_request and assign_floor_down_request. The Bldg_Lift has other local events e.g. cabin_up_request, lift_move_up etc.

The Scenario of Listing 3 tests the action of requesting a floor from within a cabin of the multi-shaft lift system modelled in Fig. 3. Note that we use *with* "«formula»" to instantiate the additional parameter f to specify the requested floor for the given building lift L1.

Scenario: *Request cabin floor*

Given *class* "Bldg_Lift:L1"
Then *method* "cabin_up_request" *with* "f = 1" *is enabled*
And *method* "cabin_down_request" *with* "f = 1" *is disabled*
And *attribute* "lift_status" *is* "STATIONARY"
And *attribute* "lift_direction" *is* "UP"

When *call method* "cabin_up_request" *with* "f = 1"
Then *association* "upRequests" *is* "{1}"
And *method* "lift_start_moving" *is enabled*

When *call method* "lift_start_moving"
Then *attribute* "lift_status" *is* "MOVING"

Listing 3. Test scenario for iUML-B class diagram

6 Related Work

Our approach is inspired by the behaviour-driven development methods [15] of agile methods. Siqueira, deSousa and Silva [14] also propose using BDD with Event-B. However, they use Event-B to support the BDD process by providing it with better analyses whereas we retain focus on formal modelling using 'BDD-like' techniques to improve our model development process. The concept of acceptance testing of a formal model is perhaps unusual, however it builds on the idea of model validation via animation which has been supported for some time particularly in Event-B, with tools such as ProB [11] and BMotion Studio [10,12]. Acceptance testing is a more specific use of such validation tools where the goal is not only to validate the model but to allow the end-user or similar stakeholder to assess and accept the model as suitable for their needs.

7 Conclusion

We have developed an approach to formal modelling based on ideas from Behaviour Driven Development. We use scenarios to drive the formal model construction, verification and acceptance. We have shown how to enhance Cucumber in order to apply the acceptance tests written in the Gherkin language to the Event-B formal model and also to a model formulated using iUML-B notation. For efficient coverage we use a model-mutation based test case generator to generate scenarios for acceptance testing. Our experiments support the ideas but were somewhat neutral in the case of H1: 'scenarios help to improve the validity of the model'. Further experiments will be carried out in this area on larger and less familiar applications where tacit knowledge is less likely to confound results. For example a different modeller could develop a new feature to assess whether scenarios help to identify the scope of impact of the change in a situation where the style of the overall model is already fixed. We would also like to explore the relationship between scenario testing and verification of temporal properties such as 'does the lift eventually reach a requested floor'. This could be explored in relation to 'lifted' behaviours such as found in the multi-shaft lift where we might want to examine local liveness properties of classes. The test case generation, while having greater coverage than the manually written scenarios, did miss part of the seeded bugs depending on the selected search strategy. We believe this can be addressed by tuning the MoMuT tools and will carry out further work and experiments in this area. Our prototype tool can be found under https://github.com/tofische/cucumber-event-b. Further work is needed to develop the methods and tools to support the use of Cucumber for iUML-B. Our next applications will be in the railway domain on the Hybrid ERTMS/ETCS Level 3 [8] and in the avionics domain on an aircraft turn-around security authentication system, which are real industrial applications.

Acknowledgements. This work has been conducted within the ENABLE-S3 project that has received funding from the ECSEL Joint Undertaking under Grant Agreement no. 692455. This Joint Undertaking receives support from the European Unions HORIZON 2020 research and innovation programme and Austria, Denmark, Germany, Finland, Czech Republic, Italy, Spain, Portugal, Poland, Ireland, Belgium, France, Netherlands, United Kingdom, Slovakia, Norway.

ENABLE-S3 is funded by the Austrian Federal Ministry of Transport, Innovation and Technology (BMVIT) under the program "ICT of the Future" between May 2016 and April 2019. More information is at https://iktderzukunft.at/en/.

We also thank Thorsten Tarrach (Austrian Institute of Technology, Vienna, Austria) for his assistance with MoMuT.

References

1. Abrial, J.R.: Modeling in Event-B: System and Software Engineering. Cambridge University Press, Cambridge (2010)
2. Abrial, J.R., Butler, M., Hallerstede, S., Hoang, T.S., Mehta, F., Voisin, L.: Rodin: an open toolset for modelling and reasoning in Event-B. Softw. Tools Technol. Transf. **12**(6), 447–466 (2010)

3. Back, R.J.R., Sere, K.: Stepwise refinement of action systems. In: van de Snepscheut, J.L.A. (ed.) MPC 1989. LNCS, vol. 375, pp. 115–138. Springer, Heidelberg (1989). https://doi.org/10.1007/3-540-51305-1_7
4. Dghyam, D., Hoang, T.S., Snook, C.: Requirements document, scenarios, and models for lift examples, May 2018. https://doi.org/10.5258/SOTON/D0604
5. Dijkstra, E.W.: Guarded commands, nondeterminacy and formal derivation of programs. Commun. ACM **18**(8), 453–457 (1975)
6. Fellner, A., Krenn, W., Schlick, R., Tarrach, T., Weissenbacher, G.: Model-based, mutation-driven test case generation via heuristic-guided branching search. In: Proceedings of the 15th ACM-IEEE International Conference on Formal Methods and Models for System Design, pp. 56–66. ACM (2017)
7. Hoang, T.S.: An introduction to the Event-B modelling method. In: Romanovsky, A., Thomas, M. (eds.) Industrial Deployment of System Engineering Methods, pp. 211–236. Springer, Heidelberg (2013). https://doi.org/10.1007/978-3-642-33170-1
8. Hoang, T.S., Butler, M., Reichl, K.: The hybrid ERTMS/ETCS level 3 case study. In: Butler, M., Raschke, A., Hoang, T.S., Reichl, K. (eds.) ABZ 2018. LNCS, vol. 10817, pp. 251–261. Springer, Cham (2018). https://doi.org/10.1007/978-3-319-91271-4_17
9. Krenn, W., Schlick, R., Aichernig, B.K.: Mapping UML to labeled transition systems for test-case generation. In: de Boer, F.S., Bonsangue, M.M., Hallerstede, S., Leuschel, M. (eds.) FMCO 2009. LNCS, vol. 6286, pp. 186–207. Springer, Heidelberg (2010). https://doi.org/10.1007/978-3-642-17071-3_10
10. Ladenberger, L., Bendisposto, J., Leuschel, M.: Visualising Event-B models with B-motion studio. In: Alpuente, M., Cook, B., Joubert, C. (eds.) FMICS 2009. LNCS, vol. 5825, pp. 202–204. Springer, Heidelberg (2009). https://doi.org/10.1007/978-3-642-04570-7_17
11. Leuschel, M., Butler, M.: ProB: an automated analysis toolset for the B method. Softw. Tools Technol. Transf. (STTT) **10**(2), 185–203 (2008)
12. Ladenberger, L.: BMotion studio for ProB project website, January 2016. http://stups.hhu.de/ProB/w/BMotion_Studio
13. Said, M.Y., Butler, M., Snook, C.: A method of refinement in UML-B. Softw. Syst. Model. **14**(4), 1557–1580 (2015). https://doi.org/10.1007/s10270-013-0391-z
14. Siqueira, F.L., de Sousa, T.C., Silva, P.S.M.: Using BDD and SBVR to refine business goals into an Event-B model: a research idea. In: 2017 IEEE/ACM 5th International FME Workshop on Formal Methods in Software Engineering (FormaliSE), pp. 31–36, May 2017
15. Smart, J.F.: BDD in Action: Behavior-Driven Development for the Whole Software Life cycle. Manning Publications Company, Shelter Island (2014)
16. Snook, C., Butler, M.: UML-B: formal modeling and design aided by UML. ACM Trans. Softw. Eng. Methodol. **15**(1), 92–122 (2006). https://doi.org/10.1145/1125808.1125811
17. Solis, C., Wang, X.: A study of the characteristics of behaviour driven development. In: 2011 37th EUROMICRO Conference on Software Engineering and Advanced Applications, pp. 383–387, August 2011
18. Wynne, M., Hellesøy, A.: The Cucumber Book: Behaviour-Driven Development for Testers and Developers. Pragmatic Programmers LLC, Raleigh (2012)

The Foul Adversary: Formal Models

Naipeng Dong[1(✉)] and Tim Muller[2]

[1] National University of Singapore, Singapore, Singapore
dcsdn@nus.edu.sg
[2] University of Oxford, Oxford, UK

Abstract. In classical notions of privacy in computer security, users attempt to keep their data private. A user that is bribed, extorted or blackmailed (i.e., *coerced*) may not do so. To get a general model of coercion, we strengthen the Dolev-Yao adversary with the ability to coerce others, to the *foul adversary*. We show that, depending on the setting, subtly different abilities should be assigned to the adversary – whereas existing approaches are one-size-fits-all. The variations of the foul adversary are formalised and we provide a hierarchical relation in their strength. We further interpret the adversary models using several examples.

1 Introduction

Privacy is increasingly important in Internet-based services. A new privacy notion - *enforced privacy* - arose, which assumes users reveal private information due to *coercion*, e.g., bribery or extortion [14]. Vote-buying, bribed doctors and rigged auctions are real-life examples of voters/doctors/bidders revealing information that should be private, which harm the system's desired properties e.g., fairness [12,15,17]. In domains like e-voting, e-auction and e-health, coercion must be prevented [3,10,20]; the systems should enforce a user's privacy even when the user reveals his private information. The basic idea is that if a system provides a way for the coerced user to mislead the attacker, then the adversary cannot distinguish whether the provided information is true, and thus the system enforces privacy of the user [12,16,24]. Note that bribed, extorted or blackmailed users differ from compromised users (e.g., [5]) - a coerced user is assumed to lie to the attacker if possible whereas a compromised user is an extension of the attacker, and thus totally controlled by the attacker.

There are cryptographic protocols that ensure enforced privacy [3,10,20,26,27]. As the design of cryptographic protocols is well-known to be error-prone and flaws in such protocols are often subtle and counter-intuitive, formal verification is an important step before implementation. There are multiple ways to formalise enforced privacy. Currently, a standard method (proposed by Benaloh and Tuinstra [6] and later symbolically formalised by Delaune et al. [12]) is to encode a privacy property as the formal equivalent of "even if the user gives up his private information, the (Dolev-Yao [13]) adversary cannot be sure that this

J. Sun and M. Sun (Eds.): ICFEM 2018, LNCS 11232, pp. 37–53, 2018.
https://doi.org/10.1007/978-3-030-02450-5_3

really is his private information". This method does not generalise to security properties other than privacy. We propose an alternative method, which is to keep the security/privacy property unaltered ("the adversary cannot know the user's private information"), but to verify it under an adversary that has the power to coerce; the *foul* adversary.

Our approach philosophically differs from the existing approaches. The existing approaches enhance the security requirements (privacy becomes enforced privacy) of the system in question. Our approach is the first to allow reasoning about coercion even in absence of a concrete security system or protocol. We give the attacker the ability to (try to) coerce whenever he desires. Like any attacker, he has the capability of reasoning about his knowledge, and inserting it into a protocol; the only difference is that there may now be coerced data in his knowledge. Our approach is rooted in similar formal techniques, meaning automated verification is also feasible.

The main advantage of the standard method [12] is that it already has some tool support (e.g., ProVerif [7]), and there are various case-studies using the method [4,15,17]. The advantages of our proposed method are: (1) it generalises to security properties other than privacy, (2) it allows a greater degree of fine-tuning, and (3) it makes the assumptions of coercion explicit. To illustrate why it pays to have assumptions explicit: The voting protocol in [12] makes an implicit assumption that it suffices to keep the vote of the user enforced private. However, as Küsters et al. [24] point out, the fact that a person voted at all may need to be enforced private. Küsters et al. [24] have an alternative proposal for enforced privacy. We discuss both methodologies in Sect. 2.

To motivate our alternative approach to coercion, take a frivolous example (more technical and relevant examples are given later) where residents are to be protected against potentially violent burglars. At a burglary, a burglar may threaten a resident to enter a code to disable the alarm. A duress code (or panic code) is a code that disables the sirens and lights, making it appear the alarm is disabled, but in reality notifies the police that a burglar is coercing a resident. When the system ensures that the residents have the code, then the alarm is coercion resistant[1] [8]. The precise details matter when the system allows cases where the residents never received the duress code, or where the residents never configured the duress code. We refer to this issue as the user knowledge aspect, as the crucial question is whether it is sufficient when a user could know something, or whether he actually needs to know it. Moreover, if the burglars are sufficiently notorious, then residents may forgo using their duress code, as they fear retribution from the burglar even after their arrest. We refer to this issue as the dynamics aspect, as the crucial question is how potential futures

[1] Or at least somewhat coercion resistant. If the burglar is aware of the existence of a duress code, he could elicit two codes that turn off the alarm, knowing that one of the two must be the real code, and decrease the odds of a silent alarm from 100% to 50%. A burglar would typically still be deterred with a 50% probability of a silent alarm going off. We do not further investigate probabilistic scenarios.

influence the present. The user knowledge aspect and the dynamics aspect are orthogonal issues, which can be individually fine-tuned in our approach.

Contributions. We formalise and investigate a family of adversaries – *foul adversaries* – that extend the Dolev-Yao adversary with the ability to coerce. There are two orthogonal aspects that determine the strength of the foul adversaries, the user knowledge aspect (weak or strong) and the dynamic aspect (static, conservative, aggressive or extended). We prove a hierarchy of these 8 (2×4) different foul adversaries, and illustrate the foul adversaries using practical examples.

Paper Organization. In Sect. 2, we introduce the context of our approach. In Sect. 3, we define the core of our foul adversary in the form of knowledge and reasoning. In Sect. 4, we introduce the notion of security systems and further formalise the variants of the foul adversary. Then we introduce examples to illustrate our approach and to concretely link it to security systems, in Sect. 5. Finally, we conclude in Sect. 6.

2 Coercion

Coercion involves an adversary forcing a user to say (or do) something against their will. However, unlike a controlled user, these coerced users may say (or do) something else without the adversary noticing. All definitions explicitly deal with the fact that users only actually say (or do) what the adversary demands when the adversary can distinguish if the user does not comply.

Currently, there is research on coercion in the literature and defending against coercion in protocol design. We discuss these approaches and their successes below, in *Existing Methods.* The approaches have in common that they see coercion as part of the security requirements. In *Foul Adversary,* we discuss the exact differences resulting from making coercion part of the adversary's abilities.

Existing Methods. The requirement to prevent coercion was first proposed in e-voting systems [6]. Cryptographic e-voting protocols have been proposed to meet this requirement (e.g., [26,27]). To formally verify these protocols, formalisations of enforced privacy in e-voting were proposed to capture the requirements, for instance quantitative receipt-freeness and coercion-resistance [22], coercion-resistance in game-based provable security style [25], coercion-resistance using epistemic approach [24], and receipt-free and coercion-resistance using process algebras, e.g., in the applied pi calculus [10] and in CSP [21]. Later, the enforced privacy requirements have been found in other domains, such as e-auctions [3] and e-health [10]. Formalisations of enforced privacy properties in e-auctions and e-health have also been proposed, following the framework in the applied pi calculus [15,17,22]. Thus, systems wherein coercion may occur are a growing phenomenon, occurring in many new security domains.

The definition of enforced privacy by Delaune et al. [11] is particularly influential, as it is the first symbolic formal definition of enforced privacy that is generalised over protocols. The definition, however, did not generalise nicely over different domains, as it was specifically intended for e-voting. Voters may be bribed to vote for a certain candidate, and receive benefits only if they can prove that they voted for that candidate. Thus, it is not sufficient that the adversary cannot invade your privacy and obtain a proof of your vote, but the protocol must prevent users from providing the proof to the adversary.

Assume that there is a user that honestly forwards all data honestly and correctly to the adversary. Presumably the user's privacy is broken if he actually does this. If there exists an alternative behaviour for the user, that looks exactly the same to the adversary but now it does not break the user's privacy, then the user can "cheat" the adversary. By behaving in the alternative way, the user does not break its privacy, but the adversary cannot tell that the user is not being honest. Therefore, the user cannot prove that it broke its own privacy, and the adversary has no reason to believe that the user actually broke his own privacy. When this is the case, Delaune et al. say that enforced privacy holds. As pointed out by Backes et al. [4] and Küsters et al. [24], the definition by Delaune et al. does not capture certain protocols (such as [23,26]) and certain attacks (abstention attacks). To tackle the problem, Backes et al. [4] improved the definition. However, these definitions depend on specific protocol structures (as pointed out by Küsters et al. [24]). Küsters et al. [24] proposed a more general epistemic definition following the same basic idea. This approach requires reasoning on voter's goals and strategies. In addition, the above mentioned work focuses on a specific domain - e-voting.

Foul Adversary. We have the following assumption: Users only want to cooperate with the foul adversary when it is impossible to merely pretend to cooperate. This is a high-level assumption shared by all of the variations of the foul adversary model (and shared by the existing enforced properties [4,12,15,17]). The exact meaning of that abstract assumption is difficult to pin down. In fact, we argue that the precise interpretation depends on the context, and that a variety of models is necessary.

Another assumption is a standard assumption, namely that a system is secure if and only if no attacker can perform an attack. This means that we can ignore, without loss of generality, those attackers that are strictly weaker than some other attackers. Concretely, we can ignore attackers that coerce at the wrong time, for the wrong data, or do not realise they can coerce for data. For example, a foul adversary may not know whether a user knows some coercible data, but choose to try to coerce anyway, and gain knowledge if the user does (and punish unfairly if he does not).

There are two aspects on which we divide the foul adversaries: On the requirements for a user to cheat, and on the role of time in coercion. First, we use the duress code example from the introduction to illustrate the first aspect. Then, we introduce an informal example to illustrate the time aspect (see Sect. 5.1). We formalise the distinctions between the foul adversaries in the following sections.

3 Knowledge

In modern formalisms (such as Tamarin [29], the applied pi calculus [2], etc.), for the analysis of security properties under the Dolev-Yao adversary, it is possible but not necessary to reason explicitly about the knowledge of users (or even about users at all). Here, we explicitly model the users and their knowledge, to make the assumptions explicit.

Moreover, the fact that we explicitly reason about adversary knowledge is a core concept in our approach. We argue that some subtleties simply cannot be captured by a model that does not take knowledge into account. In this section, we create a model of knowledge and reasoning using coercion. We do not take learning (dynamic knowledge) into account, until Sect. 4. Our model of knowledge is similar to other definitions in symbolic security (e.g., [9,29]).

3.1 Preliminaries

A common way to reason about knowledge is epistemic modal logic [19]. However, an epistemic agent has perfect reasoning capabilities, allowing him to solve computationally hard problems. The (Dolev-Yao or foul) adversary is not capable of solving computationally hard problems. Hence, in the context of security protocol modelling, we need an alternative model of knowledge. We take Cortier and Kremer [9]'s model of the Dolev-Yao knowledge and reasoning as our starting point. In their model, a user knows something iff he can derive it from one of the facts in his core knowledge.

We adopt a symbolic approach [2,13,29], meaning that we adopt the ideal properties of the cryptographic primitives. Messages that a user and an adversary know can be modelled as the following (e.g. in [2,9]):

- There exists a countable set of *names* $\mathcal{N}$, an countable set of *variables* $\mathcal{V}$, and a countable set of *signatures* Σ – a set of function symbols with arities.
- A *term* in $\mathcal{T}(\mathcal{N}, \mathcal{V}, \Sigma)$ is either a name from $\mathcal{N}$, a variable from $\mathcal{V}$, or $\mathsf{f}(M_1, \ldots, M_n)$ where f is an n-ary function in Σ and all M_i $(0 \le i \le n)$ are terms in $\mathcal{T}(\mathcal{N}, \mathcal{V}, \Sigma)$.
- The variables in a term M are denoted by $\delta(M)$. A term is *ground* when $\delta(M) = \emptyset$. Ground terms are called *data* and denoted as $\mathcal{T}(\mathcal{N}, \Sigma)$. Replacing a variable x in term M with a ground term d is an *instantiation*, denoted by $M\{d/x\}$. We use θ to represent instantiation of a set of variables, $\delta(\theta)$ to denote the variables, and $\varphi(\theta)$ to denote the data to replace the variables[2].
- Properties of cryptographic primitives are captured by an *equational theory* E, where E is a set of equations of terms of the form $M =_E N$, where $M, N \in \mathcal{T}(\mathcal{N}, \mathcal{V}, \Sigma)$.

The derivation rules are provided by an axiomatization, such as found in [30] and in [1,9]. We axiomatize the reasoning of the users (the Dolev-Yao adversary

[2] Only our notion of instantiation differs from the standard, as we disallow names to be substituted, and we disallow variables to be substituted into a formula.

$$A\frac{x \in X}{X \vdash x} \quad B\frac{X \vdash y \quad x =_E y}{X \vdash x} \quad F\frac{X \vdash x_0, \ldots, x_n \quad f \in \Sigma}{X \vdash f(x_0, \ldots, x_n)}$$

Fig. 1. Standard knowledge reasoning rules.

in particular) with the rules in Fig. 1. We may refer to axiom A as the axiom of core knowledge, to axiom B as the axiom of equality and to axiom F as the axiom of function application. If there exists a derivation with premise X and conclusion y under axioms A, B and F, and a specified equational theory E, then we may write $X \vdash_{DY} y$. The statement $X \vdash_{DY} y$ means that an agent with core knowledge X has y in his knowledge. $\vdash_{DY}$ models the reasoning ability of the Dolev-Yao adversary. Let $\mathcal{X}$ be a set of sets of knowledge, and Y be a set of knowledge, we may write $\mathcal{X} \vdash_{DY} Y$ to mean $\forall_{y \in Y} \exists_{X \in \mathcal{X}} (X \vdash_{DY} y)$.

3.2 Weak Coercion

As mentioned before, one of the two aspects on which we distinguish the adversary's power, is user knowledge. The distinction between the weak and strong variants is that the former uses weak coercion, and the latter uses strong coercion. The definitions of weak coercion and strong coercion are similar, but weak coercion is simpler. Here, we define weak coercion, and in Sect. 3.3 we show how strong coercion differs.

Weak coercion is based on a notion of verifiability and a notion of elicitation. Given an equation which can only be satisfied with data d, then d is called verifiable under that equation. Elicitation models obtaining information by coercion. In particular, if d is verifiable under an equation that the foul adversary can construct, and a user has d, then the foul adversary can ask the user to provide d, which he must provide as the foul adversary can verify it. Elicitation is modelled as a derivation rule, where the adversary elicits data whenever necessary.

Verifiability. Verifiability is a property of data. For example, if you receive a hashed message, then there is only one original message that would give you that hash (assuming an idealised hash function without collision). In this case, we say that the original message is verifiable under the hashed message. More precisely, let the hashed message be $h(m)$ and m the original, then the equation $h(x) =_E h(m)$ can only be satisfied when $x =_E m$. Thus $h(x)\theta =_E h(m)\theta$ holds, only if θ replaces x by m (note that m is not a variable, and cannot be instantiated). This forms the basis of the definition.

We obtain the following formal definition of verifiability of D (a set of data) under two given terms M, N:

$$V^{M,N}(D) \text{ iff } \exists_{\theta:\varphi(\theta)=D \wedge M\theta =_E N\theta} \left(\nexists_{\theta':\delta(\theta')=\delta(\theta) \wedge D \neq_E \varphi(\theta')} (M\theta' =_E N\theta') \right).$$

The formula states that D is verifiable under M, N, when there exists an instantiation θ (of D onto variables that occur in M, N), such that M and N are

$$C\frac{\mathcal{C}_{\mathbf{K}}(D),\ A \vdash_{DY} M,\ A \vdash_{DY} N,\ V^{M,N}(D)}{(A, \mathbf{K}) \vdash_{\xi} D}$$

Fig. 2. Knowledge reasoning rule concerning elicitation.

equivalent and there is no instantiation θ' (of other data than D onto the same variables) that equates M and N. Thus, if the user is challenged to give the correct data to equate M and N, then the user cannot provide any other data than D (or data that equates to D)[3].

Elicitation. The foul adversary can gain knowledge by coercion – elicitation. A set of data D is elicitable if the coercible users can derive it (i.e., when the users *know* it). Formally, given the set of core knowledge $\mathbf{K}$ of coercible users, that a set of data D is elicitable (denoted as $\mathcal{C}_{\mathbf{K}}(D)$) is defined as:

$$\mathcal{C}_{\mathbf{K}}(D) \text{ iff } \forall d \in D, \exists_{K \in \mathbf{K}}(K \vdash_{DY} d).$$

When D is elicitable and the adversary can derive some terms under which D is verifiable, then the user has no choice but to provide D truthfully. This is the intuition behind the elicitation rule, which is modelled as a derivation rule, meaning that elicitation is just a way for the adversary to gain knowledge.

Since the question of whether D is elicitable depends on the knowledge of the users, it is unavoidable that the elicitation rule does not merely depend on the adversary's (core) knowledge. The premises of elicitation are the core knowledges of the users, and the core knowledge of the adversary. If the adversary can construct terms M, N, such that data d is verifiable under M, N, then the adversary can coerce d from users that know the data d. This is directly codified in the coercion rule, in Fig. 2.

In Fig. 2, $\mathcal{C}_{\mathbf{K}}(D)$ ensures that D can actually be provided by the coerced users, $A \vdash_{DY} M$ (or N) ensures that the adversary can actually construct two terms M (or N) from his core knowledge A – note that he uses variables here – and finally $V^{M,N}(D)$ ensures that misrepresenting D is impossible for the coerced users. Then the adversary with knowledge A can coerce the users with knowledge $\mathbf{K}$ for data D. Note that as mentioned in Sect. 2, to coerce for d, the adversary need not know that the coerced user knows d.

3.3 Strong Coercion

Strong coercion is highly similar to weak coercion. The verification rule is liberalised, and some data which is not verifiable in weak coercion may now be

[3] The domain of θ has not been restricted in the formula. Note that we can add a condition $\delta(\theta) \subseteq \delta(M) \cup \delta(N)$ without loss of generality. If there were a variable $x \in \delta(\theta), x \notin \delta(M) \cup \delta(N)$, then $M\theta =_E N\theta$ implies $M\theta' =_E N\theta'$, for all θ' that are equal to θ except on where x maps to. In that case, the condition $\nexists \ldots$ is trivially false. Therefore, we can limit our θ to those with only variables also in M or N.

$$C_s \frac{\mathcal{C}_{\mathbf{K}}(D),\ A \vdash_{DY} M,\ A \vdash_{DY} N,\ V_{\mathbf{K}}^{M,N}(D)}{(A, \mathbf{K}) \vdash_{\zeta_s} D}$$

Fig. 3. Knowledge reasoning rule concerning strong coercion.

verifiable. The verification rule now takes into account the core knowledge(s) of the user(s) that need to cheat the adversary. If the users do not actually know the data needed to cheat the adversary, then they cannot cheat the adversary, meaning the data remains verifiable.

More precisely, data D may not be verifiable under M, N, due to the existence of some $D' \neq_E D$ that fits the same equation. In reality, the existence of such D' may not help the user, if he is unable to construct it. For example, if $h(k) =_E h(k')$, then the adversary, who saw the hash $h(k)$, may construct $M = h(k)$ and $N = h(x)$, and is not able to coerce for k this way, since k' satisfies the equation too. However, if the user cannot actually derive k', then he still has no choice but to provide k to satisfy the equation. In this section, we make minimal changes to weak coercion to obtain strong coercion.

Verifiability. Using the notion of instantiation, we obtain the formal definition of verifiability of D under M, N for coerced users with core knowledges $\mathbf{K}$:

$$V_{\mathbf{K}}^{M,N}(D) \text{ iff } \exists_{\theta:\varphi(\theta)=D \wedge M\theta =_E N\theta} \left(\nexists_{\theta':\delta(\theta')=\delta(\theta) \wedge D \neq_E \varphi(\theta')} \left(\mathbf{K} \vdash_{DY} \varphi(\theta') \wedge M\theta' =_E N\theta' \right) \right).$$

Strong verifiability is identical to weak verifiability, except for the additional expression $\mathbf{K} \vdash_{DY} \varphi(\theta')$ in the not-exists, which expresses the additional requirement that the user actually knows how to construct the deception.

Proposition 1. *$V^{M,N}(D)$ implies $V_{\mathbf{K}}^{M,N}(D)$.*

Proof. If θ' exists in strong verifiability, then it exists in weak verifiability.

Elicitation. Strong coercion is a simple adaptation from weak coercion, where we use strong verifiability rather than weak verifiability; see Fig. 3.

4 Behaviour

In this section, we use a crude model of the dynamics of the systems. We assert that all users follow some protocol, which determines what actions they may perform. The adversary can also perform actions, depending on his knowledge. The effect of the actions is deterministic, meaning that the consequences of an action are fixed. This allows us to use the extensive form (explicit) representation of a system, where traces and states are equivalent notions. We formalise this representation in Sect. 4.1.

In Sect. 4.2, we introduce the four variations of the dynamic aspect: static, conservative, aggressive and extended foul adversaries. We show the relationships between the different adversaries that we have introduced, in Sect. 4.3.

4.1 Preliminaries

A system is $(S, \mathcal{A}, \mathcal{I}, s^0, U, \mathsf{K}_0)$ where S is a set of states, $\mathcal{A}$ is a set of actions of the form $\mathsf{keyword}(u, v, d)$ where $\mathsf{keyword} \in \{\mathsf{public}, \mathsf{private}, \mathsf{block}, \mathsf{insert}\}$, u is the (alleged) sender, v is the (alleged) receiver, $d : \mathcal{T}(\mathcal{N}, \mathcal{V}, \Sigma)$ is the communicated data, $\mathcal{I} : S \times \mathcal{A} \times S$ is a deterministic[4] set of transitions forming a tree[5], s^0 is the initial state at the root of the tree, U is a set of users (coerced users $U_{\mathcal{C}}$ are a subset of U) and $\mathsf{K}_0 : U \cup \{e\} \to \wp(\mathcal{T}(\mathcal{N}, \mathcal{V}, \Sigma))$ is an assignment of initial core knowledge to the users. As a consequence of this definition, every state is uniquely identified by the sequence of actions leading to it. Hence, we may simply write $[a_1, \ldots, a_n]$ to refer to the state s_n which has the property that $s^0 \xrightarrow{a_1} s_1, \ldots, s_{n-1} \xrightarrow{a_n} s_n$.

Users behave according to some protocol specification, which dictates their actions. Users can send $\mathsf{s}(w, d)$ and receive $\mathsf{r}(w, d)$ public messages d to/from w, and send $\mathsf{ps}(w, d)$ and receive $\mathsf{pr}(w, d)$ privately messages d to/from w under certain circumstances. Users do not introduce variables, only terms, if a user sends a variable, it is a variable it received by the adversary. Let $\pi_u(s)$ be a projection of the global state to the user state, and let $\rho^s_u(a)$ mean that action a is enabled at user state $\pi_u(s)$. A transition

- $s \xrightarrow{\mathsf{public}(u,v,\tau)} t$ exists iff $\rho^s_u(\mathsf{s}(v, \tau))$, $\rho^s_v(\mathsf{r}(u, \tau))$,
- $s \xrightarrow{\mathsf{private}(u,v,\tau)} t$ exists iff $\rho^s_u(\mathsf{ps}(v, \tau))$, $\rho^s_v(\mathsf{pr}(u, \tau))$,
- $s \xrightarrow{\mathsf{block}(u,v,\tau)} t$ exists iff $\rho^s_u(\mathsf{s}(v, \tau))$, and
- $s \xrightarrow{\mathsf{insert}(u,v,\tau)} t$ exists iff $\rho^s_v(\mathsf{r}(u, \tau))$ and the adversary knows τ with $\tau \in \mathcal{T}(\mathcal{N}, \mathcal{V}, \Sigma)$ (That the adversary knows τ is later formally defined as a series of $s \Vdash \tau$ distinguished by the superscripts of $\Vdash$ which depends on the adversary model).

Thus, in the extensive form representation, a private communication can happen only if both parties can privately communicate. Similarly for public communication. However, in addition, the adversary can block a public communication – pretending to be the receiver – or insert a public communication (provided the adversary knows the content of the communication) – pretending to be the sender. These are standard assumptions in the Dolev-Yao model, which is our starting point.

At every state, the users and the adversary have some knowledge. The knowledge consists of a core knowledge, and the ability to reason. We define $\kappa^u(s)$ as a function that gives the core knowledge of u in state s.

- $\kappa^u(s^0) = \mathsf{K}_0(u)$, for all users;
- $\kappa^v(t) = \kappa^v(s) \cup \{\tau\}$ when $s \xrightarrow{\mathsf{public}(u,v,\tau)} t$, $s \xrightarrow{\mathsf{private}(u,v,\tau)} t$ or $s \xrightarrow{\mathsf{insert}(u,v,\tau)} t$;

[4] Given state s and action a, there is at most one state t such that $s \xrightarrow{a} t$.

[5] Due to knowledge monotonicity, it is important that the system is represented in the extensive form of a tree (potentially infinite).

- $\kappa^e(t) = \kappa^e(s) \cup \{\tau\}$ when $s \xrightarrow{\mathsf{public}(u,v,\tau)} t$ or $s \xrightarrow{\mathsf{block}(u,v,\tau)} t$; and
- $\kappa^v(t) = \kappa^v(s)$ for all other users.

Due to the fact that we use extensive form representation, we have uniquely defined the knowledge of all users in all states. We write $\xrightarrow{a}_{\mathsf{D}}$ if the message in a is data; i.e. if it does not contain variables.

4.2 Formal Models of Foul Adversaries

Here we introduce the static, conservative, aggressive and extended foul adversaries, that differ in how they treat the dynamic aspect.

Static Foul Adversary. The static foul adversary models a situation in which the foul adversary only has power over the coerced users in the present. An example is a street robber that wants to obtain your PIN code, if you manage to cheat the street robber, then he cannot punish you later. All that matters is that the data is not currently verifiable.

Let $\Vdash^S_S$ be the weakest relationship satisfying,

1. in state $s \in S$, for $\mathbf{K} = \{\kappa^{u_i}(s) | u_i \in U_C\})$ and $A = \kappa^e(s)$, if $(A, \mathbf{K}) \vdash_{\varsigma_s} d$, then $s \Vdash^S_S d$; and
2. $\forall s \to s' \in \mathcal{I}$, $s \Vdash^S_S d \implies s' \Vdash^S_S d$.

The strong static foul adversary (SSFA) is an adversary that uses $\Vdash^S_S$ as derivation relation.

Condition 1 simply encodes that the static foul adversary can elicit information in a state that allows him to elicit information. Condition 2 is a modelling trick. Without condition 2, it is possible that data d becomes unverifiable due to the user learning a cheat. However, we can assume without loss of generality that the adversary had sufficient foresight to elicit d when it was possible. We address this issue by simply defining the reasoning to be monotonic.

The relation $\Vdash^W_S$ is defined similarly, using $\vdash_\varsigma$ rather than $\vdash_{\varsigma_s}$. The weak static foul adversary (WSFA) is an adversary that uses $\Vdash^W_S$ as derivation relation. Here, the monotonicity condition (condition 2) is superfluous, as the adversary knowledge is trivially monotonic using only condition 1 (since data cannot become unverifiable).

Conservative Foul Adversary. The conservative foul adversary models a situation in which the foul adversary is not willing to coerce unless it is sure it can follow up on its threats. An example is a mafioso who values his reputation of following up on threats more than breaking the security property. This typically occurs in scenarios where the stakes of the individual users are relatively low.

Let $\Vdash^S_C$ be the weakest relationship satisfying,

1. in state $s \in S$, for $\mathbf{K} = \{\kappa^{u_i}(s) | u_i \in U_C\}$ and $A = \kappa^e(s)$, if $(A, \mathbf{K}) \vdash_{\varsigma_s} d$, then $s \Vdash^S_C d$;

2. $\forall s \rightarrow s' \in \mathcal{I}$, $s \Vdash^{S}_{C} d \implies s' \Vdash^{S}_{C} d$; and
3. $\forall s \rightarrow_{\mathsf{D}} s' \in \mathcal{I}$ and $\mathcal{C}_{\mathbf{K}}(\{d\})$ for $\mathbf{K} = \{\kappa^{u_i}(s) | u_i \in U_{\mathcal{C}}\}$, $s' \Vdash^{S}_{C} d \implies s \Vdash^{S}_{C} d$.

The strong conservative foul adversary (SCFA) is an adversary that uses $\Vdash^{S}_{C}$ as derivation relation.

Condition 3 states that if for all (non-imaginary) futures, the foul adversary can verify data d, then the user has no choice to surrender d, provided he has d. The subscript D (in $\rightarrow_{\mathsf{D}}$) ensures that the future is not imaginary, as it disallows variables in the messages – restricting to communications with actual data.

The relation $\Vdash^{W}_{C}$ is defined similarly, using $\vdash_{\varsigma}$ rather than $\vdash_{\varsigma_s}$. The weak conservative foul adversary (WCFA) is an adversary that uses $\Vdash^{W}_{C}$ as derivation relation. Again, monotonicity is superfluous here.

Aggressive Foul Adversary. The aggressive foul adversary models a situation in which the user wants to avoid crossing the foul adversary at all costs. This is the typical dynamic version of the foul adversary, applicable to voting systems, where the foul adversary may punish users after the results came in.

Let $\Vdash^{S}_{A}$ be the weakest relationship satisfying,

1. in state $s \in S$, for $\mathbf{K} = \{\kappa^{u_i}(s) | u_i \in U_{\mathcal{C}}\})$ and $A = \kappa^{e}(s)$, if $(A, \mathbf{K}) \vdash_{\varsigma_s} d$, then $s \Vdash^{S}_{A} d$;
2. $\forall s \rightarrow s' \in \mathcal{I}$, $s \Vdash^{S}_{A} d \implies s' \Vdash^{S}_{A} d$; and
3. $\exists s \rightarrow_{\mathsf{D}} s' \in \mathcal{I}$ and $\mathcal{C}_{\mathbf{K}}(\{d\})$ for $\mathbf{K} = \{\kappa^{u_i}(s) | u_i \in U_{\mathcal{C}}\}$, $s' \Vdash^{S}_{A} d \implies s \Vdash^{S}_{A} d$.

The strong aggressive foul adversary (SAFA) is an adversary that uses $\Vdash^{S}_{A}$ as derivation relation.

Condition 3 is changed to an existential property, which states that if in some (non-imaginary) futures, the foul adversary can verify data d, then the user has no choice to surrender d, provided he has d. Again, we are only considering real data, not imaginary communications.

The relation $\Vdash^{W}_{A}$ is defined similarly, using $\vdash_{\varsigma}$ rather than $\vdash_{\varsigma_s}$. The weak aggressive foul adversary (WAFA) is an adversary using $\Vdash^{W}_{A}$ as derivation relation.

Extended Foul Adversary. The aggressive foul adversary also models a situation in which the user wants to avoid crossing the foul adversary at all costs, but furthermore, the adversary cares more about not being cheated than about the actual security property at hand. In particular, it involves scenarios where the adversary coerces for data which he can only verify because he coerced for the data in the first place.

Let $\Vdash^{S}_{E}$ be the weakest relationship satisfying,

1. in state $s \in S$, for $\mathbf{K} = \{\kappa^{u_i}(s) | u_i \in U_{\mathcal{C}}\})$ and $A = \kappa^{e}(s)$, if $(A, \mathbf{K}) \vdash_{\varsigma_s} d$, then $s \Vdash^{S}_{E} d$;
2. $\forall s \rightarrow s' \in \mathcal{I}$, $s \Vdash^{S}_{E} d \implies s' \Vdash^{S}_{E} d$; and
3. $\exists s \rightarrow s' \in \mathcal{I}$ and $\mathcal{C}_{\mathbf{K}}(\{d\})$ for $\mathbf{K} = \{\kappa^{u_i}(s) | u_i \in U_{\mathcal{C}}\}$, $s' \Vdash^{S}_{E} d \implies s \Vdash^{S}_{E} d$.

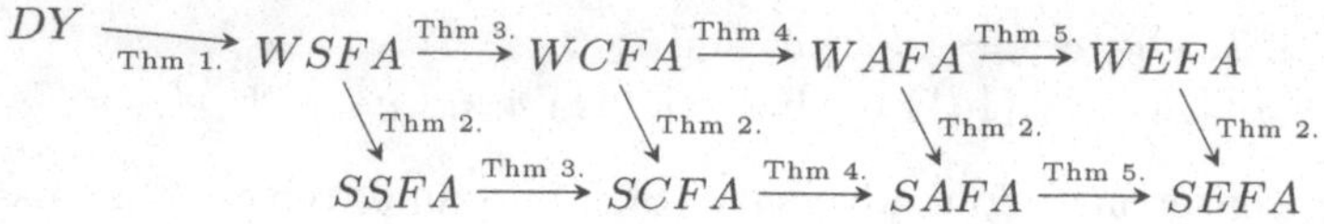

$$DY \xrightarrow[\text{Thm 1.}]{} WSFA \xrightarrow{\text{Thm 3.}} WCFA \xrightarrow{\text{Thm 4.}} WAFA \xrightarrow{\text{Thm 5.}} WEFA$$

$$WSFA \searrow^{\text{Thm 2.}} SSFA, \quad WCFA \searrow^{\text{Thm 2.}} SCFA, \quad WAFA \searrow^{\text{Thm 2.}} SAFA, \quad WEFA \searrow^{\text{Thm 2.}} SEFA$$

$$SSFA \xrightarrow{\text{Thm 3.}} SCFA \xrightarrow{\text{Thm 4.}} SAFA \xrightarrow{\text{Thm 5.}} SEFA$$

Fig. 4. Relations of adversary models.

The strong extended foul adversary (SEFA) is an adversary that uses $\Vdash^{S}_{E}$ as derivation relation.

Condition 3 is changed to allow imaginary futures. In addition to non-imaginary future states, it may be useful for the adversary to send a variable (imaginary communication). The users process the received variable, and output a function of that variable. The adversary can then use that output term to construct an equation to verify the data.

The relation $\Vdash^{W}_{E}$ is defined similarly, using $\vdash_{\varsigma}$ rather than $\vdash_{\varsigma_s}$. The weak extended foul adversary (WEFA) is an adversary using $\Vdash^{W}_{E}$ as derivation relation.

4.3 Hierarchy

The relations between the foul adversaries are shown in Fig. 4. We say adversary A is stronger than adversary B (denoted as $B \to A$), if a protocol satisfies a property w.r.t. A, then protocol satisfies the property w.r.t. B, i.e., $B \vdash d \implies A \vdash d$. In Fig. 4, from left to right the adversary is getting stronger, because the ability of a stronger adversary contains all the ability of a weaker adversary. The adversaries in the second row is stronger than the corresponding one in the first row. The theorems in the figure and their proofs can be found in [18].

5 Example Systems

The notions that we have introduced were, by design, of a high level of abstraction. In this section, we introduce examples to make the ideas more concrete, and to link our approach to security systems and protocols. Our notion of coercion allows other security properties than privacy, in Sect. 5.1, we use the common property of secrecy. We also apply out approach to privacy, in Sect. 5.2. In this section, we do not encode all properties formally into the formalism, for brevity's sake. We merely codify the relevant elements of the examples, and rely on common sense for the details. Even fairly simple systems and protocols would require pages of specification, when defined rigorously.

5.1 Examples on (Enforced) Secrecy

Special Symmetric Encryption. Let the equational theory support a special symmetric encryption, meaning that $\mathsf{enc}(\mathsf{dec}(m, k), k) =_E m$ and $\mathsf{dec}(\mathsf{enc}(m, k), k) =_E m$ are in the equational theory. There are two honest (and coercible) users, the sender u and the receiver v communicating on public channels, and a foul adversary e. The user u contains states s_u, s'_u and the transition $(s_u \xrightarrow{\mathsf{s}(v,\mathsf{enc}(m,k))} s'_u)$ and user v contains at least the states s_v, s'_v and the transition $(s_v \xrightarrow{\mathsf{r}(u,x)} s'_v)$. The system at least contains the transition $s \rightarrow s'$ where in state s', v gains knowledge $\mathsf{enc}(m,k)$. Furthermore, a state s'' exists with $(s \rightarrow s'')$ where in state s'', the adversary gains knowledge $\mathsf{enc}(m,k)$. The reasoning abilities of u and v are $\vdash_{DY}$ and that of the adversary depends on the foul adversary model, e.g., $\Vdash^S_S$ in the case of static foul adversary. The initial knowledge is f, such that $\mathsf{f}(u) = \{m,k\}$, $\mathsf{f}(v) = \{k\}$ and $f(e) = \emptyset$.

We are interested in the secrecy of m, meaning that the correctness of the protocol is determined by the reachability of a state t where $t \Vdash^S_S m$.

The core knowledge of the adversary is initially empty, and the adversary receives at most one message, $\mathsf{enc}(m,k)$ in state s''. The largest core knowledge that the adversary can achieve is, therefore, $\{\mathsf{enc}(m,k)\}$. We can neither coerce for m nor for k, since the user can generate m' and k', such that $\mathsf{enc}(m,k) =_E \mathsf{enc}(m',k')$. In particular for arbitrary k', let $m' = \mathsf{dec}(\mathsf{enc}(m,k),k')$, in which case $\mathsf{enc}(m',k') =_E \mathsf{enc}(\mathsf{dec}(\mathsf{enc}(m,k),k'),k') =_E \mathsf{enc}(m,k)$. Formally, m or k cannot be verified: since encryption and decryption are the only functions, whenever two terms $M\theta =_E N\theta$ holds for m and k, it also holds for some m' and k', due to the equational theory.

Encryption of Natural Language. Take the same scenario as sketched in the previous example. We add a constant c and a unary function e to the equational theory, with $\mathsf{e}(m) =_E \mathsf{c}$ only for a subset of terms T ($m \in T$), representing those messages that are valid English texts. Dissimilar to the previous example, we cannot conclude that the protocol that sends $\mathsf{enc}(m,k)$ (with $m \in T$) is safe under the foul adversary, as the fact that $\mathsf{enc}(m,k) =_E \mathsf{enc}(\mathsf{dec}(\mathsf{enc}(m,k),k'),k')$ is no longer sufficient to prevent coercion, due to that an arbitrary k' leads to non-readable messages, assuming the probability of $k' \in T$ is negligible. The foul adversary can add a test $\mathsf{e}(\_) =_E \mathsf{c}$, which holds for m, but not for an arbitrary $m' =_E \mathsf{dec}(\mathsf{enc}(m,k),k')$. Formally, there exists $\mathsf{e}(\mathsf{dec}(\mathsf{enc}(y,x),x))\{k/x\}\{m/y\} =_E \mathsf{c}$ (serving as the relation $M\theta =_E N\theta$ in rule C in Fig. 2 or rule C_s in Fig. 3), that only holds for m and k, but not holds for arbitrary m' and k'.

Interestingly, together the last two examples imply that the same encryption method is coercion resistant when containing random data, but not coercion resistant when it contains natural language.

Note that under Dolev-Yao adversary, secrecy of m is satisfied, because there is no way for the Dolev-Yao adversary to obtain the key. Thus, this example shows that static foul adversary is strictly stronger than Dolev-Yao adversary.

Coercion with Delayed Verification. Take the same scenario as in the previous example, but let the adversary initially know m'. Furthermore, upon receiving the first term x, the receiver will respond with $\mathsf{dec}(x,k)$. In an honest run, the received term will be $\mathsf{enc}(m,k)$, meaning that the response is m.

Suppose the adversary wants to replace m in the message with m'. That is, the adversary needs to insert the message $\mathsf{enc}(m', k)$ to the receiver, and thus he needs to know $\mathsf{enc}(m', k)$ before the receiver outputs anything. Since the static foul adversary cannot look ahead, the adversary cannot know k (and thus $\mathsf{enc}(m', k)$) before the receiver sending the response, as the adversary does not have enough information to verify them. It means that the static foul adversary cannot insert the message $\mathsf{enc}(m', k)$ to the receiver before the receiver outputs anything. The dynamic foul adversary, however, can look ahead. Since there is a trace where the adversary will know m, and be able to verify k using $\mathsf{enc}(m, \_) = \mathsf{enc}(m, k)$. That, in turn, means that the adversary can coerce for k in the initial state. Hence, the adversary knows k in the initial state, and can construct and insert $\mathsf{enc}(m', k)$ before the receiver outputs anything.

5.2 Examples on (Enforced) Privacy

Enforced privacy properties such as receipt-freeness and coercion-resistance are important requirements in e-voting. We use a simplified well-known e-voting protocol to show how enforced privacy properties can be formalised with respect to the foul adversary. This simplified protocol is the voting phase of the Okamoto e-voting protocol [28][6].

Two voters V_1 and V_2 have initial knowledge $\{V_1, V_2, C, v_1, r_1\}$ and $\{V_1, V_2, C, v_2, r_2\}$ respectively, where v_1 and v_2 are their votes, r_1 and r_2 are two random numbers for the commitment, C is the vote-collector. The two voters send the committed votes first over public channels, then send privately the opening information (r_1 and r_2 respectively), and finally receive the voting result; modelled as follows.

$$s^0_{V_1} \xrightarrow{\mathsf{s}(C,(\mathsf{com}(v_1,r_1)))} s_{V_1} \xrightarrow{\mathsf{ps}(C,(\mathsf{com}(v_1,r_1),r_1))} s'_{V_1} \xrightarrow{\mathsf{r}(C,((v_1,v_2),(m_1,m_2)))} s''_{V_1},$$
$$s^0_{V_2} \xrightarrow{\mathsf{s}(C,(\mathsf{com}(v_2,r_2),r_2))} s_{V_2} \xrightarrow{\mathsf{ps}(C,(\mathsf{com}(v_2,r_2),r_2))} s'_{V_2} \xrightarrow{\mathsf{r}(C,((v_1,v_2),(m_1,m_2)))} s''_{V_2}.$$

The vote-collector C's initial knowledge is $\{V_1, V_2, C\}$. C reads in the votes and the opening information, and sends out the voting results. One possible trace of C is as follows.

$$s^0_C \xrightarrow{\mathsf{r}(V_1,\mathsf{com}(v_1,r_1))} s^1_C \xrightarrow{\mathsf{pr}(V_1,(\mathsf{com}(v_1,r_1),r_1))} s^2_C \xrightarrow{\mathsf{r}(V_2,(\mathsf{com}(v_2,r_2))} s^3_C$$
$$\xrightarrow{\mathsf{pr}(V_2,(\mathsf{com}(v_2,r_2),r_2))} s^4_C \xrightarrow{\mathsf{s}(V_1,((v_1,v_2),(m_1,m_2)))} s^5_C \xrightarrow{\mathsf{s}(V_2,((v_1,v_2),(m_1,m_2)))} s^6_C.$$

Assuming s^0 is the initial state, with $\kappa^e(s^0) = \{V_1, V_2, C\}$. The following transitions are eligible: $s^0 \xrightarrow{\mathsf{block}(V_1,C,(\mathsf{com}(v_1,r_1)))} s^1 \xrightarrow{\mathsf{insert}(V_1,C,(\mathsf{com}(v_1,r_1)))} s^2 \xrightarrow{\mathsf{private}(V_1,C,(\mathsf{com}(v_1,r_1),r_1))} s^3 \xrightarrow{\mathsf{public}(V_2,C,(\mathsf{com}(v_2,r_2)))} s^3 \xrightarrow{\mathsf{private}(V_2,C,(\mathsf{com}(v_2,r_2),r_2))} s^5 \xrightarrow{\mathsf{block}(C,V_1,((v_1,v_2),(m_1,m_2)))} s^6$. The adversary knowledge in state s^1 is $\kappa^e(s^1) = \kappa^e(s^0) \cup \{\mathsf{com}(v_1, r_1)\}$, since the public message from V_1 to C is blocked by e.

[6] For the simplicity of presentation, we ignore some functionalities, such as signature, registration and verifiability, and focus only on the critical part for enforced privacy.

Vote privacy is formalized as $V_1\{c_1/v_1\}|V_2\{c_2/v_2\} \sim V_1\{c_2/v_1\}|V_2\{c_1/v_2\}$, where '$\sim$' is indistinguishability of left side (V_1 votes for c_1 and V_2 votes for c_2) and right side (V_1 votes for c_2 and V_2 votes for c_1) and '|' denotes parallel composition (following the definition in [12]). When $v_1 \neq v_2$, the property is satisfied - the left situation and right situation of '$\sim$' lead to the same voting result, and the adversary cannot distinguish.

However, if the adversary can coerce V_1 for the vote v_1 and the random number r_1, then the property does not hold anymore. In state s^1 we have ($\mathbf{K} = \{V_1, V_2, C, v_1, r_1\}$, $\kappa^e(s^1) = \{V_1, V_2, C, M_1\}$ and $M_1 = \mathsf{com}(v_1, r_1)$),

$$\frac{\mathcal{C}_{\mathbf{K}}(\{v_1, r_1\}), A \vdash_{DY} M_1, \exists_{\{v_1/x\}\{v_2/y\} \wedge M_1 =_E \mathsf{com}(x,y)} \nexists_{v',r'} (M_1 =_E \mathsf{com}(v', r'))}{(A, \mathbf{K}) \vdash_{\zeta} \{v_1, r_1\}}.$$

Hence, in the left side situation, the adversary can verify that V_1 votes for c_1, since v_1 is substituted with c_1, whereas at the right side, the adversary verifies that V_1 votes for c_2 (since $\{c_2/v_1\}$). That is, enforced privacy is broken.

By replacing bit commitment with trap-door bit commitment $\mathsf{tdcom}(v, r, td)$, the rule does not hold anymore, because for $M_1 =_E \mathsf{com}(v_1, r_1, td), \exists r' : M_1 =_E \mathsf{com}(v_1, r', td')$. When the adversary coerces for both r_1 and td_1, although the adversary can elicit r_1 and td_1 for the case of V_1 voting for c_1, since V_1 can also derive r' and td' such that $M_1 =_E \mathsf{com}(v_2, r', td')$, the adversary can also elicit r' and td' for the case of V_1 voting for c_2. Hence, M_1 can be opened as c_1 and c_2. This holds on both sides of the equations; thus enforced privacy is not broken in this way. Of course, to prove the enforced privacy property is satisfied in this case, one needs to consider all branches and all states, often using tool support.

6 Conclusions

In the paper, we propose the idea of modelling an adversary with the ability to coerce – the foul adversary. This contrasts the standard approach of modelling coercion resistance as a security requirement. Knowledge and reasoning are key points in the foul adversary, which is highlighted by the fact that elicitation is the main power of the foul adversaries. Elicitation is built upon the notion of verification, if only one piece of data fits the equation, then the foul adversary obtains the data. We show that reasoning about coercion itself can be just as important, as we have shown by example that different contexts may require different models of the adversary. For the next step, we are planning to implement a verification tool that embedded the foul adversary to facilitate the automatic verification of enforced privacy of complex case studies.

References

1. Abadi, M., Cortier, V.: Deciding knowledge in security protocols under equational theories. Theor. Comput. Sci. **367**(1–2), 2–32 (2006)
2. Abadi, M., Fournet, C.: Mobile values, new names, and secure communication. In: Proceedings of 28th Symposium on Principles of Programming Languages, pp. 104–115. ACM (2001)
3. Abe, M., Suzuki, K.: Receipt-free sealed-bid auction. In: Chan, A.H., Gligor, V. (eds.) ISC 2002. LNCS, vol. 2433, pp. 191–199. Springer, Heidelberg (2002). https://doi.org/10.1007/3-540-45811-5_14
4. Backes, M., Hritcu, C., Maffei, M.: Automated verification of remote electronic voting protocols in the applied pi-calculus. In: Proceedings of 21st IEEE Computer Security Foundations Symposium, pp. 195–209. IEEE CS (2008)
5. Basin, D., Cremers, C.: Modeling and analyzing security in the presence of compromising adversaries. In: Gritzalis, D., Preneel, B., Theoharidou, M. (eds.) ESORICS 2010. LNCS, vol. 6345, pp. 340–356. Springer, Heidelberg (2010). https://doi.org/10.1007/978-3-642-15497-3_21
6. Benaloh, J., Tuinstra, D.: Receipt-free secret-ballot elections (extended abstract). In: Proceedings of 26th Symposium on Theory of Computing, pp. 544–553. ACM (1994)
7. Blanchet, B.: An efficient cryptographic protocol verifier based on prolog rules. In: Proceedings of 14th IEEE Computer Security Foundations Workshop, pp. 82–96. IEEE CS (2001)
8. Clark, J., Hengartner, U.: Panic passwords: authenticating under duress. HotSec **8**, 8 (2008)
9. Cortier, V., Kremer, S.: Formal models and techniques for analyzing security protocols: a tutorial. Found. Trends Program. Lang. **1**(3), 151–267 (2014)
10. De Decker, B., Layouni, M., Vangheluwe, H., Verslype, K.: A privacy-preserving ehealth protocol compliant with the belgian healthcare system. In: Mjølsnes, S.F., Mauw, S., Katsikas, S.K. (eds.) EuroPKI 2008. LNCS, vol. 5057, pp. 118–133. Springer, Heidelberg (2008). https://doi.org/10.1007/978-3-540-69485-4_9
11. Delaune, S., Kremer, S., Ryan, M.: Coercion-resistance and receipt-freeness in electronic voting. In: Proceedings of 19th IEEE Computer Security Foundations Workshop, pp. 28–42. IEEE CS (2006)
12. Delaune, S., Kremer, S., Ryan, M.D.: Verifying privacy-type properties of electronic voting protocols. J. Comput. Secur. **17**(4), 435–487 (2009)
13. Dolev, D., Yao, A.C.-C.: On the security of public key protocols. IEEE Trans. Inf. Theory **29**(2), 198–207 (1983)
14. Dong, N., Jonker, H., Pang, J.: Challenges in eHealth: from enabling to enforcing privacy. In: Liu, Z., Wassyng, A. (eds.) FHIES 2011. LNCS, vol. 7151, pp. 195–206. Springer, Heidelberg (2012). https://doi.org/10.1007/978-3-642-32355-3_12
15. Dong, N., Jonker, H., Pang, J.: Formal analysis of privacy in an ehealth protocol. In: Foresti, S., Yung, M., Martinelli, F. (eds.) ESORICS 2012. LNCS, vol. 7459, pp. 325–342. Springer, Heidelberg (2012). https://doi.org/10.1007/978-3-642-33167-1_19
16. Dong, N., Jonker, H., Pang, J.: Enforcing privacy in the presence of others: notions, formalisations and relations. In: Crampton, J., Jajodia, S., Mayes, K. (eds.) ESORICS 2013. LNCS, vol. 8134, pp. 499–516. Springer, Heidelberg (2013). https://doi.org/10.1007/978-3-642-40203-6_28

17. Dong, N., Jonker, H.L., Pang, J.: Formal modelling and analysis of receipt-free auction protocols in the applied pi. Comput. Secur. **65**, 405–432 (2017)
18. Dong, N., Muller, T.: The foul adversary: formal models. https://sites.google.com/view/foul-adversary/home
19. Fagin, R.: Reasoning About Knowledge. MIT Press, Cambridge (1995)
20. Fujioka, A., Okamoto, T., Ohta, K.: A practical secret voting scheme for large scale elections. In: Seberry, J., Zheng, Y. (eds.) AUSCRYPT 1992. LNCS, vol. 718, pp. 244–251. Springer, Heidelberg (1993). https://doi.org/10.1007/3-540-57220-1_66
21. Heather, J., Schneider, S.: A formal framework for modelling coercion resistance and receipt freeness. In: Giannakopoulou, D., Méry, D. (eds.) FM 2012. LNCS, vol. 7436, pp. 217–231. Springer, Heidelberg (2012). https://doi.org/10.1007/978-3-642-32759-9_19
22. Jonker, H.L., Pang, J., Mauw, S.: A formal framework for quantifying voter-controlled privacy. J. Algorithms Cogn. Inform. Log. **64**(2–3), 89–105 (2009)
23. Juels, A., Catalano, D., Jakobsson, M.: Coercion-resistant electronic elections. In: Proceedings of 4th ACM Workshop on Privacy in the Electronic Society, pp. 61–70. ACM (2005)
24. Küsters, R., Truderung, T.: An epistemic approach to coercion-resistance for electronic voting protocols. In: Proceedings of 30th IEEE Symposium on Security and Privacy, pp. 251–266. IEEE CS (2009)
25. Küsters, R., Truderung, T., Vogt, A.: A game-based definition of coercion-resistance and its applications. In: Proceedings of 23rd IEEE Computer Security Foundations Symposium, pp. 122–136. IEEE CS (2010)
26. Lee, B., Boyd, C., Dawson, E., Kim, K., Yang, J., Yoo, S.: Providing receipt-freeness in mixnet-based voting protocols. In: Lim, J.-I., Lee, D.-H. (eds.) ICISC 2003. LNCS, vol. 2971, pp. 245–258. Springer, Heidelberg (2004). https://doi.org/10.1007/978-3-540-24691-6_19
27. Okamoto, T.: An electronic voting scheme. In: Terashima, N., Altman, E. (eds.) Advanced IT Tools. IFIPAICT, pp. 21–30. Springer, Boston (1996). https://doi.org/10.1007/978-0-387-34979-4_3
28. Okamoto, T.: Receipt-free electronic voting schemes for large scale elections. In: Christianson, B., Crispo, B., Lomas, M., Roe, M. (eds.) Security Protocols 1997. LNCS, vol. 1361, pp. 25–35. Springer, Heidelberg (1998). https://doi.org/10.1007/BFb0028157
29. Schmidt, B., Meier, S., Cremers, C.J.F., Basin, D.A.: Automated analysis of Diffie-Hellman protocols and advanced security properties. In: Proceedings of 25th IEEE Computer Security Foundations Symposium, pp. 78–94. IEEE CS (2012)
30. Schneider, S.: Security properties and CSP. In: Proceedings of IEEE Symposium on Security and Privacy, pp. 174–187. IEEE CS (1996)

The Miles Before Formal Methods - A Case Study on Modeling and Analyzing a Passenger Lift System

Teck Ping Khoo[1(✉)] and Jun Sun[2]

[1] TÜV SÜD Asia Pacific Pte Ltd, Singapore, Singapore
teckping_khoo@mymail.sutd.edu.sg

[2] Singapore University of Technology and Design, Singapore, Singapore

Abstract. Cyber-Physical Systems (CPS) pervade our everyday lives. As users, we need assurances that such systems satisfy requirements on safety, reliability, security and interoperability. CPS presents a major challenge for formal analysis because of their complexity, physical dependencies and non-linearity, and for smart CPS - the ability to improve their behavior over time. Existing approaches on analyzing CPS (e.g., model checking and model-based testing) often assume the existence of a system model. Such approaches have limited application in practice as the models often do not exist. In this work, we report our experience on applying a three-step approach to analyzing a practical CPS: a passenger lift system in a commercial building. The three steps are (1) determining the right level of system abstraction, (2) building the model automatically using grammatical inference, and (3) analyzing the model. The inferred model is in the form of a probabilistic deterministic real time automaton, which allows us to verify the system against properties demanded by the lift requirement. The resulting models form the basis of formal analysis and potentially other approaches. We believe that our approach and experience are applicable to other CPSs.

1 Introduction

Recently, intensive research has been directed at Cyber-Physical Systems (CPS). CPS are systems which harness closed loop feedback from physical processes via a communication network to computational resources running smart algorithms [1]. Examples of CPS include autonomous vehicles, smart medical services, and smart manufacturing. Increasingly, these systems pervade our everyday lives and as users, we need assurances that such systems have been properly analyzed to exacting standards for safety, reliability, security and interoperability.

As these modern industrial and consumer systems become more complex, the practice of analyzing such systems for conformance to specific properties needs to evolve in tandem. For instance, smart CPS often have machine learning capabilities and therefore their operation can improve over time. Conventional analysis approaches break down for such systems due to the high complexity of

J. Sun and M. Sun (Eds.): ICFEM 2018, LNCS 11232, pp. 54–69, 2018.
https://doi.org/10.1007/978-3-030-02450-5_4

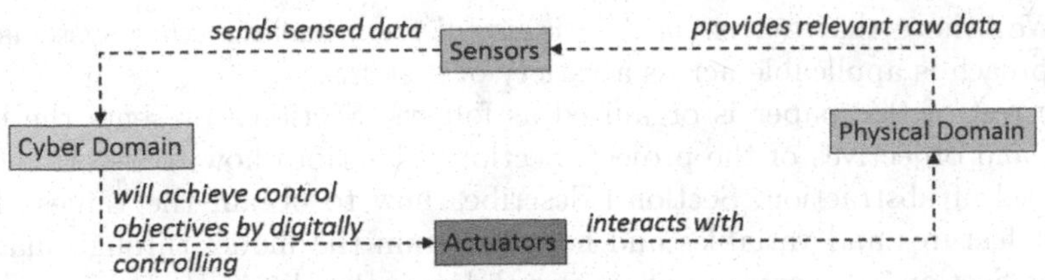

Fig. 1. Cyber-physical systems

the systems. For instance, Model Based Testing (MBT) [2] is the modeling of systems for the purpose of testing, and it is an accepted testing methodology. However, it is not applicable unless we can build a model of the system. Similarly, alternative system analysis techniques like model checking [3] and theorem proving [4] require the availability of a system model. Current modeling methods are highly systems-specific and manual. Significant time and effort must be invested to build a proper model of the system. Furthermore, whenever a change is made to the system, the model must be updated or re-built. *This limits the widespread adoption of model-based system analysis techniques.*

While it might be possible to manually model conventional systems, modeling CPS is extremely challenging if not impossible. Figure 1 shows an overall architecture of a typical CPS. In order to analyze the system, we must model the cyber-domain (i.e., the digital control algorithms implemented in the control software or programmable logic controllers) and, with greater difficulty, the physical-domain (i.e., the continuous evolution of physical processes like air pressure and temperature). Existing literatures [5] on manual modeling and then analyzing CPS are thus limited to simple CPS which are far from real world systems. In order to achieve industrial adoption of model-based analysis techniques, it is desirable to have a systematic process of modeling (which ideally could be automated) which is applicable across a wide range of CPS. Furthermore, there must be a way of convincing users that the system model truly represents the system (via some form of validation).

In this work, we report our experience on applying a structured approach to obtain a model of a real-world lift system automatically, which is subsequently subject to formal analysis. Our approach has three main steps. Firstly, we determine the level of system abstraction, which is essential for model building. The right level of abstraction is derived based on the analysis objective with the help from domain experts. Secondly, once important features and variables are identified in the first step, we develop data-driven approaches of obtaining values of features and variables from the actual system, based on sensing techniques. We remark that sensors provide only low-level system information (like instant acceleration or air pressure). To derive high-level features and variables, often domain expertise is required. Lastly, we validate the model so as to have certain confidence that the model reflects the actual system. Applying the above-mentioned approach, we are able to build a model of the lift system which is now in place for model-based testing and model checking in a commercial company in Singapore. We believe that our experience is useful for modeling other systems and our approach is applicable across a variety of systems.

The rest of this paper is organized as follows. Section 2 presents the background and objectives of the project. Section 3 describes how to determine the right level of abstraction. Section 4 describes how to obtain the values of the relevant features and variables and how to obtain the model through machine learning. Section 5 presents our effort on validating the obtained model. Section 6 provides details of how we used the model to verify some lift properties. Section 7 reviews related work. Lastly, Sect. 8 concludes with a discussion on how to generalize our approach to other systems.

2 Background and Objectives

Our study was motivated by news of frequent elevator breakdowns in Singapore over the past year. According to [6], there are more than 60,000 elevators in Singapore. About 24,000 are in high-rise public housing. Many of these elevators were installed more than 20 years ago and are likely to require more maintenance. Elevator maintenance has not been able to keep up with the failure rate. The problem is exacerbated by the shortage of skilled technicians in this sector. Conventional elevator maintenance is conducted at fixed intervals, e.g., at least once a month as legally required by Singapore [7]. This may not be enough to prevent elevators with latent faults from breaking down.

According to [8], in the years 2013 to 2016, there were about 20 to 30 reported lift breakdowns in Singapore public housing estates out of every 1,000 lifts per month. This works out to an average of 480 lift breakdowns a month, and this figure does not include breakdowns in commercial and private lifts. Such breakdowns lead to downtime, and unfortunately, casualties in some cases. In most cases, the breakdown is due to wear and tear. For others, the lifts fail due to misuse, for example due to passengers jamming of the lift doors to keep them open [9]. It is therefore valuable to design a system which can continuously monitor the main mechanical characteristics of a lift. More importantly, it would be invaluable if we could obtain certain kind of the lift model (based on the monitored data) so that we can analyze the lift status (e.g., check whether vital properties are satisfied) or even "predict" lift breakdowns.

We seek a model with the following capabilities:

1. It must be able to provide predictions about future states of the system. We must be able to infer meaningful system states from the model and be able to somehow extend them into the future.
2. The level of abstraction of the model must be well-chosen, such that the use of existing tools for model analysis poses no issues.
3. It must be suitably acceptable for human comprehension and belief that the model is indeed representative of the real system. There is no point deriving an incomprehensible model of an already complex system. Such a model poses difficulties for system stakeholders to believe that it truly represents the real system.

4. Some means to derive the model fully or semi automatically must be developed, without which the entire model building exercise cannot be scaled to a realistic large number of real systems for widespread adoption. This automation can be achieved only after doing the needed ground work to capture meaningful events from the CPS. The model should be easy to update based on the latest available data as well.

The system under test is a fully operational passenger lift in a commercial building. We determined the key system parameters to model, mounted sensors in the lift to capture raw data, and investigated how to infer the needed parameters from the raw data. Concurrently, we validated the model and adjusted the way the data was collected, to achieve the highest possible correlation between the model and the real system. We made use of *Real Time Identification from Positive Samples (RTI+)* [16], an algorithm to construct a *Probabilistic Deterministic Real Time Automata (PDRTA)* [16] from timed words. RTI+ was applied to the lift data to construct a PDRTA, which was subsequently used to verify some lift properties using a model checker called *Process Analysis Toolkit (PAT)* [18]. We found these results to be realistic and consistent, and believe that this approach can be generalized to other systems. Although properties can be verified directly on the traces obtained, using a model checker to verify properties on the model provides the probability that a specific property hold. Abstracting traces into a model at various points of time also provides a snapshot of the system over time. This opens up the possibility of model comparison for anomaly detection or predictive maintenance.

3 Determining the Right Level of Abstraction

Lift modeling is a complex endeavor due to the large numbers of inter-connected systems working together. The lift controller accepts inputs from all the call buttons on all the lift landings, as well as from within the lift car. An appropriate program runs within the lift controller to command the lift to go to specific floors based on the sequence of floor requests. Safeguards need to be built into the lift controller to prevent unsafe situations, such as allowing the lift car to stop in between floors or allowing the lift doors to open while the lift is traveling. It is therefore critical that key system parameters are identified for the purpose of system modeling - to prevent missing the right parameters which reflect system status, and to avoid capturing unimportant ones which obfuscate the model.

This work aims to automate model-building based on expert knowledge, i.e. digitizing the expert. Indeed, zooming in on the key system parameters is not a trivial task, as only professional lift inspectors or technicians have this knowledge. The layman will not have any knowledge of specific lift components which are system-critical but are usually hidden within the system. Identifying the right level of abstraction is a general problem in system modeling. It is common to fall into the trap of aiming to "model everything". A good model must capture the key system parameters and yet remain as simple as possible - this is a

Table 1. Determining the key parameters via areas of maintenance

Area of maintenance	Lift motion status	Door state
1. Door open control		X
2. Door protective devices		X
3. Lift car doors and lift landing doors		X
7. Movement of lift car	X	
16. Controller and electrical system	X	X
17. Guide shoes or rollers of lift car and counterweight	X	
18. Safety gear	X	
19. All lift parts	X	X

common aim for all forms of modeling. Available sources of knowledge for system abstraction are expert knowledge, and system standards. Expert knowledge is often built on a thorough knowledge and understanding of the system design and operation, whether in normal or exceptional modes. System standards are important as a way of knowing what to abstract, as the standards indicate which aspect of the system needs regular monitoring or standard conformance.

From a standard checklist for lift inspection [10], lift speed and door opening and closing speeds are important certification parameters as they are measured in many checks. Lift doors cause the majority of lift issues as they open and close at least twice with every trip. This is corroborated by news of lift breakdowns [11]. In the Singapore context, in view of the numerous lift incidents mentioned earlier, the Singapore Government strengthened the Building Maintenance and Strata Management (Lift, Escalator and Building Maintenance) Regulations in 2016 [12]. This lift safety standard stipulates 20 areas of maintenance for lifts and 10 for escalators. The first area of maintenance for lifts pertains to "Door open control" [13]. The standard specifies that "When lift car doors and lift landing doors are opened and the button controlling the opening of those doors is pressed, the opened lift car doors and lift landing doors must stay open." It goes on to specify that "When lift car doors and lift landing doors are partially closed and the button controlling the opening of those doors is pressed, the partially closed lift car doors and lift landing doors must reopen." Nine out of these 20 areas of maintenance points to the need to monitor the *lift motion status* and *door states*. Table 1 provides an indication of how monitoring these parameters can address the nine areas of maintenance.

Internal institutional lift experts have also provided a list of lift parameters to monitor, with the lift motion status and door states having the highest priorities. Given that lift motion status and door status are important, we need some means to define and capture *events* representing these parameters from the lift sensor data. Based on Table 1, the following events which represents the system parameter changes are defined:

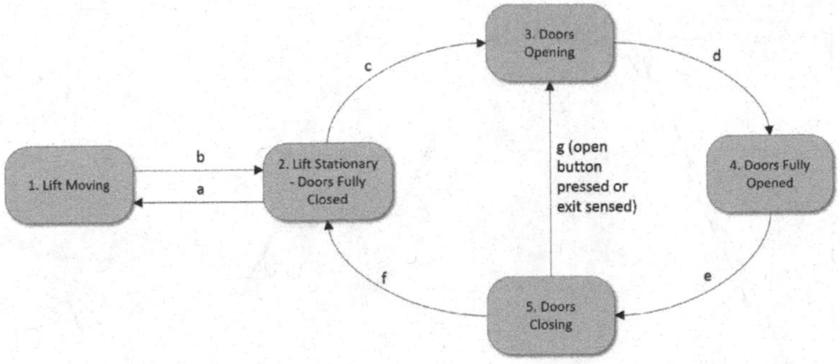

Fig. 2. Key events to capture

- a = lift starts moving, b = lift stops moving, c = doors start opening
- d = doors stop opening, e = doors start closing, f = doors stop closing

The definition of these events form the inputs to available tools for model-building, which shall be covered in a later section. These events are also shown in the state transition diagram in Fig. 2 for illustration. These events effectively define the level of abstraction, i.e., we aim to build a model which precisely captures the system behaviors in terms of these critical events.

4 Obtaining the Model Automatically

In this section, we present our approach on obtaining the model automatically. As established, the model must include lift motion status and door states. The *Vertical Transportation Handbook* [14] provides the *up peak traffic* scenario, where all passengers arrive at the lobby and wish to go up. If the model is to represent such a scenario, the lift and doors speeds need to be precisely captured, as this scenario mostly comprise lift and door motion. Modern lift systems are digital and readily store this information. However, systems which are already installed, and which are most likely to give problems, may have already been installed for over a decade. Such systems are likely to be analog systems and it is difficult to capture such info from such systems. Moreover, for model-based verification to be widely adopted, access to the system logs cannot be assumed. Non-intrusive sensing technology is therefore the best way to get these data from a wide variety of systems.

4.1 Lift Motion Inference

In this case study, we do not have access to the lift controller. This is typical as such access is usually restricted to the lift manufacturer or maintenance crew. Therefore system logs cannot be used for analysis. Sensors must be mounted in the lift to capture data which can be used to infer the needed parameters. The first identified key system parameter is lift motion status. Motion is usually

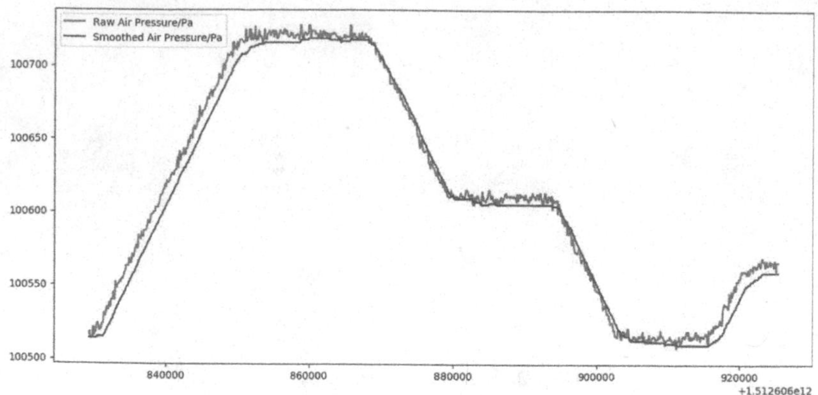

Fig. 3. The raw and smoothed air pressure as measured from the lift

detected using linear accelerometers. When vertical linear acceleration is zero, it can mean that the lift speed is not changing (constant speed, can be zero speed or non-zero speed). Positive vertical acceleration means that the lift is changing its speed from 0 to non-zero (starting from rest). Negative values mean the speed is changing from non-zero to 0 (coming to a rest). In practice, it was discovered that noise in the readings is severe. We make the simple observation that the lift only moves vertically, and select the barometer as the sensor of choice. The barometer measures air pressure, which decreases as the lift is moving upwards and increases as it is moving downwards. It remains level when the lift is at rest, as long as the weather conditions remain constant. The barometer was observed to be able to measure a change in air pressure even when only one floor is traveled.

To infer lift motion from air pressure, we make use of the physical law that air pressure is constant at a fixed height. The sensed raw air pressure is noisy, and we make use of exponential weighted smoothing with a smoothing factor $\alpha = 0.1$ to get a smoother curve, which is needed for accurate lift motion inference. This is illustrated in Fig. 3.

An algorithm was used to infer whether the lift is moving or not. A moving window of air pressure values is maintained. if the difference between the maximum and minimum values is less than a set threshold, the lift is taken to be stationary, otherwise it is taken to be moving. Based on inspection of the inferred lift motion state superimposed on the air pressure, we compensate the motion detection by some time for more accurate motion detection. This is illustrated in Fig. 4. In this figure, the high value of motion inference indicates lift is moving, while the low value indicates that the lift is not moving.

4.2 Door State Inference

The second identified key system parameter is the door state. The magnetometer is the sensor of choice. This sensor needs to be mounted on the lift door frame

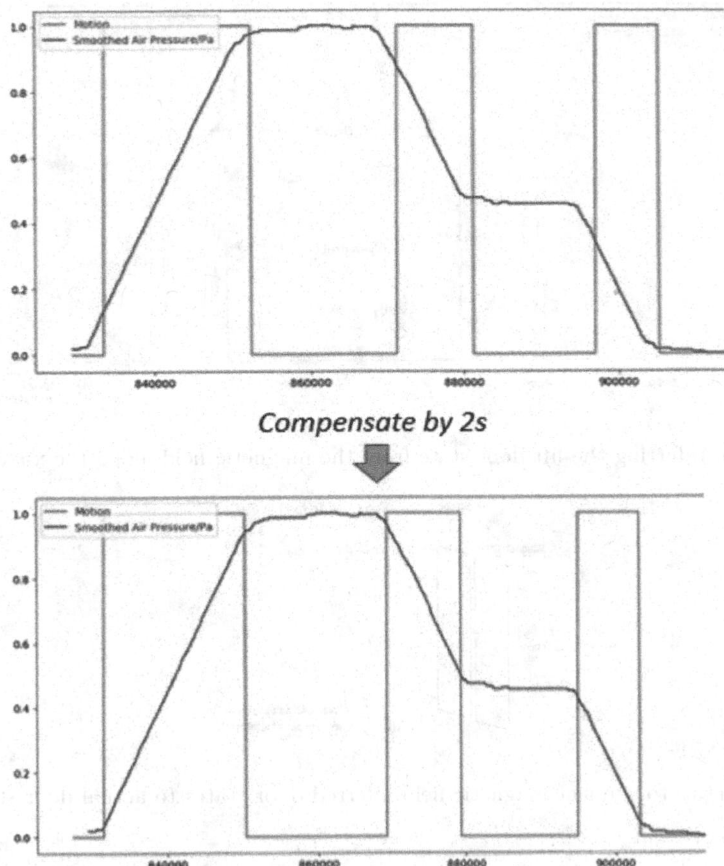

Fig. 4. Timing compensation for more accurate motion inference. Note that the motion inference on the top appears to be delayed - therefore we compensate the timing by 2 s based on inspection to get the more accurate motion inference on the bottom

close to a magnet which was mounted on the lift door. An algorithm was devised to derive the door states from the magnetic field along the x-axis. A moving window of magnetic field values is maintained. If the difference between the maximum and minimum values is less than a set threshold, the door is either fully closed or fully opened. This depends on whether the magnetic field value is close to a fixed threshold selected in the middle of the two fully opened and fully closed levels. The trend (whether rising or falling) of the magnetic field is used to differentiate door opening or closing. Figure 5 shows the derived door states based on this approach.

While the inference of the door states using the algorithm appears to be accurate, validating that the inference is correct has to be done. Photographic evidence of the door states was used to compensate for timing differences between the sensed door state and actual door states. A Windows PC and its web-cam

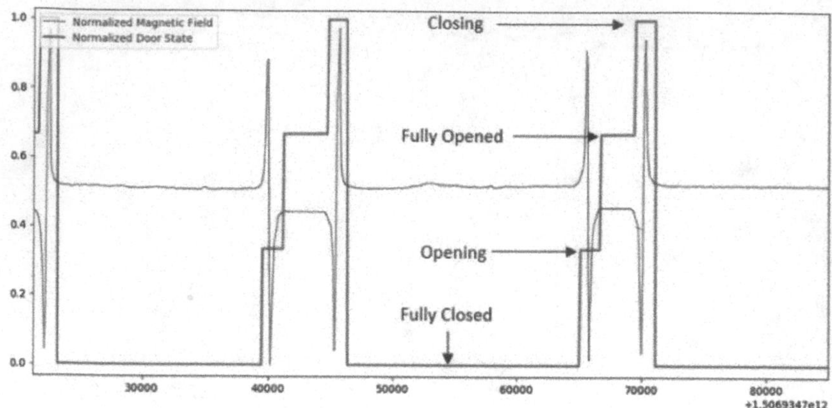

Fig. 5. Inferring the lift door state from the magnetic field along the x-axis

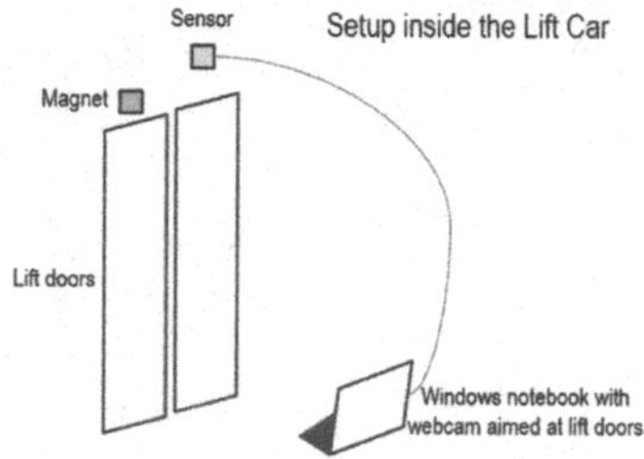

Fig. 6. Setup to connect magnetic field-inferred door states to actual door states

was used to take one picture of the doors with each data sample, and to name the image using the time-stamp and inferred door state. Figure 6 describes the setup. The average timing compensations for lift door state inference were discovered after comparing the photos with the inferred door states. Figure 7 shows the discovered timing compensations.

With the above-described set up, we are now able to systematically monitor the relevant lift status, i.e., in terms of the events defined in the previous section, which subsequently allows us to build a model of the system.

4.3 Constructing a Probabilistic Deterministic Real Time Automata (PDRTA)

The passenger lift system must be suitably modeled. The selected model must be expressive enough to characterize the system's parameters, such as the time needed for the lift to start moving and then to stop moving. Another such parameter is the door opening and closing times. Therefore, the model must provide at least one clock which keeps track of the time delay from one event to the next. Timed Automata (TA [15]) with clocks are suitable in this aspect. Given that the data to create the model is from real systems, they will contain noise.

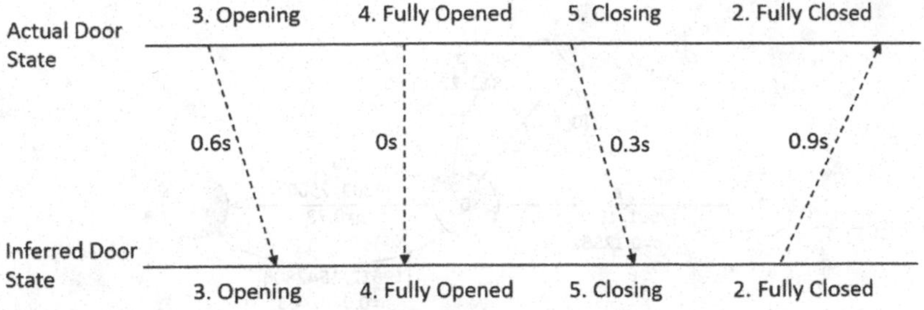

Fig. 7. Discovered timing compensations for the door state inference

The model must therefore include probabilities of specific sequences of events to handle this noise, and to perform statistical reasoning.

The automated construction of a model from event logs is the subject of study in the field of grammatical induction. Verwer *et al.* in [16] developed the Real Time Identification from Positive Samples (RTI+) algorithm to construct a Probabilistic Deterministic Real Time Automata (PDRTA) from timed strings. RTI+ first constructs a Timed Augmented Prefix Tree Acceptor (TAPTA) from all the samples. The traces of each sample follow a unique path in the TAPTA. The goal of the algorithm is to reduce the TAPTA such that the resulting model maximizes the likelihood of observing the samples, and is the smallest possible. RTI+ performs state merging, splitting and coloring using a red-blue framework. At each iteration of the algorithm, hypothesis testing is conducted at a specific level of significance to decide if state merging, splitting or coloring should be done. The timing guards are derived from state splitting. A *Likelihood Ratio test* is used to determine if a merge/split is to be performed at every iteration. A Likelihood Ratio test statistic is evaluated and hypothesis testing is conducted at a specific level of significance. The probability of a transition is derived by assigning a probability distribution over time, which is modeled using histograms. The reader is encouraged to refer to [16] for details. The use of a PDRTA to model the lift is suitable, and we applied the PDRTA learning algorithm for this project.

Time stamped events labeled as a, b, c, d, e, f were collected over five full days from Tuesday 3 October to Saturday 7 October 2017. A typical event trace is $a, b, c, d, e, f, a, b, c, d, a, b, c, d, e, f$. It is important that each timed word starts with the same initial state and does not stop abruptly, as far as possible. For example the word a, b, c captures the door starting to open but no events about the door closing. In line with these requirements, a timed word must start with the symbol a and contains only one a. A timed word therefore represents the lift moving, then stopping, then having its doors doing an arbitrary number of actions, all before it starts moving again.

There are 6,518 timed words in the data. 1,025 words were randomly chosen to build the PDRTA using RTI+. Software in the form of a C++ implementation of RTI+ was downloaded from [17]. This software was used to run the RTI+ algorithm using the likelihood ratio method 5% level of significance. The

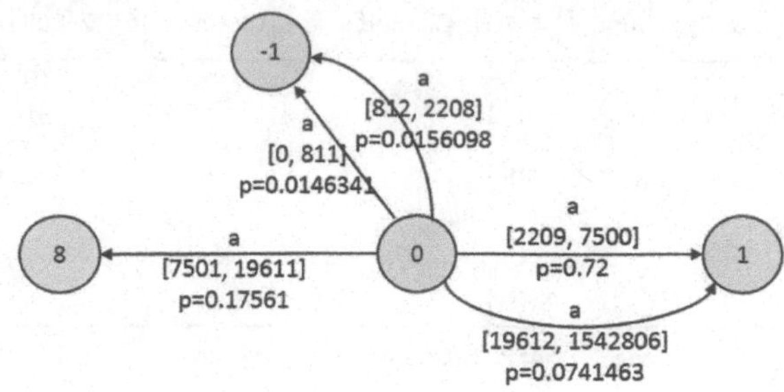

Fig. 8. Part of the discovered PDRTA

resulting PDRTA contains 18 states and 42 transitions. On a Windows 7 notebook with an Intel i5 processor at 2.3 GHz and 16 GB of RAM, the execution time was short, at less than 5 s. Figure 8 shows part of the discovered PDRTA. Only outgoing transitions from *State 0* are shown. Each transition shows the symbol, delay range and probability.

5 Validating the Obtained Model

The proposed approach learns a model from data - it is important that the model is validated. This is in contrast to models which are created from pure expert understanding as the experts' knowledge of the system should already provide some basis to conclude that the model is valid.

We see threats to validity on two fronts - the data used to build the model must be validated to ensure that it connects to reality, and inferred system parameters from the data must be checked to at least ensure that it makes sense. As mentioned in the previous sections, the data was validated as part of the model building process. The lift motion was validated empirically with domain knowledge. In this case, it can be assumed that air pressure is sufficiently constant at a constant height above sea level. The lift door states inferred by magnetic field were validated by photographic evidence.

Key lift parameters were evaluated over five days from Tuesday 3 October 2017 to Saturday 7 October 2017. The results are tabulated in Table 2.

From Table 2, we see that the number of trips on Tuesday to Friday, which were all working days, were fairly consistent averaging at around 1550. There is a noticeable and expected smaller number of trips of 268 on the Saturday, which was a non-working day. Similarly, the number and proportion of normal and abnormal door cycles were consistent across all the weekdays. A normal operation cycle is the event trace *abcdef*, which corresponds to a lift moving, then stopping, and then the doors opening and closing without any interruption. The mean and median door opening times were all very close, with a very low standard deviation of about 70 ms. The same applies for the door closing times. This provides confidence that the setup were able to capture the door states robustly and consistently.

Table 2. Key lift parameters over five days

	Tue 3/10/17	Wed 4/10/17	Thu 5/10/17	Fri 6/10/17	Sat 7/10/17
Number of traces (Trips)	1623	1551	1575	1503	268
Number of normal operation cycles (abcdef)	1339	1309	1314	1246	197
Number of abnormal operation cycles	284	242	261	257	71
Mean door opening time/ms	2290	2288	2281	2290	2271
Median door opening time/ms	2299	2299	2298	2299	2285
Standard deviation door opening time/ms	76	71	79	70	69
Mean door closing time/ms	2832	2827	2828	2831	2832
Median door closing time/ms	2805	2805	2805	2803	2812
Standard deviation door closing time/ms	94	101	116	85	61

6 Verifying Properties

With the model built after the previous steps, we are now ready to verify the built model so as to check whether crucial properties correlated to lift safety standards are satisfied. Note that our model contains not only realtime but also probability. The Process Analysis Toolkit (PAT) [18] is thus adopted to perform model verification on the PDRTA. PAT is a framework which supports composing, simulating and reasoning of concurrent, real-time systems and other possible domains. It comes with a well-designed GUI, featured model editor and animated simulator. Additionally, PAT implements various model checking techniques supporting different properties such as deadlock-freeness, divergence-freeness, reachability, LTL properties with fairness assumptions, refinement checking and probabilistic model checking.

We use the PTCSP module in PAT, which supports a modeling language expressive enough to capture PDRTA models. In order to model check a property, we must model the property precisely in PAT as well. For instance, in order to verify the property "the lift door must not open while the lift is moving", we design the following process.

$$Property = a \rightarrow c \rightarrow b \rightarrow fail \rightarrow Skip$$

where $fail$ is a special event denoting violation of the property. The system is modeled as a parallel composition of the PDRTA model and process *Property*. PAT is then applied to compute the probability of $fail$ occurring, which in this case is the probability of the violation of the property. We similarly model a set of other 5 safety properties.

Table 3. Summary of verification results by PAT

Property	Results	Time (s)	Memory (KB)
1	Invalid	<1	32776
2	Invalid	<1	32686
3	$0.13267 < p < 0.13268$	<1	32817
4	Invalid	<1	32661
5	Invalid	<1	33014
6	$0.86644 < p < 0.86644$	<1	33169
7	Invalid	<1	33055

Table 3 summarizes the verification results where the first column shows the property number, the second column shows the verification results using PAT's verification engine for Markov Decision Processes (MDP) with time abstraction, the third column shows the verification time needed, and the last column shows PAT's estimated consumed memory. Note that the result could be a probability range if the property could be satisfied.

For all verification results, the process for modeling the property captures the negation of the property, i.e., *unwanted behavior*. PAT thus returns *invalid* if the property is always satisfied. Property 1 pertains to passenger safety, i.e., the lift door must not start opening while the lift is traveling. Property 2 pertains to lift travel, i.e., the lift must start and stop within one second. Property 4 pertains to lift door functionality, i.e., the lift door opening time must not be less than 2 s. Property 5 pertains to lift door functionality, i.e., the lift door opening time must not be more than 2.4 s. Property 7 pertains to lift door functionality, i.e., the lift door closing time must not be more than 3 s. All of these safety properties have been verified.

Property 3 pertains to the duration from the lift start moving to the lift stop moving, i.e., we test if this duration can take longer than 100 s, which is a realistic upper bound for a building with five levels. PAT returns a probability of 0.13267 that this property is violated. We account for this result by inspecting the model, and discovered that there is one transition with the symbol a having a delay of between 0 and *1542806* with probability of 0.0741463. Indeed, the delay of 1542806 occurs in many of the other transitions and appear to be the result of RTI+ being unable to find those transitions with delays less than this value. This behavior is consistent with RTI+ inferring the PDRTA using a top-down approach. The low probability of violation of 0.13267 is accounted for by the low probability of this transition (0.0741463). This suggests that this property is the result of imprecise learning, i.e., a kind of false alarm.

Property 6 pertains to lift door functionality, i.e., the lift door closing time must not be less than 2 s. PAT's results suggest that there is a probability of 0.8664 that this property is violated. We account for this result by inspecting the model, and discovered that there are two high probability transitions with the symbol f having a delay between 0 and *1542806*. The transition probabilities are both high at 0.96092 and 0.981818. The high probability of violation of 0.86644 is accounted for by the high probability of these transitions (0.96092 and 0.981818). We note that in this instance, while RTI+ inferred the model correctly, RTI+ could have inferred the PDRTA with more timing precision, as the delay window is between 0 and 1542806 is the largest possible in the entire model. This is thus found to be a false alarm.

7 Related Work

In this work, we report our experience in applying a structured approach to modeling a passenger lift for the purpose of model-based verification. The resulting model is to be used for verifying expected properties of the lift as recovered from the relevant lift safety and maintenance standards, for the lift owners to decide if the lift is about to fail, and if so, the probability. This section covers related work about modeling techniques for creating models with similar use cases.

Related work exists which applies formal techniques to CPS. In [5], the authors developed a methodology for formally verifying a CPS. Physical measurements were compared against a formal description of required CPS behavior, in an attempt to discover bugs.

In [20], predictive maintenance of a railroad network was done using large amounts of sensor data. These sensors include temperature, strain, vision, infrared, weight and impact, sensors. This was combined with failure information, servicing records and information about the types of trains using the network. Techniques applied correlation analysis, causal analysis, time series analysis. Machine learning, in this case, Support Vector Machine (SVM) was applied to automatically derive rules to build models capable of predicting failures.

In [21], the authors used a multi-classifier machine learning approach for predictive maintenance, and applied it to semiconductor manufacturing. The authors put forth the point that in predictive maintenance, maintenance is carried out using a gauge of the health of machinery. This gauge is derived from past data, specifically defined health factors, statistic inference methods, and specific engineering approaches.

As far as we know, we are the first to apply the RTI+ algorithm on a passenger lift system, and to use the model to verify some expected system properties. In [16], Verwer created the RTI+ algorithm to learn a model of driving behavior, in an effort to recommend the right engine settings to optimize fuel efficiency. Elevators are not commonly targeted for modeling research. An example is [21], where the authors used differential equations to model the mechanical properties of an elevator, in a bid to discover the optimal elevator settings by simulation.

8 Conclusion

With the successful application of the proposed approach to model a lift, we believe that this approach can be applied to CPSs. Care needs to be exercised on identifying the right events to capture, be they from the cyber or from the physical domain. Once the right events are identified, the rest of the modeling effort rests mainly on applying sound engineering practices to capture the data robustly. The positive data (meaning the system is operating normally) should then be fed into the algorithm with the right settings to derive the system model.

One key step towards generalizing the approach to other CPS is to further automate the model validation process. Using the case study presented here as an example, the lift motion can be captured by linear accelerometer and cross validated with motion inferred by air pressure field. The door states can be inferred by computer vision and cross validated with states inferred by magnetic field. After cross validation, the discovered model must be updated if necessary based on the findings of these tests.

Acknowledgement. We thank Dr. Martin Saerbeck, Dr. Kenneth Zhu, Ms. Sohyeon Jin and Ms. Yifan Jia for their support in the technical aspects of this paper. We thank Mr Sanjay Kharb for his expert views on actual lift operations and legal requirements.

References

1. Lee, E.A.: The past, present and future of cyber-physical systems: a focus on models. Sensors **15**, 4837–4869 (2015). https://doi.org/10.3390/s150304837
2. Pretschner, A.: Model-based testing. In: Proceedings of 27th International Conference on Software Engineering, ICSE 2005, Saint Louis, MO, USA, pp. 722-723 (2005). https://doi.org/10.1109/ICSE.2005.1553582
3. Clarke, E.M.: The birth of model checking. In: Grumberg, O., Veith, H. (eds.) 25 Years of Model Checking. LNCS, vol. 5000, pp. 1–26. Springer, Heidelberg (2008). https://doi.org/10.1007/978-3-540-69850-0_1
4. Klein, G., Gamboa, R.: J. Autom. Reason. **56**, 201 (2016). https://doi.org/10.1007/s10817-016-9363-7
5. Woehrle, M., Lampka, K., Thiele, L.: Conformance testing for cyber-physical systems. ACM Trans. Embed. Comput. Syst. **11**(4), 1–23 (2012). Article 84. https://doi.org/10.1145/2362336.2362351
6. Building and Construction Authority (2018). Lift Safety. https://www.bca.gov.sg/LiftSafety/lift.html. Accessed
7. The Government Gazette, Electronic Edition Building Maintenance and Strata Management Act (Chapter 30c) Building Maintenance and Strata Management (lift, escalator and building maintenance) regulations 2016 arrangement of regulations. https://www.bca.gov.sg/LiftSafety/others/BMSM(Lift_Escalator_BM)Regs_2016.pdf. Accessed 21 May 2018
8. Ming, T.E.: Town councils to set aside more money for lift maintenance (2016). http://www.todayonline.com/singapore/average-monthly-lift-breakdown-rate-has-fallen-lawrence-wong. Accessed 19 Jan 2018
9. Heng, L.: Parliament Discusses... Lift breakdowns (2016). http://www.tnp.sg/news/singapore/parliament-discusses-lift-breakdowns. Accessed 12 Jan 2018

10. Testing and Commissioning Procedure for Lift, Escalator and Passenger Conveyor Installation in Government Buildings of the Hong Kong Special Administrative Region 2012 Edition. https://www.archsd.gov.hk/media/11431/e212.pdf. Accessed 16 May 2018
11. Lim, M.Z.: Lift issues plague BTO premium flats (2017). http://www.tnp.sg/news/singapore/lift-issues-plague-bto-premium-flats. Accessed 12 Jan 2018
12. Ong, J.: BCA tightens requirements for lift and escalator maintenance (2016). https://www.channelnewsasia.com/news/singapore/bca-tightens-requirements-for-lift-and-escalator-maintenance-7901654. Accessed 22 Jan 2018
13. Building and Construction Authority: BCA announces details of tightened lift maintenance regime and new escalator safety regulations (2016). https://www.bca.gov.sg/newsroom/others/Release_LiftEscalator_Regulations_080716.pdf. Accessed 21 May 2018
14. Strakosch, G.R., Caporale, R.S.: 4. Incoming Traffic, The Vertical Transportation Handbook. Wiley, Hobokent (2010)
15. Alur, R., Dill, D.: The theory of timed automata. In: de Bakker, J.W., Huizing, C., de Roever, W.P., Rozenberg, G. (eds.) REX 1991. LNCS, vol. 600, pp. 45–73. Springer, Heidelberg (1992). https://doi.org/10.1007/BFb0031987
16. Verwer, S.: Efficient identification of timed automata: theory and practice. Ph.D. dissertation. TU Delft, Delft University of Technology, July 2010. https://repository.tudelft.nl/islandora/object/uuid:61d9f199-7b01-45be.../download Accessed 14 May 2018
17. Sicco Verwer, July 2010. http://www.cs.ru.nl/sicco/software.htm Accessed 14 May 2018
18. Sun, J., Liu, Y., Dong, J.S., Pang, J.: PAT: towards flexible verification under fairness. In: Bouajjani, A., Maler, O. (eds.) CAV 2009. LNCS, vol. 5643, pp. 709–714. Springer, Heidelberg (2009). https://doi.org/10.1007/978-3-642-02658-4_59
19. National University of Singapore: PAT: Process Analysis Toolkit (2014). http://pat.comp.nus.edu.sg/ Accessed 17 May 2018
20. Li, H.: Improving rail network velocity: a machine learning approach to predictive maintenance. Transp. Res. Part C: Emerg. Technol. **50**(1), 17–26 (2014). https://doi.org/10.1145/1188913
21. Susto, G.A., Schirru, A., Pampuri, S., McLoone, S., Beghi, A.: Machine learning for predictive maintenance: a multiple classifier approach. IEEE Trans. Ind. Inform. **11**(3), 812–820 (2015)
22. Vladic, J., Djokic, R., Kljajin, M., Karakasic, M.: Modelling and simulations of elevator dynamic behaviour, March 2011. ISSN 1330-3651. https://hrcak.srce.hr/file/107016. Accessed 16 July 2018

PAR: A Practicable Formal Method and Its Supporting Platform

Jinyun Xue(✉), Yujun Zheng, Qimin Hu, Zhen You, Wuping Xie, and Zhuo Cheng

State International S&T Cooperation Base of Networked Supporting Software, Jiangxi Normal University, Nanchang 330022, China
jinyun@vip.sina.com

Abstract. The use of formal methods can significantly improve the reliability, correctness and efficiency of software development. Although formal methods has been invented for more than 40 years, but academia and industry do not have a unified understanding of what are formal methods and its essential characteristics. Formal methods has not been recognized and widely applied by academia and industry. The authors of this paper have long been engaged in the study of the essential features of Formal methods. The authors propose a new definition: **Formal methods are a strict technology based on mathematics and tool support for software and hardware system, including high-level abstract specification, modeling language and different levels of model transformation tools.** Based on this definition, this paper develops a practicable formal methods and its supporting platform, called ***PAR method*** and ***PAR platform***, *short for PAR.* PAR consists of the following elements: requirement modeling language SNL, algorithm modeling language Radl, abstract program modeling language Apla, a set of rules for the model transformation and a set of automatic transformation tools from requirement models to algorithm models, to abstract program models and to executable programs. The goal of the transformations is to generate executable program. The elements embody 6 innovative ideas given in Sect. 2. There are two kinds of applications of PAR. One is that many nontrivial algorithms and programs have been developed formally. Another is formal developing several safety-critical information systems.

Keywords: Formal methods · Par platform · Modeling language
Model transformation · Formal specification

1 Introduction

The use of Formal methods can significantly improve the reliability, correctness and efficiency of software development [4]. Although Formal methods has

This work was funded by the NSF of China under Grant No. 61662036, 61472167, 61462041, 61272075, 61020106009, 60773054, 60573080, 60273092, 69983003, 69783006; MOST of China Grant No. 2008DFA11940, 2003CCA02800.

J. Sun and M. Sun (Eds.): ICFEM 2018, LNCS 11232, pp. 70–86, 2018.
https://doi.org/10.1007/978-3-030-02450-5_5

been invented for more than 40 years [1,3,5,14], but academia and industry do not have a unified understanding of what is Formal methods and its essential characteristics. Woodcock [22] thought "formal methods are mathematical techniques, often sup-ported by tools, for developing software and hardware systems". Bjørners opinion [4] is "by a formal method we shall understand a method whose techniques and tools can be explained in mathematics". The definition by Wikipedia [45] is "formal methods are a particular kind of mathematically based techniques for the specification, development and verification of software and hardware systems". For these reasons, Formal methods has not been recognized and widely applied by academia and industry. Gargantini [8] thought "many practitioners are still reluctant to adopt formal methods. Besides the well-known lack of training, this skepticism is mainly due to: the complex notations; the lack of easy to-use tools supporting a developer during the life cycle activities of system development". Bjørner said [4] that when ask ourselves the question: Have formal methods for software development in the current sense been successful? Our answer is, regretfully, no! He thought "The academic and industry obstacles can be overcome. Still, a main reason for formal methods not being picked up, and hence "more" successful, is the lack of scalable and practical tool support."

The above situation shows that the main reason for the failure of Formal methods to be applied in large scale is that the language provided by the existing formal methods is very complex and difficult to learn. The tools for supporting formal methods are simple and cannot provide effective help for the users of the methods. We think the main reason for this is that the degree of abstraction-level of formal languages is not high enough. On formal methods support tool, people are not clear about its main goal. At present, the support tool of formal methods can only form a formal verification for the related components developed by software (program). It's far from enough.

The authors of this paper have long been engaged in the study of the essential features of formal methods. The authors propose a new definition: **Formal methods are a strict technology based on mathematics and tool support for software and hardware system, including high-level abstract specification, modeling language and different levels of model transformation tools. The specification and modeling language should be as abstract as possible and reflect different levels of abstraction according to the characteristics of software and hardware. All models and model transformation tools should be verified formally or automatically.**

Based on this definition, this paper develops a practicable formal methods and its supporting platform, called PAR method and PAR platform, short for PAR. PAR consists of the following elements: requirement modeling language SNL, algorithm modeling language Radl, abstract program modeling language Apla, a set of rules for the model transformation and a set of automatic transformation tools between requirement model, algorithm model, abstract program model and executable program. The goal of the transformations is to generate executable program. One of the distinct features of the PAR platform is the agile genericity mechanisms. In PAR not only a value, a data type and an ADT can be generic parameter, and a computing-action (including operator, method, function and procedure, transaction, subsystem and web service, etc.) can be generic parameter also. The elements embody 6 innovative ideas given in the Sect. 2.

The first one is that many nontrivial algorithms and programs have been developed formally, formal derivation or formal proof, including graph algorithms [29], travel tree algorithms [32], array section algorithms [25,26], Knuths famous hard problem of cyclic permutation [10,24,33]. The abstract Hopcroft-Tarjan planarity algorithm was described in Apla. The Apla program was transformed by PAR platform to C++ code that can correctly test the planarity and generate improved planar embedding [10]. A more convincing example is formal development of Knuth's challenging program that converts a binary fraction to decimal fraction with certain condition [13,27,28].

The second one is to develop several safety-critical information systems, including shuttle transportation problems [36], discrete optimization algorithm design [37], fire evacuation [38], population classification in earthquakes [39], Emergency railway transportation planning [40], active services support for disaster rescue [41], Airline passenger profiling [42] and Industrial Accident Early Warning [43], etc. A general distributed transaction processing system is implemented in PAR and used in student information management system [23].

In Sect. 2, we give a brief description of key ideas and innovative techniques of PAR. The third Section describes the main elements of PAR method and PAR. Two kinds of applications of PAR and two cases study described in Sect. 4. Related work is described in Sect. 5. Finally, conclusions and future research are presented.

2 Key Ideas and Innovative Techniques of PAR

Compared with other formal methods and program generating system, say B method [1], RAISE [18], Kestrelwares [19], Orc [6,12,16], rCOS, [15,21], NDAUTO [44] and NDADAS [44], etc.,s the PAR method and PAR platform have following innovative techniques.

2.1 A Unified Approach for Designing Algorithm Based on Quantifier Transformation

The efficiency of an algorithm is mainly influenced by the method of algorithm design and implementation, the data structures and programming language of describing algorithm. In PAR [26], we put emphasis on the method of algorithm design and implementation. In general, it is easier to design algorithms using enumeration or exhaustive search, but the algorithms have low efficiency; in contrast, it is more difficult to design efficient algorithm using effective design method. Generally speaking, using traditional method, e.g. dynamic programming, greedy, divide-and-conquer, etc., one can get efficient algorithm, but the difficult is in choosing suitable one. Since implementing algorithm using iteration has higher efficiency than using recursion, we stick to iteration rather than recursion in our methodology. We generalize the recurrence relation concept of a sequence of numbers (difference equation) to problem solving sequence and propose a unified approach for designing algorithmic program [26]. It covers several existed algorithm design techniques including divide-and-conquer, dynamic programming, greedy, enumeration and some nameless methods. The designer of algorithms using PAR method can partly avoid the difficulty in making choice among various existed design methods. Using the approach, we have formally developed many nontrivial algorithmic programs, including graph algorithms [29], travel tree algorithms [32].

2.2 A New Representation of Algorithms

The most important notion in PAR is recurrence relation of problem solving sequence, short for recurrence. Based on the recurrence relation, the structure of an algorithm is defined as follows [23,24]:

ALGORITHM: ⟨algorithm name⟩
SPECIFICATION: ⟨algorithm specification⟩
BEGIN: ⟨initialization of variables and function in the recurrence⟩
TERMINATION: ⟨termination condition of the recurrence⟩
A_I: ⟨algorithm invariant⟩
RECUR: ⟨set of recurrences⟩
END

We get a new representation of algorithm, mainly a set of recurrences and initiations. That is exactly a set of mathematical formulae and is easy for formal proof and derivation. It characterizes main idea of an efficient algorithm and is more precise and simple than the representation of algorithm in natural language, flowchart and program. **The Radl expressions have referential transparency and make the formal derivation of algorithms possible. The particular merit of the new representation of algorithm is easiness of understanding and demonstrating the ingenuity and correctness of an algorithm.**

2.3 The New Techniques About Loop Invariants

The recursive program corresponding to recursive algorithm can be developed directly based on the recurrence relation. We just pay main attention on developing the program corresponding to iterative algorithm. The key for developing correct iterative program is loop invariant. This is recognized by not only the advocator of formal methods of design algorithms and programs but also some specialist of algorithm design, for example, Kingston, Baase, etc. However, the existing standard strategies for developing loop invariants are only suitable for some simple problems. There are many complicated algorithms and programs that cannot get satisfying loop invariants using these techniques. This leads to that many computer scientists doubt the possibility of deriving or proving algorithms and programs using loop invariant. In [25], we exposed new properties of loop invariant and presented the new definition of loop invariant and two new strategies for developing it. Following is the new definition and one of the two new strategies.

The new definition and strategies are quite powerful, especially in using the recursive definition technique of new strategy to develop the loop invariant of an iteration program with inherent recursive property. Using the new techniques, we have formally proved and derived many nontrivial algorithmic programs, including graph algorithms, travel tree algorithms, sorting algorithms, array section algorithms and some numeric algorithms. A convincing example is formal development of Knuth's challenging program that converts a binary fraction to decimal fraction with certain conditions [13,27,28].

2.4 Genericity for Modeling

The generic mechanisms in executable programming languages such as Java and C++ play an important role in increasing the reusability and reliability of software and efficiency of software development. However, how to apply genericity to modeling language is rarely successful, although generic mechanism such as classifier templates, operation templates and package templates is provided in Unified Modeling language. Due to the complexity of UML itself and the difficulty of use, the wide application of genericity in MDE is seriously affected. To solve the above problems, the author of this paper proposes a generic modeling language mechanism implexmented in PAR [34]. One of the distinct features of the PAR platform is the agile genericity mechanisms. In PAR not only a value, a data type and an ADT can be generic parameter, and a computing-action (including operator, method, function and procedure, transaction, subsystem and web service, etc.) can be generic parameter too.

2.5 The New Techniques for Generating Database Application Program

In Radl and Apla, accessing to database is an expression of abstract operations rather than SQL statements. The expression is much simpler and shorter than SQL statement. It gives us one methodology to develop the database application system with high reliability and productivity. This makes formal derivation or proof of a database application program possible.

2.6 Distributed Transaction Processing in PAR

The popularization and application of advanced technologies such as cloud computing, big data and information system make computer software more and more complex, and the reliability and development efficiency of software cannot be guaranteed. The distributed transaction processing technology can be widely used in software development. Here, an abstract language mechanism of concurrent distributed transaction processing is proposed and integrated into the Apla modeling language. The expanded Apla language of the platform is called Apla+. Based on Apla+, a general transaction processing system is implemented [23]. It is very easy and convenient to build abstract general transaction processing programs and then convert them into Java and other executable language programs. Because the strict correctness of abstract programs can be proved by the standard program proving method, the reliability of the transaction processing system is improved. This paper introduces the whole process of transaction processing program design and code generation through a typical example.

3 Main Elements in PAR

PAR method given in [25,26] is a formal methods. It provides the methodology that supports formal development of algorithmic programs described using some executable language; say Ada, Java, C++ and C#, from their formal specification. The Forming of PAR is a long term research plan and been supported by a series of national research foundations including NSFC and 863 High-Tech program.

3.1 Data Type and Action in PAR

3.1.1 Standard Data Type

The standard data type referred to in this article is the data type set in the common executable programming language such as C++ and Java, character type, floating point type, Boolean type and so on.

3.1.2 Predefined Composed Data Type

These type types are stored in the component library in the form of abstract data type (ADT) designed by the system designer, and can be used as standard data types. The system predefines set, List, bag, binary tree, graph, relational data and other predefined data types. The two implementations of each predefined data were predefined.x

3.1.3 Self-defined Abstract Data Type (ADT)

The PAR platform provides an abstract data type language mechanism defined self for building system models. The above three data types can be used as generic parameters of modeling language.

3.1.4 Standard Action

Standard actions are operators in common executable programming language.

- ▶ Numeric operators: $+, -, *, /, \%$
- ▶ Logic operators: $\wedge, \vee, \equiv, \urcorner, \Box$
- ▶ Comparison Operator$>, \geq, <, \leq, =$

3.1.5 Self-defined Action

User defined action self: Subprogram, function, procedure, method, subsystem, transaction, service, thread, etc.

The above two actions can be used as generic parameters of modeling language.

3.1.6 Pre-defined Action

In PAR, the predefined action including several quantifiers. See Sect. 3.3.

3.2 Formal Modeling Language Radl

3.2.1 Requirement Modeling

Using the data types and actions provided in the Radl modeling language, we can describe the formal requirements of various typical algorithms and applications. Based on these formalized requirements, we can make use of the change rules of quantifier and other logical expressions to realize the system function refinement and data refinement, and get a system model which is closer to the executable program language model. That is the algorithm model and the abstract program design model.

3.2.2 Algorithm Modeling

Radl was designed for the description of algorithm specifications, transformation rules for deriving algorithms and algorithms itself. We presented a set of abstract notations for expressing pre-defined abstract data type, say array, set, sequence, binary tree and graph, etc. The motivation of developing these mathematics-oriented notations is aimed at making specification transformation, algorithm derivation and program proof like operating traditional mathematical formula. The most important notion in PAR method is *recurrence relation of problem solving sequence*, short for *recurrence*. Based on the recurrence, the core of an algorithm is defined as a set of recurrences, see Sect. 2.2.

The Radl expressions have referential transparency that makes the formal derivation of algorithms possible. Radl was designed for the description of algorithm specifications, transformation rules for deriving algorithms and algorithms itself. We presented a set of abstract notations for expressing pre-defined data type, say array, set, list, tree, graph and database, etc. Radl provides a user-defined mechanism for abstract data type.

3.3 Rules of Specification Transformation

Most of specification transformation rules are quantifier properties and are proved in [15,16]. Following are used in this paper. Let θ be an binary operator and big θ be the quantifier of operator θ, then,

$$(\theta\ i : r(i) : f(i)) \tag{1}$$

Means the quantity of $f(i)$ where i range over $r(i)$. We write the quantifier of binary operator $+$, $\bullet$, $\wedge$, $\vee$, $\Diamond$ (minimum), $\blacklozenge$ (maximum), $\cap$ (intersection),

$\cup$ (union) and $\uparrow$ as $\sum, \prod, \forall, \exists, \Diamond, \blacklozenge, \cap, \cup$ and $\uparrow$. Obviously operator $+, \bullet, \wedge, \vee, \Diamond, \blacklozenge, \cap, \cup$ are associative and commutative and their quantifier θ have following properties:

(a) Multi-dummies

$$(\theta\ i, j : r(i) \wedge s(i, j) : f(i, j)) = (\theta\ i : r(i) : (\theta\ j : s(i, j) : f(i, j))) \quad (2)$$

(b) Split with no overlap

$$(\theta\ i : r(i) : f(i)) = (\theta\ i : r(i) \wedge b(i) : f(i))\ \theta\ (\theta\ i : r(i) \wedge \neg b(i) : f(i)) \quad (3)$$

(c) One point split

$$(\theta\ i : 0 \leq i < n + 1 : f(i)) = (\theta\ i : 0 \leq i < n : f(i))\ \theta\ f(n) \quad (4)$$

(d) Generalized Associativity and Commutativity

$$(\theta\ i : r(i) : s(i) \theta\ f(i)) = (\theta\ i : r(i) : s(i))\ \theta\ (\theta\ i : r(i) : f(i)) \quad (5)$$

3.4 Modeling Language Apla

The purpose of developing Apla is to implement functional abstract and data abstract in program development perfectly, so that any Apla program is simple enough and is ease for understanding, formal derivation or proof. It is also ease to transform into some OOP language programs, say C++, C#, and Java, etc.

Apla is a object-based programming with convenient generics. The purpose of developing Apla is to implement functional abstract and data abstract in program development perfectly so that any Apla program is simple enough and is ease for understanding, formal derivation or proof. It is also ease to transform into some OOP language programs, say C++, Java, C# etc... Apla and Radl have same standard procedures and functions. The data types and Pre-defined ADTs and are also same. We borrow some control structure from Dijkstras Guarded Command Language, but restrict the nondeterminism.

3.5 Generic Constructions [34]

3.5.1 Type Region and Type Variable

In Radl and Apla, we define the set of types that satisfy some properties as type region and a type parameter in a program unit as type variable. The syntax of the type region declaration is as follows:

$$some\ type\ =\ \{set\ of\ types\ satisfied\ some\ properties\};$$

3.5.2 Action Region and Action Variable

We define the set of all action that satisfy some properties as action region and an action parameter in a program unit as action variable. The syntax of the action region declaration is similar with type region. The action can be the predefined operators of Apla and defined procedures, functions and services by users.

$$Action\ region:\ someaction\ =\ \{set\ of\ actions\ satisfied\ some\ properties\};$$

3.5.3 ADT Region and ADT Variable

The ADT consists of the set of data and the set of operations. The model of ADT can be a algebra system. We define the set of all ADT that satisfy some properties as ADT region and an ADT parameter in a program unit as ADT variable. The syntax of the action region declaration is similar with type region.

$$ADT\ region:\ someadt\ =\ \{set\ of\ ADT\ satisfied\ some\ properties\};$$

3.6 Mechanism of Distributed Transaction Processing

Following is two components described using Java, where running of Transaction-Thread will make PAR enter concurrent and distributer environment, DistTransaction is used to implement distributed transaction process. Following operation appeared in Radl and Apla that make PAR implement simply Distributed Transaction Processing.

TransactionThread: component of transaction processing thread;
DistTransaction: distributed transaction processing component;
commit
rollback
exception
TransactionThread: component of transaction processing thread;

3.7 Automatic Model Transformation Tools

Radl algorithms and Apla programs are simple enough and ease for formal derivation and proof. But, it cannot be executed in a computer. Therefore, we developed the PAR platform that consists of 5 automatic transformation tools of algorithms or programs. One of them would be able to transform a Radl algorithm into Apla program. Others may transform Apla programs to the programs of target language, says C++ and Java, etc. Based on the PAR platform, the efficiency of developing algorithms and program and reliability of the programs are increased obviously.

3.8 Correctness of Model and Correctness of Model Transformation

3.8.1 Correctness of Model

The model defined in this paper can be refined by manual refinement of the requirement model, and then the algorithm model, abstract program model and executable language program model can be obtained in turn. These models can also be automatically generated by model automatic converters. Such models can be based on the definition of loop invariant and development strategy given

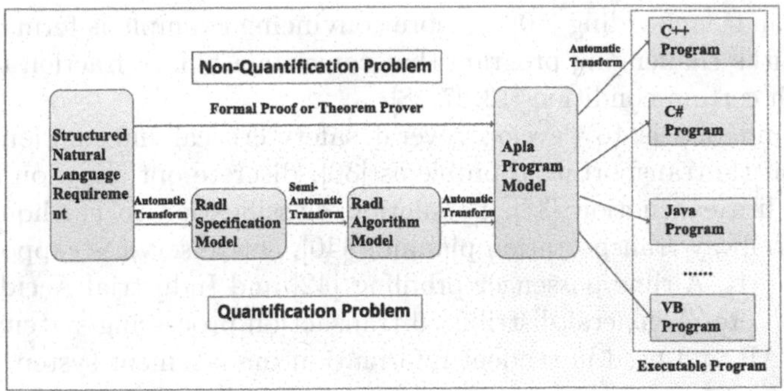

Fig. 1. Architecture of PAR platform

by Xue [25], using Dijkstra-Gries standard algorithm and program correctness proof method, formalized or automatically proved the relevant algorithms and program correctly. It can also be calculated the reliability of the program by software testing method.

3.8.2 Correctness of Model Transformation

The correctness of model transformation directly affects the correctness of the model. The correctness of model transformation can guarantee the correctness of the algorithm and program generated by the transformation. To prove the correctness of the model transformation, it is necessary to use the knowledge of category theory.

3.9 Architecture of PAR Platform

The architecture of PAR Platform is show in Fig. 1. There are two ways to generate codes. The first way is for processing quantification problem. PAR Platform can transform SNL requirement model to Radl specification model, then to Radl algorithm model, and to Apla abstract program model, finally to executable program. The second way is for processing non-quantification problem. Users can directly design Apla program manually and give it's formal proof, then transform it to executable program.

4 Applications and Case Studies

4.1 There are Two Kinds of Applications of PAR

The first one is that many nontrivial algorithms and programs have been developed formally, formal derivation or formal proof, including graph algorithms [29], travel tree algorithms [32], array section algorithms [25,26], Knuths famous hard problem of cyclic permutation [10,24,33]. The abstract Hopcroft-Tarjan planarity algorithm was described in Apla. The Apla program was transformed by PAR platform to C++ code that can correctly test the planarity and generate improved planar embedding [10]. A more convincing example is formal development of Knuths challenging program that converts a binary fraction to decimal fraction with certain condition [13,27,28].

The second one is to develop several safety-critical information systems, including shuttle transportation problems [36], discrete optimization algorithm design [37], fire evacuation [38], population classification in earthquakes [39], Emergency railway transportation planning [40], active services support for disaster rescue [41], Airline passenger profiling [42] and Industrial Accident Early Warning [43], etc. A general distributed transaction processing system is implemented in PAR and used in student information management system [23].

4.2 Case Studies

The case studies consists of two typical nontrivial examples. One is a simple problem, but the solution in not. Another is one Apla program section that comes from a student information management system.

The Cubes of the First n Natural Numbers. Given is an integer n, $0 \leq n$. Develop a program to store in array $b[0 \ldots n-1]$ the cubes of the first n natural numbers. Thus, upon termination, for each $i, 0 \leq i < n, a[i] = i^3$. The program may not use exponentiation, multiplication, or division, only use addition and subtraction.

The problem seems quite simple but in my teaching experience no student is be able to solve the problem correctly. Even more, no student is able to understand the correctness of the program after we show them the final solution. Here, we develop the algorithm and the program based on PAR method.

■ **Step 1.** Describe the formal functional specification of an algorithmic problem using Radl;

AQ1: Given is an integer $n, 0 \leq n$

AR1: $(i : 0 \leq i < n : a(i) = i^3)$

For satisfying the postcondition AR2, we repeat following two steps:

■ **Step 2.** Partition the problem into a couple of subproblems each of which has the same structure with the original problem;

■ **Step 3.** Formally derive the algorithm from the formal functional specification. The algorithm is described using Radl and represented by recurrences and initialization;

Based on the postcondition AR2 and algebra law, we have

$a(i+1) = (i+1)^3 = i^3 + 3i^2 + 3i + 1$ [Partition the problem]

Let $a(i) = i^3$

Then $a(i+1) = a(i) + 3i^2 + 3i + 1$ [Derive the recurrence]

For computing $3i^2$

Let $b(i) = 3i^2$

Then $b(i+1) = 3(i+1)^2 = 3i^2 + 6i + 3$ [Partition the problem]

$\quad = b(i) + 6i + 3$ [Derive the recurrence]

For computing $6i$

Let $c(i) = 6i$

Then $c(i+1) = 6(i+1) = 6i + 6 = c(i) + 6$..............(1)
$b(i+1) = b(i) + c(i) + 3$..............(2)
For computing $3i$
Let $d(i) = 3i$
Then $d(i+1) = 3i + 3 = d(i) + 3$..............(3)
$a(i+1) = a(i) + b(i) + d(i) + 1$..............(4)

Obviously, the algorithm invariant **AI1** is

AI1: $a(i) = i^3 \wedge b(i) = 3i^2 \wedge d(i) = 3i \wedge c(i) = 6i \wedge 0 \leq i < n$

Combining recurrence (1)–(4), then assign the initial value to each function, we got the algorithm for solving the problem:

```
ALGORITHM: Cube
SPECIFICATION: {AQ1; AR1}
{AI1}
RANGE: 0 ≤ i < n
BEGIN: i := 0 : a(i) = 0 : b(i) = 0 : c(i) = 0 : d(i) = 0;
RECUR: a(i + 1) = a(i) + b(i) + d(i) + 1;
       b(i + 1) = b(i) + c(i) + 3
       c(i + 1) = c(i) + 6;
       d(i + 1) = d(i) + 3;
END
```

■ **Step 4.** Develop loop invariant directly based on our new strategy [23] straightforward; Considering the algorithm, we need an array variable, say a, to store the cube of integer i ; simple b, c, d to store the value of function b(i), c(i), d(i). According to our definition [23], the loop invariant of a loop program is an assertion that reflects verification law of each variable in the loop. Thus, we have the loop invariant:

LI.1: $a(i) = i^3 \wedge b(i) = 3i^2 \wedge d(i) = 3i \wedge c(i) = 6i \wedge 0 \leq i < n$

■ **Step 5.** Based on the loop invariant, transform the Radl algorithm and algorithm specification to Apla program and program specification mechanically or automatically;

In this example, the program specification $\{PQ1; PR1\}$ is same as the algorithm specification $\{AQ1; AR1\}$. We transform the algorithm and algorithm invariant into Apla program as follows:

```
PROGRAM: Cube
{PQ1; PR1}
i := 0 : a(i) = 0 : b(i) = 0 : c(i) = 0 : d(i) = 0;
{LI.1}
DO i ≠ n − 1 → a(i + 1) = a(i) + b + d + 1;
               b = b + c + 3
               c = c + 6;
               d = d + 3;
OD
```

This program was described using Extended Guarded Command Language (Apla), but it cannot be run on a computer. For getting an executable program, we must do:

■ **Step 6.** Transform the Apla program to an executable language program, say Ada, C++, Java, etc. mechanically or automatically.

Apla Program Section for Information Processing. The problem is to connect the student database and to get student name from the database, to store the names into an array, then to store and sort the data in the array to the binary tree according to inorder and dictionary order.

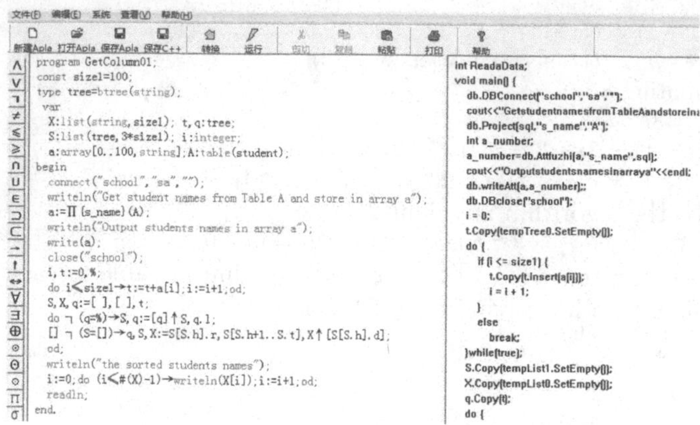

Fig. 2. Apla and C++ Program section for accessing and sorting student names

The Apla program of solving the problem is in the left part of the Fig. 2. The right part of the Fig. 2 is the corresponding C++ code generated by automatic model transforming tools. Observing the Apla program is quite short, only 32 lines, but C++ code has 330 lines. The Apla program access the student name from student database, then to build the binary tree stored by inorder, then to store the node data according to inorder tree walk. The student name in the array is ordered according a nondecreasing sequence.

This example show us 3 points: the abstract lever of Apla is very high; the Apla program is ease to read; the correctness of Apla program is quite ease to verifying. The details showed in [32].

5 Related Work

The PAR method and PAR platform is a unified and systematic approach for formal development of algorithm and programs. There are some similar formal approaches with ours.

Program calculus, this approach is the most famous formal methods for developing algorithm and program, which was created by Dijkstra [7] and developed into practical techniques by Gries [9], Backhouse et al. [3]. The approach treats program and algorithm as same thing. A program is developed hand-in-hand with its loop invariant and proof of correct-ness. Our development of the algorithm and program has some similarity with theirs. However our emphasis is different: we separate algorithm, represented by recurrence, from program, then pay special attention on formal derivation of algorithm rather than program calculus. The algorithm represented by recurrence relation is exactly a set of mathematical formula and has mathematical transparency. Therefore, it can be produced directly by formal derivation based on some simple mathematical tools. After getting correct algorithm represented by recurrence, trans-forming it into correct program is a trivial work. The work can be done mechanically. It is possible to develop a software system to finish it automatically. However, using calculus approach, one derive program by weakening program specification. The program statement cannot be produced directly by formal derivation because it has no mathematical transparency. There is a big gap between weakened program specification and program. It is difficult to remove the gap mechanically and automatically.

B method [1], **RAISE** [18], **Kestrelwares** [19], **Orc** [6,12,16], **rCOS**, [15,21], **NDAUTO** [44] and **NDADAS** [44], etc., Comparing with those formal methods and program generating system, PAR method and PAR platform have following innovative techniques that described in Sect. 2: 2.1 A Unified Approach for Designing Algorithm Based on Quantifier Transformation; 2.2 A New Representation of Algorithms; 2.3 The New Techniques About Loop Invariants; 2.4 Generosity for Modeling; 2.5 The new techniques for generating database application program; 2.6 Distributed Transaction Processing In PAR.

6 Conclusion and Future Work

1. On the basis of the study of the essential features of formal methods, this paper focuses on overcoming complex, difficult to understand and inconvenient for application in the existing formal methods specification and design language. We put forward a new formal methods definition. Based on the definition, we research successful and practical formal methods and support platform, namely the PAR method and PAR Platform. PAR method and the PAR platform have been successfully applied in the formal development of complex algorithms and information processing software. The effect is remarkable, which proves the correctness and effectiveness of the new definition of formal method proposed in this paper.
2. The paper describes the effectiveness of the 6 innovative theories and techniques given in Sect. 2.2. These innovative theories and techniques, which guarantee the advanced and innovative nature of the PAR and PAR platforms, and become the theoretical and technical basis for the realization of the PAR platform, and can also effectively carry out the development and promotion of the development of formal software.
3. The formal methods proposed and implemented by PAR have been applied in the formalized development of complex algorithms and programs. It has solved a number of international problems and has important theoretical value. Using the PAR method and the PAR platform, many Safety-Critical information processing systems have been developed, in the actual earthquake, fire, and aviation accidents. The success of disaster rescue work proves that PAR has great practical application value.
4. The formal methods of software development and the model driven engineering MDE have their own advantages and disadvantages in practical application. Combining these two methods can serve as a complement to each other and will effectively promote the renewal and development of software development methods. We will work in this area.

Acknowledgments. At first, our thanks go to anonymous reviewers for helpful suggestion and comments that changed the presentation of this paper.

Our warm thanks go also to Prof. David Gries for his kind encouragement and suggestions. His academic thought deeply influenced our research team.

We would like to thank Xu Wensheng, Zuo Zhengkang, Shi Haihe, Wang ChangJing, who attended the previous work of the project.

References

1. Abrial, J.-R.: The B Book - Assigning Programs to Meanings. Cambridge University Press, Cambridge (1996)
2. Adesina, O.: Integrating formal methods with model-driven engineering. In: International Conference on Model-Driven Engineering Languages and Systems, Ottawa, Canada (2015)
3. Backhouse, R.C.: Program Construction and Verification. Prentice Hall International, London (1986)
4. Bjørner, D., Havelund, K.: 40 years of formal methods: some obstacles and some possibilities? In: Jones, C., Pihlajasaari, P., Sun, J. (eds.) FM 2014. LNCS, vol. 8442, pp. 42–61. Springer, Cham (2014). https://doi.org/10.1007/978-3-319-06410-9_4
5. Clarke, E.M., Wing, J.M.: Formal methods: state of the art and future directions. ACM Comput. Surv. **28**(4), 626–643 (1996)
6. Cook, W., Misra, J.: Structured interacting computations. In: Wirsing, M., Banâtre, J.-P., Hölzl, M., Rauschmayer, A. (eds.) Software-Intensive Systems and New Computing Paradigms. LNCS, vol. 5380, pp. 139–145. Springer, Heidelberg (2008). https://doi.org/10.1007/978-3-540-89437-7_9
7. Dijkstra, E.W.: A Discipline of Programming. Prentice Hall, Upper Saddle River (1976)
8. Gargantini, G., Riccobene, A.E., Scandurra, P.: Combining formal methods and MDE techniques for model-driven system design and analysis. Int. J. Adv. Softw. **3**(1 and 2), 1–18 (2010)
9. Gries, D.: The Science of Programming. Springer, New York (1981). https://doi.org/10.1007/978-1-4612-5983-1
10. Gries, D., Xue, J.: Generating a random permutation. In: BIT28, vol. 10 pp. 569–572 (1988)
11. Gries, D., Xue, J.: The hopcroft-tarjan plannarity algorithm presentations and improvements. TR88-906, CS Department of Cornell University, pp. 1–20 (1988)
12. Kitchin, D., Quark, A., Cook, W., Misra, J.: The Orc programming language. In: Lee, D., Lopes, A., Poetzsch-Heffter, A. (eds.) FMOODS/FORTE -2009. LNCS, vol. 5522, pp. 1–25. Springer, Heidelberg (2009). https://doi.org/10.1007/978-3-642-02138-1_1
13. Knuth, D.: A simple program whose proof isn't. In: Beauty is Our Business. A Birthday Salute to E.W. Dijkstra (1990). (Ed. by, W.H.J. Feijen et al.)
14. Jones, C.B.: Systematic Software Development Using VDM. Prentice-Hall International, New York (1986)
15. Liu, Z., Morisset, C., Stolz, V.: rCOS: Theory and tool for component-based model driven development. In: Arbab, F., Sirjani, M. (eds.) FSEN 2009. LNCS, vol. 5961, pp. 62–80. Springer, Heidelberg (2010). https://doi.org/10.1007/978-3-642-11623-0_3

16. Misra, J., Cook, W.R.: Computation orchestration: a basis for wide-area computing. J. Softw. Syst. Model. (2017)
17. Paull, M.C.: Algorithm Design—A Recursion Transformation Framework. Wiley, New York (1987)
18. RAISE. http://spd-web.terma.com/Projects/raise
19. Smith, D.R.: KIDS: a semiautomatic program development system. IEEE Trans. Softw. Eng. **16**(9), 1024–1043 (1990)
20. Spivey, J.M.: Introducing Z: A Specification Language and Its Formal Semantics. Combridge University Press, New York (1988)
21. Ke, W., Li, X., Liu, Z., Stolz, V.: rCOS: A formal model-driven engineering method for component-based software. Fronti. Comput. Sci. China **6**(1), 17–39 (2012)
22. Woodcock, J., Larsen, P.G., Bicarregui, J., Fitzgerald, J.: Formal methods: practice and experience. ACM Comput. Surv. **41**(4), 19 (2009)
23. Xia, J., Xue, J.: Design and implementation of concurrent distributed transaction in modeling language Apla. In: NCTCS (2018, to appear)
24. Xue, J., Gries, D.: Developing a linear algorithm for cubing a cycle permutation. Sci. Comput. Program. **11**, 161–165 (1988)
25. Xue, J.: Two new strategies for developing loop invariants and its applications. J. Comput. Sci. Technol **8**(3), 147–154 (1993)
26. Xue, J.: A unified approach for developing efficient algorithmic programs. J. Comput. Sci. Technol. **12**(4), 314–329 (1997)
27. Xue, J., Davis, R.: A simple program whose derivation and proof is also. In: First IEEE International Conference On Formal Engineering Method (1997)
28. Xue, J., Davis, R.: A derivation and proof of Knuths binary to decimal program. In: Software: Concepts and Tools, vol. 12, pp. 149–156 (1997)
29. Xue, J.: Formal derivation of graph algorithmic programs using partition and recur. J. Comput. Sci. Technol. **13**(6), 553–561 (1998)
30. Xue, J.: A practicable approach for formal development of algorithmic programs. In: International Symposium on Future Software Technology (ISFST-1999), Masami Noro, October 1999
31. Xue, J.Y.: Developing the generic path algorithmic program and its instantiations using PAR method. In: The Second Asia Workshop On Programming Languages and Systems, Korea (2001)
32. Xue, J.: PAR method and its supporting platform. In: International Workshop on Formal Method for Developing Software, Annual Report, Macao: UNU-IIST, no. 348 (2006)
33. Xue, J., Yang, B., Zuo, Z.: A linear in-situ algorithm for the power of cyclic permutation. In: Preparata, F.P., Wu, X., Yin, J. (eds.) FAW 2008. LNCS, vol. 5059, pp. 113–123. Springer, Heidelberg (2008). https://doi.org/10.1007/978-3-540-69311-6_14
34. Xue, J.: Genericity in PAR platform. In: Liu, S., Duan, Z. (eds.) SOFL+MSVL 2015. LNCS, vol. 9559, pp. 3–14. Springer, Cham (2016). https://doi.org/10.1007/978-3-319-31220-0_1
35. Xue, J.: PAR: a model driven engineering platform for generating algorithms and software. In: Symposium on Programming: Logics, Models, Algorithms and Concurrency to recognize Jayadev Misra's Accomplishments, University of Texas, 29th and 30th April 2016. https://www.cs.utexas.edu/symposium
36. Zheng, Y.J., Xue, J.Y.: A simple Greedy algorithm for a class of shuttle transportation problems. Opt. Lett. **3**(4), 491–497 (2009)
37. Zheng, Y.J., Xue, J.Y.: A problem reduction based approach to discrete optimization algorithm design. Computing **88**(1–2), 31–54 (2010)

38. Zheng, Y.J., Ling, H.F., Xue, J.Y., Chen, S.Y.: Population classification in fire evacuation: a multiobjective particle swarm optimization approach. IEEE Trans. Evol. Comput. **18**(1), 70–81 (2014)
39. Zheng, Y.J., Ling, H.F., Chen, S.Y., Xue, J.Y.: A hybrid neuro-fuzzy network based on differential biogeography-based optimization for online population classification in earthquakes. IEEE Trans. Fuzzy Syst. **23**(4), 1070–1083 (2014)
40. Zheng, Y.J., Zhang, M.X., Ling, H.F., Chen, S.Y.: Emergency railway transportation planning using a hyperheuristic approach. IEEE Trans. Intell. Transp. Syst. **16**(1), 321–329 (2015)
41. Zheng, Y.J., Chen, Q.Z., Ling, H.F., Xue, J.Y.: Rescue wings: mobile computing and active services support for disaster rescue. IEEE Trans. Serv. Compt. **9**(4), 594–607 (2016)
42. Zheng, Y.J., Sheng, W.G., Sun, X.-M., Chen, S.Y.: Airline passenger profiling based on fuzzy deep machine learning. IEEE Trans. Neural Netw. Learn. Syst. **28**(12), 2911–2923 (2017)
43. Zheng, Y.J., Chen, S.-Y., Yu, X., Xue, J.-Y.: A pythagorean-type fuzzy deep denoising auto-encoder for industrial accident early warning. IEEE Trans. Fuzzy Syst. **25**(6), 1561–1575 (2017)
44. Xu, J.: The Automation of software. IEEE Trans. Syst. (1993). Qinghua Published Company
45. Formal methods C Wikipedia. https://en.wikipedia.org/wiki/Formal_methods

Verification

Deductive Verification of Hybrid Control Systems Modeled in Simulink with KeYmaera X

Timm Liebrenz[(✉)], Paula Herber, and Sabine Glesner

Software and Embedded Systems Engineering, Technische Universität Berlin, Berlin, Germany
{timm.liebrenz,paula.herber,sabine.glesner}@tu-berlin.de

Abstract. Hybrid control systems are, due to their ever-increasing complexity, more and more developed in model-driven design languages like Simulink. At the same time, they are often used in safety-critical applications like automotive or medical systems. Ensuring the correctness of Simulink models is challenging, as their semantics is only informally defined. There exist some approaches to formalize the Simulink semantics, however, most of them are restricted to a discrete subset. To overcome this problem, we present an approach to map the informally defined execution semantics of *hybrid* Simulink models into the formally well-defined semantics of differential dynamic logic (d$\mathcal{L}$). In doing so, we provide a formal foundation for Simulink, and we enable deductive formal verification of hybrid Simulink models with an interactive theorem prover for hybrid systems, namely KeYmaera X. Our approach supports a large subset of Simulink, including time-discrete and time-continuous blocks, and generates compact and comprehensible d$\mathcal{L}$ models fully-automatically. We show the applicability of our approach with a temperature control system and an industrial case study of a multi-object distance warner.

Keywords: Hybrid systems · Formal verification
Model-driven development

1 Introduction

The complexity of embedded systems is steadily increasing. To cope with this problem, model-driven design is widely used for their development. One commonly used model-based design language for hybrid control systems is Simulink [15]. Simulink enables fast and efficient design of dynamic systems, and comes with mature tool support for graphical editing, simulation, and automated code generation. While simulation enables validation of the system behavior for a given set of input scenarios, it is not sufficient for safety-critical systems, such as cars or medical devices, where faulty behavior can cause injuries or even threaten human lives. Formal verification can provide guarantees about crucial

J. Sun and M. Sun (Eds.): ICFEM 2018, LNCS 11232, pp. 89–105, 2018.
https://doi.org/10.1007/978-3-030-02450-5_6

system properties for all possible input scenarios. However, the semantics of Simulink is only informally defined, which impedes formal verification. There exist some approaches to formalize the Simulink semantics and thus to enable formal verification [2,11,22]. However, most of them are restricted to a discrete subset. The few approaches that support both time-discrete and time-continuous behavior are restricted to very special classes of hybrid systems [5].

In this paper, we present an approach for deductive formal verification of hybrid control systems modeled in Simulink. The key idea of our approach is that we map the informally defined semantics of Simulink into the formally well-defined semantics of differential dynamic logic (d$\mathcal{L}$) [21]. This has four major advantages: First, with our mapping, we precisely and unambiguously capture the Simulink semantics and thus define a formal semantics for Simulink. Second, we enable a fully-automatic transformation of given Simulink models into d$\mathcal{L}$ models. Third, our transformation supports both time-discrete and time-continuous Simulink blocks, and thus is applicable to a broad range of hybrid control systems modeled in Simulink. Fourth, the resulting d$\mathcal{L}$ models enable the machine-assisted deductive verification of safety properties of given Simulink models for all possible input scenarios using the interactive theorem prover KeYmaera X [9]. Our transformation keeps the structure of the Simulink model transparent to the designer by mapping stateful Simulink blocks into equivalent d$\mathcal{L}$ variables.

The rest of this paper is structured as follows: In Sect. 2, we introduce Simulink and d$\mathcal{L}$. We discuss related work in Sect. 3. In Sect. 4, we present our transformation from Simulink into d$\mathcal{L}$. We illustrate our approach with a hybrid temperature control system in Sect. 5 and demonstrate its practical applicability with an industrial case study in Sect. 6. In Sect. 7, we conclude our paper.

2 Preliminaries

In this section, we introduce the preliminaries for the remainder of this paper.

2.1 Simulink

MATLAB/Simulink [15] enables modeling and simulation of hybrid control systems. The basic building elements are blocks that have input and output ports. Signals connect these ports. There are different kinds of blocks, e.g., direct feedthrough, time-discrete, time-continuous, and control flow blocks.

Figure 1 shows a temperature control system modeled in Simulink. It is designed for an operation room and allows fine-granular temperature control: it takes a heating value (*HeatOn*) and a cooling value (*HeatOff*) as input, which are real values that represent the temperature gradient, and adjusts the current temperature accordingly. The desired temperature is defined as a constant block *Tdes*. In a feedback loop, a *Switch* block determines whether a heating or cooling value is used. The output temperature (*Tout*) is calculated by integrating the input values over (continuous) time with the *Integrator* block, and the result is

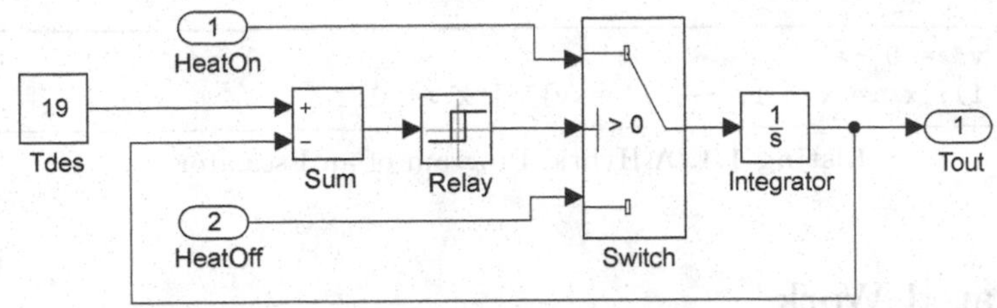

Fig. 1. Simulink model

used to control the *Switch*. The control signal is relayed (*Relay*) to avoid rapid switching, i.e. only if the output temperature deviates from the desired temperature by more than a given min or max value, the control signal changes. We use this example in Sect. 5 to illustrate our approach.

2.2 KeYmaera X

KeYmaera X is a theorem prover for deductive verification of hybrid systems that are modeled in differential dynamic logic (d$\mathcal{L}$). Systems in d$\mathcal{L}$ are modeled as hybrid programs, which can model time-discrete as well as time-continuous behavior. The main language elements of a hybrid program α are the following: Let α and β be hybrid programs, x a variable, θ an arithmetic expression and H a first-order formula. The *sequential composition* $\alpha; \beta$ connects two hybrid programs so that α is executed before β. The *nondeterministic choice* $\alpha \cup \beta$ (or α ++ β) allows for a branch in the execution, where either α or β can be executed. A *nondeterministic repetition* α^* repeats an inner program α an arbitrary number of times. With a *discrete assignment* $x := \theta$ a value given by θ is assigned to variable x. A *nondeterministic assignment* $x := *$ assigns an arbitrary value to the variable x. In a *continuous evolution* $(x'_1 = \theta_1, \dots x'_n = \theta_n \,\&\, H)$, the variables x_i evolve according to the given gradient θ_i as long as the invariant H holds, which is also called the evolution domain. Note that the evolution may stop at any time. If a *test formula* $?H$ is given, the execution continues only if it holds.

To specify requirements, d$\mathcal{L}$ supports the modality operators $[\alpha]\phi$ and $\langle\alpha\rangle\phi$, where ϕ is a d$\mathcal{L}$ formula. The modality $[\cdot]$ is true if ϕ is true after all runs of α. The modality $\langle\cdot\rangle$ is true if ϕ is true after at least one run of α.

Listing 1.1 shows a hybrid program that models a person on an escalator [18]. The variable x denotes the position of the person and v the speed of the escalator. The person can step down $(x := x - 1)$ if it is not already at the bottom $(x > 1)$, or move up with speed v for an arbitrary time $(x' = v)$. This can be repeated an arbitrary number of times $(\{\cdot\}^*)$. The specification $[\cdot]$ requires that under the precondition $x \geq 2 \wedge v \geq 0$, after all possible executions, $x \geq 0$.

```
x >= 2 & v >= 0 ->
{[{?(x > 1); x := x - 1; ++ {x' = v}}*] x >= 0}
```

Listing 1.1. A Hybrid Program of an Escalator

3 Related Work

In this section, we first discuss approaches for formal verification of general hybrid systems. Then, we discuss formal verification approaches for Simulink.

Hybrid System Verification. A widely used formalism for the verification of hybrid systems are hybrid automata [1]. Hybrid automata have gained wide attention in the hybrid systems community, and many verification approaches for hybrid systems have been based upon this formalism [8, 10]. The disadvantage of all model checking techniques is, however, the construction of the state space of the underlying model, which is exponential in the number of concurrent processes. As a consequence, model checking approaches typically do not scale for larger systems. In [19, 20], the authors present a contract-based approach for the verification of hybrid systems. System components together with their contracts are specified in d$\mathcal{L}$ and are then semi-automatically verified using KeYmaera X. By providing deductive verification techniques, KeYmaera X provides a promising approach that scales better than model checking based approaches for many systems. In particular, by arguing with invariants as an abstraction of the complete system behavior, KeYmaera X has the potential to avoid an exhaustive exploration of the state space. However, the system design and the contracts must be provided as a formal model in d$\mathcal{L}$, which typically requires a high expertise as well as a high manual effort. In practice, complex systems are often developed in languages like Simulink, where the semantics is informally defined. This impedes the verification process and requires either a manual development of a formal model or a transformation into a formally well-defined language.

Simulink Formalization and Verification. Most existing approaches for formal verification of Simulink transform Simulink models into some formal representation. For example, in [2], the authors present a transformation of Simulink models into Why3 to enable deductive verification [7]. In [11], Simulink models are transformed into the UCLID verification system [13], and thus enable Satisfiability Modulo Theory (SMT) solving for the verification of safety properties. In [22], Boogie [3] is used as formal representation, and the SMT solver Z3 [6] for formal verification. However, all of these approaches only consider a discrete subset of Simulink and are not applicable for hybrid systems. In [23], a toolbox for the simulation of hybrid equations in Simulink is presented. However, this approach only allows the simulation of systems and does not provide means to formally verify them for arbitrary input scenarios. In [5], the tool CheckMate for modeling and verification of hybrid automata in Simulink is presented. They provide special blocks to model and verify polyhedral invariant hybrid automata (PIHA). However, this approach can only be applied for a special class of hybrid systems and requires the use of specialized blocks. Thus, it is not applicable for most industrial Simulink models. Most closely related to our approach is the approach presented in [17], where a transformation from Simulink into a specific hybrid automata dialect (SpaceEx) is proposed. This enables the use of reachability algorithms for hybrid automata. However, concurrency is modeled using parallel composition of hybrid automata, so the state space is exponential in the number of concurrent blocks. In the work of [4], a synchronous language that incorporates the use of ordinary differential equations is presented. They present how different Simulink blocks can be expressed in the Zelus language. However, they do not provide means to verify systems models. Finally, The MathWorks provides the Simulink Design Verifier [16], which provides model checking as well as abstract interpretation techniques. However, the Design Verifier is only applicable for time-discrete Simulink models, and its scalability is limited [11], as it is based on an exploration of exponential state spaces.

With our approach, we enable deductive (and thus potentially scalable) verification of *hybrid* control systems modeled in Simulink with the hybrid theorem prover KeYmaera X.

4 From Simulink to Differential Dynamic Logic

In this section, we present our mapping from the informal execution semantics of Simulink into the formally well-defined semantics of $d\mathcal{L}$, and an automatic transformation from Simulink models into equivalent $d\mathcal{L}$ representations. With our fully-automatic transformation, the developer only needs to provide a Simulink model and a requirements specification (in $d\mathcal{L}$), and can then use KeYmaera X to interactively prove safety properties, as shown in Fig. 2.

Our approach for the transformation from Simulink to $d\mathcal{L}$ is twofold: First, we define transformation rules that map the semantics of individual Simulink blocks to $d\mathcal{L}$. Second, we compose the individual blocks into a $d\mathcal{L}$ representation that precisely captures the semantics of the original model. Our key idea to faithfully model the exact data, control, and timing dependencies of the original model is to introduce discrete state variables for time-discrete blocks that keep an inner state, continuous evolutions to model time-continuous blocks, and to use a sophisticated macro mechanism to represent stateless behavior, e.g. port connections, arithmetic calculations, and, in particular, control flow. Since all macros are fully expanded during the transformation, our macro mechanism does not introduce additional variables in the final $d\mathcal{L}$ model, and since we keep the structure of the original model transparent to the designer using prefixing, the resulting models are compact and comprehensible.

In the following subsection, we define the Simulink subset we support with our approach. Then, in Sect. 4.2 we present our transformation rules for individual blocks. In Sect. 4.3, we present our algorithm for automatic system composition.

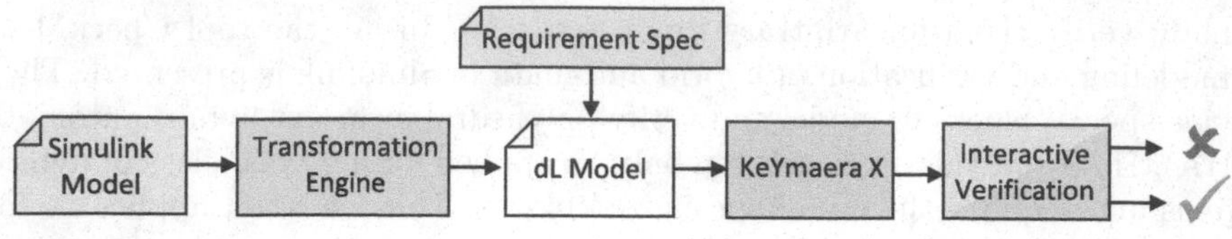

Fig. 2. Verification approach

4.1 Assumptions

We require a given Simulink model to fulfill the following assumptions.

1. No algebraic loops are used.
2. No S Function blocks are used.
3. No external scripts or libraries are used.

If all three assumptions are met, we can automatically transform a given hybrid control system in Simulink into a hybrid program in d$\mathcal{L}$. Note that many industrial Simulink models meet these requirements. Note also that some additional assumptions on the concrete block set are imposed by the current state of our implementation, which can be easily extended with further blocks, i.e., a transformation rule for a (continuous) integrator block is conceptually the same as that for a (continuous) sine wave block.

4.2 Transformation Rules

In this subsection, we define transformation rules for individual blocks and illustrate our approach with showcases for different block groups. Each transformation rule defines the semantics of a given block as a tuple (M, β), where M is a set of macros, and β a hybrid program that describes the behavior of the block. Each macro $m \in M$ consists of an expression id that is replaced by another expression e during the transformation process. To denote that such a macro is applied to a hybrid program α, we write $\alpha[id \leftarrow e]$. A hybrid program β consists of assignments and continuous evolutions as introduced in Sect. 2.2. Note that the hybrid programs for individual blocks may be incomplete in the sense that some variables are undefined (e.g., the input of the current block). These undefined variables are replaced by macros of other blocks during the transformation process. As a preparation for our transformation rules, we assign a unique identifier to each output port of every block. These identifiers are also used for the input ports to which the output ports are connected. Note that we add all transformed behavior in a nondeterministic loop. This enables us to consider the behavior of changing streams of values and not only single values.

Inports. Inports connect a system to an environment and provide incoming signals. Our transformation rule for Inports is shown in the first row of Table 1.

Table 1. Showcase transformation rules

Simulink block		**Macros and d$\mathcal{L}$ representation**

Inport	1 → *out*	$M : \{\alpha[out \leftarrow input]\}$
		β : `{ input := *;`
		`?(input <= IN_MAX & input >= IN_MIN);`
		`}`

Sum	in_1 → op_1 ⋮ in_n → op_n → *out*	$M : \{\alpha[out \leftarrow 0\, op_1(in_1) op_2(in_2) ... op_n(in_n)]\}$ β : `{}`

Unit Delay	*in* → $\frac{1}{z}$ → *out*	$M : \{\alpha[out \leftarrow output]\}$
		β : `{ ?(steptime >= STEPSIZE);`
		`output := state;`
		`state := in;`
		`++`
		`?(steptime < STEPSIZE);`
		`}`

Switch	in_1, c_{in}, in_2 → c_{switch} → *out*	$M : \{\alpha[out \Leftarrow \{(in_1, c_{switch}), (in_2, \neg c_{switch})\}]\}$
		$=$ `{ { ?(`c_{switch}`);`
		$\alpha[out \leftarrow in_1, c_{switch}]$;
		`++`
		`?(`$\neg c_{switch}$`);`
		$\alpha[out \leftarrow in_2, \neg c_{switch}]$;
		`} }`
		β : `{}`

Integrator	*in* → $\frac{1}{s}$ → *out*	$M : \{\alpha[out \leftarrow s]\}$ β : `{s' = in}`

There, we introduce a d$\mathcal{L}$ variable *input* for the provided signal, and define a macro that replaces all occurrences of the unique identifier assigned to the output port of a given Inport block (*out*) with *input*. The hybrid program β that models an Inport block consists of two parts: First, to model arbitrary inputs, we use a *nondeterministic assignment*. Second, if the requirements contain information on bounds for input signals, a *test formula* is added to the hybrid program, which defines the range of the possible values.

Direct Feedthrough Blocks. Direct feedthrough blocks, e.g. arithmetic or logic blocks, do not have an inner state and write their results directly to their output ports. To model this, we create a macro that performs the operation defined by the semantics of a given block. As an example, the transformation rule of the *Sum* block is shown in the second row of Table 1. Note that all macros are fully expanded in the final d$\mathcal{L}$ model, that is, for the *Sum* block rule shown in the second row of Table 1, all occurrences of *out* will be replaced by the combination of all inputs in_i with the operators op_i defined by the parameter of the block (which might be '+' or '−' for a Sum block). Note that the input variables in_i are replaced by other expressions resulting from the transformation rules of the preceding blocks during the transformation process.

Time-Discrete Blocks. Blocks with time-discrete behavior, e.g. Unit Delay and Discrete Integrator, are blocks with an inner state that changes only at given sample times. The transformation rule for the *Unit Delay* block is shown in the third row of Table 1. There, the input value `in` is stored in an inner state and yielded at the output with a delay of one cycle. The variable `state` represents the inner state of the Unit Delay block, and `output` the delayed output. To model discrete steps, we introduce a constant `STEPSIZE` that captures a given sample time and a continuous variable *steptime*. Discrete state variables are only updated if *steptime* is equal to `STEPSIZE`, otherwise no behavior is added. To model time, we add *steptime* to the continuous evolution of the system with a derivative of 1. To consider each discrete step, we add `steptime <= STEPSIZE` to the evolution domain. We update all outputs of time-discrete blocks at the beginning of the evaluation of discrete steps. After all discrete assignments, we reset *steptime* to zero, if `steptime >= STEPSIZE`.

Control Flow Blocks. Control flow blocks, e.g. the *Switch* block, change the control flow of the system. This may create a discrete jump in time-continuous behavior. To transform control flow blocks, we introduce a new kind of macro, namely conditional macros. The idea of a conditional macro is that we make the macro mechanism dependent on control flow conditions. To this end, we first define an extended replacement function $\alpha[id \leftarrow e, c]$, which replaces id with e in a hybrid program α as above and additionally adds the condition c to all evolution domains (invariants) in α. A *conditional macro* is given by $\alpha[id \Leftarrow CM]$, where id is the identifier that should be replaced and CM is a set of conditional replacements (e_i, c_i) The expansion of a conditional macro is defined as follows:

$$\begin{aligned}\alpha[id \Leftarrow CM] &= \alpha[id \Leftarrow \{(e_1, c_1), ..., (e_n, c_n)\}] \\ &= \texttt{\{ ?(}c_1\texttt{); } \alpha[id \leftarrow e_1, c_1]\texttt{; ++ ... ++ ?(}c_n\texttt{); } \alpha[id \leftarrow e_n, c_n]\texttt{; \}}\end{aligned}$$

A conditional macro creates a nondeterministic choice, where a hybrid program α that contains id is split into multiple cases (one case for each condition c_i). In each case with condition c_i, id is replaced by the corresponding e_i. We illustrate the use of conditional macros with the transformation rule for a *Switch* block in the fourth row of Table 1. The Switch has three input signals, namely a control input c_{in} and two data inputs c_1 and c_2, one output signal out, and an internal condition c_{switch}. If the control input c_{in} fulfills the condition c_{switch} the first data input in_1 is written to out, otherwise the second data input in_2 is written to out. Note that the switch condition c_{switch} is of the form $c_{in} \sim C$ with $\sim \in \{>, \geq, \neq\}$ and C a constant Simulink expression. This concept to handle control flow can be easily adapted for other control flow blocks. Note that our conditional macro mechanism may introduce more cases than necessary.

To increase the readability of the transformed program, our implementation of conditional macros only creates nondeterministic choices for assignments and evolutions where *id* actually occurs.

Time-Continuous Blocks. According to the Simulink simulation semantics, time-continuous blocks, e.g. Integrator, Ramp and Sine Wave blocks, are executed concurrently. To capture this in our transformation, we combine the evolution of all state variables of all time-continuous blocks into one continuous evolution. Note that this continuous evolution also contains a variable for the simulation time. Note also that the continuous evolutions may be split by conditional macros. Still, each choice then contains all continuous state variables. We illustrate our transformation rule for time-continuous blocks with the *Integrator* block in the bottom row of Table 1. The Integrator block takes the input signal in and integrates it over time. This means that it models the differential equation $s(t) = \int_0^t in(\tau)\,d\tau$, which is equivalent to $\frac{ds(t)}{dt} = in(t)$, where s is the inner state of the integrator.

4.3 Model Composition

In the previous subsections, we have defined transformation rules for a broad range of Simulink blocks, including blocks with time-discrete and time-continuous behavior. In this subsection, we present our approach for the transformation of hybrid control systems that may consist of an arbitrary number of direct feedthrough, time-discrete, control flow and time-continuous blocks into d$\mathcal{L}$. The main challenge in combining the individual block transformation rules defined above is to precisely capture the interactions between blocks.

```
VariableDeclarations
Preconditions & Initializations ->
[ { ... }* ] Postcondition
```

Listing 1.2. Structure of a transformed model

To capture the combined behavior of a given hybrid control system modeled in Simulink, we introduce one global simulation loop, which is modeled as a *nondeterministic repetition* in d$\mathcal{L}$, and comprises both discrete assignments and continuous evolutions, as shown in Listing 1.2. The *Variable Declarations* contain all variables and constants that are used in the system. *Preconditions* are derived from the system requirements. In the *Initializations* section, initial values are assigned to variables and constants. The global simulation loop comprises the transformed system behavior, namely time-discrete behavior, additional assignments, e.g. assignments to variables that are used to influence the control flow and the time-continuous behavior, and continuous evolutions. Lastly, the *Postcondition* captures the properties that should be met according to the requirements specification. Note that in d$\mathcal{L}$, whenever a loop is left, it may or may not be executed again. Whenever the loop may terminate, all verification goals must hold to ensure correct system behavior. Thus, we verify that the postconditions always hold, independent of the number of system runs.

Transformation Algorithm. Our transformation algorithm walks through a given Simulink model, applies the transformation rules defined above, and incrementally builds a hybrid program. During the transformation process, each block is translated into a set of macros and a hybrid program consisting of assignments and/or continuous evolutions. The macros are collected, while the hybrid program is appended sequentially to the program in the simulation loop. When all blocks are translated, the macros are expanded. To ensure that all dependencies are correctly considered, we handle all time-discrete stateful blocks in the correct order, i.e. we start with blocks that have no inputs and then recursively handle all blocks where all input blocks have already been translated. Since direct feedthrough and stateless blocks are transformed using our macro mechanism, the transformation is not dependent on the order of these blocks. With our assumption that the system does not contain algebraic loops, each feedback loop in the original Simulink model contains at least one stateful block and this algorithm always terminates. Note that we flatten all subsystems at the beginning of the transformation and use prefixing to keep the structure of the original Simulink model transparent to the developer.

Discrete Jumps in Continuous Evolutions and Zero-Crossing Semantics. In Simulink, blocks are executed in time steps and the signals are calculated for each step. If the results of a calculation indicate a zero-crossing that causes a change in the system behavior, e.g. the condition at a Switch changes, smaller time-steps are used to find the best approximation of the time where the Switch block switches. In d$\mathcal{L}$, the default continuous evolutions can evolve an arbitrary amount of time. To enable the detection of switch points in continuous evolutions, we provide two additional rules for conditional macros: First, we create a new nondeterministic choice for each continuous evolution. Second, we add the corresponding conditions to the evolution domain. Together, this ensures that the continuous evolutions can only evolve as long as this control flow does not change. We extend the continuous evolutions in our transformation with $smallStep \leq EPS$ to ensure that control flow changes are evaluated with at most a delay of a given ϵ (EPS). Note that we also add the condition $steptime \leq STEPSIZE$ to the evolution domain of all continuous evolutions to ensure that discrete assignments take place each time the steptime elapses.

5 Illustrating Example: Temperature Control System

In this section, we illustrate our transformation from Simulink to d$\mathcal{L}$ using the temperature control system shown in Fig. 1. We have fully implemented our transformation from Simulink to d$\mathcal{L}$ in Java using the MeMo framework [12], which provides a parser for Simulink and an intermediate representation that enables easy access to elements of Simulink models. We have fully automatically transformed the temperature control system into an equivalent d$\mathcal{L}$ representation in only a few seconds. For this model we have verified two crucial properties using KeYmaera X, namely that it keeps the temperature in a certain range and that we avoid rapid switching, i.e. there is a minimal distance between each switching. The interactive verification within KeYmaera X took approximately 2 hours for the correct temperature range and approximately 8 hours for the absence of rapid switching. The necessary manual interactions include the addition of preconditions as well as the definition of loop invariants. Thanks to the tactics available in KeYmaera X, a re-execution of these proofs just takes a few minutes (if we provide the necessary conditions and invariants).

In the following, we first present the d$\mathcal{L}$ model resulting from the fully-automatic transformation process. Then, we illustrate the interactive verification process in KeYmaera X and discuss the necessary manual interactions.

5.1 Transformation to d$\mathcal{L}$

The transformation of our example system (Fig. 1) yields three simple and two conditional macros:

$$\begin{aligned} Integrator\_out &\leftarrow Integrator\_state \\ Sum\_out &\leftarrow Tdes\_out - Integrator\_out \\ Tdes\_out &\leftarrow Tdes \end{aligned}$$

$$\begin{aligned} Switch\_out \Leftarrow &\{(HeatOn\_out, Relay\_out > 0), (HeatOff\_out, Relay\_out \leq 0)\} \\ Relay\_out \Leftarrow &\{(Relay\_state, Sum\_out > Relay\_max), \\ &(Relay\_state, Sum\_out < Relay\_min), \\ &(Relay\_state, Sum\_out \geq Relay\_min \wedge Sum\_out \leq Relay\_max)\} \end{aligned}$$

Note that the conditional macro for the *Relay* block uses identical replacements in all three cases. This is due to the semantics of the Relay block, which prescribes that in all cases, the internally kept state is forwarded to its output. Still, the distinction between the three cases is necessary in order to enforce correct switching behavior. It is complemented with a discrete assignment to the internal state of the Relay block with 0 or 1, depending on the input value.

The full hybrid program in d$\mathcal{L}$ (without initial conditions and variable declarations) is shown in Listing 1.3. For brevity and simplicity of presentation, we omit prefixing and refer to the internal state of stateful blocks and to the output of stateless blocks with the block name (i.e., we use *Integrator* for *Integrator_s* and *HeatOn* for *HeatOn_out*).

The only discrete assignments (Lines 2–6) are generated for the *Relay* block, whose internal state is set to 1.0 or 0.0 depending on the deviation of the current temperature from the desired value of 19.0 degree celsius. For the continuous evolution (Lines 7–29), we distinguish all cases where the switching or relay behavior of the system changes. We use the corresponding conditions both as conditions in the evolution and as evolution domain. This ensures that whenever a switching or relay condition changes, the simulation loop is restarted and all conditions are newly evaluated. Note that we disjunct the evolution domain with $smallStep \leq EPS$ to allow for numerical approximations, i.e. to allow values to evolve a small step further than defined by the sample time. In each case, we have three continuous evolutions (e.g. Line 9): the simulation time *simTime* and the *smallStep* time evolve with a gradient of 1, and the *Integrator* evolves with *HeatOn* or *HeatOff*, depending on the current control flow conditions.

```
1  {smallStep:=0.0; OutPort1:=Integrator; HeatOn:=*; HeatOff:=*;
2    {?(Tdes-Integrator>=0.5); Relay:=1.0;
3    ++
4     ?(Tdes-Integrator<=-0.5); Relay:=0.0;
5    ++
6     ?((Tdes-Integrator<0.5) & (Tdes-Integrator>-0.5));
7    }{?((Tdes-Integrator>=0.5) & (Relay>0.0));
8     {simTime' = 1.0, Integrator' = HeatOn, smallStep' = 1.0
9     & ((Tdes-Integrator>=0.5) & (Relay>0.0)) | (smallStep<=EPS)}
10   ++
11    ?((Tdes-Integrator>=0.5) & (Relay<=0.0));
12    {..., Integrator' = HeatOff, ...
13    & ((Tdes-Integrator>=0.5) & (Relay<=0.0))|...}
14   ++
15    ?((Tdes-Integrator<=-0.5) & (Relay>0.0));
16    {..., Integrator' = HeatOn, ...
17    & ((Tdes-Integrator<=-0.5) & (Relay>0.0))|...}
18   ++
19    ?((Tdes-Integrator<=-0.5) & (Relay<=0.0));
20    {..., Integrator' = HeatOff, ...
21    & ((Tdes-Integrator<=-0.5) & (Relay<=0.0))|...}
22   ++
23    ?((Tdes-Integrator<0.5) & (Tdes-Integrator>-0.5) & (Relay>0.0));
24    {..., Integrator' = HeatOn, ...
25    & ((Tdes-Integrator<0.5) & (Tdes-Integrator>-0.5) & (Relay>0.0))|...}
26   ++
27    ?((Tdes-Integrator<0.5) & (Tdes-Integrator>-0.5) & (Relay<=0.0));
28    {.., Integrator' = HeatOff, ...
29    & ((Tdes-Integrator<0.5) & (Tdes-Integrator>-0.5) & (Relay<=0.0))|...}
30   }}*
```

Listing 1.3. Temperature Control System in d$\mathcal{L}$

5.2 Verification with KeYmaera X

To illustrate the interactive verification process in KeYmaera X, we have verified that our temperature control system keeps the temperature, which is given by the output value of *Integrator*, in a certain range around the desired temperature, and that we avoid rapid switching.

Correct Temperature Range. To show that the temperature control system keeps the temperature in a certain range of $\Delta \in \mathbb{R}$ around the desired value $Tdes \in \mathbb{R}$, we have defined the following property:

$$[\cdot]\, Tdes - \Delta \leq Integrator \leq Tdes + \Delta$$

We use the modal box operator to prove that this property holds after each simulation step. In the following, we set $Tdes = 19$ and $\Delta = 1$. To verify that our desired property holds as a loop invariant, we use loop induction. This yields the following proof goals:

$$HeatOn{\cdot}t + Integrator \geq 18, HeatOn \cdot t + Integrator \leq 20$$
$$HeatOff{\cdot}t + Integrator \geq 18, HeatOff \cdot t + Integrator \leq 20$$

where $t \in \mathbb{R}$ is a small step, e.g. defined for the first subgoal as: $t \geq 0 \wedge \forall \tau (0 \leq \tau \leq t \rightarrow 19.0 - (HeatOn \cdot \tau + Integrator) \geq 0.5 | \tau + smallStep \leq EPS)$.

These proof goals show us that the input values *HeatOn* and *HeatOff* need to provide a non-negative heating value respectively a negative cooling value. To resolve these goals and finally, to prove the desired property, we have manually added the following preconditions:

$$0 \leq HeatOn \leq 20 \wedge -20 \leq HeatOff \leq 0$$

This means that we can verify that the system keeps the temperature in the desired range for all possible input scenarios where the values of *HeatOn* and *HeatOff* are restricted by 20 respectively −20. The desired property can be shown automatically using the *Auto* tactic in KeYMaera X. Overall, the only manual interactions necessary are the introduction of the desired property as loop invariant and two additional preconditions.

Absence of Rapid Switching. To show that our temperature control system avoids rapid switching we have defined a constant *MIN*, which defines the required minimal distance between two switching actions. In addition, we have introduced two additional time variables *relayOnTime* and *relayOffTime*, which are reset whenever the *Relay* is set to 1.0 or 0.0, respectively. Then, we have defined the absence of rapid switching with the following property:

$$[\cdot]\, Relay = 0.0 \rightarrow relayOnTime \geq MIN \wedge Relay = 1.0 \rightarrow relayOffTime \geq MIN$$

Again, the modal box operator defines that the property should be true after all runs of a given hybrid program. We have again introduced the property as a loop invariant to ensure that it holds before and after each simulation step. In addition, we have manually inserted the following loop invariants:

$$Tdes - Integrator + HeatOff \cdot relayOffTime \leq -0.5$$
$$Tdes - Integrator + HeatOn \cdot relayOnTime \geq 0.5$$
$$Relay = 1.0 \rightarrow Tdes - Integrator > -0.5$$
$$Relay = 0.0 \rightarrow Tdes - Integrator < 0.5$$

Note that we do not assume that these loop invariants hold, but rather verify them as an intermediate verification step to help KeYmaera X find a proof for our desired property. We have included all loop invariants also as preconditions. In addition, we have manually added the following preconditions:

$$MIN = 0.01$$
$$relayOnTime \geq MIN \wedge relayOffTime \leq MIN$$
$$(-1.0/MIN) \leq HeatOff < 0.0 \wedge 0.0 < HeatOn \leq (1.0/MIN)$$

This means that we can verify the absence of rapid switching for all possible input scenarios where the values of *HeatOn* and *HeatOff* are restricted to a certain range. For example, if the minimal distance between two switching actions is 0.01, *HeatOn* should be lower than 100 and *HeatOff* greater than −100. Again, the desired property can be shown using the *Auto* tactic. Overall, the only manual interactions necessary are the introduction of the postcondition as loop invariant, four additional loop invariants, and four additional preconditions.

6 Evaluation

To evaluate the applicability of our approach, we have used a multi-object distance warner system provided by our partners from the automotive industry. A time-discrete variant of this case study was also used in [11], but they were not able to cope with the original hybrid version. In our evaluation, we have used the original hybrid version, and used our transformation for the core component of the system, namely a distance calculator, which comprises 18 blocks (including 5 time-discrete, 1 time-continuous, and 3 control flow blocks) and 23 signal lines. We have used KeYmaera X to prove two properties of the system, namely that no overflow can occur and that the distance increases if a positive relative speed is measured and decreases if a negative relative speed is measured.

Absence of Overflows. To verify the absence of overflows, we have introduced global constants *MINVAL* and *MAXVAL*. As shown in [11], the original model actually produces an overflow. To produce a counter-example that demonstrates this faulty behavior, we used the following requirements specification:

$$< \cdot > Integrator < MINVAL \vee Integrator > MAXVAL$$

For the interactive verification with KeYmaera X, we were able to produce a counter-example in 20 min. An automatic execution of the generated proof rules takes 5 min. To prevent the overflow, we have changed the integrator in the model to a bounded integrator, which holds its output value if it would rise above or fall below specified values. With the corrected model, we have then shown the absence of overflows using the following requirements specification:

$$[\cdot]\, Integrator \geq MINVAL \wedge Integrator \leq MAXVAL$$

We have verified this specification interactively in KeYmaera X in 21 min. An automatic execution of the generated proof rules takes 11 min.

Increasing and Decreasing Distance. A major advantage of our approach is that we can not only verify static properties like the absence of overflows, but also dynamic properties, i.e., dynamic relations between inputs and outputs. To illustrate this, we have verified that, under the condition that there is no zero crossing during the current measurement cycle time, a positive relative speed measurement causes an increase in the calculated distance at the output.

$$[\cdot]\, gainPrevious > 0 \land noZeroCrossing \implies relativeDistance \geq 0$$

An analogous formula can be used for a negative relative speed and a decreasing distance. To enable the proof, we have added state variables, which store the current sign and detect whether a zero crossing occurred. To not change the system behavior, we only add hybrid programs that are assignments to these new variables or nondeterministic choices of the form $\{?(c); \alpha; ++?(!c); \beta; \}$, where c is a condition, and α and β are hybrid programs of the just defined form or empty. We were able to prove the desired properties with KeYmaera X interactively in 7 h. An automatic execution of the generated proof rules takes 76 min.

7 Conclusion

In this paper, we have presented a novel approach for the deductive formal verification of hybrid control systems modeled in Simulink. The key idea is threefold: Firstly, we map the informally defined Simulink semantics to the formally well-defined semantics of differential dynamic logic ($d\mathcal{L}$). Secondly, we use an expressive macro mechanism to efficiently capture stateless behavior and arithmetic or logic expressions. Thirdly, we precisely capture discrete as well as continuous behavior in a nondeterministic repetitive simulation loop that combines discrete assignments and continuous evolutions. By using the box modality [.], we ensure that all possible behaviors are captured. We have presented a fully-automatic transformation from Simulink into $d\mathcal{L}$, and we have shown how the resulting $d\mathcal{L}$ model can semi-automatically be verified with the interactive theorem prover KeYmaera X. With the use of KeYmaera X, we are able to prove safety and correctness properties of hybrid control systems for all possible input scenarios.

The main idea of our transformation is twofold: (1) We provide transformation rules for individual blocks, which precisely capture the block semantics in $d\mathcal{L}$. (2) We provide a transformation algorithm that takes a Simulink model as input and yields a semantically equivalent $d\mathcal{L}$ representation. Our transformation approach supports true hybrid systems, i.e. it supports time-discrete, time-continuous and control flow blocks and takes their timing and interactions into account. To cope with discrete jumps in continuous behavior, we introduce a small time step behavior to model a maximum delay between the change of a value and the next step in which the control flow is updated. We have demonstrated the applicability of our approach by verifying crucial properties of a hybrid temperature control system and an industrial case study, namely a multi-object distance warner, using KeYmaera X.

In future work, we plan to increase the scalability of our approach by using contracts together with a service-oriented design approach for Simulink [14]. Furthermore, we plan to automatically generate verification goals for the absence of some industrially relevant error classes, e.g. overflows and division by zero.

References

1. Alur, R., Courcoubetis, C., Henzinger, T.A., Ho, P.-H.: Hybrid automata: an algorithmic approach to the specification and verification of hybrid systems. In: Grossman, R.L., Nerode, A., Ravn, A.P., Rischel, H. (eds.) HS 1991-1992. LNCS, vol. 736, pp. 209–229. Springer, Heidelberg (1993). https://doi.org/10.1007/3-540-57318-6_30
2. Araiza-Illan, D., Eder, K., Richards, A.: Formal verification of control systems' properties with theorem proving. In: 2014 UKACC International Conference on Control (CONTROL), pp. 244–249. IEEE (2014)
3. Barnett, M., Chang, B.-Y.E., DeLine, R., Jacobs, B., Leino, K.R.M.: Boogie: a modular reusable verifier for object-oriented programs. In: de Boer, F.S., Bonsangue, M.M., Graf, S., de Roever, W.-P. (eds.) FMCO 2005. LNCS, vol. 4111, pp. 364–387. Springer, Heidelberg (2006). https://doi.org/10.1007/11804192_17
4. Bourke, T., Carcenac, F., Colaço, J.L., Pagano, B., Pasteur, C., Pouzet, M.: A synchronous look at the Simulink standard library. In: ACM Transactions on Embedded Computing Systems (TECS), vol. 16, p. 176. ACM (2017)
5. Chutinan, A., Krogh, B.H.: Computational techniques for hybrid system verification. IEEE Trans. Autom. Control **48**, 64–75 (2003)
6. de Moura, L., Bjørner, N.: Z3: an efficient SMT solver. In: Ramakrishnan, C.R., Rehof, J. (eds.) TACAS 2008. LNCS, vol. 4963, pp. 337–340. Springer, Heidelberg (2008). https://doi.org/10.1007/978-3-540-78800-3_24
7. Filliâtre, J.-C., Paskevich, A.: Why3—where programs meet provers. In: Felleisen, M., Gardner, P. (eds.) ESOP 2013. LNCS, vol. 7792, pp. 125–128. Springer, Heidelberg (2013). https://doi.org/10.1007/978-3-642-37036-6_8
8. Frehse, G.: PHAVer: algorithmic verification of hybrid systems past HyTech. In: Morari, M., Thiele, L. (eds.) HSCC 2005. LNCS, vol. 3414, pp. 258–273. Springer, Heidelberg (2005). https://doi.org/10.1007/978-3-540-31954-2_17
9. Fulton, N., Mitsch, S., Quesel, J.-D., Völp, M., Platzer, A.: KeYmaera X: an axiomatic tactical theorem prover for hybrid systems. In: Felty, A.P., Middeldorp, A. (eds.) CADE 2015. LNCS (LNAI), vol. 9195, pp. 527–538. Springer, Cham (2015). https://doi.org/10.1007/978-3-319-21401-6_36
10. Henzinger, T.A., Ho, P.-H., Wong-Toi, H.: HyTech: a model checker for hybrid systems. In: Grumberg, O. (ed.) CAV 1997. LNCS, vol. 1254, pp. 460–463. Springer, Heidelberg (1997). https://doi.org/10.1007/3-540-63166-6_48
11. Herber, P., Reicherdt, R., Bittner, P.: Bit-precise formal verification of discrete-time MATLAB/Simulink models using SMT solving. In: 2013 Proceedings of the International Conference on Embedded Software (EMSOFT), pp. 1–10. IEEE (2013)
12. Hu, W., Wegener, J., Stürmer, I., Reicherdt, R., Salecker, E., Glesner, S.: MeMo-methods of model quality. In: MBEES, pp. 127–132 (2011)
13. Lahiri, S.K., Seshia, S.A.: The UCLID decision procedure. In: Alur, R., Peled, D.A. (eds.) CAV 2004. LNCS, vol. 3114, pp. 475–478. Springer, Heidelberg (2004). https://doi.org/10.1007/978-3-540-27813-9_40

14. Liebrenz, T., Herber, P., Göthel, T., Glesner, S.: Towards service-oriented design of hybrid systems modeled in Simulink. In: 2017 IEEE 41st Annual Computer Software and Applications Conference (COMPSAC), vol. 2, pp. 469–474. IEEE (2017)
15. MathWorks: MATLAB Simulink (www.mathworks.com/products/simulink.html)
16. MathWorks: White Paper: Code Verification and Run-Time Error Detection Through Abstract Interpretation. Technical report (2008)
17. Minopoli, S., Frehse, G.: SL2SX translator: from Simulink to SpaceEx models. In: Proceedings of the 19th International Conference on Hybrid Systems: Computation and Control, pp. 93–98. ACM (2016)
18. Mitsch, S., Platzer, A.: The KeYmaera X proof IDE: concepts on usability in hybrid systems theorem proving. In: 3rd Workshop on Formal Integrated Development Environment. Electronic Proceedings in Theoretical Computer Science, vol. 240, pp. 67–81. Open Publishing Association (2017)
19. Müller, A., Mitsch, S., Retschitzegger, W., Schwinger, W., Platzer, A.: A component-based approach to hybrid systems safety verification. In: Ábrahám, E., Huisman, M. (eds.) IFM 2016. LNCS, vol. 9681, pp. 441–456. Springer, Cham (2016). https://doi.org/10.1007/978-3-319-33693-0_28
20. Müller, A., Mitsch, S., Retschitzegger, W., Schwinger, W., Platzer, A.: Change and delay contracts for hybrid system component verification. In: Huisman, M., Rubin, J. (eds.) FASE 2017. LNCS, vol. 10202, pp. 134–151. Springer, Heidelberg (2017). https://doi.org/10.1007/978-3-662-54494-5_8
21. Platzer, A.: Differential dynamic logic for hybrid systems. J. Autom. Reason. **41**, 143–189 (2008)
22. Reicherdt, R., Glesner, S.: Formal verification of discrete-time MATLAB/Simulink models using Boogie. In: Giannakopoulou, D., Salaün, G. (eds.) SEFM 2014. LNCS, vol. 8702, pp. 190–204. Springer, Cham (2014). https://doi.org/10.1007/978-3-319-10431-7_14
23. Sanfelice, R., Copp, D., Nanez, P.: A toolbox for simulation of hybrid systems in MATLAB/Simulink: Hybrid Equations (HyEQ) toolbox. In: Proceedings of the 16th International Conference on Hybrid Systems: Computation and Control, pp. 101–106. ACM (2013)

Verification of Strong Nash-equilibrium for Probabilistic BAR Systems

Dileepa Fernando[1(✉)], Naipeng Dong[1], Cyrille Jegourel[2], and Jin Song Dong[1,3]

[1] National University of Singapore, Singapore, Singapore
fdileepa@comp.nus.edu.sg, {dcsdn,dcsdjs}@nus.edu.sg

[2] Singapore University of Technology and Design, Singapore, Singapore
jegourelcyrille@yahoo.fr

[3] Griffith University, Nathan, Australia

Abstract. Verifying whether rational participants in a BAR system (a distributed system including *Byzantine*, *Altruistic* and *Rational* participants) would deviate from the specified behaviour is important but challenging. Existing works consider this as Nash-equilibrium verification in a multi-player game. If the game is probabilistic and non-terminating, verifying whether a coalition of rational players would deviate becomes even more challenging. There is no automatic verification algorithm to address it. In this article, we propose a formalization to capture that coalitions of rational players do not deviate, following the concept of Strong Nash-equilibrium (SNE) in game-theory, and propose a model checking algorithm to automatically verify SNE of non-terminating probabilistic BAR systems. We implemented a prototype and evaluated the algorithm in three case studies.

1 Introduction

In general, most real-world systems involve collaboration of many distributed parties, e.g., Internet routing [20], peer-to-peer file sharing [3], cooperative backup [14], etc. In these systems, agents are assumed to follow the rules or specifications in the system designs. These rules/specifications may have to be followed over infinite times, e.g. in operating systems [17] and medical computing [7].

In such non-terminating concurrent multi-agent systems a particular agent may deviate from the system specifications to maximise its self-interest. Following the motto "Unity makes strength", self-interested agents may also deviate as coalitions to improve their individual rewards simultaneously. For example, miners in block-chain form coalitions to reduce the cost of breaking block-chain security (i.e. increase profit) [11]. It is thus natural to consider the system as a game[1] in which self-interested agents are rational players, implying that an agent cooperates only if it improves her benefit.

[1] Here, *game* refers to the atomic concept of Game Theory, defined as the study of mathematical models of conflict and cooperation between intelligent and rational decision-maker agents.

J. Sun and M. Sun (Eds.): ICFEM 2018, LNCS 11232, pp. 106–123, 2018.
https://doi.org/10.1007/978-3-030-02450-5_7

However, rational behaviours are not the only source of deviation from the specifications. Some devices may not work properly for other reasons than self-interest. The interacting components of a large system may be designed by different companies, that increases the probability of incompatibility or misconfiguration. Some devices may also have been intentionally designed to be malicious, in the sense that they aim more at the failures of other agents than the maximisation of their own rewards. Such agents/devices are named as Byzantine players in the game. Though a system is unlikely to work correctly in the presence of misconfigured agents, little has been done to verify such "damaged" system.

Byzantine-Altruistic-Rational (BAR)[2] models have been introduced in [2] in order to analyse the systems with selfish and "broken" agents. Later it has been extended in two directions: (1) Applying to probabilistic systems (PBAR) [9]; (2) Considering coalitions of rational players [16]. In this work we consider the combination - coalition of rational players in PBAR systems.

Verifying whether rational players deviate from the system specification in a BAR system is challenging due to the exhaustive strategy space of rational players. In PBAR, verification becomes even more challenging as the introduction of probabilities makes the calculations more complex. Moreover, in non-terminating PBAR, the convergence of rewards is not guaranteed. Especially, we consider the coalitions of rational players which require to reason about both group interest and individual interest.

Verification techniques like model checking have been used to guarantee whether a system satisfies some arbitrary properties derived from the specifications. For example, in the secret sharing protocol [10], model checking is used to guarantee that a secret is fairly distributed among entities that cooperate according to specified rules. Model checking algorithms are proposed to verify BAR [15], PBAR with stopping games [9] and BAR with a specific coalition [16]. However, there is no algorithm to automatically analyse coalitions in PBAR systems.

Contributions. We propose a formalization of Strong Nash Equilibrium (SNE) [19] to capture that any rational player or their coalition would not deviate from the specified behaviour in non-terminating probabilistic BAR systems (Sect. 5). We propose an approximation algorithm to automatically verify SNE (Sect. 6). We implement the algorithm as a prototype and evaluate the algorithm using case studies (Sect. 7).

2 Related Work

Nash-equilibrium. We observe two directions of research on Nash-equilibrium (NE): (1) Learning NE-strategy, e.g., in planning [18] and social behaviour analysis [13], where the environment and other players are dynamic; (2) analysing NE, where the environment and player behaviours are pre-defined, such as a PBAR

[2] In BAR model, the agents are divided in three categories, altruistic, rational or Byzantine. Only altruistic agents follow the system specification.

system in this work. In analysing NE, we observe 3 sub-directions, namely, computing NE, e.g., PRALINE [4], finding optimal strategy of rational players, e.g., PRISM-games [5] and verifying NE, e.g. EAGLE [21]. Verifying NE is further divided into two categories: applying to games with 0 or 1 rewards e.g., [21], and applying to games with cumulative reward objectives e.g., [15]. BAR system verification resides in the later category.

Model Checking for NE. The tool EAGLE [21] and PRALINE [4] only handle non-probabilistic games. The closest to our work is PRISM-games 2.0 [12], which performs multi-objective optimal strategy synthesis for rational coalitions in probabilistic games. However, PRISM-games 2.0 does not handle non-terminating games with discounted long-run rewards (A detailed comparison is presented in Sect. 7.1).

Verification of BAR Systems. The approach in [15] is only applicable for non-probabilistic BAR systems. Later, the work [9] extends it for probabilistic BAR systems stopping with probability 1; while the work [16] extends it with coalition but only considering coalitions with an agreed group reward. Our work combines both extensions in the concept level and further extends them to (1) probabilistic BAR systems in general (without the constraint to stop with probability (1) and (2) considering multi-objectives (individual interests in a coalition) rather than simply considering them as one agent/player.

3 Running Example

We illustrate a PBAR system using a simplified/artificial version of pricing game that is well-known in economics. Assume that sellers simultaneously set their prices for one type of product for an year. Buyers buy from the sellers who offer the cheapest price. The market share is thus divided equally between the sellers who offer the cheapest price. The profit of a seller in an year is the price times his market share for the year. The sellers make an agreement to reset the prices at the beginning of each year according to an agreed probabilistic distribution. A seller is altruistic if she follows the agreement, Byzantine if she chooses her price non-deterministically, rational if he chooses the price that maximizes her long-term profit. This game is played for infinite long time and the profit decreases each year at a rate β (to simulate the inflation or product depreciation).

For simplicity, we assume there are 3 sellers (d_1, d_2 and d_3) and 3 prices (p, $2p$ and $3p$), where p is a positive number. Initially, the sellers' prices are empty denoted as $\langle \perp, \perp, \perp \rangle$ respectively. The agreed price distribution is: resetting the price at p with probability 0.9 and resetting the price at $2p$ and $3p$ with probability 0.05 respectively. We assume d_1 and d_2 can be altruistic or rational and d_3 is Byzantine.

Reward Calculation Illustration. In the scenario that d_1 and d_2 are both rational, for a given year, assume d_1 and d_2 decide to set the price at p and d_3

decides to set the price at $2p$, then the prices for the first year are $\langle p, p, 2p\rangle$. Since buyers choose to buy at the lowest price, the buyers buy from d_1 and d_2. Assuming the total market share is 1, the market share for d_1, d_2 and d_3 is thus 1/2, 1/2, and 0 respectively. Hence, the profits for the sellers for the first year is $\langle 1/2 \times p, 1/2 \times p, 0 \times p\rangle = \langle p/2, p/2, 0\rangle$. The profits of other years can be calculated in the same way. Given a trace specifying the price decisions of the sellers of each chronological year, we can calculate the profit of a seller, denoted as $\mathit{profit}_1, \mathit{profit}_2, \mathit{profit}_3, \cdots$. Since in the long-run, the actual profit for each seller decreases by β, the long-term profit for a seller following the trace is

$$\mathit{profit}_1 + \mathit{profit}_2 * \beta + \mathit{profit}_3 * \beta^2 + \cdots = \Sigma_{t=1}^{\infty} \mathit{profit}_t * \beta^t.$$

4 PBAR System Specification

Given n players, we denote the set of Byzantine players as Z and denote the non-Byzantine set as Z'. A PBAR-system can be formally represented as follows.

Definition 1. *Given a set of n players and a subset Z of Byzantine players, a PBAR-system is a tuple $\mathcal{M} = (S, I, A, T, P, H)$, where*

- *S is a set of states,*
- *I is the set of initial states,*
- *$A = \Gamma_1 \times \Gamma_2 \times \cdots \times \Gamma_n$ is a set of actions, where Γ_i is player i's local action set.*
- *$T : S \times A \rightarrow S$ specifies the transition function,*
- *$P : S \times A \times \mathbb{P}(Z') \rightarrow [0, 1]$ specifies the probability of taking an action at a state, given a set of altruistic players, which is a subset of non-Byzantine players. $\mathbb{P}(Z')$ is the power set of Z'. A subset of non-Byzantine players is an element in $\mathbb{P}(Z')$.*
- *$H : \langle H_1(s, a), \ldots, H_n(s, a)\rangle$ where, $H_i : S \times A \rightarrow \mathcal{R}$ is the reward function of player i.*

Running Example Specification. According to the example specification, we have $n = 3$ and $Z = \{d_3\}$. A state represents the price combination of the sellers. Therefore there are 28 states in total, including $\{\langle t_1, t_2, t_3\rangle | t_1, t_2, t_3 \in \{p, 2p, 3p\}\}$ (27 states) and the initial state $\langle \bot, \bot, \bot\rangle$. The actions represent the chosen price $A = \{\langle \gamma_1, \gamma_2, \gamma_3\rangle | \gamma_1, \gamma_2, \gamma_3 \in \{p, 2p, 3p\}\}$. Since from any state it is possible to choose a price combination to go to any other state, the state transitions are edges in the complete graph of the 27 states, plus the edges from the initial state to each other states. The probability function is as follows: Since d_3 is Byzantine, the possible sets of altruistic players are $\emptyset$, $\{d_1\}$, $\{d_2\}$ and $\{d_1, d_2\}$. According to the probabilistic distribution of altruistic players' actions (only altruistic players follow the probabilistic distribution), we have for any $s \in S$ and $\langle \gamma_1, \gamma_2, \gamma_3\rangle \in A$, when only d_1 is altruistic[3],

$$P(s, \langle \gamma_1, \gamma_2, \gamma_3\rangle, \{d_1\}) = \begin{cases} 0.9 & \text{if } \gamma_1 = p \\ 0.05 & \text{if } \gamma_1 = 2p \text{ or } \gamma_1 = 3p. \end{cases}$$

[3] We do not need to consider the case of $\emptyset$ as there is no probability in this case.

By replacing γ_1 with γ_2, d_1 with d_2 in the above equation, we obtain $P(s, \langle\gamma_1, \gamma_2, \gamma_3\rangle, \{d_2\})$. When both d_1 and d_2 are altruistic,

$$P(s, \langle\gamma_1, \gamma_2, \gamma_3\rangle, \{d_1, d_2\}) = \begin{cases} 0.81 & \text{if } \gamma_1 = p \wedge \gamma_2 = p \\ 0.045 & \text{if } \gamma_1 = p \wedge \gamma_2 = 2p \text{ or } \gamma_1 = 2p \wedge \gamma_2 = p \text{ or} \\ & \quad \gamma_1 = p \wedge \gamma_2 = 3p \text{ or } \gamma_1 = 3p \wedge \gamma_2 = p \\ 0.0025 & \text{otherwise (4 cases).} \end{cases}$$

The pay-off function H is defined as $\langle H_1(s, a), H_2(s, a), H_3(s, a)\rangle$ where $a = \langle\gamma_1, \gamma_2, \gamma_3\rangle$,

$$H_i(s, \langle\gamma_1, \gamma_2, \gamma_3\rangle) = \begin{cases} \gamma_i * \frac{1}{m} & \text{if } \gamma_i = \min\{\gamma_1, \gamma_2, \gamma_3\} \\ & m \text{ is the number of minimum prices in } \langle\gamma_1, \gamma_2, \gamma_3\rangle \\ 0 & \text{otherwise.} \end{cases}$$

5 Formalizing Strong Nash-equilibrium

On top of the specification of a PBAR system, which captures the behaviour of altruistic, rational and Byzantine players, we now formalise the concept of Strong Nash-equilibrium (SNE) [19], capturing that coalition of rational players would not deviate from the specified altruistic behaviour for better pay-off in a PBAR system.

Intuitively, given a set of Byzantine players Z, for any coalition C ($C \subseteq Z'$), we compare the pay-off gained by the players in the coalition when they behave altruistically, named as the *altruistic game-reward*, and the maximum pay-off gained by the players in the coalition when they deviate, named as the *rational game-reward*. Only if a coalition's rational game-reward is better than the altruistic game-reward (i.e. at least one player in the coalition gets better reward while the other do not lose reward), then the coalition would deviate from the altruistic behaviours. In the following part, we show how to formalise/calculate the two types of rewards.

Given a PBAR system $\mathcal{M} = (S, I, A, T, P, H)$, a path is an action sequence $\pi = \pi_a^0, \ldots, \pi_a^{|\pi|-1}$ ($|\pi|$ can be infinite) where, $\pi_a^l \in A$ is the action at step l. π corresponds to a valid state sequence $\pi_s^0, \ldots, \pi_s^{|\pi|-1}$ where validity is captured by transition function T ($T(\pi_s^l, \pi_a^l) = \pi_s^{l+1}$ $0 \leq l \leq |\pi| - 1$). We denote the set of paths starting from a state s with length k as $\Pi^k(s)$.

In non-terminating systems, both altruistic game-reward and rational game-reward are accumulated in infinite steps starting from the same initial state. To avoid the reward getting infinite and thus not comparable, we use the discounted pay-off, as shown in calculating the long-term pay-off in the running example. Thus, the pay-off of player i following path π is $\mathsf{R}_i(\pi) = H_i(\pi_s^0, \pi_a^0) + H_i(\pi_s^1, \pi_a^1)\beta + \ldots + H_i(\pi_s^{k-1}, \pi_a^{k-1})\beta^{k-1}$.

However, $\mathsf{R}_i(\pi)$ cannot be directly used in the formalisation of SNE. First, we need to consider the Byzantine players in the context of PBAR. Since Byzantine players behave arbitrarily, for a given sequence of joint actions of players in C (a strategy of C), there may be various paths due to the Byzantine players' s choices. Among these paths, we assume that the coalition always consider its minimum pay-off, which captures the guaranteed pay-off of the coalition no matter how the Byzantine players behave. To calculate the guaranteed pay-off, we define two basic concepts: (1) *a joint action sequence of a set of players Λ following a path π* is $\mathsf{P}^{\pi}_{\Lambda} = \mathsf{p}(\pi^0_a, \Lambda), \cdots, \mathsf{p}(\pi^{|\pi|-1}_a, \Lambda)$ with $\mathsf{p}(\langle\gamma_1, \ldots, \gamma_n\rangle, \{\lambda_1, \ldots, \lambda_l\}) = \langle\gamma_{\lambda_1}, \ldots, \gamma_{\lambda_l}\rangle$, $\Lambda = \{\lambda_1 \ldots, \lambda_l\}$ (λ_i is the index of the player)[4]; and (2) *a joint action choice of length k (possibly infinite) for a set of players $\Lambda = \{\lambda_1 \ldots, \lambda_l\}$* is defined as $\Sigma^k_\Lambda = \alpha^1, \ldots, \alpha^k$, where $\alpha^l = \langle\gamma^l_{\lambda_1}, \ldots, \gamma^l_{\lambda_l}\rangle$ is the joint action choice at step l. Given a starting state s and a joint action choice Σ^k_Λ, there may be a set of multiple paths adhering the joint action choice, denoted as $\Phi(s, \Sigma^k_\Lambda) = \{\pi | \pi \in \Pi^k(s), \mathsf{P}^{\pi}_{\Lambda} = \Sigma^k_\Lambda\}$. Given a starting state s, if we fix a joint action choice of non-Byzantine players Z', the resulting subset of paths will only contain the paths that vary due to the choices of Byzantine players, denoted as $\Phi(s, \Sigma^k_{Z'})$ (i.e., $\Lambda = Z'$). In the set $\Phi(s, \Sigma^k_{Z'})$, for a player $i \in Z'$, we first calculate its pay-off of each path and then choose the minimum pay-off. The result is the guaranteed pay-off of i starting from s of length k, given a fixed non-Byzantine players' choice $\Sigma^k_{Z'}$. Formally,

$$u_{i,Z}(s, \Sigma^k_{Z'}) = \min\{\mathsf{R}_i(\pi) | \pi \in \Phi(s, \Sigma^k_{Z'})\}.$$

Second, due to the probabilistic behaviour of altruistic players, the system is probabilistic with multiple paths, and thus the pay-off of a player is always the expected pay-off, i.e., the pay-off of a path weighted by the probability of the path being taken. That is, if we release the constrain of fixing non-Byzantine players' choice to only fixing the rational/coalition[5] players' choice (Σ^k_C), for each player i, we will obtain a set of guaranteed pay-offs $\{u_{i,Z}(s, \Sigma^k_{Z'}) | \mathsf{P}^{\Sigma^k_{Z'}}_C = \Sigma^k_C\}$. Since the values in the set vary due to the probabilistic choice of altruistic players, they follow the same probabilistic distribution of altruistic players' joint choice. Thus we calculate the expected the pay-off of i by multiplying each value in the set with its corresponding probability and then adding up the results. Formally, the expected guaranteed pay-off of player i is

$$v_{i,Z}(s, \Sigma^k_C) = E(u_{i,Z}(s, \Sigma^k_{Z'}) | \mathsf{P}^{\Sigma^k_{Z'}}_C = \Sigma^k_C).$$

This prepares us to calculate the altruistic and the rational game-reward for players in a coalition. We finally release the constraint of a specified joint action choice of players in the coalition, and there will be the following two cases.

- Altruistic: When the players in C behave altruistically, due to their probabilistic behaviour, when releasing the constraint of a given joint action choice of C, there is a set of $v_{i,Z}(s, \Sigma^k_C)$ values which follow a probabilistic distribution. We calculate the expected value of them, which captures the player i's reward starting from state s with length k, when considering all the possible behaviours of Byzantine and altruistic players' behaviours,

$$U^k_{i,Z}(s) = E(v_{i,Z}(s, \Sigma^k_C) | \forall \Sigma^k_C).$$

[4] Essentially, $\mathsf{P}^{\pi}_{\Lambda}$ projects each action to a part of it.

[5] Note that the rational players are exactly players in the coalition, capturing that the rational players assume the unknown players (not in C) are altruistic by default.

- Rational: When the players in C are rational, they follow a joint action choice (the best strategy) that leads to the best rewards, denoted as Υ. When the coalition only contains one player i, Υ can be easily calculated as the maximum value in the set $O = \{v_{i,Z}(s, \Sigma_C^k) | \forall \Sigma_C^k\}$, capturing that i chooses her actions that lead to the best rewards. When the coalition contains multiple players, we will need to find the best pay-off which is non-trivial, since the best choice for one player may not be the best choice for other players in the coalition (discussed in the next Section). No matter which case, Υ is one value in the set O, i.e., $\Upsilon = v_{i,Z}(s, \Sigma_C^k)$ for some Σ_C^k.

To summarise, when s is an initial state and k is infinite, $U_{i,Z}^k(s)$ is i's altruistic game-reward; and the player i's ration game-reward will be $\Upsilon = v_{i,Z}(s, \Sigma_C^k)$ for some Σ_C^k.

Note that differing from the coalition in [16], we do not consider the entire coalition as a single agent/player. That is, if, to achieve the best rational game-reward, it requires some players to sacrifice their pay-off (i.e., some players lose pay-off following the coalition while others in the coalition gain), this coalition will not be valid, since each player in the coalition is rational. In this work, we say a coalition would deviate if for every player in the coalition, the rational game-reward is no less than the altruistic game-reward, i.e., all players do not lose. One last point is that, we introduce a parameter ϵ to quantify the least significant reward gain for deviation (i.e., a player in a coalition gains if his rational game-reward in the coalition is greater than ϵ plus his altruistic game-reward). This allows us to capture a variety of SNE parametrised by $\epsilon(> 0)$. As a side effect, we can achieve better termination of automatic verification by enlarging ϵ [15].

Therefore, a system satisfying ϵ-SNE is formalised as follows, capturing that there is NOT a joint action (Σ_C^∞) choice such that the coalition would deviate.

Definition 2 (ϵ-Strong Nash Equilibrium). *Let $\epsilon > 0$. A PBAR system $\mathcal{M} = (S, I, A, T, P, H)$ with Byzantine players Z is ϵ-SNE if $\forall C \subseteq Z', \nexists \Sigma_C^\infty$, s.t. $\forall i' \in C$, $\forall s \in I$,*

$$U_{i',Z}^\infty(s) + \epsilon < v_{i',Z}(s, \Sigma_C^\infty).$$

SNE in the Running Example. We illustrate the above ideas using the running example, by calculating the reward for the first year and the entire game-reward for two cases: coalition with size 1 and with size 2.

Calculating First Year Profits. As shown in Sect. 3, in the first year, given a fixed choice of d_1 and d_2 (non-Byzantine players), there are three pay-offs of d_1 (respectively d_2), depending on the choice of d_3. We choose the minimum value, i.e., the guaranteed pay-off of d_1 (respectively d_2). The guaranteed pay-offs of d_1 and d_2 and their corresponding action choices are shown in Table 1[6].

[6] In this example, it happens (uncommonly) that given any fixed choice of d_1 and d_2, that d_3 chooses the lowest price p leads to the guaranteed pay-off of d_1 and d_2 in every case.

Table 1. Guaranteed profit of d_1

Action choice	$\langle 2p, 2p, p\rangle$	$\langle 2p, 3p, p\rangle$	$\langle 2p, p, p\rangle$
Guaranteed pay-offs ($\langle d_1, d_2, d_3\rangle$)	$\langle 0, 0, p\rangle$	$\langle 0, 0, p\rangle$	$\langle 0, p/2, p/2\rangle$
Action choice	$\langle 3p, 2p, p\rangle$	$\langle 3p, 3p, p\rangle$	$\langle 3p, p, p\rangle$
Guaranteed pay-offs ($\langle d_1, d_2, d_3\rangle$)	$\langle 0, 0, p\rangle$	$\langle 0, 0, p\rangle$	$\langle 0, p/2, p/2\rangle$
Action choice	$\langle p, 2p, p\rangle$	$\langle p, 3p, p\rangle$	$\langle p, p, p\rangle$
Guaranteed pay-offs($\langle d_1, d_2, d_3\rangle$)	$\langle p/2, 0, p/2\rangle$	$\langle p/2, 0, p/2\rangle$	$\langle p/3, p/3, p/3\rangle$

Consider d_1, we first calculate her pay-off when she is altruistic. Since altruistic sellers' behaviour is probabilistic, we calculate the expected guaranteed pay-off of d_1, i.e., d_1's pay-off for each action choice (see Table 1) times its probability, $p/2 \times 0.9 \times 0.05 + p/2 \times 0.9 \times 0.05 + p/3 \times 0.9 \times 0.9 = 0.315p$. That is, $U^1_{1,\{3\}}(\langle \perp, \perp, \perp\rangle) = 0.315p$.

Second, we calculate the pay-off of d_1 when she is rational. In this case, she plays the action which gives her the maximum profit. For example, since d_3's action is always p, if d_2 also chooses p, there are three choices for d_1 (the first column in Table 1). d_1 chooses action p which gives pay-off $p/2$, since the other actions provide 0 pay-off. In this example, it happens that the best strategy for d_1 is always playing p, no matter how d_2 acts. Since d_2 is altruistic, the choice of d_2 is probabilistic. Therefore, the pay-off of d_1 is the expected pay-off depending on the choice of d_2, which is $p/2 \times 0.05 + p/2 \times 0.05 + p/3 \times 0.9 = 0.35p$. That is for any $\Sigma^1_{\{1\}}$, $v_{1,\{3\}}(\langle \perp, \perp, \perp\rangle, \Sigma^1_{\{1\}}) \leq 0.35p$.

Since d_1 and d_2 are symmetric, the pay-off of d_2 is exactly the same as d_1. When d_2 is altruistic, her pay-off is $U^1_{2,\{3\}}(\langle \perp, \perp, \perp\rangle) = 0.315p$; and when d_2 is rational, $\forall \Sigma^1_{\{2\}}, v_{2,\{3\}}(\langle \perp, \perp, \perp\rangle, \Sigma^1_{\{2\}}) \leq 0.35p$.

Therefore, when $\epsilon \leq 0.035p$, $U^1_{i,\{3\}}(\langle p, p, p\rangle) + \epsilon < v_{i,\{3\}}(\langle p, p, p\rangle, \Sigma^1_{\{i\}})$ for both d_1 and d_2. That is, d_1 and d_2 would deviate and thus the game is not a SNE for coalitions of size 1 with path of length 1.

Coalition of d_1 and d_2. According to Table 1, both d_1 and d_2 choosing the action p in which d_1 and d_2 gain $p/3$ individually, which is better than being altruistic which gains $0.315p$. When $\epsilon \leq (p/3 - 0.315p)$, d_1 and d_2 both deviate. In this particular case, the coalition deviation corresponds to their individual deviation.

Calculating Game Profits. Assuming $\beta = 0.5$, in this example, since the pay-offs for each year are the same as in the first year, the long-term game-reward for d_1 and d_2 when they are altruistic and rational (without coalition) are as follows ($i \in \{1, 2\}$ to indicate d_1 and d_2 respectively): $U_{i,\{3\}}(\langle \perp, \perp, \perp\rangle) = 0.315p + 0.315p\beta + \ldots = \frac{0.315p}{1-\beta}$, and $\forall \Sigma^\infty_{\{i\}}, v_{i,\{3\}}(\langle \perp, \perp, \perp\rangle, \Sigma^\infty_{\{i\}}) \leq 0.35p + 0.35p\beta + \ldots = \frac{0.35p}{1-\beta}$. Thus SNE with $\epsilon \leq \frac{0.035p}{1-\beta}$ is violated for coalitions size 1. When d_1 and d_2 form a coalition, similarly, the best joint action is both d_1 and d_2 choosing p. Each seller's long-term game-reward is $v_{i,\{3\}}(\langle \perp, \perp, \perp\rangle, \Sigma^\infty_{\{1,2\}}) = \frac{p/3}{1-\beta}$ for $i \in \{1, 2\}$.

The coalition would deviate when $\epsilon \leq \frac{(p/3-0.315p)}{1-\beta}$, since $U_{i,\{3\}}(\langle\bot,\bot,\bot\rangle)+\epsilon \leq v_{i,\{3\}}(\langle\bot,\bot,\bot\rangle, \Sigma^{\infty}_{\{1,2\}})$.

Note that in this example, it happens that the actions maximizing the game-reward coincide with the best actions in each year. However, this is not always true in general. In many cases, the best strategy leading to the best long-term game-reward may not be the best action in each step. Automated verification is particularly useful in such cases.

6 Verification Algorithm

6.1 Reduction

Verifying ϵ-SNE is equivalent to finding the negation of the ϵ-SNE conditions defined in Definition 2, i.e., finding a joint action choice of some coalition so that the players in the coalition deviate. If such a joint action choice exists, then ϵ-SNE is violated. Thus the verification problem can be reduced to a multi-objective optimization problem of finding the existence of feasible joint action choices.

The negation of Definition 2 is as follows: For some coalitions $C \subseteq Z'$ there exist Σ^{∞}_{C}, for all $i \in C$, $s \in I$, $v_{i,Z}(s, \Sigma^{\infty}_{C}) - U_{i,Z}(s) > \epsilon$. The verification of the above inequality can be reduced to the following multi-objective optimization problem:

$\underset{\Sigma^{\infty}_{C}}{\text{maximize}}$	**objective:** $v_{i,Z}(s, \Sigma^{\infty}_{C}) - U_{i,Z}(s)\ \forall i \in C$
subject to	**constraints:** $v_{i,Z}(s, \Sigma^{\infty}_{C}) - U_{i,Z}(s) > \epsilon\ \forall i \in C$

Given a fixed Σ^{∞}_{C} and $s \in I$, the objectives of players in C form an objective vector of n-dimensions ($n = |C|$) where each dimension represents each player's objective. Depending on different Σ^{∞}_{C} and $s \in I$, there is a set of objective vectors. In multi-objective optimization, we say that vector $\boldsymbol{x}$ dominates vector $\boldsymbol{y}$ if the value of each dimension of $\boldsymbol{x}$ is no less than the corresponding value of $\boldsymbol{y}$. Thus the constraints can be represented by a vector $\boldsymbol{x}$ dominates the vector $\langle\epsilon,\ldots,\epsilon\rangle$. The verification of ϵ-SNE is now reduced to find whether there exists a vector which dominates $\langle\epsilon,\ldots\epsilon\rangle$ or not. Non-existence of this vector is equivalent to SNE. To find the vector satisfying the constraint, it is sufficient to compare $\langle\epsilon,\ldots,\epsilon\rangle$ with the set of vectors which are not dominated by any other vectors, which is exactly finding a solution for the optimization problem. Each vector can be considered as a point in a n-dimensional space. The set of vectors that are not dominated by any other vectors form a curve, called Pareto-curve in the n-dimensional space. Verification of ϵ-SNE can be reduced to checking whether or not a point in the Pareto-curve dominates $\langle\epsilon,\ldots,\epsilon\rangle$.

6.2 Approximation

In order to find a point which dominates $\langle\epsilon,\ldots,\epsilon\rangle$, one has to enumerate the points on the Pareto curve w.r.t all the strategy combinations (potentially infinite), which may not be feasible in some cases. For simplicity, we choose only the coalition strategies corresponding to the optimal value of a single objective function which can be proven to be Pareto optimal strategies in multi-objective function [6]. The single objective function is a linear combination of each player's individual objectives parametrised by α as follows: $\alpha = \langle\alpha_1,\ldots\alpha_{|C|}\rangle$ such that $\alpha_i \in [0,1]$ and $\Sigma_{i=1}^{|C|}\alpha_i = 1$. Thus the linear combination is $\Sigma_{i=1}^{|C|}\alpha_i(v_{i,Z}(s,\Sigma_C^\infty) - U_{i,Z}(s))$. The Pareto-curve is approximated by the optimal objective vectors (corresponding to linear combinations) generated by various α values.

Since $U_{i,Z}(s)$ is a constant for a given i, s and Z, we can simplify the previous linear combination formula into $\Sigma_{i=1}^{|C|}\alpha_i(v_{i,Z}(s,\Sigma_C^\infty))$, which is named as the *joint objective function.* With a configuration C, Z and s, given an α, there is an optimal joint action that maximizes the joint objective function which can be denoted as $\sigma^m = argmax\{\Sigma_{i=1}^{|C|}\alpha_i(v_{i,Z}(s,\Sigma_C^\infty))\}$. With a joint action choice σ^m, we can reverse to the original vector representing $v_{i,Z}(s,\Sigma_C^\infty) - U_{i,Z}(s)$ for each player i in C. This vector corresponds to a point in the Pareto curve. If the vector dominates $\langle\epsilon,\ldots,\epsilon\rangle$, this joint action choice is a strategy for the coalition to deviate.

Yet, another issue is that in general, the pay-off of each player (one value in each vector) cannot be calculated as an exact value due to the infinite length. Therefore, we approximate the pay-offs in a vector with some error bound $(\Xi_{u,i}(t) + \Xi_{v,i}(t))$ (uncertainty level) which leads to a region (named as uncertain region) rather than a point in the Pareto curve. For example, Fig. 1, given a joint action choice σ^m for t steps (dot t), there is the shaded area between two parallel dotted lines (the gradient is determined by α) representing the possible joint action choices that lead to the optimal rewards in infinite steps. Each point in this area is a vector $\langle V_{1,Z,C,\alpha}^\infty(s)\text{-}U_{1,Z}(s),\ldots,V_{i,Z,C,\alpha}^\infty(s)\text{-}U_{i,Z}(s)\rangle(i\in C)$. For each i, we find the points that correspond to the lowest $V_{i,Z,C,\alpha}^\infty(s)\text{-}U_{i,Z}(s)$. For each such point ($l$), we calculate the uncertainty region that contains the points that dominate l (the triangular darker region). This region must contain some point which is not dominated by any point in the shaded area (For proofs see [8]). This region decreases when increasing t. We can choose $k = \min(t)$ s.t. every

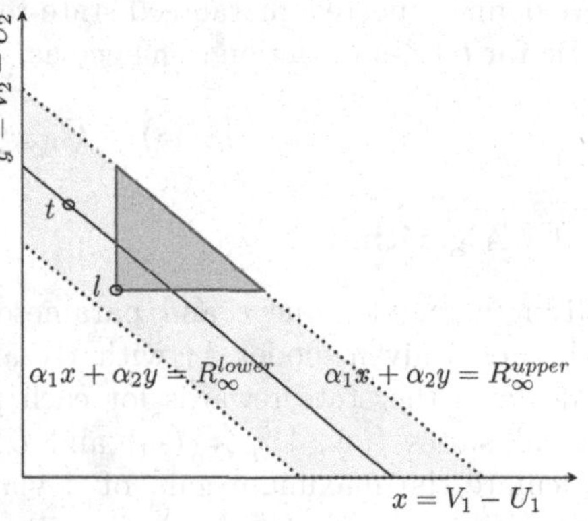

Fig. 1. Uncertain regions

dimension i of a point in the uncertainty region is bounded by parameter δ. We provide details about finding k in our proof [8].

6.3 Calculation of Rewards

We calculate the rewards for all players $i \in C$ in k steps as follows. Let $L = Z' \backslash C$, we first initialize the reward for 0 steps: $V^0_{i,Z,C,\alpha}(s) = 0$, and $U^0_{i,Z}(s) = 0$. Then we iteratively calculate the guaranteed state-reward (we refer to the game-reward starting from a state s as a state reward) for player i for a given non-Byzantine action combination $\langle a_C, a_L\rangle$[7] in $t+1$-steps starting from state s for a joint-objective function parameterized by α, in order to determine the optimal action combination. The above guaranteed state-reward is denoted by $g^t_{i,Z,\alpha}$, thus

$$g^{t+1}_{i,Z,\alpha}(s, \langle a_C, a_L\rangle) = \{min_{a_Z \in A_Z}((H_i(s,a) + \beta_i V^t_{i,Z,C,\alpha}(s'))|a = \langle a_C, a_Z, a_L\rangle, T(s,a) = s')\}.$$

Expected guaranteed state-reward of player i for joint action a_C for the last action in $t+1$-step action sequence is $v^{t+1}_{i,Z,\alpha}(s, a_C) = E_{a_L \in A_L}(g^{t+1}_{i,Z,\alpha}(s, \langle a_C, a_L\rangle))$.

We define expected guaranteed state-reward of player i in rational coalition C for $t+1$-step action sequence as,

$$V^{t+1}_{i,Z,C,\alpha}(s) = v^{t+1}_{i,Z,\alpha}(s, a^m_C),$$
$$\text{where } a^m_C = argmax\{\{\Sigma^{|C|}_{i=1}\alpha_i(v_{i,Z,\alpha}(s, a'_C))\} \mid a'_C \text{ is enabled at } s\}.$$

We define expected guaranteed state-reward of i when all coalitions C are altruistic for $t+1$-step action sequence as,

$$U^{t+1}_{i,Z}(s) = E_{a_{Z'} \in A_{Z'}}(g^{t+1}_{i,Z,\alpha}(s, a_{Z'})).$$

6.4 Algorithm

Given a regret value ϵ and parameter δ, we propose Algorithm 1 to decide whether a given model $\mathcal{M}$ with Byzantine players Z satisfies SNE. Line 1–6 calculates the state rewards for each player i (not in Z) in k steps from the initial states (i.e., $V^k_{i,Z,C,\alpha}(s_0)$ and $U^k_{i,Z}(s_0)$, $s_0 \in I$). Using the results, we calculate the maximum gain of deviating in k steps (denoted as $\Delta_{i,\alpha}$), i.e., $max(V^k_{i,Z,C,\alpha}(s_0) - U^k_{i,Z}(s_0))$ (line 7). Then we use $\Delta_{i,\alpha}$ and the error bound $\Xi_{u,i}(k) + \Xi_{v,i}(k)$ to approximate the gain of deviating in infinite steps and obtain its lower and upper bounds (line 8). The final step is to decide the relation between the bounds and ϵ according to Definition 1. Given an α, the bounds of all players form the uncertainty region like in Fig. 1. If all points in the uncertainty region dominate $\langle\epsilon, \ldots, \epsilon\rangle$, we have $\epsilon_1(i,\alpha) > \epsilon, \forall i$, meaning that there is a strategy for C to deviate and gain more than ϵ, then $\mathcal{M}$ does not satisfy ϵ-SNE (line 9–10). If all the points in the uncertainty region are dominated by $\langle\epsilon, \ldots, \epsilon\rangle$ ($\epsilon_2(i,\alpha) \leq \epsilon, \forall i$), then there is no joint action choice of C can deviate and gain, and thus the algorithm returns SNE (line 11–12). Otherwise, we are

[7] a_C is short for $\mathsf{p}(a, C)$, a_L is short hand for $\mathsf{p}(a, L)$.

Algorithm 1. $isSNE$(game $\mathcal{M}$, set Z, double ϵ, δ)

1: **Let** $s \in S$, $C \in Z'$ $a_C \in A_C$,$L = Z' \setminus C$, $i \in C$
2: **Let** k, $2(\Xi_{u,i}(k) + \Xi_{v,i}(k)) \leq \delta$, $\alpha_i \in (0, 1)$
3: $V^0_{i,Z,C,\alpha}(s) \leftarrow 0; U^0_{i,Z}(s) \leftarrow 0;$
4: **for** t=1 **to** k **do**
5:     Update $U^t_{i,Z}(s)$,$V^t_{i,Z,C,\alpha}(s)$
6: **end for**
7: $\Delta_{i,\alpha} \leftarrow \max\{V^k_{i,Z,C,\alpha}(s) - U^k_{i,Z}(s) | s \in I\}$
8: $\epsilon_1(i, \alpha) \leftarrow \Delta_{i,\alpha} - \Xi_{u,i}(k) - \Xi_{v,i}(k)$; $\epsilon_2(i, \alpha) \leftarrow \Delta_{i,\alpha} + \Xi_{u,i}(k) + \Xi_{v,i}(k)$
9: **if** $(\epsilon_1(i, \alpha) > \epsilon \; \forall i \in C)$ **then**
10:     **return** NOT SNE
11: **else if** $(\epsilon_2(i, \alpha) \leq \epsilon, \forall i \in C)$ **then**
12:     **return** ϵ-SNE
13: **else if** $((\epsilon_1(i, \alpha) \leq \epsilon \; \forall i \in C)$,
$(\exists i \in C \; \epsilon_1(i, \alpha) \leq \epsilon \leq \epsilon_2(i, \alpha)))$ **then**
14:     **return** $\epsilon + \delta$-SNE
15: **else**
16:     $\delta^* \leftarrow \max\{(\epsilon_2(i) - \epsilon)\mathbb{1}(\epsilon_2(i) > \epsilon) | i \in C\}$
17:     **return** UNDECIDED
18: **end if**

uncertain about the domination relation, therefore we enlarge the regret value by δ, which will lead to an easier decision (line 13–14). If by refining regret value, we still cannot decide, we try a different α value (line 15–18). Given β and δ, the algorithm has complexity $O(|S| * |A|)$ where $|S|$ and $|A|$ are the sizes of state space and the action space.

7 Evaluation

In this section we evaluate our model and algorithm in three aspects: efficiency, scalability and applicability. (1) We illustrate the efficiency of our algorithm by comparing with existing tools - PRISM-games in particular. We use the job scheduling as an example as it is representative of many real-world problems while being easy to illustrate. (2) To show the scalability of our algorithm, we take the apple-picking game as an illustration. The apple-picking game is a practical game that has been used to perform analysis in the game theory domain. Especially, it engages all elements that we would like to illustrate - probabilistic infinite game with rational players that may potentially form coalitions. (3) We apply our algorithm to a real-world scenario - analysing a probabilistic secret sharing scheme. The secret sharing scheme is an important building block in many security critical systems. Being a multi-party computation scheme, rational and Byzantine participants are key concepts. Moreover, it has been proved that probability is essential in the secret sharing scheme to counter the rational behaviour of participants [1]. Particularly, the secret sharing scheme we analyse considers coalitions.

7.1 Comparison with PRISM-games - Job Scheduling Case Study

As mentioned in Sect. 2, the most relevant work to ours is PRISM-games 2.0 [12], since it also handles NE in probabilistic game with coalitions under adversarial behaviour. However, it does not support infinite games. Moreover, it does not directly support SNE verification. In order to be able to adopt PRISM-games for PBAR verification, one has to apply some modelling tricks. We make the following modelling effort in using PRISM-games for verifying PBAR: first, we limited the game length/steps and encoded the discount factor in each state; second, we model different player configurations separately and each forms a model. In each model, we compute the optimal rational/altruistic rewards for the limited length using PRISM-games. Then we compare the rewards for all models to see whether SNE is satisfied. We use the following job scheduling game (adapted from [15] by adding probability) to show the comparison with our algorithm.

Job Scheduling. Suppose there are m jobs $J = \{J_1, \cdots, J_m\}$ each of which consists of a set of tasks; and there are q tasks $T = \{T_0, \cdots, T_q\}$. A system, comprising n workers, specifies a sequence of tasks for each worker. A task sequence for worker i is denoted as $\mathcal{T}_i = \langle \tau(i, 0), \cdots, \tau(i, l_i) \rangle$, where $l_i + 1$ is the length of the task sequence. A set of tasks form a job, denoted by the function $\eta : J \rightarrow \mathbb{P}(T)$. Once a job is completed, the rewards are granted to the workers who finished the tasks that compose the job. When a worker finishes a task, she can choose to wait for her reward with probability 0.6 and not to wait with probability 0.4. Once she gets the rewards or decides not to wait, she can start the next task with probability 0.6, take a rest with probability 0.2 or skip the next task with probability 0.2. After finishing all tasks in the sequence (i.e., after finishing $\tau(i, l_i)$), a worker repeats the sequence of tasks from the beginning (i.e., task $\tau(i, 0)$). Taking a task consumes the rewards (i.e., getting negative rewards). If more than one worker finish the same task which finishes some job, all of them will be rewarded. A worker deviates from the system by not following the probabilistic distribution.

Experimental Results. Given a set of Byzantine players Z, let $\epsilon = 1.1$ and $\delta = 0.1$, we verify SNE for different configurations of jobs and players. We run the verification using our algorithm and PRISM-games using a 64-bit x-86 Intel machine with 2.40 GHz processor and 8 GB RAM. The experimental results are shown in Table 2. For the simplicity of representation, we use $|Z|$ to represent all the possible configurations with the same length of Z in Table 2, since in this example, the verification results for the same $|Z|$ are the same, due to symmetry of players' behaviour. For PRISM-games, we set the game length of each model as 9. From Table 2, we can see that PRISM-games throws out-of memory error in the model building phase even with a limited game length of 9 (with the same corresponding the values of ϵ and δ in each test configuration). The PRISM-games model can be found in [8]. As PRISM-games is not designed for PBAR, auxiliary variables are needed in modelling, which makes the model complicated and thus causes the out-of memory errors in generating the model.

Table 2. Experimental results for job assignment

Configuration			Coalition #1-ϵ	Coalition #1-$\epsilon+\delta$	Coalition #2-ϵ	CPU (sec)	Our algorithm		PRISM-games	
Players	Jobs	$\lvert Z\rvert$					States	Transitions	States	Transitions
3	2	1	FAIL	PASS	PASS	0.891	3^6	3^9	451625	OutofMemory
3	3	1	FAIL	PASS	PASS	0.971	3^6	3^9	554134	OutofMemory
4	2	1	FAIL	PASS	PASS	40.453	3^8	3^{12}	OutofMemory	OutofMemory
4	2	2	FAIL	PASS	PASS	31.046	3^8	3^{12}	OutofMemory	OutofMemory
4	3	1	FAIL	PASS	PASS	49.53	3^8	3^{12}	OutofMemory	OutofMemory
4	3	2	FAIL	PASS	PASS	37.507	3^8	3^{12}	OutofMemory	OutofMemory

7.2 Evaluating Scalability - Apple-Picking Game

The apple-picking game is initially proposed in [13]. This game is easy to understand while has large state space. We use this game to test the scalability of our algorithm, by setting the parameter values that lead to certain limit of the algorithm execution.

Apple-Picking Game. Assume there are 3 players, each player has 2 life points. In each round, there is a set of apples (fixed to 4 for the evaluation) and the number decreases with a discount in each round. The number needs not to be an integer (i.e., this is an infinite game). In each round, a player chooses to shoot others or not. The set of apples are equally shared among the survivors at the end of each round. If a player is shot once, her life point decreases by 1. When a player's life point reaches 0, the player dies, but will reborn in 3 rounds. Each player i also has a confidence value towards another player j, denoted as c_{ij}. c_{ij} reduces by 1 when j shoots i, and increases by 1 every 3 rounds with the cap 2. This case study is a general abstraction of many real-world systems in which agents must find compromise between sharing limited resources, e.g., price fighting. In this game, an analyst may want to know whether a strategy is optimal for every player, for example, shooting based on trust - a player i chooses not to shoot with probability w/q, where w is her maximum confidence value ($Max(c_{ij})$, $i \neq j$) and q is her total confidence value (Σc_{ij}, $i \neq j$), and chooses to shoot with $1-w/q$. Player i chooses to shoot j with probability c_{ij}/q.

Experimental Results. We model apple picking game as a PBAR-system (defined in Sect. 4). The model contains 3^{15} states and 4^3 transactions. We verified it using the proposed algorithm with $\epsilon = 1.1$ and $\delta = 0.1$, and the result is shown in Table 3.

In the experiment, we considered two scenarios: the presence ($|Z| = 1$ one of the players is Byzantine) or absence ($|Z| = 0$) of a Byzantine player. The algorithm returns "PASS" for ϵ-SNE at the presence of Byzantine player and returns FAIL at the absence of Byzantine player. This result suggests that coalition deviation is only profitable when no player is Byzantine. Moreover, when there is no Byzantine player, the system satisfies $\epsilon + \delta$-SNE when coalition size is 1 but fails when coalition size is 2. This suggests that it is profitable to form a

Table 3. Experimental results for apple game

$\|Z\|$	Coalition size	ϵ-SNE	$\epsilon + \delta$-SNE	No. states	No. transactions
1	1	PASS	PASS	3^{15}	4^3
0	1	FAIL	PASS	3^{15}	4^3
1	2	PASS	PASS	3^{15}	4^3
0	2	FAIL	FAIL	3^{15}	4^3

coalition, when there is no Byzantine players. With the CPU configuration 10-core Intel Xeon E5-2630 v4 machine with 2.2 GHz processor and 64GB RAM, the verification time for each of the test cases exceeds 4 h, which indicates the practical limit of the scalability in terms of states and transitions.

7.3 Applicability - Secret Sharing Protocol ADGH06

A secret sharing protocol is a scheme for distributing a secret among a group of participants, each of whom has a share of the secret, and only a sufficient number of shares together can reconstruct the secret. It has been widely used in security related systems e.g., homomorphic secure computation. The most well-known secret sharing protocol is Shamir's secret sharing scheme. However, it is has been proved to not work when there are rational agents, and thus a new scheme with probability is introduced to counter the rational-fault [10]. However, this scheme only considers a single agent's deviation. Hence a new version of the probabilistic secret sharing protocol (ADGH06) is proposed which is able to tolerant to k coalitions of rational agents [1].

Description. In the ADGH06 secret sharing protocol, a secret is encoded as $g(0)$ of an $m-1$ degree polynomial g (defined by a mediator), and it's shares are $g(i)$ which are distributed to each agent i ($i \neq 0$). In order to reconstruct the secret, agents broadcast their secret shares and use interpolation to recover $g(0)$. In details, the protocol repeats the following actions in a stage t until all of agents know the secret.

Each stage consists of 3 phases.

phase 1. A mediator collects *ack* from each agent for stage t.

phase 2. The mediator calculates a binary random variable b^t at stage t (the probability of $b^t = 1$ is α and the probability of $b^t = 0$ is $1 - \alpha$), produces $l^t = b^t.g + h^t$ (h^t is a random polynomial s.t. $h^t(0) = 0$), and sends $l^t(i)$ to agent i.

phase 3. All the agents broadcast their shares to other agents.

Agent i's altruistic strategy is sending its share to all the other agents and reconstruct $l^t(0)$. If i does not receive sufficient number of shares from other agents, then cheating is detected and protocol stops. If $l^t(0) \neq 0$ then $l^t(0)$ is the secret and i gets the reward. If $l^t(0) = 0$ meaning that this round does not count for that the mediator chose meaningless shares (the secret cannot be

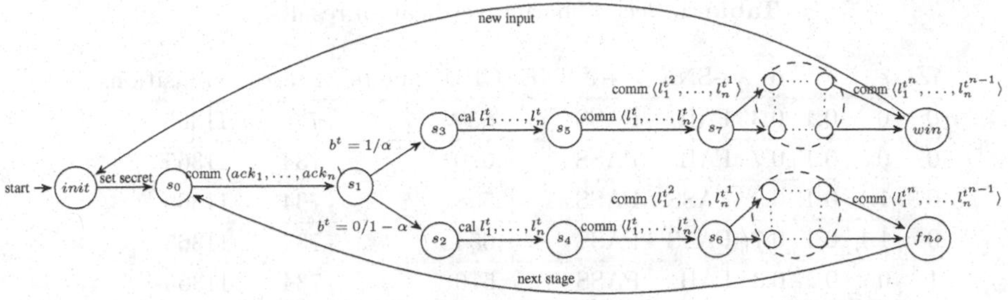

Fig. 2. All altruistic configuration.

reconstructed even with all the shares), then i proceeds to the next stage (rerunning the above actions). When all the agents follow the protocol, all of them can reconstruct $g(0)$ with $\frac{1}{\alpha}$ expected number of stages.

In better evaluate our algorithm, we introduce Byzantine agent and extend the protocol to a non-terminating one (i.e. secret sharing procedure is repeated). We also introduce a discount factor to capture that the value of the secret decreases over time.

Modelling. Due to space limit, it is impossible to show the entire model of the protocol, which captures all configurations. Here in Fig. 2, we show a projection/part of the model representing the configuration when all agents are altruistic. Probabilities α and $1 - \alpha$ are for mediator producing a meaningful polynomial or not. Probabilities of the other transitions is 1. Reward is only given when there is a transition to a *win* state, where each agent receive all the shares. The rational and Byzantine agents deviate by not sharing or sharing a wrong share. In addition, the rational agents deviate by guessing the secret when not all shares are received and when the mediator chooses meaningless shares, instead of stopping the protocol or restarting the protocol in the altruistic setting. The probability of an rational agent guess correct is p_1, while guessing wrong is $1 - p_1$ (due to the design of the polynomial g). Each rational player has one chance to use the guessed result to obtain the reward. Therefore, the larger the coalition size is, the bigger the chance of getting reward. The rational deviation is defined in [1].

Verification Results. Let the discount factor be $\beta = 0.5$ and the number of agents be $n = 4$, we verified the system using the same configuration as in Sect. 7.1. We considered two cases, with a Byzantine agent ($|Z| = 1$) and without Byzantine agents ($|Z| = 0$) (The original scheme does not claimed to be resilient to Byzantine faults). When there is no Byzantine players, the verification result (Table 4) shows that with higher regret allowance (ϵ), rational deviations become less profitable (with the same δ and α). Adding a Byzantine agent does not change the result in current parameters.

Table 4. Secret sharing verification results

|Z|	ϵ	δ	α	ϵ-SNE	$\epsilon + \delta$-SNE	CPU-time (s)	States	Transitions
0	0	0.1	0.3	FAIL	PASS	.658	734	11365
0	0	0.1	0.7	FAIL	PASS	.620	734	11365
0	1.1	0.1	0.3	PASS	PASS	.598	734	11365
0	1.1	0.1	0.7	PASS	PASS	.654	734	11365
1	0	0.1	0.3	FAIL	PASS	.576	734	11365
1	0	0.1	0.7	FAIL	PASS	.585	734	11365
1	1.1	0.1	0.3	PASS	PASS	.665	734	11365
1	1.1	0.1	0.7	PASS	PASS	.626	734	11365

8 Conclusion

We aim to decide whether a rational agent in a probabilistic system would follow the specified behaviour in the presence of mis-configured agents. We express this problem as verifying whether the system is a SNE. We proposed a verification algorithm for non-terminating games and proved its correctness. We implemented our algorithm and evaluated using three case studies. Having a running time linear to the size of the state space times the action space, large number of players may consequently slow down the termination of our algorithm. We plan to provide in a future work optimisation and alternative methods to overcome this problem.

Acknowledgement. This research is supported by the National Research Foundation, Prime Minister's Office, Singapore under its Corporate Laboratory@University Scheme, National University of Singapore, and Singapore Telecommunications Ltd.

References

1. Abraham, I., Dolev, D., Gonen, R., Halpern, J.: Distributed computing meets game theory: robust mechanisms for rational secret sharing and multiparty computation. In: Proceedings of 25th Annual ACM Symposium on Principles of Distributed Computing, pp. 53–62 (2006)
2. Aiyer, A., Alvisi, L., Clement, A., Dahlin, M., Martin, J.P., Porth, C.: BAR fault tolerance for cooperative services. In: Proceedings of 20th ACM Symposium on Operating Systems Principles, pp. 45–58 (2005)
3. Backes, M., Ciobotaru, O., Krohmer, A.: RatFish: a file sharing protocol provably secure against rational users. In: Gritzalis, D., Preneel, B., Theoharidou, M. (eds.) ESORICS 2010. LNCS, vol. 6345, pp. 607–625. Springer, Heidelberg (2010). https://doi.org/10.1007/978-3-642-15497-3_37
4. Brenguier, R.: PRALINE: a tool for computing nash equilibria in concurrent games. In: Sharygina, N., Veith, H. (eds.) CAV 2013. LNCS, vol. 8044, pp. 890–895. Springer, Heidelberg (2013). https://doi.org/10.1007/978-3-642-39799-8_63

5. Chen, T., Forejt, V., Kwiatkowska, M., Parker, D., Simaitis, A.: PRISM-games: a model checker for stochastic multi-player games. In: Piterman, N., Smolka, S.A. (eds.) TACAS 2013. LNCS, vol. 7795, pp. 185–191. Springer, Heidelberg (2013). https://doi.org/10.1007/978-3-642-36742-7_13
6. Coello, C.C.: A comprehensive survey of evolutionary-based multiobjective optimization techniques. Knowl. Inf. Syst. **1**(3), 129–156 (1999)
7. Diamond, G., Rozanski, A., Steuer, M.: Playing doctor: application of game theory to medical decision-making. J. Chron. Diseases **39**, 669–677 (1986)
8. Fernando, D., Dong, N., Jegourel, C., Dong, J.: Verification of strong Nash-equilibrium in probabilistic BAR systems(extended with proof). https://sites.google.com/view/verify-pbar
9. Fernando, D., Dong, N., Jegourel, C., Dong, J.: Verification of Nash-equilibrium for probabilistic BAR systems. In: ICECCS, pp. 53–62 (2016)
10. Halpern, J., Teague, V.: Rational secret sharing and multiparty computation: extended abstract. In: Proceedings of 36th Annual ACM Symposium on Theory of Computing, pp. 623–632 (2004)
11. Kiayias, A., Koutsoupias, E., Kyropoulou, M., Tselekounis, Y.: Blockchain mining games. In: Proceedings of 2016 ACM Conference on Economics and Computation, pp. 365–382 (2016)
12. Kwiatkowska, M., Parker, D., Wiltsche, C.: PRISM-games 2.0: a tool for multi-objective strategy synthesis for stochastic games. In: Tools and Algorithms for the Construction and Analysis of Systems, pp. 560–566 (2016)
13. Leibo, J., Zambaldi, V., Lanctot, M., Marecki, J., Graepel, T.: Multi-agent reinforcement learning in sequential social dilemmas. In: Proceedings of 16th Conference on Autonomous Agents and MultiAgent Systems, pp. 464–473 (2017)
14. Lillibridge, M., Elnikety, S., Birrell, A., Burrows, M., Isard, M.: A cooperative internet backup scheme. In: Proceedings of the General Track: 2003 USENIX Annual Technical Conference, pp. 29–41 (2003)
15. Mari, F., et al.: Model checking Nash equilibria in MAD distributed systems. In: Formal Methods in Computer-Aided Design, pp. 1–8 (2008)
16. Mari, F., et al.: Model checking coalition Nash equilibria in MAD distributed systems. In: Guerraoui, R., Petit, F. (eds.) SSS 2009. LNCS, vol. 5873, pp. 531–546. Springer, Heidelberg (2009). https://doi.org/10.1007/978-3-642-05118-0_37
17. McNaughton, R.: Infinite games played on finite graphs. Ann. Pure Appl. Log. **65**(2), 149–184 (1993)
18. Mouaddib, A.I., Boussard, M., Bouzid, M.: Towards a formal framework for multi-objective multiagent planning. In: Proceedings of 6th International Joint Conference on Autonomous Agents and Multiagent Systems, p. 123 (2007)
19. Shinohara, R.: Coalition-proof equilibria in a voluntary participation game. Int. J. Game Theory **39**(4), 603–615 (2010)
20. Shneidman, J., Parkes, D.C.: Specification faithfulness in networks with rational nodes. In: Proceedings of 23rd Annual ACM Symposium on Principles of Distributed Computing, pp. 88–97 (2004)
21. Toumi, A., Gutierrez, J., Wooldridge, M.: A tool for the automated verification of Nash equilibria in concurrent games. In: Leucker, M., Rueda, C., Valencia, F.D. (eds.) ICTAC 2015. LNCS, vol. 9399, pp. 583–594. Springer, Cham (2015). https://doi.org/10.1007/978-3-319-25150-9_34

Model Checking of C++ Programs Under the x86-TSO Memory Model

Vladimír Štill(✉) and Jiří Barnat

Faculty of Informatics, Masaryk University, Brno, Czech Republic
{xstill,xbarnat}@mail.muni.cz

Abstract. In this work, we present an extension of the DIVINE model checker that allows for analysis of C and C++ programs under the x86-TSO relaxed memory model. We use an approach in which the program to be verified is first transformed, so that it itself encodes the relaxed memory behavior, and after that it is verified by an explicit-state model checker supporting only the standard sequentially consistent memory. The novelty of our approach is in a careful design of an encoding of x86-TSO operations so that the nondeterminism introduced by the relaxed memory simulation is minimized. In particular, we allow for nondeterminism only in connection with memory fences and load operations of those memory addresses that were written to by a preceding store. We evaluate and compare our approach with the state-of-the-art bounded model checker CBMC and stateless model checker Nidhugg. For the comparison we employ SV-COMP concurrency benchmarks that do not exhibit data nondeterminism, and we show that our solution built on top of the explicit-state model checker outperforms both of the other tools. The implementation is publicly available as an open source software.

1 Introduction

Almost all contemporary processors exhibit relaxed memory behavior, which is caused by cache hierarchies, instruction reordering, and speculative execution. This, together with the rise of parallel programs, means that programmers often have to deal with the added complexity of programming under relaxed memory. The behavior of relaxed memory can be highly unintuitive even on x86 processors, which have stronger memory model than most other architectures. Therefore, programmers often have to decide whether to stay relatively safe with higher level synchronization constructs such as mutexes, or whether to tap to the full power of the architecture and risk subtle unintuitive behavior of relaxed memory accesses. For these reasons, it is highly desirable to have robust tools for finding bugs in programs running under relaxed memory.

This work has been partially supported by the Czech Science Foundation grant No. 18-02177S and by Red Hat, Inc.

J. Sun and M. Sun (Eds.): ICFEM 2018, LNCS 11232, pp. 124–140, 2018.
https://doi.org/10.1007/978-3-030-02450-5_8

Our aim is primarily to help with the development of lock-free data structures and algorithms. Instead of using higher level synchronization techniques such as mutexes, lock-free programs use low-level atomic operations provided by the hardware or programming language to ensure correct results. This way, lock-free programs can exploit the full power of the architecture they target, but they are also harder to design, as the ordering of operations in the program has to be considered very carefully. We believe that by providing a usable validation procedure for lock-free programs, more programmers will find courage to develop fast and correct programs.

Sadly, conventional validation and verification techniques often fail to detect errors caused by relaxed memory. Many of these techniques work best for deterministic, single-threaded programs, and techniques applicable to parallel programs often assume the memory is *sequentially consistent*. With sequentially consistent memory, any memory action is immediately visible to all processors and cores in the system, there is no observable caching or instruction reordering. That is, an execution of a parallel program under sequential consistency is an interleaving of actions of its threads [25]. Recently, many techniques for analysis and verification which take relaxed memory into account have been developed, and research in this field is still pretty active. In this work, we are adding a new technique which we hope will make the analysis of C and C++ programs targeting x86 processors easier.

Our technique is built on top of DIVINE, an explicit-state model checker for C and C++ programs [8]. DIVINE targets both sequential and parallel programs and can check a range of safety properties such as assertion safety and memory safety. We extend DIVINE with the support for the x86-TSO memory model [34] which describes the relaxed behavior of x86 and x86_64 processors. Due to the prevalence of the Intel and AMD processors with the x86_64 architecture, the x86-TSO memory model is a prime target for program analysis. It is also relatively strong and therefore underapproximates most of the other memory models – any error which is observable on x86-TSO is going to manifest itself under the more relaxed POWER or ARM memory models.

To verify a program under x86-TSO, we first transform it by encoding the semantics of the relaxed memory into the program itself, i.e. the resulting transformed program itself simulates nondeterministically relaxed memory operations. To reveal an error related to the relaxed memory behavior, it is then enough to verify the transformed program with a regular model checker supporting only the standard sequentially consistent memory.

In this paper we introduce a new way of encoding the relaxed memory behaviour into the program. Our new encoding introduces low amount of nondeterminism, which is the key attribute that allows us to tackle model checking of nontrivial programs efficiently. In particular, we achieve this by delaying nondeterministic choices arising from x86-TSO as long as possible. Our approach is based on the standard operational semantic of x86-TSO with store buffers, but it removes entries from the store buffer only when a load or a fence occurs (or if the store buffer is bounded and full). Furthermore, in loads we only remove those entries from store buffers that relate to the address being loaded, even if there are some older entries in the store buffer.

The rest of the paper is structured as follows: Sect. 2 contains preliminaries for our work, namely information about relaxed memory models in general and the x86-TSO memory model in particular, and about DIVINE. Section 3 then presents our contribution, details about its implementation, and integration with the rest of DIVINE. Section 4 provides evaluation results which compare DIVINE to Nidhugg [1] and CBMC [14] on a range of benchmarks from SV-COMP [9]. Section 5 summarizes related work and Sect. 6 concludes this work.

2 Preliminaries

2.1 Relaxed Memory Models

The relaxed behavior of processors arises from optimizations in cache consistency protocols and observable effects of instructions reordering and speculation. The effect of this behavior is that memory-manipulating instructions can appear to be executed in a different order than the order in which they appear in the binary, and their effect can even appear to be in different order on different threads. For efficiency reasons, virtually all modern processors (except for very simple ones in microcontrollers) exhibit relaxed behavior. The extent of this relaxation is dependent on the processor architecture (e.g., x86, ARM, POWER) but also on the concrete processor model. Furthermore, the actual behavior of the processor is often not precisely described by the processor vendor [34]. To abstract from the details of particular processor models, *relaxed memory models* are used to describe (often formally) behavior of processor architectures. Examples of relaxed memory models of modern processors are the memory model of x86 and x86_64 CPUs described formally as x86-TSO [34] and the multiple variants of POWER [27,33] and ARM [5,19,31] memory models.

For the description of a memory model, it is sufficient to consider operations which affect the memory. These operations include loads (reading of data from the memory to a register in the processor), stores (writing of data from a register to the memory), memory barriers (which constrain memory relaxation), and atomic compound operations (read-modify-write operations and compare-and-swap operation).

2.2 The x86-TSO Memory Model

The x86-TSO is very similar to the SPARC Total Store Order (TSO) memory model [35]. It does not reorder stores with each other, and it also does not reorder loads with other loads. The only relaxation allowed by x86-TSO is that store can appear to be executed later than a load which succeeds it. The memory model does not give any limit on how long a store can be delayed. An example of non-intuitive execution of a simple program under x86-TSO can be found in Fig. 1.

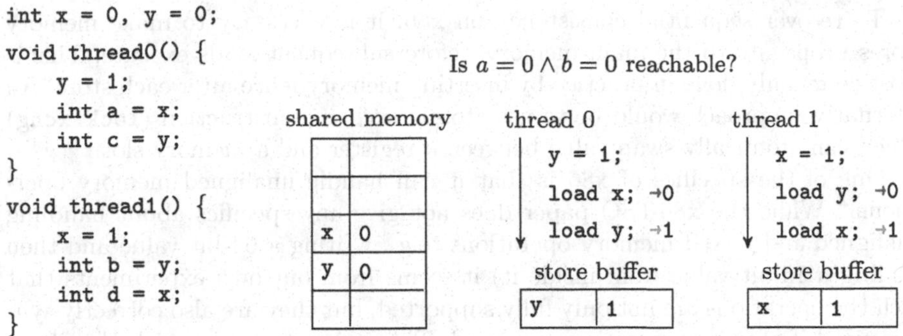

Fig. 1. A demonstration of the x86-TSO memory model. The thread 0 stores 1 to variable y and then loads variables x and y. The thread 1 stores 1 to x and then loads y and x. Intuitively, we would expect it to be impossible for $a = 0$ and $b = 0$ to both be true at the end of the execution, as there is no interleaving of thread actions which would produce such a result. However, under x86-TSO, the stores are cached in the store buffers (marked red). A load consults only shared memory and the store buffer of the given thread, which means it can load data from the memory and ignore newer values from the other thread (blue). Therefore a and b will contain old values from the memory. On the other hand, c and d will contain local values from the store buffers (locally read values are marked green). (Color figure online)

The operational semantics of x86-TSO is described by Sewell et al. in [34]. The corresponding machine has hardware threads (or cores), each with associated local store buffer, a shared memory subsystem, and a shared memory lock. Store buffers are first-in-first out caches into which store entries are saved before they are propagated to the shared memory. Load instructions first attempt to read from the store buffer of the given thread, and only if they are not succesful, they read from the shared memory. Store instructions push a new entry to the local store buffer. Atomic instructions include various read-modify-write instructions, e.g. atomic arithmetic operations (which take memory address and a constant),[1] or compare-and-swap instruction.[2] All atomic instructions use the shared memory lock so that only one such instruction can be executed at a given time, regardless of the number of hardware threads in the machine. Furthermore, atomic instructions flush the store buffer of their thread before they release the lock. This means that effects of atomic operations are immediately visible, i.e., atomics are sequentially consistent on x86-TSO. On top of these instructions, x86-TSO has a full memory barrier (`mfence`) which flushes the store buffer of the thread that executed it.[3]

[1] These instructions have the `lock` prefix in the assembly, for example `lock xadd` for atomic addition.

[2] `lock cmpxchg`.

[3] There are two more fence instructions in the x86 instruction set, but according to [34] they are not relevant to normal program execution.

To recover sequential consistency on x86, it is necessary to make memory stores propagate to the main memory before subsequent loads execute. This is most commonly done in practice by inserting memory fence after each store. An alternative approach would be to use atomic exchange instruction (`lock xchg`) which can atomically swap value between a register and a memory slot.

One of the specifics of x86 is that it can handle unaligned memory operations.[4] While the x86-TSO paper does not give any specifics about handling unaligned and mixed memory operations (e.g., writing a 64-bit value and then reading a 16-bit value from inside it) it seems from our own experiments that such the operations are not only fully supported, but they are also correctly synchronized if atomic instructions are used. This is in agreement with the aforementioned operational semantics of x86-TSO in which all the atomic operations share a single global lock.

2.3 DIVINE

DIVINE is an explicit-state model checker for C and C++ code that utilizes the clang compiler to translate the input program into the LLVM bitcode. This bitcode is then instrumented and interpreted by DIVINE's execution engine, DiVM. The complete workflow is illustrated in Fig. 2. DIVINE focuses on both parallel and sequential programs and is capable of finding a wide range of problems such as memory corruptions, assertion violations, and deadlocks caused by improper use of mutexes. DIVINE also has very good support for C and C++, which it achieves by employing of the standard clang compiler, and the libc++ standard library. Moreover, a few custom-built libraries are provided to enable full support of C++14 and C11 [8,37]. To efficiently handle parallel programs, DIVINE employs state space reductions and has a graph based representation of program memory. More details about the internal architecture of DIVINE can be found in [32].

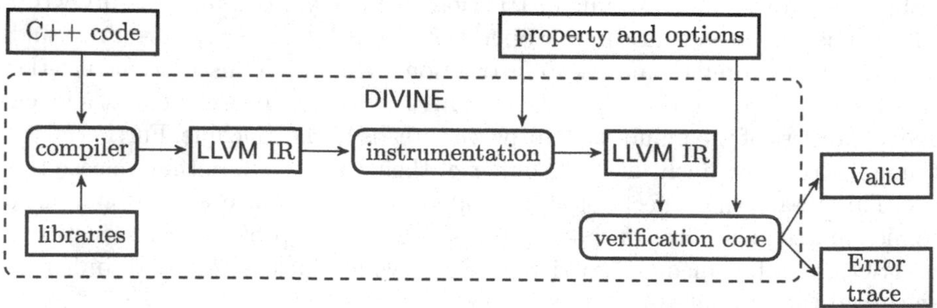

Fig. 2. Verification workflow of DIVINE when it is given a C++ file as an input. Boxes with rounded corners represent stages of input processing.

[4] Other architectures, for example ARM, require loaded values to be aligned, usually so that the address is divisible by the value size.

2.4 Relaxed Memory in C/C++ and LLVM

There are several ways in which C and C++ code can use atomic instructions and fences. These include inline assembly, compiler-provided intrinsic functions, and (since C11 and C++11) standard atomic variables and operations. While the constructs used to define atomic variables differ between C and C++, the memory model itself is the same for C11 and C++11. The C and C++ atomics are designed so that programmers can use the full potential of most platforms: the atomic operations are parametrized by a *memory order* which constrains how instructions can be reordered. The compiler is responsible for emitting assembly code which makes sure these ordering requirements are met. From the point of x86-TSO, all memory orderings except for sequential consistency amount to unconstrained execution, as such they exhibit non-atomic memory accesses.

When the C or C++ code is compiled to LLVM bitcode, the intrinsic functions and the standard atomic operations of the high-level programming language are mapped in the very same way to the corresponding LLVM instructions. The semantics of LLVM memory operations mostly copies the C++ memory model and behavior of the C++ atomic operations.

3 x86-TSO in DIVINE

DIVINE does not natively support relaxed memory, and we decided not to complicate the already complex execution engine and memory representation with a simulation of relaxed behavior. Instead, we encode the relaxed behavior into the program itself on the level of LLVM intermediate representation. The modified program running under sequential consistency simulates all x86-TSO runs of the original program, up to some bound on the number of stores which can be delayed. The program transformation is rather similar to the one presented in our previous work in [36]. The main novelty is in the way of simulation of x86-TSO which produces significantly less nondeterminism and therefore substantial efficiency improvements.

3.1 Simulation of the x86-TSO Memory Model

The most straight-forward way of simulating x86-TSO is to add store buffers to the program and flush them nondeterministically, for example using a dedicated flusher thread which flushes one entry at a time and interleaves freely with all other threads. We used this technique in [36]. This approach does, however, create many redundant interleavings as the flusher thread can flush an entry at any point, regardless of whether or not it is going to produce a run with a different memory access ordering, i.e. without any respect to the fact whether the flushed value is going to be read or not.

To alleviate this problem, it is possible to delay the choice whether to flush an entry from a store buffer to the point when the first load tries to read a buffered address. Only when such a load is detected, all possible ways the store buffers could have been flushed are simulated. In this case, the load can trigger flushing from any of the store buffers, to simulate that they could have been flushed before the load. To further improve the performance, only entries relevant to the loaded address are be affected by the flushing. These are the entries with matching addresses and any entries which precede them in the corresponding store buffers (that are flushed before them to maintain the store order).

A disadvantage of this approach is that there are too many ways in which a store buffer entry can be flushed, especially if this entry is not the oldest in its store buffer, or if there are entries concerning the same addresses in multiple store buffers. All of these cases can cause many entries to be flushed, often with a multitude of interleavings of entries from different store buffers which has to be simulated.

Therefore, we propose a *delayed flushing*: entries in the store buffers can be kept in the store buffer after newer entries were flushed if they are marked as *flushed*. Such the entries behave as if they were already written to the main memory, but can still be reordered with entries in other store buffers. That is, when there is a flushed entry for a given location in any store buffer, the value stored in the memory is irrelevant as any load will either read the flushed entry or entry from the other store buffer (which can be written after the flushed entry). Flushed entries make it possible to remove store buffer entries out of order while preserving total store order. This way a load only affects entries from the matching addresses and not their predecessors in the store order. This improvement is demonstrated in Figs. 3, 4 and 5.

DIVINE handles C and C++ code by translating it to LLVM and instrumenting it (see Fig. 2 for DIVINE's workflow). The support for relaxed memory is added in the instrumentation step, by replacing memory operations with calls to functions which simulate relaxed behavior. Essentially, all loads, stores, atomic instructions, and fences are replaced by calls to the appropriate functions.

All of the x86-TSO-simulating functions are implemented so that they are executed atomically by DIVINE (i.e., not interleaved). The most complex of these is the load operation. It first finds all entries with overlap the loaded address (*matching entries*) and out of these matching entries, it nondeterministically selects entries which will be written before the load (*selected entries*). All matching entries marked as flushed have to be selected for writing. Similarly, all matching entries which occur in a store buffer before a selected entry also have to be selected. Out of the selected entries, one is selected to be written last – this will be the entry read by the load. Next, selected entries are written, and all nonmatching entries which precede them are marked as flushed. Finally, the load is performed, either from the local store buffer if matching entry exists there, or from the shared memory.

The remaining functions are relatively straightforward – stores push a new entry to the store buffer, possibly evicting the last entry from the store buffer if the store buffer exceeds its size bound; fences flush all entries from the store buffer of the calling thread; atomic operations are basically a combination of a load, store, and a fence. The only intricate part of these operations is that if an

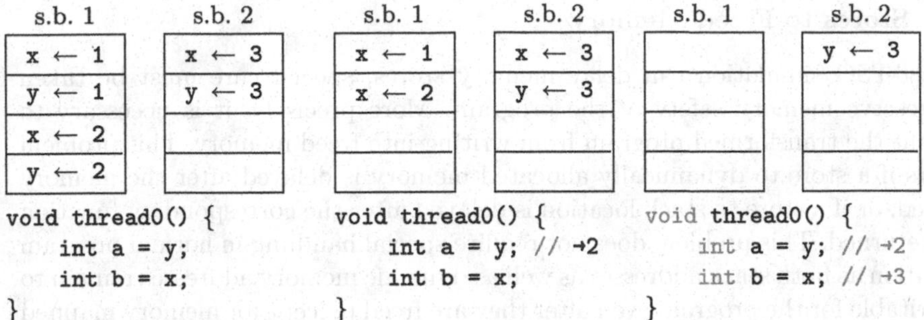

Fig. 3. Suppose `thread0` is about to execute with the displayed contents of store buffers of two other threads and suppose it had nondeterministically chosen to load value 2 from `y` (denoted by green in the figure). The entries at the top of the store buffers are the oldest entries. (Color figure online)

Fig. 4. At this point, `x` entries of store buffer 1 are marked as flushed (orange) and the `y ← 1` entry was removed as it was succeeded by the used entry `y ← 2`. The thread had nondeterministically selected to load `x` from store buffer 2. (Color figure online)

Fig. 5. In the load of `x`, all `x` entries were evicted from the buffers – all the flushed entries for `x` (which were not selected) had to be dropped before `x ← 3` was propagated to the memory. The last entry (`y ← 3`) will remain in the store buffer if `y` will never be loaded in the program again.

entry is flushed out of the store buffer, the entries from other store buffers which involve the same memory location can also be non-deterministically flushed (to simulate they could have been flushed before the given entry). This flushing is similar to flushing performed in load. An example which shows a series of loads can be found in Figs. 3, 4 and 5.

We will now argue that this way of implementing x86-TSO is correct. First, the nondeterminism in selecting entries to be flushed before a load serves the same purpose as the nondeterminism in the flusher thread of the more conventional implementation. The only difference is that in the flusher-thread scenario the entries are flushed in order, while in our new approach we are selecting only from the matching entries. Therefore, the difference between the two approaches is only on those entries which are not loaded by the load causing the flush, hence cannot be observed by the load. However, any entry which would be flushed before the selected entries in the flusher-thread approach is now marked with the flushed flag. This flag makes sure that such an entry will be flushed before an address which matches it is loaded, and therefore it behaves as if it was flushed. This way, the in-thread store order is maintained.

3.2 Stores to Freed Memory

As x86-TSO simulation can delay memory stores, special care must be taken to preserve memory safety of the program. More precisely, it is necessary to prevent the transformed program from writing into freed memory. This problem occurs if a store to dynamically allocated memory is delayed after the memory is freed, or if a store to stack location is delayed after the corresponding function had returned. This problem does not require special handling in normal program execution as both stack addresses as well as dynamic memory addresses remain to be writable for the program even after they are freed (except for memory mapped files, but these have to be released by a system call which includes sufficiently strong memory barrier).

To solve the problem of freed memory, it is necessary to evict store buffer entries which correspond to the freed memory just before the memory is freed. For entries not marked as flushed, this eviction concerns only store buffer of the thread which freed the memory. If some other thread attempted to write to the freed memory, this is an error as there is insufficient synchronization between the freeing and the store to the memory. However, corresponding entries marked as flushed should be evicted from all store buffers, as these entries correspond to changes which should have been already written to the shared memory. The program transformation takes care of inserting code to evict entries corresponding to freed memory from the store buffer.

3.3 Integration with Other Parts of DIVINE

The integration of x86-TSO simulation with the rest of DIVINE is rather straightforward. No changes are required in the DIVINE's execution engine or state space exploration algorithms. As for the libraries shipped with DIVINE, only minor tweaks were required. The `pthread` implementation had to be modified to add full memory barrier both at the beginning and at the end of every synchronizing functions. This corresponds to barriers present in the implementations used for normal execution, `pthread` mutexes and other primitives have to guarantee sequential consistency of the guarded operations (provided all accesses are properly guarded).

The DIVINE's operating system, DiOS, is used to implement low-level threading as well as simulation of various filesystem APIs [8]. We had to add memory barrier into the system call entry which hands control to DiOS. DiOS itself does not use relaxed memory simulation – the implementation of x86-TSO operations detects that the code is executed in the kernel mode and bypasses store buffers. In this way, the entire DiOS executes as if under sequential consistency. This synchronization is easily justifiable – system calls require a memory barrier or kernel lock in most operating systems.

3.4 Improvements

We have implemented two further optimizations of our x86-TSO simulation.

Static Local Variable Detection. Accesses of local variables which are not accessible to other threads need not use store buffering. For this reason, we have inserted a static analysis pass which annotates accesses to local memory before the x86-TSO instrumentation. The instrumentation ignores such annotated accesses. The static analysis can detect most local variables which are never accessed using pointers.

Dynamic Local Memory Detection. DIVINE can also dynamically detect if the given memory object is shared between threads (i.e., it is accessible from global variables or stacks of more then one thread). Using this information, it is possible to dynamically bypass store buffers for operations with non-shared memory objects. This optimization is correct even though the shared status of memory can change during its lifetime. A memory object o can become shared only when its address is written to some memory object s which is already shared (or o can become shared transitively through a series of pointers and intermediate objects). For this to happen, there has to be a store to the already shared object s, and this store has to be propagated to other threads. Once the store of the address of o is executed and written to the store buffer, o becomes shared, and any newer stores into it will go through the store buffer. Furthermore, once this store is propagated, any store which happened before turning o into a shared object also had to be propagated as x86-TSO does not reorder stores. Therefore, there is no reason to put stores to o through the store buffer if o is not shared. This optimization is not correct for memory models which allow store reordering – for such memory models, we would need to know that the object will never be shared during its lifetime.

3.5 Bounding the Size of Store Buffers

The complexity of analysis of programs under the x86-TSO memory model is high. From the theoretical point of view, we know due to Atig et al. [6] that reachability for programs with finite-state threads which run under TSO is decidable, but non-primitive recursive (it is in PSPACE for sequential consistency). The proof uses the so called SPARC TSO memory model [35] that is very similar to x86-TSO. However, the proof of decidability does not translate well to an efficient decision procedure, and real-world programs are much more complex than the finite-state systems used in the decidability proof.

For this reason, we would need to introduce unbounded store buffers to properly verify real-world programs. Unfortunately, this can be impractical, especially for programs which do not terminate. Therefore, our program transformation inserts store buffers of limited size, limiting thus the number of store operations that can be delayed at any given time. The size of the store buffers is fully configurable, and it currently defaults to 32, a value probably high enough to discover most bugs which can be observed on a real hardware.

Our implementation also supports the store buffers of unlimited size (when size is set to 0). In this mode, programs with infinite loops that write into shared memory will not have finite state space. Therefore, DIVINE will not terminate unless it discovers an error in the program. Verification with unbounded buffers will still terminate for terminating programs and for all programs with errors.

4 Evaluation

The implementation is available at https://divine.fi.muni.cz/2018/x86tso/, together with information about how to use it. We compared our implementation with the stateless model checker Nidhugg [1] and the bounded model checker CBMC [14,24]. For evaluation we used SV-COMP benchmarks from the Concurrency category [9], excluding benchmarks with data nondeterminism[5] as our focus is on performance of relaxed memory analysis, not on handling of nondeterministic values. Furthermore, due to the limitation of stateless model checking with DPOR, Nidhugg cannot handle data nondeterminism at all. There are 55 benchmarks in total.

The evaluation was performed on a machine with 2 dual core Intel Xeon 5130 processors running at 2 GHz with 16 GB of RAM. Each tool was running with memory limit set to 10 GB and time limit set to 1 h. The tools were not limited in the number of CPUs they can use.

We have used CBMC version 5.8 with the option `--mm tso`. Since there is no official release of Nidhugg, we have used version 0.2 from git, commit id `375c554` with `-tso` option to enable relaxed memory support and inserted a definition of the `__VERIFIER_error` function. For DIVINE, we have used the `--svcomp` option to enable support for SV-COMP atomic sections (which are supported by default by CBMC and Nidhugg), and we disabled nondeterministic memory failure by using the `divine check` command (SV-COMP does not consider the possibility of allocation failure). To enable x86-TSO analysis, `--relaxed-memory tso` is used for DIVINE.[6] The buffer bound was the default value (32) unless stated otherwise.

Table 1. Comparison of the default configuration of DIVINE with CBMC and Nidhugg.

	CBMC	Nidhugg	DIVINE
Finished	21	25	27
TSO bugs	3	3	9
Unique	5	3	5

Table 1 compares performance of the default configuration of DIVINE with the remaining tools. The line "finished" shows the total number of benchmarks for which the verification task finished with the given limits. From these the line

[5] I.e., all the benchmarks which contain calls to functions of the `__VERIFIER_nondet_*` family were excluded.

[6] The complete invocation is `divine check --svcomp --relaxed-memory tso BENCH.c`.

"TSO bugs" shows the number of errors caused by relaxed memory in benchmarks which were not supposed to contain any bugs under sequential consistency. All discovered errors were manually checked to really be observable under the x86-TSO memory model. Finally, "unique" shows the number of benchmarks solved only by the given tool and not the other two. There were only 8 benchmarks solved by all three tools, all of them without any errors found.

Table 2. Comparison of various configurations of DIVINE. The "base" version uses none of the improvements from Sect. 3.4. The configurations marked with "s" add the static local variable optimization, while the configurations marked with "d" add the dynamic detection of non-shared memory objects. The "+sdu" configuration has both optimizations enabled and it has unbounded buffers. Finally, the "+sd4" has buffer bound set to 4 entries instead of the default 32 entries. The default version is "+sd".

	Base	+s	+d	+sd	+sdu	+sd4
Finished	26	26	27	27	27	27
TSO bugs	8	8	9	9	9	9

Table 3. Comparison of various versions of DIVINE on benchmarks on the 26 which all the versions finished. For the description of these versions, please refer to Table 2.

	Base	+s	+d	+sd	+sdu	+sd4
States	252 k	263 k	250 k	231 k	206 k	296 k
Time	2:14:49	2:17:13	1:09:23	1:05:05	0:58:28	1:24:59

Table 2 shows effects of buffer size bound and improvements described in Sect. 3.4. It can be seen that all versions perform very similarly, only one more benchmark was solved by the versions with dynamic shared object detection (the remaining solved benchmarks were the same for all versions). The number of solved benchmarks remains the same regardless of used store buffer bound.

Table 3 offers more detailed look at the 26 benchmarks solved by all versions of DIVINE. It shows the aggregate differences in state space sizes and solving times. It can be seen that the dynamic shared object detection improves performance significantly. Interestingly, we can see that of the 3 versions which differ only in store buffer size ("+sd", "+sdu", and "+sd4"), the unbounded version performs the best. We expect this to be caused by the nondeterminism in flushing the excessive entries out of the store buffer when the bound is reached – this can trigger flushing of matching entries from other store buffers and therefore increase nondeterminism.

5 Related Work

There are numerous techniques for analysis of programs with respect to relaxed memory.

Verification of Absence of SC Violations. For these methods, the question is whether a program, when running under a relaxed memory model, exhibits any runs not possible under sequential consistency. This problem is explored under many names, e.g. (TSO-)safety [12], robustness [11,16], stability [4], and monitoring of sequential consistency [13]. A similar techniques are used in [40] to detect data races in Java programs. A related problem of correspondence between a parallel and sequential implementation of a data structure is explored in [29]. Some of these techniques can also be used to insert memory fences into the programs to recover sequential consistency.

Neither of these techniques is directly comparable to our method. For these techniques, a program is incorrect if it exhibits relaxed behavior, while for us, it is incorrect if it violates specification (e.g., assertion safety and memory safety). In practice, the appearance of relaxed behavior is often not a problem, provided the overall behavior of the data structure or algorithm matches desired specification. In many lock-free data structures, a relaxed behavior is essential to achieving high performance.

Direct Analysis Techniques. There are multiple methods for analysis of relaxed memory models based on program transformation. In [3] a transformation-based technique for the x86, POWER, and ARM memory models is presented. Another approach to program transformation is taken in [7], in this case, the transformation uses context switch bounding but not buffer bounding, and it uses additional copies for shared variables for TSO simulation. In [2] the context-bounded analysis using transformation is applied to the POWER memory model. Our work in [36] presents a transformation of LLVM bitcode to simulate buffer-bounded x86-TSO runs; compared to this work it has significantly less efficient implementation of the x86-TSO simulation.

A stateless model checking [20] approach to the analysis of programs running under the C++11 memory model (except for the release-consume synchronization) is presented in [28]. In [41] the authors focus mostly on modeling of TSO and PSO and its interplay with dynamic partial order reduction (DPOR, [18]). They combine modeling of thread scheduling nondeterminism and memory model nondeterminism using store buffers to a common framework by adding shadow thread for each store buffer which is responsible for flushing contents of this buffer to the memory. Another approach to combining TSO and PSO analysis with stateless model checking is presented in [1]. The advantage of this approach is that for a program without relaxed behavior it should produce no additional traces compared to sequential consistency. Another approach to stateless model checking is taken in [23], which uses execution graphs to explore all behavior of a C/C++ program under a modified C++11 memory model without exploring its interleaving directly.

So far, all of the described techniques used some kind of bounding to achieve efficiency – either bounding number of reordered operations, number of context switches, or number of iterations of loops. An unbounded approach to verification of programs under TSO is presented in [26]. It uses store buffers represented by automata and leverages cycle iteration acceleration to get a representation of store buffers on paths which would form cycles if values in store buffers were disregarded. It does not, however, target any real-world programming language. Instead, it targets a modified Promela language [21]. Another unbounded approach is presented in [10] – it introduces TSO behaviors lazily by iterative refinement, and while it is not complete, it should eventually find all errors.

Other Methods. In [30], the SPARC hierarchy of memory models (TSO, PSO, RMO) is modeled using encoding from assembly to Murφ [17]. In [22] an explicit state model checker for C# programs (supporting subset of C#/.NET bytecode) which uses the .NET memory model is presented. The verifier first verifies program under SC and then it explores additional runs allowed under the .NET memory model. The implementation of the exploration algorithm uses a list of delayed instructions to implement instruction reordering. The work [15] presents verification of (potentially infinite state space) programs under TSO and PSO (with bounded store buffers) using predicate abstraction.

A completely different approach is taken in [38]. This work introduces a separation logic GPS, which allows proving properties about programs using (a fragment of) the C11 memory model. That is, this work is intended for manual proving of properties of parallel programs, not for automatic verification. The memory model is not complete; it lacks relaxed and consume-release accesses. Another fragment of the C11 memory model is targeted by the RSL separation logic introduced in [39].

6 Conclusion

We showed that by careful design of simulation of relaxed memory behaviour we can use the standard model checker supporting only the sequential consistency to efficiently detect relaxed memory errors in programs that are otherwise correct under sequentially consistent memory. Moreover, according to our experimental evaluation, our explicit-state model checking approach outperforms a state-of-the-art stateless model checker as well as bounded model checker, which is actually quite an unexpected result. We also show that many of the used benchmarks can be solved only by one or two of the three evaluated tools, which highlights the importance of employing different approaches to analysis of programs under relaxed memory. Finally, we show that for terminating programs, our approach is viable both with bounded and unbounded store buffer size.

References

1. Abdulla, P.A., Aronis, S., Atig, M.F., Jonsson, B., Leonardsson, C., Sagonas, K.: Stateless model checking for TSO and PSO. In: Baier, C., Tinelli, C. (eds.) TACAS 2015. LNCS, vol. 9035, pp. 353–367. Springer, Heidelberg (2015). https://doi.org/10.1007/978-3-662-46681-0_28
2. Abdulla, P.A., Atig, M.F., Bouajjani, A., Ngo, T.P.: Context-bounded analysis for POWER. In: Legay, A., Margaria, T. (eds.) TACAS 2017. LNCS, vol. 10206, pp. 56–74. Springer, Heidelberg (2017). https://doi.org/10.1007/978-3-662-54580-5_4
3. Alglave, J., Kroening, D., Nimal, V., Tautschnig, M.: Software verification for weak memory via program transformation. In: Felleisen, M., Gardner, P. (eds.) ESOP 2013. LNCS, vol. 7792, pp. 512–532. Springer, Heidelberg (2013). https://doi.org/10.1007/978-3-642-37036-6_28
4. Alglave, J., Maranget, L.: Stability in weak memory models. In: Gopalakrishnan, G., Qadeer, S. (eds.) CAV 2011. LNCS, vol. 6806, pp. 50–66. Springer, Heidelberg (2011). https://doi.org/10.1007/978-3-642-22110-1_6
5. Alglave, J., Maranget, L., Tautschnig, M.: Herding cats: modelling, simulation, testing, and data mining for weak memory. ACM Trans. Program. Lang. Syst. **36**(2), 7:1–7:74 (2014)
6. Atig, M.F., Bouajjani, A., Burckhardt, S., Musuvathi, M.: On the verification problem for weak memory models. In: POPL, pp. 7–18. ACM, New York (2010)
7. Atig, M.F., Bouajjani, A., Parlato, G.: Getting rid of store-buffers in TSO analysis. In: Gopalakrishnan, G., Qadeer, S. (eds.) CAV 2011. LNCS, vol. 6806, pp. 99–115. Springer, Heidelberg (2011). https://doi.org/10.1007/978-3-642-22110-1_9
8. Baranová, Z., et al.: Model checking of C and C++ with DIVINE 4. In: D'Souza, D., Narayan Kumar, K. (eds.) ATVA 2017. LNCS, vol. 10482, pp. 201–207. Springer, Cham (2017). https://doi.org/10.1007/978-3-319-68167-2_14
9. Beyer, D.: Software verification with validation of results. In: Legay, A., Margaria, T. (eds.) TACAS 2017. LNCS, vol. 10206, pp. 331–349. Springer, Heidelberg (2017). https://doi.org/10.1007/978-3-662-54580-5_20
10. Bouajjani, A., Calin, G., Derevenetc, E., Meyer, R.: Lazy TSO reachability. In: Egyed, A., Schaefer, I. (eds.) FASE 2015. LNCS, vol. 9033, pp. 267–282. Springer, Heidelberg (2015). https://doi.org/10.1007/978-3-662-46675-9_18
11. Bouajjani, A., Derevenetc, E., Meyer, R.: Checking and enforcing robustness against TSO. In: Felleisen, M., Gardner, P. (eds.) ESOP 2013. LNCS, vol. 7792, pp. 533–553. Springer, Heidelberg (2013). https://doi.org/10.1007/978-3-642-37036-6_29
12. Burckhardt, S., Musuvathi, M.: Effective program verification for relaxed memory models. In: Gupta, A., Malik, S. (eds.) CAV 2008. LNCS, vol. 5123, pp. 107–120. Springer, Heidelberg (2008). https://doi.org/10.1007/978-3-540-70545-1_12
13. Burnim, J., Sen, K., Stergiou, C.: Sound and complete monitoring of sequential consistency for relaxed memory models. In: Abdulla, P.A., Leino, K.R.M. (eds.) TACAS 2011. LNCS, vol. 6605, pp. 11–25. Springer, Heidelberg (2011). https://doi.org/10.1007/978-3-642-19835-9_3
14. Clarke, E., Kroening, D., Lerda, F.: A tool for checking ANSI-C programs. In: Jensen, K., Podelski, A. (eds.) TACAS 2004. LNCS, vol. 2988, pp. 168–176. Springer, Heidelberg (2004). https://doi.org/10.1007/978-3-540-24730-2_15
15. Dan, A.M., Meshman, Y., Vechev, M., Yahav, E.: Predicate abstraction for relaxed memory models. In: Logozzo, F., Fähndrich, M. (eds.) SAS 2013. LNCS, vol. 7935, pp. 84–104. Springer, Heidelberg (2013). https://doi.org/10.1007/978-3-642-38856-9_7

16. Derevenetc, E., Meyer, R.: Robustness against power is PSpace-complete. In: Esparza, J., Fraigniaud, P., Husfeldt, T., Koutsoupias, E. (eds.) ICALP 2014. LNCS, vol. 8573, pp. 158–170. Springer, Heidelberg (2014). https://doi.org/10.1007/978-3-662-43951-7_14
17. Dill, D.L.: The Mur ϕ verification system. In: Alur, R., Henzinger, T.A. (eds.) CAV 1996. LNCS, vol. 1102, pp. 390–393. Springer, Heidelberg (1996). https://doi.org/10.1007/3-540-61474-5_86
18. Flanagan, C., Godefroid, P.: Dynamic partial-order reduction for model checking software. In: POPL, pp. 110–121. ACM, New York (2005)
19. Flur, S., et al.: Modelling the ARMv8 architecture, operationally: concurrency and ISA. In: POPL, pp. 608–621. ACM, New York (2016)
20. Godefroid, P.: Model checking for programming languages using VeriSoft. In: POPL, pp. 174–186. ACM, New York (1997)
21. Holzmann, G.J.: The model checker SPIN. IEEE Trans. Softw. Eng. **23**(5), 279–295 (1997)
22. Huynh, T.Q., Roychoudhury, A.: A memory model sensitive checker for C#. In: Misra, J., Nipkow, T., Sekerinski, E. (eds.) FM 2006. LNCS, vol. 4085, pp. 476–491. Springer, Heidelberg (2006). https://doi.org/10.1007/11813040_32
23. Kokologiannakis, M., Lahav, O., Sagonas, K., Vafeiadis, V.: Effective stateless model checking for C/C++ concurrency. In: Proceedings of the ACM on Programming Languages, vol. 2, pp. 17:1–17:32, December 2017
24. Kroening, D., Tautschnig, M.: CBMC – C bounded model checker. In: Ábrahám, E., Havelund, K. (eds.) TACAS 2014. LNCS, vol. 8413, pp. 389–391. Springer, Heidelberg (2014). https://doi.org/10.1007/978-3-642-54862-8_26
25. Lamport, L.: How to make a multiprocessor computer that correctly executes multiprocess programs. IEEE Trans. Comput. **28**(9), 690–691 (1979)
26. Linden, A., Wolper, P.: An automata-based symbolic approach for verifying programs on relaxed memory models. In: van de Pol, J., Weber, M. (eds.) SPIN 2010. LNCS, vol. 6349, pp. 212–226. Springer, Heidelberg (2010). https://doi.org/10.1007/978-3-642-16164-3_16
27. Mador-Haim, S., et al.: An axiomatic memory model for POWER multiprocessors. In: Madhusudan, P., Seshia, S.A. (eds.) CAV 2012. LNCS, vol. 7358, pp. 495–512. Springer, Heidelberg (2012). https://doi.org/10.1007/978-3-642-31424-7_36
28. Norris, B., Demsky, B.: CDSchecker: checking concurrent data structures written with C/C++ atomics. In: OOPSLA, pp. 131–150. ACM, New York (2013)
29. Peizhao, O., Demsky, B.: Checking concurrent data structures under the C/C++11 memory model. SIGPLAN **52**(8), 45–59 (2017)
30. Park, S., Dill, D.L.: An executable specification, analyzer and verifier for RMO (Relaxed Memory Order). In: SPAA, pp. 34–41. ACM, New York (1995)
31. Pulte, C., Flur, S., Deacon, W., French, J., Sarkar, S., Sewell, P.: Simplifying ARM concurrency: multicopy-atomic axiomatic and operational models for ARMv8. In: Proceedings of the ACM on Programming Languages, vol. 2, pp. 19:1–19:29, December 2017
32. Ročkai, P., Štill, V., Černá, I., Barnat, J.: DiVM: model checking with LLVM and graph memory. J. Syst. Softw. **143**, 1–13 (2018)
33. Sarkar, S., Sewell, P., Alglave, J., Maranget, L., Williams, D.: Understanding POWER multiprocessors. In: PLDI, pp. 175–186. ACM, New York (2011)
34. Sewell, P., Sarkar, S., Owens, S., Nardelli, F.Z., Myreen, M.O.: X86-TSO: a rigorous and usable programmer's model for x86 multiprocessors. Commun. ACM **53**(7), 89–97 (2010)

35. CORPORATE SPARC International, Inc.: The SPARC Architecture Manual (Version 9). Prentice-Hall Inc, Upper Saddle River (1994)
36. Štill, V., Ročkai, P., Barnat, J.: Weak memory models as LLVM-to-LLVM transformations. In: Kofroň, J., Vojnar, T. (eds.) MEMICS 2015. LNCS, vol. 9548, pp. 144–155. Springer, Cham (2016). https://doi.org/10.1007/978-3-319-29817-7_13
37. Štill, V., Ročkai, P., Barnat, J.: Using off-the-shelf exception support components in C++ verification. In: QRS, pp. 54–64. IEEE, July 2017
38. Turon, A., Vafeiadis, V., Dreyer, D.: GPS: navigating weak memory with ghosts, protocols, and separation. In: OOPSLA, pp. 691–707. ACM, New York (2014)
39. Vafeiadis, V., Narayan, C.: Relaxed separation logic: a program logic for C11 concurrency. In: OOPSLA, pp. 867–884. ACM, New York (2013)
40. Yang, Y., Gopalakrishnan, G., Lindstrom, G.: Memory-model-sensitive data race analysis. In: Davies, J., Schulte, W., Barnett, M. (eds.) ICFEM 2004. LNCS, vol. 3308, pp. 30–45. Springer, Heidelberg (2004). https://doi.org/10.1007/978-3-540-30482-1_11
41. Zhang, N., Kusano, M., Wang, C.: Dynamic partial order reduction for relaxed memory models. In: PLDI, pp. 250–259. ACM, New York (2015)

Network Systems

Modeling and Verifying NDN Access Control Using CSP

Yuan Fei and Huibiao Zhu(✉)

Shanghai Key Laboratory of Trustworthy Computing,
School of Computer Science and Software Engineering,
East China Normal University, Shanghai, China
hbzhu@sei.ecnu.edu.cn

Abstract. Named Data Networking (NDN) is a new promising architecture of information-centric networking. NDN could not reuse the existing access control solutions designed for the IP architecture due to their fundamental difference of design, as well as NDNs caching property. As a result, several access control solutions have been proposed for NDN. One of them is specially for both closed and open environment. In this paper, we make the very first attempt to model and verify several important properties of NDN access control. We adopt CSP (Communicating Sequential Processes) to model the NDN access control proposed by Hamdane et al., as well as their security properties. By feeding the models into the model checker PAT (Process Analysis Toolkit), we have verified that the NDN access control cannot prevent the NK key pair faking and the data leakage with the appearance of intruders. We introduce a new method to solve these issues. Considering the situation when the entities are invaded, we also improve our method to make the NDN access control strong enough to maintain the property of key authenticity and data security in this vulnerable situation. We hope that our study would help enhancing the adaptability and robustness of the NDN access control.

Keywords: Modeling · Verification · Named Data Networking (NDN) Access control

1 Introduction

Named Data Networking (NDN) [20] is one of the leading architectures in Information-Centric Networking (ICN) that aims to resolve the existing problems in TCP/IP Internet [1,3]. Although TCP/IP-based network has shown great resilience over the years, it cannot support the newly evolving content distribution model successfully, as users gradually pay more attention to named content rather than its location. NDN emerges as one of the promising architectures in ICN, where each packet does not carry an IP address but a data name. The data producers mean publishers and the data consumers represent subscribers in NDN. When a data consumer needs a data, it sends out an *Interest* packet with a required name of the data. According to the name, routers

J. Sun and M. Sun (Eds.): ICFEM 2018, LNCS 11232, pp. 143–159, 2018.
https://doi.org/10.1007/978-3-030-02450-5_9

forward the packets over the network, and a *Data* packet with a matching name will be returned to the consumer when it is produced by some data producer.

As an fundamental aspect of network security, access control is strongly correlated with other security services such as authenticity, auditing and authorizations [16]. Generally, the main purpose of access control is to regulate who can view or use resources in a computing environment. Traditional mechanisms of access control focus on the IP addresses of end hosts. Such host-centric access control models cannot be easily adapted into NDN. As *Data* packets are cached in *ContentStore* at NDN routers for effective data delivery, they may be obtained by the consumers without access right. New access control models are called for NDN.

Some solutions have been proposed for ICN architectures including NDN with several limits. Using data encryption is a natural and intuitive approach for building access control. Chen et al. [5] proposed an encryption and probability based access model for NDN. The bloom-filter data structure applied in this model is suitable for video streaming service, but may reduce the efficiency in other scenarios. In Misra et al. [12], content are encrypted by a symmetric data key whose dissemination is supported by Broadcast Encryption (BE). However, BE is limited to a context where the number of users is not infinite. As the prototype of NDN, CCNx introduced a simple access control solution [7], which allows the control of the rights of reading, writing and management. Unfortunately, its lazy revocation produces a possible situation where a revoked entity reads protected content. To address these limits, Hamdane et al. [8] introduced a new encryption-based NDN access control.

We found that the verification of the security of NDN access control is still challenging. In this paper, we made the very first step to model and verify the NDN access control proposed in [8] using classical process algebra language CSP (Communicating Sequential Processes) [4,9]. Moreover, we also choose the model checker tool PAT (Process Analysis Toolkit) [13,18] to verify several safety and liveness properties, including deadlock freedom, data availability, key authentication and data security. The verification results demonstrate that when the intruder eavesdrops and modifies messages, the models built from the original NDN access control cannot resist the NK (node key) key pair faking and the data leakage. By introducing the digital signature method, our modified models can satisfy key authentication and data security properties. Then we introduce the scenario of invaded entity to our model, and find out that the two properties can no longer be maintained. We propose the digital certificate method and apply it in our model. Then the verification results show that our updated models regain the two properties again. Our work provides security for access control, and makes it be more adaptive to complicated network environment.

The rest of the paper is organized as follows. Section 2 gives a brief introduction of NDN access control, as well as the introduction of CSP. Section 3 is devoted to the modelling of NDN access control. In Sect. 4, we apply model checker PAT to verify deadlocks, data availability, key authentication and data security, and also give the improvement for better safety performance. Finally, Sect. 5 concludes and discusses future work.

2 Background

In this section, we introduce the NDN access control [8]. We also give a brief introduction to CSP.

2.1 NDN Access Control

Hamdane et al. propose an access control solution for NDN based on data encryption, which is valid both in closed and opened environment. Symmetric data key *DK* is used to encrypt the data produced by a writer. A pair of keys ($NK_{encryption}$, $NK_{decryption}$) is specially used to encrypt *DK*. Similar to public and private keys, $NK_{encryption}$ is used for encryption and $NK_{decryption}$ does the decryption job. However, both of them are secret.

The establishment of this access control solution is mainly based on the entities as below:

- **Readers and writers:** They correspond to users with the read and write rights respectively. Readers want to read the encrypted data. Writers are responsible for producing the encrypted data.
- **Access Control Manager (ACM):** It is introduced to control the management of the access control policy.
- **Network Nodes (NN):** They guarantee content delivery to transit message between entities and ACM.

We simplify some steps of read and write operations in [8] and only retain the processing related with keys and data. Fig. 1 illustrates the packet propagation of read and write operations in closed environments. As *NN* is only responsible to transit message to *ACM*, $Reader_i$ and $Writer_i$ are communicating with *ACM* essentially.

- **Read Operation Process**: $Reader_i$ sends the required *Data name* to *ACM* (step a.1). *ACM* replies $Reader_i$ with *Data* packet including *Data* encrypted with data key *DK* (step a.2). $Reader_i$ knows the name of data key *DK* and sends the *Interest* to *ACM* (step a.3). *ACM* uses $NK_{encryption}$ to encrypt *DK* and creates a *Data* packet to send back to $Reader_i$ (step a.4). $Reader_i$ sends the *Interest* packet carrying name of key pair ($NK_{encryption}$, $NK_{decryption}$) to *ACM* (step a.5). *ACM* returns all the hash value of public keys (step a.6). $Reader_i$ gives *ACM* with *NK name* and its hash value of public key (step a.7). *ACM* uses the related public key to encrypt $NK_{decryption}$ to produce a *Data* packet for *ACM* (step a.8).
- **Write Operation Process**: Assuming that $Writer_i$ knows the name of key pair ($NK_{encryption}$, $NK_{decryption}$) in advance, it sends an *Interest* packet containing *NK name* to *ACM* (step b.1). *ACM* returns a *Data* packet with all the hash values of public keys that *ACM* has already known (step b.2). Then $Writer_i$ recognizes its own hash and transmits it together with *NK name* as a new *Interest* to *ACM* (step b.3). *ACM* recognizes which writer it is communicating with, and uses $Writer_i$'s public key to encrypt key pair

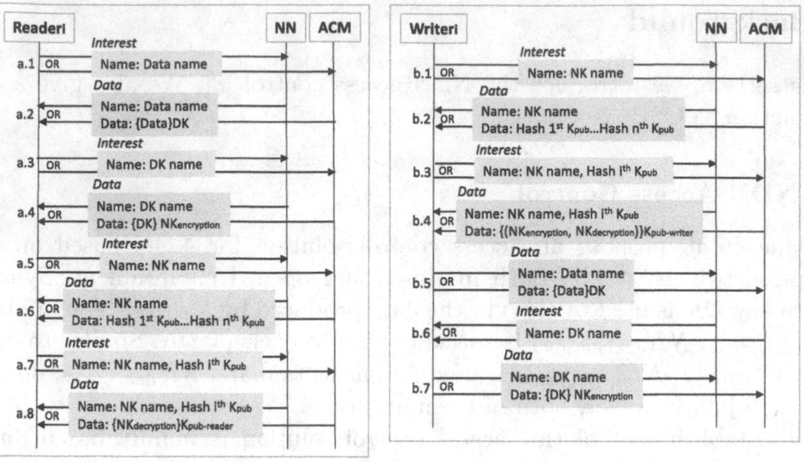

Fig. 1. Packet propagation of read and write operations in closed environments

$(NK_{encryption}, NK_{decryption})$. This is added to a new *Data* packet which is fed back to *ACM* (step b.4). Then $Writer_i$ sends *Data* encrypted with data key *DK* to *ACM* (step b.5). *ACM* learns *DK name* and sends the *Interest* to $Writer_i$ (step b.6). $Writer_i$ then uses $NK_{encryption}$ to encrypt *DK* and produces a new *Data* packet as a reply (step b.7).

2.2 A Brief Introduction of CSP

In this subsection, we give a short introduction to CSP (Communicating Sequential Processes) [4,9]. It is a process algebra proposed by Hoare in 1978. As one of the most mature formal methods, it is tailored for describing the interaction between concurrency systems by mathematical theories. Because of its well-known expressive ability, CSP has been widely used in many fields [6,11,14,15].

CSP processes are constituted by primitive processes and actions. We use the following syntax to define the processes in this paper, whereby P and Q represent processes, the alphabets $\alpha(P)$ and $\alpha(Q)$ mean the set of actions that the processes P and Q can take respectively, and a and b denote the atomic actions and c stands for the name of a channel.

$$P,Q = Skip \mid Stop \mid a \rightarrow P \mid \; c?x \rightarrow P \mid c!e \rightarrow P \mid P \Box Q \mid P \| Q \mid P ||| Q \mid P \lhd b \rhd Q \mid P;Q$$

where:

- *Skip* stands for a process which only terminates successfully.
- *Stop* represents that the process does nothing and its state is deadlock.
- $a \rightarrow P$ first performs action a, then behaves like P.
- $c?x \rightarrow P$ receives a message by the channel c and assigns it to a variable x, then does the subsequent behavior like P.

- $c!\,e \rightarrow P$ sends a message e through the channel c, then performs P.
- $P \Box Q$ acts like either P or Q and the environment decides the selection.
- $P \parallel Q$ shows the parallel composition between P and Q.
- $P|||Q$ indicates the process chooses to perform actions in P and Q randomly.
- $P \lhd b \rhd Q$ denotes if the condition b is true, the process behaves like P, otherwise, like Q.
- $P;Q$ executes P and Q sequentially.

3 Modeling NDN Access Control

3.1 Sets, Messages and Channels

In order to model the behavior between the writers/readers and the ACM in Fig. 1, we need to give the fundamental information about sets, messages and channels. We assume the existence of some sets used in the models. **Entity** set represents entities including writers, readers and ACM. **Name** set denotes NK names, Data names and DK names. **Key** set is constituted by keys. **Content** set contains the content to be encrypted. **Ack** set consists of acknowledgments.

Interest and *Data* packets transmitted between entities and internal processing procedures of entities are two core elements of modeling. With the help of the previously defined sets, we abstract them into different messages. Each message includes a tag from the set $\{msg_{int}, msg_{dat}, msg_{ack}, msg_{pro}\}$. In addition, we use the form $E(k)$ and $H(k)$ to represent the encryption and the hash of key k. The definition of messages is given as below.

$$
\begin{aligned}
MSG_{int} &= \{msg_{int}.a.b.n,\ msg_{int}.a.b.n.H(k) \mid a, b \in Entity, n \in Name, k \in Key\}\\
MSG_{dat1} &= \{msg_{dat}.a.b.n.H(k),\ msg_{dat}.a.b.n.E(k,c),\ msg_{dat}.a.b.n.c \mid\\
&\qquad a, b \in Entity, n \in Name, k \in Key, c \in Content\}\\
MSG_{dat2} &= \{msg_{dat}.a.b.n.H(k).E(k,c) \mid a, b \in Entity, n \in Name, k \in Key, c \in Content\}\\
MSG_{ack} &= \{msg_{ack}.x \mid x \in Ack\}\\
MSG_{pro} &= \{msg_{pro}.E(k_1, c_1).k,\ msg_{pro}.E(k_1, c_1).E(k_2, c_2).k,\\
&\qquad msg_{pro}.E(k_1, c_1).E(k_2, c_2).E(k_3, c_3).k \mid\\
&\qquad k, k_1, k_2, k_3 \in Key, c_1, c_2, c_3 \in Content\}\\
MSG_{out} &= MSG_{int} \cup MSG_{dat1 \cup dat2} \qquad MSG_{in} = MSG_{ack} \cup MSG_{pro}\\
MSG &= MSG_{in} \cup MSG_{out}
\end{aligned}
$$

MSG_{int} and $MSG_{dat1 \cup dat2}$ represent *Interest* packets and *Data* packets respectively. MSG_{pro} denotes the messages sent to the process specially for internal processing and MSG_{ack} represents the feedbacks produced by the process. MSG_{out} represents messages transmitted between entities. MSG_{in} denotes internal processing messages of entities.

We also give the three definitions of channels to model the communications between processes.

- channels between readers (writers) and ACM, denoted by COM_PATH:
  $ComWM$, $ComRM$

- channels of intruders who intercept readers, writers and ACM, represented by $INTRUDER\_PATH$:
  FakeWM1, FakeWM2, FakeRM1, FakeRM2
- channels of processing messages, depicted by $PROCESS\_PATH$:
  CheckNK, GetData

The declarations of channels are as below.

$$\textbf{Channel } COM\_PATH, INTRUDER\_PATH : MSG_{out}$$

$$\textbf{Channel } PROCESS\_PATH : MSG_{in}$$

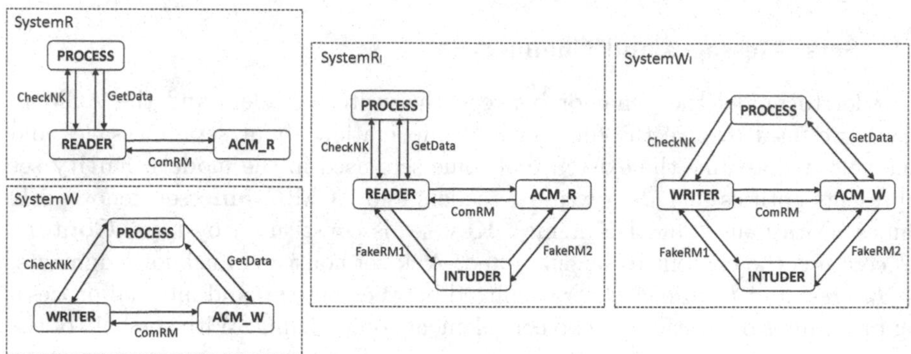

Fig. 2. Interprocess communication between processes in models

3.2 Overall Modeling

We formalize the read and write operations and consider the existence of intruders. The models are built as below.

$$\begin{aligned} SystemR =_{df}\ & READER(R, M, K, NN, ND, NDK)[|PROCESS\_PATH|]PROCESS \\ & [|COM\_PATH|]ACM\_R(R, M, DK, DATA, NK\_e, NK\_d, HL) \\ SystemW =_{df}\ & WRITER(W, M, K, NN, DK, DATA)[|PROCESS\_PATH|]PROCESS \\ & [|COM\_PATH|]ACM\_W(W, M, HL, NK\_e, NK\_d, NDK) \\ SystemR_I =_{df}\ & SystemR[|INTRUDER\_PATH|]INTUDER \\ SystemW_I =_{df}\ & SystemW[|INTRUDER\_PATH|]INTUDER \end{aligned}$$

READER and *WRITER*, as their names imply, represent the reader and the writer. ACM_R and ACM_W denote the behavior of ACM when it communicates with readers and writers respectively. *PROCESS* denotes the internal processing procedure. Considering the situation when intruders exist, we also build process *INTRUDER* to simulate the behavior of intruders who eavesdrop and modify messages.

We use $P[|A|]Q$ to denote the parallel composition of P and Q, synchronizing on the events in set A. Fig. 2 illustrates interprocess communication between processes in four models. There are several constants appeared in models, we give their meanings and their relationship with pre-defined sets in Table 1. We also list the significance of variables used in our models in Table 2.

Table 1. The relationship between involved constants and pre-defined sets

Set	Constants
Entity	R(reader), W(writer), M(ACM)
Name	NN(NK key pair name), NDK(data key name), ND(data name)
Key	K(public key), K^{-1}(private key), DK(data key), NK_e(NK$_{encryption}$), NK_d(NK$_{decryption}$), NK_e_f(fake NK$_{encryption}$), NK_d_f(fake NK$_{decryption}$)
Content	DATA(data), HL(hash list), NK_e(NK$_{encryption}$), NK_d(NK$_{decryption}$), NK_e_f(fake NK$_{encryption}$), NK_d_f(fake NK$_{decryption}$)
Ack	YES(positive feedback), NO(negative feedback)

Table 2. The relationship between involved variables and pre-defined sets

Set	Variables
Entity	r(reader), w(writer), m(ACM)
Name	nn(NK key pair name), ndk(data key name), nd(data name)
Key	k,k1,k2(public key), k^{-1},$k1^{-1}$,$k2^{-1}$(private key), dk,dk1(data key), nk_e,nk_e1(true/fake NK$_{encryption}$), nk_d(true/fake NK$_{decryption}$)
Content	data(data), hl(hash list), nk_e,nk_e1(true/fake NK$_{encryption}$), nk_d(true/fake NK$_{decryption}$)
Ack	ack,ack1(positive/negative feedback)

3.3 Reader Modeling

We first formalize process $READER_0$ to describe the behavior of a reader.

$$
\begin{aligned}
&READER_0(r, m, k, nn, nd, ndk) =_{df}\\
&Initialization\{n = false; d = false\} \rightarrow ComRM!msg_{int}.r.m.nd \rightarrow\\
&ComRM?msg_{dat}.m.r.nd.E(dk, data) \rightarrow ComRM!msg_{int}.r.m.ndk \rightarrow\\
&ComRM?msg_{dat}.m.r.ndk.E(nk\_e, dk1) \rightarrow ComRM!msg_{int}.r.m.nn \rightarrow\\
&ComRM?msg_{dat}.m.r.nn.hl \rightarrow ComRM!msg_{int}.r.m.nn.H(k1) \rightarrow\\
&ComRM?msg_{dat}.m.r.nn.H(k1).E(k1, nk\_d) \rightarrow\\
&CheckNK!msg_{pro}.E(k1, nk\_d).k^{-1} \rightarrow CheckNK?msg_{ack}.ack \rightarrow\\
&\left(\begin{array}{l}(NKFakingSuccess\{n = true\} \rightarrow SKIP)\\ \lhd(ack == YES) \rhd (NKFakingError\{n = false\} \rightarrow SKIP)\end{array}\right);\\
&GetData!msg_{pro}.E(dk, data).E(nk\_e, dk1).nk\_d \rightarrow GetData?msg_{ack}.ack1 \rightarrow\\
&\left(\begin{array}{l}(DataAcquisitionSuccess\{d = true\} \rightarrow SKIP)\\ \lhd(ack1 == YES) \rhd (DataAcquisitionError\{d = false\} \rightarrow SKIP)\end{array}\right);\\
&READER_0(r, m, k, nn, nd, ndk)
\end{aligned}
$$

Boolean variable n and d indicate that NK key pair faking and data acquisition are successful or not. First, $READER_0$ initializes the two variables. The following eight actions on channel $ComRM$ correspond to a.1–a.8 steps of Reader$_i$ in Fig. 1 in order. By channel $CheckNK$, we check whether the value carried by nk_d is faked or not. We also learn whether *Data* is obtained successfully using channel *GetData*.

In order to allow the possibility of intruder action, we need to allow the message on channel *ComRM* to be intercepted or faked. We do this via renaming. In addition, $\{|c|\}$ denotes the set of all communications over channel *c*.

$$
\begin{aligned}
&READER(r, m, k, nn, nd, ndk) =_{df}\\
&READER_0(r, m, k, nn, nd, ndk)[[\\
&ComRM?\{|ComRM|\} \leftarrow ComRM?\{|ComRM|\}, ComRM?\{|ComRM|\} \leftarrow FakeRM2?\{|ComRM|\},\\
&ComRM!\{|ComRM|\} \leftarrow ComRM!\{|ComRM|\}, ComRM!\{|ComRM|\} \leftarrow FakeRM2!\{|ComRM|\}]]
\end{aligned}
$$

READER will perform either an action on channel *ComRM* or channel *FakeRM2* whenever $READER_0$ performs a corresponding action on channel *ComRM*. Besides, *READER* and $READER_0$ perform the same action.

3.4 Writer Modeling

Process $WRITER_0$ catches the behavior of a writer.

$$
\begin{aligned}
&WRITER_0(w, m, k, nn, nd, dk, data) =_{df}\\
&Initialization\{n = false\} \rightarrow ComWM!msg_{int}.w.m.nn \rightarrow ComWM?msg_{dat}.m.w.nn.hl \rightarrow\\
&ComWM!msg_{int}.w.m.nn.H(k1) \rightarrow ComWM?msg_{dat}.m.w.nn.H(k1).E(k1, (nk\_e, nk\_d)) \rightarrow\\
&ComWM!msg_{dat}.w.m.nd.E(dk, data) \rightarrow ComWM?msg_{int}.m.w.ndk \rightarrow\\
&ComWM!msg_{dat}.w.m.ndk.E(nk\_e, dk) \rightarrow\\
&CheckNK!msg_{pro}.E(k1, (nk\_e, nk\_d)).k^{-1} \rightarrow CheckNK?msg_{ack}.ack \rightarrow\\
&\left(\begin{array}{l}(NKFakingSuccess\{n = true\} \rightarrow SKIP)\\ \lhd(ack == YES) \rhd (NKFakingError\{n = false\} \rightarrow SKIP)\end{array}\right);\\
&WRITER_0(w, m, k, nn, nd, dk, data)
\end{aligned}
$$

After initializing the variable, $WRITER_0$ performs seven actions on channel *ComWM* which correspond to b.1–b.7 steps of Writer$_i$ in Fig. 1 orderly. $WRITER_0$ checks whether the NK key pair is faked or not by channel *CheckNK*.

Using renaming, process *WRITER* supports the message on channel *ComWM* to be intercepted or faked.

$$
\begin{aligned}
&WRITER(w, m, k, nn, nd, dk, data) =_{df}\\
&WRITER_0(w, m, k, nn, nd, dk, data)[[\\
&ComWM?\{|ComWM|\} \leftarrow ComWM?\{|ComWM|\}, ComWM?\{|ComWM|\} \leftarrow FakeWM2?\{|ComWM|\},\\
&ComWM!\{|ComWM|\} \leftarrow ComWM!\{|ComWM|\}, ComWM!\{|ComWM|\} \leftarrow FakeWM2!\{|ComWM|\}]]
\end{aligned}
$$

WRITER and $WRITER_0$ perform the same action except for the actions on channel *ComWM*. When $WRITER_0$ performs an action on channel *ComWM*, *WRITER* will perform either a corresponding action on channel *ComWM* or channel *FakeWM2*.

3.5 ACM Modeling

Modeling of ACM can be divided into two processes ACM_R_0 and ACM_W_0 to simulate the function of the ACM for a reader and a writer respectively.

$$\begin{aligned}
&ACM_R_0(r, m, dk, data, nk_e, nk_d, hl) =_{df}\\
&ComRM?msg_{int}.r.m.nd \rightarrow ComRM!msg_{dat}.m.r.nd.E(dk, data) \rightarrow ComRM?msg_{int}.r.m.ndk \rightarrow\\
&ComRM!msg_{dat}.m.r.ndk.E(nk_e, dk) \rightarrow ComRM?msg_{int}.r.m.nn \rightarrow ComRM!msg_{dat}.m.r.nn.hl \rightarrow\\
&ComRM?msg_{int}.r.m.nn.H(k) \rightarrow ComRM!msg_{dat}.m.r.nn.H(k).E(k, nk_d) \rightarrow\\
&ACM_R_0(r, m, dk, data, nk_e, nk_d, hl)
\end{aligned}$$

$$\begin{aligned}
&ACM_W_0(w, m, hl, nk_e, nk_d, ndk) =_{df}\\
&Initialization\{d = false\} \rightarrow ComWM?msg_{int}.w.m.nn \rightarrow ComWM!msg_{dat}.m.w.nn.hl \rightarrow\\
&ComWM?msg_{int}.w.m.nn.H(k) \rightarrow ComWM!msg_{dat}.m.w.nn.H(k).E(k, (nk_e, nk_d)) \rightarrow\\
&ComWM?msg_{dat}.w.m.nd.E(dk, data) \rightarrow ComWM!msg_{int}.w.m.ndk \rightarrow\\
&ComWM?msg_{dat}.m.w.ndk.E(nk_e1, dk1) \rightarrow\\
&GetData!msg_{pro}.E(dk, data).E(nk_e1, dk1).nk_d \rightarrow GetData?msg_{ack}.ack \rightarrow\\
&\begin{pmatrix}(DataAcquisitionSuccess\{d = true\} \rightarrow SKIP)\\ \lhd (ack == YES) \rhd (DataAcquisitionError\{d = false\} \rightarrow SKIP)\end{pmatrix};\\
&ACM_W_0(w, m, hl, nk_e, nk_d, ndk)
\end{aligned}$$

For process ACM_R_0, the eight actions on channel *ComRM* correspond to a.1–a.8 steps of ACM in Fig. 1 in order. In process ACM_W_0, the seven actions on channel *ComWM* correspond to b.1–b.7 steps of ACM in Fig. 1 in turn. ACM_W_0 also checks whether the data can be obtained by channel *GetData*.

For simulating the intercepting and faking of messages, we apply the renaming to ACM_R_0 and ACM_W_0.

$$\begin{aligned}
&ACM_R(r, m, dk, data, nk_e, nk_d, hl) =_{df}\\
&ACM_R_0(r, m, dk, data, nk_e, nk_d, hl)[[\\
&ComRM?\{|ComRM|\} \leftarrow ComRM?\{|ComRM|\}, ComRM?\{|ComRM|\} \leftarrow FakeRM1?\{|ComRM|\},\\
&ComRM!\{|ComRM|\} \leftarrow ComRM!\{|ComRM|\}, ComRM!\{|ComRM|\} \leftarrow FakeRM1!\{|ComRM|\}]]
\end{aligned}$$

$$\begin{aligned}
&ACM_W(w, m, hl, nk_e, nk_d, ndk) =_{df}\\
&ACM_W_0(w, m, hl, nk_e, nk_d, ndk)[[\\
&ComWM?\{|ComWM|\} \leftarrow ComWM?\{|ComWM|\}, ComWM?\{|ComWM|\} \leftarrow FakeWM1?\{|ComWM|\},\\
&ComWM!\{|ComWM|\} \leftarrow ComWM!\{|ComWM|\}, ComWM!\{|ComWM|\} \leftarrow FakeWM1!\{|ComWM|\}]]
\end{aligned}$$

Whenever ACM_R_0 does an action on channel *ComRM*, *ACM_R* will does a corresponding action on channel *ComRM* or channel *FakeRM1*. *ACM_W* and ACM_W_0 perform the same action on channel *GetData*. *ACM_W* will perform either an action on channel *ComWM* or channel *FakeWM1* whenever ACM_W_0 performs a corresponding action on channel *ComWM*.

3.6 *PROCESS* Modeling

In order to simulate the internal processing, we use *PROCESS* to deal with decrypting messages and checking the decrypted messages.

$$
\begin{aligned}
&PROCESS() =_{df}\\
&CheckNK?msg_{pro}.E(k1, nk\_d).k2^{-1} \rightarrow\\
&\left(\begin{array}{l}(checkNK!msg_{ack}.YES \rightarrow PROCESS())\\ \lhd((k1 == k2)\&\&(nk\_d == NK\_d\_f)) \rhd (CheckNK!msg_{ack}.NO \rightarrow PROCESS())\end{array}\right)\\
&\square CheckNK?msg_{pro}.E(k1, (nk\_e, nk\_d)).k2^{-1} \rightarrow\\
&\left(\begin{array}{l}(CheckNK?msg_{ack}.YES \rightarrow PROCESS())\\ \lhd((k1 == k2)\&\&(nk\_e == NK\_e\_f)\&\&(nk\_d == NK\_d\_f)) \rhd (CheckNK!msg_{ack}.NO \rightarrow PROCESS())\end{array}\right)\\
&\square GetData?msg_{pro}.E(dk1, data).E(nk\_e, dk2).nk\_d \rightarrow\\
&\left(\begin{array}{l}(GetData!msg_{ack}.YES \rightarrow PROCESS())\\ \lhd((((nk\_e == NK\_e)\&\&(nk\_d == NK\_d))||((nk\_e == NK\_e\_f)\&\&(nk\_d == NK\_d\_f)))\\ \quad \&\&(dk1 == dk2)) \rhd (GetData!msg_{ack}.NO \rightarrow PROCESS())\end{array}\right)
\end{aligned}
$$

PROCESS receives one encrypted message with a decryption key by channel *CheckNK*. Then it judges whether the decryption key can decrypt the message and the decrypted message is faked or not.

Using channel *GetData*, *PROCESS* obtains two encrypted messages and a decryption key. Then it determines whether the two encrypted messages can both be decrypted orderly to get the data.

3.7 Intruder Modeling

We also consider the intruder as a process. It can intercept or fake messages in the communication on channel *ComRM* and *ComWM*. First, we define the set of facts which intruders might learn.

$$
\begin{aligned}
Fact =_{df}\ & \{R, W, M\} \cup \{NN, NDK, ND\} \cup MSG_{out} \cup \{K, K^{-1}, DK, NK\_e, NK\_d, NK\_e\_f, NK\_d\_f\}\\
& \cup \{H(K)\} \cup \{E(key, content) \mid key \in \{K, DK, NK\_e, NK\_e\_f\},\\
& \qquad content \in \{Data, DK, NK\_d, NK\_d\_f, (NK\_e, NK\_d), (NK\_e\_f, NK\_d\_f)\}\}
\end{aligned}
$$

We also need to define how the intruder can deduce from the facts that it has already learned. We write $F \mapsto f$ if fact f can be deduced from the set of facts F.

$$
\begin{array}{ll}
\{K^{-1}, E(K, content)\} \mapsto content & \{DK, E(DK, content)\} \mapsto content\\
\{NK\_d, E(NK\_e, content)\} \mapsto content & \{NK\_d\_f, E(NK\_e\_f, content)\} \mapsto content\\
\{K, content\} \mapsto E(K, content) & \{DK, content\} \mapsto E(DK, content)\\
\{NK\_e, content\} \mapsto E(NK\_e, content) & \{NK\_e\_f, content\} \mapsto E(NK\_e\_f, content)\\
F \mapsto f \wedge F \subseteq F' \Rightarrow F' \mapsto f &
\end{array}
$$

The first four rules represent decryption and the next four rules represent encryption. The final rule denotes that if the intruder can deduce fact f from the set of facts F, then f can also be deduced from a lager set F'.

We also give the definitions of how the intruders get new facts form messages:

$$Info(msg_{int}.a.b.n) =_{df} \{a, b, n\} \qquad Info(msg_{int}.a.b.n.H(k)) =_{df} \{a, b, n, H(k)\}$$
$$Info(msg_{dat}.a.b.n.H(k)) =_{df} \{a, b, n, H(k)\} \qquad Info(msg_{dat}.a.b.n.E(k, c)) =_{df} \{a, b, n, E(k, c)\}$$
$$Info(msg_{dat}.a.b.n.c) =_{df} \{a, b, n, c\} \qquad Info(msg_{dat}.a.b.n.H(k).E(k, c)) =_{df} \{a, b, n, H(k), E(k, c)\}$$

where $a,b \in Entity$, $n \in Name$, $k \in Key$, $c \in Content$.

At last, we define a channel *Deduce* to support deducing new facts.

$$\textbf{Channel } Deduce : Fact.\mathbf{P}(Fact)$$

The intruder can overhear all the messages transmitted between entities. It can deduce a new fact from ones it has already known. It can also fake some special messages to disturb communication between entities. We now give the formalization of $INTRUDER_0$ as below.

$$\begin{array}{l}
INTRUDER_0(F) =_{df} \\
\Box\Box_{m \in MSG_{out}} FakeRM1?m \rightarrow FakeRM2!m \rightarrow INTRUDER_0(F \cup Info(m)) \\
\Box\Box_{m \in (MSG_{out} \setminus MSG_{dat2})} FakeRM2?m \rightarrow FakeRM1!m \rightarrow INTRUDER_0(F \cup Info(m)) \\
\Box\Box_{m \in MSG_{dat2}} FakeRM2?m \rightarrow FakeRM1!m[[nk_d \leftarrow NK_d_f]] \rightarrow INTRUDER_0(F \cup Info(m)) \\
\Box\Box_{m \in MSG_{out}} FakeWM1?m \rightarrow FakeWM2!m \rightarrow INTRUDER_0(F \cup Info(m)) \\
\Box\Box_{m \in (MSG_{out} \setminus MSG_{dat2})} FakeWM2?m \rightarrow FakeWM1!m \rightarrow INTRUDER_0(F \cup Info(m)) \\
\Box\Box_{m \in MSG_{dat2}} FakeWM2?m \rightarrow FakeWM1!m[[(nk_e, nk_d) \leftarrow (NK_e_f, NK_d_f)]] \rightarrow INTRUDER_0(F \cup Info(m)) \\
\Box\Box_{f \in Fact, f \notin F, F \mapsto f} Initialization\{l = false\} \rightarrow Deduce.f.F \rightarrow \\
\left(\begin{array}{l} (DataLeakageSuccess\{l = true\} \rightarrow INTRUDER_0(F \cup \{f\})) \\ \lhd (f == Data) \rhd (DataLeakageError\{l = false\} \rightarrow INTRUDER_0(F \cup \{f\})) \end{array} \right)
\end{array}$$

When $INTRUDER_0$ receives a message in MSG_{dat2}, it replaces some contents in the message to imitate a fake message and sends it to the original recipient. When $INTRUDER_0$ receives other message, it just eavesdrops the message and transmits it to the original recipient. Then we can give the initial knowledge of the intruder *IK* as the parameter of $INTRUDER_0$ to build *INTRUDER*.

$$INTRUDER =_{df} INTRUDER_0(IK)$$
$$IK =_{df} \{R, W, M, K, NK\_e\_f, NK\_d\_f\}$$

4 Verification and Improvement

In this section, we show how we will verify the four properties (deadlock freedom, data availability, key authentication and data security) with the help of the model checker PAT [13,18], which has been applied in various places [10,17,19]. To perform the verification, we have implemented the formal models in PAT. According to the verification results, we also improve our models twice for better safety performance.

4.1 Properties Verification

One of the four properties is the liveness property and the remaining are safety properties. Some of them are described in Linear Temporal Logic (LTL) formula, which is commonly used to describe linear-time properties. Because the four properties will be verified for all the models in this paper, we use *System()* to represent the models. PAT supports LTL formula by using the assertion #assert *P*() |= *F* to check whether system *P*() satisfies LTL formula *F*.

Property 1: Deadlock Freedom

#assert System() deadlockfree;

We must guarantee that our models should not run into a deadlock state. PAT owns a primitive to describe this situation.

Property 2: Data Availability

#define Data_Acquisition_Success d==true;

#assert System() |= <>Data_Acquisition_Success;

The property of data availability is a liveness property. Using the "eventually" operator <> in LTL, we describe the situation that we need to confirm that the data can be transmitted to the entity requiring for it.

Property 3: Key Authentication

#define NK_Faking_Success n==true;

#assert System() |= []!NK_Faking_Success;

Once the NK key pair is faked, other security issues may appear. So we use this assertion to check whether the NK key pair can be faked successfully, using the "always" operator [] in LTL.

Property 4: Data Security

#define Data_Leakage_Success l==true;

#assert System() |= []!Data_Leakage_Success;

The security of data should be maintained, as the leakage of data will produce a bad effect. The assertion is built to check whether the data can be obtained by intruders.

Verification Result. From Table 3 we learn that model *SystemR*, *SystemW*, $SystemR_I$ and $SystemW_I$ satisfy the property of deadlock freedom. This means that our four models will not run into a deadlock state.

The verification results of data availability are valid for *SystemR* and *SystemW*. We can say that our models without intruders can assure that the entity requiring for data can get it. The verification results of data availability for $SystemR_I$ and $SystemW_I$ are invalid. These illustrate that once an intruder interferes the communication between writers/readers and the ACM, the writers and the readers cannot obtain the data any more.

The verification results of key authentication and data security for *SystemR* and *SystemW* are valid. They show that the property of key authentication and data security can be maintained without intruders. The verification results of key authentication are not valid for $SystemR_I$ and $SystemW_I$. These mean that the NK key pair can be faked successfully in our models with intruders.

Attack 1 is the counterexample of the invalid assertion result of key authenticity for *System*W$_I$. For simplicity, we only present the messages on channel *INTRUDER_PATH* in all the counterexamples.

Attack1 :

A1. W → I : W.M.NN	*A2. I → M : W.M.NN*
A3. M → I : M.W.NN.HL	*A4. I → W : M.W.NN.HL*
A5. W → I : W.M.NN.H(K)	*A6. I → M : W.M.NN.H(K)*
A7. M → I : M.W.NN.H(K).E(K,(NK_e,NK_d))	*A8. I → W : M.W.NN.H(K).E(K,(NK_e_f,NK_d_f))*

At first, the intruder just intercepts messages between the writer and the ACM (A1–A6). Then it produces a dummy message (A8) including a fake NK key pair according to the intercepted message (A7). The writer will obtain the fake NK key pair after receiving this message.

For the data security in Table 3, *System* W_I obtains the invalid result. That is to say, the intruder can get data in *System* W_I. Attack 2 shows the counterexample of the invalid assertion result of the data security for *System*W$_I$.

Attack2 :

A1. W → I : W.M.NN	*A2. I → M : W.M.NN*
A3. M → I : M.W.NN.HL	*A4. I → W : M.W.NN.HL*
A5. W → I : W.M.NN.H(K)	*A6. I → M : W.M.NN.H(K)*
A7. M → I : M.W.NN.H(K).E(K,(NK_e,NK_d))	*A8. I → W : M.W.NN.H(K).E(K,(NK_e_f,NK_d_f))*
A9. W → I : W.M.ND.E(DK,Data)	*A10. I → M : W.M.ND.E(DK,Data)*
A11. M → I : M.W.NDK	*A12. I → W : M.W.NDK*
A13. W → I : W.M.NDK.E(NK_e_f,DK)	

A1–A8 are the same as those in Attack 1. Then the intruder keeps on intercepting messages between the writer and the ACM (A9–A12). Because the writer has obtained the fake NK key pair, the intruder can acquire the data key *DK* from A13. The data key *DK* can be applied to *E(DK,Data)* acquired from A9 to get *Data*.

4.2 First Model Improvement

In order to maintain the key authentication and the data security, we introduce a method similar to digital signature. The ACM creates a special pair of key: public key K_M and private key K_M^{-1}. We assume that K_M is known by readers and writers. When producing message a.8 and message b.4 in Fig. 1, ACM uses its private key K_M^{-1} to encrypt ($NK_{encryption}$, $NK_{decryption}$) and $NK_{decryption}$ at first, like creating a digital signature. This happens before ($NK_{encryption}$, $NK_{decryption}$) and $NK_{decryption}$ are encrypted by the public key of readers and writers. When readers and writers receive these messages, they apply K_M to decrypt the digital signature in them. If the operation succeeds, we can learn that this message is sent by the ACM. The improved models are called *SystemR_Sig*, *System W_Sig*,

Table 3. Verification results of models

Model	Property			
	Deadlock freedom	Data availability	Key authentication	Data security
SystemR	*Valid*	*Valid*	*Valid*	*Valid*
SystemR_I	*Valid*	*Not Valid*	*Not Valid*	*Valid*
SystemW	*Valid*	*Valid*	*Valid*	*Valid*
SystemW_I	*Valid*	*Not Valid*	*Not Valid*	*Not Valid*
SystemR_Sig	*Valid*	*Valid*	*Valid*	*Valid*
SystemR_Sig_I	*Valid*	*Not Valid*	*Valid*	*Valid*
SystemW_Sig	*Valid*	*Valid*	*Valid*	*Valid*
SystemW_Sig_I	*Valid*	*Not Valid*	*Valid*	*Valid*
SystemR_Sig_C	*Valid*	*Not Valid*	*Valid*	*Valid*
SystemR_Sig_C_I	*Valid*	*Not Valid*	*Not Valid*	*Valid*
SystemW_Sig_C	*Valid*	*Not Valid*	*Valid*	*Valid*
SystemW_Sig_C_I	*Valid*	*Not Valid*	*Not Valid*	*Not Valid*
SystemR_Dig	*Valid*	*Valid*	*Valid*	*Valid*
SystemR_Dig_I	*Valid*	*Not Valid*	*Valid*	*Valid*
SystemW_Dig	*Valid*	*Valid*	*Valid*	*Valid*
SystemW_Dig_I	*Valid*	*Not Valid*	*Valid*	*Valid*
SystemR_Dig_C	*Valid*	*Not Valid*	*Valid*	*Valid*
SystemR_Dig_C_I	*Valid*	*Not Valid*	*Valid*	*Valid*
SystemW_Dig_C	*Valid*	*Not Valid*	*Valid*	*Valid*
SystemW_Dig_C_I	*Valid*	*Not Valid*	*Valid*	*Valid*

$SystemR\_Sig_I$ and $SystemW\_Sig_I$. Meanwhile, the specific definitions of them are in the appendix [2] due to the space limit.

According to the results in Table 3, the invalid verification results of data availability for $SystemR\_Sig_I$ and $SystemW\_Sig_I$ illustrate that intruders will affect the acquisition of data for entities. Besides, other verification results of these four properties for *SystemR_Sig*, *SystemW_Sig*, $SystemR\_Sig_I$ and $SystemW\_Sig_I$ are valid. These mean that this method can effectively guarantee that the NK key pair will not be faked and the data will not be leaked.

Another situation we considered is that the public key K_M known by readers and writers is replaced by the intruder's public key K_I. The models become more vulnerable in this situation. The modified models with invaded entities are called *SystemR_Sig_C*, *SystemW_Sig_C*, $SystemR\_\text{Sig\_C}_I$ and $SystemW\_Sig\_C_I$, which are defined in the appendix [2].

From Table 3, the assertions of *SystemR_Sig_C*, *SystemW_Sig_C*, $SystemR\_Sig\_C_I$ and $SystemW\_Sig\_C_I$ for data availability are invalid. These illustrate that the invaded reader and writer cannot get the data whether an intruder exists or not. While verifying key authentication, the assertions of $SystemR\_Sig\_C_I$ and $SystemW\_Sig\_C_I$ are invalid. This means that the NK key pair can be faked successfully when the reader and the writer are invaded. Attack 3 illustrates the counterexample of the invalid assertion result of key authentication for $SystemW\_Sig\_C_I$.

Attack3 :

A1. W → I : W.M.NN	*A2. I → M : W.M.NN*
A3. M → I : M.W.NN.HL	*A4. I → W : M.W.NN.HL*
A5. W → I : W.M.NN.H(K)	*A6. I → M : W.M.NN.H(K)*
A7. M → I : M.W.NN.H(K). $E(K,E(K_M^{-1},(NK\_e,NK\_d)))$	*A8. I → W : M.W.NN.H(K).* $E(K,E(K_I^{-1},(NK\_e\_f,NK\_d\_f)))$

In the beginning, the intruder just intercepts messages between the writer and the ACM (A1–A6). With A7 intercepted from the ACM, the intruder creates a dummy message (A8) including the fake NK key pairs private key K_I^{-1}. Because the writer is invaded, it decrypts A8 successfully and gets the fake NK key pair.

The assertion of $SystemW\_Sig\_C_I$ for data security is not valid, which indicates that the intruder can get data when the writer is invaded. Attack 4 displays the counterexample of the invalid assertion result of data security for $SystemW\_Sig\_C_I$.

Attack4 :

A1. W → I : W.M.NN	*A2. I → M : W.M.NN*
A3. M → I : M.W.NN.HL	*A4. I → W : M.W.NN.HL*
A5. W → I : W.M.NN.H(K)	*A6. I → M : W.M.NN.H(K)*
A7. M → I : M.W.NN.H(K). $E(K,E(K_M^{-1},(NK\_e,NK\_d)))$	*A8. I → W : M.W.NN.H(K).* $E(K,E(K_I^{-1},(NK\_e\_f,NK\_d\_f)))$
A9. W → I : W.M.ND.E(DK,Data)	*A10. I → M : W.M.ND.E(DK,Data)*
A11. M → I : M.W.NDK	*A12. I → W : M.W.NDK*
A13. W → I : W.M.NDK.E(NK_e_f,DK)	

A1–A8 are the same as those in Attack 3. So the writer has obtained the fake NK key pair. Then the intruder continues intercepting messages between the writer and the ACM (A9–A12). Due to A13, the intruder can acquire the data key *DK*. Finally, the data key *DK* can be applied to *E(DK,Data)* acquired from A9 to get *Data*.

4.3 Second Model Improvement

The solution for the situation above is to update the previous method by adding digital certificates. Specifically, ACM provides its public key K_M to the certificate authority (CA). CA uses its private key K_A^{-1} to encrypt K_M, which creates a digital certificate $E((K_A^{-1}),K_M)$. After doing the same operations as those in the first model improvement, we add this digital certificate to the end of message a.8 and message b.4. Assuming that readers and writers know CA's public key K_A, they will fetch the digital certificates at first when dealing with these two messages. Then they decrypt the digital certificates using K_A to get K_M, which will be compared with the public key of the ACM known by the reader/writer. If the two keys are the same, we can conclude that the public key of the ACM known by the reader/writer is the real key. Otherwise, the key is faked.

The improved new models are *SystemR_Dig*, *SystemW_Dig*, $SystemR\_Dig_I$ and $SystemW\_Dig_I$. We also give the corresponding models when the readers and the writers are invaded: *SystemR_Dig_C*, *SystemW_Dig_C*, $SystemR\_Dig\_C_I$ and $SystemW\_Dig\_C_I$. These eight models are defined in the appendix [2].

All the verification results for the eight models are valid in Table 3, except the verification results of data availability in *SystemR_Dig_C* and *SystemW_Dig_C*. The property of data availability cannot be satisfied once the entity is invaded. We can conclude that this new method can guarantee the property of key authentication and data security no matter whether the entity is invaded or not.

5 Conclusion and Future Work

In this paper, we have conducted a formal modelling and verifying NDN access control. We have formalized the read and write operations in closed environments of NDN access control using the CSP process algebra, as well as the intruders. We have used assertions to specify and verify four properties (deadlock freedom, data availability, key authentication and data security) for these models. The verification results indicate that NDN access control cannot guarantee key authentication and data security when the intruder appears. As a result, we have introduced a method similar to digital signature and verified the updated models with respect to the four properties. The new verification results turn out that our method can prevent the NK key pair faking and the data leakage. Then, we have discussed the situation that the readers and the writers are invaded, and found out that the method cannot maintain the property of key authentication and data security any more. Hence, we have updated our method by adding digital certificates. The verification results indicate that our method can avoid the fake of the NK key pair and the leakage of the data, even though the readers and the writers are invaded. Our results would hopefully help to improvement the adaptability and robustness of NDN access control. As for future work, we would like to focus on the read and write operations in open environments of the NDN access control, and consider modeling and verifying other access control solutions of NDN.

Acknowledgement. This work was partly supported by Shanghai Collaborative Innovation Center of Trustworthy Software for Internet of Things (No. ZF1213).

References

1. Ahlgren, B., Dannewitz, C., Imbrenda, C., Kutscher, D., Ohlman, B.: A survey of information-centric networking. IEEE Commun. Mag. **50**(7), 26–36 (2012)
2. Appendix of Modeling and Verifying NDN Access Control Using CSP. https://github.com/asunafy/NDNAccessControl

3. Bari, M.F., Chowdhury, S.R., Ahmed, R., Boutaba, R., Mathieu, B.: A survey of naming and routing in information-centric networks. IEEE Commun. Mag. **50**(12), 44–53 (2012)
4. Brookes, S.D., Hoare, C.A.R., Roscoe, A.W.: A theory of communicating sequential processes. J. ACM **31**(3), 560–599 (1984)
5. Chen, T., Lei, K., Xu, K.: An encryption and probability based access control model for named data networking. In: IEEE 33rd International Performance Computing and Communications Conference, IPCCC 2014, Austin, TX, USA, 5–7 December 2014, pp. 1–8 (2014)
6. Fei, Y., Zhu, H., Wu, X., Fang, H., Qin, S.: Comparative modelling and verification of Pthreads and Dthreads. J. Softw.: Evol. Process **30**(3), e1919 (2018)
7. Golle, J., Smetters, D.: CCNx access control specifications. Technical report, Xerox Palo Alto Research Center-PARC (2010)
8. Hamdane, B., Boussada, R., Elhdhili, M.E., Fatmi, S.G.E.: Towards a secure access to content in named data networking. In: 26th IEEE International Conference on Enabling Technologies: Infrastructure for Collaborative Enterprises, WETICE 2017, Poznan, Poland, June 21–23, 2017, pp. 250–255 (2017)
9. Hoare, C.A.R.: Communicating Sequential Processes. Prentice-Hall, Upper Saddle River (1985)
10. Liu, Y., Sun, J., Dong, J.S.: Developing model checkers using PAT. In: Bouajjani, A., Chin, W.-N. (eds.) ATVA 2010. LNCS, vol. 6252, pp. 371–377. Springer, Heidelberg (2010). https://doi.org/10.1007/978-3-642-15643-4_30
11. Lowe, G., Roscoe, A.W.: Using CSP to detect errors in the TMN protocol. IEEE Trans. Softw. Eng. **23**(10), 659–669 (1997)
12. Misra, S., Tourani, R., Majd, N.E.: Secure content delivery in information-centric networks: design, implementation, and analyses. In: ICN 2013, Proceedings of the 3rd, 2013 ACM SIGCOMM Workshop on Information-Centric Networking, August 12, 2013, Hong Kong, China, pp. 73–78 (2013)
13. PAT: Process Analysis Toolkit. http://pat.comp.nus.edu.sg/
14. Roscoe, A.W.: The Theory and Practice of Concurrency. Prentice Hall, Upper Saddle River (1997)
15. Roscoe, A.W.: Understanding Concurrent Systems. Texts in Computer Science. Springer, London (2010). https://doi.org/10.1007/978-1-84882-258-0
16. Samarati, P., de Vimercati, S.C.: Access control: policies, models, and mechanisms. In: Focardi, R., Gorrieri, R. (eds.) FOSAD 2000. LNCS, vol. 2171, pp. 137–196. Springer, Heidelberg (2001). https://doi.org/10.1007/3-540-45608-2_3
17. Si, Y., et al.: Model checking with fairness assumptions using PAT. Front. Comput. Sci. **8**(1), 1–16 (2014)
18. Sun, J., Liu, Y., Dong, J.S.: Model checking CSP revisited: introducing a process analysis toolkit. In: Margaria, T., Steffen, B. (eds.) ISoLA 2008. CCIS, vol. 17, pp. 307–322. Springer, Heidelberg (2008). https://doi.org/10.1007/978-3-540-88479-8_22
19. Sun, J., Liu, Y., Dong, J.S., Liu, Y., Shi, L., André, É.: Modeling and verifying hierarchical real-time systems using stateful timed CSP. ACM Trans. Softw. Eng. Methodol. **22**(1), 3 (2013)
20. Zhang, L., et al.: Named data networking (NDN) project. Technical report, NDN-0001, PARC (2010)

The Power of Synchronisation: Formal Analysis of Power Consumption in Networks of Pulse-Coupled Oscillators

Paul Gainer, Sven Linker(✉), Clare Dixon, Ullrich Hustadt, and Michael Fisher

University of Liverpool, Liverpool, UK
{p.gainer,s.linker,cldixon,u.hustadt,mfisher}@liverpool.ac.uk

Abstract. Nature-inspired synchronisation protocols have been widely adopted to achieve consensus within wireless sensor networks. We analyse the power consumption of such protocols, particularly the energy required to synchronise all nodes across a network. We use the model of bio-inspired, pulse-coupled oscillators to achieve network-wide synchronisation and provide an extended formal model of just such a protocol, enhanced with structures for recording energy usage. Exhaustive analysis is then carried out through formal verification, utilising the PRISM model-checker to calculate the resources consumed on each possible system execution. This allows us to investigate a range of parameter instantiations and the trade-offs between power consumption and time to synchronise. This provides a principled basis for the formal analysis of a broader range of large-scale network protocols.

Keywords: Probabilistic verification · Synchronisation
Wireless sensor nets

1 Introduction

Minimising power consumption is a critical design consideration for wireless sensor networks (WSNs) [1,20]. Once deployed a WSN is generally expected to function independently for long periods of time. In particular, regular battery replacement can be costly and impractical for remote sensing applications. Hence, it is important to reduce the power consumption of the individual nodes by choosing low-power hardware and/or energy efficient protocols. However, to make informed choices, it is also necessary to have good estimations of the power

This work was supported by the Sir Joseph Rotblat Alumni Scholarship at Liverpool, the EPSRC Research Programme EP/N007565/1 *Science of Sensor Systems Software* and the EPSRC Research Grant EP/L024845/1 *Verifiable Autonomy*. The authors would like to thank the Networks Sciences and Technology Initiative (NeST) of the University of Liverpool for the use of their computing facilities and David Shield for the corresponding technical support.

J. Sun and M. Sun (Eds.): ICFEM 2018, LNCS 11232, pp. 160–176, 2018.
https://doi.org/10.1007/978-3-030-02450-5_10

consumption for individual nodes. While the general power consumption of the hardware can be extracted from data sheets, estimating the overall power consumption of different protocols is more demanding.

Soua and Minet provided a general taxonomy for the analysis of wireless network protocols with respect to energy efficiency [21] by identifying the contributing factors of energy wastage, for instance packet collisions and unnecessary idling. These detrimental effects can be overcome by allocating time slots for node communication. That is, nodes in a network need to synchronise their clocks and use time slots for communication to avoid packet collisions [19,23].

Biologically inspired synchronisation protocols are well-suited for WSNs since centralised control is not required to achieve synchrony. The protocols build on the underlying mathematical model of pulse-coupled oscillators (PCOs) [15,17,18]; integrate-and-fire oscillators with pulsatile coupling, such that when an oscillator fires it induces some phase-shift response determined by a *phase response function*. Mutual interactions can lead to all oscillators firing synchronously.

In previous work [9] we used a *population model* [5,6,8] to encode information about groups of oscillators sharing the same configuration. Furthermore, we introduced *broadcast failures* where an oscillator may fail to broadcast its message. Since WSNs operate in stochastic environments under uncertainty we encoded these failures within a *probabilistic* model. Here, we extend our model with reward structures to associate different current draws with its states, thus enabling us to measure the energy consumption of the overall network. We employ the probabilistic model checker PRISM [14] to analyse the average and worst-case energy consumption for both the synchronisation of arbitrarily configured networks, and restabilisation of a network, where a subset of oscillators desynchronised. We derive a metric from the complex order parameter of Kuramoto [13]. Since exact time synchronisation in real-world scenarios is not possible, it is sufficient for all oscillators to fire within some defined time window [3].

The structure of the paper is as follows. In Sect. 2 we discuss related work, and in Sect. 3 we introduce the general PCO model, from which we derive population models. Section 4 introduces the derived synchronisation metric. The construction of the formal model used for the analysis is presented in Sect. 5. Subsequently, in Sect. 6 we evaluate the results for certain parameter instantiations and discuss their trade-offs with respect to power consumption and time to synchronise. Section 7 concludes the paper.

2 Related Work

Formal methods, in particular model checking, have been successfully used to model and analyse protocols for wireless sensor systems. Heidarian et al. used model checking to analyse clock synchronisation for medium access protocols [11]. They considered both fully-connected networks and line topologies with up to four nodes. Model checking of biologically inspired coupled oscillators has also been investigated by Bartocci et al. [2]. They present a subclass of timed automata suitable to model biological oscillators, and a model checking algorithm. However, their analysis was restricted to a network of three oscillators.

We introduced a formal population model for a network of PCOs [9], and investigated both the probability and expected time for an arbitrarily configured population of oscillators to synchronise. For very small devices with limited resources, it is important to minimise the cost of low-level functionalities, such as synchronisation. Even a floating point number may need too much memory, compared to an implementation with, for example, a four-bit vector. Hence, in our model the oscillators synchronise over a finite set of *discrete* clock values.

The oscillation cycle includes a *refractory period* at the start of the oscillation cycle where an oscillator cannot be perturbed by other firing oscillators. This corresponds to a period of time where a WSN node enters a low-power idling mode. In this work we extend this approach by introducing a metric for global power consumption and discuss refinements of the model that allows us to formally reason about much larger populations of oscillators.

Wang et al. proposed an energy-efficient strategy for the synchronisation of PCOs [22]. In contrast to our work, they consider real-valued clocks and *delay-advance phase response* functions, where both positive and negative phase shifts can occur. A result of their choice of phase response function is that synchronisation time is independent of the length of the refractory period, in contrast to our model. Furthermore, they assume that the initial phase difference between oscillators has an upper bound. They achieve synchrony for refractory periods larger than half the cycle, while our models do not always synchronise in these cases, as we do not impose a bound on the phase difference of the oscillators. We consider all possible differences in phase since we examine the energy consumption for the resynchronisation of a subset of oscillators.

Konishi and Kokame conducted an analysis of PCOs where a perceived pulse immediately resets oscillators to the start of their cycle [12]. Their goal was to maximise refractory period length, while still achieving synchronisation within some number of clock cycles. Similarly to our work, they restricted their analysis to a fully coupled network. They assumed that the protocol was implemented as part of the physical layer of the network stack by using capacitors to generate pulses, therefore their clocks were continuous and had different frequencies. We assume that the synchronisation protocol resides on a higher layer, where the clock values are discretised and oscillate with the same frequency.

3 Oscillator Model

We consider a fully-coupled network of PCOs with identical dynamics over discrete time, since homogeneous wireless sensor networks are prevalent. The *phase* of an oscillator i at time t is denoted by $\phi_i(t)$. The phase of an oscillator progresses through a sequence of discrete integer values bounded by some $T \geq 1$. The phase progression over time of a single uncoupled oscillator is determined by the successor function, where the phase increases over time until it equals T, at which point the oscillator will fire in the next moment in time and the phase will reset to one. The phase progression of an uncoupled oscillator is therefore cyclic with period T, and we refer to one cycle as an *oscillation cycle*.

When an oscillator fires, it may happen that its firing is not perceived by any of the other oscillators coupled to it. We call this a *broadcast failure* and denote its probability by $\mu \in [0,1]$. Note that μ is a global parameter, hence the chance of broadcast failure is identical for all oscillators. The occurrences of broadcast failures are statistically independent, since, the parameter μ represents detrimental effects on the communication medium itself, for example fog impairing vision, or static electricity interfering with radio messages.

When an oscillator fires, and a broadcast failure does not occur, it perturbs the phase of all oscillators to which it is coupled; we use $\alpha_i(t)$ to denote the number of all other oscillators that are coupled to i and will fire at time t. The *phase response function* is a positive increasing function $\Delta : \{1,\dots,T\} \times \mathbb{N} \times \mathbb{R}^+ \to \mathbb{N}$ that maps the phase of an oscillator i, the number of other oscillators perceived to be firing by i, and a real value defining the strength of the coupling between oscillators, to an integer value corresponding to the perturbation to phase induced by the firing of oscillators where broadcast failures did not occur.

We can introduce a refractory period into the oscillation cycle of each oscillator. A refractory period is an interval of discrete values $[1,R] \subseteq [1,T]$ where $1 \leq R \leq T$ is the size of the refractory period, such that if $\phi_i(t)$ is inside the interval, for some oscillator i at time t, then i cannot be perturbed by other oscillators to which it is coupled. If $R = 0$ then we set $[1,R] = \emptyset$, and there is no refractory period at all. The *refractory function* $\mathrm{ref} : \{1,\dots,T\} \times \mathbb{N} \to \mathbb{N}$ is defined as $\mathrm{ref}(\Phi,\delta) = \Phi$ if $\Phi \in [1,R]$, or $\mathrm{ref}(\Phi,\delta) = \Phi + \delta$ otherwise, and takes as parameters δ, the degree of perturbance to the phase of an oscillator, and Φ, the phase, and increases the phase by δ if Φ is outside of the refractory period.

The phase evolution of an oscillator i over time is then defined as follows, where the *update function* and *firing predicate*, respectively denote the updated phase of oscillator i at time t in the next moment in time, and the firing of oscillator i at time t,

$$update_i(t) = 1 + \mathrm{ref}(\phi_i(t), \Delta(\phi_i(t), \alpha_i(t), \epsilon)), \qquad fire_i(t) = update_i(t) > T,$$

$$\phi_i(t+1) = \begin{cases} 1 & \text{if } fire_i(t) \\ update_i(t) & \text{otherwise.} \end{cases}$$

3.1 Population Model

Let Δ be a phase response function for a network of N identical oscillators, where each oscillator is coupled to all other oscillators, and where the coupling strength is given by ϵ. Each oscillator has a phase in $1,\dots,T$, and a refractory period defined by R. The probability of broadcast failure in the network is $\mu \in [0,1]$. We define a *population model* of the network as $\mathcal{S} = (\Delta, N, T, R, \epsilon, \mu)$. Oscillators in our model have identical dynamics, and two oscillators are indistinguishable if they share the same phase. We therefore encode the global state of the model as a tuple $\langle k_1,\dots,k_T \rangle$ where each k_Φ is the number of oscillators with phase Φ.

A *global state* of $\mathcal{S}$ is a T-tuple $\sigma \in \{0, \ldots, N\}^T$, where $\sigma = \langle k_1, \ldots, k_T \rangle$ and $\sum_{\Phi=1}^{T} k_\Phi = N$. We denote by $\Gamma(\mathcal{S})$ the set of all global states of $\mathcal{S}$, and will simply use Γ when $\mathcal{S}$ is clear from the context. Figure 1 shows four global states of a population model of $N = 8$ oscillators with $T = 10$ discrete values for their phase and a refractory period of length $R = 2$. For example $\sigma_0 = \langle 2, 1, 0, 0, 5, 0, 0, 0, 0, 0 \rangle$ is the global state where two oscillators have a phase of one, one oscillator has a phase of two, and five oscillators have a phase of five. The starred node indicates the number of oscillators with phase ten that will fire in the next moment in time, while the shaded nodes indicate oscillators with phases that lie within the refractory period (one and two). If no oscillators have some phase Φ then we omit the 0 in the corresponding node.

We distinguish between states where one or more oscillators are about to fire, and states where no oscillators will fire at all. We refer to these states as *firing states* and *non-firing* states respectively. Given a population model $\mathcal{S}$, a global state $\langle k_1, \ldots, k_T \rangle \in \Gamma$ is a *firing state* if, and only if, $k_T > 0$. We respectively denote the sets of firing and non-firing states of $\mathcal{S}$ by $\Gamma^{\mathsf{F}}(\mathcal{S})$ and $\Gamma^{\mathsf{NF}}(\mathcal{S})$.

3.2 Successor States

We now define how the global state of a population model evolves over time. Since our population model encodes uncertainty in the form of broadcast failures, firing states may have more than one possible successor state. We denote the transition from a firing state σ to a possible successor state σ' by $\sigma \to \sigma'$. With every firing state $\sigma \in \Gamma^{\mathsf{F}}$ we associate a non-empty set of *failure vectors*, where each failure vector is a tuple of broadcast failures that could occur in σ. A *failure vector* is a T-tuple where the Φth element denotes the number of broadcast failures that occur for all oscillators with phase Φ. If the Φth element is $\star$ then no oscillators with a phase of Φ fired. We denote the set of all possible failure vectors by $\mathcal{F}$. Oscillators with phase less than T may fire due to being perturbed by the firing of oscillators with a phase of T. This is discussed in detail later in this section. We refer the reader to [9] for a detailed description of failure vector calculations.

A non-firing state will always have exactly one successor state, as there is no oscillator that is about to fire. Therefore, the phase of every oscillator is simply updated by one in the next time step, until one or more oscillators fire and perturb the phase of other oscillators. Given a sequence of global states $\sigma_0, \sigma_1, \ldots, \sigma_{n-1}, \sigma_n$ where $\sigma_0, \ldots \sigma_{n-1} \in \Gamma^{\mathsf{NF}}$ and $\sigma_n \in \Gamma^{\mathsf{F}}$, we omit transitions between σ_i and σ_{i+1} for $0 \leq i < n$, and instead introduce a direct transition from the first non-firing state σ_0 to the next firing state σ_n in the sequence. This is a refinement of the model presented in [9]. While the state space remains the same the number of transitions in the model is substantially decreased. Hence the time and resources required to check desirable properties are reduced. We denote the single successor σ' of a non-firing state σ by $\overrightarrow{\text{succ}}(\sigma)$. For example, in Fig. 1 we have $\overrightarrow{\text{succ}}(\sigma_0) = \sigma_1$.

For real deployments of protocols for synchronisation the effect of one or more oscillators firing may cause other oscillators to which they are coupled to fire in

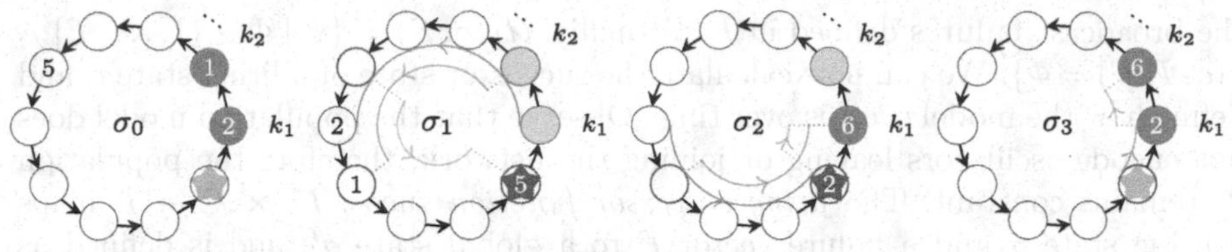

Fig. 1. Evolution of the global state over four discrete time steps.

turn. This may then cause further oscillators to fire, and so forth, and we refer to this event as a *chain reaction*. When a chain reaction occurs it can lead to multiple groups of oscillators being triggered to fire and being *absorbed* by the initial group of firing oscillators. These chain reactions are usually near-instantaneous events. Since we model the oscillation cycle as a progression through a number of discrete states, we choose to encode chain reactions by updating the phases of all perturbed oscillators in a single time step. Since we only consider fully-connected topologies, any oscillators sharing the same phase will always perceive the same number of other oscillators firing.

For the global state σ_1 of Fig. 1 we can see that five oscillators will fire in the next moment in time. In the successor state σ_2, the single oscillator with a phase of seven in σ_1 perceives the firing of the five oscillators. The induced perturbation causes the single oscillator to also fire and therefore be absorbed by the group of five. The remaining two oscillators with a phase of six in σ_1 perceive six oscillators to be firing, but the induced perturbation is insufficient to cause them to also fire, and they instead update their phases to ten.

With every firing state we have by definition that at least one oscillator is about to fire in the next time step. Since the firing of this oscillator may, or may not, result in a broadcast failure we can see that at least two failure vectors will be associated with any firing state, and that additional failure vectors will be associated with firing states where more than one oscillator is about to fire. Given a firing state σ and a failure vector F associated with that state, we can compute the successor of σ. For each phase $\Phi \in \{1, \ldots, T\}$ we calculate the number of oscillators with a phase greater than Φ perceived to be firing by oscillators with phase Φ. We simultaneously calculate $\mathit{update}^{\Phi}(\sigma, F)$, the updated phase of oscillators with phase Φ, and $\mathit{fire}^{\Phi}(\sigma, F)$, the predicate indicating whether or not oscillators with phase Φ fired. Details of these constructions are given in [9].

We can then define the function that maps phase values to their updated values in the next moment in time. Since we do not distinguish between oscillators with the same phase we only calculate a single updated value for their phase. The *phase transition function* $\tau : \Gamma^{\mathsf{F}} \times \{1, \ldots, T\} \times \mathcal{F} \to \mathbb{N}$ maps a firing state σ, a phase Φ, and a failure vector F for σ, to the updated phase in the next moment in time, with respect to the broadcast failures defined in F, and is defined as $\tau(\sigma, \Phi, F) = 1$ if $\mathit{fire}^{\Phi}(\sigma, F)$, and $\tau(\sigma, \Phi, F) = \mathit{update}^{\Phi}(\sigma, F)$ otherwise.

Let $\mathcal{U}_{\Phi}(\sigma, F)$ be the set of phase values Ψ where all oscillators with phase Ψ in σ will have the updated phase Φ in the next time step, with respect to the broadcast failures defined in F. Formally, $\mathcal{U}_\Phi(\sigma, F) = \{\Psi \mid \Phi \in \{1, \dots, T\} \wedge \tau(\sigma, \Psi, F) = \Phi\}$. We can now calculate the successor state of a firing state σ and define how the model evolves over time. Observe that the population model does not encode oscillators leaving or joining the network, therefore the population N remains constant. The *firing successor function* $\overrightarrow{\text{succ}} : \Gamma^{\mathsf{F}} \times \mathcal{F} \to \Gamma$ maps a firing state σ and a failure vector F to a global state σ', and is defined as $\overrightarrow{\text{succ}}(\langle k_1, \dots, k_T \rangle, F) = \langle k'_1, \dots, k'_T \rangle$, where $k'_\Phi = \sum_{\Psi \in \mathcal{U}_\Phi(\sigma, F)} k_\Psi$ for $1 \leq \Phi \leq T$.

3.3 Transition Probabilities

We now define the probabilities that will label the transitions in our model. Given a global state $\sigma \in \Gamma$, if σ is a non-firing state then it has exactly one successor state. If σ is a firing state then to construct the set of possible successor states we must first construct $\mathcal{F}_\sigma$, the set of all possible failure vectors for σ. Given a global state $\sigma \in \Gamma$ we define $next(\sigma)$, the set of all successor states of σ, as

$$next(\sigma) = \begin{cases} \{\overrightarrow{\text{succ}}(\sigma, F) \mid F \in \mathcal{F}_\sigma\} & \text{if } \sigma \in \Gamma^{\mathsf{F}} \\ \{\overrightarrow{\twoheadrightarrow}\!\!\!\!\text{succ}(\sigma)\} & \text{if } \sigma \in \Gamma^{\mathsf{NF}}. \end{cases}$$

For every non-firing state $\sigma \in \Gamma^{\mathsf{NF}}$ we have $|next(\sigma)| = 1$, since there is always exactly one successor state $\overset{\twoheadrightarrow}{\text{succ}}(\sigma)$, and we label the transition from σ to $\overset{\twoheadrightarrow}{\text{succ}}(\sigma)$ with probability one. We now consider each firing state $\sigma = \langle k_1, \dots, k_n \rangle \in \Gamma^{\mathsf{F}}$, and for every successor $\overrightarrow{\text{succ}}(\sigma, F) \in next(\sigma)$, we calculate the probability that will label $\sigma \to \overrightarrow{\text{succ}}(\sigma, F)$. Recalling that μ is the probability of a broadcast failure occurring, let $\mathsf{PMF} : \{1, \dots, N\}^2 \to [0, 1]$ be a probability mass function where $\mathsf{PMF}(k, f) = \mu^f (1-\mu)^{k-f} \binom{k}{f}$ is the probability that f broadcast failures occur given that k oscillators fire. Then let $\mathsf{PFV} : \Gamma^{\mathsf{F}} \times \mathcal{F} \to [0, 1]$ be the function mapping a firing state $\sigma = \langle k_1, \dots, k_T \rangle$ and a failure vector $F = \langle f_1, \dots, f_T \rangle \in \mathcal{F}$ to the probability of the failures in F occurring in σ, given by

$$\mathsf{PFV}(\sigma, F) = \prod_{\Phi=1}^{T} \begin{cases} \mathsf{PMF}(k_\Phi, f_\Phi) & \text{if } f_\Phi \neq \star \\ 1 & \text{otherwise.} \end{cases}$$

We can now describe the evolution of the global state over time. A *run* of a population model $\mathcal{S}$ is an infinite sequence $\sigma_0, \sigma_1, \sigma_2, \cdots$, where σ_0 is called the *initial state*, and $\sigma_{i+1} \in next(\sigma_i)$ for all $i \geq 0$.

4 Synchronisation and Metrics

Given a population model $\mathcal{S} = (\Delta, N, T, R, \epsilon, \mu)$, and a global state $\sigma \in \Gamma$, we say that σ is *synchronised* if all oscillators in σ share the same phase. We say that a run of the model $\sigma_0, \sigma_1, \sigma_2, \cdots$ *synchronises* if there exists an $i > 0$ such that σ_i is synchronised. Note that if a state σ_i is synchronised then any successor state σ_{i+1} of σ_i will also be synchronised.

We can extend this binary notion of synchrony by introducing a *phase coherence* metric for the level of synchrony of a global state. Our metric is derived from the *order parameter* introduced by Kuramoto [13] as a measure of synchrony for a population of coupled oscillators. If we consider the phases of the oscillators as positions on the unit circle in the complex plane we can represent the positions as complex numbers with magnitude 1. The function $p^{\mathbb{C}} : \{1, \ldots, T\} \rightarrow \mathbb{C}$ maps a phase value to its corresponding position on the unit circle in the complex plane, and is defined as $p^{\mathbb{C}}(\Phi) = e^{i\theta_\Phi}$, where $\theta_\Phi = \frac{2\pi}{T}(\Phi - 1)$.

A measure of synchrony r can then be obtained by calculating the magnitude of the complex number corresponding to the mean of the phase positions. A global state has a maximal value of $r = 1$ when all oscillators are synchronised and share the same phase Φ, mapped to the position defined by $p^{\mathbb{C}}(\Phi)$. It then follows that the mean position is also $p^{\mathbb{C}}(\Phi)$ and $|p^{\mathbb{C}}(\Phi)| = 1$. A global state has a minimal value of $r = 0$ when all of the positions mapped to the phases of the oscillators are uniformly distributed around the unit circle, or arranged such that their positions achieve mutual counterpoise. The *phase coherence function* $\mathsf{PCF} : \Gamma \rightarrow [0, 1]$ maps a global state to a real value in the interval $[0, 1]$, and is given by

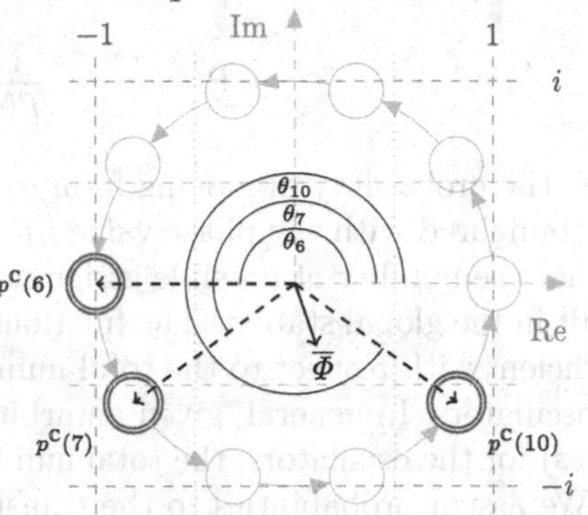

Fig. 2. Argand diagram of the phase positions for global state $\sigma_1 = \langle 0, 0, 0, 0, 0, 2, 1, 0, 0, 5 \rangle$.

$$\mathsf{PCF}(\langle k_1, \ldots, k_T \rangle) = \left| \frac{1}{N} \sum_{\Phi=1}^{T} k_\Phi p^{\mathbb{C}}(\Phi) \right|.$$

Note that for any synchronised global state σ we have that $\mathsf{PCF}(\sigma) = 1$, since all oscillators in σ share the same phase.

Figure 2 shows a plot on the complex plane of the positions of the phases for $N = 8$, $T = 10$, and the global state $\sigma_1 = \langle 0, 0, 0, 0, 0, 2, 1, 0, 0, 5 \rangle$. The phase positions are given by $p^{\mathbb{C}}(6) = e^{i\pi}$ for 2 oscillators with phase 6, $p^{\mathbb{C}}(7) = e^{\frac{6i\pi}{5}}$ for 1 oscillator with phase 7, and $p^{\mathbb{C}}(10) = e^{\frac{9i\pi}{5}}$ for 5 oscillators with phase 10. We can then determine the phase coherence as $\mathsf{PCF}(\sigma) = |\frac{1}{8}(2e^{i\pi} + e^{\frac{6i\pi}{5}} + 5e^{\frac{9i\pi}{5}})| = 0.4671$. The mean phase position is indicated on the diagram by $\overline{\Phi}$.

5 Model Construction

We use Prism [14] to formally verify properties of our model. Given a probabilistic model of a system, Prism can be used to reason about temporal and probabilistic properties of the input model, by checking requirements expressed in a suitable formalism against all possible runs of the model. We define our input models as *discrete time Markov chains* (DTMCs). A DTMC is a tuple $(Q, \sigma_I, \mathsf{P})$

where Q is a set of states, $\sigma_I \in Q$ is the initial state, and $\mathsf{P} : Q \times Q \to [0,1]$ is the function mapping pairs of states (q, q') to the probability with which a transition from q to q' occurs, where $\sum_{q' \in Q} \mathsf{P}(q, q') = 1$ for all $q \in Q$.

Given a population model $\mathcal{S} = (\Delta, N, T, R, \epsilon, \mu)$ we construct a DTMC $D(\mathcal{S}) = (Q, \sigma_I, \mathsf{P})$. We define the set of states Q to be $\Gamma(\mathcal{S}) \cup \{\sigma_I\}$, where σ_I is the initial state of the DTMC. In the initial state all oscillators are *unconfigured*. That is, oscillators have not yet been assigned a value for their phase. For each $\sigma = \langle k_1, \ldots, k_T \rangle \in Q \setminus \{\sigma_I\}$ we define

$$\mathsf{P}(\sigma_I, \sigma) = \frac{1}{T^N} \binom{N}{k_1, \ldots, k_T}$$

to be the probability of moving from σ_I to a state where k_i arbitrary oscillators are configured with the phase value i for $1 \leq i \leq T$. The multinomial coefficient defines the number of possible assignments of phases to distinct oscillators that result in the global state σ. The fractional coefficient normalises the multinomial coefficient with respect to the total number of possible assignments of phases to all oscillators. In general, given an arbitrary set of initial configurations (global states) for the oscillators, the total number of possible phase assignments is T^N.

We assign probabilities to the transitions as follows: for every $\sigma \in Q \setminus \{\sigma_I\}$ we consider each $\sigma' \in Q \setminus \{\sigma_I\}$ where $\sigma' = \overrightarrow{\mathrm{succ}}(\sigma, F)$ for some $F \in \mathcal{F}_\sigma$, and set $\mathsf{P}(\sigma, \sigma') = \mathsf{PFV}(\sigma, F)$. For all other $\sigma \in Q \setminus \{\sigma_I\}$ and $\sigma' \in Q$, where $\sigma \neq \sigma'$ and $\sigma' \notin \mathit{next}(\sigma)$, we set $\mathsf{P}(\sigma, \sigma') = 0$.

To facilitate the analysis of parameterwise-different population models we provide a Python script that allows the user to define ranges for N, T, R, ϵ, and μ. The script then automatically generates a model for each set of parameter values, checks given properties in the model using PRISM, and writes user specified output to a file which can be used by statistical analysis tools.[1]

5.1 Reward Structures

We can annotate DTMCs with information about rewards (or costs) by using a *reward structure*. A reward structure is a pair of functions, $\rho_Q : Q \to \mathbb{R}$ and $\rho_{\mathsf{P}} : Q \times Q \to \mathbb{R}$, that respectively map states and transitions to real values. By calculating the expected value of these rewards we can reason about quantitative properties of the models. For a network of WSN nodes we are interested in the time taken to achieve a synchronised state and the power consumption of the network. Given a population model $\mathcal{S} = (\Delta, N, T, R, \epsilon, \mu)$, and its corresponding DTMC $D(\mathcal{S}) = (Q, \sigma_I, \mathsf{P})$, we define the following reward structures:

Synchronisation Time. We are interested in the average and maximum time taken for a population model to synchronise. By accumulating the reward along a path until some synchronised global state is reached we obtain a measure of

[1] The scripts, along with the verification results, can be found at https://github.com/PaulGainer/mc-bio-synch/tree/master/energy-analysis.

the time taken to synchronise. Recall that we omit transitions between non-firing states; instead a transition is taken to the next global state where one or more oscillators do fire. For each transition from a firing state σ to some successor state σ', we define $\rho_{\mathsf{P}}(\sigma, \sigma') = \frac{1}{T}$. Given a non-firing state σ, let δ be the highest phase of any oscillator in that state. Hence, $T - \delta$ is the number of omitted transitions where no oscillators fire. Then, for each transition from σ to some successor state σ', we define $\rho_{\mathsf{P}}(\sigma, \sigma') = \frac{T-\delta}{T}$. In this way we obtain a measure of synchronisation time in cycles for a population model.

Power Consumption. Let I_{id}, I_{rx}, and I_{tx} be the current draw in amperes for the idle, receive, and transmit modes, V be the voltage, C be the length of the oscillation cycle in seconds, and M_t be the time taken to transmit a synchronisation message in seconds. The power consumption in Watt-hours of one node for one discrete step within its refractory period, that is, the oscillator is in the idle mode, is $W_{id} = \frac{I_{id} V C}{3600 T}$. Similarly, if the oscillator is outside of the refractory period, that is, it is in the receive mode, the corresponding power consumption is defined by $W_{rx} = \frac{I_{rx} V C}{3600 T}$. Finally, let $W_{tx} = \frac{I_{tx} V M_t}{3600}$ be the power consumption in Watt-hours to transmit one synchronisation message. The power consumption of the network consists of the power necessary to transmit the synchronisation messages, and that of the oscillators in the idle and receive modes.

For synchronisation messages, we consider each firing state σ, and assign a reward of $\rho_{\mathsf{P}}(\sigma, \sigma') = k_1 W_{tx}$ to every transition from σ to a successor state $\sigma' = \langle k_1, \ldots, k_T \rangle$. This corresponds to the total power consumption for the transmission of k_1 synchronisation messages. For each firing state $\sigma = \langle k_1, \ldots, k_T \rangle$, the total power consumption for oscillators in the idle and receive modes is

$$\rho_Q(\sigma) = \sum_{\Phi=1}^{R} k_\Phi W_{id} + \sum_{\Phi=R+1}^{T} k_\Phi W_{rx} ,$$

where R denotes the length of the refractory period. From a non firing state σ the power consumed by the network to reach the next firing state is equivalent to the accumulation of the power consumption of the network in σ and any successive non-firing states that are omitted in the transition from σ to $\overrightarrow{\mathrm{succ}}(\sigma)$. For a non firing state $\sigma = \langle k_1, \ldots, k_T \rangle$ and maximal phase $\delta = \max\{\Phi \mid \Phi \in \{1, \ldots T\} \wedge k_\Phi > 0\}$ of any oscillator in that state, we define the reward as

$$\rho_Q(\sigma) = \sum_{j=0}^{(T-\delta)-1} \left(\sum_{\Phi=1}^{R-j} k_\Phi W_{id} + \sum_{\Phi=(R+1)-j}^{\delta} k_\Phi W_{rx} \right) .$$

The formula accumulates the power consumption over σ and subsequent $(T - \delta) - 1$ non-firing states, where the left and right summands accumulate the power consumption of nodes within, and outside of the refractory period, respectively.

5.2 Restabilisation

A network of oscillators is *restabilising* if it has reached a synchronised state, synchrony has been lost due to the occurrence of some external event, and

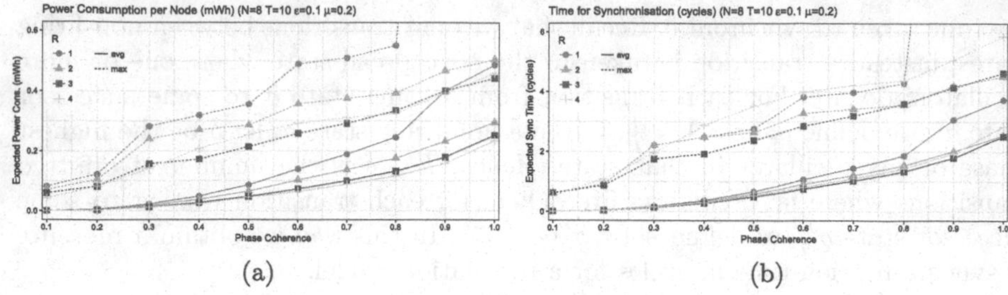

(a) (b)

Fig. 3. Power/time per node to achieve synchronisation

the network must then again achieve synchrony. We could, for instance, imagine the introduction of additional nodes with arbitrary phases to an established and synchronised network. While such a change is not explicitly encoded within our model, we can represent it by partitioning the set of oscillators into two subsets. We define the parameter U to be the number of oscillators with arbitrary phase values that have been introduced into a network of $N - U$ synchronised oscillators, or to be the number of oscillators in a network of N oscillators whose clocks have reset to an arbitrary value, where $U \in \mathbb{N}$ and $1 \leq U < N$. Destabilising U oscillators in this way results in configurations where *at least* $N - U$ oscillators are synchronised, since the destabilised oscillators may coincidentally be assigned the phase of the synchronised group. We can restrict the set of initial configurations by identifying the set $\Gamma_U = \{\langle k_1, \ldots, k_T \rangle \mid \langle k_1, \ldots, k_T \rangle \in \Gamma \text{ and } k_i \geq N - U \text{ for some } 1 \leq i \leq T\}$, where each $\sigma \in \Gamma_U$ is a configuration for the phases such that at least $N - U$ oscillators share some phase and the remaining oscillators have arbitrary phase values. As we decrease the value of U we also decrease the number of initial configurations for the phases of the oscillators. Since our model does not encode the loss or addition of oscillators we can observe that all global states where there are less than $N - U$ oscillators sharing the same phase are unreachable by any run of the system beginning in some state in Γ_U.

6 Evaluation

In this section, we present the model checking results for instantiations of the model given in the previous section. To that end, we instantiate the phase response function presented in Sect. 3 for a specific synchronisation model, and vary the length of the refractory period R, coupling constant ϵ, and the probability μ of broadcast failures. We use a synchronisation model where the perturbation induced by the firing of other oscillators is linear in the phase of the perturbed oscillator and the number of firing oscillators [15]. That is, $\Delta(\Phi, \alpha, \epsilon) = [\Phi \cdot \alpha \cdot \epsilon]$, where $[\_]$ denotes rounding of a value to the nearest integer. The coupling constant determines the slope of the linear dependency.

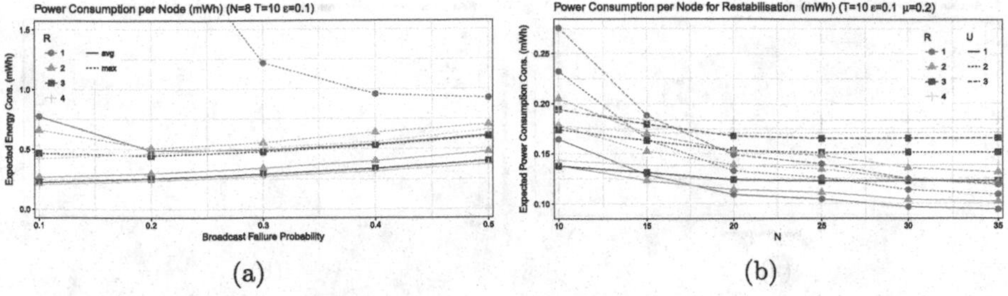

(a)

(b)

Fig. 4. Power consumption in relation to broadcast failure probability and average power consumption for resynchronisation to network size

For many experiments we set $\epsilon = 0.1$ and $\mu = 0.2$. We could have conducted analyses for different values for these parameters. For a real system, the probability μ of broadcast failure occurrence is highly dependent on the deployment environment. For deployments in benign environments we would expect a relatively low rate of failure, for instance a WSN within city limits under controlled conditions, whilst a comparably high rate of failure would be expected in harsh environments such as a network of off-shore sensors below sea level. The coupling constant ϵ is a parameter of the system itself. Our results suggest that higher values for ϵ are always beneficial, however this is because we restrict our analysis to fully connected networks. High values for ϵ may be detrimental when considering different topologies, since firing nodes may perturb synchronised subcomponents of a network. However we defer such an analysis to future work.

As an example we analyse the power consumption for values taken from the datasheet of the *MICAz* mote [16]. For the transmit, receive and idling mode, we assume $I_{tx} = 17.4$ mA, $I_{rx} = 19{,}7$ mA, and $I_{id} = 20\,\mu$A, respectively. Furthermore, we assume that the oscillators use a voltage of 3.0 V. To analyse our models, we use the model checker PRISM [14] and specify the properties of interest in PCTL [10] extended with reward operators, allowing us to compute expected rewards for the reward structures defined in Sect. 5.1. For simplicity, we will omit the name of the reward structures when expressing properties.

Synchronisation of a Whole Network. We analyse the power consumption and time for a fully connected network of eight oscillators with a cycle period of $T = 10$ to synchronise. Increasing the granularity of the cycle period, or the size of the network, beyond these values leads to models where it is infeasible to check properties due to time and memory constraints[2]. However, compared to our previous work [9], we were able to increase the network size.

Figures 3a and b show both the average and maximal power consumption per node (in mWh) and time (in cycles) needed to synchronise, in relation to the

[2] While most individual model checking runs finished within a minute, the cumulative model checking time over all analysed models was very large. The results shown in Fig. 3a already amount to 80 distinct runs.

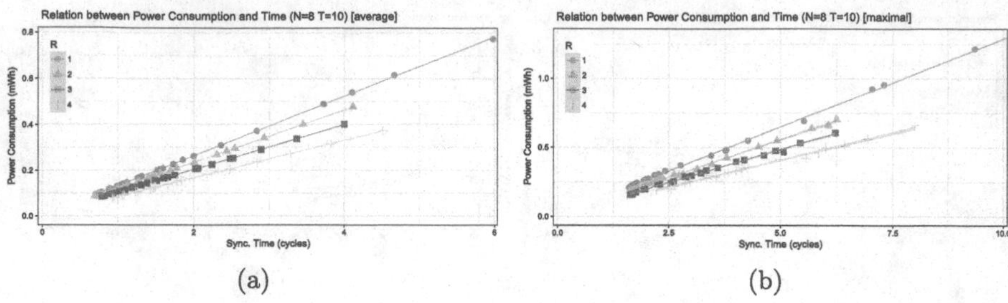

Fig. 5. Avg. (Max.) power consumption to Avg. (Max.) time for synchrony

phase coherence of the network with respect to different lengths of the refractory period, where $\epsilon = 0.1$ and $\mu = 0.2$. That is, they show how much power is consumed (time is needed, resp.) for a system in an arbitrary state to reach a state where some degree of phase coherence has been achieved. The corresponding PCTL properties are $\mathbf{R}^{\mathsf{avg}}_{=?}[\mathbf{F}\,\mathsf{coherent}_\lambda]$ and $\mathbf{R}^{\mathsf{max}}_{=?}[\mathbf{F}\,\mathsf{coherent}_\lambda]$, where $\mathsf{coherent}_\lambda$ is a predicate that holds for any state σ with $\mathsf{PCF}(\sigma) \geq \lambda$, and $\mathbf{R}^{\mathsf{avg}}$ and $\mathbf{R}^{\mathsf{max}}$ refer to the average and maximal reward accumulation respectively[3].

The much larger values obtained for $R = 1$ and phase coherence ≥ 0.9 are not shown here, to avoid distortion of the figures. The energy consumption for these values is roughly 2.4 mWh, while the time needed is around 19 cycles. Observe that we only show values for the refractory period R with $R < \frac{T}{2}$. For larger values of R not all runs synchronise [9], resulting in an infinitely large reward being accumulated for both the maximal and average cases. We do not provide results for the minimal power consumption (or time) as it is always zero, since we consider all initial configurations (global states) for oscillator phases. In particular, we consider the runs where the initial state is already synchronised.

As expected when starting from an arbitrary state, the time and power consumption increases monotonically with the order of synchrony to be achieved. On average, networks with longer refractory periods require less power for synchronisation, and take less time to achieve it. The only exception is that the average time to achieve synchrony with a refractory period of four is higher than for two and three. However, if lower phase coherence is sufficient then this trend is stable. In contrast, the maximal power consumption of networks with $R = 4$ is consistently higher than of networks with $R = 3$. In addition, the maximal time needed to achieve synchrony for networks with $R = 4$ is higher than for lower refractory periods, except when the phase coherence is greater than or equal to 0.9. We find that networks with a refractory period of three will need the smallest amount of time to synchronise, regardless of whether we consider the maximal or average values. Furthermore, the average power consumption for full synchronisation (phase coherence one) differs only slightly between $R = 3$ and $R = 4$ (less than 0.3 mWh). Hence, for the given example, $R = 3$ gives the best results. These relationships are stable even for different broadcast failure

[3] Within PRISM this can be achieved by using the *filter* construct.

probabilities μ, while the concrete values increase only slightly, as illustrated in Fig. 4a, which shows the power consumption for different μ when $\epsilon = 0.1$.

The general relationship between power consumption and time needed to synchronise is shown in Figs. 5a and b. Within these figures, we do not distinguish between different coupling constants and broadcast failure probabilities. We omit the two values for $R = 1$, $\epsilon = 0.1$ and $\mu \in \{0.1, 0.2\}$ in Fig. 5b to avoid distortion of the graph, since the low coupling strength and low probability of broadcast failure leads to longer synchronisation times and hence higher power consumption. While this might seem surprising it has been shown that uncertainty in discrete systems often aids convergence [7,9].

The relationship between power consumption and time to synchronise is linear, and the slope of the relation decreases for higher refractory periods. While the linearity is almost perfect for the average values, the maximal values have larger variation. The figures again suggest that $R = 3$ is a sensible and reliable choice, since it provides the best stability of power consumption and time to synchronise. In particular, if the broadcast failure probability changes, the variations are less severe for $R = 3$ than for other refractory periods.

Resynchronisation of a Small Number of Nodes. We now analyse the power consumption if the number of redeployed nodes is small compared to the size of the network. The approach presented in Sect. 5.2 allows us to significantly increase the network size. In particular, the smallest network we analyse is already larger than that in the analysis above, while the largest is almost five times as large. This is possible because the model has a much smaller number of initial states.

The average power consumption per node for networks of size $10, 15, \ldots, 35$, where the oscillators are coupled with strength $\epsilon = 0.1$, and broadcast failure probability $\mu = 0.2$, is shown in Fig. 4b. The corresponding PCTL property is $\mathbf{R}^{\mathsf{avg}}_{=?}[\mathbf{F}\ \mathsf{coherent}_1]$, that is, we are only interested in the power consumption until the system is fully synchronised. The solid lines denote the results for a single redeployed node, while the dashed lines represent the results for the redeployment of two and three nodes, respectively. As expected, the more nodes need to resynchronise, the more energy is consumed. However, we can also extract that for higher refractory periods, the amount of energy needed is more or less stable, in particular, in case $R = 4$, which is already invariant for more than ten nodes. For smaller refractory periods, increasing the network size, decreases the average energy consumption. This behaviour can be explained as follows. The linear synchronisation model implies that oscillators with a higher phase value will be activated more and thus are more likely to fire. Hence, in general a larger network will force the node to resynchronise faster. The refractory period determines how large the network has to be for this effect to stabilise.

7 Conclusion

We presented a formal model to analyse power consumption in fully connected networks of PCOs. To that end, we extended an existing model for synchrony convergence with a reward structure to reflect the energy consumption of wireless sensor nodes. Furthermore, we showed how to mitigate the state-space explosion typically encountered when model-checking. In particular, the model can be reduced by collapsing sequences of transitions where there are no interactions between oscillators. When investigating the restabilisation of a small number of oscillators in a network we can reduce the state space significantly, since only a small subset of the initial states needs to be considered. We used these techniques to analyse the power consumption for synchronisation and restabilisation of a network of MICAz motes, using the pulse-coupled oscillator model developed by Mirollo and Strogatz [17] with a linear phase response function. By using our model we were able to extend the size of the network compared with previous work [9] and discuss trade-offs between the time and power needed to synchronise for different lengths of the refractory period (or duty cycle).

Results obtained using these techniques can be used by designers of WSNs to estimate the overall energy efficiency of a network during its design phase. Unnecessary energy consumption can be identified and rectified before network deployment. Also, our results provide guidance for estimating the battery life of a network depending on the anticipated frequency of restabilisations. Of course, these considerations only hold for the maintenance task of synchronisation. The energy consumption of the functional behaviour has to be examined separately.

It is clear that our approach is inhibited by the usual limitation of exact probabilistic model checking for large-scale systems. We could overcome this by using approximated techniques, such as statistical model checking, or approaches based on fluid-flow approximation extended with rewards [4]. This would, of course, come at the expense of precision. An investigation of such a trade-off is deferred to future work. Our current approach is restricted to fully connected networks of oscillators. While this is sufficient to analyse the behaviour of strongly connected components within a network, further investigation is needed to assess different network topologies. To that end, we could use several interconnected population models thus modelling the interactions of the networks subcomponents. Furthermore, topologies that change over time are of particular interest. However, it is not obvious how we could extend our approach to consider such dynamic networks. The work of Lucarelli and Wang may serve as a starting point for further investigations [15]. Stochastic node failure, as well as more subtle models of energy consumption, present significant opportunities for future extensions. For example, in some cases, repeatedly powering nodes on and off over short periods of time might use considerably more power than leaving them on throughout.

References

1. Albers, S.: Energy-efficient algorithms. Commun. ACM **53**(5), 86–96 (2010)
2. Bartocci, E., Corradini, F., Merelli, E., Tesei, L.: Detecting synchronisation of biological oscillators by model checking. Theor. Comput. Sci. **411**(20), 1999–2018 (2010)
3. Bojic, I., Lipic, T., Kusek, M.: Scalability issues of firefly-based self-synchronization in collective adaptive systems. In: Proceedings of SASOW 2014, pp. 68–73. IEEE (2014)

4. Bortolussi, L., Hillston, J.: Efficient checking of individual rewards properties in Markov population models. In: QAPL 2015. EPTCS, vol. 194, pp. 32–47. Open Publishing Association (2015)
5. Donaldson, A.F., Miller, A.: Symmetry reduction for probabilistic model checking using generic representatives. In: Graf, S., Zhang, W. (eds.) ATVA 2006. LNCS, vol. 4218, pp. 9–23. Springer, Heidelberg (2006). https://doi.org/10.1007/11901914_4
6. Emerson, E.A., Trefler, R.J.: From asymmetry to full symmetry: new techniques for symmetry reduction in model checking. In: Pierre, L., Kropf, T. (eds.) CHARME 1999. LNCS, vol. 1703, pp. 142–157. Springer, Heidelberg (1999). https://doi.org/10.1007/3-540-48153-2_12
7. Fatès, N.: Remarks on the cellular automaton global synchronisation problem. In: Kari, J. (ed.) AUTOMATA 2015. LNCS, vol. 9099, pp. 113–126. Springer, Heidelberg (2015). https://doi.org/10.1007/978-3-662-47221-7_9
8. Gainer, P., Dixon, C., Hustadt, U.: Probabilistic model checking of ant-based positionless swarming. In: Alboul, L., Damian, D., Aitken, J.M.M. (eds.) TAROS 2016. LNCS (LNAI), vol. 9716, pp. 127–138. Springer, Cham (2016). https://doi.org/10.1007/978-3-319-40379-3_13
9. Gainer, P., Linker, S., Dixon, C., Hustadt, U., Fisher, M.: Investigating parametric influence on discrete synchronisation protocols using quantitative model checking. In: Bertrand, N., Bortolussi, L. (eds.) QEST 2017. LNCS, vol. 10503, pp. 224–239. Springer, Cham (2017). https://doi.org/10.1007/978-3-319-66335-7_14
10. Hansson, H., Jonsson, B.: A logic for reasoning about time and reliability. FAC **6**(5), 512–535 (1994)
11. Heidarian, F., Schmaltz, J., Vaandrager, F.: Analysis of a clock synchronization protocol for wireless sensor networks. Theor. Comput. Sci. **413**(1), 87–105 (2012)
12. Konishi, K., Kokame, H.: Synchronization of pulse-coupled oscillators with a refractory period and frequency distribution for a wireless sensor network. Chaos: Interdisciplinary J. Nonlinear Sci. **18**(3) (2008)
13. Kuramoto, Y.: Self-entrainment of a population of coupled non-linear oscillators. In: Araki, H. (ed.) International Symposium on Mathematical Problems in Theoretical Physics. LNP, vol. 39, pp. 420–422. Springer, Heidelberg (1975)
14. Kwiatkowska, M., Norman, G., Parker, D.: PRISM 4.0: verification of probabilistic real-time systems. In: Gopalakrishnan, G., Qadeer, S. (eds.) CAV 2011. LNCS, vol. 6806, pp. 585–591. Springer, Heidelberg (2011). https://doi.org/10.1007/978-3-642-22110-1_47
15. Lucarelli, D., Wang, I.J., et al.: Decentralized synchronization protocols with nearest neighbor communication. In: Proceedings of SenSys 2004, pp. 62–68. ACM (2004)
16. MEMSIC Inc.: MICAz datasheet. www.memsic.com/userfiles/files/Datasheets/WSN/micaz_datasheet-t.pdf. Accessed 15 Jan 2018
17. Mirollo, R.E., Strogatz, S.H.: Synchronization of pulse-coupled biological oscillators. SIAM J. Appl. Math. **50**(6), 1645–1662 (1990)
18. Peskin, C.: Mathematical aspects of heart physiology. Courant Lecture Notes , Courant Institute of Mathematical Sciences, New York University (1975)
19. Rhee, I.K., Lee, J., Kim, J., Serpedin, E., Wu, Y.C.: Clock synchronization in wireless sensor networks: an overview. Sensors **9**(1), 56–85 (2009)
20. Rhee, S., Seetharam, D., Liu, S.: Techniques for minimizing power consumption in low data-rate wireless sensor networks. In: Proceedings of WCNC 2004, pp. 1727–1731. IEEE (2004)
21. Soua, R., Minet, P.: A survey on energy efficient techniques in wireless sensor networks. In: Proceedings of WMNC 2011, pp. 1–9. IEEE (2011)

22. Wang, Y., Nuñez, F., Doyle, F.J.: Energy-efficient pulse-coupled synchronization strategy design for wireless sensor networks through reduced idle listening. IEEE Trans. Sig. Process. **60**(10), 5293–5306 (2012)
23. Yick, J., Mukherjee, B., Ghosal, D.: Wireless sensor network survey. Comput. Netw. **52**(12), 2292–2330 (2008)

CDGDroid: Android Malware Detection Based on Deep Learning Using CFG and DFG

Zhiwu Xu[1,2(✉)], Kerong Ren[1], Shengchao Qin[3,1], and Florin Craciun[4]

[1] College of Computer Science and Software Engineering, Shenzhen University, Shenzhen, China
xuzhiwu@szu.edu.cn, renkerong99@foxmail.com

[2] National Engineering Laboratory for Big Data System Computing Technology, Shenzhen University, Shenzhen, China

[3] School of Computing, Media and the Arts, Teesside University, Middlesbrough, UK
shengchao.qin@gmail.com

[4] Faculty of Mathematics and Computer Science, Babes-Bolyai University, Cluj-Napoca, Romania
craciunf@cs.ubbcluj.ro

Abstract. Android malware has become a serious threat in our daily digital life, and thus there is a pressing need to effectively detect or defend against them. Recent techniques have relied on the extraction of lightweight syntactic features that are suitable for machine learning classification, but despite of their promising results, the features they extract are often too simple to characterise Android applications, and thus may be insufficient when used to detect Android malware. In this paper, we propose CDGDroid, an effective approach for Android malware detection based on deep learning. We use the semantics graph representations, that is, control flow graph, data flow graph, and their possible combinations, as the features to characterise Android applications. We encode the graphs into matrices, and use them to train the classification model via Convolutional Neural Network (CNN). We have conducted some experiments on Marvin, Drebin, VirusShare and ContagioDump datasets to evaluate our approach and have identified that the classification model taking the horizontal combination of CFG and DFG as features offers the best performance in terms of accuracy among all combinations. We have also conducted experiments to compare our approach against Yeganeh Safaei et al.'s approach, Allix et al.'s approach, Drebin and many anti-virus tools gathered in VirusTotal, and the experimental results have confirmed that our classification model gives a better performance than the others.

1 Introduction

According to a report from IDC [1], Android is the most popular platform for mobile devices, with almost 85% of the market share in the first quarter of

J. Sun and M. Sun (Eds.): ICFEM 2018, LNCS 11232, pp. 177–193, 2018.
https://doi.org/10.1007/978-3-030-02450-5_11

2017. Unfortunately, the increasing adoption of Android comes with the growing prevalence of Android malware. A report from security firm G DATA [2] shows that a new instance of Android malware pops up nearly every 10 seconds. Consequently, Android malware has become a serious threat for our daily life, and thus there is a pressing need to effectively mitigate or defend against them.

To protect legitimate users from the threat, many approaches and tools to detect Android malware have been proposed over the past decade. These approaches can be summarised into two categories, namely, the approach based on program analysis techniques and the approach based on machine learning techniques. The first approach aims to identify the malicious code patterns in Android applications, through either static analysis [3–5] or dynamic analysis [6–8]. But the high overhead and the rapid evolution of Android malware make this approach no longer effective. Recently, various machine learning techniques like support vector machine, decision tree and deep learning have been proposed for detecting Android malware [9–14]. This approach constructs a learning-based classification model through a (big) dataset. The key of this approach is to seek out an appropriate feature set, such as permissions, APIs, and opcodes. However, despite of their promising results, the features that are considered by most existing work based on machine learning are often too simple to characterise Android applications (e.g., lack of either control flow information or data flow information) or non-robust (e.g., prone to suffering from the poisoning attack) [15], and thus may be insufficient to help detect Android malware.

In this paper, we propose CDGDroid, an effective approach to detecting Android malware based on deep learning. Different from most existing work based on machine learning, we use two classic semantic representations of programs in program analysis techniques, namely, control flow graphs and data flow graphs, as the features to characterise Android applications. Generally, graphs offer a natural way to model the sequence of activities that occur in a program. Hence they serve as amenable data-structures for detecting malware through identifying suspicious activity sequences. In particular, a control flow graph reflects what a program intends to behave (*e.g.*, opcodes) as well as how it behaves (*e.g.*, possible execution paths), such that malware behaviour patterns can be captured easily by this feature. For example, Geinimi samples share the similar control flow graphs. On the other hand, a data flow graph represents the data dependencies between a number of operations, and thus can help in detecting malware involving sensitive or network data, like HippoSMS and RogueSppush that send and block SMS message in the background.

Our approach consists of two phases: the first phase aims to learn a classification model from an existing dataset; and the second phase uses this model to detect new, unseen malicious and normal applications. In detail, we extract control flow graphs and data flow graphs in the instruction level from applications, which are collected through static analysis on the *smali* files (*i.e.*, Dalvik executions) in applications. Both intra-procedural analysis and inter-procedural analysis are considered for these two graphs. We then encode control flow graphs and data flow graphs into matrices, where only the opcodes are preserved. Meanwhile, their possible combination modes of control flow graph and data flow graph are considered as well: two graphs are combined either via the matrix addition (called the *vertical* mode) or via the matrix extension (called the *horizontal* mode). Finally, the encoded matrices are fed into the classification model for training or testing. We use a convolutional neural network (CNN for short), a new frontier in machine learning that has successfully been applied to analyse visual imagery (*i.e.*, matrix data), to build our model.

Several experiments have been conducted to evaluate our approach. We first conduct 10-fold cross validation experiments to see the effectiveness of CFG and DFG in malware detection. We have found that the classification model with the horizontal combination of CFG and DFG as features performs the best, with the *F1 score* (a measure of a test's accuracy, see Sect. 3.1) 98.722%. We also run our model on datasets consisting of new, unknown samples. The experimental results have shown that our classification model is capable of detecting some fresh malware. Finally, we also conduct some experiments to compare our approach with Yeganeh Safaei et al.'s approach [14], Allix et al.'s approach [12], Drebin [16] and most of anti-virus tools gathered in VirusTotal [17]. The results have confirmed that our classification model has a better performance in terms of accuracy than the others.

In summary, our contributions are as follows:

- We have proposed an approach to detecting Android malware based on deep learning, using two classic semantic representations in program analysis techniques, namely, control flow graph and data flow graph.
- We have conducted several experiments, which demonstrate that our approach is viable and effective to detect Android malware, and has a better performance than a number of existing anti-virus tools in terms of accuracy.

The remainder of this paper is organised as follows. Section 2 describes our approach, followed by the experimental results in Sect. 3. Section 4 presents the related work, followed by some concluding remarks in Sect. 5.

2 Approach

In this section, we present our approach CDGDroid, an effective approach to detecting Android malware based on deep learning, using control flow graph (CFG for short) and data flow graph (DFG for short). Figure 1 shows the framework of our approach, which consists of two phases: the *training* phase (marked by arrows with solid line) and the *testing* phase (marked by arrows with broken line). The training phase aims to train a classification model from an existing dataset containing normal applications and malware samples, and the testing phase uses the trained model to detect malware from new, unseen Android applications. In detail, we first use Apktool [18] to disassemble the applications in the given dataset and collect the *smali* files from each application. We then perform static analysis on these *smali* files to extract CFGs and DFGs, which are further encoded into matrices with known categories, yielding a training data set.

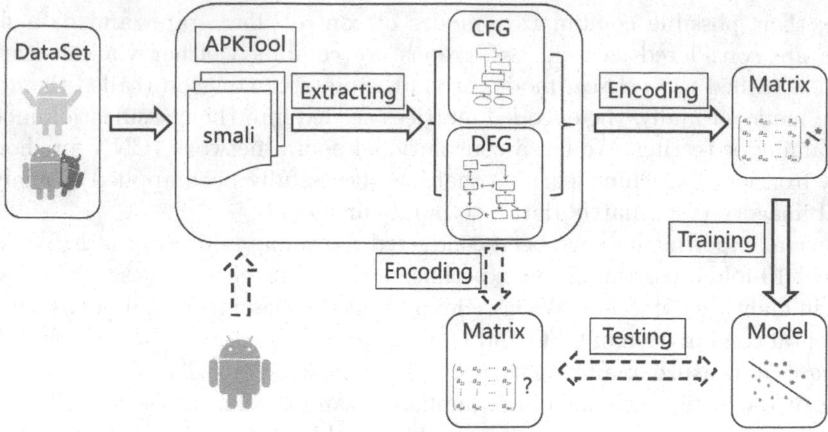

Fig. 1. Framework of our approach

Based on this training set, we train a classification model via CNN. Next, we perform the similar analysis on unseen Android applications to extract their feature matrices and then use the trained model to learn their categories. To conclude, our approach involves three tasks: (*i*) graph extracting; (*ii*) graph encoding; (*iii*) model training. In what follows, we depict each task of our approach in detail.

2.1 Graph Extracting

This section is devoted to CFG and DFG extraction from an application in the instruction level, which consists of three steps: pre-processing, CFG extraction, and DFG extraction.

Pre-processing. Android applications are distributed in markets in the form of APK. An APK is a compressed archive of Dalvik bytecode for execution, resources, assets, certificates, and an XML manifest file. Among them, the Dalvik bytecode for execution, namely, the file named *classes.dex*[1], will be extracted for further analysis.

For ease of extracting CFGs and DFGs, we leverage the disassembler Apktool [18] to disassemble the *dex* files. After disassembling, the *dex* files are converted to *smali* files, which give us the readable code in the *smali* language. We use *smali* code, instead of *Java* code, is because the disassembling is lossless in that the *smali* files support the full functionality of the original *dex* files.

CFG Extracting. There are several tools for generating CFGs for *smali* files, such as androguard and Smali-CFGs. Unfortunately, the CFGs generated by these existing tools are either lack of inter-procedural control flow, or not suitable for further analysis for us (*e.g.*, it is not easy to analyse CFG in the xgmml or

[1] There may be several additional *dex* files with the name "classes*i*.dex" in large APKs.

PNG format). Therefore we implement CDGDroid with the CFG extracting based on the *smali* files.

To begin with, we give a definition of *graph*, which is used to describe both CFG and DFG.

Definition 1. *A graph G is a quadruple* (N, E, S, F)*, where N is a finite set of nodes,* $E \subseteq N \times N$ *is a finite set of edges,* $S \subseteq N$ *is the set of starting nodes, and* $F \subseteq N$ *is the set of exiting nodes.*

Generally, a *smali* file contains the definition of a separate class, either a general class or an inner class, in the *Java* source code. So we construct the CFGs method by method for each *smali* file.

To do this, we first identify all the instructions in a method, yielding a graph *cfg* with the instructions as nodes and the first instruction as the starting node. This is different from existing tools, which take *block*s (*i.e.*, a straight-line piece of code without any jump instructions or jump targets) as basic nodes. Next, we complete this graph *cfg* by connecting the control flows (*e.g.*, a jump instruction and its targets) and identifying all the exiting nodes (*i.e.*, the reachable nodes without any out edges).

For inter-procedural analysis, we first construct a function call graph fcg by identifying the instructions starting with "invoke" or "execute"[2]. Based on this graph, we then connect the calling node with the start node of the callee method's CFG as well as the exiting nodes of the callee method's CFG with the successors of the calling node.

DFG Extracting. The DFG extracting is based on the CFG we extracted above. It is known that Dalvik is a register-based virtual machine, where most of the values are moved from memory into registers for access. So we will consider for DFG the data dependence relations between instructions via registers, including parameter registers.

Our construction of DFG is based on a variant of classic reaching definition analysis on *smali*, which is shown in Algorithm 1. This algorithm takes the CFG of a function f as input and then returns the reaching definition mapping D, which records the entry definitions (*i.e.*, *in*) and the exit definitions (*i.e.*, *out*) for each instruction. Note that, due to the inter-procedural analysis, we also take the initial definitions of parameters (*i.e.*, instructions starting with ".parameter") into account (Line 5).

Next, we extract the def-use relations as the edges of DFG, that is, if an instruction i uses a register r, whose value may come from the definition in the instruction j, then there is an edge from i to j. Algorithm 2 gives the detail of extracting. This algorithm takes the CFG of a function f as input and then returns the DFG for f, where Algorithm 1 is invoked to gather the def-use relations.

Similar to the CFG extracting, we also take the inter-procedural analysis into account via the function call graph *fcg*. In more detail, we connect the

[2] For simplicity, Java reflection, callbacks and multi-threading are not considered at present.

Algorithm 1. Reaching Definition Algorithm $RD(cfg)$

Input: CFG *cfg* of a target function f

Output: the reaching definition mapping D

```
for each node n ∈ cfg.N do
    D(n).in = ∅ and D(n).out = ∅
end for
for each starting node e ∈ cfg.S do
    enqueue e in q and add the initial definition of each parameter p_i into D(e).in
end for
while q ≠ ∅ do
    n = dequeue q
    if n is a definition with r then
        D(n).out = {(r : n)} ∪ (D(n).in − {(r : _)})
    else
        D(n).out = D(n).in
    end if
    for all nodes s in successors(n) do
        (oi, ou) = D(s) and D(s).in = D(s).in ∪ D(n).out
        if D(s).in ≠ oi and s not in q then
            enqueue s into q
        end if
    end for
end while
return D
```

Algorithm 2. DFG Extracting Algorithm $DFG(cfg)$

Input: CFG *cfg* of a target function

Output: DFG *dfg* of the function

```
D = RD(cfg)
dfg.N = cfg.N, dfg.E = ∅, dfg.S = ∅ and dfg.F = ∅
for each node n ∈ cfg.N do
    for each register r used by n do
        for each definition d of r in D(n).in do
            dfg.E = dfg.E ∪ {(d, n)}
            if d is the initial definition of a parameter then
                dfg.S = dfg.S ∪ {n}
            end if
            if n is the exiting node then
                dfg.F = dfg.F ∪ {d}
            end if
        end for
    end for
end for
return dfg
```

instructions that involved the definitions of arguments in the calling node with the start nodes of the callee method's DFG as well as the exiting nodes of the callee method's DFG with the special successor of the calling node (*i.e.*, an instruction starting with "move-result") if it exists.

2.2 Graph Encoding

It is straightforward to represent a graph as a matrix, such as the adjacency matrix. For a (simple) method, the adjacency matrix of the CFG is fine, but it could be very large for an application, even a small one. This is mainly due to the large number of nodes. Similar to existing work [14], we abstract each instruction as its opcode, for example, the instruction "invoke-virtual v0, Ljava/lang/Object;->toString();" is abstracted as "invoke-virtual". In particular, we consider all the 222 opcodes in total listed in Android Dalvik-bytecode list [19].

In more detail, given a CFG (or DFG) g, we encode it into a matrix A with size 222×222 as follows: for each edge $(n_1, n_2) \in g.E$, we add the element $A[op(n_1)][op(n_2)]$ by 1, where A is initialised as a zero matrix with size 222×222 and $op(n)$ returns the opcode of the node n. Similarly, we accumulatively add all the encoded matrices of CFGs (resp. DFG) extracted from an application as its CFG matrix (resp. DFG matrix), denoted as A_{cfg} (resp. A_{dfg}). Moreover, due to the sparseness, we also add the matrix encoded from the control-flow (resp. data-flow) edges connected by the inter-procedural analysis (*i.e.*, the function call graph *fcg*) into A_{cfg} (resp. A_{dfg}). The resulting matrix is denoted as A_{scfg} (resp. A_{sdfg}), so as to differentiate from the matrix A_{cfg} (resp. A_{dfg}) above.

We also consider the combination of CFG and DFG. Firstly, as a program dependence graph, we combines these two graphs together into a graph. So the first mode, called the *vertical* one, is to combine these two graphs together via the matrix addition (denoted as $A_{cfg} + A_{dfg}$), that is, the vertical combination of A_{cfg} and A_{dfg} is a matrix A such that for each $i \in [1, 222]$ and $j \in [1, 222]$

$$A[i][j] = A_{cfg}[i][j] + A_{dfg}[i][j]$$

Secondly, we also would like to use them as different features, just like multi-views [20]. So the second mode, called the *horizontal* one, combines them via the matrix extension (denoted as $A_{cfg} \oplus A_{dfg}$). The resulting matrix A is of size 444×222[3] instead, and satisfies that for each $i \in [1, 444]$ and $j \in [1, 222]$

$$A[i][j] = \begin{cases} A_{cfg}[i][j] & \text{if} 1 \leq i \leq 222 \\ A_{dfg}[i-222][j] & \text{otherwise} \end{cases}$$

2.3 Model Training

CNN is a new frontier in machine learning that has successfully been applied to analyse visual imagery (*i.e.*, matrix data). So we use CNN to train our model.

[3] The alternative extension with size 222×444 is fine as well.

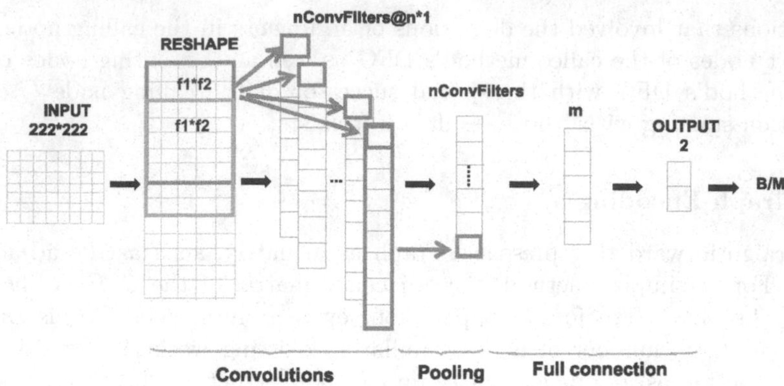

Fig. 2. Structure of our network model

In detail, we use the *Sequential* container to build our network model, which consists of 4 main layers, namely, a convolution layer with a reshape, a pooling layer and two fully connected layers, and uses the negative log likelihood criterion to compute a gradient. Note that, the reshape prior to convolution is used to reduce the number of parameters and thus save the training time. Figure 2 shows the structure of our network model.

3 Experiments

In this section, we conduct a series of experiments to evaluate our approach. Firstly, we conduct a set of cross-validation experiments to see the effectiveness of CFG and DFG in malware detection. Secondly, to test our approach's ability to detect unknown samples, we run our model on a dataset consisting of fresh samples. Finally, we also conduct some experiments to compare our approach with some existing Android malware detecting tools.

3.1 Dataset and Evaluative Criteria

We collect the samples mainly from four datasets, namely, Marvin [21], Drebin [16], VirusShare [22], and ContagioDump [23]. The Marvin dataset contains a training set (with 50501 benign samples and 7406 malware samples) and a testing set (with 25495 benign samples and 3166 malware samples). The other three datasets, Drebin, VirusShare and ContagioDump[4], contain only malware samples, with 5560, 11080 and 1150 samples, respectively. We also collect 1771 applications from Mi App Store [24], which pass the detecting of most anti-virus tools gathered in VirusTotal [17] and thus are considered as benign samples.

To quantitatively validate the experimental results, we use the following performance measures. *Accuracy* is the most intuitive performance measure and it

[4] Only the malware samples whose creation dates are in 2018 are collected.

is simply a ratio of correctly predicted observation to the total observations. *Precision* is the ratio of correctly predicted positive observations to the total predicted positive observations, and *Recall* is the ratio of correctly predicted positive observations to all observations in actual class. *F1 score* is the weighted average of *Precision* and *Recall*, that is, (2·*Precision*·*Recall*)/(*Precision*+*Recall*). *AUC* is the area under ROC curve, which is (arguably) the best way to summarize its performance in a single number. Intuitively, the higher the measures above, the better the classifier.

3.2 Experiments on Different Features

In this section, we first conduct experiments to evaluate how CFG and DFG contribute to the effectiveness of malware detection. We then run experiments to see how the combination modes affect the malware detection.

CFG and DFG. We separately use the feature matrices A_{cfg}, A_{scfg}, A_{dfg} and A_{sdfg} to train the classification model on the dataset consisting of the training set of Marvin, Drebin and VirusShare, where *10-fold cross validation* is employed. In addition, we also consider traditional CFGs [5] based on *blocks* and encode them into matrices (called as A_{tcfg}) in a similar way, where all the blocks without jumps are abstracted as a special node. More specifically, only nodes involving "control" are preserved in A_{tcfg}, yielding a matrix with size 32 × 32 (*i.e.*, 31 "control" opcodes and 1 special node for the other nodes). The experimental results are given in Table 1.

Table 1. Results on different feature matrices

Feature	Precision	Accuracy	Recall	F1 Score	AUC
A_{cfg}	99.833%	99.400%	94.691%	97.195%	0.999
A_{scfg}	100.000%	99.194%	92.704%	96.214%	0.999
A_{dfg}	99.869%	99.613%	96.620%	98.218%	0.999
A_{sdfg}	99.835%	99.470%	95.370%	97.552%	0.999
A_{tcfg}	99.842%	95.568%	59.981%	74.941%	0.993

The results show that all the features are effective in detecting malware, with *accuracy* larger than 95.5%, *precision* larger than 99.8%, and *AUC* larger than 0.99. Compared with CFG, the feature DFG performs better, both for intra-procedural analysis (1.053% higher in *F1 score*) and inter-procedural analysis (1.391% higher in *F1 score*). A possible reason is that DFGs are built on CFGs such that DFGs would, in some sense, contain some "control flow" information. Rather surprisingly, the graphs with inter-procedural analysis perform worse than the ones without. More specifically, the *F1 score* of A_{cfg} is

[5] For convenience, we do not consider the inter-procedural analysis for traditional CFGs, since the instructions for method calling are abstracted as the special node.

1.020% higher than the one of A_{scfg}, although the *precision* of A_{cfg} is better than the one of A_{scfg}; and A_{dfg} is 0.683% better than A_{sdfg} in term of *F1 score*. There are two possible reasons behind this: (1) the ignoring of callbacks and multi-threading makes the function call graphs incomplete; (2) accumulating the matrices extracted from inter-procedural analysis and the ones from intra-procedural analysis together might have lost the differences between them, thus make against the model.

In addition, we have found that the *AUC* of A_{tcfg} is 0.993, which is pretty high, and thus also demonstrates that "control flow" information is capable of facilitating detect malware. Moreover, the *precision* and the *accuracy* of A_{tcfg} are quite close to the ones of A_{cfg} and A_{dfg}, although the *recall* and *F1 score* are not so high. We may take *block*s into account to improve A_{tcfg} as shown in [12], which is left as future work. As A_{tcfg} is much simpler than A_{cfg} and A_{dfg}, we believe that A_{tcfg} can be used as a feature of models on-device.

Combination Modes. In these experiments, we use the feature matrix $A_{cfg} + A_{dfg}$ and $A_{cfg} \oplus A_{dfg}$ to train the model on the same dataset as above, respectively. Note that, as shown in the experiments above, the graphs without inter-procedural analysis perform better, so we do not consider A_{scfg} and A_{sdfg} here. The experimental results are shown in Table 2.

Table 2. Results on different modes

Feature	Precision	Accuracy	Recall	F1 Score	AUC
$A_{cfg} + A_{dfg}$	99.770%	99.536%	96.020%	97.859%	0.999
$A_{cfg} \oplus A_{dfg}$	99.903%	99.721%	97.568%	98.722%	0.999

From the results, we can see that the horizontal combination $A_{cfg} \oplus A_{dfg}$ performs better than both A_{cfg} and A_{dfg}, and thus the horizontal combination can improve the detection. While the vertical combination $A_{cfg} + A_{dfg}$ performs better than A_{cfg} but worse than A_{dfg}. That is to say, the vertical combination may make against the detecting model. Similar to inter-procedural analysis, a possible reason is that the vertical combination, *i.e.*, adding CFGs and DFGs together, could lose their differences.

3.3 Experiments on Unknown Samples

To test the viability of the proposed approach to detect unknown samples, we run our model trained with the feature matrix $A_{cfg} \oplus A_{dfg}$ respectively on two datasets: the first one comes from the testing set of Marvin, and the second one consists of the new malware samples from ContagioDump, whose creation date is in 2018. The experimental results are shown in Table 3.

It can be seen from the results that the proposed CDGDroid is capable of detecting some fresh malware. In detail, CDGDroid performs on the testing set of

Table 3. Results on other dataset

Dataset	Precision	Accuracy	Recall	F1 Score
Marvin	99.649%	99.822%	98.737%	99.191%
ContagioDump	100.000%	72.870%	72.870%	84.301%

Marvin quite well, with the *precision* 99.649%, the *accuracy* 99.822%, the *recall* 98.737% and the *F1 score* 99.191%. And for ContagioDump dataset, there are 72.870% malware samples that can be detected by CDGDroid. ContagioDump comprises only malware samples, so the *precision* of detection is 100%. Compared with the testing set of Marvin, the performance of CDGDroid is a little worse. One main reason is that the samples in ContagioDump are collected *later* than the ones in the training set (*i.e.*, Marvin, Drebin and VirusShare), that is, the samples in ContagioDump are *genuinely new*.

3.4 Comparison Against Malware Detecting Tools

In this section, we present experiments to compare our approach with some recent tools, namely, Yeganeh Safaei et al.'s approach [14] (based on CNN), Allix et al.'s approach [12] (using CFG), Drebin [16] (using 8 other features), and VirusTotal [17] (gathering a variety of anti-virus tools).

DODroid. Yeganeh Safaei et al. [14] recently proposed an Android malware detection system based on a deep convolutional neural network, using the raw opcode sequence as features. We dub this system "DODroid" (Deep Opcode). As both CDGDroid and DODroid use CNN to build the classification model, we conduct experiments to compare CDGDroid against DODroid. In detail, we use the same training dataset (*i.e.*, the training set of Marvin) to train both CDGDroid and DODroid, and then use the same testing dataset (*i.e.*, the testing set of Marvin) to test these two models. The experimental results are shown in Table 4.

Table 4. Comparison against DODroid

Tool	Precision	Accuracy	Recall	F1 Score
CDGDroid	99.903%	99.721%	97.568%	98.722%
DODroid	98.396%	99.067%	93.137%	95.695%

It can be seen from the results that CDGDroid outperforms DODroid. Regardless of the slight differences of two CNN models, the results also show that CFG and DFG are more effective than opcodes in malware detection, that is, *control flows* and *data flows* can help in detecting malware.

CSBD. Allix et al. [12] proposed another scalable approach using structural features, namely textual representations of the CFGs. Here we compare our approach against the re-implementation of Allix et al.'s approach from [25], where Random Forest is used to train the classifier and this approach is referred as CFG-Signature Based Detection (CSBD). So we also refer this approach as CSBD here. The experiments are similar to the ones of DODroid. The experimental results are shown in Table 5.

Table 5. Comparison against CSBD

Tool	Precision	Accuracy	Recall	F1 Score
CDGDroid	99.903%	99.721%	97.568%	98.722%
CSBD	92.151%	99.033%	99.747%	95.799%

We can see that CSBD has a better *recall*, while CDGDroid gets a better *precision*. A main reason is that CSBD takes *block*s of CFGs as features, while CDGDroid focuses on control flow and data flow information, plus a simple *block* information (*i.e*, the adjacency information of nodes). In short, CDGDroid gets a better *F1 score* than CSBD, so we conclude that CDGDroid performs better than CSBD.

Drebin. Drebin [16] is a lightweight Android malware detecting tool based on SVM, which uses 8 different types of features, namely, hardware components, requested permissions, app components, filtered intents, restricted API calls, used permissions, suspicious API calls, and network addresses. We also conduct experiments to compare against Drebin, where we use the re-implementation of Drebin from [25] as well. The experiments are performed on the malware samples from Drebin and the benign samples from Marvin and from Mi App Store. Table 6 gives the experimental results.

Table 6. Comparison against Drebin

Tool	Precision	Accuracy	Recall	F1 Score
CDGDroid	99.781%	99.870%	98.273%	99.021%
Drebin	91.000%	99.123%	96.000%	94.000%

The results show that CDGDroid performs better than Drebin, which also indicates that the features we consider (*i.e.* CFG and DFG) are quite effective in malware detection, with respective to the 8 features used in Drebin.

VirusTotal. VirusTotal [17] is a free online malware detecting website, which gathers a variety of anti-virus tools. For comparison, we design a crawler to automatically upload the samples in the testing set of Marvin into VirusTotal for further detecting by those anti-virus tools, which lasts almost one week. The results are shown in Table 7, where those tools with too few responds from VirusTotal are filter out.

Table 7. Comparison against anti-virus tools in VirusTotal

Tool	Precision	Accuracy	Recall	F1 Score	Tool	Precision	Accuracy	Recall	F1 Score
CDGDroid	99.649%	99.822%	98.737%	99.191%	Kaspersky	98.434%	99.789%	99.683%	99.050%
Avast	98.509%	99.746%	99.201%	98.850%	DrWeb	96.427%	99.370%	98.025%	97.220%
Jiangmin	97.682%	99.318%	96.134%	96.900%	Qihoo-360	96.013%	99.490%	97.556%	96.780%
GData	94.057%	99.252%	99.553%	96.730%	Emsisoft	94.050%	99.250%	99.550%	96.720%
TrendMicro	97.900%	99.198%	94.694%	96.270%	Sophos	91.998%	98.956%	99.169%	95.450%
BitDefender	94.049%	98.831%	95.431%	94.740%	Alibaba	89.973%	99.121%	98.793%	94.180%
F-Secure	90.808%	98.480%	96.151%	93.400%	QuickHeal	88.296%	98.433%	99.055%	93.370%
NOD32	87.182%	98.277%	99.621%	92.990%	Ikarus	86.414%	98.250%	99.743%	92.600%
Arcabit	89.076%	98.607%	92.393%	90.700%	K7GW	85.283%	98.414%	96.400%	90.500%
Tencent	83.100%	98.447%	98.843%	90.290%	Comodo	92.557%	97.777%	86.808%	89.590%
Symantec	92.101%	97.776%	87.198%	89.580%	VBA32	99.960%	97.791%	80.152%	88.970%
Fortinet	85.522%	97.414%	92.254%	88.760%	AVware	77.629%	97.791%	99.627%	87.260%
Avira	77.929%	97.528%	96.038%	86.040%	Antiy-AVL	89.085%	96.807%	81.067%	84.890%
AegisLab	76.108%	97.182%	94.857%	84.450%	Microsoft	99.956%	96.990%	72.820%	84.260%
NANO	70.888%	96.648%	97.934%	82.240%	Cyren	65.584%	95.868%	99.737%	79.130%
VIPRE	93.002%	95.590%	65.046%	76.550%	F-Prot	78.086%	94.639%	71.920%	74.880%
McAfee	80.799%	93.392%	53.167%	64.130%	AVG	81.474%	93.337%	51.707%	63.260%
AhnLab-V3	85.445%	92.747%	49.817%	62.940%	McAfee-GW	92.244%	93.216%	42.424%	58.120%
TotalDefense	99.810%	92.399%	33.228%	49.860%					

From the results, we can see that our tool CDGDroid outperforms most of anti-virus tools. In particular, our tool CDGDroid gets the best *accuracy* (99.822%) and the best *F1 score* (99.191%). Although there are 3 (resp. 12) tools having a better *precision* (resp. *recall*) than CDGDroid, the gaps of *precision* (resp. *recall*) between CDGDroid and these tools are quite small.

4 Related Work

Over the past decade, there are a lot of research work for Android malware detection. Here we only review some related and recent ones, namely, graph based detection and deep learning based detection.

Graph Based Detection. Sahs and Khan [9] proposed a machine learning-based system which extracts features from control flow graphs of applications. Allix et al. [12] devised several machine learning classifiers that rely on a set of features which are textual representations of the control flow graphs of applications. DroidMiner [10] digs malicious behavioral patterns from a two-level behavioural graph representation built on control-flow graphs and call graphs.

AppContext [26] extracts the contextual information of security-sensitive activities along with structural information through reduced inter-procedure control-flow graphs, and CWLK [25] is a similar approach, which extracts the information through call graphs and inter-procedural control-flow graphs. DroidOL [13] is an online machine learning based framework, which extracts features from inter-procedural control-flow sub-graphs. MKLDroid [20] integrates context-aware multiple views to detect Android malware, where all views are built from inter-procedural control flow graphs. However, most of these approaches only consider control flow properties, leaving data flow properties out of consideration.

Data flow analysis is also adopted in malware detection. Flowdroid [3] and Amandroid [4] are two state-of-the-art data flow analysis tools for Android. Andriatsimandefitra and Tong [27] proposed to use system flow graphs, constructed from the log of an information flow monitor, to characterise malware samples. DroidSIFT [28] takes a weighted contextual (security-related) API dependency graph as semantics feature sets and use graph similarity metrics to detect malware. DroidADDMiner [11] is a machine learning based system that extracts features based on data dependency between sensitive APIs. However, all these tools rely on heavyweight data flow analyses.

There are some approaches that take both control flow and data flow properties into account. Apposcopy [29] and ASTROID [30] detect Android malware via signature matching on program graphs, including certain control- and data-flow properties. CASANDRA [31] extracts features from contextual API dependency graphs, containing structural information and contextual information. Different from these approaches, we use deep learning to build our classification model.

Some other graphs are used to detect Android malware as well, such as function call graphs [32–34], permission event graphs [35], component topology graph [36].

Deep Learning Based Detection. Droid-Sec [37] and DroidDetector [38] used the deep belief network (DBN) to build the classification model, taking required permission, sensitive API and dynamic behaviour as features. Droiddeep [39] built the model by DBN as well, but used some more features (e.g., actions and components). DroidDelver [40] and DroidDeepLearner [41] are another two models built on DBN, where permissions and API calls were taken as features. Mclaughlin [14] designed the detection systems by Convolutional Neural Network (CNN), using opcode sequences as features. Nix and Zhang [42] and MalDozer [43] also built the system by CNN, but used system API call sequences as features. Deep4MalDroid [44] is a deep learning framework (*i.e.*, Stacked AutoEncoders) resting on the system call graphs extracted by dynamic analysis from Android applications. Nauman et al. [45] applied several deep learning models including fully connected, convolutional and recurrent neural networks as well as autoencoders and deep belief networks to detect Android malware, using the eight features proposed in [16]. DeepFlow [46] identified malware directly from the data flows in the Android application based deep learning.

Most of these approach consider neither control flow nor data flow information (except DeepFlow), while our approach takes both control and data flow graphs into account.

5 Conclusion

In this work, we have proposed an Android malware detection approach based on CNN, using control flow graph (CFG) and data flow graph (DFG). To evaluate the proposed approach, we have carried out some interesting experiments. Through experiments, we have found that the classification model with the horizontal combination of CFG and DFG as features performs the best. The experimental results have also demonstrated that our classification model is capable of detecting some fresh malware, and has a better performance than Yeganeh Safaei et al.'s work, Drebin and most of anti-virus tools gathered in VirusTotal.

As for future work, we may consider a better function call graph to improve the approach. We can use other program graphs, such as program dependence graphs, to train the model. We can also leverage N-Gram to extract program traces with length N as features. More experiments on malware anti-detecting techniques (*i.e.*, obfuscation techniques) are under consideration.

Acknowledgements. The authors would like to thank the anonymous reviewers for their helpful comments. This work was partially supported by the National Natural Science Foundation of China under Grants No. 61502308 and 61772347, Science and Technology Foundation of Shenzhen City under Grant No. JCYJ20170302153712968, Project 2016050 supported by SZU R/D Fund and Natural Science Foundation of SZU (Grant No. 827-000200).

References

1. Report from IDC. http://www.idc.com/promo/smartphone-market-share/os
2. Report from G DATA (2017). https://www.gdatasoftware.com/blog/2017/04/29712-8-400-new-android-malware-samples-every-day
3. Arzt, S., et al.: Flowdroid: precise context, flow, field, object-sensitive and lifecycle-aware taint analysis for android apps. In: PLDI 2014, pp. 259–269 (2014)
4. Wei, F., Roy, S., Ou, X.: Amandroid: a precise and general inter-component data flow analysis framework for security vetting of android apps. In: CCS 2014, pp. 1329–1341 (2014)
5. Enck, W., et al.: TaintDroid: an information-flow tracking system for realtime privacy monitoring on smartphones. In: OSDI 2014, pp. 393–407 (2014)
6. Enck, W., Ongtang, M., Mcdaniel, P.: On lightweight mobile phone application certification. In: CCS 2009, pp. 235–245 (2009)
7. Felt, A., et al.: Android permissions demystified. In: CCS 2011, pp. 627–638 (2011)
8. Grace, M., et al.: Riskranker: scalable and accurate zero-day android malware detection. In: MobiSys 2012, pp. 281–294 (2012)
9. Sahs, J., Khan, L.: A machine learning approach to android malware detection. In: EISIC 2012, pp. 141–147 (2012)

10. Yang, C., Xu, Z., Gu, G., Yegneswaran, V., Porras, P.: DroidMiner: automated mining and characterization of fine-grained malicious behaviors in android applications. In: Kutyłowski, M., Vaidya, J. (eds.) ESORICS 2014. LNCS, vol. 8712, pp. 163–182. Springer, Cham (2014). https://doi.org/10.1007/978-3-319-11203-9_10
11. Li, Y., Shen, T., Sun, X., Pan, X., Mao, B.: Detection, classification and characterization of android malware using API data dependency. In: Thuraisingham, B., Wang, X.F., Yegneswaran, V. (eds.) SecureComm 2015. LNICST, vol. 164, pp. 23–40. Springer, Cham (2015). https://doi.org/10.1007/978-3-319-28865-9_2
12. Allix, K., et al.: Empirical assessment of machine learning-based malware detectors for android. Empirical Softw. Eng. **21**(1), 183–211 (2016)
13. Narayanan, A., Liu, Y., Chen, L., Liu, J.: Adaptive and scalable android malware detection through online learning. In: IJCNN 2016, pp. 157–175 (2016)
14. Mclaughlin, N., et al.: Deep android malware detection. In: CODASPY 2017, pp. 301–308 (2017)
15. Chen, S., et al.: Automated poisoning attacks and defenses in malware detection systems: an adversarial machine learning approach. Comput. Secur. **73**, 326–344 (2017)
16. Arp, D., et al.: DREBIN: effective and explainable detection of android malware in your pocket. In: NDSS 2014 (2014)
17. VirusTotal. https://www.virustotal.com
18. Wiśniewski, R., Tumbleson, C.: Apktool: a tool for reverse engineering Android APK files. https://ibotpeaches.github.io/Apktool/
19. Dalvik Bytecode. https://source.android.com/devices/tech/dalvik/dalvik-bytecode
20. Narayanan, A., Chandramohan, M., Chen, L., Liu, Y.: A multi-view context-aware approach to android malware detection and malicious code localization. Empirical Softw. Eng. **23**(3), 1222–1274 (2017)
21. Lindorfer, M., Neugschwandtner, M., Platzer, C.: Marvin: Efficient and comprehensive mobile app classification through static and dynamic analysis. In: ComSAC 2015, pp. 422–433 (2015)
22. VirusShare. https://virusshare.com/
23. Contagiodump. http://contagiodump.blogspot.com/
24. Mi App Store. https://dev.mi.com/en
25. Narayanan, A., et al.: Contextual Weisfeiler-Lehman graph kernel for malware detection. In: IJCNN 2016, pp. 4701–4708 (2016)
26. Yang, W., et al.: Appcontext: differentiating malicious and benign mobile app behaviors using context. In: ICSE 2015, pp. 303–313 (2015)
27. Andriatsimandefitra, R., Tong, V.V.T.: Capturing android malware behaviour using system flow graph. In: Au, M.H., Carminati, B., Kuo, C.-C.J. (eds.) NSS 2014. LNCS, vol. 8792, pp. 534–541. Springer, Cham (2014). https://doi.org/10.1007/978-3-319-11698-3_43
28. Zhang, M., Duan, Y., Yin, H., Zhao, Z.: Semantics-aware android malware classification using weighted contextual API dependency graphs. In: CCS 2014, pp. 1105–1116 (2014)
29. Feng, Y., Anand, S., Dillig, L., Aiken, A.: Apposcopy: semantics-based detection of android malware through static analysis. In: FSE 2014, pp. 576–587 (2014)
30. Feng, Y., et al.: Automated synthesis of semantic malware signatures using maximum satisfiability. CoRR, abs/1608.06254 (2016)
31. Narayanan, A., Chandramohan, M., Chen, L., Liu, Y.: Context-aware, adaptive and scalable android malware detection through online learning (extended version). CoRR, abs/1706.00947 (2017)

32. Gascon, H., Yamaguchi, F., Arp, D., Rieck, K.: Structural detection of android malware using embedded call graphs. In: AISec 2013, pp. 45–54 (2013)
33. Du, Y., Wang, J., Li, Q.: An android malware detection approach using community structures of weighted function call graphs. IEEE Access **PP**(99), 1 (2017)
34. Fan, M., et al.: Frequent subgraph based familial classification of android malware. In: ISSRE 2016, pp. 24–35 (2016)
35. Chen, K., et al.: Contextual policy enforcement in android applications with permission event graphs. Heredity **110**(6), 586 (2013)
36. Shen, T., et al.: Detect android malware variants using component based topology graph. In: TrustCom 2014, pp. 406–413 (2014)
37. Yuan, Z., Lu, Y., Wang, Z., Xue, Y.: Droid-Sec: deep learning in android malware detection. In: SIGCOMM 2014, pp. 371–372 (2014)
38. Yuan, Z., Lu, Y., Xue, Y.: Droiddetector: android malware characterization and detection using deep learning. Tsinghua Sci. Technol. **21**(1), 114–123 (2016)
39. Su, X., Zhang, D., Li, W., Zhao, K.: A deep learning approach to android malware feature learning and detection. In: TrustCom 2016, pp. 244–251 (2016)
40. Hou, S., Saas, A., Ye, Y., Chen, L.: DroidDelver: an android malware detection system using deep belief network based on API call blocks. In: Song, S., Tong, Y. (eds.) WAIM 2016. LNCS, vol. 9998, pp. 54–66. Springer, Cham (2016). https://doi.org/10.1007/978-3-319-47121-1_5
41. Wang, Z., Cai, J., Cheng, S., Li, W.: Droiddeeplearner: identifying android malware using deep learning. In: Sarnoff 2016, pp. 160–165 (2016)
42. Nix, R., Zhang, J.: Classification of android apps and malware using deep neural networks. In: IJCNN 2017, pp. 1871–1878 (2017)
43. Karbab, E., Debbabi, M., Derhab, A., Mouheb, D.: Maldozer: automatic framework for android malware detection using deep learning. Digit. Invest. **24**, S48–S59 (2018)
44. Hou, S., Saas, A., Chen, L., Ye, Y.: Deep4maldroid: a deep learning framework for android malware detection based on Linux kernel system call graphs. In: WIW 2017, pp. 104–111 (2017)
45. Nauman, M., Tanveer, T., Khan, S., Syed, T.: Deep neural architectures for large scale android malware analysis. Cluster Comput. 1–20 (2017)
46. Zhu, D., et al.: Deepflow: deep learning-based malware detection by mining android application for abnormal usage of sensitive data. In: ISCC 2017, pp. 438–443, July 2017

Type Theory

Strongly Typed Numerical Computations

Matthieu Martel[(✉)]

Laboratoire de Mathématiques et Physique (LAMPS),
Université de Perpignan Via Domitia, Perpignan, France
matthieu.martel@univ-perp.fr

Abstract. It is well-known that numerical computations may sometimes lead to wrong results because of roundoff errors. We propose an ML-like type system (strong, implicit, polymorphic) for numerical computations in finite precision, in which the type of an expression carries information on its accuracy. We use dependent types and a type inference which, from the user point of view, acts like ML type inference. Basically, our type system accepts expressions for which it may ensure a certain accuracy on the result of the evaluation and it rejects expressions for which a minimal accuracy on the result of the evaluation cannot be inferred. The soundness of the type system is ensured by a subject reduction theorem and we show that our type system is able to type implementations of usual simple numerical algorithms.

1 Introduction

It is well-known that numerical computations may sometimes lead to wrong results because of the accumulation of roundoff errors [8]. Recently, much work has been done to detect these accuracy errors in finite precision computations [1], by static [6,9,18] or dynamic [7] analysis, to find the least data formats needed to ensure a certain accuracy (precision tuning) [11,12,17] and to optimize the accuracy by program transformation [5,14]. All these techniques are used late in the software development cycle, once the programs are entirely written.

In this article, we aim at exploring a different direction. We aim at detecting and correcting numerical accuracy errors at software development time, i.e. during the programming phase. From a software engineering point of view, the advantages of our approach are many since it is well-known that late bug detection is time and money consuming. We also aim at using intensively used techniques recognized for their ability to discard run-time errors. This choice is motivated by efficiency reasons as well as for end-user adoption reasons.

We propose an ML-like type system (strong, implicit, polymorphic [15]) for numerical computations in which the type of an arithmetic expression carries information on its accuracy. We use dependent types [16] and a type inference

This work is supported by the Office for Naval Research Global under Grant NICOP N62909-18-1-2068 (Tycoon project). https://www.onr.navy.mil/en/Science-Technology/ONR-Global.

J. Sun and M. Sun (Eds.): ICFEM 2018, LNCS 11232, pp. 197–214, 2018.
https://doi.org/10.1007/978-3-030-02450-5_12

which, from the user point of view, acts like ML [13] type inference [15] even if it slightly differs in its implementation. While type systems have been widely used to prevent a large variety of software bugs, to our knowledge, no type system has been targeted to address numerical accuracy issues in finite precision computations. Basically, our type system accepts expressions for which it may ensure a certain accuracy on the result of the evaluation and it rejects expressions for which a minimal accuracy on the result of the evaluation cannot be inferred.

Let us insist on the fact that we use a dependent type system. Consequently, the type corresponding to a function of some argument x depends on the type of x itself. The soundness of our type system relies on a subject reduction theorem introduced in Sect. 4. Based on an instrumented operational semantics computing both the finite precision and exact results of a numerical computation, this theorem shows that the error on the result of the evaluation of some expression e is less than the error predicted by the type of e. Obviously, as any non-trivial type system, our type system is not complete and rejects certain programs that would not produce unbounded numerical errors. Our type system has been implemented in a prototype language Numl and we show that, in practice, our type system is expressive enough to type implementations of usual simple numerical algorithms [2] such as the ones of Sect. 5. Let us also mention that our type system represents a new application of dependent type theory motivated by applicative needs. Indeed, dependent types arise naturally in our context since accuracy depends on values.

This article is organized as follows. Section 2 introduces informally our type system and shows how it is used in our implementation of a ML-like programming language, Numl. The formal definition of the types and of the inference rules are given in Sect. 3. A soundness theorem is given in Sect. 4. Section 5 presents experimental results and Sect. 6 concludes.

2 Programming with Types for Numerical Accuracy

In this section, we present informally how our type system works throughout a programming sequence in our language, Numl. First of all, we use real numbers $\mathsf{r}\{s, u, p\}$ where r is the value itself, and $\{s, u, p\}$ the format of r. The format of a real number is made of a sign $s \in \mathsf{Sign}$ and integers $u, p \in \mathsf{Int}$ such that u is the unit in the first place of r, written $\mathsf{ufp}(\mathsf{r})$ and p the precision (i.e. the number of digits of the number). For inputs, p is either explicitly specified by the user or set by default by the system. For outputs, p is inferred by the type system. We have $\mathsf{Sign} = \{0, \oplus, \ominus, \top\}$ and $\mathsf{sign}(\mathsf{r}) = 0$ if $\mathsf{r} = 0$, $\mathsf{sign}(\mathsf{r}) = \oplus$ if $\mathsf{r} > 0$ and $\mathsf{sign}(\mathsf{r}) = \ominus$ if $\mathsf{r} < 0$. The set Sign is equipped with the partial order relation $\prec \subseteq \mathsf{Sign} \times \mathsf{Sign}$ defined by $0 \prec \oplus$, $0 \prec \ominus$, $\oplus \prec \top$ and $\ominus \prec \top$. The ufp of a number x is

$$\mathsf{ufp}(x) = \min\left\{i \in \mathbb{N} \ : \ 2^{i+1} > x\right\} = \lfloor \log_2(x) \rfloor. \tag{1}$$

The term p defines the precision of r. Let $\varepsilon(\mathsf{r})$ be the absolute error on r, we assume that $\varepsilon(\mathsf{r}) < 2^{u-p+1}$. The errors on the numerical constants arising in programs are specified by the user or determined by default by the system.

Format	Name	p	e bits	e_{min}	e_{max}
Binary16	Half precision	11	5	−14	+15
Binary32	Single precision	24	8	−126	+127
Binary64	Double precision	53	11	−1122	+1223
Binary128	Quadruple precision	113	15	−16382	+16383

Fig. 1. Basic binary IEEE754 formats.

The errors on the computed values can be inferred by propagation of the initial errors. Similarly to Eq. (1), we also define the *u*nit in the *l*ast *p*lace (ulp) used later in this article. The ulp of a number of precision p is defined by

$$\mathsf{ulp}(x) = \mathsf{ufp}(x) - p + 1. \tag{2}$$

For example, the type of 1.234 is $\mathtt{real}\{+, 0, 53\}$ since $\mathsf{ufp}(1.234) = 0$ and since we assume that, by default, the real numbers have the same precision as in the IEEE754 double precision floating-point format [1] (see Fig. 1). Other formats may be specified by the programmer, as in the example below. Let us also mention that our type system is independent of a given computer arithmetic. The interpreter only needs to implement the formats given by the type system, using floating-point numbers, fixed-point numbers [10], multiple precision numbers[1], etc. in order to ensure that the finite precision operations are computed exactly. The special case of IEEE754 floating-point arithmetic, which introduces additional errors due to the roundoff on results of operations can also be treated by modifying slightly the equations of Sect. 3.

```
> 1.234 ;; (* precision of 53 bits by default *)
- : real{+,0,53} = 1.234000000000000

> 1.234{4};; (* precision of 4 bits specified by the user *)
- : real{+,0,4} = 1.2
```

Notice that, in `Numl`, the type information is used by the pretty printer to display only the correct digits of a number and a bound on the roundoff error.

Note that accuracy is not a property of a number but a number that states how closely a particular finite-precision number matches some ideal true value. For example, using the basis $\beta = 10$ for the sake of simplicity, the floating-point value 3.149 represents π with an accuracy of 3. It itself has a precision of 4. It represents the real number 3.14903 with an accuracy of 4. As in `ML`, our type system admits parameterized types [15].

```
> let f = fun x -> x + 1.0 ;;
val f : real{'a,'b,'c} -> real{<expr>,<expr>,<expr>} = <fun>

> verbose true ;;
- : unit = ()

> f ;;
- : real{'a,'b,'c} -> real{(SignPlus 'a 'b 1 0),((max 'b 0) +_ (sigma+ 'a 1)),
((((max 'b 0) +_ (sigma+ 'a 1)) -_ (max ('b -_ 'c) -53))-_ (iota ('b -_ 'c) -53))} = <fun>
```

[1] https://gmplib.org/.

In the example above, the type of `f` is a function of an argument whose parameterized type is `real{'a, 'b, 'c}`, where `'a`, `'b` and `'c` are three type variables. The return type of the function `f` is `Real`$\{e_0, e_1, e_2\}$ where e_0, e_1 and e_2 are arithmetic expressions containing the variables `'a`, `'b` and `'c`. By default these expressions are not displayed by the system (just like higher order values are not explicitly displayed in ML implementations) but we may enforce the system to print them. In `Numl`, we write `+`, `-`, `*` and `/` for the operators over real numbers. Integer expressions have type `int` and we write `+_`, `-_`, `*_` and `/_` for the elementary operators over integers. The expressions arising in the type of `f` are explained in Sect. 3. As shown below, various applications of `f` yield results of various types, depending on the type of the argument.

```
> f 1.234 ;;
- : real{+,1,53} = 2.234000000000000

> f 1.234{4} ;;
- : real{+,1,5} = 2.2
```

If the interpreter detects that the result of some computation has no significant digit, then an error is raised. For example, it is well-known that in IEEE754 double precision $(10^{16}+1)-10^{16}=0$. Our type system rejects this computation.

```
> (1.0e15 + 1.0) - 1.0e15 ;;
- : real{+,50,54} = 1.0

> (1.0e16 + 1.0) - 1.0e16 ;;
Error: The computed value has no significant digit. Its ufp is 0 but the ulp of the
certified value is 1
```

Last but not least, our type system accepts recursive functions. For example, we have:

```
> let rec g x = if x < 1.0 then x else g (x * 0.07) ;;
val g : real{+,0,53} -> real{+,0,53} = <fun>

> g 1.0 ;;
- : real{+,0,53} = 0.07000000000000

> g 2.0 ;;
Error: This expression has type real{+,1,53} but an expression was expected of type
real{+,0,53}
```

In the above session, the type system unifies the return type of the function with the type of the conditional. The types of the `then` and `else` branches also need to be unified. Then the return type is `real{+,0,53}` which corresponds to the type of the value `1.0` used in the `then` branch. The type system also unifies the return type with the type of the argument since the function is recursive. Finally, we obtain that the type of `g` is `real{+,0,53} -> real{+,0,53}`. As a consequence, we cannot call `g` with an argument whose ufp is greater than $\mathsf{ufp}(1.0)=0$. To overcome this limitation, we introduce new comparison operations for real numbers. While the standard comparison operator < has type `'a -> 'a -> bool`, the operator <{s,u,p} has type `real{s,u,p} -> real{s,u,p} -> bool`. In other words, the compared value are cast in the format $\{s,u,p\}$ before performing the comparison. Now we can write the code:

```
> let rec g x = if x <{*,10,15} 1.0 then x else g (x * 0.07) ;;
val g : real{*,10,15} -> real{*,10,15} = <fun>

> g 2.0 ;;
- : real{*,10,15} = 0.1

> g 456.7 ;;
- : real{*,10,15} = 0.1

> g 4567.8 ;;
Error: This expression has type real{+,12,53} but an expression was expected of
type real{*,10,15}
```

Interestingly, unstable functions (for which the initial errors grow with the number of iterations) are not typable. This is a desirable property of our system.

```
> let rec h n = if (n=0) then 1.0 else 3.33 * (h (n -_ 1)) ;;
Error: This expression has type real{+,-1,-1} but an expression was expected of
type real{+,-3,-1}
```

Stable computations should be always accepted by our type system. Obviously, this is not the case and, as any non-trivial type system, our type system rejects some correct programs. The challenge is then to accept enough programs to be useful from an end-user point of view. We end this section by showing another example representative of what our type system accepts. More examples are given later in this article, in Sect. 5. The example below deals with the implementation of the Taylor series $\frac{1}{1-x} = \sum_{n \geq 0} x^n$. The implementation gives rise to a simple recursion, as shown in the programming session below.

```
> let rec taylor x{*,-1,25} xn i n = if (i > n) then 0.0{*,10,20}
                                      else xn + (taylor x (x * xn) (i +_ 1) n) ;;

val taylor : real{*,-1,25} -> real{*,10,20} -> int -> int -> real{*,10,20} = <fun>

> taylor 0.2 1.0 0 5;;
- : real{*,10,20} = 1.2499 +/- 0.0009765625
```

Obviously, our type system computes the propagation of the errors due to finite precision but does not take care of the method error intrinsic to the implemented algorithm (the Taylor series instead of the exact formula $\frac{1}{1-x}$ in our case.) All the programming sessions introduced above as well as the additional examples of Sect. 5 are fully interactive in our system, Numl, i.e. the type judgments are obtained instantaneously (about 0.01 s in average following our measurements) including the most complicated ones.

3 The Type System

In this section, we introduce the formal definition of our type system for numerical accuracy. First, in Sect. 3.1, we define the syntax of expressions and types and we introduce a set of inference rules. Then we define in Sect. 3.2 the types of the primitives for the operators among real numbers (addition, product, etc.) These types are crucial in our system since they encode the propagation of the numerical accuracy information.

$$\frac{}{\Gamma \vdash \mathtt{i} : \mathtt{int}} \ (\text{INT}) \qquad \frac{}{\Gamma \vdash \mathtt{b} : \mathtt{bool}} \ (\text{BOOL})$$

$$\frac{\mathsf{sign}(\mathtt{r}) \prec s \quad \mathsf{ufp}(\mathtt{r}) \le u}{\Gamma \vdash \mathtt{r\{s,u,p\}} : \mathtt{real\{s,u,p\}}} \ (\text{REAL}) \qquad \frac{\Gamma(\mathtt{id}) = t}{\Gamma \vdash \mathtt{id} : t} \ (\text{ID})$$

$$\frac{\Gamma \vdash e_0 : \mathtt{bool} \qquad \Gamma \vdash e_1 : t_1 \qquad \Gamma \vdash e_2 : t_2 \qquad t = t_1 \sqcup t_2}{\Gamma \vdash \mathtt{if}\ e_0\ \mathtt{then}\ e_1\ \mathtt{else}\ e_2 : t} \ (\text{COND})$$

$$\frac{\Gamma, x : t_1 \vdash e : t_2}{\Gamma \vdash \lambda x.e : \Pi x : t_1.t_2} \ (\text{ABS}) \qquad \frac{\Gamma, x : t_1, f : \Pi.y : t_1.t_2 \vdash e : t_2 \quad y \text{ not free in } t_2}{\Gamma \vdash \mathtt{rec}\ f\ x.e : \Pi x : t_1.t_2} \ (\text{REC})$$

$$\frac{\Gamma \vdash e_1 : \Pi x : t_0.t_1 \qquad \Gamma \vdash e_2 : t_2 \qquad t_2 \sqsubseteq t_0}{\Gamma \vdash e_1\ e_2 : t_1[x \mapsto e_2]} \ (\text{APP})$$

Fig. 2. Typing rules for our language.

3.1 Expressions, Types and Inference Rules

In this section, we introduce the expressions, types and typing rules for our language. For the sake of simplicity, the syntax introduced hereafter uses notations *à la* lambda calculus instead of the ML-like syntax employed in Sect. 2. In our system, expressions and types are mutually dependent. They are defined inductively using the grammar of Eq. (3).

$$\begin{array}{rl} \mathsf{Expr} \ni e ::= & \mathtt{r}\{s,u,p\} \in \mathsf{Real}_{u,p} \mid \mathtt{i} \in \mathsf{Int} \mid \mathtt{b} \in \mathsf{Bool} \mid \mathtt{id} \in \mathsf{Id} \\ & \mid \mathtt{if}\ e_0\ \mathtt{then}\ e_1\ \mathtt{else}\ e_2 \mid \lambda x.e \mid e_0\ e_1 \mid \mathtt{rec}\ f\ x.e \mid t \\ \mathsf{Typ} \ni t ::= & \mid \mathtt{int} \mid \mathtt{bool} \mid \mathtt{real}\{i_0, i_1, i_2\} \mid \alpha \mid \Pi x : e_0.e_1 \\ \mathsf{IExp} \ni i ::= & \mid \mathtt{int} \mid \mathsf{op} \in \mathsf{Id_I} \mid \alpha \mid i_0\ i_1 \end{array} \tag{3}$$

In Eq. (3), the e terms correspond to expressions. Constants are integers $\mathtt{i} \in \mathsf{Int}$, booleans $\mathsf{b} \in \mathsf{Bool}$ and real numbers $\mathtt{r}\{s,u,p\}$ where r is the value itself, $s \in \mathsf{Sign}$ is the sign as defined in Sect. 2 and $u, p \in \mathsf{Int}$ the ufp (see Eq. (1)) and precision of $\mathtt{r}$. For inputs, the precision p is given by the user by means of annotations or chosen by default by the system. Then p is inferred for the outputs of programs. The term p defines the precision of r. Let $\varepsilon(\mathsf{r})$ be the absolute error on r, we assume that

$$\varepsilon(\mathsf{r}) < 2^{u-p+1}. \tag{4}$$

The errors on the numerical constants arising in programs are specified by the user or determined by default by the system. The errors on the computed values can be inferred by propagation of the initial errors.

In Eq. (3), identifiers belong to the set Id and we assume a set of pre-defined identifiers $+, -, \times, \le, =, \ldots$ related to primitives for the logical and arithmetic operations. We write $+$, $-$, $\times$ and $\div$ the operations on real numbers and $+_{-}$, $-_{-}$, $\times_{-}$ and $\div_{-}$ the operations among integers. The language also admits conditionals, functions $\lambda x.e$, applications $e_0\ e_1$ and recursive functions $\mathtt{rec}\ f\ x.e$ where f is the name of the function, x the parameter and e the body. The language of

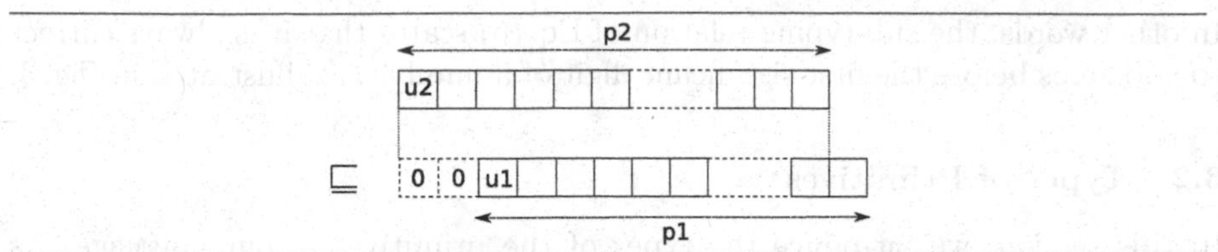

Fig. 3. The sub-typing relation $\sqsubseteq$ of Eq. (6).

expressions also includes type expressions t defined by the second production of the grammar of Eq. (3).

The definition of expressions and type is mutually recursive. Type variables are denoted α, β, ... and $\Pi x : e_0.e_1$ is used to introduce dependent types [16]. Let us notice that our language does not explicitly contain function types $t_0 \rightarrow t_1$ since they are encoded by means of dependent types. Let $\equiv$ denote the syntactic equivalence, we have

$$t_0 \rightarrow t_1 \equiv \Pi x : t_0.t_1 \quad \text{with } x \text{ not free in } t_1. \tag{5}$$

For convenience, we also write $\lambda x_0.x_1 \ldots x_n.e$ instead of $\lambda x_0.\lambda x_1 \ldots \lambda x_n.e$ and $\Pi x_0 : t_0.x_1 : t_1 \ldots x_n : t_n.e$ instead of $\Pi x_0 : t_0.\Pi x_1 : t_1 \ldots \Pi x_n : t_n.e$.

The types of constants are `int`, `bool` and $\texttt{real}\{i_0, i_1, i_2\}$ where i_0, i_1 and i_2 are integer expressions denoting the format of the real number. Integer expressions of $\mathsf{IExpr} \subseteq \mathsf{Expr}$ are a subset of expressions made of integer numbers, integer primitives of $\mathsf{Id}_\mathsf{I} \subseteq \mathsf{Id}$ (such as $+\_$, $\times\_$, etc.), type variables and applications. Note that this definition restricts significantly the set of expressions which may be written inside `real` types.

The typing rules for our system are given in Fig. 2. These rules are mostly classical. The type judgment $\Gamma \vdash e : t$ means that in the type environment Γ, the expression e has type t. A type environment $\Gamma : \mathsf{Id} \rightarrow \mathsf{Typ}$ maps identifiers to types. We write $\Gamma\, x : t$ the environment Γ in which the variable x has type t. The typing rules (Int) and (Bool) are trivial. Rule (Real) states that the type of a real number `r{s,u,p}` is `real{s,u,p}` assuming that the actual sign of `r` is less than s and that the ufp of `r` is less than u. Following Rule (Id), an identifier `id` has type t if $\Gamma(\texttt{id}) = t$. Rules (Cond), (Abs) and (Rec) are standard rules for conditionals and abstractions respectively. The rule for application, (App), requires that the first expression e_1 has type $\Pi x : t_0.t_1$ (which is equivalent to $t_0 \rightarrow t_1$ if x is not free in t_1) and that the argument e_2 has some type $t_2 \sqsubseteq t_0$. The sub-typing relation $\sqsubset$ is introduced for real numbers. Intuitively, we want to allow the argument of some function to have a smaller ulp than what we would require if we used $t_0 = t_2$ in Rule (App), provided that the precision p remains as good with t_2 as with t_0. This relaxation allows to type more terms without invalidating the type judgments. Formally, the relation $\sqsubseteq$ is defined by

$$\texttt{real}\{\texttt{s}_1, \texttt{u}_1, \texttt{p}_1\} \sqsubseteq \texttt{real}\{\texttt{s}_2, \texttt{u}_2, \texttt{p}_2\} \iff s_1 \sqsubseteq s_2 \wedge u_2 \geq u_1 \wedge p_2 \leq u_2 - u_1 + p_1. \tag{6}$$

In other words, the sub-typing relation of Eq. (6) states that it is always correct to add zeros before the first significant digit of a number, as illustrated in Fig. 3.

3.2 Types of Primitives

In this section, we introduce the types of the primitives of our language. As mentioned earlier, the arithmetic and logic operators are viewed as functional constants of the language. The type of a primitive for an arithmetic operation among integers $*_{\_} \in \{+_{\_}, -_{\_}, \times_{\_}, \div_{\_}\}$ is

$$t_{*_{\_}} = \Pi x : \mathtt{int}.y : \mathtt{int}.\mathtt{int}. \tag{7}$$

The type of comparison operators $\bowtie \in \{=, \neq, <, >, \leq, \geq\}$ are polymorphic with the restriction that they reject the type $\mathtt{real}\{\mathtt{s},\mathtt{u},\mathtt{p}\}$ which necessitates special comparison operators:

$$t_{\bowtie} = \Pi x : \alpha.y : \alpha.\mathtt{bool} \quad \alpha \neq \mathtt{real}\{\mathtt{s},\mathtt{u},\mathtt{p}\}. \tag{8}$$

For real numbers, we use comparisons at a given accuracy defined by the operators $\bowtie_{\{u,p\}} \in \{<_{\{u,p\}}, >_{\{u,p\}}\}$. We have

$$t_{\bowtie_{\{u,p\}}} = \Pi \mathtt{s} : \mathtt{int}, \mathtt{u} : \mathtt{int}, \mathtt{p} : \mathtt{int}.\mathtt{real}\{\mathtt{s},\mathtt{u},\mathtt{p}+1\} \rightarrow \mathtt{real}\{\mathtt{s},\mathtt{u},\mathtt{p}+1\} \rightarrow \mathtt{bool}.$$

Notice that the operands of a comparison $\bowtie_{\{u,p\}}$ must have $p+1$ bits of accuracy. This is to avoid unstable tests, as detailed in the proof of Lemma 3 in Sect. 4. An unstable test is a comparison between two approximate values such that the result of the comparison is altered by the approximation error. For instance, if we reuse an example of Sect. 2, in IEEE754 double precision, the condition $10^{16} + 1 = 10^{16}$ evaluates to `true`. We need to avoid such situations in our language in order to preserve our subject reduction theorem (we need the control-flow be the same in the finite precision and exact semantics). Let us also note that our language does not provide an equality relation $=_{\{u,p\}}$ for `real` values. Again this is to avoid unstable tests. Given values x and y of type $\mathtt{real}\{\mathtt{s},\mathtt{u},\mathtt{p}\}$, the programmer is invited to use $|x - y| < 2^{u-p+1}$ instead of $x = y$ in order to get rid of the perturbations of the finite precision arithmetic.

The types of primitives for real arithmetic operators are fundamental in our system since they encode the propagation of the numerical accuracy information. They are defined in Figs. 4 and 5. The type t_* of some operation $* \in \{+, -, \times, \div\}$ is a pi-type with takes six arguments $\mathtt{s}_1, \mathtt{u}_1, \mathtt{p}_1, \mathtt{s}_2, \mathtt{u}_2$ and $\mathtt{p}_2$ of type `int` corresponding to the sign, `ufp` and precision of the two operands of $*$ and which produces a type $\mathtt{real}\{\mathtt{s}_1,\mathtt{u}_1,\mathtt{p}_1\} \rightarrow \mathtt{real}\{\mathtt{s}_2,\mathtt{u}_2,\mathtt{p}_2\} \rightarrow \mathtt{real}\{\mathcal{S}_*(\mathtt{s}_1,\mathtt{s}_2), \mathcal{U}_*(\mathtt{s}_1,\mathtt{u}_1,\mathtt{s}_2,\mathtt{u}_2), \mathcal{P}_*(\mathtt{u}_1,\mathtt{p}_1,\mathtt{u}_2,\mathtt{p}_2)\}$ where $\mathcal{S}_*$, $\mathcal{U}_*$ and $\mathcal{P}_*$ are functions which compute the sign, `ufp` and precision of the result of the operation $*$ in function of $\mathtt{s}_1, \mathtt{u}_1, \mathtt{p}_1, \mathtt{s}_2, \mathtt{u}_2$ and $\mathtt{p}_2$. These functions extend the functions used in [12].

The functions $\mathcal{S}_*$ determine the sign of the result of an operation in function of the signs of the operands and, for additions and subtractions, in function of the `ufp` of the operands. The functions $\mathcal{U}_*$ compute the `ufp` of the result. Notice that $\mathcal{U}_+$ and $\mathcal{U}_-$ use the functions σ_+ and σ_-, respectively. These functions are

$$
\begin{array}{c}
\mathtt{t}_* = \Pi \mathtt{s}_1 : \mathtt{int}, \mathtt{u}_1 : \mathtt{int}, \mathtt{p}_1 : \mathtt{int}, \mathtt{s}_2 : \mathtt{int}, \mathtt{u}_2 : \mathtt{int}, \mathtt{p}_2 : \mathtt{int}. \\
\mathtt{real}\{\mathtt{s}_1, \mathtt{u}_1, \mathtt{p}_1\} \rightarrow \mathtt{real}\{\mathtt{s}_2, \mathtt{u}_2, \mathtt{p}_2\} \\
\rightarrow \mathtt{real}\{\mathcal{S}_*(\mathtt{s}_1, \mathtt{u}_1, \mathtt{s}_2, \mathtt{u}_2), \mathcal{U}_*(\mathtt{s}_1, \mathtt{u}_1, \mathtt{s}_2, \mathtt{u}_2), \mathcal{P}_*(\mathtt{s}_1, \mathtt{u}_1, \mathtt{p}_1, \mathtt{s}_2, \mathtt{u}_2, \mathtt{p}_2)\}
\end{array}
$$

$$
\begin{aligned}
\mathcal{U}_+(\mathtt{s}_1, \mathtt{u}_1, \mathtt{s}_2, \mathtt{u}_2)) &= \max(\mathtt{u}_1, \mathtt{u}_2) + \sigma_+(\mathtt{s}_1, \mathtt{s}_2) \\
\mathcal{P}_+(\mathtt{s}_1, \mathtt{u}_1, \mathtt{p}_1, \mathtt{s}_2, \mathtt{u}_2, \mathtt{p}_2) &= \max(\mathtt{u}_1, \mathtt{u}_2) + \sigma_+(\mathtt{s}_1, \mathtt{s}_2) - \\
&\quad \max(\mathtt{u}_1 - \mathtt{p}_1, \mathtt{u}_2 - \mathtt{p}_2) - \iota(\mathtt{u}_1 - \mathtt{p}_1, \mathtt{u}_2 - \mathtt{p}_2) \\
\mathcal{U}_-(\mathtt{s}_1, \mathtt{u}_1, \mathtt{s}_2, \mathtt{u}_2)) &= \max(\mathtt{u}_1, \mathtt{u}_2) + \sigma_-(\mathtt{s}_1, \mathtt{s}_2) \\
\mathcal{P}_-(\mathtt{s}_1, \mathtt{u}_1, \mathtt{p}_1, \mathtt{s}_2, \mathtt{u}_2, \mathtt{p}_2) &= \max(\mathtt{u}_1, \mathtt{u}_2) + \sigma_-(\mathtt{s}_1, \mathtt{s}_2) - \\
&\quad \max(\mathtt{u}_1 - \mathtt{p}_1, \mathtt{u}_2 - \mathtt{p}_2) - \iota(\mathtt{u}_1 - \mathtt{p}_1, \mathtt{u}_2 - \mathtt{p}_2) \\
\mathcal{U}_\times(\mathtt{s}_1, \mathtt{u}_1, \mathtt{s}_2, \mathtt{u}_2)) &= \mathtt{u}_1 + \mathtt{u}_2 + 1 \\
\mathcal{P}_\times(\mathtt{s}_1, \mathtt{u}_1, \mathtt{p}_1, \mathtt{s}_2, \mathtt{u}_2, \mathtt{p}_2) &= \mathtt{u}_1 + \mathtt{u}_2 + 1 - \\
&\quad \max(\mathtt{u}_1 + \mathtt{u}_2 + 1 - \mathtt{p}_1, \mathtt{u}_1 + \mathtt{u}_2 + 1 - \mathtt{p}_2) - \iota(\mathtt{p}_1, \mathtt{p}_2) \\
\mathcal{U}_\div(\mathtt{s}_1, \mathtt{u}_1, \mathtt{s}_2, \mathtt{u}_2)) &= \mathtt{u}_1 - \mathtt{u}_2 + 1 \\
\mathcal{P}_\div(\mathtt{s}_1, \mathtt{u}_1, \mathtt{p}_1, \mathtt{s}_2, \mathtt{u}_2, \mathtt{p}_2) &= \mathcal{P}_\times(\mathtt{u}_1, \mathtt{p}_1, \mathtt{u}_2, \mathtt{p}_2) - 1 \qquad \iota(x, y) = \begin{cases} 1 \text{ if } x = y, \\ 0 \text{ otherwise.} \end{cases}
\end{aligned}
$$

Fig. 4. Types of the primitives corresponding to the elementary arithmetic operations $* \in \{+, -, \times, \div\}$. The functions $\mathcal{S}_*$ and σ_* are defined in Fig. 5.

defined in the bottom right corner of Fig. 5 to increment the ufp of the result of some addition or subtraction in the relevant cases only. For example if a and b are two positive real numbers then $\mathsf{ufp}(a+b)$ is possibly $\max\big(\mathsf{ufp}(a), \mathsf{ufp}(b)\big) + 1$ but if $a > 0$ and $b < 0$ then $\mathsf{ufp}(a+b)$ is not greater than $\max\big(\mathsf{ufp}(a), \mathsf{ufp}(b)\big)$. The functions $\mathcal{P}_*$ compute the precision of the result. Basically, they compute the number of bits between the ufp and the ulp of the result.

We end this section by exhibiting some properties of the functions $\mathcal{P}_*$. Let $\varepsilon(x)$ denote the error on $x \in \mathsf{Real}_{u,p}$. We have $\varepsilon(x) < 2^{u-p+1} = \mathsf{ulp}(x)$. Let us start with addition. Lemma 1 relates the accuracy of the operands to the accuracy of the result of an addition between two values x and y. Lemma 2 is similar to Lemma 1 for product.

Lemma 1. *Let x and y be two values such that $\varepsilon(x) < 2^{u_1-p_1+1}$ and $\varepsilon(y) < 2^{u_2-p_2+1}$. Let $z = x + y$, $u = \mathcal{U}_+(s_1, u_1, s_2, u_2)$ and $p = \mathcal{P}_+(s_1, u_1, p_1, s_2, u_2, p_2)$. Then $\varepsilon(z) < 2^{u-p+1}$.*

Proof. The errors on addition may be bounded by $e_+ = \varepsilon(x) + \varepsilon(y)$. Then the most significant bit of the error has weight $\mathsf{ufp}(e_+)$ and the accuracy of the result is $p = \mathsf{ufp}(x+y) - \mathsf{ufp}(e_+)$. Let $u = \mathsf{ufp}(x+y) = \max(u_1, u_2) + \sigma_+(s_1, s_2) = \mathcal{U}_+(s_1, u_1, s_2, u_2)$. We need to over-approximate e_+ in order to ensure p. We have $\varepsilon(x) < 2^{u_1-p_1+1}$ and $\varepsilon(y) < 2^{u_2-p_2+1}$ and, consequently, $e_+ < 2^{u_1-p_1+1} + 2^{u_2-p_2+1}$. We introduce the function $\iota(x, y)$ also defined in Fig. 4 and which is equal to 1 if $x = y$ and 0 otherwise. We have

$$
\begin{aligned}
\mathsf{ufp}(e_+) &< \max(u_1 - p_1 + 1, u_2 - p_2 + 1) + \iota(u_1 - p_1, u_2 - p_2) \\
&\le \max(u_1 - p_1, u_2 - p_2) + \iota(u_1 - p_1, u_2 - p_2)
\end{aligned}
$$

Let us write $p = \max(u_1 - p_1, u_2 - p_2) - \iota(u_1 - p_1, u_2 - p_2) = \mathcal{P}_+(s_1, u_1, p_1 s_2, u_2, p_2)$. We conclude that $u = \mathcal{U}_+(s_1, u_1, s_2, u_2)$, $p = \mathcal{P}_+(s_1, u_1, p_1 s_2, u_2, p_2)$ and $\varepsilon(z) < 2^{u-p+1}$. □

$\mathcal{S}_+$

s1\s2	0	+	−	⊤
0	0	+	−	⊤
+	+	+	+ if $u_1 < u_2$ − if $u_2 < u_1$ ⊤ otherwise	⊤
−	−	+ if $u_2 < u_1$ − if $u_1 < u_2$ ⊤ otherwise	−	⊤
⊤	⊤	⊤	⊤	⊤

$\mathcal{S}_\times$ and $\mathcal{S}_\div$

s1\s2	0	+	−	⊤
0	0	0	0	0
+	0	+	−	⊤
−	0	−	+	⊤
⊤	0	⊤	⊤	⊤

$\mathcal{S}_-$

s1\s2	0	+	−	⊤
0	0	−	+	⊤
+	+	− if $u_1 < u_2$ + if $u_2 < u_1$ ⊤ otherwise	+	⊤
−	−	−	− if $u_2 < u_1$ + if $u_1 < u_2$ ⊤ otherwise	⊤
⊤	⊤	⊤	⊤	⊤

σ_+

	0	+	−	⊤
0	0	0	0	0
+	0	1	0	1
−	0	0	1	1
⊤	0	1	1	1

σ_-

	0	+	−	⊤
0	0	0	0	0
+	0	0	1	1
−	0	1	0	1
⊤	0	1	1	1

Fig. 5. Operators used in the types of the primitives of Fig. 4.

Lemma 2. *Let x and y be two values such that $\varepsilon(x) < 2^{u_1-p_1+1}$ and $\varepsilon(y) < 2^{u_2-p_2+1}$. Let $z = x \times y$, $u = \mathcal{U}_\times(s_1,u_1,s_2,u_2)$ and $p = \mathcal{P}_\times(s_1,u_1,p_1,s_2,u_2,p_2)$. Then $\varepsilon(z) < 2^{u-p+1}$.*

Proof. For product, we have $p = \mathsf{ufp}(x \times y) - \mathsf{ufp}(e_\times)$ with $e_\times = x \cdot \varepsilon(y) + y \cdot \varepsilon(x) + \varepsilon(x) \cdot \varepsilon(y)$. Let $u = u_1 + u_2 + 1 = \mathcal{U}_\times(s_1,u_1,s_2,u_2)$. We have, by definition of ufp, $2^{u_1} \le x < 2^{u_1+1}$ and $2^{u_2} \le y < 2^{u_2+1}$. Then $e_\times$ may be bounded by

$$\begin{aligned} e_\times &< 2^{u_1+1} \cdot 2^{u_2-p_2+1} + 2^{p_2+1} \cdot 2^{u_1-p_1+1} + 2^{u_1-p_1+1} \cdot 2^{u_2-p_2+1} \\ &= 2^{u_1+u_2-p_2+2} + 2^{u_1+u_2-p_1+2} + 2^{u_1+u_2-p_1-p_2+2}. \end{aligned} \tag{9}$$

Since $u_1+u_2-p_1-p_2+2 < u_1+u_2-p_1+2$ and $u_1+u_2-p_1-p_2+2 < u_1+u_2-p_2+2$, we may get rid of the last term of Eq. (9) and we obtain that

$$\begin{aligned} \mathsf{ufp}(e_\times) &< \max(u_1+u_2-p_1+2, u_1+u_2-p_2+2) + \iota(p_1,p_2) \\ &\le \max(u_1+u_2-p_1+1, u_1+u_2-p_2+1) + \iota(p_1,p_2). \end{aligned}$$

Let us write $p = \max(u_1+u_2-p_1+1, u_1+u_2-p_2+1) - \iota(p_1,p_2) = \mathcal{P}_\times(s_1,u_1,p_1 s_2,u_2,p_2)$. Then $u = \mathcal{U}_\times(s_1,u_1,s_2,u_2)$, $p = \mathcal{P}_\times(s_1,u_1,p_1 s_2,u_2,p_2)$ and $\varepsilon(z) < 2^{u-p+1}$. □

Note that, by reasoning on the exponents of the values, the constraints resulting from a product become linear. The equations for subtraction and division

$$\frac{|\mathtt{r} - v_{\mathbb{F}}| < 2^{u-p+1} \quad \mathsf{ufp}(\mathtt{r}) \leq u \quad \mathsf{sign}(v_{\mathbb{F}}) \prec s}{\mathtt{r\{s,u,p\}} \rightarrow_{\mathbb{F}} v_{\mathbb{F}}} \text{ (FVal)} \qquad \frac{v_{\mathbb{R}} = \mathtt{r}}{\mathtt{r\{s,u,p\}} \rightarrow_{\mathbb{R}} v_{\mathbb{R}}} \text{ (RVal)}$$

$$\frac{e_0 \rightarrow e_0'}{e_0 * e_1 \rightarrow e_0' * e_1} \text{ (Op1)} \qquad \frac{e_1 \rightarrow e_1'}{v * e_1 \rightarrow v * e_1'} \text{ (Op2)} \qquad * \in \{+, -, \times, \div, +_{-}, -_{-}, \times_{-}, \div_{-}\}$$

$$\frac{v = v_0 * v_1}{v_0 * v_1 \rightarrow v} \text{ (Op)} \qquad * \in \{+, -, \times, \div, +_{-}, -_{-}, \times_{-}, \div_{-}\} \qquad \mathtt{rec}\ f\ x.e \rightarrow \lambda x.e\langle \mathtt{rec}\ f\ x.e/f\rangle \text{ (REC)}$$

$$\frac{e_0 \rightarrow e_0'}{e_0 \bowtie e_1 \rightarrow e_0' \bowtie e_1} \text{ (Cmp1)} \qquad \frac{e_1 \rightarrow e_1'}{v \bowtie e_1 \rightarrow v \bowtie e_1'} \text{ (Cmp2)} \qquad \bowtie \in \{<_{\{u,p\}}, >_{\{u,p\}}, <, >\}$$

$$\frac{b = (2^{u-p+1} \bowtie v_1^{\mathbb{F}} - v_0^{\mathbb{F}})}{v_0 \bowtie_{\{u,p\}} v_1 \rightarrow_{\mathbb{F}} b} \text{ (FCmp)} \qquad \frac{b = (v_0 \bowtie v_1)}{v_0 \bowtie_{\{u,p\}} v_1 \rightarrow_{\mathbb{R}} b} \text{ (RCmp)} \qquad \bowtie \in \{<_{\{u,p\}}, >_{\{u,p\}}\}$$

$$\frac{e_1 \rightarrow e_1'}{e_0\ e_1 \rightarrow e_0\ e_1'} \text{ (App1)} \qquad \frac{e_0 \rightarrow e_0'}{e_0\ v \rightarrow e_0'\ v} \text{ (App2)} \qquad (\lambda x.e)\ v \rightarrow e\langle v/x\rangle \text{ (Red)}$$

$$\frac{b = v_0 \bowtie v_1}{v_0 \bowtie v_1 \rightarrow b} \quad \bowtie \in \{=, \neq, <, >, \leq, \geq\} \qquad \frac{e_0 \rightarrow e_0'}{\mathtt{if}\ e_0\ \mathtt{then}\ e_1\ \mathtt{else}\ e_2 \rightarrow \mathtt{if}\ e_0'\ \mathtt{then}\ e_1\ \mathtt{else}\ e_2} \text{ (Cond)}$$

$$\frac{v = \mathtt{true}}{\mathtt{if}\ v\ \mathtt{then}\ e_1\ \mathtt{else}\ e_2 \rightarrow e_1} \text{ (CondTrue)} \qquad \frac{v = \mathtt{false}}{\mathtt{if}\ v\ \mathtt{then}\ e_1\ \mathtt{else}\ e_2 \rightarrow e_2} \text{ (CondFalse)}$$

Fig. 6. Operational semantics for our language.

are almost identical to the equations for addition and product, respectively. We conclude this section with the following theorem which summarize the properties of the types of the result of the four elementary operations.

Theorem 1. *Let x and y be two values such that $\varepsilon(x) < 2^{u_1-p_1+1}$ and $\varepsilon(y) < 2^{u_2-p_2+1}$ and let $* \in \{+, -, \times, \div\}$ be an elementary operation. Let $z = x * y$, $u = \mathcal{U}_*(s_1, u_1, s_2, u_2)$ and $p = \mathcal{P}_*(s_1, u_1, p_1, s_2, u_2, p_2)$. Then $\varepsilon(z) < 2^{u+p-1}$.*

Proof. The cases of addition and product correspond to Lemmas 1 and 2, respectively. The cases of subtraction and division are similar. □

`Numl` uses a modified Hindley-Milner type inference algorithm. Linear constraints among integers are generated (even for non linear expressions). They are solved space limitation reasons, the details of this algorithm are out of the scope of this article.

4 Soundness of the Type System

In this section, we introduce a subject reduction theorem proving the consistency of our type system. We use two operational semantics $\rightarrow_{\mathbb{F}}$ and $\rightarrow_{\mathbb{R}}$ for the finite precision and exact arithmetics, respectively. The exact semantics is used for proofs. Obviously, in practice, only the finite precision semantics is implemented. We write $\rightarrow$ whenever a reduction rule holds for both $\rightarrow_{\mathbb{F}}$ and $\rightarrow_{\mathbb{R}}$ (in this case, we assume that the same semantics $\rightarrow_{\mathbb{F}}$ or $\rightarrow_{\mathbb{R}}$ is used in the lower and upper parts of the same sequent). Both semantics are displayed in Fig. 6. They concern the subset of the language of Eq. (3) which do not deal with types.

$$\begin{aligned} \mathsf{EvalExpr} \ni e ::= \; & \mathtt{r}\{s,u,p\} \in \mathsf{Real}_{u,p} \mid \mathtt{i} \in \mathsf{Int} \mid \mathtt{b} \in \mathsf{Bool} \mid \mathtt{id} \in \mathsf{Id} \\ & \mid \mathtt{if}\ e_0\ \mathtt{then}\ e_1\ \mathtt{else}\ e_2 \mid \lambda x.e \mid e_0\ e_1 \mid \mathtt{rec}\ f\ x.e \mid e_0\ *\ e_1 \end{aligned} \quad (10)$$

In Eq. (10), $*$ denotes an arithmetic operator $* \in \{+,-,\times,\div,+_{\_},-_{\_},\times_{\_},\div_{\_}\}$. In Fig. 6, Rule (FVAL) of $\rightarrow_{\mathbb{F}}$ transforms a syntactic element describing a real number $\mathtt{r}\{\mathtt{s},\mathtt{u},\mathtt{p}\}$ in a certain format into a value $v_{\mathbb{F}}$. The finite precision value $v_{\mathbb{F}}$ is an approximation of $\mathtt{r}$ with an error less than the ulp of $\mathtt{r}\{\mathtt{s},\mathtt{u},\mathtt{p}\}$. In the semantics $\rightarrow_{\mathbb{R}}$, the real number $\mathtt{r}\{\mathtt{s},\mathtt{u},\mathtt{p}\}$ simply produces the value $\mathtt{r}$ without any approximation by Rule (RVal). Rules (Op1) and (Op2) evaluate the operands of some binary operation and Rule (Op) performs an operation $* \in \{+,-,\times,\div,+_{\_},-_{\_},\times_{\_},\div_{\_}\}$ between two values v_0 and v_1.

Rules (Cmp1), (Cmp2) and (ACmp) deal with comparisons. They are similar to Rules (Op1), (Op2) and (Op) described earlier. Note that the operators $<$, $>$, $=$, $\neq$ concerned by Rule (ACmp) are polymorphic except that they do not accept arguments of type `real`. Rules (FCmp) and (RCmp) are for the comparison of `real` values. Rule (FCmp) is designed to avoid unstable tests by requiring that the distance between the two compared values is greater than the ulp of the format in which the comparison is done. With this requirement, a condition cannot be invalidated by the roundoff errors. Let us also note that, with this definition, $x <_{u,p} y \not\Rightarrow y >_{u,p} x$ or $x >_{u,p} y \not\Rightarrow y <_{u,p} x$. For the semantics $\rightarrow_{\mathbb{R}}$, Rule (RCmp) simply compares the exact values.

The other rules are standard and are identical in $\rightarrow_{\mathbb{F}}$ and $\rightarrow_{\mathbb{R}}$. Rules (App1), (App2) and (Red) are for applications and Rule (Rec) is for recursive functions. We write $e\langle v/x\rangle$ the term e in which v has been substituted to the free occurrences of x. Rules (Cond), (CondTrue) and (CondFalse) are for conditionals.

The rest of this section is dedicated to our subject reduction theorem. First of all, we need to relate the traces of $\rightarrow_{\mathbb{F}}$ and $\rightarrow_{\mathbb{R}}$. We introduce new judgments

$$\Gamma \models (e_{\mathbb{F}}, e_{\mathbb{R}}) \;:\; t. \quad (11)$$

Intuitively, Eq. (11) means that expression $e_{\mathbb{F}}$ simulates $e_{\mathbb{R}}$ up to accuracy t. In this case, $e_{\mathbb{F}}$ is syntactically equivalent to $e_{\mathbb{R}}$ up to the values which, in $e_{\mathbb{F}}$, are approximations of the values of $e_{\mathbb{R}}$. The value of the approximation is given by type t.

Formally, $\models$ is defined in Fig. 7. These rules are similar to the typing rules of Fig. 2 excepted that they operate on pairs $(e_{\mathbb{F}}, e_{\mathbb{R}})$. They are also designed for the language of Eq. (10) and, consequently, deal with the elementary arithmetic operations $+$, $-$, $\times$ and $\div$ as well as the comparison operators. The difference between the rules of Figs. 2 and 7 is in Rule (VReal) which states that a `real` value $v_{\mathbb{R}}$ is correctly simulated by a value $v_{\mathbb{F}}$ up to accuracy $\mathtt{real}\{\mathtt{s},\mathtt{u},\mathtt{p}\}$ if

$$\frac{}{\Gamma \models (\mathtt{i},\mathtt{i}) : \mathtt{int}} \ (\textsc{Int}) \qquad \frac{}{\Gamma \models (\mathtt{b},\mathtt{b}) : \mathtt{bool}} \ (\textsc{Bool}) \qquad \frac{\Gamma(\mathtt{id}) = t}{\Gamma \models (\mathtt{id},\mathtt{id}) \ : \ t} \ (\textsc{Id})$$

$$\frac{\mathsf{sign}(\mathtt{r}) \prec s \quad \mathsf{ufp}(\mathtt{r}) \leq u}{\Gamma \models (\mathtt{r\{s,u,p\}},\mathtt{r\{s,u,p\}}) \ : \ \mathtt{real\{s,u,p\}}} \ (\textsc{SReal}) \qquad \frac{|v_{\mathbb{R}} - v_{\mathbb{F}}| < 2^{u-p+1}}{\Gamma \models (v_{\mathbb{F}}, v_{\mathbb{R}}) \ : \ \mathtt{real\{s,u,p\}}} \ (\textsc{VReal})$$

$$\frac{\Gamma \models (e_{1\mathbb{F}}, e_{1\mathbb{R}}) : \mathtt{real\{s_1,u_1,p_1\}} \qquad \Gamma \models (e_{2\mathbb{F}}, e_{2\mathbb{R}}) : \mathtt{real\{s_1,u_1,p_1\}} \qquad * \in \{+,-,\times,\div\}}{\Gamma \models (e_{1\mathbb{F}} * e_{2\mathbb{F}}, e_{1\mathbb{R}} * e_{2\mathbb{R}}) : \mathtt{real}\{\mathcal{S}_*(\mathtt{s_1,u_1,s_2,u_2}), \mathcal{U}_*(\mathtt{s_1,u_1,s_2,u_2}), \mathcal{P}_*(\mathtt{s_1,u_1,p_1,s_2,u_2,p_2})\}} \ (\textsc{ROp})$$

$$\frac{\Gamma \models (e_{1\mathbb{F}}, e_{1\mathbb{R}}) : \mathtt{real\{s_1,u,p+1\}} \qquad \Gamma \models (e_{2\mathbb{F}}, e_{2\mathbb{R}}) : \mathtt{real\{s_1,u,p+1\}} \qquad * \in \{<,>\}}{\Gamma \models (e_{1\mathbb{F}} \bowtie_{u,p} e_{2\mathbb{F}}, e_{1\mathbb{R}} \bowtie_{u,p} e_{2\mathbb{R}}) : \mathtt{bool}} \ (\textsc{RCmp})$$

$$\frac{\Gamma \models (e_{1\mathbb{F}}, e_{1\mathbb{R}}) : \mathtt{int} \qquad \Gamma \models (e_{2\mathbb{F}}, e_{2\mathbb{R}}) : \mathtt{int} \qquad *_{-} \in \{+_{-}, -_{-}, \times_{-}, \div_{-}\}}{\Gamma \models (e_{1\mathbb{F}} *_{-} e_{2\mathbb{F}}, e_{1\mathbb{R}} *_{-} e_{2\mathbb{R}}) : \mathtt{int}} \ (\textsc{IntOp})$$

$$\frac{\Gamma \models (e_{1\mathbb{F}}, e_{1\mathbb{R}}) : t \qquad \Gamma \models (e_{2\mathbb{F}}, e_{2\mathbb{R}}) : t \qquad t \neq \mathtt{real\{s,u,p\}} \qquad \bowtie \in \{=,\neq,<,>,\leq,\geq\}}{\Gamma \models (e_{1\mathbb{F}} \bowtie e_{2\mathbb{F}}, e_{1\mathbb{R}} \bowtie e_{2\mathbb{R}}) : \mathtt{bool}} \ (\textsc{ACmp})$$

$$\frac{\Gamma \models (e_{0\mathbb{F}}, e_{0\mathbb{R}}) \ : \ \mathtt{bool} \qquad \Gamma \models (e_{1\mathbb{F}}, e_{1\mathbb{R}}) \ : \ t_1 \qquad \Gamma \models (e_{2\mathbb{F}}, e_{2\mathbb{R}}) \ : \ t_2 \qquad t = t_1 \sqcup t_2}{\Gamma \models (\mathtt{if}\ e_{0\mathbb{F}}\ \mathtt{then}\ e_{\mathbb{F}}1\ \mathtt{else}\ e_{2\mathbb{F}}, \mathtt{if}\ e_{0\mathbb{R}}\ \mathtt{then}\ e_{1\mathbb{R}}\ \mathtt{else}\ e_{2\mathbb{R}}) \ : \ t} \ (\textsc{Cond})$$

$$\frac{\Gamma, x : t_1 \models (e_{\mathbb{F}}, e_{\mathbb{R}}) : t_2}{\Gamma \models (\lambda x.e_{\mathbb{F}}, \lambda x.e_{\mathbb{R}}) : \Pi x : t_1.t_2} \ (\textsc{Abs}) \qquad \frac{\Gamma, x : t_1, f : \Pi.y : t_1.t_2 \models (e_{\mathbb{F}}, e_{\mathbb{R}}) : t_2}{\Gamma \models (\mathtt{rec}\ f\ x.e_{\mathbb{F}}, \mathtt{rec}\ f\ x.e_{\mathbb{R}}) : \Pi x : t_1.t_2} \ (\textsc{Rec})$$

$$\frac{\Gamma \models (e_{1\mathbb{F}}, e_{1\mathbb{R}}) : \Pi x : t_0.t_1 \qquad \Gamma \models (e_{2\mathbb{F}}, e_{2\mathbb{R}}) : t_2 \qquad t_2 \sqsubseteq t_0}{\Gamma \models (e_{1\mathbb{F}}\ e_{2\mathbb{F}}, e_{1\mathbb{R}}\ e_{2\mathbb{R}}) : t_1[x \mapsto e_2]} \ (\textsc{App})$$

Fig. 7. Simulation relation $\models$ used in our subject reduction theorem.

$|v_{\mathbb{R}} - v_{\mathbb{F}}| < 2^{u-p+1}$. It is easy to show, by examination of the rules of Figs. 2 and 7 that

$$\Gamma \models (e_{\mathbb{F}}, e_{\mathbb{R}}) \ : \ t \Longrightarrow \Gamma \vdash e_{\mathbb{F}} \ : \ t. \tag{12}$$

We introduce now Lemma 3 which asserts the soundness of the type system for one reduction step. Basically, this lemma states that types are preserved by reduction and that concerning the values of type `real`, the distance between the finite precision value and the exact value is less than the ulp given by the type.

Lemma 3 (Weak subject reduction). *If* $\Gamma \models (e_{\mathbb{F}}, e_{\mathbb{R}}) \ : t$ *and if* $e_{\mathbb{F}} \rightarrow_{\mathbb{F}} e'_{\mathbb{F}}$ *and* $e_{\mathbb{R}} \rightarrow_{\mathbb{R}} e'_{\mathbb{R}}$ *then* $\Gamma \models (e'_{\mathbb{F}}, e'_{\mathbb{R}}) \ : t$.

Proof. By induction on the structure of expressions and case examination on the possible transition rules of Fig. 6.

- If $e_{\mathbb{F}} \equiv e_{\mathbb{R}} \equiv \mathtt{r\{s,u,p\}}$ then $\Gamma \models (\mathtt{r\{s,u,p\}}, \mathtt{r\{s,u,p\}}) \ : \ \mathtt{real\{s,u,p\}}$ and, from the reduction rules (FVal) and (RVal) of Fig. 6, $\mathtt{r\{s,u,p\}} \rightarrow_{\mathbb{F}} v_{\mathbb{F}}$ and $\mathtt{r\{s,u,p\}} \rightarrow_{\mathbb{R}} v_{\mathbb{R}}$ with $|v_{\mathbb{F}} - v_{\mathbb{R}}| < 2^{u-p+1}$. So $\Gamma \models (v_{\mathbb{F}}, v_{\mathbb{R}}) \ : \ \mathtt{real\{s,u,p\}}$.

- If $e_{\mathbb{F}} \equiv e_{0\mathbb{F}} * e_{1\mathbb{F}}$ and $e_{\mathbb{R}} \equiv e_{0\mathbb{R}} * e_{1\mathbb{R}}$ then several cases must be distinguished.
  - If $e_{\mathbb{F}} \equiv v_{0\mathbb{F}} \ * \ v_{1\mathbb{F}}$ and $e_{\mathbb{R}} \equiv v_{0\mathbb{R}} \ * \ v_{1\mathbb{R}}$ then, by induction hypothesis, $\Gamma \models (v_{0\mathbb{F}}, v_{0\mathbb{R}}) \ : \mathtt{real}\{\mathtt{s}_0, \mathtt{u}_0, \mathtt{p}_0\}$, $\Gamma \models (v_{1\mathbb{F}}, v_{1\mathbb{R}}) \ : \mathtt{real}\{\mathtt{s}_1, \mathtt{u}_1, \mathtt{p}_1\}$ and, consequently, from Rule (VREAL),

$$|v_{0\mathbb{R}} - v_{0\mathbb{F}}| < 2^{u_0 - p_0 + 1} \quad \text{and} \quad |v_{1\mathbb{R}} - v_{1\mathbb{F}}| < 2^{u_1 - p_1 + 1}. \tag{13}$$

  Following Fig. 4, the type t of e is

$$\begin{aligned} t = \big(&\Pi \mathtt{s}_1 : \mathtt{int}, \mathtt{u}_1 : \mathtt{int}, \mathtt{p}_1 : \mathtt{int}, \mathtt{s}_2 : \mathtt{int}, \mathtt{u}_2 : \mathtt{int}, \mathtt{p}_2 : \mathtt{int}. \\ &\quad \mathtt{real}\{\mathtt{s}_1, \mathtt{u}_1, \mathtt{p}_1\} \to \mathtt{real}\{\mathtt{s}_2, \mathtt{u}_2, \mathtt{p}_2\} \to \\ &\quad \to \mathtt{real}\{\mathcal{S}_*(\mathtt{s}_1, \mathtt{u}_1, \mathtt{s}_2, \mathtt{u}_2), \mathcal{U}_*(\mathtt{s}_1, \mathtt{u}_1, \mathtt{s}_2, \mathtt{u}_2), \mathcal{P}_*(\mathtt{s}_1, \mathtt{u}_1, \mathtt{p}_1, \mathtt{s}_2, \mathtt{u}_2, \mathtt{p}_2)\} \\ &\big) \ \mathtt{s}_1 \ \mathtt{u}_1 \ \mathtt{p}_1 \ \mathtt{s}_2 \ \mathtt{u}_2 \ \mathtt{p}_2, \\ =\ & \mathtt{real}\{\mathcal{S}_*(\mathtt{s}_1, \mathtt{u}_1, \mathtt{s}_2, \mathtt{u}_2), \mathcal{U}_*(\mathtt{s}_1, \mathtt{u}_1, \mathtt{s}_2, \mathtt{u}_2), \mathcal{P}_*(\mathtt{s}_1, \mathtt{u}_1, \mathtt{p}_1, \mathtt{s}_2, \mathtt{u}_2, \mathtt{p}_2)\} \\ =\ & \mathtt{real}\{\mathtt{s}, \mathtt{u}, \mathtt{p}\} \end{aligned}$$

  By Rule (OP), $e \to_{\mathbb{F}} v_{\mathbb{F}}$ and $e \to_{\mathbb{R}} v_{\mathbb{R}}$ and, by Theorem 1, with the assumptions of Eq. (13), we know that $|v_{\mathbb{R}} - v_{\mathbb{F}}| < 2^{u-p+1}$. Consequently, $\Gamma \models (v_{\mathbb{F}}, v_{\mathbb{R}}) \ : \ \mathtt{real}\{\mathtt{s}, \mathtt{u}, \mathtt{p}\}$.
  - If $e_{\mathbb{F}} \equiv v_{0\mathbb{F}} \ * \ v_{1\mathbb{F}}$ and $e_{\mathbb{R}} \equiv v_{0\mathbb{R}} \ * \ v_{1\mathbb{R}}$ with $\Gamma \models (v_0, v_1) \ \mathtt{int}$ then, by Rule (Op), $e \to (v, v)$ and, by Eq. (7), $\Gamma \vdash v \ \mathtt{int}$. If $e \equiv e_0 * e_1$ then, by Rule (Op1), $e \to e_0 * e_1'$ and we conclude by induction hypothesis. The case $e \equiv e_0 * \ v_1$ is similar to the former one.
- If $e_{\mathbb{F}} \equiv e_{0\mathbb{F}} \bowtie_{u,p} e_{1\mathbb{F}}$ and $e_{\mathbb{R}} \equiv e_{0\mathbb{R}} \bowtie_{u,p} e_{1\mathbb{R}}$ then several cases have to be examined.
  - If $e_{\mathbb{F}} \equiv v_{0\mathbb{F}} \bowtie_{u,p} v_{1\mathbb{F}}$ and $e_{\mathbb{R}} \equiv v_{0\mathbb{R}} \bowtie_{u,p} v_{1\mathbb{R}}$ then by rules (FCmp) and (RCmp) $e_{\mathbb{F}} \to_{\mathbb{F}} b_{\mathbb{F}}$, $e_{\mathbb{R}} \to_{\mathbb{R}} b_{\mathbb{R}}$ with $b_{\mathbb{F}} = v_{0\mathbb{F}} - v_{1\mathbb{F}} \bowtie_{\{u,p\}} 2^{u-p+1}$ and $b_{\mathbb{R}} = v_{0\mathbb{R}} - v_{1\mathbb{R}} \bowtie_{\{u,p\}} 0$. By rule (RCmp) of Fig. 7, $\Gamma \models (v_{0\mathbb{F}}, v_{1\mathbb{F}}) \ \mathtt{real}\{\mathtt{s}, \mathtt{u}, \mathtt{p}\}$ and $\Gamma \models (v_{0\mathbb{R}}, v_{1\mathbb{R}}) \ \mathtt{real}\{\mathtt{s}, \mathtt{u}, \mathtt{p}\}$. Consequently, $|v_{0\mathbb{R}} - v_{0\mathbb{F}}| < 2^{u-p+1}$ and $|v_{1\mathbb{R}} - v_{1\mathbb{F}}| < 2^{u-p+1}$. By combining the former equations, we obtain that $|(v_{0\mathbb{R}} - v_{1\mathbb{R}}) - (v_{0\mathbb{F}} - v_{1\mathbb{F}})| < 2^{u-p}$. Consequently, $b_{\mathbb{F}} = b_{\mathbb{R}}$ and we conclude that $\Gamma \models (b_{\mathbb{F}}, b_{\mathbb{R}}) \ \mathtt{bool}$.
  - The other cases for $e_{\mathbb{F}} \equiv e_{0\mathbb{F}} \bowtie_{u,p} e_{1\mathbb{F}}$ are similar to the cases $e_{\mathbb{F}} \equiv v_{0\mathbb{F}} * v_{1\mathbb{F}}$ examined previously.
- The other cases simply follow the structure of the terms, by application of the induction hypothesis. □

Let $\to_{\mathbb{F}}^*$ (resp. $\to_{\mathbb{R}}^*$) denote the reflexive transitive closure of $\to_{\mathbb{F}}$ (resp. $\to_{\mathbb{R}}$). Theorem 2 expresses the soundness of our type system for sequences of reduction of arbitrary length.

Theorem 2 (Subject reduction). *If $\Gamma \models (e_{\mathbb{F}}, e_{\mathbb{R}}) : t$ and if $e_{\mathbb{F}} \to_{\mathbb{F}}^* e_{\mathbb{F}}'$ and $e_{\mathbb{R}} \to_{\mathbb{R}}^* e_{\mathbb{R}}'$ then $\Gamma \models (e_{\mathbb{F}}', e_{\mathbb{R}}') : t$.*

Proof. By induction on the length of the reduction sequence, using Lemma 3. □

Theorem 2 asserts the soundness of our type system. It states that the evaluation of an expression of type $\mathtt{real}\{\mathtt{s}, \mathtt{u}, \mathtt{p}\}$ yields a result of accuracy 2^{u-p+1}.

5 Experiments

In this section, we report some experiments showing how our type system behaves in practice. Section 5.1 presents Numl implementations of usual mathematical formulas while Sect. 5.2 introduce a larger example demonstrating the expressive power of our type system.

5.1 Usual Mathematical Formulas

Our first examples concern usual mathematical formulas, to compute the volume of geometrical objects or formulas related to polynomials. These examples aim at showing that usual mathematical formulas are typable in our system. We start with the volume of the sphere and of the cone.

```
> let sphere r = (4.0 / 3.0) * 3.1415926{+,1,20} * r * r * r ;;
val sphere : real{'a,'b,'c} -> real{<expr>,<expr>,<expr>} = <fun>

> sphere 1.0 ;;
- : real{+,7,20} = 4.188

> let cone r h = (3.1415926{+,1,20} * r * r* h) / 3.0 ;;
val cone : real{'a,'b,'c} -> real{'a,'b,'c}
           -> real{<expr>,<expr>,<expr>} = <fun>

> cone 1.0 1.0 ;;
- : real{+,4,20} = 1.0472
```

We repeatedly define the function sphere with more precision in order to show the impact on the accuracy of the results. Note that the results now have 15 digits instead of the former 5 digits.

```
> let sphere r = (4.0 / 3.0) * 3.1415926535897932{+,1,53} * r * r * r ;;
val sphere : real{'a,'b,'c} -> real{<expr>,<expr>,<expr>} = <fun>

> sphere 1.0 ;;
- : real{+,7,52} = 4.1887902047863
```

The next examples concern polynomials. We start with the computation of the discriminant of a second degree polynomial.

```
> let discriminant a b c = b * b - 4.0 * a * c ;;
val discriminant : real{'a,'b,'c} -> real{'d,'e,'f} -> real{'g,'h,'i}
                   -> real{<expr>,<expr>,<expr>} = <fun>

> discriminant 2.0 -11.0 15.0 ;;
- : real{+,8,52} = 1.000000000000
```

Our last example concerning usual formulas is the Taylor series development of the sine function. In the code below, observe that the accuracy of the result is correlated to the accuracy of the argument. As mentioned in Sect. 2, error methods are neglected, only the errors due to the finite precision are calculated (indeed, $\sin\frac{\pi}{8} = 0.382683432\ldots$).

```
let sin x = x - ((x * x * x) / 3.0) + ((x * x * x * x * x) / 120.0) ;;
val sin : real{'a,'b,'c} -> real{<expr>,<expr>,<expr>} = <fun>

> sin (3.14{1,6} / 8.0) ;;
- : real{*,0,6} = 0.3

> sin (3.14159{1,18} / 8.0) ;;
- : real{*,0,18} = 0.37259
```

5.2 Newton-Raphson Method

In this section, we introduce a larger example to compute the zero of a function using the Newton-Raphson method. This example, which involves several higher order functions, shows the expressiveness of our type system. In the programming session below, we first define a higher order function `deriv` which takes as argument a function and computes its numerical derivative at a given point. Then we define a function `g` and compute the value of its derivative at point 2.0. Next, by partial application, we build a function computing the derivative of `g` at any point. Finally, we define a function `newton` which searches the zero of a function. The `newton` function is also an higher order function taking as argument the function for which a zero has to be found and its derivative.

```
> let deriv f x h = ((f (x + h)) - (f x)) / h ;;
val deriv : (real{<expr>,<expr>,<expr>} -> real{'a,'b,'c})
            -> real{<expr>,<expr>,<expr>} -> real{'d,'e,'f}
            -> real{<expr>,<expr>,<expr>} = <fun>

> let g x = (x*x) - (5.0*x) + 6.0 ;;
val g : real{'a,'b,'c} -> real{<expr>,<expr>,<expr>} = <fun>

> deriv g 2.0 0.01 ;;
- : real{*,5,51} = -0.9900000000000

> let gprime x = deriv g x 0.01 ;;
val gprime : real{<expr>,<expr>,<expr>} -> real{<expr>,<expr>,<expr>} = <fun>

> let rec newton x xold f fprime = if ((abs (x-xold))<0.01{*,10,20}) then x
                                   else newton (x-((f x)/(fprime x))) x f fprime ;;
val newton : real{*,10,21} -> real{0,10,20} -> (real{*,10,21} -> real{'a,'b,'c})
            -> (real{*,10,21} -> real{'d,'e,'f}) -> real{*,10,21} = <fun>

> newton 9.0 0.0 g gprime ;;
- : real{*,10,21} = 3.0001
```

We call the `newton` function with our function `g` and its derivative computed by partial application of the `deriv` function. We obtain a root of our polynomial `g` with a guaranteed accuracy. Note that while Newton-Raphson method converges quadratically in the reals, numerical errors may perturb the process [4].

6 Conclusion

In this article, we have introduced a dependent type system able to infer the accuracy of numerical computations. Our type system allows one to type non-trivial programs corresponding to implementations of classical numerical analysis methods. Unstable computations are rejected by the type system. The consistency of typed programs is ensured by a subject reduction theorem. To our knowledge, this is the first type system dedicated to numerical accuracy. We believe that this approach has many advantages going from early debugging to compiler optimizations. Indeed, we believe that the usual type `float` proposed by usual `ML` implementations, and which is a simple clone of the type `int`, is too poor for numerical computations. We also believe that this approach is a credible alternative to static analysis techniques for numerical precision [6,9,18]. For the developer, our type system introduces few changes in the programming style, limited to giving the accuracy of the inputs of the accuracy of comparisons to allow the typing of certain recursive functions.

A first perspective to the present work is the implementation of a compiler for `Numl`. We aim at using the type information to select the most appropriate formats (the IEEE754 formats of Fig. 1, multiple precisions numbers of the GMP library when needed or requested by the user or fixed-point numbers.) In the longer term, we also aim at introducing safe compile-time optimizations based on type preservation: an expression may be safely (from the accuracy point of view) substituted to another expression as long as both expressions are mathematically equivalent and that the new expression has a greater type than the older one in the sense of Eq. (6). Finally, a second perspective is to integrate our type system into other applicative languages. In particular, it would be of great interest to have such a type system inside a language used to build critical embedded systems such as the synchronous language `Lustre` [3]. In this context numerical accuracy requirements are strong and difficult to obtain. Our type system could be integrated naturally inside `Lustre` or similar languages.

References

1. ANSI/IEEE: IEEE Standard for Binary Floating-point Arithmetic (2008)
2. Atkinson, K.: An Introduction to Numerical Analysis, 2nd edn. Wiley, Hoboken (1989)
3. Caspi, P., Pilaud, D., Halbwachs, N., Plaice, J.: LUSTRE: a declarative language for programming synchronous systems. In: POPL, pp. 178–188. ACM Press (1987)
4. Damouche, N., Martel, M., Chapoutot, A.: Impact of accuracy optimization on the convergence of numerical iterative methods. In: Falaschi, M. (ed.) LOPSTR 2015. LNCS, vol. 9527, pp. 143–160. Springer, Cham (2015). https://doi.org/10.1007/978-3-319-27436-2_9
5. Damouche, N., Martel, M., Chapoutot, A.: Improving the numerical accuracy of programs by automatic transformation. STTT **19**(4), 427–448 (2017)
6. Darulova, E., Kuncak, V.: Sound compilation of reals. In: POPL 2014, pp. 235–248. ACM (2014)
7. Denis, C., de Oliveira Castro, P., Petit, E.: Verificarlo: checking floating point accuracy through Monte Carlo arithmetic. In: ARITH 2016, pp. 55–62. IEEE (2016)
8. Franco, A.D., Guo, H., Rubio-González, C.: A comprehensive study of real-world numerical bug characteristics. In: ASE, pp. 509–519. IEEE (2017)

9. Goubault, E.: Static analysis by abstract interpretation of numerical programs and systems, and FLUCTUAT. In: Logozzo, F., Fähndrich, M. (eds.) SAS 2013. LNCS, vol. 7935, pp. 1–3. Springer, Heidelberg (2013). https://doi.org/10.1007/978-3-642-38856-9_1
10. Mentor Graphics Algorithmic C Datatypes, Software Version 2.6 edn. (2011). http://www.mentor.com/esl/catapult/algorithmic
11. Lam, M.O., Hollingsworth, J.K., de Supinski, B.R., LeGendre, M.P.: Automatically adapting programs for mixed-precision floating-point computation. In: Supercomputing, ICS 2013, pp. 369–378. ACM (2013)
12. Martel, M.: Floating-point format inference in mixed-precision. In: Barrett, C., Davies, M., Kahsai, T. (eds.) NFM 2017. LNCS, vol. 10227, pp. 230–246. Springer, Cham (2017). https://doi.org/10.1007/978-3-319-57288-8_16
13. Milner, R., Harper, R., MacQueen, D., Tofte, M.: The Definition of Standard ML. MIT Press, Cambridge (1997)
14. Panchekha, P., Sanchez-Stern, A., Wilcox, J.R., Tatlock, Z.: Automatically improving accuracy for floating point expressions. In: PLDI, pp. 1–11. ACM (2015)
15. Pierce, B.C.: Types and Programming Languages. MIT Press, Cambridge (2002)
16. Pierce, B.C. (ed.): Advanced Topics in Types and Programming Languages. MIT Press, Cambridge (2004)
17. Rubio-Gonzalez, C., et al.: Precimonious: tuning assistant for floating-point precision. In: HPCNSA, pp. 27:1–27:12. ACM (2013)
18. Solovyev, A., Jacobsen, C., Rakamarić, Z., Gopalakrishnan, G.: Rigorous estimation of floating-point round-off errors with symbolic taylor expansions. In: Bjørner, N., de Boer, F. (eds.) FM 2015. LNCS, vol. 9109, pp. 532–550. Springer, Cham (2015). https://doi.org/10.1007/978-3-319-19249-9_33

Type Capabilities for Object-Oriented Programming Languages

Xi Wu[1(✉)], Yi Lu[2], Patrick A. Meiring[1], Ian J. Hayes[1], and Larissa A. Meinicke[1]

[1] School of ITEE, The University of Queensland, Brisbane 4072, Australia
{xi.wu,p.meiring,l.meinicke}@uq.edu.au, Ian.Hayes@itee.uq.edu.au
[2] Oracle Labs, Brisbane 4000, Australia
yi.x.lu@oracle.com

Abstract. Capabilities are used to control access to system resources. In modern programming languages that execute code with different levels of trust in the same process, the propagation of such capabilities must be controlled so that they cannot unintentionally be obtained by unauthorised code. In this paper, we present a statically-checked type system for object-oriented programming languages which guarantees that capabilities are restricted to authorised code. Capabilities are regarded as types that are granted to code based on a user-defined policy file (similar to that used by Java). In order to provide a finer-grained access control, the type system supports parameterised capabilities to more precisely identify system resources. The approach is illustrated using file-access examples.

Keywords: Capability-based security · Access control
Authorisation · Parameterisation · Programming language

1 Introduction

The concept of capability-based security [5,16], in which a capability is regarded as a communicable and unforgeable token of authority, has been used in operating systems. A process inside the system, which possesses a capability, is authorised to use the referenced object according to the operations that are specified on that capability. In this model, the acquisition of capabilities is limited by authorisation at the process-level, and forgery is prevented by storing capabilities in a memory region protected from direct application writes. Capabilities can be shared, but only through operating system APIs, which can enforce the correct passing of capabilities based on the Principle Of Least Privilege (POLP) [15]. In operating systems, processes are mostly isolated (i.e., run in different memory spaces and can only communicate via restricted channels), and so it is relatively straight-forward to ensure that capabilities are not leaked to unauthorised processes.

The goal of our work is provide access control at the programming-language level using a capability-based approach. However, although capabilities may also be used at the application (i.e. programming language) level to control access to

J. Sun and M. Sun (Eds.): ICFEM 2018, LNCS 11232, pp. 215–230, 2018.
https://doi.org/10.1007/978-3-030-02450-5_13

resources, their use in this context is complicated by the fact that both trusted and untrusted code may be executing *within* the same process, and so it is necessary to control the flow of capabilities within the same process itself. This is challenging because of the use of shared memory and pointers, and the level of interaction between trusted and untrusted code. In this context, *language-based security* [7,14] approaches may be used to prevent vulnerabilities that are not addressed by process-based access control at the operating system level.

One of the main approaches to handling capabilities in programming languages is the object capability model. It was first proposed by Dennis and Horn [1] and is currently supported by secure programming languages such as E [11], Joe-E [9,10] and Caja [12,17]. In this model, a capability is regarded as a reference to an object, which may be used to invoke operations on that object. Such capabilities can only be obtained through a pre-existing chain of references. It provides modularity in code design and ensures reliable encapsulation in code implementation. However, this references-as-capabilities model does not provide an explicit authorisation mechanism or enforce security guarantees.

Java [3] is an object-oriented programming language. It has an access control model for guarding access to resources which relies on programmer discipline to insert security checks, which are then performed at runtime [2,8]. It makes use of a capability-like notion for access to some resources. For example, the class *FileOutputStream* in the Java Class Library (JCL) is like a capability to write to a file in the sense that permission-checking is performed in the constructor of the class. After the class has been instantiated, no further permission checks are required to use the operations of the class, like the *write* method. The Java access control model provides an approach to prevent confused deputy attacks [4] (e.g., unauthorised code accesses security-sensitive code by calling authorised code). However, it is not sufficient to track the propagation of capabilities, which means that Java does not guarantee that capabilities are not obtained and used by unauthorised code.

Capability-based access to Java resources was proposed recently by Hayes et al. [6] with the aim of preventing security flaws as well as tightening security management for access to resources both within JCL and Java applications. In this work, a capability can be viewed as an object with a restricted interface, which contains a set of operations that can be invoked by holders of the capability. In other words, a capability encapsulates what one can do with a resource. For example, a capability *OutCap* with a method *write* for output access to a stream is declared as follows:

capability OutCap { **void** write (**int** b); }

Access to this capability is restricted to code that has a corresponding permission, e.g. permission *write*. The philosophy behind capabilities is that code can only access a resource if it is given an explicit capability to do so: no other access is permitted. Once a capability is created, it has a more restrictive dynamic type than its implementing class and access to the full facilities of the implementing class (e.g., via down casting) is precluded. Thus, classes implementing capabilities are not directly accessible to users and hence cannot be overridden. In this way, only capabilities are open to exploit by untrusted code.

In the original approach proposed by Hayes et al. [6], no solutions were proposed for controlling the propagation of capabilities. The example in Listing 1 demonstrates how this can lead to capabilities escaping to unauthorised code. In the listing, the class *AuthorisedCode* is assumed to have the permissions required to use the file access capability (*FileAccessCap*), and to write to output streams (*OutCap*), while the class *UnauthorisedCode* does not. Because *UnauthorisedCode* does not have the permission to write to streams it cannot directly request the capability *OutCap*. However, this does not prevent the authorised code passing an instance of this capability to the unauthorised code as a parameter in a method call.

Listing 1. Capabilities may escape to unauthorised code

```
public class AuthorisedCode {
  public static void main (String[] args) throws Exception {
    FileAccessCap fileAccess = new RandomAccessFileManager();
    UnauthorisedCode uc = new UnauthorisedCode();
    OutCap out = fileAccess.requestOutCap (filename);
    uc.use(out);
  }
}
public class UnauthorisedCode {
  public void use (OutCap out){
    out.write(temp);
  }
}
```

In practice, permissions granted to a class are parameterised using the targets on which a certain action is allowed. For example, a class that has the permission to write to files may either have: unlimited access to modify any file on the system (denoted "*"); access to modify only files in a particular directory (e.g. "dir/*"); or only a particular file, (e.g. "dir/a.txt") etc. In the original Capability model proposed in [6], there was no mechanism to limit a capability to be used on a particular target. For example, in Listing 1, either the capability *OutCap* is granted to a class, or it is not. There is no way to restrict *OutCap* to only be used to write to a particular file.

Contributions. In this paper, our aim is to adapt capabilities to object-oriented programming languages in a way that (i) controls their propagation, and (ii) allows them to be parameterised in a way that limits their use to particular targets, so that they more closely correspond to the fine-grained permissions that are typically granted to classes.

We use the term "type capabilities" to analogize the term "object capabilities" that restrict capabilities at runtime. The key insight of our work is that, by providing explicit code-level authorisation via a user-defined policy file, we enforce a security guarantee at compile time that capabilities can only be obtained by authorised code. The main contributions are summarized as follows:

Table 1. Syntax of a Java-like language with parameterised capabilities

$CB ::= \textbf{capability } cb(\widetilde{n}) \textbf{ extends } \overline{cb(\widetilde{n})}\ \{\overline{dec}\}$	(*capabilities*)
$C\ ::= \textbf{class } \mathrm{c}(\widetilde{n}) \textbf{ extends } \mathrm{c}(\widetilde{n}) \textbf{ implements } \overline{cb(\widetilde{n})}\ \{\overline{\tau f}; \overline{M}\}$	(*classes*)
$M\ ::= dec\{s\}$	(*methods*)
$dec ::= m(\overline{\tau\, x})$	(*declarations*)
$s\ ::= x = e \mid x.f = x \mid s;\ s \mid x.m(\overline{x}) \mid \textbf{if } x \textbf{ then } s \textbf{ else } s$	(*statements*)
$\mathrm{e}\ ::= \mathrm{x} \mid \mathrm{x.f} \mid \textbf{new } c(\widetilde{\sigma}) \mid (\tau)\, e$	(*expressions*)
$\tau\ ::= \textbf{int} \mid c(\widetilde{\sigma}) \mid cb(\widetilde{\sigma})$	(*types*)
$\sigma\ ::= n \mid \kappa$	(*parameters*)

* We present a type system to enforce the proper use of capabilities by type checking. Capabilities are regarded as types so that we can control the propagation of capabilities by controlling the visibility of their types.
* We provide a security guarantee statically at compile time, reducing the possibility of errors in code as well as runtime overhead. In particular, we guarantee that a method on an object can only be invoked if: (1) the static type of that object is granted to the calling class, and (2) the runtime type of the object is a subtype of its static type.
* We introduce capability types that are parameterised by strings, denoting the targets on which they can be used. It provides a finer-grained access control and identifies system resources more precisely.

Organization. Section 2 gives the abstract syntax of parameterised capabilities for a Java-like core language. In Sect. 3, we illustrate how to enforce the proper use of capabilities statically by a type system and apply our approach on an example of Java file access. Section 4 presents the big-step operational semantics as well as the subject reduction theorem with a security guarantee before we conclude our paper and point out some future directions in Sect. 5.

2 A Java-Like Language with Parameterised Capabilities

Built on the model of capabilities described by Hayes et al. [6], a Java-like core language with parameterised capabilities is shown in Table 1. We choose a minimal set of features that still gives a Java-like feel to the language, i.e., classes, capabilities, inheritance, instance methods and fields, method override, dynamic dispatch and object creation.

In the syntax, the metavariables cb and c range over capability names and class names respectively; f and m range over field names and method names; x ranges over variables, n ranges over final string variables as type parameter names and κ stands for string literals. Names for capabilities, classes, fields and variables are unique in their corresponding defining scopes. For simplicity, we use the notation $\overline{x}$ as a shorthand for the sequence $x_1; ...; x_n$, in which n stands for the length of the sequence and we use semicolon to denote the concatenation of sequences. A sequence can be empty.

A *capability CB*, defined by a new keyword capability, consists of a set of method declarations and it may extend other capabilities. A *class C* is composed of a sequence of fields $\overline{f}$ as well as a sequence of methods $\overline{M}$. We abbreviate sequences of pairs as $\overline{\tau\, f}$ for $\tau_1\, f_1; ...; \tau_n\, f_n$. A class has one super class and may implement a sequence of capabilities. Both capabilities and classes can be parameterised by a string parameter, which limits the targets that these capabilities or classes can be used on. The notation $\widetilde{n}$ (a sequence containing zero or one element) represents that the parameter n is optional: if the parameter is absent then the capabilities or classes can be used on any target.

A *method M* is a declaration *dec*, representing the method signature, followed by a method body s. A method *declaration dec* with the form of $m(\overline{\tau\ x})$ contains the method name m as well as a list of parameters with types. We assume methods are not overloaded, that is, they are distinguished via their names rather than their signatures.

A *statement s* is distinguished from an *expression* since it does not contain return values. It can be an assignment $x = e$, a field assignment $x.f = x$, a sequential composition $s; s$, a conditional choice **if** x **then** s **else** s or a parameterised method invocation $x.m(\overline{x})$. An *expression e* can be a variable x, a class field $x.f$ or a creation expression **new** $c(\widetilde{\sigma})$, which creates a new object of class c with a type parameter $\widetilde{\sigma}$. It can also be a type cast $(\tau)\ e$, which stands for casting the type of the expression e into type τ. A *type* τ can be an integer **int**, a class type $c(\widetilde{\sigma})$ or a capability type $cb(\widetilde{\sigma})$. σ is a string type parameter, which may be a final string variable or a string literal.

A *program P* is a triple (CT, CBT, s) of a class table, a capability table and a statement used as the program entry point. A class table CT is a mapping from class names to class declarations. Similarly, a capability table CBT is a mapping from capability names to capability declarations. For simplicity, the semantic rules in Sects. 3 and 4 are written with respect to a fixed program P including a fixed class table CT and a fixed capability table CBT. We assume that for every class c (including class **Object**) appearing in CT, we have $c \in dom(CT)$ and we simply write"**class** $c(\widetilde{n})$..." to abbreviate $CT(c) =$ **class** $c(\widetilde{n})$.... Likewise, for every capability cb appearing in CBT, we have $cb \in dom(CBT)$ and we use "**capability** $cb(\widetilde{n})$..." to abbreviate $CBT(cb) =$ **capability** $cb(\widetilde{n})$....

Example. The parameterised capability for output access to a stream is given in Listing 2, as well as its implementing class and an application class.

Classes implementing a parameterised capability are also parameterised with the same *string* variable. Class $OutCapImp(n)$ in Listing 2 implements the capability $OutCap(n)$, which provides a method to write a file. We assume the implementing class always has at least one constructor (maybe by default) taking n as its parameter, hence the instantiation of the class is restricted to the specific target file name. For example, in Listing 2, the class *Application* instantiates

Listing 2. The parameterised capability for file output stream

```
capability OutCap(n){ write(int b) }

class OutCapImp(n) implements OutCap(n){
    OutCapImp(n) { ... }; // open the file on path 'n'
    write(int b) { ... }
}
class Application{
    main() {
        OutCap("dir/A.txt") out = new OutCapImp("dir/A.txt")
    }
}
```

OutCap with the string ***"dir/A.txt"***, restricting the instance *out* to only write to the text file "A.txt" under the directory *dir*.

3 Static Semantics

In this section, we give a set of inference rules to formalize the static semantics of our type system. Based on a user-defined policy file, we control type visibility to avoid capabilities escaping to unauthorised code, and to restrict the targets that these capabilities can be used on.

Table 2. Subtyping rules

$$\tau <: \tau \qquad \frac{cb'_i(\widetilde{n}'_i) \in \overline{cb'(\widetilde{n}')} \quad \textbf{capability}\ cb(\widetilde{n})\ \textbf{extends}\ \overline{cb'(\widetilde{n}')}\ \{...\} \quad |\widetilde{\sigma}| = |\widetilde{n}| \quad \widetilde{\sigma}'_i = \text{truncate}(\widetilde{\sigma}, |\widetilde{n}'_i|)}{cb(\widetilde{\sigma}) <: cb'_i(\widetilde{\sigma}'_i)}$$

$$\frac{\tau_1 <: \tau_2 \quad \tau_2 <: \tau_3}{\tau_1 <: \tau_3} \qquad \frac{c \neq \textbf{Object} \quad \textbf{class}\ c(\widetilde{n})\ \textbf{extends}\ c'(\widetilde{n}') ...\ \{...\} \quad |\widetilde{\sigma}| = |\widetilde{n}| \quad \widetilde{\sigma}' = \text{truncate}(\widetilde{\sigma}, |\widetilde{n}'|)}{c(\widetilde{\sigma}) <: c'(\widetilde{\sigma}')}$$

$$\frac{cb_i(\widetilde{n}_i) \in \overline{cb(\widetilde{n})} \quad \textbf{class}\ c(\widetilde{n})\ \textbf{extends}\ c'(\widetilde{n}')\ \textbf{implements}\ \overline{cb(\widetilde{n})}\ \{...\} \quad |\widetilde{\sigma}| = |\widetilde{n}| \quad \widetilde{\sigma}_i = \text{truncate}(\widetilde{\sigma}, |\widetilde{n}_i|)}{c(\widetilde{\sigma}) <: cb_i(\widetilde{\sigma}_i)}$$

3.1 Subtyping Rules and Look up Functions

Subtyping rules are given in Table 2. They include the reflexive and transitive closure of the direct subclass (and subcapability) relations. If a class $c(\widetilde{n})$ implements a capability $cb(\widetilde{n})$, for all instantiations $\widetilde{\sigma}$ of parameter $\widetilde{n}$, $c(\widetilde{\sigma})$ is also a

Table 3. Look up functions on fields and methods

$$\text{fields}(\textbf{Object}) = \bullet \quad \text{methods}(\textbf{Object}) = \bullet \quad \text{methodsigs}(\textbf{Object}) = \bullet$$

$$\frac{\textbf{class}\; c(\widetilde{n})\;\textbf{extends}\; c'(\widetilde{n}')\;\{\overline{\tau_0\, f;}\;\overline{m(\overline{\tau\, x})\{s\}}\} \quad c \neq \textbf{Object} \quad \widetilde{\sigma}' = \text{truncate}(\widetilde{\sigma}, |\widetilde{n}'|)}{\begin{array}{c}\text{fields}(c(\widetilde{\sigma})) = \text{fields}(c'(\widetilde{\sigma}')) \oplus \{\overline{f \mapsto \tau_{0}{}_{[\widetilde{n\backslash\sigma}]}}\} \\ \text{methods}(c(\widetilde{\sigma})) = \text{methods}(c'(\widetilde{\sigma}')) \oplus \{\overline{m \mapsto (c(\widetilde{\sigma}), (\overline{\tau_{[\widetilde{n\backslash\sigma}]}\, x})\{s_{[\widetilde{n\backslash\sigma}]}\})}\} \\ \text{methodsigs}(c(\widetilde{\sigma})) = \text{methodsigs}(c'(\widetilde{\sigma}')) \oplus \{\overline{m \mapsto (\overline{\tau_{[\widetilde{n\backslash\sigma}]}})}\}\end{array}}$$

$$\frac{\textbf{capability}\; cb(\widetilde{n})\;\textbf{extends}\;\overline{cb'(\widetilde{n}')}\;\{\overline{m(\overline{\tau\, x})}\} \quad \overline{\widetilde{\sigma}' = \text{truncate}(\widetilde{\sigma}, |\widetilde{n}'|)}}{\text{methodsigs}(cb(\widetilde{\sigma})) = \overline{\text{methodsigs}(cb'(\widetilde{\sigma}'))} \oplus \{\overline{m \mapsto (\overline{\tau_{[\widetilde{n\backslash\sigma}]}})}\}}$$

subtype of $cb(\widetilde{\sigma})$. Here, the sequence of the substitution value $\widetilde{\sigma}$ has the same length as the one of the string parameter $\widetilde{n}$ (denoted as $|\widetilde{\sigma}| = |\widetilde{n}|$). The rules use the function *truncate*, which shortens a sequence to the given length, to generalise instantiation to cases where classes (or capabilities) extend other classes (or capabilities) with fewer (i.e., zero) type parameters.

Table 3 gives the look up functions for accessing field and method definitions and declarations. The function *fields* is used to look up all field definitions (as a mapping from field names to types) in a class, including any field inherited from its superclass(es). The functions *methodsigs* and *methods* return mappings from method names to the method signatures and declarations (respectively) of methods in a type. Specifically, the function *methods* provides a tuple for each method, which is composed of the class type ($c(\widetilde{\sigma})$) that defined the method body as well as the method definition (of form $(\overline{\tau\, x})\{s\}$). We use the operator $\oplus$ to denote the addition of two mappings, where elements in the right-hand side mapping override (take precedence over) elements in the left-hand side mapping. The notation $t_{[\widetilde{n\backslash\sigma}]}$ denotes the substitution of any reference to type parameter n for σ within the preceding term t.

3.2 Well-Formedness and Typing Rules

A user-defined policy file Σ is a mapping from a class c (or a capability cb) to the set $\mathcal{G}$ of permissions (i.e., well-formed capabilities and well-formed classes) granted to that class (or capability). The transitive closure $\mathcal{G}^+$ of the set $\mathcal{G}$ can be found in Definition 1. It is defined with respect to $\preceq$, which is a partial order relation on strings. For example, "dir/A.txt" $\preceq$ "dir/*" and "dir/*" $\preceq$ "*".

Definition 1 (Transitive Closure of $\mathcal{G}$). *For the permission set $\mathcal{G}$ of a class (or a capability), class c, capability cb, types τ and τ', string literals κ and κ', and type parameter name n, the transitive closure of $\mathcal{G}$, denoted as $\mathcal{G}^+$, is defined as follows: (1) if $\tau \in \mathcal{G}$, then we have $\tau \in \mathcal{G}^+$; (2) if $\tau \in \mathcal{G}$ and $\tau <: \tau'$, then*

Table 4. Well-formedness rules for program, capabilities and classes

All rules are shown with respect to a fixed program $P = (CT, CBT, s)$.

Program

$$\frac{\mathcal{G} \vdash s \quad \forall\, c \in \mathrm{dom}(CT) \cdot \Sigma \vdash CT(c) \quad \forall\, cb \in \mathrm{dom}(CBT) \cdot \Sigma \vdash CBT(cb)}{\Sigma \vdash P}$$

Capabilities

$$\frac{\overline{\boldsymbol{\tau \in (\Sigma(cb))^{+}}}}{\Sigma\ cb(\widetilde{n}) \vdash m(\overline{\tau\, x})}$$

$$\frac{\begin{array}{c}\overline{\Sigma\ cb(\widetilde{n}) \vdash m_i(\overline{\tau\, x})} \quad \mathrm{referencedtypevars}(CBT(cb)) \subseteq \{\widetilde{n}\} \\ \left(\begin{array}{c}\forall\, cb_j'(\widetilde{n_j}') \in \overline{cb'(\widetilde{n}')}, \forall\, m_k \in \mathrm{dom}(\mathrm{methodsigs}(cb_j'(\widetilde{n_j}'))) \cdot \\ \mathbf{capability}\, cb_j'(\widetilde{n_j}'') \ldots \wedge \boldsymbol{\widetilde{n_j}' = \mathrm{truncate}(\widetilde{n}, |\widetilde{n_j}''|)} \wedge cb_j'(\widetilde{n_j}') \not<: cb(\widetilde{n}) \wedge \\ \mathrm{methodsigs}(cb_j'(\widetilde{n_j}'))(m_k) = \mathrm{methodsigs}(cb(\widetilde{n}))(m_k)\end{array}\right)\end{array}}{\Sigma \vdash \mathbf{capability}\ cb(\widetilde{n})\ \mathbf{extends}\ \overline{cb'(\widetilde{n}')}\{\overline{m_i(\overline{\tau\, x})}\}}$$

Classes

$$\frac{\overline{\boldsymbol{\tau \in (\Sigma(c))^{+}}} \quad \Sigma(c)\,(\overline{\tau\, x}) \vdash s}{\Sigma\ c(\widetilde{n}) \vdash m(\overline{\tau\, x})\{s\}}$$

$$\frac{\begin{array}{c}\overline{\boldsymbol{\tau_0 \in (\Sigma(c))^{+}}} \quad \overline{\Sigma\ c(\widetilde{n}) \vdash m_j(\overline{\tau\, x})\{s\}} \quad \mathrm{referencedtypevars}(CT(c)) \subseteq \{\widetilde{n}\} \\ c \neq \mathbf{Object} \quad \mathbf{class}\, c'(\widetilde{n}''') \ldots \quad \boldsymbol{\widetilde{n}' = \mathrm{truncate}(\widetilde{n}, |\widetilde{n}'''|)} \quad c'(\widetilde{n}') \not<: c(\widetilde{n}) \\ \forall\, m_q \in \mathrm{dom}(\mathrm{methodsigs}(c'(\widetilde{n}'))) \cdot \mathrm{methodsigs}(c'(\widetilde{n}'))(m_q) = \mathrm{methodsigs}(c(\widetilde{n}))(m_q) \\ \forall\, f_q \in \mathrm{dom}(\mathrm{fields}(c'(\widetilde{n}'))) \cdot \mathrm{fields}(c'(\widetilde{n}'))(f_q) = \mathrm{fields}(c(\widetilde{n}))(f_q) \\ \left(\begin{array}{c}\forall\, cb_k(\widetilde{n_k}'') \in \overline{cb(\widetilde{n}'')}, \forall\, m_o \in \mathrm{dom}(\mathrm{methodsigs}(cb_k(\widetilde{n_k}''))) \cdot \\ \mathbf{capability}\ cb_k(\widetilde{n_k}^{i}) \wedge \boldsymbol{\widetilde{n_k}'' = \mathrm{truncate}(\widetilde{n}, |\widetilde{n_k}^{i}|)} \wedge cb_k(\widetilde{n_k}'') \not<: c(\widetilde{n}) \wedge \\ \mathrm{methodsigs}(cb_k(\widetilde{n_k}''))(m_o) = \mathrm{methodsigs}(c(\widetilde{n}))(m_o)\end{array}\right)\end{array}}{\Sigma \vdash \mathbf{class}\ c(\widetilde{n})\ \mathbf{extends}\ c'(\widetilde{n}')\ \mathbf{implements}\ \overline{cb(\widetilde{n}'')}\{\overline{\tau_0\, f};\ \overline{m_j(\overline{\tau\, x})\{s\}}\}}$$

we have $\tau' \in \mathcal{G}^+$; (3) if $c(\kappa) \in \mathcal{G}$ and $\kappa' \preceq \kappa$, then we have $c(\kappa') \in \mathcal{G}^+$; (4) if $cb(\kappa) \in \mathcal{G}$ and $\kappa' \preceq \kappa$, then we have $cb(\kappa') \in \mathcal{G}^+$; (5) if $c($""$) \in \mathcal{G}$, then we have $c(n) \in \mathcal{G}^+$; (6) if $cb($"*"$) \in \mathcal{G}$, then we have $cb(n) \in \mathcal{G}^+$.*

Example. Let $\mathcal{G} = \{OutCap(\text{"dir/*"})\}$, then we have $OutCap(\text{"dir/*"}) \in \mathcal{G}^+$. Because the relation on strings "dir/A.txt" $\preceq$ "dir/*" is satisfied, according to Definition 1, we have that $OutCap(\text{"dir/A.txt"}) \in \mathcal{G}^+$. Intuitively, if the user allows the code to write any file in the directory *dir* through *OutCap*, then it implicitly allows the code to write the specific text file *A.txt* in that directory.

A typing environment Γ is a finite sequence of bindings $x : \tau$ of variables to types. For the variables in the domain of Γ, $\Gamma(x)$ is the type bound to the variable x. The typing judgement for an expression is of the form $\mathcal{G}\ \Gamma \vdash e : \tau$, which means the expression e with type τ is well-formed in the typing environment Γ, according to the permission set $\mathcal{G}$ granted to the current executing class. The type judgement for a statement is of the form $\mathcal{G}\ \Gamma \vdash s$, which is used for checking whether a statement s is well-formed or not according to the permission set $\mathcal{G}$.

Well-formedness rules for program, capabilities and classes are shown in Table 4. A program P, composed of classes and capabilities, is well-formed based on the user-defined policy file Σ (denoted as $\Sigma \vdash P$) only if all classes and capabilities are well-formed (denoted as $\forall\ c \in \text{dom}(CT) \cdot \Sigma \vdash CT(c)$ and $\forall\ cb \in \text{dom}(CBT) \cdot \Sigma \vdash CBT(cb)$ respectively), as well as the entry point statement of the program is well-formed (denoted as $\mathcal{G} \vdash s$, and $\mathcal{G}$ stands for the permission set granted to the class containing the entry point statement).

The other two group rules in Table 4 are used for checking the well-formedness of capabilities and classes respectively. Traditional well-formedness checking considers that statements of the method body are well-formed, signatures of overriding methods are compatible and there are no cycles in the transitive closure of extension relations. It also checks that the only type variable referenced inside a class or capability is the class or capability parameter n (e.g., through the function *referencedtypevars*). Besides these traditional criteria, we add the following additional criteria (highlighted in **bold**) which state a class (or capability) is well-formed only if:

* types of parameters in all method signatures are granted;
* types of all fields in the class are granted;
* capability parameters (or class parameters) should remain the same in extension (or implementation) relations.

If a type τ is granted to a capability cb (or a class c) based on the user-defined policy file Σ, then we have $\tau \in \Sigma(cb)$ (or $\tau \in \Sigma(c)$).

The typing rules for expressions and statements are shown in Table 5. As before, we highlight our additions in **bold**. The first group of rules are used for expressions. We can obtain the types of variables directly from the typing environment Γ according to the first rule (VAR) and look up the types of fields using rule (FID). Types of variables and fields are granted to the current executing class if they are given in the set $\mathcal{G}$, which stands for the set of permissions granted to the current executing class based on the user-defined policy file. Note that we leave the situation that the type of the expression is a subtype of a variable or a field to be covered by the subsumption rule (SUB). The rule (NEW) for the object creation may create an object with the parameter $\widetilde{\sigma}$ to instantiate the type parameter. The derived type of the expression should be the same as the class type (i.e., $c(\widetilde{\sigma})$). The last rule (CAST) in the first group for expressions is used to deal with the type casting in the object-oriented programming languages, which allows an expression to be cast to a granted subtype.

The next group of typing rules in Table 5 covers the rules for statements. Rule (AGN) and rule (FIDAGN) for variable assignment and field assignment are typed by ensuring that the derived type of the expression is the same as the type of the variable x or the field f. For the rule (IF), if the variable x has the type **int**, and statements s_1 and s_2 are well-formed under the typing environment

Table 5. Typing rules for expressions and statements

All rules are shown with respect to a fixed program $P = (CT, CBT, s)$.

Expressions

$$\text{(VAR)}\ \frac{\Gamma(x) = \tau \quad \tau \in \mathcal{G}^+}{\mathcal{G}\,\Gamma \vdash x : \tau} \qquad \text{(SUB)}\ \frac{\mathcal{G}\,\Gamma \vdash e : \tau' \quad \tau' <: \tau \quad \tau \in \mathcal{G}^+}{\mathcal{G}\,\Gamma \vdash e : \tau}$$

$$\text{(NEW)}\ \frac{c(\widetilde{\sigma}) \in \mathcal{G}^+}{\mathcal{G}\,\Gamma \vdash \mathbf{new}\ c(\widetilde{\sigma}) : c(\widetilde{\sigma})} \qquad \text{(CAST)}\ \frac{\mathcal{G}\,\Gamma \vdash e : \tau' \quad \tau \in \mathcal{G}^+}{\mathcal{G}\,\Gamma \vdash (\tau)\, e : \tau}$$

$$\text{(FID)}\ \frac{\Gamma(x) = \tau_0 \quad \tau_0 \in \mathcal{G}^+ \quad \text{fields}(\tau_0)(f) = \tau \quad \tau \in \mathcal{G}^+}{\mathcal{G}\,\Gamma \vdash x.f : \tau}$$

Statements

$$\text{(AGN)}\ \frac{\Gamma(x) = \tau \quad \mathcal{G}\,\Gamma \vdash e : \tau}{\mathcal{G}\,\Gamma \vdash x = e} \qquad \text{(SEQ)}\ \frac{\mathcal{G}\,\Gamma \vdash s_1 \quad \mathcal{G}\,\Gamma \vdash s_2}{\mathcal{G}\,\Gamma \vdash s_1;\ s_2}$$

$$\text{(FIDAGN)}\ \frac{\Gamma(x) = \tau_0 \quad \tau_0 \in \mathcal{G}^+ \quad \text{fields}(\tau_0)(f) = \tau \quad \mathcal{G}\,\Gamma \vdash y : \tau}{\mathcal{G}\,\Gamma \vdash x.f = y}$$

$$\text{(IF)}\ \frac{\Gamma(x) = \mathbf{int} \quad \mathcal{G}\,\Gamma \vdash s_1 \quad \mathcal{G}\,\Gamma \vdash s_2}{\mathcal{G}\,\Gamma \vdash \mathbf{if}\ x\ \mathbf{then}\ s_1\ \mathbf{else}\ s_2}$$

$$\text{(CALL)}\ \frac{\Gamma(x) = \tau_0 \quad \tau_0 \in \mathcal{G}^+ \quad \text{methodsigs}(\tau_0)(m) = (\overline{\tau_p}) \quad \overline{\mathcal{G}\,\Gamma \vdash y : \tau_p}}{\mathcal{G}\,\Gamma \vdash x.m(\overline{y})}$$

Γ and the permission set $\mathcal{G}$, then the whole statement is also well-formed under Γ and $\mathcal{G}$. To type a sequential composition, each statement needs to be typed in the typing environment Γ under the permission set $\mathcal{G}$, which is shown in rule (SEQ). The last rule (CALL) looks up the method signature and checks whether the types of the method arguments (i.e., the types of $\overline{y}$) are the same as the ones of the method parameters (e.g., $\overline{\tau_p}$).

3.3 Example Revisited

We revisit the example of Java file output access used in Sect. 2 to demonstrate the applicability of the proposed model. The capability *OutCap* and its implementation class are given in Listing 2. A combined capability *InOutCap* for both input and output access, and an application class are given in Listing 3.

The class *Application* is granted the type *InOutCap*("dir/*") and the type *OutCapImp*("dir/A.txt") as permissions by the user, thus we have that:

$$\mathcal{G} = \Sigma(\mathit{Application}) = \{\mathit{InOutCap}(\text{"dir/*"}), \mathit{OutCapImp}(\text{"dir/A.txt"})\}$$

Listing 3. Application class using file stream capabilities

```
capability InOutCap(n) extends OutCap(n){
    write(int b);
    read()
}
//grant: InOutCap("dir/*") and OutCapImp("dir/A.txt")
class Application{
    main() {
        OutCap("dir/A.txt") out = new OutCapImp("dir/A.txt");
        InOutCap("dir/A.txt") inOut = (InOutCap("dir/A.txt")) out;
        OutCap("*") out2 = (OutCap("*")) inOut //invalid
    }
}
```

We check the following three statements based on our typing rules and illustrate why the third statement in the *main* method is invalid. The first statement creates an instance of capability *OutCap*("dir/A.txt"), which passes the type checking using rules (NEW), (SUB) and (AGN) from Table 5. The inference steps are illustrated below. According to Definition 1, we have both *OutCap*("dir/A.txt") $\in \mathcal{G}^+$ and *OutCapImp*("dir/A.txt") $\in \mathcal{G}^+$.

$$\dfrac{\dfrac{\dfrac{OutCapImp(\text{"dir/A.txt"}) \in \mathcal{G}^+}{\mathcal{G}\ \Gamma \vdash new\ OutCapImp(\text{"dir/A.txt"}) : OutCapImp(\text{"dir/A.txt"})} \quad OutCapImp(\text{"dir/A.txt"}) <: OutCap(\text{"dir/A.txt"}) \quad OutCap(\text{"dir/A.txt"}) \in \mathcal{G}^+}{\mathcal{G}\ \Gamma \vdash new\ OutCapImp(\text{"dir/A.txt"}) : OutCap(\text{"dir/A.txt"})} \quad \Gamma(out) = OutCap(\text{"dir/A.txt"})}{\mathcal{G}\ \Gamma \vdash out = new\ OutCapImp(\text{"dir/A.txt"})}$$

The second statement casts the type of the instance *out* to capability *InOutCap* with the parameter "dir/A.txt". The following inference steps are given based on the rules (VAR), (CAST) and (AGN) in Table 5. Also, based on Definition 1, we can deduce that *InOutCap*("dir/A.txt") $\in \mathcal{G}^+$.

$$\dfrac{\dfrac{\dfrac{\Gamma(out) = OutCap(\text{"dir/A.txt"}) \quad OutCap(\text{"dir/A.txt"}) \in \mathcal{G}^+}{\mathcal{G}\ \Gamma \vdash out : OutCap(\text{"dir/A.txt"}) \quad InOutCap(\text{"dir/A.txt"}) \in \mathcal{G}^+}}{\mathcal{G}\ \Gamma \vdash (InOutCap(\text{"dir/A.txt"}))out : InOutCap(\text{"dir/A.txt"})} \quad \Gamma(inOut) = InOutCap(\text{"dir/A.txt"})}{\mathcal{G}\ \Gamma \vdash inOut = (InOutCap(\text{"dir/A.txt"}))out}$$

However, the third statement cannot pass the type checking as we **cannot** deduce *OutCap*("*") $\in \mathcal{G}^+$, based on Definition 1 and the types granted to *Application*.

Through controlling the type visibility, we avoid capabilities escaping to unauthorised code and restrict the targets that capabilities can access, based on a user-defined policy file. Revisiting and applying our approach to the motivating example in Sect. 1, we can find that the *UnauthorisedCode* is granted neither the type *OutCap*("dir/B.txt") nor the type *OutCap*("dir/*"), thus the declaration itself of class *UnauthorisedCode* cannot pass the well-formedness check at compile time.

4 Dynamic Semantics

In this section, we present the dynamic semantics and security-related subject reduction theorem of the type system. We show that the type-correctness of the runtime state and the security invariant are preserved over the evaluation of expressions and statements.

4.1 Operational Semantics

The dynamic semantics is devised using the big-step style operational semantics. We start by adding some additional notations to represent runtime values and states as follows.

$$e ::= ... \mid v$$
$$v ::= l^{c(\widetilde{\kappa})} \mid null \mid num$$

v is a runtime value, denoting the result of evaluating an expression. It can be an integer num, a location l labeled with its dynamic type $c(\widetilde{\kappa})$, or $null$.

We use S to stand for the stack, mapping from local variables to values (e.g., $S(x) = v$ denotes that the variable x contains the value v), and H represents the heap, mapping from locations and fields to values (e.g., $H(l^{c(\widetilde{\kappa})})(f) = v$ describes that the field f of class $c(\widetilde{\kappa})$ which is allocated at the location l on the heap contains the value v). The notation A denotes a list recording method invocation actions taken by the program. Each action is recorded as a quadruple $(c, c_i(\widetilde{\kappa_i}), \tau_r, m)$, in which c stands for the class name of the current calling class, $c_i(\widetilde{\kappa_i})$ is the class that contains the implementation of the method we are calling, τ_r is the runtime type of the object on which we are calling the method and m is the method name. The evaluation rule for expressions is of the form $c \vdash \langle e \mid S\ H\ A\rangle \rightarrow \langle v \mid S'\ H'\ A'\rangle$, which represents that in a given class c, an expression e can make a transition into a value v, and the evaluation of their side effects is shown on the stack, heap and action list. The evaluation rule for statements is in the form of $c \vdash \langle s \mid S\ H\ A\rangle \rightarrow \langle S'\ H'\ A'\rangle$, which denotes that statements are evaluated for their side effects only.

We proceed with a detailed explanation of the semantic rules for expressions and statements in Table 6. The notation $S[x \mapsto v]$ represents the update of the stack S that maps the variable x to the value v, which is similar with the update of the heap H with the form of $H[l^{c(\widetilde{\kappa})} \mapsto [f \mapsto v]]$. We use notations $dom(S)$

Table 6. Dynamic semantics for expressions and statements

Expressions

$$(\text{T-VAL})\ \frac{S(x) = v}{c \vdash \langle x \mid S\, H\, A\rangle \rightarrow \langle v \mid S\, H\, A\rangle} \qquad (\text{T-LOAD})\ \frac{S(x) = l^{c'(\overline{\kappa})} \quad H(l^{c'(\overline{\kappa})})(f) = v}{c \vdash \langle x.f \mid S\, H\, A\rangle \rightarrow \langle v \mid S\, H\, A\rangle}$$

$$(\text{T-CAST})\ \frac{c \vdash \langle e \mid S\, H\, A\rangle \rightarrow \langle l^{c'(\overline{\kappa})} \mid S\, H'\, A\rangle \quad c'(\overline{\kappa}) <: \tau}{c \vdash \langle (\tau)e \mid S\, H\, A\rangle \rightarrow \langle l^{c'(\overline{\kappa})} \mid S\, H'\, A\rangle}$$

$$(\text{T-NEW})\ \frac{l^{c'(\overline{\kappa})} \notin dom(H) \quad \text{dom}(\text{fields}(c'(\overline{\kappa}))) = \overline{f} \quad H' = H, \{l^{c'(\overline{\kappa})} \mapsto [\overline{f \mapsto \text{null}}]\}}{c \vdash \langle \textbf{new}\ c'(\overline{\kappa}) \mid S\, H\, A\rangle \rightarrow \langle l^{c'(\overline{\kappa})} \mid S\, H'\, A\rangle}$$

Statements

$$(\text{T-AGN})\ \frac{c \vdash \langle e \mid S\, H\, A\rangle \rightarrow \langle v \mid S\, H'\, A\rangle}{c \vdash \langle x = e \mid S\, H\, A\rangle \rightarrow \langle S[x \mapsto v]\, H'\, A\rangle}$$

$$(\text{T-FLD})\ \frac{c \vdash \langle y \mid S\, H\, A\rangle \rightarrow \langle v \mid S\, H\, A\rangle \quad S(x) = l^{c'(\overline{\kappa})} \quad l^{c'(\overline{\kappa})} \in \text{dom}(H)}{c \vdash \langle x.f = y \mid S\, H\, A\rangle \rightarrow \langle S\, H[l^{c'(\overline{\kappa})} \mapsto H(l^{c'(\overline{\kappa})})[f \mapsto v]]\, A\rangle}$$

$$(\text{T-CALL})\ \frac{\begin{array}{c} S(x) = l^{c'(\overline{\kappa})} \quad S(\overline{y}) = \overline{v} \quad \text{methods}(c'(\overline{\kappa}))(m) = (c_i(\overline{\kappa_i}), (\overline{\tau\, z})\{s\}) \\ c_i \vdash \langle s \mid S_0\, H\, A_0\rangle \rightarrow \langle S'\, H'\, A'\rangle \quad S_0 = \{\overline{z \mapsto v}\} \quad A_0 = A, \{c, c_i(\overline{\kappa_i}), c'(\overline{\kappa}), m\} \end{array}}{c \vdash \langle x.m(\overline{y}) \mid S\, H\, A\rangle \rightarrow \langle S\, H'\, A'\rangle}$$

$$(\text{T-THEN})\ \frac{S(x) = v \quad v > 0 \quad c \vdash \langle s_1 \mid S\, H\, A\rangle \rightarrow \langle S_1\, H_1\, A_1\rangle}{c \vdash \langle \textbf{if}\ x\ \textbf{then}\ s_1\ \textbf{else}\ s_2 \mid S\, H\, A\rangle \rightarrow \langle S_1\, H_1\, A_1\rangle}$$

$$(\text{T-ELSE})\ \frac{S(x) = v \quad v \leq 0 \quad c \vdash \langle s_2 \mid S\, H\, A\rangle \rightarrow \langle S_2\, H_2\, A_2\rangle}{c \vdash \langle \textbf{if}\ x\ \textbf{then}\ s_1\ \textbf{else}\ s_2 \mid S\, H\, A\rangle \rightarrow \langle S_2\, H_2\, A_2\rangle}$$

$$(\text{T-SEQ})\ \frac{c \vdash \langle s_1 \mid S\, H\, A\rangle \rightarrow \langle S_1\, H_1\, A_1\rangle \quad c \vdash \langle s_2 \mid S_1\, H_1\, A_1\rangle \rightarrow \langle S_2\, H_2\, A_2\rangle}{c \vdash \langle s_1;\ s_2 \mid S\, H\, A\rangle \rightarrow \langle S_2\, H_2\, A_2\rangle}$$

and $dom(H)$ to stand for the domain of the stack S and the heap H, respectively. The notation $H' = H, \{l^{c(\overline{\kappa})} \mapsto ...\}$ is used to represent an extension of heap H where $l^{c(\overline{\kappa})} \notin \text{dom}(H)$, and $A' = A, \{...\}$ is used for the extension of list A.

The first two rules (T-VAL) and (T-LOAD) evaluate variables and fields from the stack and the heap respectively. The rule (T-CAST) describes the downcasting between objects or capability variables if the runtime type is a subtype of the type to be converted to. The last rule (T-NEW) is used for an object creation, which extends the heap with the new object. All fields are initially set to null.

The remaining rules are used for statement evaluations. The rules (T-AGN) and (T-FLD) are used to update the stack and the heap respectively. Method invocation in (T-CALL) dynamically looks up the target method to be called based on the dynamic type of the object. A record of the method invocation action will be added into the action list A. The rules (T-THEN) and (T-ELSE) describe the transitions performed by the conditional choice. In particular, the rule (T-THEN) accounts for the case where the condition is true (indicated by the value of the variable x is greater than zero); whereas the rule (T-ELSE) accounts for the case where it is false. The last rule (T-SEQ) is used for evaluating the sequential composition of two statements in order, which means that statement s_2 is evaluated based on the output configuration of statement s_1.

4.2 Subject Reduction

In this section, we prove that well-formed programs are safe over subject reduction [13], which means that the type-correctness of the program state and the security invariant are preserved under evaluations.

$$\text{(CORR)}\quad \frac{\begin{array}{c}\left(\begin{array}{c}\forall x \in \mathrm{dom}(\varGamma), \tau \cdot \varGamma(x) = \tau \wedge \boldsymbol{\tau \in (\varSigma(c))^{+}} \Longrightarrow \\ x \in \mathrm{dom}(S) \wedge \exists v \cdot S(x) = v \wedge H \vdash v : \tau\end{array}\right) \\ \left(\begin{array}{c}\forall l^{c'(\widetilde{\kappa})} \in \mathrm{dom}(H), f, \tau \cdot \mathrm{fields}(c'(\widetilde{\kappa}))(f) = \tau \Longrightarrow \\ f \in \mathrm{dom}(H(l^{c'(\widetilde{\kappa})})) \wedge \exists v \cdot H(l^{c'(\widetilde{\kappa})})(f) = v \wedge H \vdash v : \tau\end{array}\right) \\ \varSigma(c)\ \varGamma \Vdash A\end{array}}{\varSigma(c)\ \varGamma \vdash S\ H\ A}$$

An additional rule (CORR) is given to illustrate the correspondence between the typing environment $\varGamma$ of type system and the configuration, including stack S and heap H, under the user-defined policy file $\varSigma$ and the current executing class c. It requires that for every variable x in $\varGamma$, a value v exists for variable x on the stack S such that v is type-correct to $\varGamma(x)$. Similarly, for every object on the heap, both the fields present, and their values, must match the object's type information. Lastly, the security invariant on the action list A must be maintained.

Definition 2 (Security Invariant). *For the action list A, user-defined policy file $\varSigma$, calling class c, class $c_i(\widetilde{\kappa_i})$ containing the method body that is called, runtime type $c'(\widetilde{\kappa})$ of the object on which the method is called and method name m, the security invariant (represented as $\varSigma(c)\ \varGamma \Vdash A$) says that:*

$$\begin{array}{c}\forall (c, c_i(\widetilde{\kappa_i}), c'(\widetilde{\kappa}), m) \in A, \exists \tau \cdot \tau \in (\varSigma(c))^{+} \wedge c'(\widetilde{\kappa}) <: \tau \wedge \\ c'(\widetilde{\kappa}) <: c_i(\widetilde{\kappa_i}) \wedge \mathrm{methodsigs}(\tau)(m) = \mathrm{methodsigs}(c_i(\widetilde{\kappa_i}))(m)\end{array}$$

The security invariant says that for all method invocation actions in A, there exists a type τ granted to the current calling class c, of which the runtime type $c'(\widetilde{\kappa})$ is a subtype. Also, the runtime type is a subtype of the type of class $c_i(\widetilde{\kappa_i})$ which contains the implementation of the method we invoked and the method signature looked up based on τ and $c_i(\widetilde{\kappa_i})$ should be the same. It provides a guarantee that each well-formed method invocation action in the action list A

can only use the types (i.e., capabilities and classes) granted to its invoking class based on the user-defined policy file, restricting capability types only to authorised code.

In order to accommodate runtime values, we add three more rules to extend our static inference rules for checking the runtime values are type correct in the context of heap H.

$$\text{(NULL)} \quad H \vdash \mathit{null} : \tau \qquad\qquad \text{(LOC)} \ \frac{l^{c(\widetilde{\kappa})} \in \text{dom}(H) \quad c(\widetilde{\kappa}) <: \tau}{H \vdash l^{c(\widetilde{\kappa})} : \tau}$$
$$\text{(NUM)} \quad H \vdash \mathit{num} : \mathbf{int}$$

The preservation theorem for subject reduction is given in Theorem 1, which presents the preservation of well-formedness and security invariant on statements. Preservation for expressions is trivial as expressions only look up values from well-formed stack or heap, thus we omit it. Theorem 1 can be proved by structural induction on the semantic derivation.

Theorem 1 (Preservation). *For any typing environment Γ, stack S, heap H, action list A, statement s, current executing class c, user-defined policy file Σ and the well-formed program P:*

$$\left.\begin{array}{r} \Sigma \vdash P \\ \Sigma(c)\ \Gamma \vdash s \\ \Sigma(c)\ \Gamma \vdash S\ H\ A \\ c \vdash \langle s | S\ H\ A\rangle \rightarrow \langle S'\ H'\ A'\rangle \end{array}\right\} \Longrightarrow \Sigma(c)\ \Gamma \vdash S'\ H'\ A'$$

5 Conclusion and Future Work

Existing authorisation mechanisms used in programming languages like Java are not effective in controlling interactions between different parts of code within the same process. In this paper, we tackled the problem of adapting capabilities to programming languages for providing authorisation to code. We regarded capabilities as types and presented a statically-checked type system to enforce the proper use of capabilities by controlling the type visibility at compile time, providing a security guarantee that restricts capabilities (i.e., the access to resources) only to authorised code. We also introduced parameterised capability types to provide a finer-grained access control and to identify system resources more precisely. We applied our model on file-access examples.

Future directions for our research include building a prototype implementation of the type system, and validating its usability by applying it to real-world case studies. Other possible directions include extending the language with even richer parameterisation to increase its expressiveness, and adding more language features (e.g., method overloading, return values and exceptions) to improve the quality of our formalism.

Acknowledgements. The research presented here is supported by Australian Research Council Linkage Grant LP140100700 in collaboration with Oracle Labs Australia.

References

1. Dennis, J.B., van Horn, E.C.: Programming semantics for multiprogrammed computations. Commun. ACM **9**(3), 143–155 (1966)
2. Gong, L., Ellison, G., Dageforde, M.: Inside Java 2 Platform Security: Architecture, API Design, and Implementation, Second edn. Addison Wesley, Boston (2003)
3. Gosling, J., Joy, B., Steele, G., Bracha, G., Buckley, A., Smith, D.: The Java language specification: Java SE 10 edition, 20 February 2018. https://docs.oracle.com/javase/specs/jls/se10/html/index.html. Accessed 27 Sept 2018
4. Hardy, N.: The confused deputy: (or why capabilities might have been invented). SIGOPS Oper. Syst. Rev. **22**(4), 36–38 (1988)
5. Hardy, N.: KeyKOS architecture. Oper. Syst. Rev. **19**(4), 8–25 (1985)
6. Hayes, I.J., Wu, X., Meinicke, L.A.: Capabilities for Java: secure access to resources. In: Chang, B.-Y.E. (ed.) APLAS 2017. LNCS, vol. 10695, pp. 67–84. Springer, Cham (2017). https://doi.org/10.1007/978-3-319-71237-6_4
7. Kozen, D.: Language-based security. In: Kutyłowski, M., Pacholski, L., Wierzbicki, T. (eds.) MFCS 1999. LNCS, vol. 1672, pp. 284–298. Springer, Heidelberg (1999). https://doi.org/10.1007/3-540-48340-3_26
8. Gong, L., Mueller, M., Prafullchandra, H., Schemers, R.: Going beyond the sandbox: an overview of the new security architecture in the Java development Kit 1.2. In: Proceedings of 1st USENIX Symposium on Internet Technologies and Systems, USITS 1997. USENIX (1997)
9. Mettler, A., Wagner, D.: The Joe-E language specification, version 1.0. Technical report EECS-2008-91, University of California, Berkeley, August 2008
10. Mettler, A., Wagner, D., Close, T.: Joe-E: a security-oriented subset of Java. In: Proceedings of the Symposium on Network and Distributed System Security, NDSS 2010. The Internet Society (2010)
11. Miller, M.S.: Robust composition: towards a unified approach to access control and concurrency control. Ph.D. thesis, Johns Hopkins University (2006)
12. Miller, M.S., Samuel, M., Laurie, B., Awad, I., Stay, M.: Caja: safe active content in sanitized JavaScript, 7 June 2008. https://storage.googleapis.com/google-code-archive-downloads/v2/code.google.com/google-caja/caja-spec-2008-06-07.pdf. Accessed 27 Sept 2018
13. Pierce, B.C.: Types and Programming Languages. MIT Press, Cambridge (2002)
14. Sabelfeld, A., Myers, A.C.: Language-based information-flow security. IEEE J. Sel. Areas Commun. **21**(1), 5–19 (2003)
15. Saltzer, J.H., Schroeder, M.D.: The protection of information in computer systems. Proc. IEEE **63**(9), 1278–1308 (1975)
16. Shapiro, J.S., Smith, J.M., Farber, D.J.: EROS: a fast capability system. In: Proceedings of 17th ACM Symposium on Operating System Principles, SOSP 1999, pp. 170–185. ACM (1999)
17. Google Caja Team: Google-Caja: a source-to-source translator for securing JavaScript-based web. http://code.google.com/p/google-caja/. Accessed 27 Sept 2018

Capabilities: Effects for Free

Aaron Craig[1], Alex Potanin[1(✉)], Lindsay Groves[1], and Jonathan Aldrich[2]

[1] School of Engineering and Computer Science, Victoria University of Wellington, Wellington, New Zealand
{aaron.craig,alex,lindsay}@ecs.vuw.ac.nz

[2] School of Computer Science, Carnegie Mellon University, Pittsburgh, USA
jonathan.aldrich@cs.cmu.edu

Abstract. Object capabilities are increasingly used to reason informally about the properties of secure systems. But can capabilities also aid in *formal* reasoning? To answer this question, we examine a calculus that uses effects to capture resource use and extend it to support capability-based reasoning. We demonstrate that capabilities provide a way to reason about effects: we can bound the effects of an expression based on the capabilities to which it has access. This reasoning is "free" in that it relies only on type-checking (not effect-checking), does not require the programmer to add effect annotations within the expression, and does not require the expression to be analysed for its effects. Our result sheds light on the essence of what capabilities provide and suggests ways of integrating lightweight capability-based reasoning into languages.

1 Introduction

Capabilities have been recently gaining attention as a promising mechanism for controlling access to resources, particularly in object-oriented languages and systems [4–6, 16]. A *capability* is an unforgeable token that can be used by its bearer to perform some operation on a resource [3]. In a *capability-safe* language, all resources must be accessed through object capabilities, and a resource-access capability must be obtained from an object that already has it: "only connectivity begets connectivity" [16]. For example, a `logger` component that provides a logging service would need to be initialised with an object capability providing the ability to append to the log file.

Capability-safe languages prohibit the *ambient authority* [17] that is present in non-capability-safe languages. An implementation of a `logger` in Java, for example, does not need to be initialised with a log file capability, as it can simply import the appropriate file-access library and open the log file for appending by itself. But critically, a malicious implementation could also delete the log, read from another file, or exfiltrate logging information over the network. Other mechanisms such as sandboxing can be used to limit the damage of such malicious components, but recent work has found that Java's sandbox (for instance) is difficult to use and therefore often misused [1, 11].

In practice, reasoning about resource use in capability-based systems is mostly done informally. But if capabilities are useful for *informal* reasoning, shouldn't they also aid in *formal* reasoning? Recent work by Drossopoulou et al. [6] sheds some light on this question by presenting a logic that formalizes capability-based reasoning about trust

J. Sun and M. Sun (Eds.): ICFEM 2018, LNCS 11232, pp. 231–247, 2018.
https://doi.org/10.1007/978-3-030-02450-5_14

between objects. Two other trains of work, rather than formalise capability-based reasoning itself, reason about how capabilities may be used: Dimoulas et al. [5] developed a formalism for reasoning about which components may use a capability and which may influence (perhaps indirectly) the use of a capability, while Devriese et al. [4] formulate an effect parametricity theorem that limits the effects of an object based on the capabilities it possesses, and then use logical relations to reason about capability use in higher-order settings. Overall, this prior work presents new formal systems for reasoning about capability use, or reasoning about new properties using capabilities.

We are interested in a different question: can capabilities be used to enhance formal reasoning that is currently done without relying on capabilities? In other words, what value do capabilities add to existing formal reasoning approaches?

To answer this question, we decided to pick a simple and practical formal reasoning system, and see if capability-based reasoning could help. A natural choice for our investigation is effect systems [18]. Effect systems are a relatively simple formal reasoning approach, which augment type systems with the ability to reason about dynamic effects—and keeping things simple will help to highlight the difference made by capabilities. Effects also have an intuitive link to capabilities: in a system that uses capabilities to protect resources, an expression can only have an effect on a resource if it is given a capability to do so.

One challenge to the wider adoption of effect systems is their annotation overhead [19]. For example, Java's checked exception system, which is a kind of effect system, is often criticised for being cumbersome [8]. While effect inference can be used to reduce the annotations required [9], understanding error messages that arise through effect inference requires a detailed understanding of the internal structure of the code, not just its interface. Capabilities are a promising alternative for reducing the overhead of effect annotations, as suggested by the following example:

```
import log : String -> Unit with effect File.write
e
```

Fig. 1. Declaring an effect

Our examples are written in a capability-safe language supporting first-class, object-like modules, similar to *Wyvern* [14], in which expressions declare what capabilities they need to execute. In this case, an expression `e` must be passed a function of type `String` → `Unit`,[1] which incurs no more than the effect `File.write` when invoked. This function is bound to the name `log` inside `e`.

What can we say about the effects that evaluating `e` will have on resources, such as the file system or network? Because we are in a capability-safe language, `e` has no ambient authority, so the only way it could have any effects is via the `log` function given to it. Since the `log` function is annotated as having no more than the `File.write` effect, this is an upper-bound on the effects of `e`. Note we only required that `e` obeys the rules of capability safety. We did not require it to have effect annotations, and we didn't

[1] `Unit` is a singleton type, like `void` in C and Java.

analyse its structure, as an effect inference would. Also note that e might be arbitrarily large, perhaps consisting of an entire program we have downloaded from a source we trust enough to write to a log, but not enough to access any other resources. Thus in this scenario, capabilities can be used to reason "for free" about the effects of a large body of code (e), based on a few annotations on the components it imports (log).

This example illustrates the central intuition of this paper: in a capability-safe setting, the effects of an unannotated expression can be bounded by the effects latent in the variables that are in scope. In the remainder of this paper, we formalise these ideas in a capability calculus (CC; Sect. 2). Along the way we must generalise this intuition: what if log takes a higher-order argument? If e evaluates, not to unit, but to a function, what can we say about its effects? We then show how CC can model practical situations by encoding a range of Wyvern-like programs Sect. 3). A more thorough discussion, including a proof of soundness is given in an accompanying technical report [2].

2 Capability Calculus (CC)

While the current resurgence of interest in capabilities is primarily focused on object-oriented languages, for simplicity our formal definitions build on a typed lambda calculus with a simple notion of capabilities and their operations. CC permits the nesting of unannotated code inside annotated code in a controlled, capability-safe manner using the import form from Fig. 1. This allows us to reason about unannotated code by inspecting what capabilities are passed into it from its unannotated surroundings.

Allowing effect-annotated and unannotated code to be mixed helps reduce the cognitive overhead on developers, allowing them to prototype in the unannotated sublanguage and incrementally add annotations as they are needed. Reasoning about unannotated code is difficult in general. Figure 2 demonstrates why: apply takes a function *f* as input and executes it, but the effects of *f* depend on its implementation. Without more information, there is no way to know what effects might be incurred by apply.

```
def apply(f: Unit → Unit):
    f()
```

Fig. 2. What effects can apply incur?

Consider another scenario, where a developer must decide whether or not to use the logger functor defined in Fig. 3. This functor takes two capabilities as input, File and Socket.[2] It instantiates an object-like module that has a single, unannotated log method with access to these capabilities. The type of this object-like module is Logger, which is assumed to be defined elsewhere.

How can we determine what effects will be incurred if Logger.log is invoked? One approach is to manually[3] examine its source code, but this is tedious and error-prone.

[2] Note that the resource literal is File, while the type of the resource literal is {File}.

[3] or automatically—but if the automation produces an unexpected result we must fall back to manual reasoning to understand why.

```
module def logger(f:{File},s:{Socket}):Logger
def log(x: Unit): Unit
  ...
```

Fig. 3. In a capability-safe setting, `logger` can only exercise authority over the `File` and `Socket` capabilities given to it.

In many real-world situations, the source code may be obfuscated or unavailable. A capability-based argument can do better, since a `Logger` can only exercise the authority it is explicitly given. In this case, the `logger` functor must be given `File` and `Socket`, so an upper bound on the effects of the `Logger` it instantiates will be the set of all operations on those resources, $\{\texttt{File}.*, \texttt{Socket}.*\}$. Knowing the `Logger` could perform arbitrary reads and writes to `File`, or communicate with `Socket`, the developer decides this implementation cannot be trusted and does not use it.

To model this situation in CC, we add a new `import` expression that selects what authority ε_s the unannotated code may exercise. In the above example, the expected least authority of `Logger` is $\{\texttt{File.append}\}$, so that is what the corresponding `import` would select. The type system can then check whether the capabilities being passed into the unannotated code exceed ε_s. If it accepts, then ε_s is a safe upper bound on the effects of the unannotated code. This is the key result: when unannotated code is nested inside annotated code, capability-safety enables us to make a safe inference about its effects by examining what capabilities are being passed in by the annotated code.

2.1 Grammar (CC)

The grammar of CC has rules for annotated code and analogous rules for unannotated code. To distinguish the two, we put a hat above annotated types, expressions, and contexts. $\hat{e}$, $\hat{\tau}$, and $\hat{\Gamma}$ are annotated, while e, τ, and Γ are unannotated. The rules for unannotated programs and their types are given in Fig. 4. Unannotated types τ are built using $\rightarrow$ and sets of resources $\{\bar{r}\}$. An unannotated context Γ maps variables to unannotated types. The syntax for invoking an operation on a resource is $e.\pi$. Resource literals and operations are drawn from fixed sets R (containing, e.g. `File`, `Socket`) and Π (containing, e.g. `write`, `read`).

Because our focus is on tracking what effects happen, i.e. whether particular operations are invoked on particular resources, we make the following simplifying assumptions: first, any operation may be called on any resource literal; and second, all operations take no inputs and return `unit`.

Rules for annotated programs and their types are shown in Fig. 5. The first main difference is that the $\rightarrow_\varepsilon$ type constructor has a subscript ε, which is a set of effects that functions of that type may incur. The other main difference is the new expression form, $\texttt{import}(\varepsilon_s)\ x = \hat{e}\ \texttt{in}\ e$, where e is some unannotated code and $\hat{e}$ is a capability being passed to it; we call $\hat{e}$ an import. For simplicity, we assume there is only ever one import. Note the definition not only allows resource literals to be imported, but also effectful functions. Inside e, $\hat{e}$ is bound to the variable x. ε_s is the maximum authority that e is allowed to exercise (its "selected authority"). For

$$
\begin{array}{llr}
e ::= & & exprs: \\
\mid & x & variable \\
\mid & v & value \\
\mid & e\,e & application \\
\mid & e.\pi & operation \\
v ::= & & values: \\
\mid & r & resource\ literal \\
\mid & \lambda x : \tau.e & abstraction
\end{array}
\qquad
\begin{array}{llr}
\tau ::= & & types: \\
\mid & \{\bar{r}\} & resource\ set \\
\mid & \tau \rightarrow \tau & function \\
\Gamma ::= & & type\ ctx: \\
\mid & \varnothing & empty\ ctx \\
\mid & \Gamma, x : \tau & binding \\
\varepsilon ::= & & effects: \\
\mid & \{\overline{r.\pi}\} & effect\ set
\end{array}
$$

Fig. 4. Unannotated programs and types in CC.

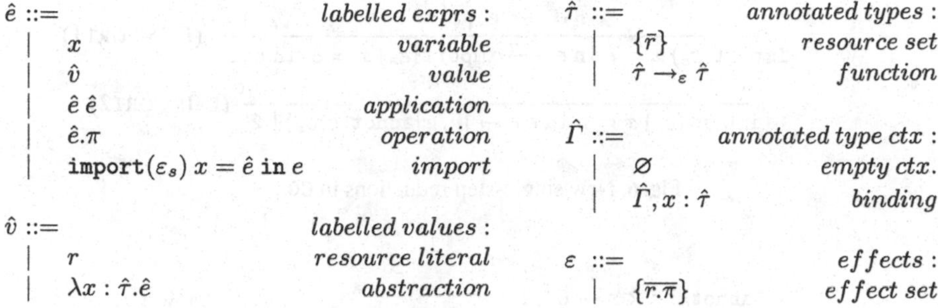

Fig. 5. Annotated programs and types in CC.

example, suppose an unannotated `Logger`, which requires `File`, is expected to only append to a file, but has an implementation which writes. This would be the expression `import(File.append)` $x =$ `File in` λy : `Unit. x.write`. The `import` expression is the only way to mix annotated and unannotated code, because it is the only situation in which we can say something interesting about the effects of unannotated code. For the rest of our discussion of CC, we will only be interested in unannotated code when it is encapsulated by an `import` expression.

Capability safety prohibits ambient authority. CC meets this requirement by forbidding the use of resource literals directly inside an `import` expression (though they can still be passed in as a capability via the binding variable x). We could have enforced this syntactically, but we choose to do it using the typing rule for `import` in Sect. 2.3.

2.2 Semantics (CC)

The rules for CC are natural extensions of the simply-typed lambda calculus, so for brevity we only give the rules for `import` (see Fig. 6). Reductions are defined on annotated expressions, using the notation $\hat{e} \longrightarrow \hat{e}' \mid \varepsilon'$, which means that $\hat{e}$ is reduced to $\hat{e}'$ in a single step, incurring the set of effects ε'. To execute the unannotated code inside an `import` expression, we recursively annotate its components with the selected authority ε_s. While it is meaningful to execute unannotated code, we only care about it inside `import` expressions, so do not bother to give rules for this.

E-IMPORT1 reduces the capability being imported. When it has been reduced to a value $\hat{v}$, E-IMPORT2 annotates e with the selected authority ε—this is $\texttt{annot}(e, \varepsilon)$—and substitutes the import $\hat{v}$ for its name x in e—this is $[\hat{v}/x]\texttt{annot}(e, \varepsilon)$.

$\texttt{annot}(e, \varepsilon)$ is the expression obtained by recursively annotating the parts of e with the set of effects ε. A definition is given in Fig. 7, with versions defined on expressions and types. Later we will need to annotate contexts, so the definition is given here. Note that annot operates on a purely syntatic level. Nothing prevents us from annotating a program with something unsafe, so any use of annot must be justified.

$$\boxed{\hat{e} \longrightarrow \hat{e} \mid \varepsilon}$$

$$\frac{\hat{e} \longrightarrow \hat{e}' \mid \varepsilon'}{\texttt{import}(\varepsilon_s)\; x = \hat{e} \;\texttt{in}\; e \longrightarrow \texttt{import}(\varepsilon_s)\; x = \hat{e}' \;\texttt{in}\; e \mid \varepsilon'} \quad \text{(E-IMPORT1)}$$

$$\frac{}{\texttt{import}(\varepsilon_s)\; x = \hat{v} \;\texttt{in}\; e \longrightarrow [\hat{v}/x]\texttt{annot}(e, \varepsilon_s) \mid \varnothing} \quad \text{(E-IMPORT2)}$$

Fig. 6. New single-step reductions in CC.

$$\begin{aligned}
&\texttt{annot} :: e \times \varepsilon \rightarrow \hat{e}\\
&\texttt{annot}(r, _) = r\\
&\texttt{annot}(\lambda x : \tau_1.e, \varepsilon) = \lambda x : \texttt{annot}(\tau_1, \varepsilon).\texttt{annot}(e, \varepsilon)\\
&\texttt{annot}(e_1\; e_2, \varepsilon) = \texttt{annot}(e_1, \varepsilon)\; \texttt{annot}(e_2, \varepsilon)\\
&\texttt{annot}(e_1.\pi, \varepsilon) = \texttt{annot}(e_1, \varepsilon).\pi
\end{aligned}$$

$$\begin{aligned}
&\texttt{annot} :: \tau \times \varepsilon \rightarrow \hat{\tau}\\
&\texttt{annot}(\{\bar{r}\}, _) = \{\bar{r}\}\\
&\texttt{annot}(\tau_1 \rightarrow \tau_2, \varepsilon) = \texttt{annot}(\tau_1, \varepsilon) \rightarrow_\varepsilon \texttt{annot}(\tau_2, \varepsilon).
\end{aligned}$$

$$\begin{aligned}
&\texttt{annot} :: \Gamma \times \varepsilon \rightarrow \hat{\Gamma}\\
&\texttt{annot}(\varnothing, _) = \varnothing\\
&\texttt{annot}(\Gamma, x : \tau, \varepsilon) = \texttt{annot}(\Gamma, \varepsilon), x : \texttt{annot}(\tau, \varepsilon)
\end{aligned}$$

Fig. 7. Definition of annot.

2.3 Static Rules (CC)

Terms can be annotated or unannotated, so we need to be able to recognise when either is well-typed. We do not reason about the effects of unannotated code directly, so judgements involving them only ascribe a type to an expression, with the form $\Gamma \vdash e : \tau$. Subtyping judgements have the form $\tau <: \tau$. Because these rules are essentially those of the simply-typed lambda calculus, we do not list them here.

Judgements involving annotated terms have the form $\hat{\Gamma} \vdash \hat{e} : \hat{\tau}\;\texttt{with}\;\varepsilon$, meaning that when $\hat{e}$ is evaluated, it reduces to a value of type $\hat{\tau}$, incurring no more than the effects in ε. Most of the rules are analogous to those of the simply-typed lambda calculus; these ones are given in Fig. 8. Note that the rule for typing an operation call,

$$\boxed{\Gamma \vdash e : \tau \texttt{ with } \varepsilon}$$

$$\frac{}{\Gamma, x : \tau \vdash x : \tau \texttt{ with } \varnothing} \ (\varepsilon\text{-VAR}) \qquad \frac{}{\Gamma, r : \{r\} \vdash r : \{r\} \texttt{ with } \varnothing} \ (\varepsilon\text{-RESOURCE})$$

$$\frac{\Gamma, x : \tau_2 \vdash e : \tau_3 \texttt{ with } \varepsilon_3}{\Gamma \vdash \lambda x : \tau_2.e : \tau_2 \rightarrow_{\varepsilon_3} \tau_3 \texttt{ with } \varnothing} \ (\varepsilon\text{-ABS}) \qquad \frac{\Gamma \vdash e_1 : \tau_2 \rightarrow_\varepsilon \tau_3 \texttt{ with } \varepsilon_1 \quad \Gamma \vdash e_2 : \tau_2 \texttt{ with } \varepsilon_2}{\Gamma \vdash e_1\, e_2 : \tau_3 \texttt{ with } \varepsilon_1 \cup \varepsilon_2 \cup \varepsilon} \ (\varepsilon\text{-APP})$$

$$\frac{\Gamma \vdash e : \{\bar{r}\}}{\Gamma \vdash e.\pi : \texttt{Unit with } \{\bar{r}.\pi\}} \ (\varepsilon\text{-OPERCALL}) \qquad \frac{\Gamma \vdash e : \tau \texttt{ with } \varepsilon \quad \tau <: \tau' \quad \varepsilon \subseteq \varepsilon'}{\Gamma \vdash e : \tau' \texttt{ with } \varepsilon'} \ (\varepsilon\text{-SUBSUME})$$

$$\boxed{\Gamma \vdash e : \tau \texttt{ with } \varepsilon}$$

$$\frac{\tau_1' <: \tau_1 \quad \tau_2 <: \tau_2' \quad \varepsilon \subseteq \varepsilon'}{\tau_1 \rightarrow_\varepsilon \tau_2 <: \tau_1' \rightarrow_{\varepsilon'} \tau_2'} \ (\text{S-ARROW}) \qquad \frac{r \in r_1 \implies r \in r_2}{\{\bar{r}_1\} <: \{\bar{r}_2\}} \ (\text{S-RESOURCE})$$

Fig. 8. Type-and-effect and subtyping judgements in CC.

$$\begin{aligned}&\texttt{erase} :: \hat{\tau} \rightarrow \tau\\ &\texttt{erase}(\{\bar{r}\}) = \{\bar{r}\}\\ &\texttt{erase}(\hat{\tau}_1 \rightarrow_\varepsilon \hat{\tau}_2) = \texttt{erase}(\hat{\tau}_1) \rightarrow \texttt{erase}(\hat{\tau}_2)\end{aligned}$$

Fig. 9. Definition of erase.

ε-OPERCALL, types the expression as Unit, following our simplifying assumption that all operations return Unit.

There is one rule left, for typing import. Since it is a complicated rule, we will start with a simplified (but incorrect) version, and spend the rest of the section building up to the final version.

To begin, typing $\texttt{import}(\varepsilon_s)\ x = \hat{e}\ \texttt{in}\ e$ in a context $\hat{\Gamma}$ requires us to know that $\hat{e}$ is well-typed, so we add the premise $\hat{\Gamma} \vdash \hat{e} : \hat{\tau}\ \texttt{with}\ \varepsilon_1$. e is only allowed to use what authority has been explicitly given to it (i.e. the capability $\hat{e}$, bound to x). To ensure this, we require that e can be typechecked using only one binding, $x : \hat{\tau}$, which binds x to the type of the capability being imported. Typing e in this restricted environment means it cannot use any other capabilities, thus prohibiting the exercise of ambient authority.

There is a problem though: e is unannotated, while $\hat{\tau}$ is annotated, and there is no rule for typechecking unannotated code in an annotated context. To get around this, we define a function erase in Fig. 9, which removes the annotations from a type. We can then add $x : \texttt{erase}(\hat{\tau}) \vdash e : \tau$ as a premise.

The first version of ε-IMPORT is given in Fig. 10. Since $\texttt{import}(\varepsilon_s)\ x = \hat{v}\ \texttt{in}\ e$ reduces to $[\hat{v}/x]\texttt{annot}(e, \varepsilon_s)$ by E-IMPORT2, its ascribed type is $\texttt{annot}(\tau, \varepsilon)$, which is the type of the unannotated code e, annotated with its selected authority ε_s. The effects of reducing the import are $\varepsilon_1 \cup \varepsilon_s$—the former happens when the imported capability

$$\frac{\hat{\Gamma} \vdash \hat{e} : \hat{\tau}\ \texttt{with}\ \varepsilon_1 \quad x : \texttt{erase}(\hat{\tau}) \vdash e : \tau}{\hat{\Gamma} \vdash \texttt{import}(\varepsilon_s)\ x = \hat{e}\ \texttt{in}\ e : \texttt{annot}(\tau, \varepsilon_s)\ \texttt{with}\ \varepsilon_s \cup \varepsilon_1} \quad (\varepsilon\text{-IMPORT1-BAD})$$

Fig. 10. A first (incorrect) rule for type-and-effect checking `import` expressions.

is reduced to a value, while the latter happens when the body of the `import` expression is annotated and executed.

This first rule is incomplete, since any capability can be passed to the unannotated code e, even if it has effects that weren't declared in ε_s. To avoid this, we define a function `effects`, which collects the set of effects that an (annotated) type captures. For example, {`File`} captures every operation on `File`, so `effects`({`File`}) = {`File`.∗}. A first (but not yet correct) definition of this is given in Fig. 11. We then add the premise $\texttt{effects}(\hat{\tau}) \subseteq \varepsilon_s$, which restricts imported capabilities to only those with effects selected in ε_s. The updated rule for typing `import` is given in Fig. 12.

$$\begin{aligned}&\texttt{effects} :: \hat{\tau} \to \varepsilon\\&\texttt{effects}(\{\bar{r}\}) = \{r.\pi \mid r \in \bar{r}, \pi \in \Pi\}\\&\texttt{effects}(\hat{\tau}_1 \to_\varepsilon \hat{\tau}_2) = \texttt{effects}(\hat{\tau}_1) \cup \varepsilon \cup \texttt{effects}(\hat{\tau}_2)\end{aligned}$$

Fig. 11. A first (incorrect) definition of `effects`.

$$\frac{\hat{\Gamma} \vdash \hat{e} : \hat{\tau}\ \texttt{with}\ \varepsilon_1 \quad x : \texttt{erase}(\hat{\tau}) \vdash e : \tau \quad \texttt{effects}(\hat{\tau}) \subseteq \varepsilon_s}{\hat{\Gamma} \vdash \texttt{import}(\varepsilon_s)\ x = \hat{e}\ \texttt{in}\ e : \texttt{annot}(\tau, \varepsilon_s)\ \texttt{with}\ \varepsilon \cup \varepsilon_1} \quad (\varepsilon\text{-IMPORT2-BAD})$$

Fig. 12. A second (still incorrect) rule for type-and-effect checking `import` expressions.

There are still issues with this second rule, as the annotations on one import can be broken by another import. To illustrate, consider Fig. 13 where two[4] capabilities are imported. This program imports a function go which, when given a `Unit` $\to_\varnothing$ `Unit` function with no effects, will execute it. The other import is `File`. The unannotated code creates a `Unit` → `Unit` function which writes to `File` and passes it to go, which subsequently incurs `File.write`.

```
import({File.*})
  go = λx: Unit →∅ Unit. x unit
  f = File
in
  go (λy: Unit. f.write)
```

Fig. 13. Permitting multiple imports will break ε-IMPORT2.

[4] Our formalisation only permits a single capability to be imported, but this discussion leads to a generalisation needed for the rules to be safe when multiple capabilities can be imported. In any case, importing multiple capabilities can be handled with an encoding of pairs.

In the world of annotated code, it is not possible to pass a file-writing function to go, but because the judgement $x : \texttt{erase}(\hat{\tau}) \vdash e : \tau$ discards the annotations on go, and since the file-writing function has type $\texttt{unit} \rightarrow \texttt{unit}$, the unannotated world accepts it. Although the unannotated code is allowed to incur this effect, since its selected authority is $\{\texttt{File.}*\}$, this nonetheless violates the type signature of go. We want to prevent this.

If go had the type $\texttt{Unit} \rightarrow_{\{\texttt{File.write}\}} \texttt{Unit}$, Fig. 13 would be safely rejected. However, a modified program where a file-reading function is passed to go would have the same issue. go is only safe when it expects every effect that the unannotated code might pass to it. To ensure this is the case, we shall require imported capabilities to have the authority to incur every effect in ε_s. To achieve greater control in how we say this, we split the definitions of `effects` into two separate functions, `effects` and `ho-effects`. The latter is for higher-order effects, which are those effects not captured directly in the function body, but rather are possible because of what is passed into the function as an argument. If values of $\hat{\tau}$ possess a capability that can be used to incur the effect $r.\pi$, then $r.\pi \in \texttt{effects}(\hat{\tau})$. If values of $\hat{\tau}$ can incur $r.\pi$, but need to be given the capability (as a function argument) by someone else to do so, then $r.\pi \in \texttt{ho-effects}(\hat{\tau})$. Definitions are given in Fig. 14.

$$\begin{aligned}
&\texttt{effects} :: \hat{\tau} \rightarrow \varepsilon \\
&\texttt{effects}(\{\bar{r}\}) = \{r.\pi \mid r \in \bar{r}, \pi \in \Pi\} \\
&\texttt{effects}(\hat{\tau}_1 \rightarrow_\varepsilon \hat{\tau}_2) = \texttt{ho-effects}(\hat{\tau}_1) \cup \varepsilon \cup \texttt{effects}(\hat{\tau}_2) \\
\\
&\texttt{ho-effects} :: \hat{\tau} \rightarrow \varepsilon \\
&\texttt{ho-effects}(\{\bar{r}\}) = \varnothing \\
&\texttt{ho-effects}(\hat{\tau}_1 \rightarrow_\varepsilon \hat{\tau}_2) = \texttt{effects}(\hat{\tau}_1) \cup \texttt{ho-effects}(\hat{\tau}_2)
\end{aligned}$$

Fig. 14. Effect functions (corrected).

Both `effects` and `ho-effects` are mutually recursive, with base cases for resource types. Any effect can be directly incurred by a resource on itself, hence $\texttt{effects}(\{\bar{r}\}) = \{r.\pi \mid r \in \bar{r}, \pi \in \Pi\}$. A resource cannot be used to indirectly invoke some other effect, so $\texttt{ho-effects}(\{\bar{r}\}) = \varnothing$. The mutual recursion echoes the subtyping rule for functions: recall that functions are contravariant in their input type and covariant in their output; likewise, both functions recurse on the input-type using the other function, and recurse on the output-type using the same function.

In light of these new definitions, we still require $\texttt{effects}(\hat{\tau}) \subseteq \varepsilon_s$—unannotated code must select any effect its capabilities can incur—but we add a new premise $\varepsilon_s \subseteq \texttt{ho-effects}(\hat{\tau})$, which requires any higher-order effect of the imported capabilities to be declared in ε_s. Put another way, the imported capabilities must be expecting every effect they could be given by the unannotated code (which is at most ε_s). The counterexample from Fig. 13 is now rejected, because $\texttt{ho-effects}((\texttt{Unit} \rightarrow_\varnothing \texttt{Unit}) \rightarrow_\varnothing \texttt{Unit}) = \varnothing$, but $\texttt{effects}(\texttt{File}) = \{\texttt{File.}*\} \not\subseteq \varnothing$.

This is *still* not sufficient! Consider $\varepsilon_s \subseteq \texttt{ho-effects}(\hat{\tau}_1 \rightarrow_{\varepsilon'} \hat{\tau}_2)$. Expanding the definition of `ho-effects`, this is the same as $\varepsilon_s \subseteq \texttt{effects}(\hat{\tau}_1) \cup \texttt{ho-effects}(\hat{\tau}_2)$. Let $r.\pi \in \varepsilon_s$ and suppose $r.\pi \in \texttt{effects}(\hat{\tau}_1)$, but $r.\pi \notin \texttt{ho-effects}(\hat{\tau}_2)$. Then

$\varepsilon_s \subseteq \texttt{effects}(\hat{\tau}_1) \cup \texttt{ho-effects}(\hat{\tau}_2)$ is still true, but $\hat{\tau}_2$ is not expecting $r.\pi$. If $\hat{\tau}_2$ is a function, unannotated code could violate its annotations by passing it a capability for $r.\pi$, even though $r.\pi$ is not a higher-order effect of $\hat{\tau}_2$.

The cause of this issue is that $\subseteq$ does not distribute over $\cup$. We want a relation like $\varepsilon_s \subseteq \texttt{effects}(\hat{\tau}_1) \cup \texttt{ho-effects}(\hat{\tau}_2)$, which also implies $\varepsilon_s \subseteq \texttt{effects}(\hat{\tau}_1)$ and $\varepsilon_s \subseteq \texttt{effects}(\hat{\tau}_2)$. Figure 15 defines this: safe is a distributive version of $\varepsilon_s \subseteq \texttt{effects}(\hat{\tau})$ and ho-safe is a distributive version of $\varepsilon_s \subseteq \texttt{ho-effects}(\hat{\tau})$. An amended version of ε-IMPORT is given in Fig. 16, with a new premise $\texttt{ho-safe}(\hat{\tau}, \varepsilon_s)$, capturing the notion that imported capabilities must be expecting the effects they could be passed by the unannotated code (which is at most ε_s).

$\boxed{\texttt{safe}(\hat{\tau}, \varepsilon)}$

$$\frac{}{\texttt{safe}(\{\bar{r}\}, \varepsilon)} \text{ (SAFE-RESOURCE)} \qquad \frac{\varepsilon \subseteq \varepsilon' \quad \texttt{ho-safe}(\hat{\tau}_1, \varepsilon) \quad \texttt{safe}(\hat{\tau}_2, \varepsilon)}{\texttt{safe}(\hat{\tau}_1 \rightarrow_{\varepsilon'} \hat{\tau}_2, \varepsilon)} \text{ (SAFE-ARROW)}$$

$\boxed{\texttt{ho-safe}(\hat{\tau}, \varepsilon)}$

$$\frac{}{\texttt{ho-safe}(\{\bar{r}\}, \varepsilon)} \text{ (HOSAFE-RESOURCE)} \qquad \frac{\texttt{safe}(\hat{\tau}_1, \varepsilon) \quad \texttt{ho-safe}(\hat{\tau}_2, \varepsilon)}{\texttt{ho-safe}(\hat{\tau}_1 \rightarrow_{\varepsilon'} \hat{\tau}_2, \varepsilon)} \text{ (HOSAFE-ARROW)}$$

Fig. 15. Safety judgements in CC.

$$\frac{\begin{array}{c}\hat{\Gamma} \vdash \hat{e} : \hat{\tau} \texttt{ with } \varepsilon_1 \quad \texttt{effects}(\hat{\tau}) \subseteq \varepsilon_s \\ \texttt{ho-safe}(\hat{\tau}, \varepsilon_s) \quad x : \texttt{erase}(\hat{\tau}) \vdash e : \tau\end{array}}{\hat{\Gamma} \vdash \texttt{import}(\varepsilon_s)\ x = \hat{e} \texttt{ in } e : \texttt{annot}(\tau, \varepsilon_s) \texttt{ with } \varepsilon \cup \varepsilon_1} \text{ (ε-IMPORT3-BAD)}$$

Fig. 16. A third (still incorrect) rule for type-and-effect checking import expressions.

The premises so far restrict what authority can be selected by unannotated code, but consider the example $\hat{e} = \texttt{import}(\varnothing)\ x = \texttt{unit in } \lambda f : \texttt{File. f.write}$. The unannotated code selects no capabilities and returns a function which takes File and incurs File.write. This satisfies the premises in ε-IMPORT3, but its type would be the pure function $\{\texttt{File}\} \rightarrow_{\varnothing} \texttt{Unit}$.

Speaking more generally, suppose the unannotated code evaluates to a function of type f, which is annotated to $\texttt{annot}(f, \varepsilon_s)$. Suppose $\texttt{annot}(f, \varepsilon_s)$ is invoked at a later point, back in the annotated world, incurring $r.\pi$. What is the source of $r.\pi$? If $r.\pi$ was selected by the import expression surrounding f, it is safe for $\texttt{annot}(f, \varepsilon_s)$ to incur this effect. Otherwise, $\texttt{annot}(f, \varepsilon_s)$ may have been passed, as an argument, a capability to do $r.\pi$, in which case $r.\pi$ is a higher-order effect of $\texttt{annot}(f, \varepsilon_s)$. If the argument is a function, then $r.\pi \in \varepsilon_s$ by the soundness of our calculus. But if the argument is a resource literal r, then $\texttt{annot}(f, \varepsilon_s)$ could exercise $r.\pi$ without declaring it in ε_s—this we do not yet account for.

To make ε_s contain every effect captured by resources passed into $\texttt{annot}(f, \varepsilon_s)$ as arguments, we inspect f for resource types. For example, if the unannotated code evaluates to a function of type $\{\texttt{File}\} \rightarrow \texttt{Unit}$, we need $\{\texttt{File.*}\} \in \varepsilon_s$. To do this, we add a new premise $\texttt{ho-effects}(\texttt{annot}(\tau, \varnothing)) \subseteq \varepsilon_s$. Because ho-effects is only defined on annotated types, we first annotate τ with $\varnothing$, and since we are only inspecting the resources passed into f as arguments, our choice of annotation doesn't matter.

Now we can handle the example from before. The unannotated code types via the judgement $x : \texttt{Unit} \vdash \lambda f : \{\texttt{File}\}.\ \texttt{f.write} : \{\texttt{File}\} \rightarrow \texttt{Unit}$. Its higher-order effects are $\texttt{ho-effects}(\texttt{annot}(\{\texttt{File}\} \rightarrow \texttt{Unit}, \varnothing)) = \{\texttt{File.*}\}$, but $\{\texttt{File.*}\} \not\subseteq \varnothing$, so the example is safely rejected.

The final version of ε-IMPORT is given in Fig. 17. With it, we can now model the example from the beginning of this section, where the Logger selects the File capability and exposes an unannotated function log with type $\texttt{Unit} \rightarrow \texttt{Unit}$ and implementation e. The expected least authority of Logger is $\{\texttt{File.append}\}$, so its corresponding import expression would be $\texttt{import}(\texttt{File.append})\ f = \texttt{File in } \lambda x : \texttt{Unit}.\ e$. The imported capability is $f = \texttt{File}$, which has type $\{\texttt{File}\}$, and $\texttt{effects}(\{\texttt{File}\}) = \{\texttt{File.*}\} \not\subseteq \{\texttt{File.append}\}$, so this example safely rejects: Logger.log has authority to do anything with File, and its implementation e might be violating its stipulated least authority $\{\texttt{File.append}\}$.

$$\frac{\begin{array}{c}\texttt{effects}(\hat{\tau}) \cup \texttt{ho-effects}(\texttt{annot}(\tau, \varnothing)) \subseteq \varepsilon_s \\ \hat{\Gamma} \vdash \hat{e} : \hat{\tau}\ \texttt{with}\ \varepsilon_1 \quad \texttt{ho-safe}(\hat{\tau}, \varepsilon_s) \quad x : \texttt{erase}(\hat{\tau}) \vdash e : \tau\end{array}}{\hat{\Gamma} \vdash \texttt{import}(\varepsilon_s)\ x = \hat{e}\ \texttt{in}\ e : \texttt{annot}(\tau, \varepsilon_s)\ \texttt{with}\ \varepsilon_s \cup \varepsilon_1}\ (\varepsilon\text{-IMPORT})$$

Fig. 17. The final rule for typing imports.

3 Applications

In this section, we examine a number of scenarios to show how capabilities can help developers reason about the effects and behaviour of code. In each story we will discuss some Wyvern code before translating it to CC and explaining how its rules apply. By doing this, we hope to convince the reader of the benefits of capability-based reasoning, and that CC captures the intuitive properties of capability-safe languages like Wyvern.

3.1 Unannotated Client

A logger module, when given File, exposes a log function which incurs the effect File.append. The client module, possessing the logger module, exposes an unannotated function run. While logger has been annotated, client has not. If client.run is executed, what effects might it have? Code for this example is given below.

```
module def logger(f: {File}):Logger
def log(): Unit with {File.append} =
  f.append(''message logged'')
```

```
module def client(logger: Logger)
def run(): Unit =
  logger.log()
```

```
require File
instantiate logger(File)
instantiate client(logger)
client.run()
```

A translation into CC is given below. Lines 1–3 and 5–8 define `MakeLogger` and `MakeClient`, which instantiate the `logger` and `client` modules respectively (represented as functions). Lines 10–14 define `MakeMain`, which returns a function which, when executed, instantiates all other modules and invokes the code in the body of `main`. Program execution begins on line 16, where `main` is given the initial capabilities (just `File` in this case).

```
1  let MakeLogger =
2    (λf: File.
3      λx: Unit. f.append) in
4
5  let MakeClient =
6    (λlogger: Unit →{File.append} Unit.
7      import(File.append) l = logger in
8        λx: Unit. l unit) in
9
10 let MakeMain =
11   (λf: File.
12       let loggerModule = MakeLogger f in
13       let clientModule = MakeClient loggerModule in
14       clientModule unit) in
15
16 MakeMain File
```

The interesting part is on line 7, where the unannotated code selects $\{\texttt{File.append}\}$ as its authority. This matches the effects of `logger`, i.e. $\texttt{effects}(\texttt{Unit} \rightarrow_{\{\texttt{File.append}\}} \texttt{Unit}) = \{\texttt{File.append}\}$. The unannotated code typechecks by ε-IMPORT, approximating its effects as $\{\texttt{File.append}\}$.

3.2 Unannotated Library

The next example inverts the roles of the last scenario. Now, the annotated `client` wants to use the unannotated `logger`, which captures `File` and exposes a single function `log`, which incurs the `File.append` effect. The implementation of `client.run` executes `logger.log`; it is annotated with $\varnothing$, so this violates its interface.

```
module def logger(f: {File}): Logger
def log(): Unit =
    f.append(''message logged'')
```

```
module def client(logger: Logger)
def run(): Unit with {File.append} =
   logger.log()
```

```
require File
instantiate logger(File)
instantiate client(logger)
client.run()
```

The translation is given below. On lines 3–4, the unannotated code is wrapped in an `import` expression selecting {`File.append`} as its authority. The implementation of `logger` actually abides by this, but since it captures `File` it could, in general, do anything to `File`; therefore, ε-IMPORT rejects this example. Formally, the imported capability has the type {`File`}, but $\texttt{effects}(\{\texttt{File}\}) = \{\texttt{File.*}\} \not\subseteq \{\texttt{File.append}\}$. The only way for this to typecheck would be to annotate `client.run` as having every effect on `File`.

```
1  let MakeLogger =
2    (λf: File.
3      import(File.append) f = f in
4        λx: Unit. f.append) in
5
6  let MakeClient =
7    (λlogger: Logger.
8      λx: Unit. logger unit) in
9
10 let MakeMain =
11   (λf: File.
12     let loggerModule = MakeLogger f in
13     let clientModule = MakeClient loggerModule in
14     clientModule unit) in
15
16 MakeMain File
```

3.3 Higher-Order Effects

Here, `Main` gains its functionality from a plugin. Plugins might be written by third-parties, so we may not be able to view their source code, but still want to reason about the authority they exercise. In this example, `plugin` has access to `File`, but its interface does not permit it to perform any operations on `File`. It tries to subvert this by wrapping `File` inside a function and passing it to `malicious`, which invokes `File.read` in a higher-order manner in an unannotated context.

```
module malicious
def log(f: Unit → Unit): Unit
   f()
```

```
module plugin
import malicious
def run(f: {File}): Unit with ∅
  malicious.log(λx:Unit. f.read)
```

```
require File
import plugin
plugin.run(File)
```

This example shows how higher-order effects can obfuscate potential security risks. On line 3 of `malicious`, the argument to `log` has type `Unit` → `Unit`. The body of `log` types with the T-rules, which do not approximate effects. It is not clear from inspecting the unannotated code that a `File.read` will be incurred. To realise this requires one to examine the source code of both `plugin` and `malicious`.

A translation is given below. On lines 2–3, the `malicious` code selects its authority as ∅, to be consistent with the annotation on `plugin.run`. ε-IMPORT safely rejects this: when the unannotated code is annotated with ∅, it has type {`File`} $\rightarrow_{\varnothing}$ `Unit`, but the higher-order effects of this type are {`File.`∗}, which are not contained in the selected authority ∅.

```
1  let malicious =
2    (import(∅) y=unit in
3      λf: Unit → Unit. f()) in
4
5  let plugin =
6    (λf: {File}.
7      malicious(λx:Unit. f.read)) in
8
9  let MakeMain =
10   (λf: {File}.
11     plugin f) in
12
13 MakeMain File
```

To get this example to typecheck, the program would have to be rewritten to explicitly say that plugins can exercise arbitrary authority over `File`, by changing the selected authority of `import` and the annotation on `plugin.run`.

3.4 Resource Leak

This is another example which obfuscates an unsafe effect by invoking it in a higher-order manner. The setup is the same, except the function which `plugin` passes to `malicious` now returns `File` when invoked. `malicious` uses this function to obtain `File` and directly invokes `read` upon it, violating the declared purity of `plugin`.

```
module malicious
def log(f: Unit → File):Unit
  f().read
```

```
module plugin
import malicious
def run(f: {File}): Unit with ∅
  malicious.log(λx:Unit. f)
```

```
require File
import plugin
plugin.run(File)
```

The translation is given below. The unannotated code in `malicious` is on lines 5–6. It has selected authority is ∅, to be consistent with the annotation on `plugin`. Nothing is being imported, so the `import` binds y to `unit`. This example is rejected by ε-IMPORT because the premise $\varepsilon = \texttt{effects}(\hat{\tau}) \cup \texttt{ho-effects}(\texttt{annot}(\tau, \varepsilon))$ is not satisfied. In this case, $\varepsilon = \varnothing$ and $\tau = (\texttt{Unit} \rightarrow \{\texttt{File}\}) \rightarrow \texttt{Unit}$. Then $\texttt{annot}(\tau, \varepsilon) = (\texttt{Unit} \rightarrow_{\varnothing} \{\texttt{File}\}) \rightarrow_{\varnothing} \texttt{Unit}$ and $\texttt{ho-effects}(\texttt{annot}(\tau, \varepsilon)) = \{\texttt{File}.*\}$. Thus, the premise cannot be satisfied and the example is safely rejected.

```
1  let malicious =
2    (import(∅) y=unit in
3      λf: Unit → {File}. f().read) in
4
5  let plugin =
6    (λf: {File}.
7      malicious(λx:Unit. f)) in
8
9  let MakeMain =
10   (λf: {File}.
11     plugin f) in
12
13 MakeMain File
```

4 Conclusions

We introduced CC, a lambda calculus with a simple notion of resources and their operations, which allows unannotated code to be nested inside annotated code with a new `import` construct. Its capability-safe design enables us to safely reason about the effects of unannotated code by inspecting what capabilities are passed into it by its annotated surroundings. Such an approach allows code to be incrementally annotated, giving developers a balance between safety and convenience, alleviating the verbosity that has discouraged widespread adoption of effect systems [19].

More broadly, our results demonstrate that the most basic form of capability-based reasoning—that you can infer what code can do based on what capabilities are passed to it—is not only useful for informal reasoning, but can improve formal reasoning about code by reducing the necessary annotation overhead.

4.1 Related Work

While much related work has already been discussed as part of the presentation, here we cover some additional strands related to capabilities and effects.

Capabilities were introduced by [3] to control which processes had permission to access which resources in an operating system. These ideas were adapted to the programming language setting, particularly by Miller [17], whose object-capability model constrains how permissions may proliferate among objects in a distributed system. [13] formalised the notion of a capability-safe language and showed that a subset of Caja (a Javascript implementation) is capability-safe. Miller's object-capability model has been applied to more heavyweight systems, such as [6], which formalises the notion of trust in a Hoare logic. Capability-safety parallels have been explored in the operating systems literature, where similar restrictions on dynamic loading and resource access [7] enable static, lightweight analyses to enforce privilege separation [12].

The original effect system by [10] was used to determine what expressions could safely execute in parallel. Subsequent applications include determining what functions a program might invoke [21] and what regions in memory might be accessed or updated during execution [20]. In these systems, "effects" are performed upon "regions"; in ours, "operations" are performed upon "resources". CC also distinguishes between unannotated and annotated code; only the latter will type-and-effect-check. Another capability-based effect system is the one by [4], who use effect polymorphism and possible world semantics to express behavioural invariants on data structures. CC is not as expressive, since it only inspects how capabilities are passed around a program, but the resulting formalism and theory is much more lightweight. Ongoing work with the Wyvern programming language includes an effect system which partially builds on ideas from this paper [15].

4.2 Future Work

Our system only models capabilities which manipulate system resources. This definition could be generalised to track other sorts of effects, such as stateful updates. Resources and their operations are fixed throughout runtime, but we could imagine them being created and destroyed at runtime. Finally, other future work could incorporate polymorphic types and effects.

References

1. Coker, Z., Maass, M., Ding, T., Le Goues, C., Sunshine, J.: Evaluating the flexibility of the Java sandbox. In: Proceedings of the 31st Annual Computer Security Applications Conference, ACSAC 2015, USA, pp. 1–10 (2015)
2. Craig, A., Potanin, A., Groves, L., Aldrich, J.: Capabilities: effects for free. Technical report, School of Engineering and Computer Science, Victoria University of Wellington, Wellington, New Zealand (2018). https://ecs.victoria.ac.nz/Main/TechnicalReportSeries
3. Dennis, J.B., Van Horn, E.C.: Programming semantics for multiprogrammed computations. Commun. ACM **9**(3), 143–155 (1966)
4. Devriese, D., Birkedal, L., Piessens, F.: Reasoning about object capabilities with logical relations and effect parametricity. In: IEEE European Symposium on Security and Privacy (2016)
5. Dimoulas, C., Moore, S., Askarov, A., Chong, S.: Declarative policies for capability control. In: Computer Security Foundations Symposium (2014)

6. Drossopoulou, S., Noble, J., Miller, M.S., Murray, T.: Reasoning about risk and trust in an open world. In: ECOOP, pp. 451–475 (2007)
7. Hunt, G., et al.: Sealing OS processes to improve dependability and safety. SIGOPS OS Rev. **41**(3), 341–354 (2007)
8. Kiniry, J.R.: Exceptions in Java and Eiffel: two extremes in exception design and application. In: Dony, C., Knudsen, J.L., Romanovsky, A., Tripathi, A. (eds.) Advanced Topics in Exception Handling Techniques. LNCS, vol. 4119, pp. 288–300. Springer, Heidelberg (2006). https://doi.org/10.1007/11818502_16
9. Leijen, D.: Koka: programming with row polymorphic effect types. In: Mathematically Structured Functional Programming 2014. EPTCS, March 2014
10. Lucassen, J.M., Gifford, D.K.: Polymorphic effect systems. In: POPL, POPL 1988, USA, pp. 47–57 (1988)
11. Maass, M.: A theory and tools for applying sandboxes effectively. Ph.D. thesis, Carnegie Mellon University (2016)
12. Madhavapeddy, A., et al.: Unikernels: library operating systems for the cloud. SIGPLAN Not. **48**(4), 461–472 (2013)
13. Maffeis, S., Mitchell, J.C., Taly, A.: Object capabilities and isolation of untrusted web applications. In: Proceedings of the 2010 IEEE Symposium on Security and Privacy, SP 2010, pp. 125–140. IEEE Computer Society (2010)
14. Melicher, D., Shi, Y., Potanin, A., Aldrich, J.: A capability-based module system. In: 31st European Conference on Object-Oriented Programming (ECOOP 2017), pp 20:1–20:27 (2017). Article No. 20
15. Melicher, D., Shi, Y., Zhao, V., Potanin, A., Aldrich, J.: Using object capabilities and effects to build an authority-safe module system: poster. In: Proceedings of the 5th Annual Symposium and Bootcamp on Hot Topics in the Science of Security, HoTSoS 2018, Raleigh, North Carolina, USA, 10–11 April 2018
16. Miller, M., Yee, K.P., Shapiro, J.: Capability myths demolished. Technical report SRL2003-02, Systems Research Laboratory, Johns Hopkins University (2003)
17. Miller, M.S.: Robust composition: towards a unified approach to access control and concurrency control. Ph.D. thesis, Johns Hopkins University (2006)
18. Nielson, F., Nielson, H.R.: Type and effect systems. In: Olderog, E.-R., Steffen, B. (eds.) Correct System Design. LNCS, vol. 1710, pp. 114–136. Springer, Heidelberg (1999). https://doi.org/10.1007/3-540-48092-7_6
19. Rytz, L., Odersky, M., Haller, P.: Lightweight polymorphic effects. In: Noble, J. (ed.) ECOOP 2012. LNCS, vol. 7313, pp. 258–282. Springer, Heidelberg (2012). https://doi.org/10.1007/978-3-642-31057-7_13
20. Talpin, J.P., Jouvelot, P.: The type and effect discipline. Inf. Comput. **111**(2), 245–296 (1994)
21. Tang, Y.M.: Control-flow analysis by effect systems and abstract interpretation. Ph.D. thesis, Ecole des Mines de Paris (1994)

Theorem Proving

A Framework for Interactive Verification of Architectural Design Patterns in Isabelle/HOL

Diego Marmsoler(✉)

Technische Universität München, Munich, Germany
diego.marmsoler@tum.de

Abstract. Architectural design patterns capture architectural design experience and are an important tool in software engineering to support the conceptualization and analysis of architectures. They constrain different aspects of an architecture and usually guarantee some corresponding properties for architectures implementing them. Verifying such patterns requires proving that the constraints imposed by the pattern indeed lead to architectures which satisfy the corresponding guarantee. Due to the abstract nature of patterns, verification is often done by means of interactive theorem proving and requires detailed knowledge about the underlying model, limiting its application to experts of this model. Moreover, proving properties for different patterns usually involves repetitive proof steps, leading to proofs which are difficult to maintain. To address these problems, we developed a framework that supports the interactive verification of architectural design patterns in Isabelle/HOL. The framework implements a model for dynamic architectures as well as a corresponding calculus in terms of two Isabelle/HOL theories and consists of roughly 3 500 lines of Isabelle/HOL proof script. To evaluate our framework, we applied it for the verification of four different architectural design patterns and compared the overall amount of proof code to the code contributed by the framework. Our results suggest that the framework has the potential to significantly reduce the amount of proof code required for the verification of patterns and thus to address the problems mentioned above.

Keywords: Architectural design pattern
Interactive theorem proving · Architecture verification
Configuration trace · Co-inductive list · Isabelle/HOL

1 Introduction

Architectural design patterns (ADPs) are an important tool in software engineering for the conceptualization and analysis of software systems. They capture architectural design experience and are regarded as the 'Grand Tool' for designing a software systems architecture [1]. ADPs usually constrain the design of an

J. Sun and M. Sun (Eds.): ICFEM 2018, LNCS 11232, pp. 251–269, 2018.
https://doi.org/10.1007/978-3-030-02450-5_15

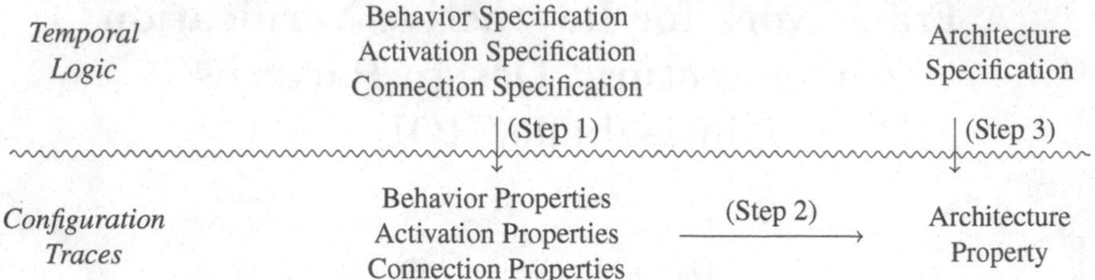

Fig. 1. Interactive verification of architectural design patterns.

architecture: the types of components, the activation/deactivation of components of a certain type, and connections between active components. In return, they guarantee certain safety/liveness properties for architectures implementing the pattern [2]. Verifying ADPs requires to verify whether the constraints imposed by them indeed lead to the claimed guarantees. Due to the abstract nature of patterns, verification is often done by means of interactive theorem proving [3]. The corresponding process is summarized in Fig. 1: The specification of an ADP is given in terms of temporal logic formulæ to express the constraints on the behavior of components as well as on their activation/deactivation and interconnection. In addition, the pattern's guarantee is specified in terms of a temporal logic formula over the architecture as a whole. To verify the pattern, one has to interpret the specification at the model level in terms of different sets of configuration traces (Step 1) and show that the intersection of these properties leads to a property (Step 2) which corresponds to the claimed guarantee (Step 3).

Problem Description. First attempts to verify different patterns revealed that reasoning about a pattern's specification imposes the following challenges:

- The interpretation of the specification (Step 1) and verification results (Step 3) requires deep knowledge about the model of configuration traces.
- The proof of the guarantee itself (Step 2) requires many repetitive steps which are similar for every ADP.

These problems have two negative consequences on the verification of ADPs:

- The required expertise limits the practical applicability of the approach: verification is restricted to experts of the model.
- The repetitive nature of the proofs increases the effort to verify a pattern in the first place as well as to maintain verification results in the long run.

Approach. In order to address the problems identified above, we developed a framework to support the interactive verification of patterns at a more abstract level: we implemented the model of configuration traces [4,5] as well as a corresponding calculus [6,7] to support reasoning about component behavior, in Isabelle/HOL [8]. The implementation consists of two theories amounting to roughly 3 500 lines of Isabelle/HOL proof script and is available online via the archive of formal proofs [9].

Evaluation. To evaluate the framework, we first applied it for the verification of four different ADPs: a variant of the *Singleton*, the *Publisher-Subscriber*, and the *Blackboard* pattern as well as a pattern for *Blockchain* architectures. Then, we calculated the overall number of proof lines for each of the patterns and compared it to the number of lines contributed by the framework. The corresponding theories are again available online as a separate entry in the archive of formal proofs [10] and consist of another 3 500 lines of Isabelle/HOL proof script.

Contributions. With this paper, we report on the results obtained from our development. Thus, its major contributions can be summarized as follows:

- It *describes* the *framework* itself: the major definitions and corresponding theorems as well as its interface in terms of an Isabelle/HOL locale [11].
- It *demonstrates* the *use of the framework* in terms of a running example.
- It *presents* and *discusses* the data obtained from the *evaluation* of the framework.

Overview. The remainder of the paper is organized as follows: In Sect. 2, we provide some background for our work. Therefore, we first describe our formal model of architectures (Sect. 2.1). Then, we introduce the Blackboard pattern as our running example (Sect. 2.2). Finally, we provide some general background on Isabelle/HOL for readers who are not familiar with it (Sect. 2.3). In Sect. 3, we then present our framework. Therefore, we first provide an overview of the major definitions and theorems and then we demonstrate its usage in terms of our running example. We continue with a discussion about the evaluation of the framework and the obtained results in Sect. 4. Finally, we discuss related work in Sect. 5 and conclude with a brief outlook and a description of next steps in Sect. 6.

2 Background

In the following, we provide some background for our work. Therefore, we first introduce the formal model of architectures on which our approach is based on. Then, we introduce a variant of the Blackboard pattern which serves as a running example. Finally, we provide some background on Isabelle/HOL for readers not familiar with it.

2.1 A Model of Dynamic Architectures

Since some architectural patterns involve dynamic aspects, such as component activation and deactivation, as well as architecture reconfiguration, our framework is based on a model of dynamic architectures. In our model, such an architecture is represented by *a set* of so-called *configuration traces* [4,5], i.e., streams [12] of architecture snapshots. An *architecture snapshot* represents the state of an architecture at some point in time: active components with their ports valuated by messages and connections between the ports of these components.

Figure 2 depicts the first three snapshots of a conceptual representation of an exemplary configuration trace: components are represented by gray rectangles and their ports by empty (input) and filled (output) circles, port valuations are represented by assignments of sets of messages (numbers or characters) to the corresponding port, and connections between ports are represented by solid lines between the ports.

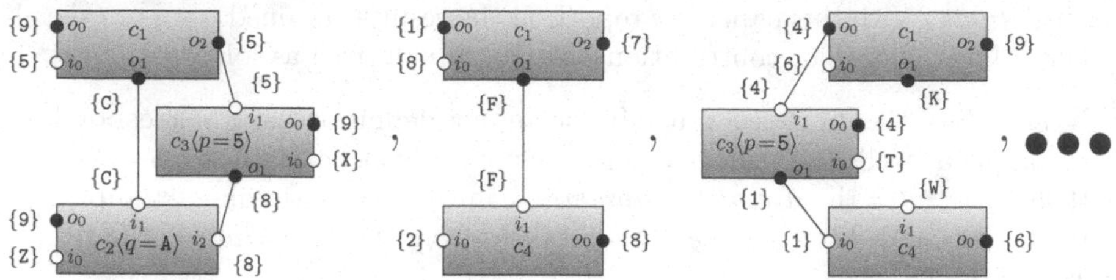

Fig. 2. Conceptual representation of a configuration trace.

Composition is modeled in terms of *behavior projection* which can be used to extract the behavior of a single component out of a given configuration trace. Given *valid* behavior for each component in terms of streams of valuations of the component's ports, composition of components results in a set of configuration traces, such that the behavior of each component (obtained through projection) is a valid behavior for that component.

2.2 A Pattern for Blackboard Architectures

Throughout the paper, we shall use a variant of the Blackboard pattern [1,2,13] to demonstrate our ideas. Blackboard architectures are usually found in systems which work on some collaborative problem solving task. Thereby, it is desired to design an architecture which can solve a complex problem (such as solving a logical equation composed of several sub formulas connected by logical operators) by breaking it down into simpler sub problems (such as solving the corresponding sub formulas) which can be solved and assembled to a solution for the original problem.

In the following, we specify the pattern in terms of sets of configuration traces. Therefore, we first specify the types of involved messages in terms of abstract data types [14,15]. Then, we specify component types in two steps: first, we graphically specify a set of interfaces using so-called *configuration diagrams* [16]. Then, we specify assertions about the behavior of components in terms of so-called *behavior trace assertions*, i.e., linear temporal logic formulæ [17] using port names as free variables. Finally, we add architectural assertions to specify component activation and deactivation as well as connection reconfiguration. Architectural assertions are specified using so-called *configuration trace assertions*, i.e., linear temporal logic formulæ using component variables and some designated predicates to express component activation ($\|\_\|$) and connections between ports of components ($\_.\_ \rightsquigarrow \_.\_$).

Data Types. Blackboard architectures work with *problems* and *solutions* for them. Figure 3a provides an algebraic specification for the corresponding data types. We denote by $\mathtt{PROB}$ the set of all problems and by $\mathtt{SOL}$ the set of all solutions. Complex problems consist of *subproblems* which can be complex themselves. To solve a problem, its subproblems have to be solved first. Therefore, we assume the existence of a *subproblem relation* $\prec \subseteq \mathtt{PROB} \times \mathtt{PROB}$. For complex problems, this relation may not be known in advance. Indeed, one of the benefits of a Blackboard architecture is that a problem can be solved also without knowing this relation in advance. However, the subproblem relation has to be well-founded (a partial order with no infinite decreasing chains) (Eq. (1)) for a problem to be solvable. In particular, we do not allow for cycles in the transitive closure of $\prec$. While there may be different approaches to solve a problem (i.e. several ways to split a problem into subproblems), we assume that the final solution for a problem is always unique. Thus, we postulate the existence of a function $solve\colon \mathtt{PROB} \rightarrow \mathtt{SOL}$ which assigns the *correct* solution to each problem. Note, however, that this function is not known in advance and it is one of the reasons of using this pattern to calculate this function.

Component Types. Two types of components are common for Blackboard architectures: blackboards and knowledge sources. The corresponding interfaces are specified by the configuration diagram depicted in Fig. 3c. The types of data which can be exchanged through each of the ports is given by the corresponding

DTSpec ProbSol	**imports** SET
$\prec$:	$\mathtt{PROB} \times \mathtt{PROB}$
solve:	$\mathtt{PROB} \rightarrow \mathtt{SOL}$
well-founded($\prec$)	(1)

(a) Data Type Specification.

PSpec BBPorts	**imports** ProbSol
rp:	$\mathtt{PROB} \times \wp(\mathtt{PROB})$
ns, *cs*:	$\mathtt{PROB} \times \mathtt{SOL}$
op, *prob*:	$\mathtt{PROB}$

(b) Port Specification.

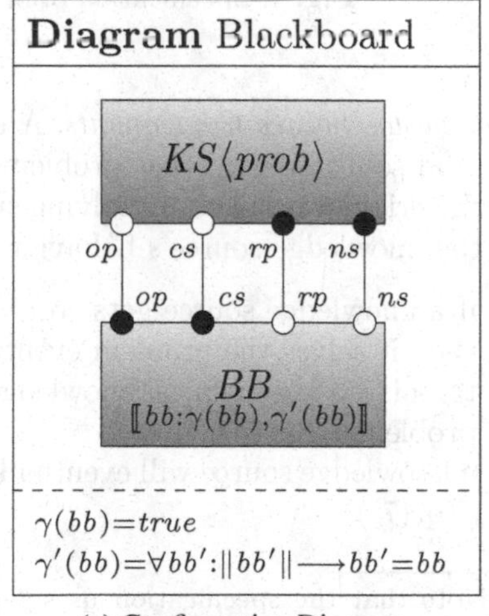

(c) Configuration Diagram.

Fig. 3. Specification of a Blackboard architecture.

port specification (Fig. 3b). Since each component of type knowledge sources can solve only certain problems, knowledge sources are parametrized by a problem *prob*. In the following, we specify the behavior of components of each of the two types.

Blackboard Components. A Blackboard provides the *current state* towards solving the original problem and forwards problems and solutions from knowledge sources. Figure 4 provides a specification of the blackboard's behavior in terms of three behavior trace assertions[1]:

- if a solution to a subproblem is received on its input, then it is eventually provided at its output (Eq. 2).
- if solving a problem requires a set of subproblems to be solved first, those problems are eventually provided at its output (Eq. (3)).
- a problem is provided as long as it is not solved (Eq. (4)).

BSpec Blackboard — **for** *BB* **of** Blackboard

flex	p:	PROB
	P:	PROB SET
rig	p':	PROB
	s':	SOL

$$\square\Big(\big(p', s'\big) \in ns \longrightarrow \diamondsuit\big((p', s') \in cs\big)\Big) \tag{2}$$

$$\square\Big(\big(p, P\big) \in rp \longrightarrow \big(\forall p' \in P\colon \ (\diamondsuit(p' \in op))\big)\Big) \tag{3}$$

$$\square\Big(p' \in op \longrightarrow \big(p' \in op\ \mathcal{W}\ (p', solve(p')) \in cs\big)\Big) \tag{4}$$

Fig. 4. Specification of behavior for blackboard components.

Knowledge Source Components. A knowledge source receives open problems via *op* and solutions for other problems via *cs*. It might contribute to the solution of the original problem by solving subproblems. Figure 5 provides a specification of the knowledge source's behavior in terms of three behavior trace assertions:

- if a knowledge source gets correct solutions for all the required subproblems, then it solves the problem eventually (Eq. (5)).
- to solve a problem, a knowledge source requires solutions only for smaller problems (Eq. (6)).
- a knowledge source will eventually communicate if it is able to solve a problem (Eq. (7)).

[1] Note that the specification uses *flexible* and *rigid* variables: while the former are newly interpreted at each point in time, the latter keep their value over time. Moreover, it uses the *weak* until operator which is defined as follows: $\gamma'\ \mathcal{W}\ \gamma \stackrel{\text{def}}{=} \square(\gamma') \vee (\gamma'\ \mathcal{U}\ \gamma)$.

BSpec Knowledge Source		**for** $KS\langle prob\rangle$ **of** Blackboard
flex	p:	PROB
	P:	$\wp$(PROB)
rig	p':	PROB

$$\Box\Big(\forall (prob, P) \in rp\colon \big((\forall p' \in P\colon \Diamond(p', solve(p')) \in cs) \longrightarrow \Diamond(prob, solve(prob)) \in ns\big)\Big) \quad (5)$$

$$\Box\Big(\forall (prob, P) \in rp\colon \forall p \in P\colon p \prec prob\Big) \quad (6)$$

$$\Box\Big(prob \in op \longrightarrow \Diamond(\exists P\colon (prob, P) \in rp)\Big) \quad (7)$$

Fig. 5. Specification of behavior for knowledge source components.

Architectural Constraints. Architectural constraints for the Blackboard pattern are described by the configuration diagram in Fig. 3c: The '$[\![bb\colon \gamma(bb), \gamma'(bb)]\!]$' annotation for a blackboard interface provides lower and upper bounds for the activation of blackboard components

- With $\gamma(bb) = true$, we require that a blackboard component is always activated.
- With $\gamma'(bb) = \forall bb'\colon \|bb'\| \longrightarrow bb' = bb$, we require that a blackboard component is unique.

Thus, we require a *unique* blackboard component to be always activated. The absence of annotations for *KS* interfaces, on the other hand, allows knowledge source components to be de-/activated over time. The *solid* connections between the ports denote a constraint requiring that the ports of a knowledge source component are connected with the corresponding ports of a blackboard component as depicted, whenever both components are active. Note that many knowledge sources may be active at each point in time, in which case every knowledge source is connected to the blackboard as depicted in the diagram.

The constraints introduced by the configuration diagram are refined by an additional configuration trace assertions provided in Fig. 6: By Eq. (8) we require that whenever a knowledge source obtains a request to solve a problem which it is able to solve, the knowledge source will stay active until that problem is solved ($ks'_{p'}$ denotes a knowledge source which is able to solve problem p').

ASpec Blackboard		**for** Blackboard
rig	ks':	$KS\langle prob\rangle$
	p':	PROB

$$\Box\Big(\|ks'_{p'}\| \wedge p' \in ks'.op \longrightarrow \big(\|ks'_{p'}\| \;\mathcal{W}\; \|ks'_{p'}\| \wedge (p', solve(p')) \in ks'.ns\big)\Big) \quad (8)$$

Fig. 6. Specification of activation constraints for Blackboard architectures.

2.3 Isabelle/HOL

Isabelle is an LCF-style [18] theorem prover based on Standard ML [19]. It provides a so-called meta-logic on which different object logics are based. Isabelle/HOL is one of them, implementing higher-order logic for Isabelle. It integrates a prover IDE and comes with an extensive library of theories from various domains. New theories are then developed by defining terms of a certain type and deriving theorems from these definitions. To support the specification of theories, Isabelle/HOL provides tools for the specification of (co)datatypes [20] and (co)recursive functions. To support the verification of theorems, Isabelle/HOL provides a structured proof language called Isabelle/Isar [21] and a set of logical reasoners to verify correctness of single proof steps. For the development of our framework, two additional features of Isabelle are important: coinductive lists and locales.

Coinductive Lists. In order to implement the model of configuration traces in Isabelle/HOL, we relied on Lochbihler's theory of coinductive (lazy) lists [22]. In his theory, Lochbihler formalized lazy lists using Isabelle/HOL's coinductive datatype package and provides definitions and properties for many important concepts such as filtering elements from infinite lists to create new lists.

Locales. In Isabelle, modularization of theories is supported through the notion of locales [11]. A locale consists of a list of type and function parameters and corresponding assumptions about them. Locales can extend other locales and may be instantiated by concrete definitions of the corresponding parameters.

3 IPV: A Framework for Interactive Pattern Verification

Figure 7 provides an overview of our framework for the interactive verification of architectural design patterns: The framework consists of two Isabelle/HOL theories which are available through the archive of formal proofs [9]:

`Configuration_Traces` imports theory `Coinductive_List` and provides a formalization of the model described in Sect. 2.1 in terms of lazy lists.

`Dynamic_Architecture_Calculus` imports theory `Configuration_Traces`, provides operators for the specification of component behavior, and implements a calculus to reason about component behavior [7] specified using these operators.

Moreover, the framework provides an interface to these theories in terms of an Isabelle/HOL locale [11] `dynamic_component`. The locale requires definitions for certain concepts of the model (Step 1) and then provides customized operators for the specification of component behavior (Step 2) and rules to support reasoning about such specifications (Step 3). A pattern theory may use the framework by instantiating the locale for every type of component involved in the pattern. Then, the behavior of each component type is specified using the specification operators provided by the corresponding instantiation. Moreover, activation and connection constraints are specified for components of the different types. Finally, the pattern can be verified by using the verification rules provided by the framework.

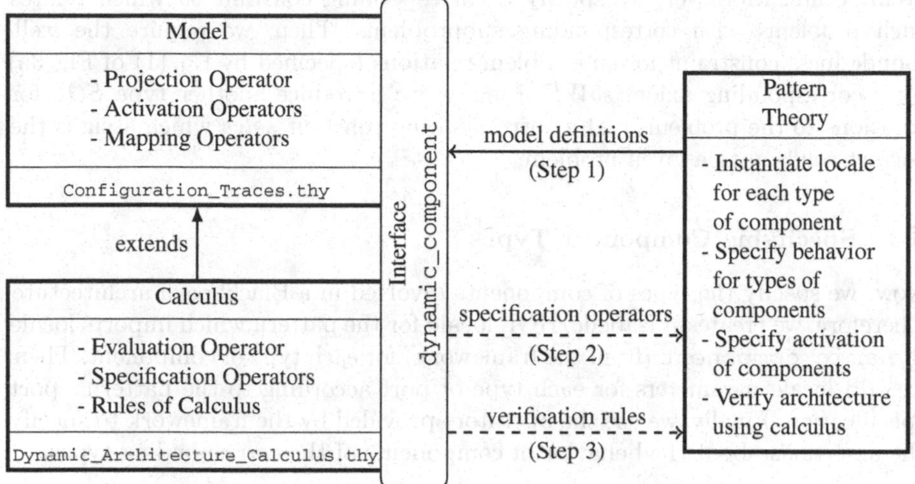

Fig. 7. Overview of IPV framework.

In the following, we demonstrate the different steps in more detail in terms of our running example. Thereby, we specify the Blackboard pattern introduced in Sect. 2.2 in Isabelle/HOL and verify a characteristic property of such architectures using the verification rules provided by the framework. The corresponding Isabelle/HOL script is provided in this paper's electronic supplementary material [23].

3.1 Creating the Theory

As a first step, we create a new Isabelle/HOL theory which imports theory `Dynamic_Architecture_Calculus` [9] from the Archive of Formal Proofs:

theory *Blackboard* **imports** *DynamicArchitectures.Dynamic-Architecture-Calculus*

Note that importing theory `Dynamic_Architecture_Calculus` is crucial here, since it provides access to locale `dynamic_component` which is used in Sect. 3.3 to specify the pattern.

3.2 Specifying Data Types

Next, we specify Isabelle/HOL datatypes for the data types required by the Blackboard pattern (specified in Fig. 3a):

```
typedecl PROB
consts sb :: (PROB × PROB) set
axiomatization where sbWF: wf sb
typedecl SOL
consts solve:: PROB ⇒ SOL
```

First, we introduce a new type *PROB* for the problems to be solved by the architecture. Moreover, we specify a corresponding constant *sb* which relates such problems with corresponding subproblems. Then, we require the well-foundedness constraint for subproblem relations (specified by Eq. (1) of Fig. 3a) by a corresponding axiom *sbWF*. Finally, we introduce another type *SOL* for solutions to the problems and a corresponding constant *solve* which assigns the correct solution to a given problem.

3.3 Specifying Component Types

Now, we specify the types of components involved in a Blackboard architecture. Therefore, we create an Isabelle/HOL locale for the pattern which imports locale `dynamic_component` (from the framework) for each type of component. Then, we add locale parameters for each type of port according to the pattern's port specification. Finally, we use the operators provided by the framework to specify the assertions about the behavior of components of the corresponding types.

Creating the Pattern's Locale. According to Sect. 2.2, a Blackboard architecture has two types of components: blackboards and knowledge sources. Thus, we create a locale `blackboard` with two instantiations of locale `dynamic_component`: *bb* and *ks*, respectively.

```
locale blackboard =
 bb: dynamic-component bbcmp bbactive +
 ks: dynamic-component kscmp ksactive
 for bbactive :: 'bid ⇒ cnf ⇒ bool (‖-‖-)
  and bbcmp :: 'bid ⇒ cnf ⇒ 'BB (σ-(-))
  and ksactive :: 'kid ⇒ cnf ⇒ bool (‖-‖-)
  and kscmp :: 'kid ⇒ cnf ⇒ 'KS (σ-(-)) +
```

Note that locale `dynamic_component` requires two parameters for each type of component: a function to denote activation of a component of the corresponding type within a given architecture snapshot, and another function to obtain a certain component from a given architecture snapshot. Thus, we specify corresponding functions to denote activation and component selection for blackboards (*bbactive* and *bbcmp*) as well as for knowledge sources (*ksactive* and *kscmp*) and pass them to the corresponding locale import. To foster readability, we also provide concrete syntax for these functions: ‖_‖ for activation and σ(_) for selection.

Importing the locale for blackboards and knowledge sources provides us with custom specification mechanisms for these types of components:

- Evaluation functions *bb.eval* and *ks.eval*, to evaluate component behavior specifications for blackboards and knowledge sources, respectively.
- Specification operators for common linear temporal logic operators such as next (*bb.nxt*/*ks.nxt*), globally (*bb.glob*/*ks.glob*), eventually (*bb.evt*/*ks.evt*), until (*bb.until*/*ks.until*), and weak until (*bb.wuntil*/*ks.wuntil*).

Moreover, importing the locale also provides us with rules to support reasoning about specifications involving these operators (in terms of Isabelle/HOL lemmata). In essence, the framework provides introduction and elimination rules for all the temporal operators combined with corresponding specifications of component activation (this amounts to roughly 35 rules for each type of component).

Specifying Ports and Parameters. As described in Sect. 2.2, each component type specifies 4 ports to exchange data with its environment. Thus, for each instance of the port types specified in Fig. 3b by one of the component types, we create one corresponding locale parameter:

```
fixes bbrp :: 'BB ⇒ (PROB × PROB set) set
 and ksrp :: 'KS ⇒ PROB × PROB set
 and bbns :: 'BB ⇒ (PROB × SOL) set
 ...
```

The parameters are modeled as functions which take a snapshot of a component of the corresponding type ('BB or 'KS) and return a set of elements according to the ports data type.

As mentioned in Sect. 2.2, each knowledge source is parametrized by a problem which it can solve. Thus, we first add a corresponding locale parameter which associates a problem with each knowledge source:

```
and prob :: 'kid ⇒ PROB
```

Moreover, we add a locale assertion which ensures that at least one knowledge source exists for each possible problem:

```
assumes
ks1: ∀p. ∃ks. p=prob ks
```

Specifying Component Behavior. Next we can specify the assertions about the behavior of the blackboard or knowledge sources as specified in Figs. 4 and 5, respectively. Note that assumptions about component behavior are specified in terms of behavior trace assertions (without considering component activation or deactivation). Thus, the specification of the corresponding locale assumptions need to be formulated using the temporal logic operators provided by the framework and described above:

and *bhvbb1*: $\bigwedge t\ t'\ bid\ p\ s.\ [\![t \in arch]\!] \Longrightarrow bb.eval\ bid\ t\ t'\ 0$
$(\Box_b\ (bb.ba\ (\lambda\ bb.\ (p,s) \in bbns\ bb) \longrightarrow^b (\Diamond_b\ (bb.ba\ (\lambda\ bb.\ (p,s) \in bbcs\ bb)))))$
...
and *bhvks1*: $\bigwedge t\ t'\ kId\ p\ P.\ [\![t \in arch;\ p = prob\ kId]\!] \Longrightarrow ks.eval\ kId\ t\ t'\ 0$
$(\Box_b\ ((ks.ba\ (\lambda\ ks.\ (p,\ P) = ksrp\ ks))\ \wedge^b$
$(\forall_b\ q.\ ((ks.pred\ (q \in P)) \longrightarrow^b (\Diamond_b\ (ks.ba\ (\lambda\ ks.\ (q,solve(q)) \in kscs\ ks)))))$
$\longrightarrow^b (\Diamond_b\ (ks.ba\ (\lambda\ ks.\ (p,solve(p)) \in ksns(ks))))))$
...

bhvbb1, for example, formalizes Eq. (2): with *bb.eval bid t t'* 0, we require that the subsequent formula is to be interpreted for a component of type blackboard (since we are using the blackboard variant of *eval*) with a certain identifier *bid* for a configuration trace *t* at time point 0. The specification of the formula itself then uses the corresponding temporal operators from the framework: *bb.glob* for globally, *bb.evt* for eventually, and *bb.ass* for basic assertions about the state of a blackboard component. Note that such basic assertions specify states of concrete components in terms of a function which take a component's state as input and returns whether it is valid or not for the time point given by the surrounding temporal specification.

bhvks1 formalizes Eq. (5): again, we use the evaluation function to access the framework and use the corresponding temporal operators to formulate the property. Since this time, however, we are formalizing a specification for knowledge sources, we need to use the corresponding instantiation for knowledge sources (*ks*).

3.4 Specifying Architectural Constraints

Finally, we can finalize the specification of the pattern by adding architectural constraints imposed by the pattern as described in Sect. 2.2. Since architectural assertions can be directly expressed over configuration traces, we do not need to use the operators provided by the framework for their specification.

Specifying Assertions About Component Activation. First, we specify assertions about the activation of blackboards and knowledge sources:

and *alwaysActive*: $\bigwedge k.\ \exists\ id{::}'bid.\ \|id\|_k$
and *unique*: $\exists\ id.\ \forall\ k.\ \forall\ id'{::}'bid.\ \|id'\|_k \longrightarrow id = id'$
and *actks*: $\bigwedge t\ n\ kid\ p.\ [\![t \in arch;\ \|kid\|_{t\ n};\ p{=}prob\ kid;\ p{\in}ksop\ (\sigma_{kid}(t\ n))]\!]$
$\Longrightarrow (\exists\ n'{\geq}n.\ \|kid\|_{t\ n'} \wedge (p,\ solve\ p) \in ksns\ (\sigma_{kid}(t\ n')) \wedge (\forall\ n''{\geq}n.\ n''{<}n' \longrightarrow \|kid\|_{t\ n''}))$
$\vee\ (\forall\ n'{\geq}n.\ (\|kid\|_{t\ n'} \wedge (\neg(p,\ solve\ p) \in ksns\ (\sigma_{kid}(t\ n')))))$

The first two assumptions formalize the activation of blackboard components as specified by the configuration diagram in Fig. 3c: with *alwaysActive* and *unique* we require a *unique* blackboard component to be *always* activated. The third assertion specifies activation of knowledge source components as expressed by the configuration trace assertion shown in Fig. 6: With *actks* we require that, whenever a knowledge source obtains a request to solve a problem which it is able to solve, the knowledge source will stay active until that problem is solved.

Specifying Assertions About Component Connection. Finally, we specify assertions about connections between component ports:

and *conn1*: $\bigwedge k\ bid.\ \|bid\|_k \Longrightarrow bbns\ (\sigma_{bid}(k)) = (\bigcup kid{\in}\{kid.\ \|kid\|_k\}.\ ksns\ (\sigma_{kid}(k)))$
...

Connections between component ports are modeled in terms of conditional equalities between the connected ports (the condition requires the components to be activated). *conn1*, for example, specifies a required connection between ports *ns* of a blackboard and *ns* of a knowledge source.

3.5 Verifying Blackboard Architectures

Finally, we can use the framework to verify the specification of the Blackboard pattern. Therefore, we first specify a desired property for Blackboard architectures as an Isabelle/HOL theorem and prove it using the verification rules provided by the framework.

A Characteristic Property for Blackboard Architectures. In the following, we specify a characteristic property for Blackboard architectures as an Isabelle/HOL theorem:

theorem *pSolved*:
fixes t **and** $t'::nat \rightarrow 'BB$ **and** p **and** $t''::nat \Rightarrow 'KS$
assumes $t{\in}arch$ **and** $\forall n.\ \forall p{\in}bbop(\sigma_{the\text{-}bb}(t\ n)).\ \exists n'{\geq}n.\ \|sKs\ p\|_{t\ n'}$
shows $\forall n.\ p{\in}bbop(\sigma_{the\text{-}bb}(t\ n)) \longrightarrow (\exists m{\geq}n.\ (p,solve(p)) \in bbcs\ (\sigma_{the\text{-}bb}(t\ m)))$

The property states that, if for each open (sub-)problem, a knowledge source which is able to solve the corresponding problem will be eventually activated, then the architecture guarantees that the original problem is indeed solved.

Verifying the Property. In the following, we demonstrate how the rules of the framework can be used to support the verification process. Therefore, we present a small excerpt from the overall proof of the above property[2]. However, since the proof relies on rule evtEA, we first briefly describe this rule and then we show how it was used in the proof.

Eventually Elimination. In general, the rule has the following form:

evtEA

$$\frac{(t,t',n)\ {}_{k}\overset{t}{\models}_{(c)} \Diamond\gamma}{\exists n' \geq \langle c \overset{n}{\vee} t\rangle \colon (t,t',n')\ {}_{k}\overset{t}{\models}_{(c)} \gamma}\ \exists i \geq n\colon \|c\|_{t(i)}$$

[2] The full proof is provided in [23].

It allows to eliminate an eventually operator from a behavior specification $\diamondsuit\gamma$ for a component c at time point n and conclude that γ holds sometimes after the last activation (before n) of component c. However, in order to be applied, the rule requires that component c is again activated in the future.

Proof Excerpt. In the following excerpt we show how the above rule is used to eliminate the eventually operator available in locale assumption *bhvks1*, obtained from Eq. (5):

```
...
1 ultimately have ks.eval (sKs p) t t'' nᵣ (◇ᵦ (ks.ba (λ ks. (p,solve(p))∈ksns(ks))))
2   using ks.impE[of sKs p t t'' nᵣ] by blast
3 with ‹∃i≥nᵣ. ‖sKs p‖ₜ ᵢ› obtain nₛ where nₛ≥⟨sKs p → t⟩nᵣ and
4   (∃i≥nₛ. ‖sKs p‖ₜ ᵢ ∧ (∀n''≥⟨sKs p ⇐ t⟩nₛ. n'' ≤ ⟨sKs p → t⟩nₛ ⟶
5     ks.eval (sKs p) t t'' n'' (ks.ba (λ ks. (p,solve(p))∈ksns(ks))))) ∨
6   ¬ (∃i≥nₛ. ‖sKs p‖ₜ ᵢ) ∧ ks.eval (sKs p) t t'' nₛ (ks.ba (λ ks. (p,solve(p))∈ksns(ks)))
7   using ks.evtEA[of nᵣ sKs p t] by blast
...
```

The excerpt starts with the fact that for a knowledge source with identifier $sKs\ p$, at some time point n_r, problem p and its solution $solve(p)$ are eventually provided at $sKs\ p's$ output port ns (lines 1 and 2). It then uses rule evtEA to obtain time point n_s for which problem p and its solution $solve(p)$ are actually provided at $sKs\ p's$ output port ns (lines 3–7). In order to do so, it uses another fact, which ensures that component $sKs\ p$ is indeed eventually activated, to discharge the side condition of rule evtEA (line 3).

4 Evaluation

In order to evaluate the framework, we used it to specify and verify four architectural design patterns: versions of the Singleton, Publisher-Subscriber, and Blackboard pattern, as well as a pattern for Blockchain architectures. The corresponding Isabelle/HOL theories are available via the archive of formal proofs and can be accessed online [10].

To investigate the frameworks potential to support the verification of architectural design patterns, we then calculated the *normalized* amount of proof code for the verification of each pattern and classified it into proof code attributed by the framework and additional proof code specific to the pattern. The collected raw data is available online [23] and summarized in Fig. 8. Figure 8a depicts the absolute amount of framework code (black) and proof code specific to the pattern (gray) for each of the four patterns. It already suggests that the framework contributes a significant amount of proof code to the overall verification. To investigate this suspicion in more detail, Fig. 8b depicts the relative amount of framework code vs. proof code specific to the pattern. It shows that, except for the Publisher-Subscriber pattern, the amount of proof code contributed by the framework amounts to at least two-thirds of the overall proof code used to verify the patterns. The data obtained for the Publisher-Subscriber pattern can be explained by the absence of behavioral constraints imposed by the pattern. For the pattern was specified in a way such that it requires only certain restrictions about the activation of components and connection between them, but no restrictions on the components actual behavioral was imposed. In summary, the data suggests that for patterns which do indeed involve constraints about component behavior, the proposed framework has the potential for significant reductions of the proof code required to verify them.

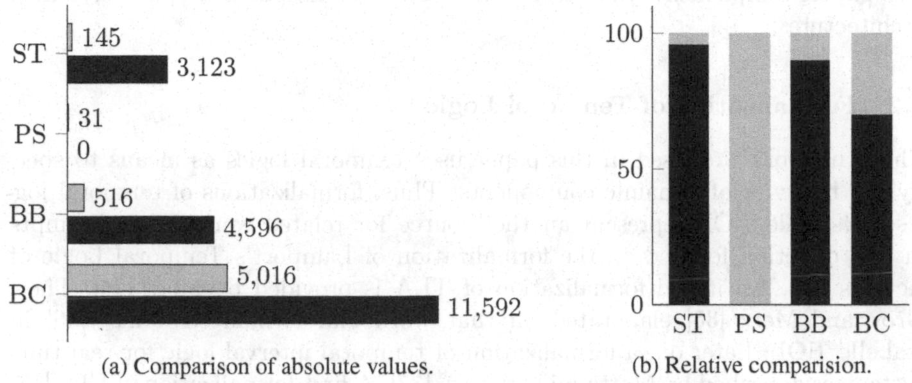

(a) Comparison of absolute values. (b) Relative comparision.

Fig. 8. Contribution of framework to overall verification.

5 Related Work

To the best of our knowledge, the framework presented in this paper is the first of its kind. Nevertheless, related work can be found in two related areas: applications of interactive theorem proving to software architectures and formalizations of temporal logics.

5.1 Interactive Theorem Proving for Software Architectures

Over the last decades, some attempts were made to apply interactive theorem proving to software architectures. One of the first attempts in this direction was done by Bergner [24]. The author proposes an approach to specify component networks and verify whether a given (runtime) component network satisfies its specification. The approach was implemented in Spectrum [25], a functional programming language which allows for axiomatic specifications of functions. Another approach comes from Fensel and Schnogge [26], which apply the KIV interactive theorem prover [27] to verify concrete architectures in the area of knowledge-based systems. Another example in this areas is the work of Spichkova [28] which provides a mapping from a FOCUS [29] specification to a corresponding Isabelle/HOL [8] theory. More recently, some attempts were made to apply interactive theorem proving to the verification of architectural connectors. Li and Sun [30], for example, apply the Coq proof assistant [31] to verify connectors specified in Reo [32].

While all these approaches apply interactive theorem proving to the verification of different aspects of software architectures, there is one major difference to our work: The above approaches mainly focus on the specification of static architectures. However, as argued in the introduction of this paper, dynamic architectures are becoming increasingly important. Thus, the work presented in this paper, complements these approaches by extending their scope to dynamic architectures.

5.2 Formalization of Temporal Logic

The framework proposed in this paper uses temporal logics as means to specify the behavior of dynamic components. Thus, formalizations of temporal logics in Isabelle/HOL represent another source for related work. First attempts in this direction focused on the formalization of Lamport's Temporal Logic of Actions [33]. An initial formalization of TLA is provided by Merz [34]. Then, Grov and Merz [35] elaborated on that work and formalized TLA* [36] in Isabelle/HOL. Later on, a formalization of temporal interval logic for real time systems is described by Mattolini and Nese [37]. A first formalization of LTL [17] in Isabelle/HOL is provided by Schimpf et al. [38] and then refined by Sickert [39].

While the above approaches all provide valuable insights into the process of formalizing temporal logics, the scope of this work is different: we are interested in combining a given temporal logic specification with a specification of component activations. To this end, we provide a calculus in terms of a set of rules which allows to reason about temporal specifications taking into consideration that states may be active or not. Thus, with our work we also complement existing work in this area.

6 Conclusion

In this paper, we described our results obtained by implementing a framework for the interactive verification of architectural design patterns (ADPs) in Isabelle/HOL:

- We described the major definitions and corresponding theorems as well as the interface to the framework.
- We demonstrate usage of the framework in terms of a running example: a dynamic version of the Blackboard pattern.
- We present and discuss the framework's evaluation in which the framework was used to specify and verify four different ADPs: a variant of the *Singleton*, the *Publisher-Subscriber*, and the *Blackboard* pattern as well as a pattern for *Blockchain* architectures.

Results. Our evaluation showed that for those patterns which involve the specification of component behavior, the framework contributed *at least* 75% of the proof code required for their verification. Moreover, the evaluation also suggested that using the framework allows reasoning at a more abstract level, thus reducing the amount of knowledge of the underlying model required for the verification of ADPs.

Implication. Based on our results, we conclude that the framework proposed in this paper has the potential to significantly reduce the amount of proof code required to verify ADPs, thus reducing the effort to develop and maintain verification results for ADPs. Moreover, reducing the necessary knowledge of the underlying model may increase practical applicability of the interactive verification of ADPs.

Vision and Outlook. Our overall research aims towards bringing interactive theorem proving closer to the software architecture community [40]. With the work presented in this paper, we provide another, important cornerstone towards this overall research agenda. However, additional work remains to be done in order to fully achieve our overall goal. In particular, future work should focus on the development of tools to support the interactive verification of patterns. Therefore, we are currently working on an implementation of our approach in Eclipse/EMF which uses the framework presented in this paper to support the interactive verification of ADPs.

Acknowledgments. We would like to thank all the people from the Isabelle mailing-list for their fast support. In particular, we would like to thank Andreas Lochbihler for his valuable support. Moreover, we would like to thank Ondřej Kunčar, Veronika Bauer, and all the anonymous reviewers of ICFEM 2018 for their comments and helpful suggestions on earlier versions of this paper.

References

1. Taylor, R.N., Medvidovic, N., Dashofy, E.M.: Software Architecture: Foundations, Theory, and Practice. Wiley, Hoboken (2009)
2. Buschmann, F., Meunier, R., Rohnert, H., Sommerlad, P., Stal, M.: Pattern-Oriented Software Architecture: A System of Patterns. Wiley, West Sussex (1996)
3. Marmsoler, D.: Hierarchical specification and verification of architecture design patterns. In: Proceedings of Fundamental Approaches to Software Engineering, FASE 2018, Thessaloniki, Greece, 14–20 April 2018 (2018)
4. Marmsoler, D., Gleirscher, M.: Specifying properties of dynamic architectures using configuration traces. In: Sampaio, A., Wang, F. (eds.) ICTAC 2016. LNCS, vol. 9965, pp. 235–254. Springer, Cham (2016). https://doi.org/10.1007/978-3-319-46750-4_14
5. Marmsoler, D., Gleirscher, M.: On activation, connection, and behavior in dynamic architectures. Sci. Ann. Comput. Sci. **26**(2), 187–248 (2016)
6. Marmsoler, D.: On the semantics of temporal specifications of component-behavior for dynamic architectures. In: 2017 International Symposium on Theoretical Aspects of Software Engineering (TASE), pp. 1–6. IEEE (2017). https://doi.org/10.1109/tase.2017.8285638

7. Marmsoler, D.: Towards a calculus for dynamic architectures. In: Hung, D., Kapur, D. (eds.) ICTAC 2017. LNCS, vol. 10580, pp. 79–99. Springer, Cham (2017). https://doi.org/10.1007/978-3-319-67729-3_6
8. Nipkow, T., Paulson, L.C., Wenzel, M. (eds.): Isabelle/HOL, vol. 2283. Springer, Heidelberg (2002). https://doi.org/10.1007/3-540-45949-9
9. Marmsoler, D.: Dynamic architectures. Archive of Formal Proofs, July 2017. http://isa-afp.org/entries/DynamicArchitectures.html
10. Marmsoler, D.: A theory of architectural design patterns. Archive of Formal Proofs, March 2018. http://isa-afp.org/entries/Architectural_Design_Patterns.html
11. Ballarin, C.: Locales and locale expressions in Isabelle/Isar. In: Berardi, S., Coppo, M., Damiani, F. (eds.) TYPES 2003. LNCS, vol. 3085, pp. 34–50. Springer, Heidelberg (2004). https://doi.org/10.1007/978-3-540-24849-1_3
12. Broy, M.: A logical basis for component-oriented software and systems engineering. Comput. J. **53**(10), 1758–1782 (2010)
13. Shaw, M., Garlan, D.: Software Architecture: Perspectives on an Emerging Discipline, vol. 1. Prentice Hall, Englewood Cliffs (1996)
14. Broy, M.: Algebraic specification of reactive systems. In: Wirsing, M., Nivat, M. (eds.) AMAST 1996. LNCS, vol. 1101, pp. 487–503. Springer, Heidelberg (1996). https://doi.org/10.1007/BFb0014335
15. Wirsing, M.: Algebraic specification. In: van Leeuwen, J. (ed.) Handbook of Theoretical Computer Science, vol. B, pp. 675–788. MIT Press, Cambridge (1990)
16. Marmsoler, D., Degenhardt, S.: Verifying patterns of dynamic architectures using model checking. In: Formal Engineering Approaches to Software Components and Architectures, FESCA@ETAPS 2017, Uppsala, Sweden, 22 April 2017, pp. 16–30 (2017)
17. Manna, Z., Pnueli, A.: The Temporal Logic of Reactive and Concurrent Systems. Springer, New York (1992). https://doi.org/10.1007/978-1-4612-0931-7
18. Gordon, M.J., Milner, A.J., Wadsworth, C.P.: Edinburgh LCF. LNCS, vol. 78. Springer, Heidelberg (1979). https://doi.org/10.1007/3-540-09724-4
19. Milner, R., Tofte, M., Harper, R.: The Definition of Standard ML. MIT Press, Cambridge (1990). Literaturverz. S. [87]–89
20. Blanchette, J.C., Hölzl, J., Lochbihler, A., Panny, L., Popescu, A., Traytel, D.: Truly modular (co)datatypes for Isabelle/HOL. In: Klein, G., Gamboa, R. (eds.) ITP 2014. LNCS, vol. 8558, pp. 93–110. Springer, Cham (2014). https://doi.org/10.1007/978-3-319-08970-6_7
21. Wenzel, M.: Isabelle/Isar - a generic framework for human-readable proof documents. From Insight to Proof - Festschrift in Honour of Andrzej Trybulec **10**(23), 277–298 (2007)
22. Lochbihler, A.: Coinduction. The Archive of Formal Proofs. http://afp.sourceforge.net/entries/Coinductive.shtml (2010)
23. Marmsoler, D.: A framework for interactive verification of architectural design patterns in Isabelle/HOL. Electronic Supplementary Material. http://www.marmsoler.com/docs/ICFEM18/
24. Bergner, K.: Spezifikation großer Objektgeflechte mit Komponentendiagrammen. Ph.D. thesis, Technische Universität München (1996)
25. Broy, M., Facchi, C., Grosu, R., et al.: The requirement and design specification language spectrum - an informal introduction. Technical report, Technische Universität München (1993)
26. Fensel, D., Schnogge, A.: Using KIV to specify and verify architectures of knowledge-based systems. In: Automated Software Engineering, pp. 71–80, November 1997

27. Reif, W.: The KIV-approach to software verification. In: Broy, M., Jähnichen, S. (eds.) KORSO: Methods, Languages, and Tools for the Construction of Correct Software. LNCS, vol. 1009, pp. 339–368. Springer, Heidelberg (1995). https://doi.org/10.1007/BFb0015471
28. Spichkova, M.: Specification and seamless verification of embedded real-time systems: FOCUS on Isabelle. Ph.D. thesis, Technical University Munich, Germany (2007)
29. Broy, M., Stolen, K.: Specification and Development of Interactive Systems: Focus on Streams, Interfaces, and Refinement. Springer, New York (2012)
30. Li, Y., Sun, M.: Modeling and analysis of component connectors in Coq. In: Fiadeiro, J.L., Liu, Z., Xue, J. (eds.) FACS 2013. LNCS, vol. 8348, pp. 273–290. Springer, Cham (2014). https://doi.org/10.1007/978-3-319-07602-7_17
31. Bertot, Y., Castéran, P.: Interactive Theorem Proving and Program Development: Coq'Art: The Calculus of Inductive Constructions. Springer, Heidelberg (2013)
32. Arbab, F.: Reo: a channel-based coordination model for component composition. Math. Struct. Comput. Sci. **14**(03), 329–366 (2004)
33. Lamport, L.: The temporal logic of actions. ACM Trans. Program. Lang. Syst. (TOPLAS) **16**(3), 872–923 (1994)
34. Merz, S.: Mechanizing TLA in Isabelle. In: Workshop on Verification in New Orientations, pp. 54–74. Citeseer (1995)
35. Grov, G., Merz, S.: A definitional encoding of TLA* in Isabelle/HOL. Archive of Formal Proofs, November 2011. http://isa-afp.org/entries/TLA.html
36. Merz, S.: A more complete TLA. In: Wing, J.M., Woodcock, J., Davies, J. (eds.) FM 1999. LNCS, vol. 1709, pp. 1226–1244. Springer, Heidelberg (1999). https://doi.org/10.1007/3-540-48118-4_15
37. Mattolini, R., Nesi, P.: An interval logic for real-time system specification. IEEE Trans. Softw. Eng. **27**(3), 208–227 (2001)
38. Schimpf, A., Merz, S., Smaus, J.-G.: Construction of Büchi Automata for LTL model checking verified in Isabelle/HOL. In: Berghofer, S., Nipkow, T., Urban, C., Wenzel, M. (eds.) TPHOLs 2009. LNCS, vol. 5674, pp. 424–439. Springer, Heidelberg (2009). https://doi.org/10.1007/978-3-642-03359-9_29
39. Sickert, S.: Linear temporal logic. Archive of Formal Proofs, March 2016. http://isa-afp.org/entries/LTL.html
40. Marmsoler, D.: Towards a theory of architectural styles. In: Proceedings of the 22nd ACM SIGSOFT International Symposium on Foundations of Software Engineering - FSE 2014, pp. 823–825. ACM Press (2014)

Formalization of Symplectic Geometry in HOL-Light

Guohui Wang[1,2,4(✉)], Yong Guan[1,3,5], Zhiping Shi[3,4,5(✉)], Qianying Zhang[1,4], Xiaojuan Li[1,3], and Yongdong Li[1]

[1] Beijing Advanced Innovation Center for Imaging Technology, Capital Normal University, Beijing, China
{ghwang,guanyong,qyzhang,lixj}@cnu.edu.cn, lydbeijing@163.com
[2] School of Mathematical Science, Capital Normal University, Beijing, China
[3] Beijing Key Laboratory of Light Industrial Robot and Safety Verification, College of Information Engineering, Capital Normal University, Beijing, China
shizp@cnu.edu.cn
[4] Beijing Center for Mathematics and Information Interdisciplinary Sciences, Capital Normal University, Beijing, China
[5] National International Science and Technology Cooperation Demonstration Base of Interdisciplinary of Electronic System Reliability and Mathematics, Capital Normal University, Beijing, China

Abstract. Symplectic geometry is a versatile geometric theory widely used in many disciplines such as analytical mechanics, geometric topology and Lie group. However, when symplectic geometry is applied in practice, the satisfaction of its preconditions is often not formally verified. Therefore, it is necessary to make verifications on symplectic geometry and its applications. The purpose of the present work is to conduct such verifications by establishing a formal theorem library in HOL-Light. For this purpose, seven basic concepts are formalized at first. Then, the properties of symplectic vector spaces and symplectic matrices are formally verified. To validate the correctness of the formalized symplectic geometry and to demonstrate its applications, formal analysis is finally made on the symplectic features of matrix optics. The present work not only lays a necessary foundation for formal verifications in this field but also extends the library of theories of the HOL-Light system. Based on this foundation, some more sophisticated symplectic geometry theories and their engineering applications can be further formalized and verified.

Keywords: Formalization · Theorem proving · Symplectic geometry Higher-order logic · HOL-Light

1 Introduction

There are three parallel branches of geometric theories, namely algebraic geometry, differential geometry and symplectic geometry. Different from the former two ones, the symplectic geometry mainly formulates the geometric and topological

J. Sun and M. Sun (Eds.): ICFEM 2018, LNCS 11232, pp. 270–283, 2018.
https://doi.org/10.1007/978-3-030-02450-5_16

properties of symplectic manifolds, which are the foundations of the Hamiltonian mechanics. As an elegant mathematical theory, the symplectic geometry was originally initiated by Hamilton in his geometrics-based formulation of analytical mechanics.

After its continuous development in the past more than one and a half centuries, the symplectic geometry has become a versatile theory. Now, it has been extended into geometric topology, Lie group and other related theories [4,5]. Besides its classical application in analytical mechanics, it is widely used in multi-disciplines such as the geometrical optics, celestial mechanics, elasticity mechanics, fluid mechanics, the mechanics-based optimal control and the symplectic algorithm based numerical computation. Different from the conventional theories in these fields, the symplectic theories provide more powerful theoretical formulations for describing physical phenomena that are related to symplectic manifolds [2,11]. For example, in the field of numerical computation, all conservative physical processes without dissipation cannot be numerically solved by the conventional Runge-Kutta algorithms, but they can be solved by the symplectic Runge-Kutta methods [1,14,17], because all these physical processes have symplectic structures, which cannot be kept unchanged by the conventional Runge-Kutta algorithms.

The symplectic geometry is a sophisticated mathematical theory. In engineering practices, it is often applied with its preconditions being satisfied incompletely or by default. Therefore, it is necessary to perform verification on its applications in the related fields. Generally, the available verification methods include experiments, simulations and formal proof. Compared with experiments and simulations, formal proof is a more rigorous verification technique, because it has completeness in logic. Now, there are two main formal proof approaches [7,22]. One is theorem proving [10,13,20] and the other is model checking [15,19]. As their names imply, theorem proving is more suitable for the problems that can be represented as formal theorems, while model checking is more applicable for those that can be described as formal models. Because the symplectic geometry contains a series of mathematical theorems, it is better to verify it through theorem proving. Now, there are several available theorem provers such as HOL-Light [8], HOL4 [16,21], Isabelle/HOL [3], ACL2 [9], Coq [12], Mizar [18], PVS [6], etc. In each prover, theorem proving can be conducted only when the associated formal theorem libraries have been established. To our knowledge, the formal theorem library of symplectic geometry has not been constructed in any existing theorem provers. Therefore, the formalization of symplectic geometry is required by the related verification work.

In the present work, a basic formalization of the symplectic geometry is established in HOL-Light. Because the symplectic vector space and symplectic transform are two representative parts of the symplectic geometry, they and their properties are formalized here. To demonstrate the application and validness of the present formalization, formal verification is further performed on some basic theories of matrix optics.

2 Preliminaries

In this section, the symplectic geometry is compared with the Euclidean geometry at first. Then, a brief introduction is given for the theorem prover HOL-Light. Finally, the formalization framework of the symplectic geometry is constructed.

2.1 Comparison Between Symplectic Geometry and Euclidean Geometry

Different from the Euclidean geometry that is mainly based on the concept of length, the symplectic geometry is established in the phase space and principally describes the area. In the Euclidean space, the scalar product of two vectors has the form of symmetry. However, in the symplectic space, each symplectic form is always anti-symmetric. In addition, Table 1 shows more specific differences between their properties.

Table 1. The properties of Euclidean and symplectic geometric theories.

Properties	Euclidean geometry	Symplectic geometry
Elements	R^n $x = (x_1, x_2, ..., x_n)$	R^{2n} $x = (x_1, x_2, ..., x_n; x_{n+1}, x_{n+2}, ..., x_{2n})$
Inner product	$(x, y) = \sum_{i=1}^{n} x_i y_i$	$[x, y] = \sum_{i=1}^{n} (x_i y_{n+i} - x_{n+i} y_i)$
Bilinear	Yes	Yes
Alternating	$(x, y) = (y, x)$	$[x, y] = -[y, x]$
Non-degenerate	Yes	Yes
Vanishing property	No $(x, x) = \|x\| > 0$	Yes $[x, x] = 0$
Metric characteristics	Length	Area

2.2 HOL-Light

HOL-Light is an interactive theorem prover that performs theorem proving in terms of higher order logic. It was developed by John Harrison when he was at the computer lab of Cambridge University. It belongs to the HOL family, whose first version HOL88 was developed by Mike Gordon at Cambridge in the 1980s. After HOL88, other versions including HOL90, HOL 98 and HOL4 were also issued successively. Compared with all other versions, HOL-Light is simpler but meanwhile more practical. Its core only consists of five basic axioms and eight primitive inference rules, which provide a necessary foundation for theorem proving. Besides, it implemented the objective CAML (OCAML) language, which is a variant of the ML programming language. By using OCAML, a large number of mathematical theorems have been formalized and the corresponding theorem libraries have also been constructed in these years.

Except for HOL-Light, there are several other prevailing theorem provers such as Coq, Isabell/HOL, Mizar and PVS. Because the Euclidean vector theory has been formalized in HOL-Light and the associated theorem library is the foundation for the formalization of symplectic geometry, HOL-Light is selected as the theorem prover here.

2.3 Formalization Framework for Symplectic Geometry

In HOL-Light, although the n-dimensional Euclidean space has been formalized, the formalization of the symplectic geometry is absent. Symplectic geometry is a versatile geometric theory widely used in many disciplines such as analytical mechanics, geometric topology and Lie group. Therefore, it will be formalized here.

The formalization framework of the symplectic geometry is shown in Fig. 1. It is seen that the theorem library of the formalized Euclidean geometry is the basic precondition for formalizing the symplectic geometry. Because the formalization of the Euclidean geometry has been provided by HOL-Light, the symplectic geometry can be directly formalized. In the present work, the symplectic vector space and matrix are formalized successively, because the former is the theoretical foundation of the latter.

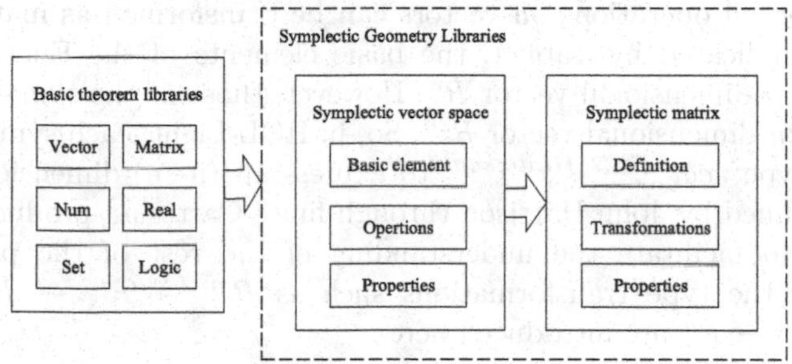

Fig. 1. The formalization framework of the symplectic geometry.

3 Formalization of Symplectic Vector Space

A symplectic vector space is a set of vectors defined over a number field, F, that has the following symplectic bilinear form: ω: $V \times V \to F$. It has four main properties:

- Bilinearity: This means that each parameter has the property of linearity.
  For u_1, u_2 and $v \in V$, there exist $a, b \in R$, such that
  $\omega(au_1 + bu_2, v) = a\omega(u_1, v) + b\omega(u_2, v)$
  For u, v_1 and $v_2 \in V$, there also exist $a, b \in R$, such that
  $\omega(u, av_1 + bv_2) = a\omega(u, v_1) + b\omega(u, v_2)$

- Zero: For $v \in V, \omega(v,v) = 0$.
- Skew-symmetry: For u and $v \in V$, $\omega(u,v) = -\omega(v,u)$.
- Nondegeneracy: For any vector $v \in V$, if $\omega(u,v) = 0$, then $u = 0$.

Furthermore, each symplectic form is a symmetric form, but not vice versa. When the basis vectors are given, each symplectic form ω can be expressed as a matrix, which is skew-symmetric, non-singular and concave. It deserves noting that the symplectic matrix here is different from the matrix that represents the transformation of a symplectic space.

The symplectic form of a standard symplectic space R_{2n} is generally a skew-symmetric and non-singular block matrix J as below

$$J = \begin{bmatrix} 0 & \mathrm{I}_n \\ -\mathrm{I}_n & 0 \end{bmatrix} \tag{1}$$

where I_n is the $n \times n$ identity matrix. Obviously, the inverse matrix of J can be represented as $J^{-1} = J^T = -J$. Each element of J generally has even dimensions. For example, $(x_1, x_2, ..., x_n; y_1, y_2, ..., y_n)$ is an element of J .

3.1 Formalization of the Basic Operations of Symplectic Vector Space

In HOL-Light, each column of an n-dimensional real-number matrix is a vector R^n. Therefore, all operations on vectors can be transformed as matrix manipulations. As indicated by Table 1, the basic elements of the Euclidean space constitute an n-dimensional vector R^n. However, those of the symplectic space constitute a $2n$-dimensional vector R^{2n}. So, in HOL-Light, each symplectic vector has the type $real^{\wedge(N,N)finite\_sum}$ to express an (n+n)-dimensional vector, which was defined by John Harrison through finite Cartesian products.

In order to facilitate the understanding of the rest of the paper, some definitions of the type transformations such as $R^m \rightarrow R^n \rightarrow R^{(m+n)}$ and $R^{(m+n)} \rightarrow R^m \rightarrow R^n$ are introduced here

Definition 1. The definition *Pastecart* is given by
$\vdash$ (pastecart : $\mathrm{A}^{\wedge\mathrm{M}} \rightarrow \mathrm{A}^{\wedge\mathrm{N}} \rightarrow \mathrm{A}^{\wedge(\mathrm{M,N})\mathrm{finite\_sum}}$) f g =
 λi. if i $\leq$ dimindex(: M) then f\$i
 else g\$(i − dimindex(: M))

Where the function *Pastecart* has an m-dimensional vector and another n-dimensional vector as inputs and then it returns an $(m+n)$-dimensional vector. In this paper, this function is used to construct a $2n$-dimensional symplectic vector from two n-dimensional vectors. The operator \$ is defined to represent the location in the vector of the element.

Definition 2. The definition *Fstcart* is given by
$\vdash$ (fstcart : $\mathrm{A}^{\wedge(\mathrm{M,N})\mathrm{finite\_sum}} \rightarrow \mathrm{A}^{\wedge\mathrm{M}}$) f = λi. f\$i

Definition 3. The definition *Sndcart* is given by
$\vdash$ (sndcart : $\mathrm{A}^{\wedge(\mathrm{M,N})\mathrm{finite\_sum}} \rightarrow \mathrm{A}^{\wedge\mathrm{N}}$) f $= \lambda$ i. f\$(i + dimindex(: M))

Where the functions *Fstcart* and *Sndcart* have the same structure. They are used to extract an m-dimensional vector and another n-dimensional vector from an $(m+n)$-dimensional vector. Specifically, for each $(m+n)$-dimensional vector, one can take out its first part, i.e., an m-element vector, using the function *Fstcart*, or get its second part, i.e., an n-element vector, using the function *Sndcart*.

Based on the theory of symplectic vector space described above, the symplectic inner product can be defined as

$$[x, y] = \sum_{i=1}^{n} (x_i\, y_{n+i} - x_{n+i}\, y_i) \tag{2}$$

Equation (2) can be formalized in HOL-Light as

Definition 4. The definition *Symplectic Inner Product* is given by
$\vdash \forall x\, y.$ sym_dot x y =
sum(1..dimindex(: N))(λi .(fstcart x\$i ∗ sndcart y\$i
−sndcart x\$i ∗ fstcart y\$i))

Where the symbol ∗ represents the multiplication between two real numbers. The function *sym_dot* has two $2n$-dimensional vectors as inputs. In the present work, *sym_dot* is used as an infix operator. For example, *sym_dot* x y is equal to x *sym_dot* y. Here, *sym_dot* outputs a real number that represents the symplectic inner product of x and y.

As indicated by Eq. (2), each symplectic structure can be represented by a block matrix J_{2n}. Because $\omega(x_i, y_j) = -\omega(y_i, x_j) = \delta_{ij}$ and $\omega(x_i, x_j) = -\omega(y_i, y_j) = 0$, the formalization of ω is

Definition 5. The definition *Symplectic Structure* ω is given by
$\vdash$ omega_Jmat : $\mathrm{real}^{\wedge(\mathrm{N,N})\mathrm{finite\_sum}\wedge(\mathrm{N,N})\mathrm{finite\_sum}}$ =
λ i j. if (1 ≤ i ∧ i ≤ dimindex(: N)
∧ (j = (i + dimindex(: N)))) then &1
else if ((dimindex(: N) + 1) ≤ i
∧ i ≤ dimindex(: (N, N)finite_sum)
∧ (j = (i − dimindex(: N)))) then −−&1
else &0

Where the symbol, −−, denotes negative numbers, while the symbol, &, means real numbers.

3.2 Formal Verification of the Properties of Symplectic Vector Spaces

In this section, definition 4 is employed to verify the four main properties of symplectic vector spaces which were given at the beginning of Sect. 3 at first. For this purpose, four formal theorems are constructed as below

Theorem 1. (*Bilinearity*) Each parameter has the property of linearity.
$\vdash \forall$ a b x1 x2 y : real^(N,N)finite_sum.
(a % x1 + b % x2) sym_dot y = a ∗ (x1 sym_dot y) + b ∗ (x1 sym_dot y) $\wedge$
$\forall$ a b x y1 y2 : real^(N,N)finite_sum.
x sym_dot (a % y1 + b % y2) = a ∗ (x sym_dot y1) + b ∗ (x sym_dot y2)

Where the symbol % denotes the product between a number and a vector and the symbol ∗ represents the multiplication between two real numbers. The *Bilinearity* property is named SYMPLECTIC_BILINEAR, which is proved by following tactics.

```
let SYMPLECTIC_BILINEAR = prove
  (`(!a b x1 x2 y : real ∧ (N,N)finite_sum. (a % x1 + b % x2) sym_dot y =
      a * (x1 sym_dot y) + b * (x2 sym_dot y)) /\
  (!a b x y1 y2 : real ∧ (N,N)finite_sum. x sym_dot (a % y1 + b % y2) =
      a * (x sym_dot y1) + b * (x sym_dot y2))`,
  CONJ_TAC THEN REPEAT GEN_TAC THEN REWRITE_TAC[sym_dot]
  THEN REWRITE_TAC[GSYM SUM_LMUL] THEN
  SIMP_TAC[FINITE_NUMSEG; GSYM SUM_ADD]
  THEN MATCH_MP_TAC SUM_EQ THEN BETA_TAC THEN
  REWRITE_TAC[FSTCART_ADD; FSTCART_MUL; SNDCART_ADD]
  THEN REWRITE_TAC[SNDCART_MUL; VECTOR_ADD_COMPONENT]
  THEN REWRITE_TAC[VECTOR_MUL_COMPONENT]
  THEN REAL_ARITH_TAC);;
```

The other three properties are given as following. The main tactics used in the certification process include REWRITE_TAC, SIMP_TAC, MATCH_MP_TAC and etc.

Theorem 2. (*Zero*) $\omega(v, v) = 0$ holds for all $v \in V$.
$\vdash \forall$ x : real^(N,N)finite_sum. x sym_dot x = &0

Theorem 3. (*Skew-symmetry*) $\omega(u, v) = -\omega(v, u)$ holds for all $u, v \in V$.
$\vdash \forall$ x y : real^(N,N)finite_sum. (x sym_dot y) = − −(y sym_dot x)

Theorem 4. (*Nondegeneracy*) $\omega(u, v) = 0$ for all $v \in V$ implies u is zero.
$\vdash \forall$ y.($\forall$x : real^(N,N)finite_sum. x sym_dot y = &0) $\Longrightarrow$ y = vec 0

The verification of the four properties demonstrates that the definition of the symplectic inner product is correct. In addition, some other key properties of symplectic vector spaces are also verified in Table 2. All the properties formalized here will be applied in the formal verification of Sect. 5.

Table 2. Some other key properties of symplectic vector spaces.

Properties	HOL Formalization	Mathematical Expressions
SYM_DOT_LADD	⊢ ∀x y z. (x + y) sym_dot z = x sym_dot z + y sym_dot z	[(x+y),z] = [x,z] + [y,z]
SYM_DOT_RADD	⊢ ∀x y z. x sym_dot (y + z) = x sym_dot y + x sym_dot z	[x,(y+z)] = [x,y] + [x,z]
SYM_DOT_LSUB	⊢ ∀x y z. (x − y) sym_dot z = x sym_dot z − y sym_dot z	[(x-y),z] = [x,z] - [y,z]
SYM_DOT_RSUB	⊢ ∀x y z. x sym_dot (y − z) = x sym_dot y − x sym_dot z	[x,(y-z)] = [x,y] - [x,z]
SYM_DOT_LMUL	⊢ ∀c x y. (c % x) sym_dot y = c ∗ (x sym_dot y)	[c×x,y] = c × [x,y]
SYM_DOT_RMUL	⊢ ∀c x y. x sym_dot (c % y) = c ∗ (x sym_dot y)	[x,c×y] = c × [x,y]
SYM_DOT_LNEG	⊢ ∀x y. (− −x) sym_dot y = − −(x sym_dot y)	[-x,y] = -[x,y]
SYM_DOT_RNEG	⊢ ∀x y. x sym_dot (− − y) = − −(x sym_dot y)	[x,-y] = -[x,y]
SYM_DOT_LZERO	⊢ ∀x. (vec 0) sym_dot x = &0	[0,x] = 0
SYM_DOT_RZERO	⊢ ∀x. x sym_dot (vec 0) = &0	[x,0] = 0
SYM_DOT_LREQ_EQ0	⊢ ∀x y . x = y ⇒ x sym_dot y = &0	∀x y. x = y ⇒ [x,y] = 0
SYM_DOT_EQ0	⊢ ∀x.(∀y. x sym_dot y = &0) ⇔ x = vec 0 ∧ ∀y.(∀x. x sym_dot y = &0) ⇔ y = vec 0	∀x.(∀y. [x,y] = 0)⇔ x = vec 0 ∧ ∀y.(∀x. [x,y] = 0) ⇔ *y* = *vec*0

4 Formalization of Symplectic Transformation

Consider a linear transform S defined in (V, ω). If $[Sa, Sb] = [a, b]$ with $a, b \in R^{2n}$, S is a symplectic transform. It can be formalized as

Definition 6. The definition *Symplectic Transformation* is given by
⊢ is_symplectic_matrix
(S : real^(N,N)finite_sum^(N,N)finite_sum) ⇔
∀a b : real^(N,N)finite_sum.(S ∗∗ a) sym_dot (S ∗∗ b) = a sym_dot b

Where the symbol ∗∗ denotes the multiplication between a matrix and a vector or two matrices.

The symplectic matrix S has real entries, i.e., $S \in R^{2n \times 2n}$. It satisfies the condition $S^T JS = J$, where S^T denotes the transposition of S and J is a non-singular and skew-symmetric matrix that has $2n \times 2n$ elements (see Eq. (1)).

Definition 6 is formalized as the following theorem:

Theorem 5. *Necessary and Sufficient Conditions for a Symplectic matrix.*
$\vdash \forall \mathrm{S} : \mathrm{real}^{\wedge(\mathrm{N,N})\mathrm{finite\_sum}\wedge(\mathrm{N,N})\mathrm{finite\_sum}}$
$\mathrm{is\_symplectic\_matrix\ S} \Leftrightarrow \mathrm{transp\ S} ** \mathrm{omega\_Jmat} ** \mathrm{S} = \mathrm{omega\_Jmat}$

In engineering applications, S is frequently a block matrix having the following form $S = \begin{bmatrix} A\,B \\ C\,D \end{bmatrix}$ where $A, B, C, D \in R^{n \times n}$. In this case, we say that S belongs to a symplectic group $sp(2n)$, i.e., $S \in sp(2n)$.

In addition, the inverse matrix of S is $S^{-1} = J^{-1} S^T J = \begin{bmatrix} D^T & -B^T \\ -C^T & A^T \end{bmatrix}$. The symplectic block matrix is then formally defined as

Definition 7. The definition *Symplectic Block Matrix* is given by
$\vdash (\mathrm{blockmatrix} : \mathrm{real}^{\wedge \mathrm{N} \wedge \mathrm{N}} \rightarrow \mathrm{real}^{\wedge \mathrm{N} \wedge \mathrm{N}} \rightarrow \mathrm{real}^{\wedge \mathrm{N} \wedge \mathrm{N}} \rightarrow \mathrm{real}^{\wedge \mathrm{N} \wedge \mathrm{N}} \rightarrow$
$\mathrm{real}^{\wedge(\mathrm{N,N})\mathrm{finite\_sum}\wedge(\mathrm{N,N})\mathrm{finite\_sum}})\ \mathrm{A\ B\ C\ D} =$
$\lambda \mathrm{i\,j.\,if}\ (1 \leq \mathrm{i} \wedge \mathrm{i} \leq \mathrm{dimindex}(:\mathrm{N}) \wedge 1 \leq \mathrm{j} \wedge \mathrm{j} \leq \mathrm{dimindex}(:\mathrm{N}))\ \mathrm{then\ A\$i\$j}$
$\mathrm{else\ if}\ (1 \leq \mathrm{i} \wedge \mathrm{i} \leq \mathrm{dimindex}(:\mathrm{N}) \wedge (\mathrm{dimindex}(:\mathrm{N}) + 1) \leq \mathrm{j} \wedge$
$\mathrm{j} \leq (\mathrm{dimindex}(:\mathrm{N}) + \mathrm{dimindex}(:\mathrm{N})))\ \mathrm{then\ B\$i\$(j - dimindex(:N))}$
$\mathrm{else\ if}\ ((\mathrm{dimindex}(:\mathrm{N}) + 1) \leq \mathrm{i} \wedge \mathrm{i} \leq (\mathrm{dimindex}(:\mathrm{N}) + \mathrm{dimindex}(:\mathrm{N})) \wedge$
$1 \leq \mathrm{j} \wedge \mathrm{j} \leq \mathrm{dimindex}(:\mathrm{N})\ \mathrm{then\ C\$(i - dimindex(:N))\$j}$
$\mathrm{else\ if}\ ((\mathrm{dimindex}(:\mathrm{N}) + 1) \leq \mathrm{i} \wedge \mathrm{i} \leq (\mathrm{dimindex}(:\mathrm{N}) + \mathrm{dimindex}(:\mathrm{N})) \wedge$
$(\mathrm{dimindex}(:\mathrm{N}) + 1) \leq \mathrm{j} \wedge \mathrm{j} \leq (\mathrm{dimindex}(:\mathrm{N}) + \mathrm{dimindex}(:\mathrm{N})))$
$\mathrm{then\ D\$(i - dimindex(:N))\$(j - dimindex(:N))}$
$\mathrm{else\ \&0}$

It can be inferred from Definition 7 and Theorem 6 that the necessary and sufficient conditions of the symplectic block matrix are

- $AB^T = BA^T, CD^T = DC^T$ and $AD^T - BC^T = I$
- $A^T C = C^T A, B^T D = D^T B$ and $A^T D - C^T B = I$

When $n = 1$, these conditions reduce to $det(S) = 1$.

After formalization, these conditions can be represented as the following theorem

Theorem 6. *Necessary and sufficient conditions for a symplectic block matrix.*
$\vdash \forall$ A B C D : real$^{\wedge N \wedge N}$.is_symplectic_matrix blockmatrix A B C D $\Leftrightarrow$
(A ∗∗ transp B = B ∗∗ transp A ∧
C ∗∗ transp D = D ∗∗ transp C ∧
A ∗∗ transp D − B ∗∗ transp C = mat 1) ∨
(transp A ∗∗ C = transp C ∗∗ A ∧
transp B ∗∗ D = transp D ∗∗ B ∧
transp A ∗∗ D − transp C ∗∗ B = mat 1)

The key properties of symplectic matrices have also been formalized in Table 3. They are useful in formal verification, because they can reduce the difference between the mathematical and formal models in reasoning.

Table 3. Formalized key properties of symplectic matrices.

Properties	HOL Formalization	Mathematical Expressions
SYM_MAT_DET_EQ1	⊢ ∀ S.is_symplectic_matrix S ⇒ det S = &1	$S \in sp(2n) \Rightarrow detS = 1$
SYM_MAT_INV	⊢ ∀ S.is_symplectic_matrix S ⇒ matrix_inv S = − − omega_Jmat ∗∗ transp S ∗∗ omega_Jmat ∧ matrix_inv S = matrix_inv omega_Jmat ∗∗ transp S ∗∗ omega_Jmat	$S \in sp(2n) \Rightarrow$ $S^{-1} = -JS'J = J^{-1}S'J$
SYM_MAT_INVM_N	⊢ ∀ M N.is_symplectic_matrix (matrix_inv M ∗∗ N) ⇔ tranps M ∗∗ omega_Jmat ∗∗ M∧ tranps N ∗∗ omega_Jmat ∗∗ N	$S = M^{-1}N \in sp(2n)$ $\Leftrightarrow M'JM = N'JN$
SYM_MAT_BOLCK_B	⊢ ∀ B : real$^{\wedge N \wedge N}$. is_symplectic_matrix blockmatrix (mat 1) B (mat 0) (mat 1) ⇔ transp B = B	$\begin{bmatrix} I & B \\ 0 & I \end{bmatrix} \in sp(2n) \Leftrightarrow B' = B$
SYM_MAT_BOLCK_C	⊢ ∀ C : real$^{\wedge N \wedge N}$. is_symplectic_matrix blockmatrix (mat 1) (mat 0) C (mat 1) ⇔ transp C = C	$\begin{bmatrix} I & 0 \\ C & I \end{bmatrix} \in sp(2n) \Leftrightarrow C' = C$
SYM_MAT_BOLCK_AD	⊢ ∀ A D : real$^{\wedge N \wedge N}$. is_symplectic_matrix blockmatrix A (mat 0) (mat 0) D ⇔ A = matrix_inv (transp D)	$\begin{bmatrix} A & 0 \\ 0 & D \end{bmatrix} \in sp(2n) \Leftrightarrow A = (D')^{-1}$

5 Application: Formal Analysis of Matrix Optics

As an application of the formalized symplectic geometry theory, formal analysis is conducted on the matrix optics in this section. The verification flowchart is shown in Fig. 2, which illustrates that three main steps are involved in the formal analysis. Firstly, the formal model is constructed for the system of matrix optics; secondly, the verification goal is set up; thirdly, theorem proving is performed to judge the consistency between the model and the specifications. The application

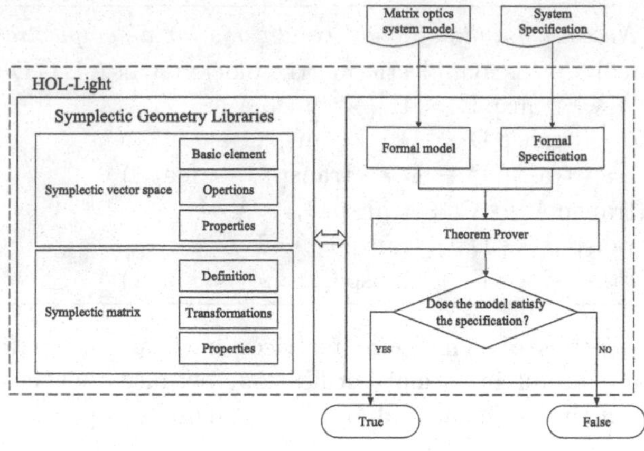

Fig. 2. The verification flowchart for the matrix optics.

not only verifies the symplectic properties of matrix optics but also validates the correctness of the present formalization of symplectic geometry.

Generally, each optical system is described by a 4 × 4 matrix as below

$$\begin{bmatrix} x_2 \\ y_2 \\ n_2 x_2' \\ n_2 y_2' \end{bmatrix} = \begin{bmatrix} a_{11} & a_{12} & b_{11} & b_{12} \\ a_{21} & a_{22} & b_{21} & b_{22} \\ c_{11} & c_{12} & d_{11} & d_{12} \\ c_{21} & c_{22} & d_{21} & d_{22} \end{bmatrix} \begin{bmatrix} x_1 \\ y_1 \\ n_1 x_1' \\ n_1 y_1' \end{bmatrix} \tag{3}$$

where $(x_1; y_1)$ is the incident plane and $(x_2; y_2)$ is the ejection plane. n_1 and n_2 represent the refractive indices of the incident and ejection spaces, respectively. Equation (3) can be rewritten into the following vector form

$$\begin{bmatrix} \overline{r}_2 \\ n_2 \overline{p}_2 \end{bmatrix} = \begin{bmatrix} A & B \\ C & D \end{bmatrix} \begin{bmatrix} \overline{r}_1 \\ n_1 \overline{p}_1 \end{bmatrix} \tag{4}$$

Assume that $det(B) \neq 0$. Then, Eq. (5) can be further recast into

$$\begin{bmatrix} n_1 \overline{p}_1 \\ n_2 \overline{p}_2 \end{bmatrix} = \begin{bmatrix} -\mathrm{B}^{-1}\mathrm{A} & \mathrm{B}^{-1} \\ \mathrm{C} - \mathrm{D}\mathrm{B}^{-1}\mathrm{A} & \mathrm{D}\mathrm{B}^{-1} \end{bmatrix} \begin{bmatrix} \overline{r}_1 \\ \overline{r}_2 \end{bmatrix} \tag{5}$$

The optical path function $L(\gamma)$ is

$$L(\gamma) = L_{axis} + \frac{1}{2}[-n_1(x_1 x_1' + y_1 y_1') + n_2(x_2 x_2' + y_2 y_2')] \tag{6}$$

where L_{axis} is the optical path along the optical axis between the incident and ejection planes.

Based on Eq. (5), one can rewrite Eq. (6) into the following vector form

$$L(\gamma) = L_{axis} + \frac{1}{2}[\overline{r}_1 \quad \overline{r}_2] \begin{bmatrix} -n_1 \overline{p}_1 \\ n_2 \overline{p}_2 \end{bmatrix} \tag{7}$$

Equation (7) can be further expressed as

$$L(\gamma) = L_{axis} + \frac{1}{2}[\overline{r}_1 \quad \overline{r}_2]\begin{bmatrix} \mathrm{B}^{-1}\mathrm{A} & -\mathrm{B}^{-1} \\ \mathrm{C}-\mathrm{D}\mathrm{B}^{-1}\mathrm{A} & \mathrm{D}\mathrm{B}^{-1} \end{bmatrix}\begin{bmatrix} \overline{r}_1 \\ \overline{r}_2 \end{bmatrix} \tag{8}$$

where $\begin{bmatrix} \mathrm{B}^{-1}\mathrm{A} & -\mathrm{B}^{-1} \\ \mathrm{C}-\mathrm{D}\mathrm{B}^{-1}\mathrm{A} & \mathrm{D}\mathrm{B}^{-1} \end{bmatrix}$ is the transformation matrix of the optical path. Denote it as M and then it is inferred that $L^T = L$ and $M^T = M$, because $L(\gamma)$ is a scalar. Finally, the following relations can be obtained

$$\begin{cases} (B^{-1}A)^T = B^{-1}A; \\ DB^{-1})^T = DB^{-1}; \\ (-B^{-1})^T = C - DB^{-1}A. \end{cases}$$

In order to prove whether the transformation matrix M satisfy the symplectic properties or not, a formal theorem is established as below

Theorem 7. *Sufficient condition for a symplectic optical matrix.*
⊢ ∀A B C D : real^N^N. invertible B ⇒
is_symplectic_matrix (blockmatrix
(matrix_inv B ∗ ∗A) (−matrix_inv B)
(C − D ∗ ∗matrix_inv B ∗ ∗A) (D ∗ ∗matrix_inv B))

This is the verification goal of the formal analysis. Some important details of the verification process are explained as below

- The assumption, $det(B) \neq 0$, is adopted here to assure that *matrix_inv B* always holds true.
- Theorem 7 is reduced by using the necessary and sufficient conditions for a symplectic block matrix in Theorem 6.
- The derivation of Theorem 7 is made quite straightforward by using the smart tactic. Such as REWRITE_TAC, ASM_SIMP_TAC, MESON_TAC and etc.
- Some theorems of matrices and vectors, including SYMMETRIC_MATRIX_INV_LMUL, MATRIX_INV_MUL_INNER, MATRIX_INV_INV and etc., which were developed by Marco Maggesi and John Harrison, are also employed in the derivation process.

Based on the above techniques, the verification goal is finally proved. This demonstrates that the transformation matrix M of the optical path formula really has a symplectic structure, or in other words, the symplectic transformation is indeed applicable for the matrix optics. The formal verification of matrix optics indicates that the formalized symplectic geometry is useful in engineering practices.

6 Conclusions

In the present work, a theorem library of symplectic geometry is established by using the vector library in HOL-light. Seven formal definitions are developed to introduce the corresponding basic concepts, based on which four typical properties of symplectic vector spaces and the necessary and sufficient conditions and some key properties of symplectic matrices are formalized. For the purpose of application, the formalized symplectic geometry is further employed to make formal analysis on matrix optics. The formal analysis not only verifies the symplectic properties of matrix optics but also validates the correctness of the present formalization of symplectic geometry.

In our future work, on one hand, some automatic reasoning tactics will be developed for the convenience of symplectic geometry based formal verification, and on the other hand, some new mathematical theorem libraries such as the theory of Poissons Bracket will be built based on the formalized symplectic geometry for the purpose of more advanced applications.

Acknowledgment. This work was supported by the National Natural Science Foundation of China (61472468, 61572331, 61602325, 61702348), the National Key Technology Research and Development Program (2015BAF13B01), National Key R&D Plan (2017YFC0806700, 2017YFB130253), the Project of the Beijing Municipal Science & Technology Commission (LJ201607) and Capital Normal University Major (key) Nurturing Project.

References

1. Antoñana, M., Makazaga, J., Murua, A.: Reducing and monitoring round-off error propagation for symplectic implicit Runge-Kutta schemes. Numer. Algorithms **76**(4), 861–880 (2017). https://doi.org/10.1007/s11075-017-0287-z. ISSN: 1572-9265
2. Besana, A., Spera, M.: On some symplectic aspects of knot framings. J. Knot Theory Ramifications **15**(07), 883–912 (2006)
3. Blanchette, J.C., Bulwahn, L., Nipkow, T.: Automatic proof and disproof in Isabelle/HOL. In: Tinelli, C., Sofronie-Stokkermans, V. (eds.) FroCoS 2011. LNCS (LNAI), vol. 6989, pp. 12–27. Springer, Heidelberg (2011). https://doi.org/10.1007/978-3-642-24364-6_2
4. Calvaruso, G., Ovando, G.P.: From almost (para)-complex structures to affine structures on lie groups. Manuscripta Math. **155**, 89–113 (2016)
5. Frejlich, P., Torres, D.M., Miranda, E.: A note on the symplectic topology of b-manifolds. J. Symplectic Geom. **15**, 719–739 (2017)
6. Gottliebsen, H., Hardy, R., Lightfoot, O., Martin, U.: Applications of real number theorem proving in PVS. Formal Aspects Comput. **25**(6), 993–1016 (2013)
7. Guo, X.L., Dutta, R.G., Mishra, P., Jin, Y.E.: Automatic code converter enhanced PCH framework for SoC trust verification. IEEE Trans. Very Large Scale Integr. Syst. **25**(12), 3390–3400 (2017)
8. Harrison, J.: HOL light: an overview. In: Berghofer, S., Nipkow, T., Urban, C., Wenzel, M. (eds.) TPHOLs 2009. LNCS, vol. 5674, pp. 60–66. Springer, Heidelberg (2009). https://doi.org/10.1007/978-3-642-03359-9_4

9. Hunt, J.W., Kaufmann, M., Moore, J.S., Slobodova, A.: Industrial hardware and software verification with ACL2. Philos. Trans. **375**(2104), 20150399 (2017)
10. Jeannin, J.B., et al.: A formally verified hybrid system for safe advisories in the next-generation airborne collision avoidance system. Int. J. Softw. Tools Technol. Transf. **230**(1), 1–25 (2015)
11. Karshon, Y., Ziltener, F.: Hamiltonian group actions on exact symplectic manifolds with proper momentum maps are standard. Trans. Am. Math. Soc. **370**, 1409–1425 (2016)
12. Li, Y., Sun, M.: Modeling and verification of component connectors in Coq, vol. 113. Elsevier North-Holland, Inc. (2015)
13. Ma, S., Shi, Z.P., Shao, Z.Z., Guan, Y., Li, L.M., Li, Y.D.: Higher-order logic formalization of conformal geometric algebra and its application in verifying a robotic manipulation algorithm. Adv. Appl. Clifford Algebras **26**(4), 1305–1330 (2016)
14. Mei, L.J., Wu, X.Y.: Symplectic exponential Runge Kutta methods for solving nonlinear Hamiltonian systems. J. Comput. Phys. **338**, 567–584 (2017)
15. Monteiro, F., Cordeiro, L., Filho, E.: ESBMC-GPU: a context-bounded model checking tool to verify CUDA programs. Sci. Comput. Program. **152**(1), 63–69 (2017)
16. Slind, K., Norrish, M.: A brief overview of HOL4. In: Mohamed, O.A., Muñoz, C., Tahar, S. (eds.) TPHOLs 2008. LNCS, vol. 5170, pp. 28–32. Springer, Heidelberg (2008). https://doi.org/10.1007/978-3-540-71067-7_6
17. Tang, W., Zhang, J.: Symplecticity-preserving continuous-stage Runge Kutta nyström methods. Appl. Math. Comput. **323**, 204–219 (2018)
18. Urban, J., Rudnicki, P., Sutcliffe, G.: ATP and presentation service for Mizar formalizations. J. Autom. Reason. **50**(2), 229–241 (2013)
19. Wei, Q.X., Jiao, J., Zhao, T.D.: Flight control system failure modeling and verification based on spin. Eng. Fail. Anal. **82**(1), 501–513 (2017)
20. Zhao, C.N., Shi, L.K., Guan, Y., Li, X.J., Shi, Z.P.: Formal modeling and verification of fractional order linear systems. ISA Trans. **62**, 87–93 (2016)
21. Zhao, C.N., Li, S.S.: Formalization of fractional order PD control systems in HOL4. Theoret. Comput. Sci. **706**(1), 22–34 (2017)
22. Zheng, X., Julien, C., Kim, M., Khurshid, S.: Perceptions on the state of the art in verification and validation in cyber-physical systems. IEEE Syst. J. **PP**(99), 1–14 (2015)

Using Theorem Provers to Increase the Precision of Dependence Analysis for Information Flow Control

Bernhard Beckert, Simon Bischof, Mihai Herda(✉), Michael Kirsten, and Marko Kleine Büning

Karlsruhe Institute of Technology (KIT), Karlsruhe, Germany
{beckert,simon.bischof,herda,kirsten}@kit.edu, marko@kleinebuening.de

Abstract. Information flow control (IFC) is a category of techniques for enforcing information flow properties. In this paper we present the *Combined Approach*, a novel IFC technique that combines a scalable system-dependence-graph-based (SDG-based) approach with a precise logic-based approach based on a theorem prover. The Combined Approach has an increased precision compared with the SDG-based approach on its own, without sacrificing its scalability. For every potential illegal information flow reported by the SDG-based approach, the *Combined Approach* automatically generates proof obligations that, if valid, prove that there is no program path for which the reported information flow can happen. These proof obligations are then relayed to the logic-based approach.

We also show how the SDG-based approach can provide additional information to the theorem prover that helps decrease the verification effort. Moreover, we present a prototypical implementation of the Combined Approach that uses the tools JOANA and KeY as the SDG-based and logic-based approach respectively.

Keywords: Information flow control · Noninterference
System dependence graph · Deductive verification

1 Introduction

When sensitive information leaks to unauthorized parties, it is often the result of bugs and errors introduced into the system during software development. An effective measure to reveal potential sources for such leakages are formal methods, which can provably detect any program instruction that may lead to such a violation of confidentiality. Whereas formal methods already experience successful applications for verifying functional properties, their adoption to security properties in larger programs still either lacks precision or scalability.

Noninterference. An established property guaranteeing confidentiality on code level is *noninterference*. Noninterference holds if no information flow from a

J. Sun and M. Sun (Eds.): ICFEM 2018, LNCS 11232, pp. 284–300, 2018.
https://doi.org/10.1007/978-3-030-02450-5_17

secret input (of *high* security) to a public output (of *low* security) of the system is possible, i.e., if and only if no secret input of a program may influence its public output. Research on secure information flow dates back to the works of Denning and Denning [5,6] and later Goguen and Meseguer [8]. In the following, we formally define the noninterference property that we want to prove using the approach described within this work. We distinguish high variables containing secret data, which should be protected, from low variables, which are publicly readable, and introduce the *low-equivalence* relation ($\sim_L$) to characterize program states that are indistinguishable for any potential attacker. A program state s is an assignment of values to program variables and program locations. We assume that the input of a program is included in the program's initial state and that the output of a program is included its final state. Two states, s and s', are low-equivalent iff all low variables in s have the same value as in s'.

Definition 1 (Noninterference). *A program P is noninterferent iff, for any initial states s_1 and s_2, the statement*

$$s_1 \sim_L s_2 \Rightarrow s_1' \sim_L s_2'$$

holds, where s_1' and s_2' are final program states after executing P in the initial states s_1 and s_2, respectively.

This means that two program executions starting in two low-equivalent states must terminate in two low-equivalent states. This guarantees that low outputs are not influenced by high inputs. Note that we restrict ourselves to terminating programs. In the rest of this work, we will refer to noninterference with respect to a given high input and a given low output simply as noninterference.

Existing Approaches. There exist various approaches and tools for checking the noninterference property of a program. In what follows, we describe the types of approaches, which we will combine in our approach.

Approaches that are based on *System Dependence Graphs* (SDGs) syntactically compute the dependences between program statements and check whether any low output syntactically depends on high input (see, for example, the JOANA tool [10]). Whereas this scales very well, such approaches over-approximate the actual dependences in the program, which may result in false alarms, since the analysis only works on the syntactical level of the program. For example, in a program such as "`l=l+h; l=l-h;`", a syntactical approach will identify a dependence between the variables `l` and `h`, even though there is in fact no (semantical) dependence between them.

Logic-based approaches (e.g., using dynamic logic for Java [3]), on the other hand, have a higher precision, i.e., they produce less false alarms, because they also consider the semantics of program statements. However, those approaches have a lower scalability. Using a logical proof calculus, the logic-based approaches' proof obligation is to show that the terminating states of two program executions are low-equivalent, assuming their two initial states are low-equivalent. False alarms only occur when the system fails to find a proof in the allotted time even though the proof obligation is valid. Proving noninterference using this approach involves simultaneously checking all execution paths for two program executions. This makes the noninterference proof harder than proving a functional property as the number of execution paths to be checked is quadratic.

Our Contribution. In this paper we present the *Combined Approach*, a novel IFC technique that combines an SDG-based approach with a logic-based approach, and in consequence achieves a higher precision than the solely SDG-based approach. The Combined Approach analyzes the dependences from security violations reported by the SDG-based approach and proves the absence of these dependences (given the program actually is noninterferent) using a theorem prover. While the deduction steps in the theorem prover may require user interaction, we automatically generate its proof obligations from the reported dependences.

Furthermore, we reduce the verification effort by enriching the generated proof obligations with information obtained from the SDG-based approach. The information relayed to the theorem prover consists of information flow contracts for the called methods, (partial) loop invariants for loops inside the verified code, and preconditions generated by a points-to analysis.

Structure of the Paper. We organize the paper as follows. Sections 2 and 3 define the SDG-based and logic-based information flow analysis techniques, respectively, used by the Combined Approach. Section 4 presents the Combined Approach. A prototypical implementation of the Combined Approach is presented in Sect. 5. Related work is discussed in Sect. 6. Finally, Sect. 7 concludes.

2 SDG-Based Information Flow Control

SDG-based information flow analyses are purely syntactic, highly scalable, and sound. However, some of the reported noninterference violations may be false alarms. While Program Dependence Graphs (PDGs) [7] and System Dependence Graphs (SDGs) [15] have been developed during the eighties, their usefulness in the context of information-flow security has been first noticed by Snelting [24] in the nineties. Decades of research in this area have resulted in JOANA, a tool that statically analyzes Java programs of up to 100k lines of code for integrity and confidentiality [9,13]. We have used JOANA for a prototype implementation of our approach.

Without loss of generality, we use the JOANA tool as an example to explain the functionality of SDG-based information-flow analysis, but our approach applies to other SDG-based analysis tools as well. The following explanation is partially based on [14], where SDG-based analysis is also used as a preprocessing step (see Sect. 6). We define SDGs for deterministic inter-procedural programs with variable assignments, branchings, loops, and function calls. Moreover, we assume that a control-flow graph (CFG) for such programs exists.

The desired noninterference property is specified by annotating which program parts correspond to sensitive (high) information and the parts where public (low) output occurs. Given these annotations, JOANA automatically builds an SDG for the program. An SDG is a directed graph consisting of interconnected Program Dependence Graphs (PDGs), where a PDG represents a single program procedure as a directed graph. More details on SDGs can be found in [15].

Nodes in the SDG represent program statements, conditions, or input parameters, and edges represent dependences between the nodes, i.e., an edge between two nodes exists if and only if the value or execution of one node may depend on the outcome of the other node. Whether an edge exists between two nodes in the SDG is determined syntactically by analyzing the control-flow graph of the analyzed program. There are roughly three types of edges in an SDG: (1) data dependence edges, representing possible direct dependences, (2) control dependences, which represent possible indirect dependences, and (3) interprocedural dependences, which represent dependences between nodes of different PDGs (other dependences have been introduced to support object orientation and multithreading, see [11]). Formal definitions for the three types of dependences can be found in [11, Chap. 2]. In the following, we give informal definitions.

A node n' is data-dependent on n if there is a program variable v that is used in n' and defined in n, and there is a path from n to n' in the CFG such that v is not redefined on any node between n and n' on that path. The standard definition of a control dependence between two nodes states that a node n' is control-dependent on a node n if the choice of the outgoing edge from n in the CFG determines whether node n' is reached. Note that it is undecidable whether a CFG path represents an actual execution path of the program, i.e., some paths in the CFG may represent executions that cannot actually take place. The CFG is thus an over-approximation of the actual program behavior. Since the dependences are defined using CFG paths, they too are an over-approximation of the actual (semantical) dependences in the program. In the rest of the paper, we refer to the program execution described by a CFG path as *execution path*. Note that an SDG path may also represent one or more actual execution paths.

Method calls are represented by special formal-in and formal-out nodes in the SDG. Formal-in nodes represent direct inputs that influence the method execution. These are the input parameters, used fields, and other classes called during execution and the class in which the method is executed. Moreover, formal-out nodes represent the influence of the method. In most cases, a formal-out node represents the method's return value. Other possibilities are that the method influences global variables, fields in other classes, or terminates with an exception.

```
int f(int x, int y) { return x; }          void caller() { ... f(a,b); ...}
```

Listing 1. Method call

As example, for function `f` in Listing 1, we have two formal-in nodes for `x` and `y`, and one formal-out node for the return value of `f`. At each method call site, there are actual-in nodes representing the arguments and actual-out nodes representing the return values. For a given method site, each actual-in node corresponds to a formal-in node of the callee and vice versa; the same holds for actual-out and formal-out nodes. Interprocedural dependences connect actual-in nodes to the corresponding formal-in nodes, and formal-out nodes to the corresponding actual-out nodes. For the call in Listing 1, there are actual-in nodes for `a` and `b`, corresponding to `f`'s formal-in nodes for `x` and `y`, respectively. The actual-out node representing the return value of `f` corresponds to the single formal-out node of `f`. For every method call we also have so-called *summary edges* in the SDG from any actual-in to any actual-out node of the method whenever the tool finds a flow from the formal-in to the formal-out node of the called method. In Listing 1, we have a flow in `f` from `x` to the return value, thus a summary edge is inserted at call site, namely from `a`'s actual-in to the single actual-out node. For a method involving many objects, there can be a huge number of actual-in and actual-out nodes and an even greater number of summary edges.

SDG-based information-flow analysis approaches, such as the one implemented by JOANA, detect illegal information flows through graph analysis, using a special form of conditional reachability analysis – *slicing* and *chopping* – at the SDG level. A forward slice of a node s consists of all nodes in SDG paths starting in s. Conversely, a backward slice of a node s consists of all nodes in SDG paths ending in s. A chop from a node s to a node t consists of all nodes on paths from s to t in the SDG and is commonly computed by calculating the backward slice for t, and then computing the forward slice for s within the subgraph induced by it. When the slicer or chopper encounters a method call site, it descends into the called method without ascending back up. However, this cannot miss any potential information flow, since for every flow through that method, a summary edge was inserted at the call site, which can be taken as a shortcut. JOANA reports a security violation whenever there exists a path from a node in the SDG that is annotated as **`high`** to a node annotated as `low`, i.e., when the chop of these two nodes is not empty. It has been proven that this approach may not miss any potential information flow, i.e., that JOANA is sound, and that any illegal information flow in the program can occur only in the execution paths determined by an SDG path from a high node to a low node [27]. Since the dependences in the SDG are over-approximations of actual dependences in the program, if no SDG path for the illegal flow is found, the program is guaranteed to be noninterferent. However, whenever there is an SDG path between a high input and a low output, the program may still be noninterferent.

3 Logic-Based Information Flow Control

Logic-based information flow analysis takes the semantics of the program language into account. The semantics of modern program languages provide a high degree of expressiveness, which must be considered when sources of illegal information leaks may be exploiting features of the program semantics. Logic provides a means for abstraction and can capture such features and moreover, using logical calculi, enables reasoning about their –direct or indirect, explicit or implicit– effects on any low program variables or locations. However, this requires a logical representation of the program together with the precise property we want to prove. Using dynamic logic [4] together with symbolic values, we can express the functional property of *partial correctness* of a program P for a precondition ϕ and a postcondition ψ by the following formula:

$$\phi \rightarrow [P]\psi$$

This means that ψ holds in all possible states in which P terminates. Since we analyze only deterministic programs, this means that either P terminates and ψ holds afterwards, or the program never terminates. Since we restrict ourselves to terminating programs, we only need to prove partial correctness in the following. Applying a logical calculus with a deductive theorem prover, we can hence symbolically execute P and attempt to prove the formula.

On this basis, we state the noninterference property based on value independence for a high variable h, a low variable l and a program P in the following way:

Definition 2 (Noninterference as value independence). *When starting* P *with arbitrary values* l*, then the value* r *of* l *– after executing* P *– is independent of the choice of* h *(note the order of the quantifiers).*

$$\forall l \; \exists r \; \forall h \; [P] \; r = l$$

However, instantiating existential quantifiers hinders automation and requires user interaction. As a mitigation, [2] established a noninterference formalization based on self-composition, effectively reducing it to a safety property. Using self-composition, the noninterference property of a program P translates to a safety property of a new program which consists of P composed with a renaming of P.

Furthermore, we need to introduce the concept of state updates [1], which capture the effects of symbolically executing program statements. We denote updates by variable assignments enclosed by curly braces, which are applied to logical terms and formulae, and thus change the program state.

We can now, based on the low-equivalence in Definition 1 from Sect. 1, extend our formalization of noninterference in Definition 3.

Definition 3 (Noninterference as self-composition with state updates).

$$\begin{aligned} \forall in_l \, \forall in_h^1 \, \forall in_h^2 \, \forall out_l^1 \, \forall out_l^2 \, \{l := in_l\}(\\ \{h := in_h^1\}[P] \, out_l^1 = l \\ \wedge \, \{h := in_h^2\}[P] \, out_l^2 = l \\ \rightarrow \, out_l^1 = out_l^2) \end{aligned}$$

Therein, we have two executions of P, one where the (high) program variable h is renamed to in_h^1, and another one where it is renamed to in_h^2. The (low) output variable l is captured in the variable out_l^1 after the first execution and in variable out_l^2 after the second one. Finally, we need to prove that both outputs

out_l^1 and out_l^2 are equivalent in the final state and assume equivalent low inputs via the variable in_l. The self-composition formula can hence be enclosed with purely universal quantifiers over the renaming variables for input and output. When trying to prove noninterference for a program P, theorem provers can now skolemize these variables and greatly reduce the necessary user interaction.

Now, when dealing with object-orientation, it is sometimes too strict to require all (low) variables and locations in the final state to be equivalent. For this matter, [23] developed a variation of noninterference using a different semantics of low-equivalence based on an object isomorphism as defined in Definition 4. Therein, for any two states s_1 and s_2, and two isomorphisms π_1 and π_2, $\pi_1(o) = \pi_2(o)$ holds if o is observable in both states s_1 and s_2.

Definition 4 (Low-equivalence with isomorphism). *Two states s, s' are low-equivalent iff they assign the same values to low variables (with L denoting the set of all low variables in state s).*

$$s \simeq_L^{\pi} s' \quad \Leftrightarrow \quad \forall v \in L\ (\pi(v^s) = v^{s'})$$

The techniques described above together with this semantics are defined and implemented in the deductive program verification tool KeY for Java [1]. It furthermore allows for more efficient noninterference proofs using modularization via the *design-by-contract* concept with an extension of the Java Modeling Language (JML) [18]. Such a contract specifies the low program variables and locations for the initial and the final state of the specified program part. The proof obligation hence requires the low elements in the final state to depend at most on the low elements in the initial state. When using the semantics for object isomorphisms, these contracts may also contain a list of fresh objects to be included in the isomorphism.

In general, the problem is undecidable and verification sometimes requires some user interaction. KeY is capable of verifying noninterference for Java programs and covers a wide range of Java features. With this toolkit, powerful specification elements are given for proving noninterference, also allowing for declassification.

4 The Combined Approach

In the following, we describe our Combined Approach on the example of proving noninterference for a given program P. The first step of the Combined Approach consists of running the SDG-based analysis to check the noninterference property for P. If there is no illegal information flow for P, we need no further action as noninterference is guaranteed to hold. If – however – the automatic SDG-based approach detects an illegal information flow, we apply the second step of the Combined Approach in order to check whether this information flow is a false positive or a genuine leak. Since the SDG-based analysis is performed as the first step, the results provided by our approach are at least as good as those of the SDG-based analysis.

The SDG-based analysis creates an SDG that models the syntactic dependences between the program parts of P. However, as explained in Sect. 2, these dependences represent an over-approximation of the actual program dependences. The goal of the Combined Approach is to use a logic-based IFC approach to prove that certain syntactic dependences in the SDG do not represent real dependences. If all syntactic dependences between the high inputs and the low outputs reported by the SDG-based analysis are proven, using the logic-based approach, to not exist semantically, then the analyzed noninterference property is proven to hold for P. We assume that the SDG-nodes corresponding to high inputs and low outputs are annotated as high and low respectively. Let N_h denote the set of all nodes annotated as high, and N_ℓ the set of all nodes annotated as low.

The SDG-based approach then returns a set of *violations*. A violation is a pair (n_h, n_ℓ) of a high node $n_h \in N_h$ and a low node $n_\ell \in N_\ell$ such that there is a path from n_h to n_ℓ in the SDG of P. We then call the set of all nodes lying on a path from n_h to n_ℓ the *violation chop* $c(n_\ell, n_h)$. To keep the notation simple, we will also use $c(n_h, n_\ell)$ for the subgraph induced by those nodes. If the set of all violation chops, denoted by C_V, is empty, the SDG-based approach guarantees noninterference. If – however – there is a false positive, C_V contains at least one chop. The idea of the Combined Approach is then to validate each violation chop $c(n_h, n_\ell) \in C_V$ and attempt to prove that the chop does not exist on the semantic level in program P. We prove this by showing that each violation chop is interrupted (see Definition 5) with the help of a logic-based approach.

Definition 5 (Unnecessary summary edge, Interrupted violation chop). *A summary edge $e = (a_i, a_o)$ is called* unnecessary *if there is no information flow from the formal-in node f_i to the formal-out node f_o corresponding to a_i and a_o, respectively.*

A violation chop is interrupted, *if we find a non-empty set S of unnecessary summary edges on this chop, such that after deleting the edges in S from the SDG, no path exists between the source and the sink of the violation chop.*

In order to show that a summary edge $e = (a_i, a_o)$ is unnecessary, a proof obligation is generated for the theorem prover of the logic-based approach. This proof obligation states that there is no information flow from the formal-in node f_i to the formal-out node f_o corresponding to the summary edge e (Sect. 5.1 contains a more precise description of the proof obligation). The proof is done for all possible contexts of the called method. If the proof is successful, we have proven that the summary edge was only inserted as a result of the over-approximation, and we can soundly delete this edge.

Note that for checking whether a violation chop is interrupted, we rely on the way the chopper works on method call sites: When deleting a summary edge, the chopper still finds the corresponding information flow in the called method because no dependence edges have been deleted there. However, since it does not ascend back to the caller and relies on the (now deleted) summary edge, the chopper proceeds in the caller as if it did not find that corresponding information flow.

Data: Set of violation chops S
Result: Noninterference guarantee or failed verification attempt
foreach *Violation chop* $C_V \in S$ **do**
  Build queue Q of summary edges in C_V, ordered by heuristics;
  while C_V *not interrupted and* Q *not empty* **do**
    Pop summary edge e from Q;
    Generate proof obligation PO for proving that e is unnecessary;
    if PO *proved with theorem prover* **then**
      Delete e from C_V;
    end
  end
end

Algorithm 1. The Combined Approach

Our approach, shown in Algorithm 1, attempts to interrupt each violation chop in C_V. For each violation chop a summary edge is taken, the appropriate information flow proof obligation is generated for the method corresponding to the summary edge, and a proof attempt is made using the theorem prover. If the proof is successful, the summary edge can then be deleted from the SDG, based on Definition 5. The order in which the summary edges are checked is established by a heuristic which is explained towards the end of this section. Note that we only need to consider summary edges that belong to a *chop* between high and low. Thus, it is sufficient to regard only a smaller subset of all summary edges. We then check whether this violation chop is interrupted. In this case we can proceed to analyze the remaining violation chops until all of them are interrupted. In case the violation chop is still not interrupted, or the proof attempt is not successful, another summary edge from the violation chop is chosen. If we are able to interrupt every violation chop by deleting unnecessary edges, our approach guarantees noninterference.

Theorem 1 (Noninterference Combined Approach). *The Combined Approach guarantees noninterference.*

Proof. Let S be the set of unnecessary summary edges that interrupt a violation chop $c(n_h, n_\ell) \in C_V$. Using the logic-based approach, we have shown for each summary edge $e = (a_i, a_o) \in S$ that the actual-out node a_o does not depend on the actual-in node a_i of that summary edge. Since each path from n_h to n_ℓ contains one such summary edge we have in fact shown that the potential dependences from n_h to n_ℓ, represented by the violation chop, do not represent real dependences. The soundness of the SDG-based approach guarantees that there are no other potential dependences from n_h to n_ℓ than the ones in the chop. Thus, proving all violation chops to be interrupted proves that the program is noninterferent. □

Note that each violation chop is guaranteed to contain at least one summary edge, namely the one corresponding to the `main` method. Generating a proof obligation for the `main` method – however – is equivalent to verifying the entire program with the theorem prover. In practice, however, programs are interprocedural and thus there are plenty of summary edges for our approach to check. Nevertheless, the verification of the `main` method with the theorem prover is still the worst case of our approach and can occur in case not enough summary edges of inner method calls can be proved to be unnecessary.

```
public int test(int high, int low) {
  int result = identity(high, low);
  return result;
}

public int identity(int h, int l) {
  l = l + h;
  l = l − h;
  return l;
}
```

Listing 2. Example program

For the example in Listing 2, when trying to show that there is no information flow from the parameter `high` to the return value of the method `test`, the SDG-based approach reports an illegal information flow, because the return value of the method `identity` is data-dependent on the parameter `h` of the same method. This is, however, a mere syntactic dependence and the reported violation is a false alarm. The reported violation chop contains only one path which contains the actual-in SDG-node representing parameter h and the actual-out SDG-node representing the return value of `identity`, connected by a summary edge as explained in Sect. 2. The Combined Approach automatically generates a proof obligation for the logic-based approach which states that the return value of `identity` does not depend on parameter `h`. By proving this, we also prove that the return value of the method `test` does not depend on the parameter `high` and thus show the noninterference of `test`. This simple example showcases a major advantage of our approach: the logic-based approach does not need to analyze the entire program, but only those parts that cannot be handled with the SDG-based approach.

Proofs with the theorem prover are often performed fully automatically, but may sometimes need auxiliary specification and user interaction. Therefore, we want to minimize the theorem prover usage as much as possible. The order in which the summary edges of the violation chops are checked has a major impact on the performance of the Combined Approach. Ideally we want to avoid proof attempts of methods that do have an information flow or of very large methods that would overwhelm the theorem prover (for example the `main` method). In order to achieve these goals, we developed several heuristics for establishing the order in which we check the summary edges with the logic-based approach. A first category of heuristics searches the code for code patterns that are likely to cause false positives by the SDG-based approach. Such patterns include code that contains array handling, arithmetic operations, or code that can throw runtime exceptions. SDG-based approaches are particularly prone to report false positives for such code, because they neither distinguish between the different array fields nor do they take the values of variables and semantics of operators into account. The second category of heuristics attempts to identify the methods that are likely to run through the theorem prover automatically. Earlier, we mentioned that it is difficult to create precise loop-invariants and thus methods without loops are assigned a higher priority. Additionally, depending on the tools used, we can exclude methods that contain programming language features that are not supported by the logic-based approach, or library methods from the analysis. A third category of heuristics tries to identify the methods that, if proven noninterferent, would bring the greatest benefit to the goal of proving the entire program noninterferent. We assign a high priority to summary edges which are *bridges* in the SDG, i.e., an edge whose removal from the SDG would result in two unconnected graphs. In case no bridge exists within the SDG, we prefer the method with the highest number of connections, i.e., the most often called method.

Due to its low scalability, the logic-based approach is more likely to handle methods that are deeper in the call graph (i.e., that call few other methods) than methods which are high in the call graph. However, the parts of the program that can disprove a reported security violation may be present in a high level method. In order to still be able to handle such cases, we automatically generate information flow contracts for the method calls occurring inside the analyzed method based on the results of the SDG-based analysis. These method calls have actual-in and actual-out SDG-nodes connected by summary edges. The generated information flow contracts state that the program parts corresponding to the actual nodes of the method call site depend at most on the actual-out nodes of the respective method call site. Due to the soundness of the SDG-based analysis, this information flow contract is also sound. However, the over-approximation done by the SDG-based analysis is also present in the contracts generated this way. Thus, using such contracts does not guarantee that the logic-based approach will successfully disprove the reported security violation, but it allows for an analysis of higher-level methods.

5 Implementation

We implemented[1] the Combined Approach using JOANA as the dependence-graph analysis tool and KeY as the theorem prover. In this section, we show how we generate the proof obligations for KeY in the form of specified Java code and also present the results of running the Combined Approach on a collection of examples that cannot be handled by JOANA alone.

5.1 Specification Generation

For the method corresponding to the summary edge selected by the heuristics, we generate an information flow method contract such that a successful proof would show that there is in fact no dependence from the formal-in to the formal-out node of the summary edge.

[1] Code available at https://git.scc.kit.edu/py8074/keyjoana.

Thus, in order to show that a summary edge $se(a_i, a_o)$ is unnecessary, we prove that there is no information flow between the corresponding formal-in node f_i and formal-out node f_o. In order to achieve this, we generate a JML specification for the appropriate method stating that f_o is determined by all formal-in nodes other than f_i, as explained in Definition 6. Note that the `determines` clause used in Definitions 7 and 8 is not part of the JML standard, and is only supported by KeY. The clause requires the expressions before the `by` keyword, evaluated in the post-state, to depend at most on the expressions after the `by` keyword, evaluated in the pre-state.

Definition 6 (Generation of the determines clause). *Let $se(a_i, a_o)$ be the summary edge to be checked, and let f_i and f_o be the formal nodes corresponding to the actual nodes a_i and a_o. Let L_i be a list of all formal-in nodes f_i' other than f_i of the method belonging to the call site of a_i and a_o. The following determines clause is added to the method contract:* `determines` f_o `\by` L_i.

Should the proof of this property succeed then it would show that f_o does not depend on f_i and therefore a_o does not depend on actual-in parameter a_i. Since there is no dependence between a_i and a_o the summary edge can be safely deleted from the violation chop.

To increase its precision, JOANA uses a points-to analysis which keeps track of the objects a reference o may point to (the points-to set of o). This information is useful, since it may show that two references cannot be aliased. We use the results of the points-to analysis to generate preconditions for the method contracts, as shown in Definition 7, thus transferring information about the context from JOANA to KeY and increasing the likelihood of a successful proof.

Definition 7 (Generation of preconditions). *Let o be a reference and P_o its points-to set. We generate the following precondition:* $\bigvee_{o' \in P_o} o = o'$

The method contracts generated this way are necessary for proving a summary edge is unnecessary, however in the general case they are not sufficient for a successful proof. If the method contains loops of any kind, the theorem prover needs loop-invariants. The automatic generation of loop-invariants is an active research field, see for example [16,21]. These approaches focus on functional loop-invariants and do not consider information flow loop-invariants.

The determines clause generated for method contracts, can be used to specify the allowed information flows of a loop. The determines clause generated for a loop invariant is similar to the one for method contracts. Because the variables from the formal-in and formal-out nodes may not directly occur in the loop some adjustments are necessary. Definition 8 shows what determines clauses are generated for loop invariants:

Definition 8 (Generation of the determines clause for loop invariants). *Let $se(a_i, a_o)$ be the summary edge to be checked, and let f_i and f_o be the formal nodes corresponding to the actual nodes a_i and a_o. Let L_i be a list of all formal-in nodes f_i' other than f_i of the method belonging to the call site of a_i and a_o. Let V_i be the set of all variables in the loop and let I_i be a list of variables in the* *method that influence f_o. The following determines clause is added to the loop invariant:* ***determines*** f_o, V_i *\by* L_i, I_i.

Note that the sets V_i and I_i can be constructed by analyzing the SDG.

5.2 Evaluation

We considered eleven examples, which cover different program structures and reasons for false positives. Each of these examples is not solvable by automated graph based approaches like JOANA. In Table 1 we have listed the eleven examples. The evaluation is split into automatic mode and interactive mode. In the automatic mode, an attempt is made to prove the generated proof obligations automatically. In the interactive mode, the theorem prover is called for all proof obligations in interactive mode. In this mode, the user can perform automatic or interactive steps and can add auxiliary specification. The column *KeY Calls* represents the number of times KeY was called to show that a summary edge is unnecessary. As can be seen in the table, in interactive mode sometimes fewer calls to KeY are necessary, as the user can better recognize which summary edges are more likely to be successfully proven as unnecessary.

The eleven examples are again divided into two groups. First, there are individual methods that cause false positives. In the method `Identity`, the high value is added and subtracted to the low variable such that the low value remains the same. There is a dependence from high to low on a syntactical level, but in reality there is none. In the method `Precondition` there is an if-condition that can never be true and the method `Excluding Statements` contains if-statements that can not both be true at the same program execution. The example `Loop Override` contains a loop which overrides the low value in the last loop execution. For this example the noninterference loop-invariant was not enough for an automated proof and further functional information had to be given by the user. The last simple method `Array Access` contains array handling code. The second group consists of programs that include these problems in different program structures. Based on the possible SDG, we regard simple flows, branching, nested summary edges and a combination of all.

The example programs are in the range of 5 to 30 lines of code. They show that the combined approach can prove programs automatically for which JOANA would generate false positives.

6 Related Work

There exist many different approaches for proving noninterference. A survey on approaches for IFC is found in [22]. In what follows, we describe some approaches that are similar to ours.

The *Hybrid Approach* [17] also aims to combine automatic dependence-graph analysis and theorem proving. The user first attempts to show noninterference using JOANA. If the user suspects the reported violation to be a false alarm, he

Table 1. List of examples

Program	*Automatic Mode*			*Interactive Mode*	
	Provable	KeY Calls	Time	Provable	KeY Calls
Individual methods					
Identity	Yes	1	5 s	Yes	1
Precondition	Yes	1	5 s	Yes	1
Excluding statements	Yes	1	5 s	Yes	1
Loop override	No	1	7 s	Yes	1
Array access	Yes	1	6 s	Yes	1
Whole programs					
KeY example	Yes	1	7 s	Yes	1
Single flow	Yes	1	6 s	Yes	1
Branching	Yes	2	10 s	Yes	2
Nested methods	Yes	2	10 s	Yes	2
Mixture	Yes	4	19 s	Yes	3
Mixture with loops	No	7	20 s	Yes	5

must identify the cause of the alarm and extend the program such that the low output is overwritten with a value that does not depend on the high input. The extended program is rechecked by JOANA, and if deemed noninterferent, KeY is used to show that the extended program computes the same low output as the original. This approach improves the precision provided by JOANA. However, there is no assistance in finding the causes of the false alarms, and the program extension must be done manually.

SDG-based approaches can also be used to identify program statements that do not contribute to a potential information flow or program execution paths that are guaranteed to not lead to an illegal information flow. This is done in [14], where the SDG-based approach is used to generate a simplified program that can then be more easily verified or tested. The approach is orthogonal to the Combined Approach presented in this paper, and the two approaches can be combined by using the approach in [14] to simplify the program for which we attempt to show that a summary edge is unnecessary.

Another combination of SDG-based approaches and theorem provers is by checking the satisfiability of the path conditions for the execution paths determined by the reported security violation [12,25]. If a path condition is unsatisfiable, then that execution path cannot lead to an illegal information flow.

Another class of approaches for information flow control are based on *type systems* [19,26]. They can have the same scalability and precision as SDG-based approaches [20], though most type systems have higher scalability but lower precision. They enforce secure information flow by assigning a security type (e.g., high or low) to the program variables and then checking whether the expressions in the program conform to the type system.

7 Conclusion

In this work, we introduced a new combined approach to prove noninterference with less user interaction while keeping the same precision. Our approach combines an automated SDG-based technique with a deductive theorem prover. We demonstrated that the noninterference properties guaranteed by the two tools are compatible and, thus, that our approach is sound. The Combined Approach has been developed tool-independently, but implemented and evaluated on a selection of examples as well as a small case study. Although the programs covered in our evaluation do not exceed 100 lines of code and could – as such – also be proven without the help of SDG-based IFC, they could – however – also be embedded in much bigger programs, which – as such – may be clearly too big for the analysis with a theorem prover.

Acknowledgements. We are grateful to the student Holger Klein for implementing the prototype. This work was supported by the German Research Foundation (DFG) under the project DeduSec (BE 2334/6-3) in the priority program "Reliably Secure Software Systems" (RS^3, SPP 1496).

References

1. Ahrendt, W., Beckert, B., Bubel, R., Hähnle, R., Schmitt, P.H., Ulbrich, M. (eds.): Deductive Software Verification - The KeY Book: From Theory to Practice. LNCS, vol. 10001. Springer, Heidelberg (2016). https://doi.org/10.1007/978-3-319-49812-6
2. Barthe, G., D'Argenio, P.R., Rezk, T.: Secure information flow by self-composition. In: 17th IEEE Computer Security Foundations Workshop, CSFW-17 2004, pp. 100–114. IEEE Computer Society (2004)
3. Beckert, B., Bruns, D., Klebanov, V., Scheben, C., Schmitt, P.H., Ulbrich, M.: Information flow in object-oriented software. In: Gupta, G., Peña, R. (eds.) LOPSTR 2013. LNCS, vol. 8901, pp. 19–37. Springer, Cham (2014). https://doi.org/10.1007/978-3-319-14125-1_2
4. Darvas, Á., Hähnle, R., Sands, D.: A theorem proving approach to analysis of secure information flow. In: Hutter, D., Ullmann, M. (eds.) SPC 2005. LNCS, vol. 3450, pp. 193–209. Springer, Heidelberg (2005). https://doi.org/10.1007/978-3-540-32004-3_20
5. Denning, D.E.: A lattice model of secure information flow. Commun. ACM **19**(5), 236–243 (1976)
6. Denning, D.E., Denning, P.J.: Certification of programs for secure information flow. Commun. ACM **20**(7), 504–513 (1977)
7. Ferrante, J., Ottenstein, K.J., Warren, J.D.: The program dependence graph and its use in optimization. ACM Trans. Program. Lang. Syst. **9**(3), 319–349 (1987)
8. Goguen, J.A., Meseguer, J.: Security policies and security models. In: Symposium on Security and Privacy (SP), pp. 11–20 (1982)

9. Graf, J., Hecker, M., Mohr, M.: Using JOANA for information flow control in Java programs - a practical guide. In: Wagner, S., Lichter, H. (eds.) Conference on Programming Languages (ATP). LNI, vol. 215, pp. 123–138. Springer, Heidelberg (2013)
10. Graf, J., Hecker, M., Mohr, M.: Using JOANA for information flow control in Java programs-a practical guide. In: Wagner, S., Lichter, H. (eds.) Software Engineering, Fachtagung des GI-Fachbereichs Softwaretechnik. LNI, vol. 215, pp. 123–138. GI (2013)
11. Hammer, C.: Information flow control for java - a comprehensive approach based on path conditions in dependence graphs. Ph.D. thesis, Universität Karlsruhe (TH), Fak. f. Informatik, July 2009. http://digbib.ubka.uni-karlsruhe.de/volltexte/1000012049
12. Hammer, C., Krinke, J., Snelting, G.: Information flow control for Java based on path conditions in dependence graphs. In: Symposium on Secure Software Engineering, pp. 87–96 (2006)
13. Hammer, C., Snelting, G.: Flow-sensitive, context-sensitive, and object-sensitive information flow control based on program dependence graphs. Int. J. Inf. Sec. **8**(6), 399–422 (2009)
14. Herda, M., Tyszberowicz, S., Beckert, B.: Using dependence graphs to assist verification and testing of information-flow properties. In: Dubois, C., Wolff, B. (eds.) TAP 2018. LNCS, vol. 10889, pp. 83–102. Springer, Cham (2018). https://doi.org/10.1007/978-3-319-92994-1_5
15. Horwitz, S., Reps, T., Binkley, D.: Interprocedural slicing using dependence graphs. Trans. Program. Lang. Syst. **12**(1), 26–60 (1990)
16. Kapur, D.: Automatically generating loop invariants using quantifier elimination. In: Baader, F., Baumgartner, P., Nieuwenhuis, R., Voronkov, A. (eds.) Deduction and Applications, 23-28 October 2005. Dagstuhl Seminar Proceedings, vol. 05431. Internationales Begegnungs- und Forschungszentrum für Informatik (IBFI), Schloss Dagstuhl, Germany (2005)
17. Küsters, R., Truderung, T., Beckert, B., Bruns, D., Kirsten, M., Mohr, M.: A hybrid approach for proving noninterference of Java programs. In: Fournet, C., Hicks, M.W., Viganò, L. (eds.) 28th Computer Security Foundations Symposium (CSF), pp. 305–319. IEEE Computer Society (2015)
18. Leavens, G.T., Kiniry, J.R., Poll, E.: A JML tutorial: modular specification and verification of functional behavior for Java. In: Damm, W., Hermanns, H. (eds.) CAV 2007. LNCS, vol. 4590, pp. 37–37. Springer, Heidelberg (2007). https://doi.org/10.1007/978-3-540-73368-3_6
19. Lortz, S., Mantel, H., Starostin, A., Bähr, T., Schneider, D., Weber, A.: Cassandra: towards a certifying app store for Android. In: ACM Workshop on Security and Privacy in Smartphones & Mobile Devices (SPSM), pp. 93–104. ACM (2014)
20. Mantel, H., Sudbrock, H.: Types vs. PDGs in information flow analysis. In: Albert, E. (ed.) LOPSTR 2012. LNCS, vol. 7844, pp. 106–121. Springer, Heidelberg (2013). https://doi.org/10.1007/978-3-642-38197-3_8
21. Rodríguez-Carbonell, E., Kapur, D.: Generating all polynomial invariants in simple loops. J. Symbolic Comput. **42**(4), 443–476 (2007)
22. Sabelfeld, A., Myers, A.C.: Language-based information-flow security. IEEE J. Sel. A. Commun. **21**(1), 5–19 (2006)
23. Scheben, C., Schmitt, P.H.: Verification of information flow properties of JAVA programs without approximations. In: Beckert, B., Damiani, F., Gurov, D. (eds.) FoVeOOS 2011. LNCS, vol. 7421, pp. 232–249. Springer, Heidelberg (2012). https://doi.org/10.1007/978-3-642-31762-0_15

24. Snelting, G.: Combining slicing and constraint solving for validation of measurement software. In: Cousot, R., Schmidt, D.A. (eds.) SAS 1996. LNCS, vol. 1145, pp. 332–348. Springer, Heidelberg (1996). https://doi.org/10.1007/3-540-61739-6_51
25. Snelting, G., Robschink, T., Krinke, J.: Efficient path conditions in dependence graphs for software safety analysis. ACM Trans. Softw. Eng. Methodol. **15**(4), 410–457 (2006)
26. Volpano, D.M., Irvine, C.E., Smith, G.: A sound type system for secure flow analysis. J. Comput. Secur. **4**(2/3), 167–188 (1996)
27. Wasserrab, D., Lohner, D.: Proving information flow noninterference by reusing a machine-checked correctness proof for slicing. In: Aderhold, M., Autexier, S., Mantel, H. (eds.) Verification Workshop (VERIFY). EPiC Series in Computing, vol. 3, pp. 141–155 (2010)

Logic and Semantics

Preserving Liveness Guarantees from Synchronous Communication to Asynchronous Unstructured Low-Level Languages

Nils Berg(✉), Thomas Göthel, Armin Danziger, and Sabine Glesner

Technische Universität Berlin, Berlin, Germany
n.berg@tu-berlin.de

Abstract. In the implementation of abstract synchronous communication in asynchronous unstructured low-level languages, e.g. using shared variables, the preservation of safety and especially liveness properties is a hitherto open problem due to inherently different abstraction levels. Our approach to overcome this problem is threefold: First, we present our notion of *handshake refinement* with which we formally prove the correctness of the implementation relation of a handshake protocol. Second, we verify the soundness of our *handshake refinement*, i.e., all safety and liveness properties are preserved to the lower level. Third, we apply our *handshake refinement* to show the correctness of *all* implementations that realize the abstract synchronous communication with the handshake protocol. To this end, we employ an exemplary language with asynchronous shared variable communication. Our approach is scalable and closes the verification gap between different abstraction levels of communication.

Keywords: Unstructured Code · Liveness properties
Handshake protocol · Formal verification · Refinement

1 Introduction

In the rigorous model-driven design of low-level implementations, formal specifications are iteratively refined until an implementation model is reached. In the subsequent transition to executable code, correctness is mostly subject to informal reasoning due to the different abstraction levels. In this paper, we consider unstructured low-level languages that are required to preserve safety and liveness properties from the formal specification. The formal verification of the relation between specification and implementation of communicating low-level code can be split in two parts: *(1)* State transformations and control flow, and *(2)* communication. While we have presented an approach for *(1)* in [7,8], in this paper we focus on the low-level implementation of communication. In particular, we do not consider the general question whether it is possible to implement synchronous communication with asynchronous means, as this was shown in

J. Sun and M. Sun (Eds.): ICFEM 2018, LNCS 11232, pp. 303–319, 2018.
https://doi.org/10.1007/978-3-030-02450-5_18

e.g. [3]. In contrast, we propose a methodology to verify that a specification using abstract synchronous communication and a concrete implementation in a low-level language using asynchronous shared variable communication have the same safety and liveness properties based on a simple handshake protocol.

In synchronous communication, sender and receiver are determined at the same time, whereas they are determined at different points in time in asynchronous communication. Thus, asynchronous communication has more decision points and a different branching behavior. The major problem is to prove preservation of liveness properties for systems with different branching behavior. To overcome this problem, we define the *handshake refinement* that enables the construction and formal verification of implementation relations for the abstract communication instruction. We show that this relation preserves safety and liveness properties. Finally, we use our notion of *handshake refinement* to show the correctness of the implementation of abstract synchronous communication with a handshake protocol in our generalized low-level language using shared variable communication. Our theorem shows that *all* implementations with this protocol are correct. This once-and-for-all approach is highly scalable and allows for compositional reasoning over shared variable communication. While the *handshake refinement* is designed for this specific handshake protocol, its concepts can be adapted to other protocols, which is left for future work.

2 Related Work

In [4], Broy and Olderog investigate the relationship between synchronous and asynchronous communication, where asynchronous communication is *buffered*, e.g. via an additional buffer process. However we do not consider high-level constructs such as buffers in our implementation language. Apart from the different abstraction level used by Broy and Olderog, their transformation from synchronous to asynchronous systems is to introduce buffers for all (previously synchronous) communication. In doing so, they lose synchronicity and the "refusal structure" of the synchronous specification, i.e. the transformation does not preserve liveness properties.

Peeters [9] models hardware, where low-level communication is synchronous (a wire from sender to recipient). They still use synchronization primitives for the implementation, and thus, does not apply to the problem we consider.

Basu et al. [1] define synchronizability of asynchronous systems. We show a similar relation, namely that it is appropriate to consider a synchronized version of the asynchronous system. The use of modeled queues is too abstract for our problem, as we aim at verifying the abstract communication construct (e.g. queue in this case) itself.

The `CSP++` framework from Gardner [6] constructs a communication backbone from a CSP (Communicating Sequential Processes) process, which can then be enriched with `C++` code. Although the idea of this framework is akin to correct by construction design, the verification of this framework itself is not addressed.

In summary, all these approaches consider either a rather high level of abstraction, or do not consider formal verification of safety and liveness properties.

Vertical Bisimulation by Rensink and Gorrieri [10] provides a congruence relation for action refinements whose implementations can interleave. They do not consider the refinement of the synchronization mechanism itself: Both source language and target language use the same CSP-like synchronization. Their definition is different from the standard bisimulation in that it keeps track of started executions of the implementations. This idea inspired our definition of the *handshake refinement*.

de Frutos Escrig et al. [5] propose *global bisimulations* to achieve associativity of nondeterministic choice. It has some similarity to our problem with split up decisions (i.e. comparing two decisions at once to two consecutive decisions), however our choices are deterministic. Moreover, it is specifically intended to be a *symmetric* relation, and our problem is asymmetric, as we consider different levels of abstraction. Therefore, the vertical bisimulation is a fitter candidate to be adapted to our problem.

3 Background

In the following, we briefly introduce CSP and the low-level language CUC (Communicating Unstructured Code) with synchronous communication which we formerly presented. We base our notion of safety and liveness on CSP and obtain compositionality for CUC by using CSP communication.

3.1 Communicating Sequential Processes (CSP)

For our specification language CUC, we consider CSP-like abstract synchronous communication (without broadcast) throughout this paper. The advantage is that we can perform proofs compositionally, which is inherited from CSP. In CSP [11], a refinement ($Spec \sqsubseteq Impl$) describes a subset relation of the behavior. The *trace* semantics ($\mathcal{T}$) records the traces and the trace refinement ensures the preservation of safety properties. The *stable failures* semantics ($\mathcal{SF}$) additionally records the refused (and by negation the possible) events at each stable state, thus allowing the stable failures refinement to ensure the preservation of liveness properties. In CSP, the notion of refinement is compositional w.r.t. contexts ($\mathcal{C}$), i.e., when only a part of the system is refined, the whole system is also in a refinement relation: $A \sqsubseteq B \Longrightarrow \mathcal{C}(A) \sqsubseteq \mathcal{C}(B)$. As parallel composition can also be part of the context $\mathcal{C}$, this allows for modular verification of concurrent systems.

3.2 Communicating Unstructured Code (CUC)

We aim at verifying safety and liveness properties of the shared variable implementation of abstract synchronous communication. To focus on the difference between abstract synchronous and low-level asynchronous communication, we choose two languages which only differ in this aspect. As the implementation language should be a low-level language with shared variable communication, we choose a low-level language with abstract synchronous communication as a specification language. To this end, we employ the language CUC. It is a generic low-level language with an abstract communication instruction, using CSP's multi-way synchronization. We introduced its operational and trace semantics in [7] and its stable failures semantics together with a Hoare calculus in [8]. The latter provides a framework to verify the stable failures refinement relation between a CSP process and a CUC program, ensuring that the CUC program preserves all safety and liveness properties of the CSP process.

We give a brief overview over CUC here, for details see [8]. The operational semantics is depicted in Fig. 1. The state σ is split into its program counter σ_{pc} and its register store σ_{rs}, *code* is a fixed set of labeled instructions. CUC has three instructions: *(1)* A nondeterministic multiple assignment (DO), which can be instantiated to actual low-level instruction, e.g. arithmetic operations. *(2)* A conditional branch (CBR) and *(3)* the communication primitive. It communicates an event nondeterministically chosen from the result of f_{ev} and then changes the state according to f_{reg}. The `comm` instruction modifies the register store to record input data. The implementation of `comm` f_{ev} f_{reg} is the subject of this paper. The communication of CUC is the same as communication in CSP: All programs offer events (in their alphabets α_i), and if multiple offer the same events, they non-deterministically choose one of them and make a synchronous step (SYNC). Non-synchronized events and τ are performed interleavingly (INTERLEAVING).

$$\frac{(\sigma_{pc}, \texttt{do}\ f) \in \mathit{code} \qquad \sigma'_{rs} \in f(\sigma_{rs}) \qquad \sigma'_{pc} = \sigma_{pc} + 1}{\sigma \xrightarrow{\tau}_{\mathit{code}} \sigma'}\ \text{DO}$$

$$\frac{(\sigma_{pc}, \texttt{cbr}\ b\ m\ n) \in \mathit{code} \qquad \sigma'_{rs} = \sigma_{rs} \qquad b\,\sigma \wedge \sigma'_{pc} = m \vee \neg b\,\sigma \wedge \sigma'_{pc} = n}{\sigma \xrightarrow{\tau}_{\mathit{code}} \sigma'}\ \text{CBR}$$

$$\frac{(\sigma_{pc}, \texttt{comm}\ f_{ev}\ f_{reg}) \in \mathit{code} \quad ev \in f_{ev}(\sigma_{rs}) \quad \sigma'_{rs} = f_{reg}(\sigma_{rs}, ev) \quad \sigma'_{pc} = \sigma_{pc} + 1}{\sigma \xrightarrow{ev}_{\mathit{code}} \sigma'}\ \text{COMM}$$

$$\frac{\sigma_1 \xrightarrow{a}_{c_1} \sigma'_1 \qquad \sigma_2 \xrightarrow{a}_{c_2} \sigma'_2 \qquad a \in \alpha_1 \cap \alpha_2}{\sigma_1 \parallel \sigma_2 \xrightarrow{a}_{(c_1\,{}_{\alpha_1}\|_{\alpha_2}\,c_2)} \sigma'_1 \parallel \sigma'_2}\ \text{SYNC}$$

INTERLEAVING-LEFT

$$\frac{\sigma_1 \xrightarrow{a}_{c_1} \sigma'_1 \qquad a \in (\alpha_1 \cup \{\tau\}) \setminus \alpha_2}{\sigma_1 \parallel \sigma_2 \xrightarrow{a}_{(c_1\,{}_{\alpha_1}\|_{\alpha_2}\,c_2)} \sigma'_1 \parallel \sigma_2}$$

INTERLEAVING-RIGHT

$$\frac{\sigma_2 \xrightarrow{a}_{c_2} \sigma'_2 \qquad a \in (\alpha_2 \cup \{\tau\}) \setminus \alpha_1}{\sigma_1 \parallel \sigma_2 \xrightarrow{a}_{(c_1\,{}_{\alpha_1}\|_{\alpha_2}\,c_2)} \sigma_1 \parallel \sigma'_2}$$

Fig. 1. Operational semantics for CUC

In the transition from synchronous to asynchronous communication, we perform a refinement based on low-level communication protocols. In this paper, we focus on a handshake protocol over shared variables and restrict the use of

CUC constructs accordingly, i.e., to use only a sender and a receiver version of `comm` and exclude communication with the environment. Additionally, we illustrate our approach with a simple protocol here, and therefore prohibit the use of external choice within a component. To restrict the communication to directed communication, we consider two restricted variants of `comm`, as defined below. Let c be a channel, x_s and x_r local registers, id the process id of the current process and ID the set of all process ids. The event $c.s.r.v$ is composed of the channel c, the ids of the sender s and the receiver r, and the transferred data value v. Finally, let $val(c.s.r.v) = v$ extract the data value of an event.

$$\texttt{comm}_s\, id\, c\, x_s := \texttt{comm}\big(\lambda\sigma.\, \{c.id.r.\sigma_{rs}(x_s) \mid r \in ID \wedge r \neq id\}\big)\big(\lambda a\, \sigma.\, \sigma\big)$$
$$\texttt{comm}_r\, id\, c\, x_r := \texttt{comm}\big(\lambda\sigma.\, \{c.s.id.v \mid s \in ID \wedge s \neq id\}\big)\big(\lambda a\, \sigma.\, \sigma(x_r := val(a))\big)$$

$\texttt{comm}_s$ offers events on its channel c, using its own id as sender, and all possible ids as receiver. The data value is the value of its local storage at x_s. After successful communication, the sender does not change its local state. $\texttt{comm}_r$ offers events on its channel c, using its own id as a receiver, all possible ids as sender, and all possible data values. After successful communication, the receiver updates its local storage at x_r to the value of the communicated event. By using events that explicitly contain the id of the sender or the receiver respectively, we enforce that senders cannot communicate among one another and the same for receivers.

In contrast to CSP and CUC, there is no environment in low-level shared variable communication. Thus, a lone `comm` in CUC should not synchronize with the environment but block. To enforce this in CUC, we only consider programs with at least two components. Furthermore, the synchronization alphabet of each concurrent program c_i is given by $\alpha_i = \{c.s.r.v \in \Sigma \mid (s \in ids(P_i) \vee r \in ids(P_i))\}$.

4 Shared Variable Semantics (SV)

In this section, we present the language *Shared Variables* (SV) and give its operational semantics. The intent of SV is to have a language with a *pure interleaving* semantics (in contrast to CUC) and to implement synchronous communication over shared variables with it. SV contains the instructions `do` f and `cbr` just like CUC, but instead of the abstract communication instruction `comm`, it contains the instructions needed for the low-level implementation of communication and synchronization over shared variables: `read`, `write` and `cas` (Compare-and-Set).

The operational semantics for SV is depicted in Fig. 2. For each component, there is a program counter σ_{pc} and a local register store σ_{rs} as in CUC. Furthermore, there is a global state Γ, which holds the values of locks, signals, and shared variables. `do` and `cbr` (as described in rules DO and CBR) have basically the same semantics as in CUC: They change the local state and the program counter, but leave the global state Γ unchanged. `cas` (as described in rules CAS-T and CAS-F) compares the value at a given address sv to a value v_1 and, if they are equal, writes the value v_2 to that address. In either case, the comparison result is written to the local register r. `write` and `read` (as described in rules WRITE and READ) transfer values from local to global storage and vice versa.

$$\frac{(\sigma_{pc}, \texttt{do}\ f) \in code \qquad \sigma'_{rs} \in f(\sigma_{rs}) \qquad \sigma'_{pc} = \sigma_{pc} + 1}{(\Gamma, \sigma) \xrightarrow{code} (\Gamma, \sigma')}\ \text{DO}$$

$$\frac{(\sigma_{pc}, \texttt{cbr}\ b\ m\ n) \in code \qquad \sigma'_{rs} = \sigma_{rs} \qquad b\,\sigma \wedge \sigma'_{pc} = m \vee \neg b\,\sigma \wedge \sigma'_{pc} = n}{(\Gamma, \sigma) \xrightarrow{code} (\Gamma, \sigma')}\ \text{CBR}$$

$$\frac{\begin{array}{c}(\sigma_{pc}, \texttt{cas}\ r\ sv\ v_1\ v_2) \in code \\ \Gamma(sv) = v_1 \qquad \Gamma' = \Gamma(sv := v_2) \qquad \sigma'_{rs} = \sigma_{rs}(r := \top) \qquad \sigma'_{pc} = \sigma_{pc} + 1\end{array}}{(\Gamma, \sigma) \xrightarrow{code} (\Gamma', \sigma')}\ \text{CAS-T}$$

$$\frac{(\sigma_{pc}, \texttt{cas}\ r\ sv\ v_1\ v_2) \in code \quad \Gamma(sv) \neq v_1 \quad \sigma'_{rs} = \sigma_{rs}(r := \bot) \quad \sigma'_{pc} = \sigma_{pc} + 1}{(\Gamma, \sigma) \xrightarrow{code} (\Gamma, \sigma')}\ \text{CAS-F}$$

$$\frac{(\sigma_{pc}, \texttt{write}\ sv\ x) \in code \quad \Gamma' = \Gamma(sv := \sigma_{rs}(x)) \quad \sigma'_{rs} = \sigma_{rs} \quad \sigma'_{pc} = \sigma_{pc} + 1}{(\Gamma, \sigma) \xrightarrow{code} (\Gamma', \sigma')}\ \text{WRITE}$$

$$\frac{(\sigma_{pc}, \texttt{read}\ x\ sv) \in code \qquad \sigma'_{rs} = \sigma_{rs}(x := \Gamma(sv)) \qquad \sigma'_{pc} = \sigma_{pc} + 1}{(\Gamma, \sigma) \xrightarrow{code} (\Gamma, \sigma')}\ \text{READ}$$

$$\frac{(\Gamma, \sigma_1) \xrightarrow{c_1} (\Gamma', \sigma'_1)}{(\Gamma, \sigma_1 \parallel \sigma_2) \xrightarrow{c_1 \parallel c_2} (\Gamma', \sigma'_1 \parallel \sigma_2)}\ \text{CON-LEFT} \qquad \frac{(\Gamma, \sigma_2) \xrightarrow{c_2} (\Gamma', \sigma'_2)}{(\Gamma, \sigma_1 \parallel \sigma_2) \xrightarrow{c_1 \parallel c_2} (\Gamma', \sigma_1 \parallel \sigma'_2)}\ \text{CON-RIGHT}$$

Fig. 2. Operational semantics for SV

Finally, the rules CON-LEFT and CON-RIGHT define the interleaving semantics: Whenever a component can take a step, the combination can take it, too. There is *no* synchronous step. In the next section, we consider how to relate the `comm` instruction and its implementation based on a simple handshake protocol.

4.1 Handshake Protocol in SV

In SV, many protocols realizing synchronous communication can be implemented. In this paper, we focus on a handshake protocol over shared variables.

send:			receive:		
	1:	**cas** hl_c m_c FREE id		1:	**cas** ss_c sr_c $\top$ $\bot$
	2:	**cbr** hl_c 3 1		2:	**cbr** ss_c 3 1
	3:	**write** sv_c x_s		3:	**read** x_r sv_c
	4:	**write** sr_c $\top$		4:	**write** fr_c $\top$
	5:	**cas** ss_c fr_c $\top$ $\bot$			
	6:	**cbr** ss_c 7 5			
	7:	**write** m_c FREE			

Fig. 3. Send and receive: implementations of the $\texttt{comm}_s$ and $\texttt{comm}_r$ instructions

$\texttt{comm}_s$ and $\texttt{comm}_r$ are implemented in SV by the constructs shown in Fig. 3 with a simple handshake protocol. The general idea is that *send* locks the channel to protect the shared variable, and synchronizes over signals with *receive*. The protocol flow is illustrated in Fig. 5. The shared variables representing the mutex and the signals are assumed to be exclusive for each channel.[1] We explain the details of the implementations of the sender and the receiver line by line:

send. (1) checks if the mutex m_c belonging to the channel is free, and if it is, writes its *id* to it. (2) If it is not free, it checks again (busy loop). Otherwise it proceeds to (3) write the data value to be sent (from the local register x_s) to the shared variable sv_c. Afterwards, it realizes a synchronization with the read process: It (4) sets the signal sr_c. Then it (5, 6) waits with a busy loop for the signal fr_c and finally (7) releases the mutex.

receive. (1, 2) waits with a busy loop for the signal sr_c. If it received the signal, it (3) reads the value from the shared variable and then (4) sets the signal fr_c.

Observe that deadlocks from CUC that are due to missing communication partners are implemented as spinlocks in SV: *send* cannot exit the busy loop (line 5, 6) without a receiver on the same channel, and *receive* cannot exit the loop (lines 1, 2) without a sender in the channel.

4.2 Definitions to Relate comm and its Implementations

To formally capture that a CUC and an SV program are syntactically the same apart from the implementation of the abstract communication, we define the *program label map*. As the implementation of the abstract communication is inserted, the following labels shift accordingly. We use this definition to define the notion of an SV program *fitting* a CUC program.

Definition 1 (Program label map). *A program label map ψ maps injectively a program label in a CUC program cuc to a corresponding program label in an SV program sv. For the formal requirements to ψ see Fig. 4.*

$$
\begin{array}{rcl}
(\ell, \mathtt{do}\ f) \in cuc^{id} & \Longleftrightarrow & (\psi(\ell), \mathtt{do}\ f) \in sv^{id} \wedge \psi(\ell+1) = \psi(\ell)+1 \\
(\ell, \mathtt{cbr}\ b\ m\ n) \in cuc^{id} & \Longleftrightarrow & (\psi(\ell), \mathtt{cbr}\ b\ \psi(m)\ \psi(n)) \in sv^{id} \\
(\ell, \mathtt{comm}_s\ id\ c\ x_s) \in cuc^{id} & \Longleftrightarrow & (\psi(\ell)+0, \mathtt{cas}\ m_c\ \text{FREE}\ id) \in sv^{id} \\
\vdots & & \vdots \\
{''} & \Longleftrightarrow & (\psi(\ell)+6, \mathtt{write}\ m_c\ \text{FREE}) \in sv^{id} \\
{''} & \Longrightarrow & \psi(\ell+1) = \psi(\ell)+7 \\
(\ell, \mathtt{comm}_r\ id\ c\ x_r) \in cuc^{id} & \Longleftrightarrow & (\psi(\ell)+0, \mathtt{cas}\ sr_c\ \top\ \bot) \in sv^{id} \\
\vdots & & \vdots \\
{''} & \Longleftrightarrow & (\psi(\ell)+3, \mathtt{write}\ fr_c\ \top) \in sv^{id} \\
{''} & \Longrightarrow & \psi(\ell+1) = \psi(\ell)+4
\end{array}
$$

Fig. 4. Requirements to a program label map ψ

[1] That mutexes and signals are only accessed from the corresponding *send* and *receive* blocks can be checked syntactically.

Definition 2 (Fitting program). *We say that an SV program sv* **fits** *a CUC program cuc, if there is a program label map ψ, mapping all the instructions from cuc to sv. Furthermore, we require the state transforming functions f of* `do` f *to only modify the variables available in cuc (i.e. not hl_c and ss_c). Similarly, the boolean conditions b of* `cbr` *instructions in cuc may only depend on variables present in cuc.*

Channel constituents group all variables that belong to a channel.

Definition 3 (Channel constituents). *The following local registers* **belong** *to a channel c: hl_c and ss_c. The following shared variables* **belong** *to a channel c: m_c, sv_c sr_c, and fr_c.*

In the following, we assume that channel constituents are unique for each channel. The registers belonging to a channel are exactly the registers that are present in *sv* but not in *cuc*. Thus, when comparing a local state of *cuc* and *sv*, we ignore those registers. We can now define *similarity* of local state, which we use to relate CUC states and SV states.

Definition 4 (Similarity w.r.t channel constituents). *Let $\sigma \mathrel{\widehat{=}} \hat{\sigma}$ denote that σ and $\hat{\sigma}$ are equal for all registers that do not belong to a channel. This equality also does not include the program counter. We say σ is* **similar** *to $\hat{\sigma}$.*

Note that $\widehat{=}$ *does* include the register into which *receive* writes the value read from the shared variable, thus receiving a value is *visible* to the $\widehat{=}$ relation.

Having defined CUC, SV and the protocol we want to verify, in the next section we define our notion of handshake refinement to formally relate CUC and SV programs, ensuring that safety and liveness properties are preserved.

5 Handshake Refinement

The idea of the *handshake refinement* is to extend usual behavioral relations of two states or processes (as in bisimulations or refinements) with a third element (the lockstate) to track the progress of the protocol execution. This enables different treatment in the relation of the same CUC state at different stages of the protocol execution. We use it to indicate which possible events of the CUC state need to be answered by the SV state. The lockstate L is a function from channel names to $\{\text{FREE}\} \uplus ID_{in} \uplus (ID \times ID)_{in} \uplus (ID \times ID)_{un} \uplus ID_{un}$. Every channel has one of five states: It can be FREE, a sender or both a sender and a receiver are in the channel, and after the communication happened, the channel will be eventually unlocked, first with both a sender and a receiver still in the channel, then only a sender. The states of the lockstate within the protocol flow are illustrated in Fig. 5 in the rectangular boxes. For each channel, the SV states and possible transitions of *send* (S, S1 to S6; on the left) and *receive* (R, R1 to R3; on the right) are depicted, and in the upper right corner also those of `do` (D) and `cbr` (C), as well as those pointing outside the code (O). N is a placeholder for O, D, C, S, or R. Dotted lines indicate the transition to the next lockstate. The dashed line marks the moment where the communication happens, i.e. all states above are in a relation to the CUC state before the communication, and those below to the CUC state after the communication has happened. The arrows over (S1), (S5'), and (R2) denote whether `cbr` will jump back to the first label or forward to the second label, based on the `cas` instruction before. Note that the transitions of *send* from S4 to S4' and S5 to S5' happen without a step from the sending component, but correspond to the transition of *receive* on the same channel from R2 to R3. We define the following shorthands for the lockstate: $id \notin L := \forall c. L(c) \neq id_{in/un} \wedge (\forall id'. L(c) \neq (id, id')_{in/un}) \wedge L(c) \neq (id', id)_{in/un})$ and $L = \emptyset := \forall c. L(c) = \text{FREE}$.

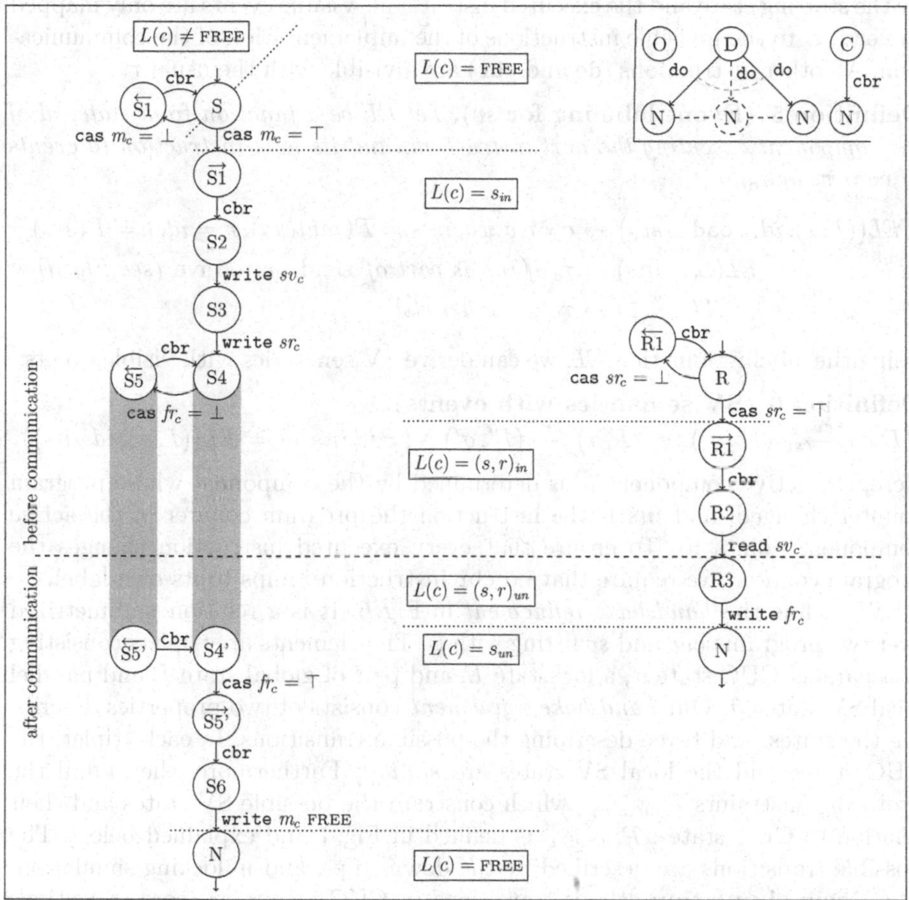

Fig. 5. The flow of the handshake protocol

To define the stable failures on SV independently of the handshake refinement, we cannot use the lockstate. In contrast to the vertical bisimulation [10], the visible event in the protocol implementation is never at the beginning of the implementation (and cannot be, as neither sender nor receiver are determined at the beginning). To overcome this problem, we introduce a special event for the invisible steps of the implementation. As the "usual" invisible event τ is already included (`do`, `cbr`), we denote the invisible instructions of the implementation of communication with τ_c. This way, we can define stable states *before* the execution of the protocol implementation, but let the refusal sets refer to events *during* the execution of the protocol implementation. This enables us to bridge the gap between abstract synchronous semantics, where the event coincides with both decision points, and the low-level asynchronous semantics, where the event happens after the second decision. To define stable failures semantics for SV, we define a labeling function mapping transitions in *sv* to events. Transitions are identified by the starting state and the executed instruction. Visible events are only mapped to `read`, τ_c to the invisible instructions of the implementation of the communication. All other instructions (`do` and `cbr`) are invisible with the usual τ.

Definition 5 (Event labeling for *sv***).** *Let EL be a function from state, id of the component executing the next instruction, and its next instruction to events of cuc,* τ*, or* τ_c*.*

$$\begin{aligned} EL((\Gamma,\_), id, \texttt{read}\_\, sv_c) &\mapsto c.s.r.v \text{ where } s = \Gamma(mutex_c), r = id, v = \Gamma(sv_c) \\ EL(\_,\_, ins) &\mapsto \tau_c \text{ if } ins \text{ is part of } \textrm{send} \text{ or } \textrm{receive} \text{ (see Fig. 3)} \\ EL(\_,\_,\_) &\mapsto \tau \qquad \text{otherwise} \end{aligned}$$

Using the labeling function *EL*, we can derive SV semantics with visible events:

Definition 6 (SV semantics with events).
$(\Gamma,\sigma) \xrightarrow{ev}_{sv} (\Gamma',\sigma') :\Leftrightarrow (\Gamma,\sigma) \xrightarrow{sv} (\Gamma',\sigma') \wedge \big(\exists id\, ins.\, ev = EL((\Gamma,\sigma), id, ins)\big)$

Here, the active component *id* is determined by the component whose program counter changed, and *ins* is the instruction the program counter of the active component points to. To ensure that every executed instruction changes the program counter, we require that no `cbr` instruction jumps to its own label.

We define the *handshake refinement* in Fig. 6. It is a relation parametrized over two programs *cuc* and *sv* fitting with ψ. The elements are triplets consisting of a parallel CUC state σ, a lockstate L, and pair of global state Γ and parallel local SV states $\hat{\sigma}$. Our *handshake refinement* consists of two properties describing the states, and three describing the possible transitions. In each triplet, the CUC states and the local SV states are *similar.* Furthermore, they fulfill the protocol constraints $\mathcal{P}_{cuc,sv,\psi}$, which constrain the possible SV states and their relation to CUC states. $\mathcal{P}_{cuc,sv,\psi}$ is defined in Fig. 7 and explained below. The possible transitions are described by the down-, up-, and unlocking-simulation. The **down-simulation** relates transitions in CUC to one or more transitions in SV. Observe that visible events only need to be answered, if the channel is FREE. This precludes triplets where the sender in SV is already decided but the CUC state still could choose a different sender. It is sound to ignore those SV states in the down-simulation, as we are only interested if the implementation (as a whole) allows and offers the same events. Although there is no "equivalent" state in CUC, all other senders were possible right before this choice of a

$\forall (\sigma, L, (\Gamma, \hat{\sigma})) \in \mathcal{B}_{cuc,sv,\psi}$. a can be visible or τ

Similar local states: $\sigma \hat{=} \hat{\sigma}$

Protocol constraints: $\mathcal{P}_{cuc,sv,\psi}(\sigma, L, (\Gamma, \hat{\sigma}))$ (see Figure 7)

Down-simulation:

$\forall\, a\, \sigma'.\, a \neq \tau \wedge L(chan(a)) = \text{FREE} \wedge \sigma \xrightarrow{a}_{cuc} \sigma' \Longrightarrow$

$\exists\, \Gamma'\, \hat{\sigma}'\, id_s\, id_r\, L'.\, (\Gamma, \hat{\sigma}) \xrightarrow{\tau_c}{}^{*}_{sv} \xrightarrow{a}_{sv} (\Gamma', \hat{\sigma}') \wedge L'(chan(a)) = (id_s, id_r)_{un} \wedge$
$(\sigma', L', (\Gamma', \hat{\sigma}')) \in \mathcal{B}_{cuc,sv,\psi}$

$\forall\, \sigma'.\, \sigma \xrightarrow{\tau}_{cuc} \sigma' \Longrightarrow$

$\exists\, \Gamma'\, \hat{\sigma}'\, L'.\, (\Gamma, \hat{\sigma}) \xrightarrow{\tau_c}{}^{*}_{sv} \xrightarrow{\tau}_{sv} (\Gamma', \hat{\sigma}') \wedge (\sigma', L', (\Gamma', \hat{\sigma}')) \in \mathcal{B}_{cuc,sv,\psi}$

Up-simulation:

$\forall (\Gamma', \hat{\sigma}').\, (\Gamma, \hat{\sigma}) \xrightarrow{\tau_c}_{sv} (\Gamma', \hat{\sigma}') \Longrightarrow \exists\, L'.\, (\sigma, L', (\Gamma', \hat{\sigma}')) \in \mathcal{B}_{cuc,sv,\psi}$

$\forall\, a\, (\Gamma', \hat{\sigma}').\, (\Gamma, \hat{\sigma}) \xrightarrow{a}_{sv} (\Gamma', \hat{\sigma}') \Longrightarrow \exists\, \sigma'\, L'.\, \sigma \xrightarrow{a}_{cuc} \sigma' \wedge (\sigma', L', (\Gamma', \hat{\sigma}')) \in \mathcal{B}_{cuc,sv,\psi}$

Unlocking-simulation:

$\exists\, c\, id_s.\, L(c) = (id_s)_{un} \vee (\exists\, id_r.\, L(c) = (id_s, id_r)_{un}) \Longrightarrow$

$\exists\, \Gamma'\, \hat{\sigma}'\, L'.\, (\Gamma, \hat{\sigma}) \xrightarrow{\tau_c}{}^{*}_{sv} (\Gamma', \hat{\sigma}') \wedge L' = L(c := \text{FREE}) \wedge (\sigma, L', (\Gamma', \hat{\sigma}')) \in \mathcal{B}_{cuc,sv,\psi}$

Fig. 6. Handshake refinement

particular sender, so we do not ignore different possible events, only the intermediate states. The **up-simulation** relates transitions in SV to transitions in CUC. τ_c events are related to zero transitions in CUC, all other events to one. Finally, the **unlocking-simulation** ensures (under simple fairness) that, after the communication has happened, the channel will be freed eventually. This allows the down-simulation to only consider states, where the channel is free. In the remainder of this paper, let $\mathcal{B}_{cuc,sv,\psi}$ denote a *handshake refinement*.

Figure 7 describes the protocol constraints $\mathcal{P}_{cuc,sv,\psi}$, which are specific to the handshake protocol at hand. They also ensure that only SV states reachable by protocol execution are included and that the lockstate reflects the current progress of the protocol execution. The overall definition is that for every channel, if the lockstate is FREE, the belonging signals must be $\perp$, and for each component, the disjunction $\mathcal{P}^{id}_{cuc,sv,\psi}$ must hold. The disjuncts describe triplets (cuc, L, sv), providing sufficient conditions to the SV state (program counter and channel related variables) and relating them to a CUC state (program counter) via ψ with the appropriate lockstate. In $\mathcal{P}^{id}_{cuc,sv,\psi}$, the lockstate also "synchronizes" the different components, i.e., excludes illegal state combinations. It follows a description of the disjuncts, from which we provide two formally.[2]

[2] For a complete formal version we refer to our Technical Report [2].

$\mathcal{P}_{cuc,sv,\psi}(\sigma, L, (\Gamma, \hat{\sigma})) := (L(c){=}\text{FREE} \Longrightarrow \neg\Gamma(sr_c) \wedge \neg\Gamma(fr_c)) \wedge \forall\, id. \mathcal{P}^{id}_{cuc,sv,\psi}(\sigma, L, (\Gamma, \hat{\sigma}))$
$\mathcal{P}^{id}_{cuc,sv,\psi}(\sigma, L, (\Gamma, \hat{\sigma})) := O \vee D \vee C \vee S \vee S1 \vee S2 \vee S3 \vee S4 \vee S5 \vee S4' \vee S5' \vee S6 \vee R \vee R1 \vee R2 \vee R3$

O, D, C Have a direct counterpart in CUC, channel variables are not a concern, $id \notin L$
D do f instruction
C cbr
S At the beginning of *send*, $id \notin L$
S1 Branch according to result of **cas** in S. If the component now has the mutex, than also the signals must be inactive.
S2 From now on in this execution of the protocol, the id of the component is in the mutex and in the lockstate.
S3 The data value to be communicated is in the shared variable.
S4 Start reading was set to $\top$ from S3 to S4. If the receiver did start, then start reading will remain $\bot$ from now on. In the first case the lockstate only contains the sender, in the second also the receiver. The first row of the formula ensures, that the SV state is mapped to a CUC state where the pc points to the appropriate **comm**.

$$(\sigma^{id}_{pc}, \mathbf{comm}_s\, id\, c\, x_s) \in cuc^{id} \wedge (\hat{\sigma}^{id}_{pc}, \mathbf{cas}\; ss_c\, fr_c\, \top\, \bot) \in sv^{id} \wedge \psi(\sigma^{id}_{pc}) + 4 = \hat{\sigma}^{id}_{pc}$$
$$\wedge\, \Gamma(m_c) = id \wedge \Gamma(sv_c) = \hat{\sigma}^{id}_{rs}(x_s) \wedge \neg\Gamma(fr_c)$$
$$\wedge\, (\Gamma(sr_c) \wedge L(c) = id_{in} \vee \neg\Gamma(sr_c) \wedge (\exists\, id_r.\, L(c) = (id, id_r)_{in}))$$

S5 Branch back to S4, as the communication has not happened yet.
S4' From now on, the communication already has happened. The lockstate is now set to unlocking. Observe, that now the SV state is in a relation with the CUC state that occurs after the communication. Therefore we need to substract 1 from the pc of the SV state, to map with ψ to **comm**.

$$(\sigma^{id}_{pc} - 1, \mathbf{comm}_s\, id\, c\, x_s) \in cuc^{id} \wedge (\hat{\sigma}^{id}_{pc}, \mathbf{cas}\; ss_c\, fr_c\, \top\, \bot) \in sv^{id} \wedge \psi(\sigma^{id}_{pc} - 1) + 4 = \hat{\sigma}^{id}_{pc}$$
$$\wedge\, \Gamma(m_c) = id \wedge \neg\Gamma(sr_c)$$
$$\wedge\, (\Gamma(fr_c) \wedge L(c) = id_{un} \vee \neg\Gamma(fr_c) \wedge (\exists\, id_r. L(c) = (id, id_r)_{un}))$$

S5' Branch according to the result of **cas** in S4'.
S6 The signals are $\bot$, in the next step the mutex and the lockstate will be free.
R At the beginning of *receive*, $id \notin L$
R1 Branch according to result of **cas** in R. If the component is now a receiver, both sender and receiver ids are in the lockstate of the channel. The state of the signals is already fixed in the disjunct of the sender where both are in the lockstate.
R2 The lockstate contains the sender and the receiver about to communicate.
R3 The lockstate still contains the sender and the receiver, but now about to unlock the channel. The SV state is now in a relation with the CUC state after the communication.

Fig. 7. Protocol restrictions

6 Preservation of Safety and Liveness Properties

In this section, we prove that our *handshake refinement* preserves safety and liveness properties of the considered CUC program *cuc* to a fitting SV program *sv*. This implies that *sv* only has behavior allowed by *cuc* (safety), and also preserves the progress (liveness). To this end, we define traces and stable failures semantics for both CUC and SV via an operational characterization and then show the stable failures refinement between *cuc* and *sv*. First, we define traces both for CUC and SV.

Definition 7 (Trace semantics). *We write* $P \stackrel{tr}{\Longrightarrow}_{cuc/sv} Q$ *to describe that there is an execution path from* P *to* Q *in cuc/sv, and during that execution the visible events in tr occur exactly in that order. We call tr the trace from* P *to* Q *over cuc/sv. Let* $\mathcal{T}(P)_{cuc/sv}$ *be all traces starting in* P *over cuc/sv.*

Not all possible SV states are legal in a *handshake refinement*, i.e., not all states are reachable by execution of the handshake protocol. We consider SV states $(\Gamma_0, \hat{\sigma}_0)$ as *initial states*, if all components of $\hat{\sigma}_0$ only point to the first instruction of *send* or *receive* (or the second, which is cbr, if it jumps back) and all mutexes are FREE and the signals are inactive ($\perp$). An empty lockstate in the *handshake refinement* $(\sigma_0, \emptyset, (\Gamma_0, \hat{\sigma}_0)) \in \mathcal{B}_{cuc,sv,\psi}$ implies those properties. Using induction on the up-simulation, we can show that every trace in $\mathcal{T}(\Gamma_0, \hat{\sigma}_0)_{sv}$ leads to a triplet in $\mathcal{B}_{cuc,sv,\psi}$ and the same trace is in $\mathcal{T}(\sigma_0)_{cuc}$ leading to the same triplet:

Lemma 1 (All *sv* **traces and their** *cuc* **counterparts are in** $\mathcal{B}_{cuc,sv,\psi}$**).**

$$(\sigma_0, \emptyset, (\Gamma_0, \hat{\sigma}_0)) \in \mathcal{B}_{cuc,sv,\psi} \wedge (\Gamma_0, \hat{\sigma}_0) \stackrel{tr}{\Longrightarrow}_{sv} (\Gamma, \hat{\sigma})$$
$$\Longrightarrow \exists \sigma\, L'.\, (\sigma, L', (\Gamma, \hat{\sigma})) \in \mathcal{B}_{cuc,sv,\psi} \wedge \sigma_0 \stackrel{tr}{\Longrightarrow}_{cuc} \sigma$$

We can directly conclude the preservation of safety properties:

Theorem 1 (Preservation of safety properties).

$$(\sigma_0, \emptyset, (\Gamma_0, \hat{\sigma}_0)) \in \mathcal{B}_{cuc,sv,\psi} \Longrightarrow \mathcal{T}(\Gamma_0, \hat{\sigma}_0)_{sv} \subseteq \mathcal{T}(\sigma_0)_{cuc}$$

Having shown that our *handshake refinement* preserves safety properties, we proceed to show that it also preserves liveness properties. We capture liveness properties using the notion of stable failures (inspired by CSP). To this end, we define the notions of stable states and refusal sets to finally define the stable failures, both for CUC and SV. We then show that the stable failures of *sv* are included in the stable failures of *cuc*. Thus, all liveness properties from *cuc* are preserved in *sv*. A state is stable if no internal transition is possible.

Definition 8 (Stable states in *cuc***).** *A state* σ *is* **stable** *in cuc* $(\sigma \downarrow_{cuc})$ *if all components either point outside the code, to* **comm**$_s$*, or to* **comm**$_r$*. Formally:*

$$\sigma \downarrow_{cuc} := \forall id.\ (\nexists ins.\ (\sigma(id)_{pc}, ins) \in cuc(id)) \vee$$
$$(\exists c.\ (\sigma(id)_{pc}, \textit{\textbf{comm}}_s\ id\ c\ x_s) \in cuc(id) \vee (\sigma(id)_{pc}, \textit{\textbf{comm}}_r\ id\ c\ x_r) \in cuc(id))$$

Refusal sets and stable failures are defined similarly to their CSP counterparts.

Definition 9 (Refusal set in *cuc***).** *A state* σ **refuses** *a set of visible events* X *in cuc, if it cannot perform any* $a \in X$*. Let* $X \subseteq \Sigma$*.*

$$\sigma\ \mathrm{ref}_{cuc}\ X := \forall a \in X.\ \neg(\sigma \stackrel{a}{\longrightarrow}_{cuc})$$

Definition 10 (Stable failures of *cuc***).** *A* **stable failure** *is a pair of a trace tr and a refusal set* X*. It denotes that there is a stable state* σ *which can be reached from the initial state init via the trace tr and refuses* X*.*

$$(tr, X) \in \mathcal{SF}_{cuc}(init) := \exists \sigma.\ init \stackrel{tr}{\Longrightarrow}_{cuc} \sigma \wedge \sigma \downarrow_{cuc} \wedge \sigma\ \mathrm{ref}_{cuc}\ X$$

Next, we define stable states, refusal sets, and stable failures for *sv*. The stable states and failures are similar to the definitions for *cuc*. The refusal sets differ, as they need to account for the invisible execution steps of the handshake protocol.

Definition 11 (Stable states in *sv***).** *A state* $(\Gamma, \hat{\sigma})$ *is* **stable** *in sv* $((\Gamma, \hat{\sigma}) \downarrow_{sv})$ *if all components either point outside the code or to the first instruction of* send *or* receive. *Formally:*

$$(\Gamma, \hat{\sigma}) \downarrow_{sv} := \forall id.\ \big(\nexists ins.\ (\hat{\sigma}(id)_{pc}, ins) \in sv(id)\big) \vee$$
$$\big(\exists c.\ (\hat{\sigma}(id)_{pc}, \texttt{cas}\ m_c\ \text{FREE}\ id) \in sv(id) \vee (\hat{\sigma}(id)_{pc}, \texttt{cas}\ sr_c\ \top\ \bot) \in sv(id)\big)$$

The stable states in *sv* coincide with the stable states in *cuc* (pointing to $\texttt{comm}_s$, $\texttt{comm}_r$ or outside of the code). They can neither make a visible event step nor a τ step, but might be able to make a τ_c step. As the visible event (i.e. `read`) occurs only in the middle of the execution of the handshake protocol, a finite number of τ_c-steps is allowed before the visible event to consider it "enabled". Assuming fairness, i.e., at any point for any component, there is a finite number of steps after which the component will make a step, possible communication happens after a finite number of τ_c-steps. Conversely, if communication is not possible, i.e., a deadlock occurs in the synchronous setting, the implementation of the handshake protocol will stay in a busy loop, thus the visible event is not reachable.

Definition 12 (Refusal set in *sv***).** *A state* **refuses** *a set of visible events in sv, if they are not reachable after a finite number of* τ_c *steps. Let* $X \subseteq \Sigma$.

$$P\ \text{ref}_{sv}\ X := \forall a \in X.\ \neg\big(P \xrightarrow{\tau_c}{}^{*}_{sv} \xrightarrow{a}_{sv}\ \big)$$

Definition 13 (Stable failures of SV) *A* **stable failure** *is a pair of a trace tr and a refusal set X. It denotes that there is a stable state* $(\Gamma, \hat{\sigma})$ *which can be reached from the initial state init via the trace tr and refuses X.*

$$(tr, X) \in \mathcal{SF}_{sv}(init) := \exists (\Gamma, \hat{\sigma}).\ init \stackrel{tr}{\Longrightarrow}_{sv} (\Gamma, \hat{\sigma}) \wedge (\Gamma, \hat{\sigma}) \downarrow_{sv} \wedge (\Gamma, \hat{\sigma})\ \text{ref}_{sv}\ X$$

To show the preservation of liveness properties, we first show two lemmas: That stable states in *sv* imply stable states in *cuc*, and the key lemma, that refusals of *sv* imply refusals of *cuc*.

Lemma 2 (Stable states in *sv* **imply stable states in** *cuc* **and** $L = \emptyset$**).**

$$\big(\sigma, L, (\Gamma, \hat{\sigma})\big) \in \mathcal{B}_{cuc,sv,\psi} \wedge (\Gamma, \hat{\sigma}) \downarrow_{sv} \Longrightarrow \sigma \downarrow_{cuc} \wedge L = \emptyset$$

Proof. As $\mathcal{B}_{cuc,sv,\psi}$ is a *handshake refinement*, $\mathcal{P}_{cuc,sv,\psi}\big(\sigma, L, (\Gamma, \hat{\sigma})\big)$ holds. In $\mathcal{P}_{cuc,sv,\psi}$ the cases where $(\Gamma, \hat{\sigma}) \downarrow_{sv}$ holds imply $\sigma \downarrow_{cuc}$ and $L = \emptyset$.

Lemma 3 (Refusals in *sv* **imply refusals in** *cuc***).**

$$\big(\sigma, L, (\Gamma, \hat{\sigma})\big) \in \mathcal{B}_{cuc,sv,\psi} \wedge (\Gamma, \hat{\sigma}) \downarrow_{sv} \Longrightarrow (\Gamma, \hat{\sigma})\ \text{ref}_{sv}\ X \Longrightarrow \sigma\ \text{ref}_{cuc}\ X$$

Proof. Using Lemma 2, we can apply the down-simulation.[3]

[3] A more detailed proof can be found in our Technical Report [2].

Theorem 2 (Preservation of liveness properties).
$$(\sigma_0, \emptyset, (\Gamma_0, \hat{\sigma}_0)) \in \mathcal{B}_{cuc,sv,\psi} \Longrightarrow \mathcal{SF}_{sv}(\Gamma_0, \hat{\sigma}_0) \subseteq \mathcal{SF}_{cuc}(\sigma_0)$$

Proof. Using the Lemmas 1, 2, and 3. (See Footnote 3)

Corollary 1 (Liveness properties without sender ID). *An adaption of the handshake protocol given in Fig. 3, where in the mutex only* TAKEN *is stored instead of the sender id, also preserves all safety and liveness properties.*

Proof. As the behavior of the protocol does not depend on the sender id being stored in the mutex, only whether the mutex is FREE or not, the behavior of the original and adapted protocols is the same, thus also the same properties are preserved. Note that the information about the sender is only needed for the proofs to reconstruct who the sender was, when the receiver reads the value. □

7 Handshake Refinement for Fitting Programs

In this section, we show that any *cuc* program and fitting *sv* program are in a *handshake refinement* relation. More specifically, we show that all sensible initial states are in a *handshake refinement* relation. This general theorem allows for a scalable approach to the verification of shared variable communication. The proof sketch can be found in [2] and is similar to bisimilarity proofs: all possible transitions of one part can be answered by its counterpart. An important difference is that the down-simulation needs to be shown ("has to answer") *only* in stable states, due to it being a refinement and not a bisimulation.

Theorem 3 (Fitting implies *handshake refinement*). *Let sv be a program fitting cuc with ψ. Then there is a* handshake refinement $\mathcal{B}_{cuc,sv,\psi}$ *containing all initial pairs, i.e., similar CUC and SV states where the program counters of each component match with ψ, all mutexes in Γ are* FREE*, all signals inactive.*

As the *handshake refinement* implies preservation of safety (Theorem 1) and liveness (Theorem 2) properties, we can now conclude with Theorem 3, that all fitting programs preserve safety and liveness properties:

Theorem 4 (Fitting implies preservation). *Let sv be a program fitting cuc with ψ. Then all safety and liveness properties from cuc are preserved to sv.*

8 Conclusion

In this paper, we have presented a method to relate abstract synchronous communication with an asynchronous handshake implementation using shared variable communication and have proved that this relation preserves safety and liveness properties. To this end, we have introduced our novel notion of *handshake refinement*, which is similar to strong bisimulation, apart from the protocol implementation, which is a refinement. It explicitly captures the state of progression through the executions of the implementations of the protocol. Moreover, we have proved in the general Theorem 4, that *all* pairs of CUC and SV programs, where the SV program results from the CUC program by replacing the abstract communication instructions with their handshake implementation, have the same safety and liveness properties. Together with a compositional method to show safety and liveness properties for CUC programs [8], we have a *compositional* framework to prove the preservation of safety and liveness properties from abstract specifications in CSP to down to low-level code, including asynchronous communication mechanisms.

Although we have presented our method for a concrete (handshake) protocol, it provides the foundation for a more generalized notion of relations between abstract synchronous and concrete asynchronous communication based on other communication/synchronization protocols. The presented protocol can be divided into four phases (which match with the four non-FREE lockstates): *(1)* registration, *(2)* before communication, *(3)* after communication, *(4)* unregistration. This is also the structure the *handshake refinement* relies upon. As the presented handshake protocol is intentionally simple, the phases are very short. Our approach can be extended to other protocols that fit in those four phases, e.g. to verify a protocol which supports a "selection on channels" (external choice in CSP). This "selection", i.e. finding a channel with a present communication partner, would happen in phase 1. This way, not only input guards, but also output guards could be supported. Overall, we have shown the preservation of liveness properties using the stable failures model. This does not consider livelocks (divergences). However, as the related CUC and SV programs are the same outside of the protocol implementation and jumps do not occur into our out of the protocol implementation, no livelocks are introduced. Inside the protocol implementation, livelocks in SV are only introduced when unsuccessfully waiting for a communication partner, in which case the CUC program was deadlocked, so no progress is eliminated.

In future work, we plan to investigate relations similar to the *handshake refinement* for different communication protocols. We are currently working on formalizing the entire presented approach in the interactive theorem prover Isabelle/HOL to guarantee the correctness of proofs and to enable the reusability of the formalization, e.g. for other protocols.

References

1. Basu, S., Bultan, T., Ouederni, M.: Synchronizability for verification of asynchronously communicating systems. In: Kuncak, V., Rybalchenko, A. (eds.) VMCAI 2012. LNCS, vol. 7148, pp. 56–71. Springer, Heidelberg (2012). https://doi.org/10.1007/978-3-642-27940-9_5
2. Berg, N., Göthel, T., Glesner, S., Danziger, A.: Technical report accompanying: preserving liveness guarantees from synchronous communication to asynchronous unstructured low-level languages. DepositOnce (2018). https://doi.org/10.14279/depositonce-7192
3. Brookes, S.D.: On the relationship of CCS and CSP. In: Diaz, J. (ed.) ICALP 1983. LNCS, vol. 154, pp. 83–96. Springer, Heidelberg (1983). https://doi.org/10.1007/BFb0036899

4. Broy, M., Olderog, R.: Trace-oriented models of concurrency. In: Handbook of Process Algebra, chap. 2. Elsevier (2001)
5. de Frutos-Escrig, D., Gregorio-Rodríguez, C.: Process equivalences as global bisimulations. JUCS **12**(11), 1521–1550 (2006)
6. Gardner, W.B.: Bridging CSP and C++ with selective formalism and executable specifications. In: Proceedings of the MEMOCODE 2003, p. 237. IEEE (2003)
7. Jähnig, N., Göthel, T., Glesner, S.: A denotational semantics for communicating unstructured code. In: Proceedings of the FESCA 2015. EPTCS, vol. 178, pp. 9–21 (2015)
8. Jähnig, N., Göthel, T., Glesner, S.: Refinement-based verification of communicating unstructured code. In: De Nicola, R., Kühn, E. (eds.) SEFM 2016. LNCS, vol. 9763, pp. 61–75. Springer, Cham (2016). https://doi.org/10.1007/978-3-319-41591-8_5
9. Peeters, A.: Implementation of handshake components. In: Abdallah, A.E., Jones, C.B., Sanders, J.W. (eds.) Communicating Sequential Processes. The First 25 Years. LNCS, vol. 3525, pp. 98–132. Springer, Heidelberg (2005). https://doi.org/10.1007/11423348_7
10. Rensink, A., Gorrieri, R.: Action refinement as an implementation relation. In: Bidoit, M., Dauchet, M. (eds.) CAAP 1997. LNCS, vol. 1214, pp. 772–786. Springer, Heidelberg (1997). https://doi.org/10.1007/BFb0030640
11. Roscoe, A.W.: Understanding Concurrent Systems. TCS. Springer, London (2010). https://doi.org/10.1007/978-1-84882-258-0

Deriving Mode Logic for Autonomous Resilient Systems

Inna Vistbakka[1(✉)], Amin Majd[1], and Elena Troubitsyna[1,2]

[1] Åbo Akademi University, Turku, Finland
{inna.vistbakka,amin.majd}@abo.fi
[2] KTH, Stockholm, Sweden
elenatro@kth.se

Abstract. Ensuring system resilience – dependability in presence of changes – is a complex engineering task. To achieve resilience, a system should not only autonomously cope with non-deterministically changing internal state and external operating conditions but also proactively reconfigure to maintain efficiency. To facilitate structuring and verifying such complex system behavior, in this paper, we demonstrate how to derive resilience-enhancing mode transition logic from the goals that the system should achieve. Our approach is formalised in Event-B that allows us to reason about resilience mechanisms at different architectural levels. We illustrate the proposed approach by an example – safe and efficient navigation of a swarm of drones.

1 Introduction

Resilience [6] is an ability of a system to deliver its services in a trustworthy way despite changes. Often resilience is reasoned about using the notion of *goals* – functional and non-functional objectives that a system should achieve [5]. Resilience can be seen as an ability of a system to reach its functional goals or maintain a required level of satisfaction of non-functional goals (e.g., efficiency).

A resilient system should autonomously, i.e., without a human intervention, recognise the changes, evaluate their impact on reachability and degree of satisfaction of goals and adapt. The adaptation process, either triggered by failures of system components or external changes, usually requires complex component coordination and system reconfiguration. Due to highly non-deterministic nature of the system and a large number of components (especially in such autonomous systems as swarms of drones), ensuring correctness of component interactions and the overall system resilience is a challenging and error-prone task.

In this paper, we propose an approach to a formal development of resilient autonomous systems. Our approach allows a developer to derive a resilience-enhancing mode logic in a structured disciplined way. We use *modes* [7] as a main mechanism to structure system behaviour. The goals, which the system should fulfil, serve as a basis for defining the mode transition logic. We formally define reachability conditions for functional goals and degree of satisfaction of non-functional ones. Changes in complying to these conditions trigger mode transitions.

J. Sun and M. Sun (Eds.): ICFEM 2018, LNCS 11232, pp. 320–336, 2018.
https://doi.org/10.1007/978-3-030-02450-5_19

We consider distributed autonomous systems that are composed of asynchronously communicating heterogeneous components – agents. Each agent has certain capabilities. Our goal reachability and degree of satisfaction conditions are defined as corresponding functions over the agent capabilities.

Since mode transitions, in general, incur complex agent coordination and system reconfiguration, we need a formal structured approach to ensure correctness of mode transition logic. In this paper, we rely on Event-B [1] – a state-based approach to correct-by-construction system development to specify and verify mode logic. We propose a specification pattern for modelling mode transitions triggered by changes in reachability and degree of satisfaction conditions.

The main development technique of Event-B – refinement – supports stepwise construction and verification of complex specifications and allows us to iteratively use the proposed pattern at different architectural levels. In the refinement process, a high-level abstract specification is incrementally augmented to unfold the entire multi-layered architecture and coordination between the components at different levels of architectural hierarchy. The approach is illustrated by an example – development of a resilient swarm of drones. Abstraction, refinement and proofs as well as automated tool support allow us to scale the formal development to such complex autonomous systems.

2 Modelling and Refinement in Event-B

Event-B is a state-based formal approach that promotes the correct-by-construction development paradigm and formal verification by theorem proving. In Event-B, a system model is specified using the notion of an *abstract state machine* [1]. An abstract state machine encapsulates the model state, represented as a collection of variables, and defines operations on the state, i.e., it describes the dynamic behaviour of a modelled system. The important system properties to be preserved are defined as model invariants. A machine usually has the accompanying component, called context. A context may include user-defined carrier sets, constants and their properties (defined as model axioms).

The dynamic behaviour of the system is defined by a collection of atomic *events*. Generally, an event has the following form:

$$\mathsf{e} \mathrel{\hat{=}} \textbf{any}\ a\ \textbf{where}\ G_e\ \textbf{then}\ R_e\ \textbf{end},$$

where e is the event's name, a is the list of local variables, and (the event *guard*) G_e is a predicate over the model state. The body of an event is defined by a *multiple* (possibly nondeterministic) assignment to the system variables. In Event-B, this assignment is semantically defined as the next-state relation R_e. The event guard defines the conditions under which the event is *enabled*, i.e., its body can be executed. If several events are enabled at the same time, any of them can be chosen for execution nondeterministically.

Event-B employs a top-down refinement-based approach to system development. A development starts from an abstract specification that nondeterministically models the most essential functional system behaviour. In a sequence of refinement steps, we gradually reduce nondeterminism and introduce detailed design decisions. In particular, we can add new events, refine old events as well as replace abstract variables by their concrete counterparts.

The consistency of Event-B models – verification of model well-formedness, invariant preservation as well as correctness of refinement steps – is demonstrated by discharging the relevant proof obligations. The Rodin platform [17] provides tool support for modelling and verification. In particular, it automatically generates all required proof obligations and attempts to discharge them. When the proof obligations cannot be discharged automatically, the user can attempt to prove them interactively using a collection of available proof tactics.

3 Resilience-Enhancing Mode Transition Logic

To achieve resilience, an autonomous system should be able to adapt to non-deterministically changing internal state and external operating conditions. In our work, we study *reconfigurability* as an essential mechanism of achieving resilience of autonomous distributed systems. Since the collaborative aspect of the component behaviour is important for our study, we adopt the agent-based approach, i.e., we consider the system components as agents and the overall system as a multi-agent system [10], correspondingly.

Agents are autonomous heterogeneous components that asynchronously communicate with each other. Each agent has a certain functionality within a system and contributes to achieving system *goals*. Goals are the functional and non-functional objectives of a system [5]. Goals constitute suitable basics for reasoning about the system behaviour and its resilience. Resilience can be seen as a property that allows the system to progress towards achieving its functional goals or maintain a required level of satisfaction of non-functional goals.

The goal-oriented framework provides us with a suitable basis for reasoning about reconfigurable autonomous systems. We formulate reconfigurability as an ability of agents to redistribute their responsibilities to ensure goal reachability or contribute to goal satisfaction. Next we discuss how notions of goals and agents can be used to reason about behaviour of an autonomous resilient system.

3.1 Reasoning About Resilience-Enhancing Mode Transitions

We assume that there is a number of main (global) goals defined for the system. Let $G = \{G_1, G_2, \ldots, G_n\}$ be a set of functional and non-functional goals that system should achieve. Goals can be decomposed into a subset of corresponding subgoals and organised hierarchically. In general, the goals can be independent and might even be seen as conflicting.

The system consists of a number of agents (components, in general). Let $A = \{a_1, a_2, , \ldots, a_m\}$ be a set of system agents. To contribute to goal achievement, the agents have to utilise their capabilities. Let $C = \{c_1, c_2, , \ldots, c_k\}$ be a set of all agent capabilities. Then, for each agent, we can define the set of its capabilities as a structure AC – *agent capabilities* – with the following property:

$$\forall\, a_i : a_i \in A \Rightarrow AC(a_i) \subseteq C.$$

Agent failures make their capabilities unavailable. In the similar way, the changes in the operating environment might prevent an agent from utilising its capabilities. Thus agent capabilities AC is a dynamic structure, i.e., during system execution a set of current agent capabilities can vary.

Based on their capabilities, the agents perform the tasks contributing to achieving the system goals. To associate such goals with the agent capabilities, we define a logical function GC – *goal reachability function* over agent capabilities:

$$GC \in T \times G \times C \rightarrow BOOL.$$

For every goal $G_i \in G$ this function determines whether or not a certain capability $c_i \in C$ is required to achieve this goal G_i.

In general, a number and types of capabilities can vary depending on system needs and overall goals. The examples of capabilities include "an ability to collect data" or "an ability to send data". As a result of agent failures or change in operational conditions, some agent capabilities might become unavailable. "Degradation" of any agent capability might also slow down or aggravate the goal achievement or goal maintenance process.

To detect any changes in overall goal achievement, we also introduce a fitness function GS – *goal satisfaction function* – that evaluates the level (degree) of the goal achievement during system functioning:

$$GS \in T \times G \times C \rightarrow REAL.$$

This function is also dynamic, i.e., its value depends on time and current available capabilities of agents that can vary during system execution.

A decrease in goal satisfaction function as well as changes of logical goal function indicate hindering achieving the desired system goals. To achieve resilience, a system should monitor its goals and reconfigure to maintain the required level of goal satisfaction. In our work we propose to use *modes* as the main mechanism for structuring the behaviour of the system [7]. Modes define coarse-grained representation of system behaviour. Changes in system states trigger a change of a mode – a mode transition. In our work, we propose to connect the states of the system agents with the goals and trigger a mode transition every time when the level of satisfaction of system goals changes. Thus the goals, which the system should fulfil, serve as a basis for defining the mode transition logic.

To achieve resilience, the system architecture should contain a monitor for detecting internal and external changes and evaluating their impact on the logical goal function or goal satisfaction function. As a result of impact evaluation, a mode transition might be triggered. We say that a mode transition is triggered whenever the following condition (*) holds:

$$(GC(t1, G_i, c_i) = TRUE \wedge GC(t2, G_i, c_i) = FALSE) \vee \\ (GS(t2, G_i, c_i) < GS(t1, G_i, c_i)), \textit{where } t1 < t2. \qquad (*)$$

Naturally, the condition (*) serves as a condition on a mode transition: when a logical goal condition on the required capability for a goal has been broken or a degree of goal satisfaction lowered from the previous monitored cycle, mode transition is triggered.

In case of a logical goal condition violation (first part of (*)), a transition to the nominal mode, will be triggered as soon as the logical goal condition on capability will be re-established. In its turn, when the goal satisfaction function again reaches the necessary (desired) level the transition back, to the nominal mode, will be triggered.

As discussed earlier, we consider reconfiguration to be the essential mechanism of achieving resilience of autonomous systems. It is triggered by the corresponding mode transition. The reconfiguration is based on reallocation of responsibilities between agents to ensure that the healthy (i.e., operational) agents can either substitute the failed ones or be utilised more efficiently to partially cover up for them. Obviously, reconfiguration requires a sophisticated agent coordination. To reason about correctness of agent coordination, we propose an Event-B specification pattern for modelling mode transitions triggered by changes in goal reachability and degree of satisfaction conditions.

3.2 Modelling Mode Transitions in Event-B

To derive a mode-structured coordination scheme for an autonomous resilient system, we rely on formal modelling in Event-B. We represent the introduced above notions and definitions in terms of the corresponding Event-B elements. Then we derive a generic specification pattern that can be used to model resilience mechanisms at different levels of abstraction.

Event-B separates the static and dynamic parts of a model, putting them into distinct yet dependent components called a *context* and a *machine*. All the static notions of our reasoning include the set of all possible goals, agents and capabilities (G, A and C, respectively) as well as different static structures defining various interdependencies between elements. The latter include (initial) values for agent capabilities, logical goal function on capabilities and goal satisfaction function (AC_init, GC_init and GS_init, correspondingly). We introduce static notions as sets and constants of a model context and define their properties as a number of context axioms. The corresponding context is presented in Fig. 1.

Context ARSystem_cnt
Sets $G, A, C, MODES, \ldots$
Constants $AC\_init, GC\_init, GS\_init, \ldots$
Axioms
...
axm4: $G \neq \varnothing$
axm5: $A \neq \varnothing$
axm6: $C \neq \varnothing$
axm7: $AC\_init \in A \rightarrow \mathbb{P}(C)$
axm8: $GC\_init \in G \times C \rightarrow BOOL$
...

Fig. 1. A generic structure of the specification pattern: context part

```
Machine ARSystem_Abs Sees ARSystem_cnt
Variables mode, AC, GC, GS_prev, GS, status, ...
Invariants mode ∈ MODES ∧ AC ∈ A → ℙ(C) ∧ GC ∈ G × C → BOOL ∧ ...
Events ...
AgentFailure ≙                               // agent failure detection
  any a_i, c_i
  where a_i ∈ A ∧ c_i ∈ AC(a_i) ∧ ...
  then AC(a_i) := AC(a_i) \ {c_i} || GC(g_i, c_i) := FALSE
  end
ModeTransition ≙                             // transition to a generic reconfiguration mode
  any a_i, c_i, g_i
  where mode=NOM ∧
     (GC_init(g_i, c_i) = TRUE ∧ GC(g_i, c_i) = FALSE) ∨ GS(g_i, c_i) < (GS_prev(g_i, c_i)) ∨ ...
  then mode:=RECONF
  end
RestoreCapability ≙                          // scheme of reconfiguration
  any a_i, g_i, c_i
  where mode=RECONF ∧ (GC(g_i, c_i) = FALSE ∧ GC_init(g_i, c_i) = TRUE)...
  then  AC(a_i) := AC(a_i) ∪ {c_i} || GC(g_i, c_i) := TRUE
  end
NominalModeTransition ≙                      // transition back to the nominal mode
  any g_i, c_i
  where mode=RECONF ∧ (GC_init(g_i, c_i) = GC(g_i, c_i) ∧ GS_prev(g_i, c_i) ≤ GS(g_i, c_i))...
  then mode:=NOM
  end
```

Fig. 2. A generic structure of the specification pattern: machine part

The system dynamics is modelled by the events in the machine of the Event-B specification. The related notions – logical goal function and goal satisfaction function, the mode transition conditions, mode transitions, agent failures etc. – are represented as model variables, invariants, predicate expressions, or specific events. *GC* and *GS* can be represented as the system variables whose values might be changed during system functioning modelled as an execution of events. The general structure of the abstract Event-B specification is shown in Fig. 2.

To model possible agent failure and, as a consequence, the loss of some agent capability, we define an event AgentFailure. This event models non-deterministic failure of a_i agent. As a result of an event execution, a capability c_i will be lost. When the monitored component detects such a change as violation of logical goal function, it triggers a dedicated mode transition. This behaviour is specified by an event ModeTranstion. Here, in the event guard, we formulate a condition on the event to fire (this condition is based on the logical expression (*) with small modifications). We check that the capability c_i, required to accomplish a goal g_i, is not available any more (or, in general, the level of fitness function has been decreased). We store the current value for goal satisfaction function in *GS* variable, while its previous value in the variable *GS_prev*. Then RestoreCapability and NominalModeTransition events model a simple case of agent reconfiguration (as a restoring of the lost capability) and a transition back to the Nominal mode.

Let us note that in this specification pattern we consider a simple case of reconfigurability – when an agent is able to restore its capability by itself (e.g., restoring communication after a transient communication failure). In more complex cases (as we will discuss in Sects. 4 and 5), reconfiguration can be based on agent cooperation, and might involve changes in relationships between agents.

The presented design Event-B pattern only reflects the main concepts of the goal-based mode transition logic and represents generic modelling solutions that can be reused in the development of resilient autonomous systems. In the next section we demonstrate how to derive mode transition logic using the proposed approach for a swarm of drones. Further, in Sect. 5, we present its Event-B development relying on the generic specification pattern described above.

4 Autonomous Swarm-Based System

The swarms of drones are increasingly used for surveillance, shipping, rescue etc. A swarm is a group of drones that, in a coordinated manner, executes a mission. For instance, a mission can be "video surveillance of a certain area". A video surveillance mission can be represented by a (generic) goal:

***G1*:** *Periodically send the images covering certain sectors of the monitored area.*

For a swarm of drones, we can identify the following generic subgoals contributing to achieving the overall goal ***G1***:

***G2*:** *Produce the payload data (e.g., images) with the required quality level.*

***G3*:** *Guarantee survivability of drones allowing them to complete the mission.*

To achieve ***G3***, we have to ensure that the following subgoals are satisfied:

***G4*:** *The drones do not prematurely deplete their batteries, i.e., they are navigated in an efficient way.*

***G5*:** *The drones do not collide with each other and static obstacles.*

***G6*:** *The drones do not collide with the unforeseen dynamically appearing objects.*

The goals are interdependent and might even be seen as conflicting, e.g., the travel distance has to be increased to guarantee safety and produce the payload data of the required quality. Hence, the controlling software should rely on sophisticated coordination mechanisms to ensure that all the goals remain satisfiable thought the mission execution.

The system architecture is presented in Fig. 3. The decision center (DC) – is an intelligent component which is responsible for generating the efficient navigation strategies according to the mission goals and preventing unsafe behaviour, i.e., it navigates the drones to avoid collisions with each other and static obstacles. DC runs high-performance machine learning and evolutionary algorithms proposed in our previous work [8,9]. They allow us to safely navigate the drones and optimise travel distance, resource consumption and quality of payload data ratio. The algorithms ensure inter-drone and drone-obstacle collision avoidance.

At each cycle DC receives the payload (e.g., imaging) and telemetry data from the swarm and processes this information and if required, generates a new routing for the swarm. The information obtained from the Dynamic Monitoring component allows DC to detect the changes in the drone swarm and in the flying zone. Such changes may invoke swarm reconfiguration and regeneration of the drone routes.

The Navigation Centre (NC) communicates with the drones by sending them the flying plan received from DC. In their turn, the drones periodically send their

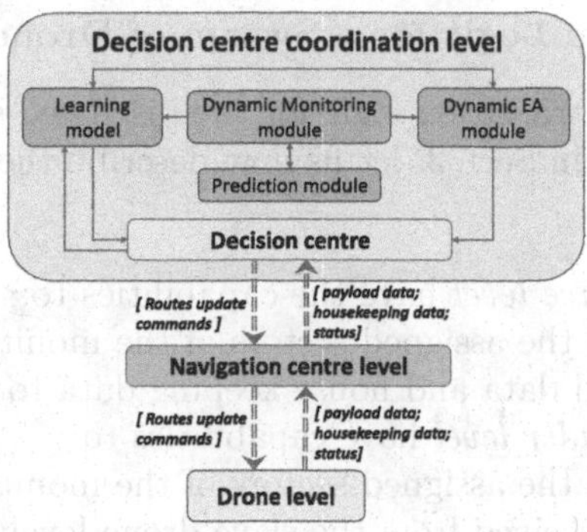

Fig. 3. Overview of a system architecture

payload and telemetry data (current status, position, battery level, etc.) to NC, which packages them, (sometimes) preprocesses and forwards to DC.

Drones communicate with NC and each other in order to achieve their individual and common goals. Since communication with NC is typically long range, it consumes significant energy. To alleviate the problem of fast energy depletion, the swarm of the drones can be organised hierarchically and form a tree-structure depending on its different capabilities: more powerful drones – *the leaders* and less powerful drones – *the slaves* – that communicate with their leaders using less power consuming means. Moreover, we distinguish a *sink* drone – a dedicated leader drone – what besides area monitoring tasks transmits data between NC and drones at the leader level. The drones of the leader level send data to the sink. Each leader has a number of slave drones and periodically gathers information from its corresponding slaves. Finally, drones of the slave level exchange information with their leaders and receive new commands. Since some drones might change their predefined routes or even fail, to maintain an efficient drone configuration, at each cycle DC assesses the current state of the swarm and might reconfigure the tree.

Moreover, each drone (at any level) has its own local collision avoidance mechanism – *drone reflexes computation module* – a module that overrides the goals received from DC and commands a drone to move away when a camera or radar of a drone detects an obstacle. When a drone detects a possible collision with an unforeseen obstacle, the reflexes computation module quickly computes a reflex movement for a drone to prevent or mitigate the collision.

The top-most layer – DC – is responsible for achieving goals ***G3*–*G5***, i.e., it controls the swarm to ensure quality, efficiency and implement *preventive* safety. The on-board drone software is responsible for satisfying goal ***G2*** and ***G6***, in the latter case implementing *defensive* safety.

Next we discuss the coordination of drones and their collaborative behaviour as well as the resilience aspect of controlling the swarm of drones.

4.1 Mode Transition Logic for a Swarm of Drones

Before deriving a mode transition logic for the discussed swarm of drones using the approach presented in Sect. 3, let us now describe the capabilities of drones of the different levels:

- The drones of the *slave level* have the capabilities to:
  - collect data from the assigned sectors of the monitored area;
  - send the collected data and house keeping data to the next drone level.
- The drones of the *leader level* have capabilities to:
  - collect data from the assigned sectors of the monitored area;
  - aggregate data received from the slave drone level;
  - send all collected data to the sink level.
- Finally, the *sink* drone has capabilities to:
  - collect data from the assigned sectors of the monitored area;
  - aggregate data received from the drones of the leader level;
  - send all collected data to NC.

Such capabilities allow a drone of any layer to achieve its goals and contribute to the overall goal achievement and maintenance. However, failures of the drones, communication loss as well as changes in the operating environment affect the level of satisfaction of the system goals as discussed in Sect. 3.

In nominal situation (called *Nominal* mode), the drones fly according to the plan issued by DC. Upon receiving new commands from DC the drones change their current routes and perform reconfiguration if it is commanded by DC. In this case, reconfiguration means that logical relationships between the drones (i.e., *sink-leader* and *leader-slave* relationships) might be changed according to a new update of a drone tree structure recalculated by DC.

Next we will analyse the factors affecting the goal satisfaction and define the corresponding mode logic that allows the system to achieve the overall system goals despite failures and deviations.

Appearing an Unpredictable Obstacle. Unpredictable obstacles appearing in a drone flying zone might prevent a drone from achieving the goal ***G6***. Thus, when a drone detects a possible collision with an unforeseen obstacle, the monitoring component evaluates the goal satisfaction function and issues a transition to the *Reflection Activation* mode. The drone reflexes computation module quickly computes a reflex movement for a drone to prevent and mitigate the collision. After the collision is avoided, the goal satisfaction function is recalculated and a transition to the *Nominal* mode is triggered.

Local Communication Failure. Each drone has capabilities to identify its local communication failure. Communication failure might prevent a drone from achieving the goal ***G2***. When a drone detects such a failure, the goal satisfaction function is recalculated and a transition to the *Local Communication Failure* mode is triggered. Upon this transition, every drone should move to reconnect with NC and reunite with a swarm. This is a self-triggered mode transition, i.e., the drones perform it independently upon detection of a failure. When a drone re-establish connection with a swarm, satisfaction function will be recalculated and a transition to the *Nominal* mode is triggered.

Slave Failure. A slave failure prevents a drone from achieving the goal ***G2***. Upon detection a slave failure (by the corresponding leader drone), the satisfaction function is recalculated and the *Slave Failure* mode is triggered. This is a local leader-triggered mode transition meaning that it does not affect other drones. The leader drone tries to re-establish connection with the failed slave drone within the time bound period and, in case of unsuccessful outcome considers this slave as failed. Further, the health status of every slave will be transmitted to the sink drone and finally will reach DC. Let us note, that if the failed slave was a candidate for the next leader then the new candidate is recalculated.

Leader Failure. In case of a leader failure (that affects achieving ***G2***), detectable by the sink drone, the sink should trigger the *Leader Failure* mode transition. The corresponding reconfiguration procedure is performed to substitute the failed leader by the predefined slave of the failed leader.

Sink Failure. NC is able to identify the health status of the sink drone. In case of a sink failure, the satisfaction function will be recalculated and NC triggers a transition to the *Sink Failure* mode. A sink failure can have severe consequences and might prevent a system from achieving all ***G1–G6*** goals. The reconfiguration is triggered to substitute the failed sink by the predefined leader. In this case, NC retransmits the DC commands to the "new" sink. Moreover, if the leader drones detect a sink failure before NC does, all healthy leaders should issue the commands to its corresponding slaves to slow down the flying speed.

Despite the small number of modes, the mode logic is complex due to the highly non-deterministic nature of the conditions triggering mode transitions. Ensuring correctness of coordinated behaviour of a collaborative swarm of drones is a challenging engineering task. To approach it in a systematic rigorous way, we rely on Event-B and its main development technique – refinement. In the next Sect. 5, we will demonstrate how to derive and verify properties of the multi-layered drone coordination in a structured rigorous way.

5 Formal Development of a Resilient Swarm of Drones

In this section, we outline the formal development of the coordinated mode logic for the discussed swarm of drones in Event-B. The full development can be found in [21]. We start from specifying the high-level general requirements and unfold the entire coordination logic in the refinement process.

Abstract Model. The initial model represents the global control cycle spanning over all layers of the architecture shown in Fig. 4. At each cycle, DC analyses the telemetry data and either maintains the previously calculated routing or generate a new one. The routing commands are transmitted from DC to NC and then from NC to the sink. Next, the sink broadcasts the received information to all the drones at the leader level. In its turn, upon receiving commands from the sink each leader further distributes the commands to its corresponding slaves.

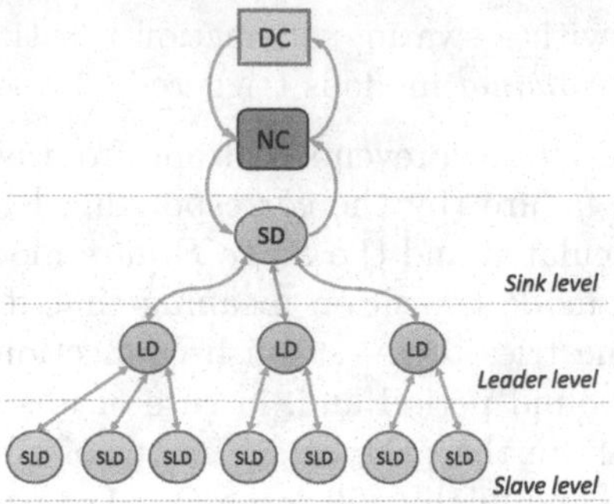

Fig. 4. System layered architecture

Once per cycle, the collected information about the monitored area and housekeeping data (e.g., battery level) are sent by slaves to their corresponding leaders. When all the required information is gathered by the leaders, they transmit data to the sink. Then the sink drone sends this information to NC and, NC forwards it to DC. DC analyses the received data and, if it is needed, issues the new commands to the drones as well as triggers the drone reconfiguration.

Next we refine the abstract model to represent the coordination required to model mode transitions in all possible nominal and off-nominal situations and the corresponding data flow.

Introducing Drones and Drone Failures. In our first refinement, we introduce a representation of the behaviour of the system components, in particular, we augment the specification by representation of drones and their failures. We model the impact of such failures on the system dynamics and resilience. In this case, reconfiguration would involve changing the relationships between drones (at every layer) in order to optimise routing, coverage, energy and safety ratio.

We distinguish the permanent drone failure (e.g., due to a physical drone damage) and transient drone failure (e.g., due to loss of communication). If a transient failure occurred then after some time a drone (of any layer) can restore the connection with the swarm and continue to function. This behaviour is modelled by the transition to the *Local Communication Failure* mode and then returning back to the *Nominal* mode.

In the case of a permanent drone failure (of any layer), the corresponding drone of the upper layer or NC will detect this failure and, eventually, DC will be notified about the loss in the swarm. In this case, the transition to the corresponding *Sink Failure*, *Leader Failure* or *Slave Failure* mode is triggered.

In case of a leader failure, as a part of reconfiguration, some predefined slave drone associated with the failed leader will become a new leader. When the other leaders detect a failure of a leader, they send the corresponding commands to their slaves to slow down their speed of the flying, until the new commands from the DC will be issued. The scheme of the leader failure reconfiguration is presented in Fig. 5.

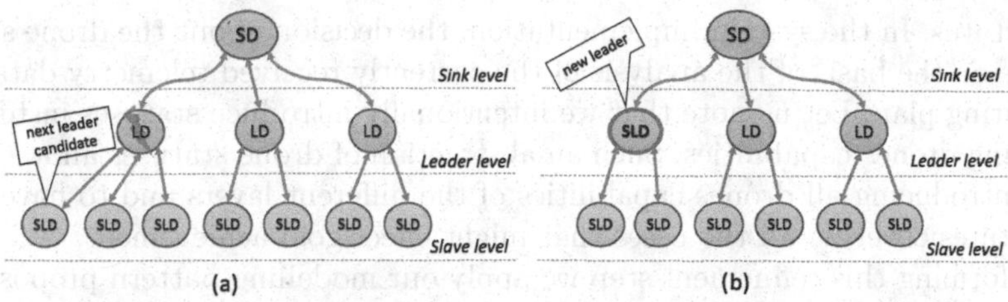

Fig. 5. Leader failure

As a result of a transition to the *Sink Failure* mode, reconfiguration of the system is also activated. Namely, the predefined leader drone becomes a new sink and the predefined slave drone replaces it by becoming a leader. The impact of the sink failure on the system architecture is represented in Fig. 6.

To model the behaviour described above, we refine our initial model by introducing a number of new variables, events and refining some abstract events. In particular, we define variables to specify the set of all drones, leaders and slaves and the sink drone (by corresponding variables *drones*, *leaders*, *slaves*, *sink*):

$$\{sink\} \cup leaders \cup slaves = drones,\ drones \subseteq SWARM.$$

Here the swarm is represented by a finite non-empty set of drones $SWARM$. It can be seen as a set that contains the ids of all drones in the swarm.

The new variable *slaves_of_leaders* established the relationship between a leader and slaves it supervises:

$$slaves\_of\_leaders \in leaders \rightarrow \mathbb{P}(slaves).$$

To model the health state of the drones, we introduce a variable *status*. It is defined as a function:

$$status \in drones \rightarrow STATUSES,$$

where $STATUSES$ is a set consisting of the constants OK, $FAILED$ and $DISCON$ representing correspondingly the nominal, failed and disconnected

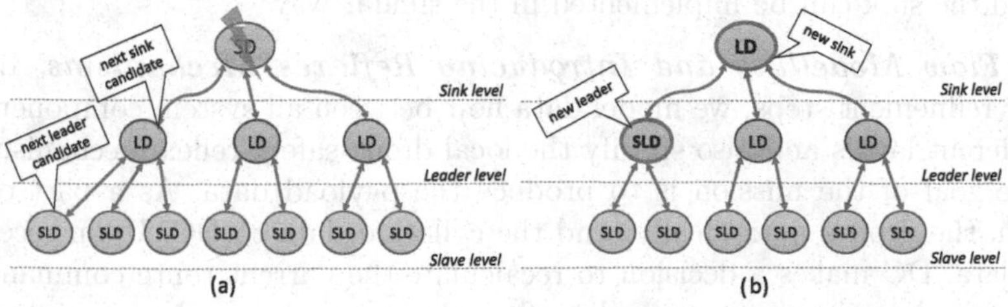

Fig. 6. Sink failure

drone status. In the system implementation, the decision about the drone status is made on the basis of the analysis of the currently received telemetry data and the routing plan. Let us note that we intentionally introduce statuses instead of modelling drones capabilities. Such an abstraction of drone statuses allows us to avoid introducing all drones capabilities of the different layers and to have only three states covering all the cases that might effect goal achievement.

Performing this refinement step we apply our modelling pattern proposed in Sect. 3. A number of new events are introduce to model possible drones failures as well as system reaction on them. We introduce SINK_Failure, SINK_discon, LEADER_Failure, etc. Upon execution of these events, the value of *status* variable is changed. As soon as a leader failure is detected, as modelled by the new event LEADER_FailureMode, then the "new" leader should be chosen from one of its slave drones (modelled by LEADER_Failure_Reconfiguration event). In this case, *slaves_of_leaders* as well as *leaders*, *slaves* and *leader_alt* variables are updated. Similarly, new events are introduced to model a slave and sink failure as well as events modelling reconfigurations and transitions back to the Nominal mode. An excerpt from the first refinement step is presented in Fig. 7.

At this refinement step we formulate and prove the correctness of coordinated reconfiguration involving all the layers of the architecture. For instance, we prove that no slaves become dispatched from some leader:

$$\forall\, sl.\ sl \in slaves \ \Rightarrow\ (\exists\, ld.\ ld \in leaders\ \wedge\ sl \in slaves\_of\_leaders(ld)).$$

Multi-level Drone Communication. The goal of our second refinement is to introduce a communication model between the sink and NC as well as between the drones. Next we discuss a simple communication scheme that can be instantiated to implement communication between the drones at any level.

Lets consider *Sink-Leader* communication. At every cycle, the sink initiates the communication with a leader. The sink checks status of a leader and if it is *OK*, then the sink sends the data via the inter-drone communication link. Upon delivery of the message, a leader updates its route commands and sends the acknowledgement to the sink. In its turn, the sink waits for the acknowledgement from a leader. Upon receiving the acknowledgement, the sink considers the data transition to be successfully completed. If no acknowledgement is received, the sink triggers the transition to *Leader Failure* mode.

The communication between the leaders and their slaves as well as between NC and the sink can be implemented in the similar way.

Data Flow Modelling and Introducing Reflexes Mechanisms. In the further refinement steps, we model data flow between all system components at the different layers and also specify the local drone safety reflex mechanisms.

The goal of the mission is to produce the payload data. As a part of the mission, the drones periodically send the collected data to DC. Upon receiving these data, DC makes a decision to recalculate the current route commands or restructure drone tree-structure. To reflect the required data flow, we introduce a number of events and variables and refine our model.

Machine SwarmOfDrones_m1 **refines** SwarmOfDrones_m0 **Sees** SwarmOfDrones_c1
Variables $phase, mode, drones, sink, leaders, slaves, status, slaves\_of\_leaders, sink\_alt, ...$
Invariants $phase \subseteq PHASES \land mode \subseteq MODES \land drones \subseteq SWARM \land leaders \subseteq drones \land$
$slaves \subseteq drones \land sink \in drones \land sink\_alt \in drones \land$
$slaves\_of\_leaders \in leaders \rightarrow \mathbb{P}(slaves) \land$
$\forall sl.\ sl \in slaves \Rightarrow (\exists ld.\ ld \in leaders \land sl \in slaves\_of\_leaders(ld)) \land$
$status \in drones \rightarrow STATUSES \land ...$
Events ...
SINK_Failure_Reconfiguration $\hat{=}$
any ld_alt, new_ld_alt, sls
where $... \land mode{=}SINK\_FAILURE\_RECONF \land status(sink){=}FAILED \land$
$status(sink\_alt) = OK \land sls{=}slaves\_of\_leader(sink\_alt) \setminus \{ld\_alt\} \land$
$ld\_alt{=}leader\_alt(sink\_alt) \land new\_ld\_alt \in sls$
then
$sink := sink\_alt$
$sink\_alt := ld\_alt$
$leaders := (leaders \setminus \{sink\_alt\}) \cup \{ld\_alt\}$
$slaves := slaves \setminus \{ld\_alt\}$
$leader\_alt(ld\_alt) := new\_ld\_alt$
$slaves\_of\_leader := (\{sink\_alt\} \lhd slaves\_of\_leader) \cup \{ld\_alt \mapsto sls\}$
end
LEADER_Failure_Reconfiguration $\hat{=}$
any $ld, ld\_alt, new\_ld\_alt, sls$
where $... \land mode = LEADER\_FAILURE\_RECONF \land ld \in leaders \land$
$sls = slaves\_of\_leader(ld) \setminus \{ld\_alt\} \land ld\_alt = leader\_alt(ld) \land$
$new\_ld\_alt \in sls \land status(ld\_alt) = OK$
then
$slaves\_of\_leader := (\{ld\} \lhd slaves\_of\_leader) \cup \{ld\_alt \mapsto sls\}$
$leader\_alt(ld\_alt) := new\_ld\_alt$
end
...

Fig. 7. The machine SwarmOfDrones_m1

Moreover, for each drone, we model possibility to react on particular hazardous situations – an unexpected appearance of an obstacle in the drone flying zone. In our proposed approach, when a drone detects a possible collision with an unforeseen obstacle, the drone safety reflex computation module quickly computes a reflex movement for the drone to prevent the collision.

To model drone safety reflex mechanisms, first we model possibility of appearing an obstacle in a drone flying zone (at any level of hierarchy). Then, upon detection an obstacle, a drone triggers mode transition to the *Reflection Activation* mode. Let us note that the drones perform this transition autonomously and independently upon detection of an obstacle. Upon triggering a transition to this "local" mode, a drone computes the best safe position and moves there. The nominal mode is restored after DC receives the update about the current drone positions and calculates the routing for the swarm. We introduce the new events Unpredictable_Obstacle and Reflection_Activation and refine the number of old events, e.g., Update_Local_Routes (omitted due to the lack of space).

6 Related Work and Conclusions

During last decades the problem of resilience and motion safety of autonomous robotic systems attracts significant research attention. A comprehensive overview of the problems associated with autonomous mobile robots is given in [18]. The analysis carried out in [20], shows that the most prominent routing schemes do not guarantee motion safety. Our approach resolves this issue and ensures not only safety but also efficiency of routing.

A layered architectural solution for robot navigation has been proposed in [3]. The authors focus on a problem of safe navigation of a vehicle in an urban environment. Similarly to our approach, they distinguish between a global route planning and a collision avoidance control. However, in their work, they focus on the safety issues associated with the navigation of a single vehicle and do not consider the problem of route optimization that is especially acute in the context of swarms of robots.

Modelling and verification of a system architecture using Event-B in the context of multi-agent and multi-robotic systems has also been investigated in works [12–14]. Moreover, in [15] we verified by proofs correctness and safety of agent interactions. In [4] the interactions between agents have been studied using goal-oriented perspective. In this work, the roles were defined as agent capabilities to perform certain tasks in order to accomplish the entire mission.

In this paper, we have presented a novel approach to formal modelling of resilient autonomous systems. Our approach allows a designer to derive the resilience-enhancing mode logic from the goals that the system should fulfil. We have considered both functional and non-functional goals and demonstrated how to define the conditions for monitoring goal reachability or degree of goal satisfaction. Using multi-agent modelling paradigm, we have demonstrated how to define such monitoring conditions as the functions over the capabilities of the system component – agents. Furthermore, we have proposed a generic Event-B specification pattern for modelling mode transitions triggered by changes in the monitored conditions at different architectural layers and demonstrated how to derive the complex mode-transition logic by refinement. The approach was illustrated by a case study – deriving mode logic of a resilient swarm of drones.

Our formal development was greatly facilitated by the Rodin platform. Reliance of refinement, proofs and powerful tool support has allowed us to derive a specification of a complex distributed system in a systematic rigorous way. The proposed technique is not constrained by the number of the architectural layers or of system components. Hence, it can potentially scale to the development of realistic autonomous systems.

In the future work, we are planing to extend our approach and focus on its communication model. Indeed, communication is a critical aspect in ensuring correct coordination and safety of the autonomous swarms of drones. To extend the communication model we can rely on our approach discussed in [19].

During the presented in this work refinement process we arrived at a centralised specification of the multi-layered swarm-based system. Our next goal can also focus on deriving its distributed implementation by refinement. We can employ modularisation facilities of Event-B [2,16] to achieve this. We can further decompose a system-level model and derive the interfaces of the drones and guarantee that their communication supports correct coordination despite unreliability of the communication channel and drones failures. To achieve it our current work can be complemented with our approaches proposed in [11,19].

References

1. Abrial, J.R.: Modeling in Event-B. Cambridge University Press, Cambridge (2010)
2. Iliasov, A., et al.: Supporting reuse in Event B development: modularisation approach. In: Frappier, M., Glässer, U., Khurshid, S., Laleau, R., Reeves, S. (eds.) ABZ 2010. LNCS, vol. 5977, pp. 174–188. Springer, Heidelberg (2010). https://doi.org/10.1007/978-3-642-11811-1_14
3. Macek, K., Govea, D.A.V., Fraichard, T., Siegwart, R.: Safe vehicle navigation in dynamic urban scenarios. In: Proceedings of 11th International IEEE Conference on Intelligent Transportation Systems, pp. 482–489. IEEE (2008)
4. Laibinis, L., Pereverzeva, I., Troubitsyna, E.: Formal reasoning about resilient goal-oriented multi-agent systems. Sci. Comput. Program. **148**, 66–87 (2017)
5. van Lamsweerde, A.: Goal-oriented requirements engineering: a guided tour. In: RE 2001, pp. 249–263. IEEE Computer Society (2001)
6. Laprie, J.: From dependability to resilience. In: 38th IEEE/IFIP International Conference on Dependable Systems and Networks, pp. G8–G9 (2008)
7. Leveson, N., Pinnel, L.D., Sandys, S.D., Koga, S., Reese, J.D.: Analyzing software specifications for mode confusion potential. In: Human Error and System Development, pp. 132–146 (1997)
8. Majd, A., Ashraf, A., Troubitsyna, E., Daneshtalab, M.: Integrating learning, optimization, and prediction for efficient navigation of swarms of drones. In: PDP 2018. IEEE (2018)
9. Majd, A., Troubitsyna, E.: Integrating safety-aware route optimisation and run-time safety monitoring in controlling swarms of drones. In: ISSRE Workshops, pp. 94–95. IEEE Computer Society (2017)
10. OMG Mobile Agents Facility (MASIF). www.omg.org
11. Pereverzeva, I., Troubitsyna, E.: Formalizing goal-oriented development of resilient cyber-physical systems. In: Alexander Romanovsky, F.I. (ed.) Trustworthy Cyber-Physical Systems Engineering, chap. 6 (2017)
12. Pereverzeva, I., Troubitsyna, E., Laibinis, L.: A case study in formal development of a fault tolerant multi-robotic system. In: Avgeriou, P. (ed.) SERENE 2012. LNCS, vol. 7527, pp. 16–31. Springer, Heidelberg (2012). https://doi.org/10.1007/978-3-642-33176-3_2
13. Pereverzeva, I., Troubitsyna, E., Laibinis, L.: Formal development of critical multi-agent systems: a refinement approach. In: EDCC 2012, pp. 156–161. IEEE Computer Society (2012)
14. Pereverzeva, I., Troubitsyna, E., Laibinis, L.: Formal goal-oriented development of resilient MAS in Event-B. In: Brorsson, M., Pinho, L.M. (eds.) Ada-Europe 2012. LNCS, vol. 7308, pp. 147–161. Springer, Heidelberg (2012). https://doi.org/10.1007/978-3-642-30598-6_11
15. Pereverzeva, I., Troubitsyna, E., Laibinis, L.: A refinement-based approach to developing critical multi-agent systems. IJCCBS **4**(1), 69–91 (2013)
16. Rodin: Modularisation Plug-in. http://wiki.event-b.org/index.php/Modularisation_Plug-in
17. Rodin: Event-B platform. http://www.event-b.org/

18. Siegwart, R., Nourbakhsh, I.R.: Introduction to Autonomous Mobile Robots. MIT Press, Cambridge (2004)
19. Tarasyuk, A., Pereverzeva, I., Troubitsyna, E., Latvala, T.: The formal derivation of mode logic for autonomous satellite flight formation. In: Koornneef, F., van Gulijk, C. (eds.) SAFECOMP 2015. LNCS, vol. 9337, pp. 29–43. Springer, Cham (2015). https://doi.org/10.1007/978-3-319-24255-2_4
20. Fraichard, Th.: A short paper about motion safety. In: Proceedings of the IEEE International Conference on Robotics and Automation. IEEE (2007)
21. Vistbakka, I., Majd, A., Troubitsyna, E.: Autonomous resilient systems: derivation of mode logic using Event-B. Technical report 1199, Turku Centre for Computer Science (2018)

UTP Semantics for BigrTiMo

Wanling Xie[1], Huibiao Zhu[1(✉)], and Shengchao Qin[2]

[1] Shanghai Key Laboratory of Trustworthy Computing, School of Computer Science and Software Engineering, East China Normal University, Shanghai, China
hbzhu@sei.ecnu.edu.cn

[2] School of Computing, University of Teesside, Middlesbrough, Tees Valley TS1 3BA, UK

Abstract. BigrTiMo [1], a process algebra that combines the rTiMo calculus [2] and the Bigraph model [3], is capable of specifying a rich variety of properties for structure-aware mobile systems. Compared with rTiMo, our BigrTiMo calculus can specify not only time, mobility and local communication, but also remote communication. In this paper, we study the semantic foundation of this highly expressive modelling language and propose a denotational semantic model for it based on Hoare and He's Unifying Theories of Programming (UTP) [4]. Compared to the standard UTP model, in addition to the communication, the novelty of the proposed UTP model in this paper covers time, location and global shared variable. Moreover, we give an example to show the contribution of BigrTiMo and illustrate how to use our semantic model and the trace-merging definition proposed in our paper under this example. We also demonstrate the proofs of some algebraic laws proposed in [1] based on our denotational semantics.

1 Introduction

With the development of cloud computing, mobile applications play an important role in modern distributed systems. Analyzing and verifying the increasing complexity of mobile applications effectively is of great significance. Ciobanu et al. [5] have first introduced a process algebra called TiMo (Timed Mobility) model for mobile systems, where it is possible to add time constraints to the basic actions (i.e., migration action and communication action) and the model of time is based on local clocks. Aman et al. [2] have extended TiMo by introducing a real-time version named rTiMo in which a global clock is used. The rTiMo processes can move between different locations of a mobile distributed system and communicate locally with other processes.

The above calculi only can model the local communication (the two communication components should be at the same location), however, in real applications, with the development of the internet, the two communication parties may not only communicate locally, but also communicate remotely (the two components can be at the different locations). In order to model the remote communications, we have extended rTiMo into BigrTiMo [1] by introducing a Bigraph model [3].

J. Sun and M. Sun (Eds.): ICFEM 2018, LNCS 11232, pp. 337–353, 2018.
https://doi.org/10.1007/978-3-030-02450-5_20

Regarding a programming language, there are four well-known methods for presenting semantics, including operational semantics, denotational semantics, algebraic semantics and deductive semantics (originally called axiomatic semantics) [6]. In [1], we have presented the operational semantics and algebraic semantics for BigrTiMo. And in this paper, we will investigate the denotational semantics which provides the mathematical meanings to programs. The approach of denotational semantics is under a purely mathematical basis, thus, it is more abstract. Compared with operational semantics, denotational semantics expresses *what a program does*. Our approach is based on Unifying Theories of Programming (UTP) proposed by Hoare and He in 1998 [4]. Compared to the standard UTP model [4], in addition to communication, the novelty of the UTP model in this paper covers time, location and global shared variable. Moreover, we give an example to show the contribution of BigrTiMo and illustrate how to use our semantic model and the trace-merging definition proposed in our paper under this example. We also demonstrate the proofs of some algebraic laws proposed in [1] based on our denotational semantics.

The remainder of this paper is organized as follows. Section 2 gives an introduction to the BigrTiMo calculus. In Sect. 3, we first present the semantic model and healthiness conditions that a BigrTiMo program should satisfy. We then explore the denotational semantics of BigrTiMo. In Sect. 4, we demonstrate the proofs of some algebraic laws based on the denotational semantics. Section 5 concludes the paper and discusses some possible future work.

2 BigrTiMo

In this section, we introduce BigrTiMo. In Sect. 2.1, we give a brief review of the bigraph. In Sect. 2.2, we introduce the syntax of BigrTiMo and give an example to show the contribution of our BigrTiMo calculus.

2.1 Review of Bigraph

A bigraph is a mathematical structure with two graphs, including a *placing graph* and a *linking graph* [3]. The placing graph is a forest which is used to model nested locality of components and the linking graph is a hypergraph that represents connectivity between components. Figure 1 illustrates an example of a bigraph. Figure 2 presents the corresponding placing and linking graphs of Fig. 1.

The encompassing rectangle represents a *region* and the grey rectangles are used to represent *holes*. Region and hole are the root and leaf node respectively in the placing graph, and enable the composition of placing graphs, e.g., a hole of a bigraph can be replaced by a region of another bigraph with the aid of composition operator defined in [3]. *Ports* are represented as black dots on the node, and are used to connect the edges or names, i.e., the node m_1 has two ports which connect to the edge e and the outer name y. The edge e and inner name x and outer name y are contained in the linking graph. We can also merge inner names and outer names using the bigraph composition operator.

We below give the definition of a bigraph.

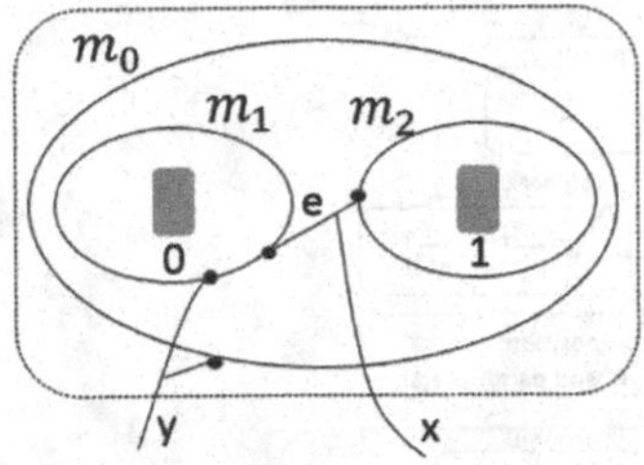

Fig. 1. Bigraph

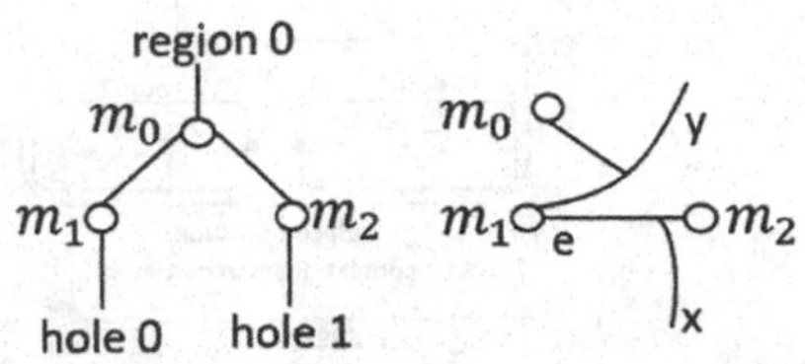

Fig. 2. Placing and linking graphs

Definition 1. *A* ***bigraph*** *is a 5-tuple* $(V, E, nupt, prnt, link)$ *where,*

- V *is the set of node identifiers and* E *is the set of edge identifiers.*
- $nupt : V \to \mathbb{N}$ *is a map that assigns their numbers of ports (i.e., a natural number) to nodes.*
- $prnt : m \uplus V \to V \uplus n$ *is the parent map which is used to assign a parent (i.e., a node or a region) to the children (i.e., a hole or a node).* $m = \{0, \ldots, |m|-1\}$ *denotes the set of holes and* $n = \{0, \ldots, |n| - 1\}$ *denotes the set of regions. The symbol* $\uplus$ *stands for the disjoint union of sets.*
- $link : X \uplus P \to E \uplus Y$ *is the link map which assigns edges and outer names to inner names and ports.* X *and* Y *denote the set of inner names and the set of outer names respectively.* P *denotes the set of ports of the bigraph and is formalized as* $P = \{(l, i) | i \in \{0, 1, \ldots, nupt(l) - 1\}\}$*, where* l *is a node in the set* V *in a bigraph. For convenience, we introduce a map* $pts : V \to \mathbb{P}(\mathbb{N})$ *that takes a node and returns the set of ports of that node.*

The bigraph stands for a specific snapshot of the world but there is no information on how it can evolve to another bigraph. Bigraph Reaction Rules (BRRs) are defined in [3] to create dynamics of bigraphs. A BRR is the form of $R \to R'$ where R and R' are bigraphs called *redex* and *reactum*, respectively. Let $r = R \to R'$ be a BRR and B a bigraph. In order to execute rule r in B we should first decompose B into $C \circ R \circ d$ where C stands for the context and d stands for the parameters inside the holes of R. We compose C with R' and with d to obtain the result B', e.g., $B = C \circ R \circ d \Rightarrow B' = C \circ R' \circ d$.

Consider a BRR **MOVE(pc0, room2)** that moves a **pc0** node from its current location to a **room2** node. Figure 3 describes the context C and parameters d where the rule is applied. A bigraph B changed to B' is illustrated at the top of Fig. 3. At the bottom of this figure, we give the decomposition of each bigraph in the context C, redex R, reactum R' and parameters d.

2.2 The Syntax of BigrTiMo

We have presented the BigrTiMo calculus in [1]. Compared with rTiMo, our BigrTiMo can model not only the location of components but also the connectivity of components. Thus, a BigrTiMo process not only can communicate

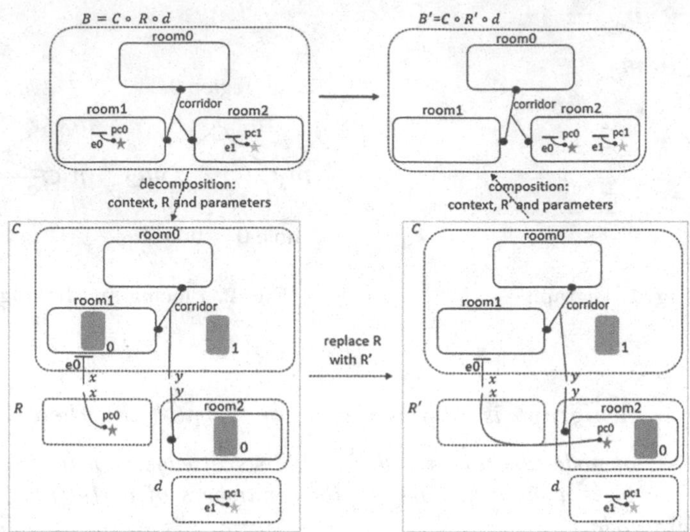

Fig. 3. Example of application of **MOVE** reaction rule

locally with other processes (like an rTiMo process), but also can communicate remotely with other processes (if the locations of the two components are connected, i.e., they share a communication link in the bigraph). In addition, a BigrTiMo process can migrate from one location to another location (if the desired location is contained in the bigraph and the current location of the process is connected to the desired location), and perform the bigraph reaction rules to update the bigraph.

The syntax of BigrTiMo is given in Table 1. In BigrTiMo, actions are controlled by using real-time constraints. Timeouts are specified by a superscript Δt. The communication channels are point-point, i.e. each connecting two processes, and synchronous. A synchronous channel with buffer size 0 sends/recieves messages synchronously and a communication $a.v$ takes place when both actions $a!\langle v\rangle$ and $a?(v)$ are enabled simultaneously. We first introduce the process parts:

1. *nil* denotes the process that terminates without taking any time.
2. $a^{\Delta t}!\langle v\rangle$ *then* P *else* Q stands for an output process. When the message v is sent via channel a successfully within t time units, the next process is P. If the communication does not happen before the timeout t, the communication attempt is aborted and the next process is Q.
3. $a^{\Delta t}?(u)$ *then* P *else* Q indicates an input process. When the process receives a message within t time units, the next process is P. If the input action does not occur before the deadline t, it gives up and switches to the process Q. The input process binds the variable u within P (but not within Q).
4. $go^{\Delta t}l$ *then* P *else* Q denotes a migration process. If the migration action happens successfully after delaying t time units, then the next process is P

located at location l. Otherwise, it switches to the alternative process Q whose location does not change.

5. $control^{\triangle t}(r)$ *then* P is an update process where r is a BRR which is performed to update the state of the shared bigraph. After delaying t time units, the update action takes place and the next process is P.
6. $P \,||\, Q$ stands for parallel composition.
7. $l[[P]]$ specifies a process P running at location l.

Table 1. BigrTiMo syntax

Process	$P, Q ::= nil$	(termination)
	$\mid a^{\triangle t}!\langle v\rangle \; then\ P\ else\ Q$	(output)
	$\mid a^{\triangle t}?(u) \; then\ P\ else\ Q$	(input)
	$\mid go^{\triangle t} l \; then\ P\ else\ Q$	(move)
	$\mid control^{\triangle t}(r) \; then\ P$	(update)
	$\mid P \,||\, Q$	(parallel composition)
Located process	$L ::= l[[P]]$	
Network	$N ::= 0 \mid L \mid L \,||\, N$	
Configuration	$G ::= empty \mid \langle N, B\rangle \mid \langle N, B\rangle \,||\, G$	

We next introduce the network and configuration parts. 0 denotes an empty network. A network can be a located process L or can be built via its component $L \,||\, N$. *empty* denotes an empty configuration. A BigrTiMo configuration is a tuple $\langle N, B\rangle$ denoted by G where N is a BigrTiMo network, B is a shared bigraph and the locations in N are all contained in the set of the node identifiers in the bigraph B. A configuration also can be built via component $\langle N, B\rangle \,||\, G$.

The shared bigraph in BigrTiMo is globally accessible and it can be read and written by different actions. In order to ensure the consistency of the shared bigraph, it can only be updated in sequential programs (i.e., $G1; G2$ denotes the behavior that runs $G1$ and $G2$ sequentially). Moreover, when programs execute atomically, sequential programs from different configurations are not allowed to execute simultaneously.

In order to support our algebraic expansion laws proposed in [1], we have presented three types of guarded choice. And we can convert every BigrTiMo program into the guarded choice form.

1. **Instantaneous Guarded Choice**
   The notation $\langle [\![\{g_1 \rightarrow N_1, \ldots, g_n \rightarrow N_n\}, B\rangle$ stands for an instantaneous guarded choice, which executes its guard g_i under the bigraph B initially and then performs the corresponding program $\langle N_i, B\rangle$ afterward. The guard g_i is an instantaneous guard which means that it takes place without any time delay, and it can be a communication guard or an event guard. A communication guard can be expressed as $a!\langle v\rangle@l$, $a?(u)@l$ or $a.[v/u]@(l, l')$, where

$a!\langle v\rangle@l$ (or $a?(u)@l$) indicates that the output (or input) action happens at location l, and $a.[v/u]@(l,l')$ denotes that the communication occurs where one communication end is from the location l and the other is from the location l', and the variable u is replaced by the message v. The event guards are $go(l')@l$ and $control(r)@l$ which represent that the migration action and update action happen at the location l, respectively.

2. **Delay Guarded Choice**
$\langle \#t \rightarrow N, B\rangle$ is a delay guarded choice and $\#t$ means delaying t time units.
3. **Hybrid Guarded Choice**
The hybrid guarded choice has the following form where the notation $\oplus$ denotes the disjointness of timed behaviors.

$$\begin{aligned}&\langle \|_{i\in I}\{g_i \rightarrow N_i\}, B\rangle\\ \oplus\ &\exists t' \in (0\ldots t) \bullet (\langle \#t' \rightarrow \|_{i\in I}\{g_i \rightarrow N_i'\}, B\rangle)\\ \oplus\ &\langle \#t \rightarrow N', B\rangle\end{aligned}$$

Example 1. Consider users with smartphones or personal computers communicating with each other. A city may contain housing area, office area and subway station and so on. Some areas may contain wireless hotspots which can be connected to the internet. If a personal computer or a smartphone is contained in a wireless hotspot it can connect to it. A user can walk from one location to anther location if the two locations are connected.

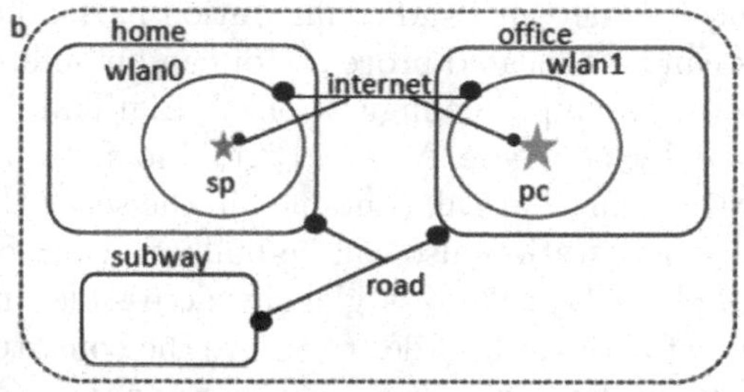

Fig. 4. The example of bigraph b (Color figure online)

Figure 4 depicts a bigraph city named b. This figure shows a city with three areas, namely *home*, $office$ and *subway*. All areas are connected with a link named *road* which models physical adjacency between the corresponding physical locations. A user can walk from *home* to *subway* (the two locations are connected with a link *road*). Some areas contain nodes $wlan0$ and $wlan1$ (white circles) which model the wireless hotspots, i.e., *home* contains $wlan0$ and $office$ contains $wlan1$. A smartphone modelled as a node *sp* (blue star) is contained in $wlan0$. A personal computer modelled as a node *pc* (grey star) is contained in $wlan1$. The nodes $wlan0$, $wlan1$, *sp* and *pc* all share a link named *internet* modelling the connectivity of the corresponding entities to the internet.

The definition of the bigraph b is showed as below.

$$
\begin{aligned}
&b = (V, E, nupt, prnt, link) \text{ where:}\\
&V = \{home, office, subway, wlan0, wlan1, sp, pc\}\\
&E = \{internet, road\}\\
&nupt(l) = 1 \,\text{where}\, l \in V\\
&prnt(l) = \begin{cases} 0, & if\ l \in \{home, office, subway\};\\ home, & if\ l = wlan0;\\ office, & if\ l = wlan1;\\ wlan0, & if\ l = sp;\\ wlan1, & if\ l = pc. \end{cases}\\
&link(p) = \begin{cases} internet, & if\ p \in \{(wlan0,0),(wlan1,0),(sp,0),(pc,0)\};\\ road, & if\ p \in \{(home,0),(office,0),(subway,0)\}. \end{cases}
\end{aligned}
$$

Consider two BigrTiMo processes *appsf* and *appbs* which are hosted at *sp* and *pc* respectively. The role of each process is described as below.

- *appsf* is a process to give instructions to a staff to receive a message (this message is used to inform the staff to go to a office) from a boss, then move to *subway*, move to *office*, connect to the internet.
- *appbs* is a process to give instructions to a boss to send a message to a staff.

The BigrTiMo syntax of the whole mobile system is:

$$\langle sp[[appsf]] \mid\mid pc[[appbs]], b\rangle.$$

The BigrTiMo syntax of two processes is as below:

$$
\begin{aligned}
appsf \ &= bs^{\Delta 1}?(u_1)\ then\ (control^{\Delta 3}(r_1)\ then\ control^{\Delta 2}(r_2)\ then\\
&\qquad control^{\Delta 1}(r_3)\ then\ nil)\ else\ nil\\
appbs \ &= bs^{\Delta 1}!\langle work\rangle\ then\ nil\ else\ nil
\end{aligned}
$$

where $r_1 = \mathbf{MOVE(sp, subway)}$, $r_2 = \mathbf{MOVE(sp, office)}$,
$r_3 = \mathbf{CONNECT(sp, wlan1)}$. □

3 Denotational Semantics of BigrTiMo

In this section, we present the denotational semantics for BigrTiMo. We use $\mathbf{beh}(\langle l[[P]], B\rangle)$ to describe the behavior of a process P running at location l in the given bigraph B after it is activated. In Sect. 3.1, we give the semantic model for BigrTiMo. In Sect. 3.2, we explore the behaviors of the basic commands. In Sect. 3.3, we investigate the behavior of the parallel composition.

3.1 The Semantic Model

In this subsection, the denotational semantic model for BigrTiMo is investigated. Similar to the semantic model for rTiMo [7], here, we also introduce a pair of variables st and st' into our semantic model in order to denote the execution state of a program. st represents the initial execution state of a program before its activation and st' stands for the final execution state of the program during the current observation. A program may have two execution states:

1. *completed state*: A program has reached the *completed state* when it terminates successfully. "$st = completed$" indicates that the previous program has terminated successfully and control passes to the current program. "$st' = completed$" indicates that the current program has terminated successfully and control passes to the next program.
2. *wait state*: A program may wait for communicating with another program via a specific channel. "$st = wait$" indicates that the predecessor of the current program is in a waiting state. Thus, the current program cannot be activated. "$st' = wait$" indicates that the current program itself is in a waiting state. Thus, the next program cannot be activated.

We describe the behavior of a program in terms of a trace of snapshots which record the sequence of the actions. In our semantic model, we introduce a variable tr to denote the trace for the sequence of the actions. Inspired by the semantic model for CSP# [8] which covers both communication and shared variables, a snapshot in our semantic model can be expressed as (t, loc, σ, κ) where:

- t indicates the time when the action takes place.
- loc records the locations at which the action takes place. And the form of loc is (l_1, l_2) or a single location l, where (l_1, l_2) means that the two components are located at l_1 and l_2 respectively (i.e., one communication end is from l_1, and the other one is from l_2). For convenience, we have $(l, l) = l$.
- σ denotes the pre-state of the shared bigraph and the action is observed under this state.
- κ denotes the observed action, including inputs/outputs, synchronous communications, migration and update. Thus, κ has the following forms:
  1. for an input/output or a synchronous communication, the form of κ is $a.v$, where a indicates the communication channel and v is the message transmitted. We define $\mathbf{Chan}(\kappa)$ to obtain the communication channel and $\mathbf{Mess}(\kappa)$ to obtain the message, i.e., if $\kappa = a.v$, then $\mathbf{Chan}(a.v) = a$ and $\mathbf{Mess}(a.v) = v$.
  2. for a migration action, κ is a desired location.
  3. for an update action, κ is a bigraph σ' which is a post-state recording the final state of the global shared bigraph after the observation. And it is used to record the observation for the sequential programs.

We use the following projections to select the components of a snapshot:

$$\pi_1((t, loc, \sigma, \kappa)) =_{df} t \qquad \pi_2((t, loc, \sigma, \kappa)) =_{df} loc$$
$$\pi_3((t, loc, \sigma, \kappa)) =_{df} \sigma \qquad \pi_4((t, loc, \sigma, \kappa)) =_{df} \kappa$$

In addition to the communication and global shared variable, our calculus has other interesting features, including time constrains and location information. Thus, the observations of a BigrTiMo program can be described by a tuple:

$$(time, time', st, st', tr, tr') \text{ where,}$$

- $time$ and $time'$ respectively denote the start point and the end point of the time interval over which the observation is recorded. We use δ to represent the length of the time interval.

  $$\delta =_{df} (time' - time)$$

  In our discrete model, we regard the length of a time interval as a non-negative real number, i.e., δ is considered as a non-negative real number.
- st represents the initial execution state of the program before its activation and st' stands for its final execution state during the current observation.
- tr represents the initial trace of a program over the interval which is passed by its predecessor. tr' stands for the final trace of a program over the interval. $tr' - tr$ denotes the sequence of snapshots contributed by the program itself during the interval.

We use the notations $\mathbf{head}(s)$ and $\mathbf{tail}(s)$ to denote the first snapshot of the trace s and the result of removing the first snapshot in the trace s, respectively.

Example 2. Let us consider the configuration in *Example* 1 in Sect. 2 again,

$$\text{where } N_1 = sp[[appsf]], \quad N_2 = pc[[appbs]], \quad G = \langle N_1 \parallel N_2, b\rangle.$$

Figure 5 shows the execution trace over the respective BRRs, where b is the initial bigraph and $b3$ is the final bigraph when the program terminates.

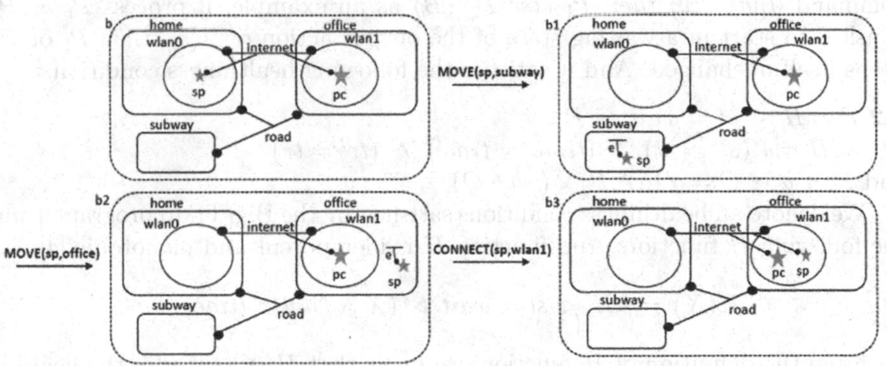

Fig. 5. Execution trace over the respective BRRs

Now we consider the trace of G. Assume that the activated time of G is at 0. According to the syntax of BigrTiMo, we know that the communication action occurs at time 0 (the two locations of the two components are connected by a communication link *internet*). After delaying three time units, the rule r_1 is performed to update the bigraph b into $b1$. After that, the rule r_2 is performed to update $b1$ into $b2$ after delaying two time units. Lastly, after delaying one time unit, the rule r_3 is performed to update $b2$ into $b3$.

A trace of $\langle N_1, b\rangle$ is given as below:

$$\langle(0, sp, b, bs.work), (3, sp, b, b1), (5, sp, b1, b2), (6, sp, b2, b3)\rangle.$$

A trace of $\langle N_2, b\rangle$ is: $\langle(0, pc, b, bs.work)\rangle$.

Hence, the one trace of G is as follows:

$$\langle(0, (sp, pc), b, bs.work), (3, sp, b, b1), (5, sp, b1, b2), (6, sp, b2, b3)\rangle. \qquad \square$$

Every program will always satisfy some given healthiness conditions which are defined as equations according to an idempotent function ϕ on predicates. And for a predicate P denoting a healthy program, we have $P = \phi(P)$.

We next consider two healthiness conditions that BigrTiMo programs should satisfy, and they are similar to the standard UTP theory [4]. In our semantic model, the variable tr is used to record the execution trace of a program, so it cannot be shortened. The variable $time$ is used to record the progress of a program and no program can ever make time go backwards, thus, it cannot be smaller. The predicate P which describes a BigrTiMo program behavior must therefore imply this fact. So it satisfies the healthiness condition **R1**.

R1 $P = P \wedge Inv(tr, time)$, where
$Inv(tr, time) =_{df} tr \preceq tr' \ \wedge \ time \leq time'$, which states that tr is a prefix of tr', and $time$ is less than or equal to $time'$.

Because of the requirement for synchronisation, a program may wait for communicating with another program via a specific channel. We take the output command $\langle l[[a^{\Delta t}!\langle v\rangle \ then \ P_1 \ else \ P_2]], B\rangle$ as an example: if process P_1 or P_2 is asked to start in a waiting state of the output action $a^{\Delta t}!\langle v\rangle$, then P_1 or P_2 keeps itself unchanged. And it satisfies the following healthiness condition.

R2 $P = \Pi \ \triangleleft \ st = wait \ \triangleright \ P$
where $\Pi =_{df} (st' = st) \ \wedge \ (time' = time) \ \wedge \ (tr' = tr)$
and $P \ \triangleleft \ b \ \triangleright \ Q =_{df} (b \wedge P) \vee (\neg b \wedge Q)$

We denote all healthiness conditions satisfied by the BigrTiMo program using the following H function. And function H is idempotent and monotonic [4].

$$H(X) =_{df} \Pi \ \triangleleft \ st = wait \ \triangleright \ (X \wedge Inv(tr, time))$$

From the definition of H function, we know that $H(X)$ satisfies the healthiness conditions **R1** and **R2**. The H function is used to define the denotational semantics for the BigrTiMo model.

3.2 Denotational Semantics of Basic Commands

We first investigate the denotational semantics of $\langle 0, B\rangle$. It is an empty configuration and its execution state, terminal time and trace all keep unchanged.

$$\mathbf{beh}(\langle 0, B\rangle) =_{df} H\left(st' = st \wedge \delta = 0 \wedge tr' = tr\right)$$

$G1; G2$ denotes the behavior that runs $G1$ and $G2$ sequentially. We now define the sequence operator for our semantic model.

Definition 2. $G1; G2 =_{df}$

$$\exists s, t, r \bullet G1[s/st', t/time', r/tr'] \ \wedge \ G2[s/st, t/time, r/tr].$$

The semantics of sequential composition is given as below:

$$\mathbf{beh}(G1; G2) =_{df} \mathbf{beh}(G1); \mathbf{beh}(G2)$$

As mentioned earlier, the guarded choice has three types: instantaneous guarded choice, delay guarded choice and hybrid guarded choice. Now we give the denotational semantics for these three types of guarded choice.

Instantaneous Guarded Choice. An instantaneous guard can be a communication guard or an event guard. The three types of the communication guard are $a!\langle v\rangle@l$, $a?(u)@l$ and $a.[v/u]@(l, l')$. The event guards are $go(l')@l$ and $control(r)@l$. The semantics of the communication guards is similar to the one in [7]. Due to space limitations, we only take the semantics of $a!\langle v\rangle@l$ as an example. And the semantics of the event guards $go(l')@l$ and $control(r)@l$ is novel in this paper.

$$\mathbf{beh}(\langle [\!]_{i\in I}\{g_i \rightarrow N_i\}, B\rangle) =_{df} \bigvee_{i\in I} \mathbf{beh}(\langle g_i \rightarrow N_i, B\rangle), \text{ where}$$

(1) if $g = a!\langle v\rangle@l$, then

$$\mathbf{beh}(\langle a!\langle v\rangle@l \rightarrow N, B\rangle) =_{df} \mathbf{beh}(\langle a!\langle v\rangle@l, B\rangle); \mathbf{beh}(\langle N, B\rangle)$$

where $\mathbf{beh}(\langle a!\langle v\rangle@l, B\rangle) =_{df} H\begin{pmatrix} st' = completed \wedge \delta = 0 \wedge \\ tr' = tr^\frown\langle(time', l, B, a.v)\rangle \end{pmatrix}$

(2) if $g = go(l')@l$, then

$$\mathbf{beh}(\langle go(l')@l \rightarrow N, B\rangle) =_{df} \mathbf{beh}(\langle go(l')@l, B\rangle); \mathbf{beh}(\langle N, B\rangle)$$

where $\mathbf{beh}(\langle go(l')@l, B\rangle) =_{df} H\begin{pmatrix} st' = completed \wedge \delta = 0 \wedge \\ tr' = tr^\frown\langle(time', l, B, l')\rangle \end{pmatrix}$

(3) if $g = control(r)@l$, then

$$\mathbf{beh}(\langle control(r)@l \rightarrow N, B\rangle) =_{df} \mathbf{beh}(\langle control(r)@l, B\rangle); \mathbf{beh}(\langle N, B'\rangle)$$

where $\mathbf{beh}(\langle control(r)@l, B\rangle) =_{df} H\begin{pmatrix} st' = completed \wedge \delta = 0 \wedge \\ tr' = tr^\frown\langle(time', l, B, B')\rangle \end{pmatrix}$

and $r = R \rightarrow R', B = C \circ R \circ d, B' = C \circ R' \circ d$.

In the semantic of $\langle control(r)@l \rightarrow N, B\rangle$, the rule r is performed to update the bigraph B into B' without any time delay. Thus, $time' = time$ and a snapshot $(time', l, B, B')$ contributed by the update action is attached to the end of the program trace.

Delay Guarded Choice. It consists of only one time delay component.

$$\mathbf{beh}(\langle \#t \rightarrow N, B\rangle) =_{df} \mathbf{beh}(\langle \#t, B\rangle); \mathbf{beh}(\langle N, B\rangle)$$

$$\text{where } \mathbf{beh}(\langle \#t, B\rangle) =_{df} H\begin{pmatrix} ((st' = wait \ \wedge \ \delta < t) \ \vee \\ (st' = completed \ \wedge \ \delta = t)) \ \wedge \ tr' = tr \end{pmatrix}$$

Hybrid Guarded Choice. The hybrid guarded choice has the following form:

$$\begin{aligned} G \ = \ & \langle \|_{i \in I}\{g_i \rightarrow N_i\}, B\rangle \\ & \oplus \exists t' \in (0 \ldots t) \bullet (\langle \#t' \rightarrow \|_{i \in I}\{g_i \rightarrow N_i'\}, B\rangle) \\ & \oplus \langle \#t \rightarrow N', B\rangle \end{aligned}$$

and the semantics of G is given below. The three branches are disjoint.

$$\mathbf{beh}(G) =_{df} \begin{pmatrix} \bigvee_{i \in I} \mathbf{beh}(\langle g_i \rightarrow N_i, B\rangle) \\ \bigvee \\ \exists t' \in (0 \ldots t) \bullet (\mathbf{beh}(\langle \#t', B\rangle); \bigvee_{i \in I} \mathbf{beh}(\langle g_i \rightarrow N_i', B\rangle)) \\ \bigvee \\ \mathbf{beh}(\langle \#t, B\rangle); \mathbf{beh}(\langle N', B\rangle) \end{pmatrix}$$

We then investigate the behavior of $\langle l[[go^{\triangle t} l' \ then \ P \ else \ Q]], B\rangle$, it indicates that if the desired location l' is contained in the set of the node identifiers in the bigraph B (denoted by V_B), as well as the location l and the desired location l' are connected in the bigraph B, then the migration action can happen successfully after delaying t time units. If the migration action takes place successfully, then the subsequent behavior of the program is the behavior of the process P at the location l' in the bigraph B. On the other hand, if the migration action does not take place, then the subsequent behavior of the program is the behavior of the process Q at the location l in the bigraph B.

$$\begin{aligned} & \mathbf{beh}(\langle l[[go^{\triangle t} l' \ then \ P \ else \ Q]], B\rangle) =_{df} \\ & \quad \mathbf{beh}(\langle \#t, B\rangle); \begin{pmatrix} (\mathbf{beh}(\langle go(l')@l, B\rangle); \mathbf{beh}(\langle l'[[P]], B\rangle)) \\ \lhd goflag \rhd \\ \mathbf{beh}(\langle l[[Q]], B\rangle) \end{pmatrix} \end{aligned}$$

where $goflag = l' \in V_B \ \wedge \ (\exists p \in pts(l).\exists p' \in pts(l').link(p) = link(p'))_B$.

In the above semantics definition, $\mathbf{beh}(\langle \#t, B\rangle)$ describes the behaviors of delaying t time units. For t time units, its trace keeps unchanged. After delaying t time units, if the boolean $goflag$ is true, then the migration action takes place and generates a snapshot attached to the end of the program trace.

The semantics of the output and input commands in our BigrTiMo is similar to the one in rTiMo [7]. Due to space limitations, here, we only take the semantic of the output command as an example.

$$\mathbf{beh}(\langle l[[a^{\Delta t}!\langle v\rangle \; then \; P \; else \; Q]], B\rangle) =_{df}$$
$$\left(\begin{array}{c} \mathbf{beh}(\langle a!\langle v\rangle @l, B\rangle); \mathbf{beh}(l[[P]], B\rangle) \\ \bigvee \\ \exists t' \in (0 \ldots t) \bullet (\mathbf{beh}(\langle \#t', B\rangle); \mathbf{beh}(\langle a!\langle v\rangle @l, B\rangle); \mathbf{beh}(l[[P]], B\rangle)) \\ \bigvee \\ \mathbf{beh}(\langle \#t, B\rangle); \mathbf{beh}(l[[Q]], B\rangle) \end{array}\right)$$

Compared to the commands proposed in [7], the novelty operator in this paper is the control command which is used to update the global shared bigraph. This command can only be executed in sequential programs, and when it executes atomically, sequential programs from different configurations are not allowed to execute simultaneously.

The control command $\langle l[[control^{\Delta t}(r) \; then \; P]], B\rangle$ performs the BRR r to update the current bigraph B. After delaying t time units, the update action takes place and the next process is P.

$$\begin{array}{l} \mathbf{beh}(\langle l[[control^{\Delta t}(r) \; then \; P]], B\rangle) =_{df} \\ \quad \mathbf{beh}(\langle \#t, B\rangle); \mathbf{beh}(\langle control(r) @l, B\rangle); \mathbf{beh}(\langle l[[P]], B'\rangle) \end{array}$$

For t time units, the update action is in a waiting state and its trace is unchanged. After delaying t time units, the update action takes place successfully and a snapshot $(time', l, B, B')$ contributed by the update action is attached to the end of the program trace.

3.3 Denotational Semantics of Parallel Composition

The parallel composition $\langle l[[P]] \parallel l'[[Q]], B\rangle$ executes the process P from l and the process Q from l' (l and l' can be same or different) under the global shared bigraph B in two ways: (1) synchronous channel output in one process takes place simultaneously with the corresponding channel input in the other process; (2) other actions of processes take place independently. The composition is described by the following definition.

$$\mathbf{beh}(\langle l[[P]] \parallel l'[[Q]], B\rangle) = \mathbf{beh}(\langle l[[P]], B\rangle) \parallel \mathbf{beh}(\langle l'[[Q]], B\rangle) \text{ where,}$$
$$\mathbf{beh}(\langle l[[P_1]], B\rangle) \parallel \mathbf{beh}(\langle l'[[P_2]], B\rangle) =_{df}$$
$$\left(\begin{array}{l} \exists st_1, st_1', st_2, st_2', time_1, time_1', time_2, time_2', tr_1, tr_1', tr_2, tr_2' \bullet \\ \qquad \mathbf{beh}(\langle l[[P_1]], B\rangle)[st_1, st_1', time_1, time_1', tr_1, tr_1' / \\ \qquad\qquad st, st', time, time', tr, tr'] \wedge \\ \qquad \mathbf{beh}(\langle l'[[P_2]], B\rangle)[st_2, st_2', time_2, time_2', tr_2, tr_2' / \\ \qquad\qquad st, st', time, time', tr, tr'] \wedge \\ \qquad Merge \end{array}\right)$$

The first two predicates in the above definition describe the two independent behaviors of the configurations $\langle l[[P_1]], B\rangle$ and $\langle l'[[P_2]], B\rangle$. The predicate $Merge$ mainly does the merging of the contributed traces of the two behavioral branches, as well as the merging of the execution states and terminal times.

We now give the definition of $Merge$.

$$Merge =_{df} \begin{pmatrix} (st_1' = completed \ \wedge \ st_2' = completed) \Rightarrow st' = completed \ \wedge \\ (st_1' = wait \ \vee \ st_2' = wait) \Rightarrow st' = wait \ \wedge \\ time' = \mathbf{max}\{time_1', time_2'\} \ \wedge \\ \exists s \in (tr_1' - tr_1) \ || \ (tr_2' - tr_2) \bullet tr' = tr^\frown s \end{pmatrix}$$

The final execution state of the behavior of the parallel composition is determined by the two parallel components together. And the terminal time of the parallel composition is the maximum between the two terminal times of the parallel components. The merging of the contributed traces of the two behaviors can be defined as follows. The result of merging two empty traces (represented as ϵ) is still empty, which is illustrated in **case-1**. If one of the two traces is empty and the other is nonempty, the result follows the nonempty one shown in **case-2**. And **case-3** shows that function $||$ is symmetric.

$$\textbf{case-1} \ \epsilon \ || \ \epsilon =_{df} \{\epsilon\} \ \ \textbf{case-2} \ s \ || \ \epsilon =_{df} \{s\} \ \ \textbf{case-3} \ s \ || \ t =_{df} t \ || \ s$$

If both traces are nonempty, then we can use the following cases to merge the two traces. We below obtain the first snapshot in the two traces respectively.

$$t_1 = \pi_1(\mathbf{head}(s)), \ l_1' = \pi_2(\mathbf{head}(s)), \ \sigma_1 = \pi_3(\mathbf{head}(s)), \ \kappa_1 = \pi_4(\mathbf{head}(s))$$
$$t_2 = \pi_1(\mathbf{head}(t)), \ l_2 = \pi_2(\mathbf{head}(t)), \ \sigma_2 = \pi_3(\mathbf{head}(t)), \ \kappa_2 = \pi_4(\mathbf{head}(t))$$

We first consider the case that $t_1 = t_2$ which means that the two actions κ_1 and κ_2 take place at the same time. The bigraph is a global shared variable, so we have $\sigma_1 = \sigma_2 = \sigma$. In this case, neither of the two actions can be an update action, since when the update action is executed, no other action can be executed at this time. Thus, we only need to consider the following two cases: (1) the two actions both are communication actions (denoted by **case-4**); (2) at least one of the two actions is not a communication action: if κ_1 is a communication action, then κ_2 should be a migration action, and if κ_1 is a migration action, then κ_2 can be a migration action or a communication action (denoted by **case-5**).

$$\textbf{case-4} \ s \ || \ t =_{df} \begin{cases} \left(\begin{pmatrix} sc^\frown(\mathbf{tail}(s) \ || \ \mathbf{tail}(t)) \\ \lhd \ \mathbf{Mess}(\kappa_1) = \mathbf{Mess}(\kappa_2) \ \rhd \emptyset \end{pmatrix} \\ \lhd \ \mathbf{Chan}(\kappa_1) = \mathbf{Chan}(\kappa_2) \ \rhd \mathrm{T} \right), & \text{if comflag} = \text{true}; \\ \mathrm{T}, & \text{otherwise.} \end{cases}$$

where $comflag = (l_1 =' l_2) \vee (\exists p \in pts(l_1) \cdot \exists p' \in pts(l_2) \cdot link(p) = link(p'))_\sigma$;
$sc = \langle (t_1, (l_1, l_2), \sigma, \kappa_1) \rangle$;
and $\mathrm{T} = \langle (t_1, l_1, \sigma, \kappa_1) \rangle^\frown(\mathbf{tail}(s) \ || \ t) \cup \langle (t_2, l_2, \sigma, \kappa_2) \rangle^\frown(s \ || \ \mathbf{tail}(t))$.

comflag = *true* means that the two communication components are at the same location described by the first predicate $l_1 = l_2$, or the locations of the two components are connected in the current bigraph σ described by the second predicate. *comflag* = *false* means that the two components cannot communicate with each other. If *comflag* = *false*, then we only need to attach **head**(s) or **head**(t) to the end of the program trace (denoted by T). If *comflag* = *true*, then we have the following descriptions.

- If **Chan**(κ_1) equals to **Chan**(κ_2) which means that the two channels are same, then we consider the messages. If **Mess**(κ_1) equals to **Mess**(κ_2) which means that the two messages are same, then a synchronization occurs and a snapshot *sc* contributed by this communication is generated. On the other hand, if the two messages are different, then the result of trace merging is empty set $\emptyset$.
- If **Chan**(κ_1) and **Chan**(κ_2) are different, then a synchronization does not happen and we only need to attach **head**(s) or **head**(t) to the end of the program trace (denoted by T).

For the case that at least one of the two actions is not a communication action, then a synchronization does not take place (denoted by T).

$$\textbf{case-5}\ s \mid\mid t =_{df} \mathrm{T}.$$

According to **case-3**, we know that function $||$ is symmetric. Thus, we only need to consider the case $t_1 < t_2$ which means that κ_1 occurs before κ_2 (denoted by **case-6**). In this case, κ_1 (or κ_2) can be a communication action, a migration action or an update action. And we only need to attach the first snapshot of s to the end of the program trace.

$$\textbf{case-6}\ s \mid\mid t =_{df} \langle (t_1, l_1, \sigma_1, \kappa_1)\rangle^\frown(\textbf{tail}(s) \mid\mid t).$$

Example 3. Let us consider the configuration in *Example* 2 in Sect. 3.1 again,

$$\text{where } N_1 = sp[[appsf]],\ \ N_2 = pc[[appbs]],\ \ G = \langle N_1 \mid\mid N_2, b\rangle.$$

As mentioned in *Example* 2, a trace of $\langle N_1, b\rangle$ is given as below:

$$s = \langle (0, sp, b, bs.work), (3, sp, b, b1), (5, sp, b1, b2), (6, sp, b2, b3)\rangle.$$

A trace of $\langle N_2, b\rangle$ is: $t = \langle (0, pc, b, bs.work)\rangle$.
According to the trace-merging definition **case-4**, we can obtain

$$s \mid\mid t = \langle (0, (sp, pc), b, bs.work)\rangle^\frown(s' \mid\mid \epsilon)$$

where $s' = \langle (3, sp, b, b1), (5, sp, b1, b2), (6, sp, b2, b3)\rangle$.

According to **case-2**, we can obtain $s' \mid\mid \epsilon = \{s'\}$.
Finally, we obtain one trace of G by merging s and t below:

$$\langle (0, (sp, pc), b, bs.work), (3, sp, b, b1), (5, sp, b1, b2), (6, sp, b2, b3)\rangle. \qquad \square$$

4 Algebraic Properties

Program properties can be expressed as algebraic laws and equations. In [1], we have presented a set of algebraic laws for BigrTiMo. Our denotational semantics in this paper can support the proofs of these laws. From these proofs, we can see that our semantics definitions are very rigorous. Due to space limitations, we only take some representative laws as examples.

(Output1) $\langle l[[a^{\Delta t}!\langle v\rangle \textit{ then } P \textit{ else } Q]], B\rangle$
$= \langle a!\langle v\rangle @l \rightarrow l[[P]], B\rangle$
$\oplus \exists t' \in (0\ldots t) \bullet (\langle \#t' \rightarrow a!\langle v\rangle @l \rightarrow l[[P]], B\rangle)$
$\oplus \langle \#t \rightarrow l[[Q]], B\rangle$, where $t > 0$.

From the law **(Output1)**, we can see that the output command can be converted into a hybrid guarded choice. And in this guarded choice, the first branch indicates that the output action occurs at the activation time of the output command. The second branch indicates that the output action takes place after delaying t' time units, where $t' \in (0\ldots t)$. And the third branch indicates that the output action does not happen before the timeout t.

Proof. By the semantics definitions for the output command and hybrid guarded choice, we know that they have the same form. Thus, this law is correct. □

$$\textbf{(Control1)}\ \langle l[[control^{\Delta t}(r) \textit{ then } P]], B\rangle = \langle \#t \rightarrow control(r)@l \rightarrow l[[P]], B\rangle$$
$$\text{where } t > 0, r = R \rightarrow R', B = C \circ R \circ d \text{ and } B' = C \circ R' \circ d.$$

From the law **(Control1)**, we can see that the control command can be converted into a delay guard followed by an instantaneous event guard, which indicates that after delaying t time units, the control action occurs successfully.

Proof. By the semantics definitions for the delay guarded choice and the instantaneous guarded choice, we have that $\textbf{beh}(\langle \#t \rightarrow control(r)@l \rightarrow l[[P]], B\rangle)$ equals to $\textbf{beh}(\langle \#t, B\rangle); \textbf{beh}(\langle control(r)@l, B\rangle); \textbf{beh}(\langle l[[P]], B'\rangle)$. According to the definition of the semantics for the control command, we see that they have the same form, so this law is correct. □

5 Conclusion

BigrTiMo is a process algebra for structure-aware mobile systems. In this paper, we have studied the denotational semantics for BigrTiMo via the concept of UTP. Compared to the standard UTP theory, in addition to communication, the novelty in our UTP model covers time, location and global shared variable. Moreover, we give an example to show the contribution of BigrTiMo and illustrate how to use our semantic model and the trace-merging definition proposed in our paper under this example. We also demonstrate the proofs of some algebraic laws based on the denotational semantics.

Recently, Hoare has proposed the challenging research topic for studying semantic linking where the starting point is from the algebra semantics [9].

Hoare and He have studied the derivation of operational semantics from the algebraic semantics [4,10]. For future work, we want to explore linking theory of the semantics for BigrTiMo.

Acknowledgments. This work was partly supported by Shanghai Collaborative Innovation Center of Trustworthy Software for Internet of Things (No. ZF1213).

References

1. Xie, W., Zhu, H., Xu, Q.: BigrTiMo - a process algebra for structure-aware mobile systems. In: ICECCS 2017, Fukuoka, Japan, 6–8 November 2017, pp. 50–59 (2017)
2. Aman, B., Ciobanu, G.: Real-time migration properties of rTiMo verified in Uppaal. In: Hierons, R.M., Merayo, M.G., Bravetti, M. (eds.) SEFM 2013. LNCS, vol. 8137, pp. 31–45. Springer, Heidelberg (2013). https://doi.org/10.1007/978-3-642-40561-7_3
3. Milner, R.: The Space and Motion of Communicating Agents. Cambridge University Press, Cambridge (2009)
4. Hoare, C.A.R., He, J.: Unifying Theories of Programming. Prentice Hall International Series in Computer Science. Prentice Hall, Upper Saddle River (1998)
5. Ciobanu, G., Koutny, M.: Timed mobility in process algebra and Petri nets. J. Log. Algebr. Program. **80**(7), 377–391 (2011)
6. Hoare, T.: Unifying semantics for concurrent programming. In: Coecke, B., Ong, L., Panangaden, P. (eds.) Computation, Logic, Games, and Quantum Foundations. The Many Facets of Samson Abramsky. LNCS, vol. 7860, pp. 139–149. Springer, Heidelberg (2013). https://doi.org/10.1007/978-3-642-38164-5_10
7. Xie, W., Xiang, S.: UTP semantics for rTiMo. In: Bowen, J.P., Zhu, H. (eds.) UTP 2016. LNCS, vol. 10134, pp. 176–196. Springer, Cham (2017). https://doi.org/10.1007/978-3-319-52228-9_9
8. Shi, L., Zhao, Y., Liu, Y., Sun, J., Dong, J.S., Qin, S.: A UTP semantics for communicating processes with shared variables. In: Groves, L., Sun, J. (eds.) ICFEM 2013. LNCS, vol. 8144, pp. 215–230. Springer, Heidelberg (2013). https://doi.org/10.1007/978-3-642-41202-8_15
9. Hoare, T., van Staden, S.: In praise of algebra. Formal Aspects Comput. **24**(4–6), 423–431 (2012)
10. He, J., Hoare, C.A.R.: From algebra to operational semantics. Inf. Process. Lett. **45**(2), 75–80 (1993)

Refinement and Transition Systems

Analysis on Strategies of Superposition Refinement of Event-B Specifications

Tsutomu Kobayashi(✉) and Fuyuki Ishikawa

National Institute of Informatics, Tokyo, Japan
{t-kobayashi,f-ishikawa}@nii.ac.jp

Abstract. The superposition refinement with the Event-B modeling method is useful because it supports construction of models in multiple abstraction levels, and thus mitigates the burden of constructing rigorous models. With such a refinement mechanism, developers can choose which subset of a target system's elements is specified in each abstraction level (refinement strategy). Although differences of refinement strategies for a model affect the complexity of modeling and verification, the effect has not been studied. We propose our automatic refinement refactoring method, which constructs abstract versions of a given Event-B model according to a refinement strategy different from the original one. We applied the refactoring method to construct various refactored versions of large Event-B models and compared them. As a result, we found that the granularity and frequently used variables are important factors for reducing the complexity. We consider the findings important to help Event-B modelers to design and change refinement strategies.

Keywords: Event-B · Refinement · Formal specifications
Design exploration

1 Introduction

Event-B [1] has been attracting strong attention. The primary advantage of Event-B is its flexible refinement mechanism to deal with the complexity of contemporary software. It supports *superposition refinement*, which enables developers to gradually introduce elements of target systems to models.

Although it is important to consider designing of Event-B refinement, existing studies lack explicit discussions on it. Because of the flexibility of superposition refinement, the design space of refinement in Event-B is large. Developers can choose the granularity and the order of introducing elements of target systems into models. Guides for designing Event-B refinement include a textbook showing good refinement design examples [1] and domain-specific guidelines [13]. However, they do not explicitly discuss refinement strategies themselves nor explain why some refinement strategies are better than others.

This work was supported by JST, ACT-I grant number JPMJPR17UA.

J. Sun and M. Sun (Eds.): ICFEM 2018, LNCS 11232, pp. 357–372, 2018.
https://doi.org/10.1007/978-3-030-02450-5_21

In our previous research, we have proposed methods for planning good refinement strategies before constructing models [6] and refactoring refinement strategies of constructed models without breaking consistency [7]. For planning, it is essentially difficult to plan concrete refinement strategies before starting modeling, and thus the support our method provides is limited. Moreover, developers often have difficulties in making design decisions before constructing and end up reconstructing models later. For refactoring, our refactoring method helps developers to construct consistent refactored models through the use of a new refinement strategy. However, developers must face the task of coming up with that strategy. In addition, the method can only be partially automated.

We tackled the problem of analyzing how to design Event-B refinement strategy by solving those problems of our previous work. First, we automated our refactoring method to support easy and flexible refactoring of refinement strategy. Second, we constructed variants of sample models by giving different refinement strategies to our tool and compared various refinement strategies.

The problem we address is novel and important. Methods on verification of refinement have been actively studied in formal methods area. However, as far as we know, design analyses of refinement that take complexity and usability into account have never been studied. From an engineering viewpoint, refinement design is equally important as verification. In fact, there have been many studies on this problem in other areas such as object-oriented design [11].

The contributions of this paper are as follows:

- Automation of our refactoring (generating additional predicates for consistency, automating proof of refactored models, and handling Event-B models)
- Evaluation on automation of refactoring
- Evaluation on effectiveness of refactoring
- Discussion on preferable refinement strategies
- Proposal of a tool-assisted design space exploration of Event-B refinement

The rest of this paper is organized as follows. First, we provide a background on Event-B in Sect. 2. Next, we explain our previous work on refactoring refinement in Event-B and our new proposal on automation of refactoring in Sect. 3. We then describe experiments for comparing various refinement strategies in Sect. 4. In Sects. 5 and 6, we discuss our methods, experiments, threats to validity, and related work. Finally, we summarize this study in Sect. 7.

2 Superposition Refinement in Event-B

2.1 Event-B and Superposition Refinement

Event-B [1] is a formal modeling method with a flexible refinement mechanism, which is designed to mitigate the complexity of contemporary software systems. Specifically, Event-B supports a special style of refinement, which is called *superposition (horizontal) refinement*. For mitigation of complexity in modeling and verification, it enables developers to gradually introduce elements of a target system to models. In other words, it helps developers to distribute the complexity over several steps. An important point of superposition refinement is that developers can design multiple ways of introduce elements.

Another style of refinement that is popular in classical formal methods is called *data (vertical) refinement*. Event-B also supports this style. This is oriented for deriving executable program codes from specifications. A typical example is conversion from a set-theoretic operation to an operation on an array. In contrast to superposition refinement, the design space of data refinement is limited. In fact, there is a semi-automated tool [9] to do data refinement.

2.2 Modeling in Event-B

In Event-B, a unit of a model (machine) consists of variables, invariants, and events. An event basically consists of guards and actions, which are necessary conditions for triggering the event and state transitions of the event, respectively.

After constructing a model, the development environment of Event-B (Rodin) generates *proof obligations* (POs), which are formulae of consistency of the model. A primary sort of PO is that an occurrence of event e does not violate an invariant i (*invariant preservation*, written as e/i/INV).

If a developer declares that a model is a refinement of another model, other sorts of POs are generated. Such POs include *guard strengthening* (GRD), which requires guards of a concrete event to be stronger than guards of corresponding events in the abstract model, and *action simulation* (SIM), which requires that concrete behavior corresponds to abstract behavior. Guard strengthening ($e_\mathrm{C}/g_\mathrm{A}$/GRD, where e_C is an event in the concrete machine and g_A is a guard of the abstract event of e_C in the abstract machine) demands that the conjunction of guards of e_C is stronger than a guard of the abstract event g_A. The (simplified) formula of $e_\mathrm{C}/g_\mathrm{A}$/GRD is $I_\mathrm{A} \wedge I_\mathrm{C} \wedge G_\mathrm{C} \Rightarrow g_\mathrm{A}$, where I_A and I_C are abstract invariants and concrete invariants, and G_C is guards of e_C. Developers can be confident with the consistency of the model by discharging all generated POs.

2.3 Example: Cars on the Bridge

We describe a variant of an Event-B example model "Cars on the Bridge" [1, Chap. 2]. It is about traffic between a mainland and an island, which are connected with a one-way bridge (Fig. 1, right). The requirements include: (R1) The number of cars outside of the mainland should not exceed the capacity (constant *cap*). (R2) When a car is going on the bridge towards the mainland, traffic lights on the mainland should prevent cars on the mainland from departing.

In Event-B, a developer first constructs an abstract model that disregards some elements of the target system. For example, Fig. 2 shows an abstract model of Cars on the Bridge (Fig. 1, left). The variable n_out is the number of cars on the island or the bridge. The invariant **inv_A1** represents requirement (R1). The event describes the behavior of a car's departure from the mainland. Various POs including mainland_out_abs/**inv_A1**/INV are generated and proved.

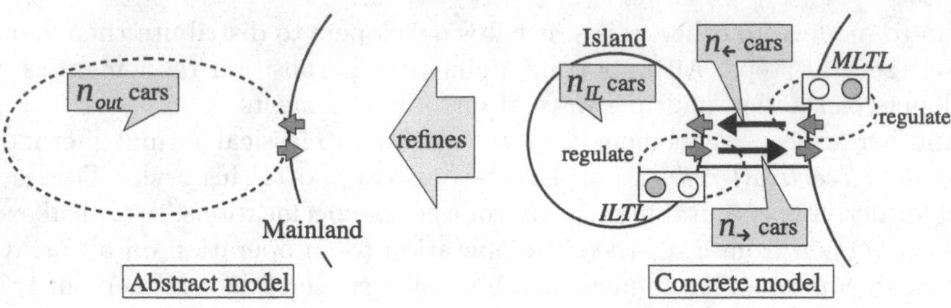

Fig. 1. Cars on the bridge example

variables: n_{out}

invariants:
inv_A1: $n_{\text{out}} \leq cap$
...

Event mainland_out_abs
when
***grd1*:** $n_{\text{out}} < cap$
then
***act1*:** $n_{\text{out}} := n_{\text{out}} + 1$
end

Fig. 2. M_{CarsA}: part of abstract model of example

After constructing an abstract model, a concrete model with more elements is constructed. For instance, Fig. 3 shows a concrete model of the example (Fig. 1, right). The number of cars on the island is n_{IL}, and the number of cars going left and right are $n_{\leftarrow}$ and $n_{\rightarrow}$, respectively. Those variables *replace* the abstract variable n_{out} (**inv_C1**). Variables of traffic lights on the mainland and the island (*MLTL* and *ILTL*) are also introduced into the model. The invariant **inv_C2** and the guard ***grd2*** satisfies the requirement (R2). In this model, the PO mainland_out_con/***grd1***/GRD is dischargeable because the its formula is:

$$(MLTL = green) \wedge (MLTL = green \Rightarrow n_{\rightarrow} = 0)$$
$$\wedge\ (n_{\leftarrow} + n_{\text{IL}} + 1 < cap) \wedge (n_{\text{out}} = n_{\leftarrow} + n_{\text{IL}} + n_{\rightarrow}) \Rightarrow n_{\text{out}} < cap.$$

variables:
$n_{\leftarrow}, n_{\text{IL}}, n_{\rightarrow}, MLTL, ILTL$

invariants:
inv_C1: $n_{\text{out}} = n_{\leftarrow} + n_{\text{IL}} + n_{\rightarrow}$
inv_C2: $MLTL = green \Rightarrow n_{\rightarrow} = 0$
...

Event mainland_out_con
refines mainland_out_abs
when
***grd2*:** $MLTL = green$
***grd3*:** $n_{\leftarrow} + n_{\text{IL}} + 1 < cap$
then
***act1*:** $n_{\leftarrow} := n_{\leftarrow} + 1$
end

Fig. 3. M_{CarsC}: part of concrete model of example

The refinement in Event-B is done in this way. First, developers blackbox traffic lights and state that "Somehow, the numbers of cars satisfy these invariants and behave like these events." They then construct a concrete model to describe that "It turned out that the cars' invariants and behaviors of the abstract model are due to traffic lights." This flexible refinement mechanism allows developers to freely design the elements introduced in each refinement step. For example, they can also introduce traffic lights before introducing cars.

Henceforth, we will use the term *refinement strategy* (RS) to mean a sequence of introduced variables in each step. We will also use the term *refinement chain* (RC) to mean a sequence of Event-B models $[M_0, M_1, \ldots, M_n]$ such that M_{i+1} refines M_i, where $0 \leq i \leq n-1$.

3 Automated Refinement Refactoring

3.1 Refinement Refactoring

We will here describe our previous work on refinement refactoring [7].

Refinement refactoring aims to improve the value of given Event-B models by changing the refinement strategy of given verified models. The refactored models have a different refinement strategy than that of the given models. By refactoring, the expression of models other than the most concrete model can be changed without changing the most concrete model, because a refinement strategy dominates the expression of models. In other words, refactoring corresponds to obtaining projection of the most concrete model onto a new state space. For example, we can improve the maintainability of a model by decomposing one refinement step into several small steps. In addition, a reusable part of an existing model can be extracted with refactoring by obtaining a projection onto a state space of reusable variables. Thus, refactoring facilitates engineering use of constructed models by obtaining a new projection of the most concrete model.

Our refactoring method receives a concrete model M and a set of variables V as input and manually produces a model $M'(V)$ (*intermediate model*) that is an abstract version of M. The input V is a subset[1] of all variables declared in the given model M and its abstract models. The output model $M'(V)$ should be consistent with M, and thus all POs (such as invariant preservation, guard strengthening, and action simulation) of $M'(V)$ should be dischargeable. Moreover, the set of variables contained in $M'(V)$ should be V. Refactoring is achieved with two operations: refinement merging and refinement decomposition. For a given refinement chain $[M_A, M_B, M_C]$, refinement merging constructs a model M_{B+C}, which refines M_A and is constructed from M_B and M_C. For a given refinement chain $[M_A, M_C]$, refinement decomposition constructs a model M_B such that $[M_A, M_B, M_C]$ is a refinement chain. By merging a refinement chain $[\ldots, M]$ and decomposing it into $[\ldots, M'(V), M]$, we can obtain a model $M'(V)$ that is written with V and consistent with M.

[1] V cannot be an arbitrary subset. See our previous work [7] for conditions of V.

The key challenge of refinement refactoring is guaranteeing consistency in refinement decomposition. A naïve approach towards refinement decomposition is *slicing*, namely constructing $M'(V)$ as a collection of parts of M that can be written with V. For example, suppose that we try to construct a model of the example disregarding the traffic lights (*MLTL* and *ILTL*). In other words, we try to construct a model that describes properties and behavior relevant to the number of cars on the bridge and the island that are controlled by the traffic lights, without describing the behavior of traffic lights. By slicing, we obtain the model $M'_{\mathrm{CarsC}}(\{n_{\leftarrow}, n_{\mathrm{IL}}, n_{\rightarrow}\})$ shown in Fig. 4. Although the model should refine M_{CarsA}, this intermediate model lacks the consistency of mainland_out_int/***grd1***/GRD, because it lacks the invariant **inv_C2** and the guard ***grd2***, which were necessary hypotheses for the consistency in the original model. Thus, slicing often drops predicates that are hypotheses of consistency proofs of the original model.

```
variables: n←, nIL, n→
```

```
invariants:
  inv_C1: nout = n← + nIL + n→
  ...
```

```
Event mainland_out_int
  refines mainland_out_abs
  when
    grd3: n← + nIL + 1 < cap
  then
    act1: n← := n← + 1
  end
```

Fig. 4. $M'_{CarsC}(\{n_{\leftarrow}, n_{\mathrm{IL}}, n_{\rightarrow}\})$: a part of intermediate model (obtained by slicing, not consistent) of example.

Our refactoring method addresses this problem by supporting the construction and addition of new predicates, which we call *complementary predicates* (CPs). CPs should be able to be expressed with variables of an intermediate model and should function as a missing hypothesis of a proof of an intermediate model. CPs can be found by analyzing a proof of the original model because they correspond to lemmas in the original proof (Sect. 2.3). For instance, in the proof of mainland_out_con/***grd1***/GRD in the original example model M_{CarsC}, there is a lemma $n_{\rightarrow} = 0$, which can be derived from hypotheses **inv_C2** and ***grd2***. This lemma can be expressed with variables $\{n_{\leftarrow}, n_{\mathrm{IL}}, n_{\rightarrow}\}$ and we can discharge the PO in the intermediate model (mainland_out_int/***grd1***/GRD) by adding this lemma to the model as a new guard of event mainland_out_int. Thus, our method achieves a consistent refinement decomposition by slicing and analyzing the original proof.

3.2 Automation with Heuristics

The method in our previous work, which include manual analysis on many proofs, is demanding and difficult. Therefore, we propose an automation of refinement refactoring by constructing the following three functionalities. **Complementary Predicates Generator.** Obtaining CPs is the most difficult and time-consuming part of manual refinement refactoring. Our method uses heuristics and Craig's interpolation (with Z3 [5]) to automate this process. **Proof Finder.** Automatic prover of Rodin cannot discharge all POs of refactored models. Our method finds parts of the original proof that correspond to the proof of refactored models and reuses them. **Merger and Slicer.** We have also developed rule-based automation of merging and slicing.

Those functionalities are implemented as a plug-in of Event-B's development environment[2]. This automation enables us to analyze the effects of refinement strategies on complexity of models and verification (Sect. 4).

Manually finding CPs is significantly difficult and demanding. To manually find a CP for a PO, a developer must find a corresponding PO in the original model, analyze the proof of it, and find hypotheses that are essential to discharge the PO and written in variables of the intermediate model. Repeating this process to find CPs for all POs of large-scale models is demanding. In addition, developers need to repeat a difficult task of deeply understanding the proofs of original models. Therefore, we made this process systematic and automatic.

Predicates sufficient for proofs in the original model can be systematically obtained as interpolants of the formulae of POs. In other words, a formula X that satisfies *hypotheses* $\Rightarrow X \Rightarrow$ *consequence* is enough to derive *consequence*. Thus, if such interpolants can be added to the intermediate model, the model becomes consistent. However, such interpolants cannot always be added to the model because X may use variables that are not in variables of the intermediate model. This is because the set of identifiers of X (an interpolant) is a subset of identifiers used in both of *hypotheses* and *consequence*. For example, mainland_out_con/***grd1***/GRD in M_{CarsC} is as follows:

$$(MLTL = green \wedge n_{\leftarrow} + n_{\mathrm{IL}} + 1 < cap \wedge (MLTL = green \Rightarrow n_{\rightarrow} = 0) \wedge n_{\mathrm{out}} = n_{\leftarrow} + n_{\mathrm{IL}} + n_{\rightarrow}) \Rightarrow n_{\mathrm{out}} < cap. \quad (1)$$

The identifiers common in the hypotheses part and the consequence part are $\{n_{\mathrm{out}}, cap\}$, but n_{out} cannot be used in the intermediate model. Thus, an interpolant of the formula of a PO of the original model cannot always be a CP.

Our method provides heuristics to convert a formula of PO into an equivalent formula such that an interpolant of the converted formula becomes a CP. The heuristic for GRD converts the original formula $I_{\mathrm{A}} \wedge I_{\mathrm{C}} \wedge G_{\mathrm{C}} \Rightarrow g_{\mathrm{A}}$ into:

$$I_{\mathrm{AB}} \wedge \tilde{I}_{\mathrm{C}} \wedge \tilde{G}_{\mathrm{C}} \Rightarrow g_{\mathrm{A}} \vee \neg \tilde{I}_{\mathrm{A}} \vee \neg I_{\mathrm{BC}} \vee \neg G_{\mathrm{BC}}, \quad (2)$$

where $\tilde{I}_{\mathrm{A}}$, $\tilde{I}_{\mathrm{C}}$, and $\tilde{G}_{\mathrm{C}}$ are abstract invariants, concrete invariants, and concrete guards that contain dropped variables, and I_{AB}, I_{BC}, G_{BC} are those that do not contain dropped variables (i.e., they are obtained by slicing). We also defined

[2] https://github.com/trarse-nii/SliceAndMerge.

heuristics for SIM and INV. For example, the heuristic converts (1) into:

$$(MLTL = green \wedge n_{\leftarrow} + n_{\mathrm{IL}} + 1 < cap \wedge (MLTL = green \Rightarrow n_{\rightarrow} = 0)) \\ \Rightarrow (n_{\mathrm{out}} < cap \vee \neg(n_{\mathrm{out}} = n_{\leftarrow} + n_{\mathrm{IL}} + n_{\rightarrow})). \tag{3}$$

The heuristics are designed so that (a) interpolants of converted formulae are always written with identifiers of the intermediate model (i.e., the interpolants can be added to the intermediate model) and (b) adding the interpolants to the intermediate model makes the model consistent. Let V_{A}, V_{B}, and V_{C} be variables of the abstract model, the intermediate model, and the concrete model, respectively. By definitions, variables of $(V_{\mathrm{A}} \backslash V_{\mathrm{B}})$ do not occur in the hypotheses part of (2) and variables of $(V_{\mathrm{C}} \backslash V_{\mathrm{B}})$ do not occur in the consequence part. Thus, the set of variables common in the hypotheses part and the consequence part is guaranteed to be a subset of V_{B}. Therefore, the interpolant can be added to the intermediate model. For instance, predicate $n_{\leftarrow} + n_{\mathrm{IL}} + n_{\rightarrow} + 1 < cap$ can be obtained as an interpolant of (3). In addition, by (2), $X \Rightarrow g_{\mathrm{A}} \vee \neg\tilde{I}_{\mathrm{A}} \vee \neg I_{\mathrm{BC}} \vee \neg G_{\mathrm{BC}}$. By strengthening the hypotheses part of this formula,

$$I_{\mathrm{A}} \wedge I_{\mathrm{B}} \wedge G_{\mathrm{B}} \wedge X \Rightarrow g_{\mathrm{A}} \vee \neg\tilde{I}_{\mathrm{A}} \vee \neg I_{\mathrm{BC}} \vee \neg G_{\mathrm{BC}},$$

where I_{B} and G_{B} are invariants and guards of the intermediate model. Since $I_{\mathrm{A}} \Rightarrow \tilde{I}_{\mathrm{A}}$, $I_{\mathrm{B}} \Rightarrow I_{\mathrm{BC}}$, and $G_{\mathrm{B}} \Rightarrow G_{\mathrm{BC}}$,

$$I_{\mathrm{A}} \wedge I_{\mathrm{B}} \wedge G_{\mathrm{B}} \wedge X \Rightarrow g_{\mathrm{A}}.$$

Thus, by adding X to the corresponding event as a guard, the GRD of the intermediate model becomes dischargeable. Therefore, our tool makes intermediate models consistent by adding interpolants of formulae converted from POs.

The proof finder aims to reuse proofs on the original model. Predicates of a model (invariants, guards, actions, etc.) related to a PO dominate the contents of the generated PO. However, the POs of a refactored model are generated from a mixture of multiple steps of original models because refactoring decomposes after merging of multiple models. Hence, it is not straightforward to find which proof on the original model should be reused to discharge POs of a refactored model. To address this problem, we added traceability information, which shows the predicates of original models used to generate a PO of a refactored model to the refactored model. The proof finder uses this traceability information to find corresponding proof in the original model and follows the same proof tree for proving a PO in the refactored model. Although the proof finder does not work for arbitrary proofs, we did not find any problems in our experiments (Sect. 4). Thus, we automated reusing the proof of an original model for verifying a refactored model by adding traceability.

4 Experiments on Models Constructed with Refactoring

4.1 Evaluation Criteria

We considered that good strategies would effectively mitigate development complexity in Event-B because the primary goal of the Event-B refinement mechanism was to mitigate such complexity. We focused on two kinds of complexities: the complexity of model itself and the complexity of verification.

Local Model Complexity. We checked *the numbers of variables, invariants, and events of each step* to evaluate the complexity of the model of each step. If a step is small, it tends to be easy to understand the step because developers can focus on a small number of elements. Therefore, we considered that the numbers should be *well-distributed over multiple steps* if developers follow a good strategy.

Proof Complexity. We checked *the number of all generated POs and the number of POs that failed to be discharged by automatic provers (manually discharged POs)* to evaluate the proof complexity. The number of manually discharged POs are checked to evaluate actual burden of proving because Rodin has automatic provers, which discharge most of the relatively simple proofs. In addition, we also considered the *local model complexity* informative to evaluate this complexity. If there is a non-dischargeable PO in a model, making modifications to a part of the model affects multiple POs. This is because POs and the contents of Event-B models are interrelated. For instance, if an invariant i needs to be modified, not only preservation of i by all events, but also GRD and SIM of related events should be checked again. Therefore, distributing model contents and POs limits the range of modification propagation, and thus reduces complexity. The number of invariants and events also affects the number of generated POs. Thus, we considered that effective strategies *distribute number of variables, invariants, events, and POs well.*

4.2 Comparison Settings and Hypotheses

As the materials, we used models [2] of a train system [1, Chap. 17] and models of an autonomous satellite flight formation system [12]. Both were constructed by modelers experienced in Event-B.

There are two important characteristics of RSs: *granularity* and *order*. For example, an RS $[\{a, b, c\}]$, which introduces three variables in one step and another RS $[\{a\}, \{b\}, \{c\}]$, which introduces them one-by-one are different in granularity. An RS $[\{a\}, \{b\}, \{c\}]$ and another RS $[\{c\}, \{b\}, \{a\}]$ are different in order of variable introduction. In an experiment we conducted, we compared strategies that differed in granularity and order to check the evaluation criteria.

To examine differences of granularity, we made the following comparisons:

Original vs. Merged. Comparison with a model constructed by merging the original models. For example, when an RC $[M_1, M_2, M_3]$ followed an RS $[\{n_{\mathrm{IL}}\}, \{n_{\leftarrow}, n_{\rightarrow}\}, \{MLTL\}]$, we constructed a model M_{1+2+3} that followed an RS $[\{n_{\mathrm{IL}}, n_{\leftarrow}, n_{\rightarrow}, MLTL\}]$ and compared $[M_1, M_2, M_3]$ and $[M_{1+2+3}]$.

Hypothesis 1: The number of POs of the merged model is less than that of the original models. This is because there is no need of checking consistencies between several steps (e.g., GRD and SIM) in the merged model. This means that decomposition adds several POs but mitigates the local model complexity.

Original vs. Decomposed. Comparing a step of original models and models constructed by decomposing the step of original models. Complementary predicates are generated and added to the model through refinement decomposition, and the complexity is affected by CPs. Therefore, to eliminate the effect of CPs, we compared decomposed models and a model constructed by re-merging the decomposed model. For instance, when the RC $[M_1, M_2, M_3]$ was given, we decomposed M_2 to construct another RC $[M_1, M_{21}, M_{22}, M_3]$ that follows an RS $[\{n_{\mathrm{IL}}\}, \{n_{\leftarrow}\}, \{n_{\rightarrow}\}, \{MLTL\}]$. We then constructed a model M_{2*} by merging M_{21} and M_{22}, and then compared (M_{21}, M_{22}) and M_{2*}. Since there are multiple ways of decompositions, we compared several of them.

Hypothesis 2: Although the sum of the number of invariants may increase due to the introduction of typing invariants[3], invariants are distributed over several steps. This also means decomposition mitigates the local model complexity. *Hypothesis 3:* The number of CPs (new guards and actions) affects the number of POs because GRD and SIM should be checked for them. However, the new GRDs and SIMs are relatively simple because CPs correspond to lemmas of original proof and thus proofs for CPs are simpler than the original proofs. This means that decomposition adds several POs, which are easily discharged by automatic provers. *Hypothesis 4:* The number of POs of the re-merged model is almost the same as that of the original model. This is because CPs are introduced as guards and actions, which do not affect the number of INVs. This means that the comparison of original models and re-merged models is fair.

To examine differences of order, we made the following comparisons:

Swapping Two Steps. Comparison with models constructed by swapping two continuous steps in the original strategy. By the same reason as Original vs. Decomposed, we used models constructed by swapping twice instead of the original models. For example, when the RC $[M_1, M_2, M_3]$ was given, we constructed another RC $[M_{S121}, M_{S122}, M_3]$ that follows an RS $[\{n_{\leftarrow}, n_{\rightarrow}\}, \{n_{\mathrm{IL}}\}, \{MLTL\}]$. We then re-swapped them to construct another RC $[M_{SS121}, M_{SS122}, M_3]$ that follows an RS $[\{n_{\mathrm{IL}}\}, \{n_{\leftarrow}, n_{\rightarrow}\}, \{MLTL\}]$, and then compared $[M_{S121}, M_{S122}, M_3]$ and $[M_{SS121}, M_{SS122}, M_3]$. We calculated standard deviation of the number of POs to compare distributions of them.

Hypothesis 5: Swapping may change the distribution of number of invariants and POs. This is because some variables are frequently used in invariants and others are rarely used. For instance, let us assume that we are going to construct models with variables $\{a, b\}$ and invariants $\{f(a), g(a, b)\}$. If we construct models by following $[\{a\}, \{b\}]$, we can distribute the invariants because $f(a)$ is introduced in the first step and $g(a, b)$ is introduced in the second step. In contrast, if we construct models by following $[\{b\}, \{a\}]$, both f and g are introduced in the second step because both depend on a. The sum of number of invariants may slightly increase due to the introduction of typing invariants. This means that orders of RSs are important.

---

[3] Rodin requires variables' typing information. Although typing information is usually inferred from normal invariants, slicing may remove such invariants. In this case, invariants of typing information (e.g., $MLTL \in COLOR$) must be newly provided.

Table 1. Merging and decomposing of results obtained for Train example.

Models	ΔV	I	ΣI	E	CP	PO	ΣPO	MPO	ΣMPO	Auto%
Tr	4, 3, 1, 1	8, 9, 3, 4	24	6,8,8,8	-	35, 63, 16, 13	127	7, 18, 6, 5	36	72%
TrM	9	24	24	8	-	110	110	32	32	71%
Tr1	4	8	8	6	-	35	35	7	7	80%
Tr1DA	1, 1, 1, 1	1, 2, 4, 5	12	3, 4, 4, 6	0, 0, 1, 0	0, 0, 13, 25	38	0, 0, 2, 5	7	82%
Tr1DMA	4	12	12	6	1	35	35	7	7	80%
Tr1DB	1, 1, 1, 1	1, 4, 3, 4	12	4, 5, 5, 6	1, 7, 1, 0	2, 26, 7, 17	52	0, 6, 1, 0	7	87%
Tr1DMB	4	12	12	6	9	36	36	8	8	78%

Reversing Multiple Steps. Comparison with models constructed by reversing steps in the original strategy. Again, we used models constructed by reversing twice instead of the original models. For instance, when the RC $[M_1, M_2, M_3]$ was given, we constructed another RC $[M_{R1}, M_{R2}, M_{R3}]$ that follows an RS $[\{MLTL\}, \{n_{\leftarrow}, n_{\rightarrow}\}, \{n_{\mathrm{IL}}\}]$. We then did reversing again to construct another RC $[M_{RR1}, M_{RR2}, M_{RR3}]$ that follows an RS $[\{n_{\mathrm{IL}}\}, \{n_{\leftarrow}, n_{\rightarrow}\}, \{MLTL\}]$, and then compared $[M_{R1}, M_{R2}, M_{R3}]$ and $[M_{RR1}, M_{RR2}, M_{RR3}]$. The hypothesis is the same as that of swapping.

4.3 Results

Due to space limitations, we omitted the results on Flight Formation Systems models, which tend to be similar to those for the Train example. The Train model and additional information are available on the Web[4].

With our automated refactoring tool, we succeeded in constructing all models and discharging all POs. This means our tool generated correct CPs. Combined with the SMT solvers plug-in of Rodin, our proof finder discharged all POs. Therefore, we conclude that our tool is appropriate for this experiment.

Table 1 shows the experiment results we obtained on granularity. Each row lists the numbers of a set of models (i.e., an RS). For example, in the original Train example (the first row "Tr"), there are four steps that introduce 4, 3, 1, and 1 variables (ΔV). Each step has 8, 9, 3, and 4 invariants (I), 24 invariants in total (ΣI). E shows events in each step, CP shows the numbers of CPs introduced in each step, PO shows the number of all POs, MPO shows manually discharged POs, and Auto% shows the rate of automatically discharged POs.

Row 2 (TrM) in Table 1 shows the results obtained for the merged model. Columns ΔV, I, and E show that TrM introduces things introduced through four steps in the original machines in one-shot. ΣPO shows that the number of POs decreased from 127 to 110 through merging. This result supports Hypothesis 1.

Rows 3–7 (Tr1*) in Table 1 show the results obtained on decomposition of the first step of the original model (the numbers are those of the first step of Tr). The first step of Tr introduces four variables: $resrt, resbl, rsrtbl$, and OCC. Row 4 (Tr1DA) shows the results obtained for a decomposed strategy that introduces $resrt$, $resbl$, $rsrtbl$, and OCC one-by-one. Row 6 (Tr1DB) shows the results

[4] http://tkoba.jp/publications/icfem2018/.

Table 2. Results obtained in swapping and reversing the Train example.

Models	ΔV	I	ΣI	E	CP	PO	σ_{PO}	MPO	σ_{MPO}	Auto%
Tr	4, 3, 1, 1	8, 9, 3, 4	24	6, 8, 8, 8	-	35, 63, 16, 13	19.9	7, 18, 6, 5	5.2	72%
TrS12	3, 4, 1, 1	4, 15, 3, 4	26	6, 8, 8, 8	0, 0, 0, 0	8, 85, 33, 13	30.5	1, 23, 9, 5	8.3	73%
TrSS12	4, 3, 1, 1	8, 13, 3, 4	28	6, 8, 8, 8	0, 0, 0, 0	36, 53, 33, 13	14.2	7, 16, 9, 5	4.1	71%
TrS23	4, 1, 3, 1	8, 2, 10, 4	24	6, 7, 8, 8	0, 5, 0, 0	35, 25, 61, 15	17.1	7, 6, 19, 6	5.5	72%
TrSS23	4, 3, 1, 1	8, 9, 3, 4	24	6, 8, 8, 8	0, 9, 0, 0	35, 65, 16, 23	18.7	7, 16, 5, 10	4.2	73%
TrS34	4, 3, 1, 1	8, 9, 1, 6	24	6, 8, 8, 8	0, 0, 4, 0	28, 45, 5, 19	20.0	7, 18, 2, 10	5.8	72%
TrSS34	4, 3, 1, 1	8, 9, 2, 6	25	6, 8, 8, 8	0, 0, 4, 0	35, 63, 7, 25	20.3	7, 18, 2, 9	5.8	72%
TrR	1, 1, 3, 4	1, 3, 6, 17	27	2, 2, 7, 8	0, 0, 1, 0	2, 7, 13, 94	37.7	0, 2, 2, 28	11.6	72%
TrRR	4, 3, 1, 1	8, 11, 5, 3	27	7, 8, 8, 8	0, 0, 1, 0	36, 49, 19, 6	16.3	9, 15, 5, 2	4.9	72%

obtained for another decomposed strategy that introduces $OCC, rsrtbl, resbl$, and $resrt$ one-by-one (i.e. in the reversed order of Tr1DA). Rows 5 and 7 (Tr1DMA and Tr1DMB) show the results obtained for a strategy constructed by merging the four steps of Tr1DA and Tr1DB, respectively.

By comparing Tr1 and others, we see no difference in the total numbers of variables and events, but an increasing number of invariants. From ΣPO, we see no significant difference from Tr1 except for Tr1DB. This is because 9 CPs (as guards) and related POs were generated by following the RS of Tr1DB ($[\{OCC\}, \{rsrtbl\}, \{resbl\}, \{resrt\}]$). As column MPO shows, these new POs were simple enough for automatic provers to discharge. We can see that we succeeded in distributing variables, invariants, and POs over several steps by decomposition. Therefore, we consider that the results support Hypotheses 2–4.

Table 2 shows the experiment results on the order in which variables are introduced. In this table, standard deviations of PO and MPO (σ_{PO} and σ_{MPO}) are shown. Row 1 (Tr) shows the results obtained with the original strategy. Rows 2–3, 4–5, 6–7 (TrSn(n + 1), TrSSn(n + 1)) show the results obtained by swapping steps 1–2, 2–3, and 3–4, respectively. Rows 8–9 (TrR, TrRR) show the results obtained by reversing. ΔV of the swapped or reversed models' strategy are simply swapped or reversed numbers of ΔV of Tr.

We see no significant differences in ΣI. It is interesting that there are steps with a large number of invariants in TrS12 (second step) and TrR (fourth step). Both of them introduce four variables introduced in the first step of the original strategy ($\{resrt, resbl, rsrtbl, OCC\}$). This is because those variables are frequently used in the invariants. It is also found that the steps with a large number of invariants (the second step of TrS12 and the fourth step of TrR) have a large number of POs (PO and MPO), and result in high standard deviations of those strategies. Thus, we consider that the result supports Hypothesis 5.

Summary. (1) Strategies with more steps have more POs in total but distribute POs well, especially if strategies are carefully chosen taking dependence into consideration. This is preferable as discussed in Sect. 4.1. (2) Due to the dependence of invariants on variables, the order in which variables are introduced affects variance of invariants and POs. In general, important variables that are written in many invariants should be introduced in early steps.

5 Discussion

5.1 Effects of Refactoring to POs

Refactoring adds several POs to the original models and also removes several POs from the original models. Generating CPs by refinement decomposition results in the generation of new POs related to the CPs. However, as CPs can be seen as lemmas, the generation of CPs helps automatic provers to discharge difficult POs. In addition, as we saw in Sect. 4.3, refinement merging removes several GRDs and SIMs.

Although changing the order of a strategy (such as swapping and reversing) involves slicing and generation of CPs, several POs are removed through it. In fact, TrR (reversed) has 116 POs but Tr (original) has 127 POs. We found that several POs about consistency between two models (such as GRD and SIM) are removed through the changing order. This is because concrete and strong guards (which were originally introduced in later steps) are introduced in early steps after changing order, and thus there is no need to strengthen them in later steps.

5.2 Dependence of Invariants on Variables

As we saw in experiments on the order of refinement strategies, dependence of invariants on variables is important for detailed analyses on complexity mitigation with refinement. The dependence is obviously problem specific. Thus, changing the order of strategy will not have much effect if the dependence is not strong.

The dependence also strongly affects whether an invariant is dropped in slicing (i.e., whether CP is generated). To analyze this, not only variables in an invariant but also the structure of the invariant is important. For example, an invariant **inv1:** $f \in a \rightarrow b$, which means that "f is a total function from a to b", limits the value of f. Although variables a and b appear in **inv1**, the values of them are not limited by **inv1**. Therefore, **inv1** can be a hypothesis in a proof related to f but it cannot be a hypothesis in a proof related to a or b. Because CP is generated by a lack of hypothesis in a proof, we need to consider whether the value of a variable is limited by an invariant.

Our future work will include detailed analyses on refactoring while taking dependence into consideration.

5.3 Use of Automated Refactoring in Development

We also consider that search for a good refinement strategy is important in development process. Automated refinement refactoring can be used to search for a desirable strategy to improve flexibility against change and actually refactor models. However, CPs generated by the current method are sometimes redundant or non-human-friendly. Therefore, we are planning to improve our CP generator so that it will not only generate correctly but also be easy to understand. Possible approaches include applying metrics of formula understandability and a method to generate simple interpolants [3].

5.4 Threats to Validity

Internal Validity Threats. Our analyses rely on artificial data constructed with our method. Thus the method, in particular the CPs it generates, may have affected the obtained results. However, we carefully designed the experiment to eliminate the effect of CPs (such as double-reversing). We also discussed how refactoring would affect POs (Sect. 5.1). Therefore, although user studies for further analyses are included in our future direction, we conclude that the analyses given in this paper are valid.

Additionally, from the experiment results obtained on changing the order of the refinement strategy, we concluded that introducing important variables in early steps is effective in reducing complexity. Although this claim seems natural, the complexity increased by refactoring in every case we examined. In other words, we didn't see any mitigation of complexity with refactoring. This is because the original models were constructed by experienced modelers in an ideal order (i.e., important variables were introduced in early steps). Therefore, we are planning to use models in which variables were introduced in a bad order to confirm the method's validity.

External Validity Threats. In terms of generalization, there may be a concern about the variations and practicality of the materials we used in the experiments. For variations, we believe our findings about granularity and order are general enough and not domain-specific. In terms of practicality, in fact, the models were constructed by experienced modelers. Although we believe the models are appropriate for examining our general findings, analyses on models constructed by inexperienced modelers would be an interesting subject for future work.

Construct Validity Threats. For the sake of simplicity, we used local model complexity and proof complexity as evaluation criteria. However, we were aware that strategies that have atomic steps (e.g., those that introduce only one variable in one step) are not optimal. Too much decomposition of refinement often causes models that lack conceptual integrity and have many meaningless POs. Thus, although our findings show that decomposing refinement steps tend to be effective, we will also consider costs of long refinement chains in our future work.

6 Related Work

There have been studies to connect Event-B models with other modeling methods and requirement analysis methods, such as UML [10] and KAOS [8]. Because such modeling methods are widely used, there have been analyses that studied the design of such models, such as decomposition into components and refinement in KAOS. In particular, in the area of object-oriented design, such studies [11] have been very active. However, by connecting Event-B models and other modeling methods and analyze models in other notations, the expressiveness of model is limited to that of other modeling notations. More importantly, analysis methods do not consider proof obligations, which need to be considered for formal refinement. Therefore, Event-B's flexible and rigorous formalism cannot be handled with such methods.

There have been case studies of Event-B modeling by experts [1,4]. The study in [4] is particularly interesting because multiple researchers have constructed different Event-B models for the same subject problem. Their models are sophisticated and good learning materials for other developers. However, they do not explain why the strategies they used are better than other possible strategies. There are also guidelines of Event-B modeling for subjects of a particular domain [13]. Although their guides are detailed, they are domain-specific and not applicable to other areas. It will be interesting to analyze more subjects of their models with our method because they are good examples of experts' models.

Our previous work [6] proposed evaluation criteria of refinement strategy based on the number of variables, and a planning method to distribute introduction of variables as much as possible. However, it is not applicable in realistic situation because the planner requires a list of invariants and variables before constructing models. In addition, the planning method is conceptual, and cannot handle details of model and POs, which are necessary in empirical analyses.

Our approach in this paper establishes a method to construct a consistent models and analyze them by automating our refactoring method. By using the automatic refactoring, we succeeded in comparing and discussing refinement strategies, considering predicates and POs by using actual Event-B models. As a result, general and domain-independent findings about refinement strategies were obtained. Our method also enables developers to search the design space of Event-B models constructed in development.

7 Conclusion and Future Work

Our goal was exploration and analysis on the design space of Event-B's flexible superposition refinement, which have never studied in the formal methods area. To this end, we provided an automatic method to construct a consistent refactored model from given models according to given refinement strategies. We defined heuristics and applied Craig's interpolation to generate predicates to resolve inconsistencies occurring through the changing of a refinement strategy. As this enabled us to flexibly change the refinement strategy of a given model, we conducted an experiment in which we compared models constructed by following various refinement strategies from the viewpoint of complexity. As a result, we found that doing fine-grained refinement and introducing frequently used variables to the model earlier are effective to reduce complexity of modeling and verification of each step. In addition, we discussed the effects that refactoring would have on complexity and dependence between predicates and variables. We conclude that our method and experiments will benefit Event-B modelers designing refinement strategies.

Our future work will primarily proceed in two directions. The first will be to analyze the relationship between dependence and refinement strategies to make our design space exploration more sophisticated. The second will be to conduct user studies and compare the result with that of our experiment to check the validity.

References

1. Abrial, J.R.: Modeling in Event-B: System and Software Engineering. Cambridge University Press, Cambridge (2010)
2. Abrial, J.-R.: Train system. http://deploy-eprints.ecs.soton.ac.uk/124/
3. Albarghouthi, A., McMillan, K.L.: Beautiful interpolants. In: Sharygina, N., Veith, H. (eds.) CAV 2013. LNCS, vol. 8044, pp. 313–329. Springer, Heidelberg (2013). https://doi.org/10.1007/978-3-642-39799-8_22
4. Boniol, F., Wiels, V.: The landing gear system case study. In: Boniol, F., Wiels, V., Ait Ameur, Y., Schewe, K.-D. (eds.) ABZ 2014. CCIS, vol. 433, pp. 1–18. Springer, Cham (2014). https://doi.org/10.1007/978-3-319-07512-9_1
5. de Moura, L., Bjørner, N.: Z3: an efficient SMT solver. In: Ramakrishnan, C.R., Rehof, J. (eds.) TACAS 2008. LNCS, vol. 4963, pp. 337–340. Springer, Heidelberg (2008). https://doi.org/10.1007/978-3-540-78800-3_24
6. Kobayashi, T., Ishikawa, F., Honiden, S.: Understanding and planning Event-B refinement through primitive rationales. In: Ait Ameur, Y., Schewe, K.D. (eds.) Abstract State Machines, Alloy, B, TLA, VDM, and Z. LNCS, vol. 8477, pp. 277–283. Springer, Heidelberg (2014). https://doi.org/10.1007/978-3-662-43652-3_24
7. Kobayashi, T., Ishikawa, F., Honiden, S.: Refactoring refinement structure of Event-B machines. In: Fitzgerald, J., Heitmeyer, C., Gnesi, S., Philippou, A. (eds.) FM 2016. LNCS, vol. 9995, pp. 444–459. Springer, Cham (2016). https://doi.org/10.1007/978-3-319-48989-6_27
8. Matoussi, A., Gervais, F., Laleau, R.: A goal-based approach to guide the design of an abstract Event-B specification. In: 16th IEEE International Conference on Engineering of Complex Computer Systems (ICECCS), pp. 139–148. IEEE (2011)
9. Requet, A.: BART: a tool for automatic refinement. In: Börger, E., Butler, M., Bowen, J.P., Boca, P. (eds.) ABZ 2008. LNCS, vol. 5238, pp. 345–345. Springer, Heidelberg (2008). https://doi.org/10.1007/978-3-540-87603-8_33
10. Said, M.Y., Butler, M., Snook, C.: Language and tool support for class and state machine refinement in UML-B. In: Cavalcanti, A., Dams, D.R. (eds.) FM 2009. LNCS, vol. 5850, pp. 579–595. Springer, Heidelberg (2009). https://doi.org/10.1007/978-3-642-05089-3_37
11. Subramanyam, R., Krishnan, M.S.: Empirical analysis of CK metrics for object-oriented design complexity: implications for software defects. IEEE Trans. Softw. Eng. **29**(4), 297–310 (2003)
12. Tarasyuk, A., Pereverzeva, I., Troubitsyna, E., Latvala, T.: The formal derivation of mode logic for autonomous satellite flight formation. In: Koornneef, F., van Gulijk, C. (eds.) SAFECOMP 2015. LNCS, vol. 9337, pp. 29–43. Springer, Cham (2015). https://doi.org/10.1007/978-3-319-24255-2_4
13. Yeganefard, S., Butler, M., Rezazadeh, A.: Evaluation of a guideline by formal modelling of cruise control system in Event-B. In: Proceedings of the Second NASA Formal Methods Symposium (NFM 2010), pp. 182–191. NASA, April 2010

Formalising Extended Finite State Machine Transition Merging

Michael Foster([✉]), Ramsay G. Taylor, Achim D. Brucker, and John Derrick

Department of Computer Science, The University of Sheffield, Regent Court, Sheffield S1 4DP, UK
{jmafoster1,r.g.taylor,a.brucker,j.derrick}@sheffield.ac.uk

Abstract. Model inference from system traces, e.g. for analysing legacy components or generating security tests for distributed components, is a common problem. *Extended Finite State Machine* (EFSM) models, managing an internal data state as a set of registers, are particularly well suited for capturing the behaviour of *stateful* components however existing inference techniques for (E)FSMs lack the ability to infer the internal state and its update functions.

In this paper, we present the underpinning formalism for an EFSM inference technique that involves the merging of transitions with updates to the internal data state. Our model is formalised in Isabelle/HOL, allowing for the machine-checked validation of transition merges and system properties.

Keywords: Model inference · State machine models · EFSM

1 Introduction

Accurate behavioural models of software systems are very valuable for development and maintenance. They are particularly useful during the testing phase where they have acted as oracles for regression testing [9] and can be used to automatically generate tests [10]. Such models are also useful in requirements engineering [5], aiding the understanding of systems.

Despite their value, models are often neglected during development. It is therefore useful to *reverse engineer* them from existing systems. There is substantial work on reverse engineering Finite State Machine (FSM) models from observations of systems including [11,13,18,20]. Most modern inference approaches begin by building a Prefix Tree Acceptor (PTA) [18], a tree-shaped automaton accepting exactly the traces observed. States and transitions are then merged where they are thought to represent the same system component.

The models produced by classical FSM inference struggle with complex systems, especially those exhibiting behaviour dependant on an internal state. Extended Finite State Machine (EFSM) inference is a promising solution to this problem. EFSM models extend traditional FSMs by providing control flow

J. Sun and M. Sun (Eds.): ICFEM 2018, LNCS 11232, pp. 373–387, 2018.
https://doi.org/10.1007/978-3-030-02450-5_22

decisions based on input values as well as persistent data storage [17]. Current EFSM inference approaches [15,19] tend to focus on guard expressions – functions that make control flow decisions based on input or data-state values – but overlook how individual transitions mutate the data state. The inference of data update functions is a key technical challenge in EFSM inference but significantly complicates the merging process.

The primary contributions of this work are as follows:

1. A formal process by which EFSM transitions with update functions may be merged.
2. The introduction of *contexts*, a scheme by which constraints on data values may be traced through EFSMs.
3. The use of contexts to prove properties and equivalence of EFSM models.

The rest of the paper is structured as follows: After a brief motivating example, Sect. 2 fixes our definition of EFSMs. Our formalism for merging EFSM transitions with update functions is introduced in Sect. 3, as is the concept of contexts. Section 4 discusses transition subsumption and how it is used in the merging process. Section 5 shows how contexts may be used to analyse properties of EFSM models. Finally, Sect. 6 concludes the paper, discussing related and future work.

1.1 Motivating Example

The inference process starts with a black-box system and observes its behaviour when presented with different inputs. From these observations, a model can be produced which reflects the observed behaviour. For example, consider a simple vending machine whose traces are exemplified in Fig. 1.

In the *actual system* the *select* operation takes one parameter: the desired drink. The *coin* operation allows the user to insert coins to pay for their drink. The output of each *coin* operation is the total amount inserted so far. Once the value reaches 100, the *vend* operation triggers the drink to be dispensed. Pressing *vend* when the total coinage inserted is less than 100 yields no output.

$$select(coke) \rightarrow coin(50)/[50] \rightarrow coin(50)/[100] \rightarrow vend()/[coke]$$
$$select(coke) \rightarrow coin(100)/[100] \rightarrow vend()/[coke]$$
$$select(pepsi) \rightarrow coin(50)/[50] \rightarrow vend() \rightarrow coin(50)/[100] \rightarrow vend()/[pepsi]$$

Fig. 1. Some observed traces of a drinks machine in which an event has the format *label*(*arguments*)/[*outputs*]. The output component is omitted if none is produced.

FSM inference processes use traces to construct a candidate model. This is done by constructing an initial PTA and iteratively merging states and transitions until an FSM model of the system similar to the one in Fig. 2 is obtained.

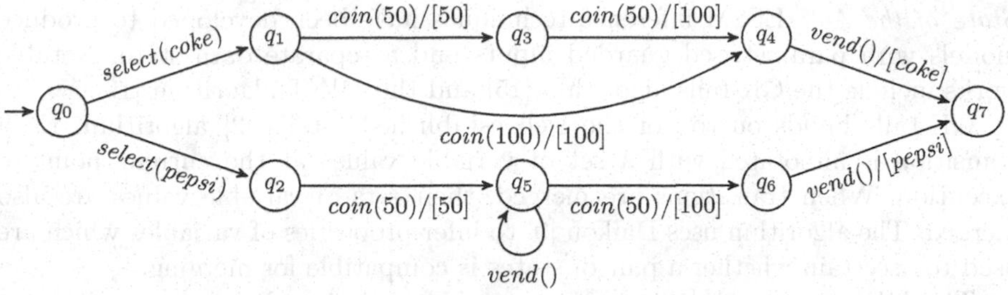

Fig. 2. A classical FSM model reflecting the traces in Fig. 1

The Problem with FSM Inference: Classical FSM inference processes produce models of the system like the one in Fig. 2. Note that transition labels are atomic so, for example, the *select(coke)* transition does not represent an event with label *select* and input *coke*, rather the transition is labelled by the literal string "select(coke)" making it a completely separate entity from the transition "select(pepsi)". This is a major problem as it means that information such as the selected drink and accrued funds must be encoded as part of the control state. Increasing product choice or the coins accepted quickly causes an explosion in model size disproportionate to the change in observable behaviour.

EFSM Inference: The FSM in Fig. 2 looks promising but is flawed because of its atomic labels. It is preferable to generate an EFSM model such as the one in Fig. 3. Here, the selected drink is stored in a register r_1 for later use in the output of the *vend* transition. A second register r_2 (initialised with 0 by the *select* transaction) keeps track of the money inserted so far. Drinks are only dispensed once this value reaches 100. This enables customers to pay for their drink with any coin in any order. This is a much more concise and faithful model of the real system.

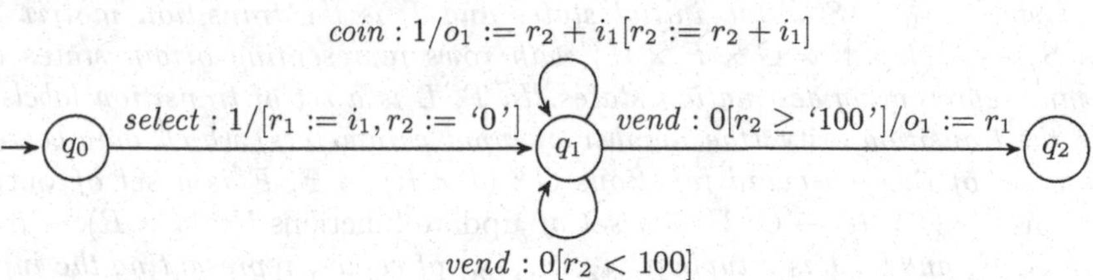

Fig. 3. An EFSM model of the simple vending machine in which transitions have the general form *label* : *arity*[*guards*]/*outputs*[*updates*]. Where a particular transition lacks guards, outputs, or updates, the relevant components are omitted.

State of the Art: EFSM inference techniques have been developed to produce models with parametrised guarded inputs and a separate data state. Notable works include the GK-tails algorithm [15] and the MINT algorithm [19].

GK-tails builds on top of the well established k-tails [2] algorithm. Each transition is annotated with a set of variable values at the current point of execution. When transitions are merged, their sets of variable values are also merged. The algorithm uses Daikon [9] to infer properties of variables which are used to ascertain whether a pair of states is compatible for merging.

The MINT approach [19] also has strong foundations but uses classifiers to determine, based on current data values, the labels of subsequent events. A key difference to GK-tails is that here data values are globally accessible so the classifiers have more data to work with. Classifiers are used not only to determine the validity of transition merges, but to detect and resolve nondeterminism.

While these techniques are valuable contributions and perform well for certain tasks, both fall short in that they fail to capture *how* data values are changed by individual transitions and are therefore unable to generate the EFSM in Fig. 3. Including data update functions as part of each transition significantly complicates the process of transition merging. This work presents a method of comparing two transitions to assess their compatibility for merging. The actual inference process is the intended subject of future work.

2 Extended Finite State Machines

To define our method, we first need to fix the format of our EFSM model. Various EFSM models are presented in the literature [4,14] as well as similar ideas under different names [3,8]. Since the aim is to automatically infer data update functions, our model affords them a more detailed treatment, combining desirable aspects of various existing models. As with classical FSM models, EFSMs are usually presented graphically like in Fig. 3.

Definition 1. *An EFSM is a tuple, (S, s_0, T) where S is a finite non-empty set of states, $s_0 \in S$ is the initial state, and T is the transition matrix $T : (S \times S) \rightarrow \mathcal{P}(L \times \mathbb{N} \times G \times F \times U)$ with rows representing origin states and columns representing destination states. In T, L is a set of transition labels. $\mathbb{N}$ gives the transition* arity *(the number of input parameters) which may be zero. G is a set of Boolean guard functions $G : (I \times R) \rightarrow \mathbb{B}$. F is a set of* output functions *$F : (I \times R) \rightarrow O$. U is a set of* update functions *$U : (I \times R) \rightarrow R$.*

In G, F, and U, I is a tuple $[i_1, i_2, \ldots, i_m]$ of values, representing the inputs of a transition which is empty if the arity is zero. Inputs do not persist across states or transitions. R is a mapping from variables $[r_1, r_2, \ldots]$, representing each register of the machine, to their values. Registers are globally accessible and persist throughout the operation of the machine. All registers are initially undefined until explicitly set by an update expression. O is a tuple $[o_1, o_2, \ldots, o_n]$ of values, which may be empty, representing the outputs of a transition.

A little syntactic sugar allows an EFSM transition from anterior state S_m to posterior state S_n to take the general form

$$S_m \xrightarrow{label:arity[g_1,\ldots,g_n]/f_1,\ldots,f_n[u_1,\ldots,u_n]} S_n$$

The first part of the transition is an atomic *label* which is the name of the event. This is followed by a colon and the *arity* of the transition, a natural number indicating the number of input parameters taken. Guard expressions g_1 to g_n are enclosed in square brackets. Next comes a slash, after which expressions f_1 to f_n define the outputs. Finally, update expressions u_1 to u_n, enclosed in square brackets, define the posterior data state. There should be at most one update function per register per transition in order to maintain consistency. For transitions without guards, outputs, or updates, the corresponding components are omitted.

Guard expressions take the current data state and a tuple of inputs and are *satisfied* if the specified conditions are met. If this is the case, the EFSM is said to have *accepted* the input. A transition cannot be taken if its guard is not satisfied. Guards operate over literals, inputs, and registers, the latter two collectively being referred to as "variables". Literals are enclosed in single quotes in order to distinguish them from variable names. Numeric values are assumed to be parsed automatically when required. Absence of a guard corresponds to the literal guard *true* which accepts any input with any data state.

Functions to compute the outputs and updates use expressions over literals and variables evaluated from the *anterior data state*. Assignment syntax $\_ := \_$ is used to identify the value being computed. As with guards, literal values are enclosed in single quotes and numeric values are parsed automatically. Registers not explicitly updated by a transition remain unchanged and are initially undefined, so cannot be used before they have been assigned.

3 A Formalism for Merging EFSM Transitions

During the inference process, a PTA is generated containing fragments such as in Fig. 4a. States with similar outgoing transitions are then merged to create a more concise model. This will likely introduce nondeterminism to the model, which can be resolved by merging the destination states of offending transitions and then the transitions themselves, arriving at something like the fragment shown in Fig. 4b. This section describes a method for merging EFSM transitions, introducing the concept of *contexts* as a record of constraints on the possible values of variables and expressions.

3.1 Method Overview

Our method uses the idea of subsumption (adapted from [15]) together with *contexts*, our scheme for recording constraints on the data state of EFSMs. The method of merging transitions with identical origin and destination states can be

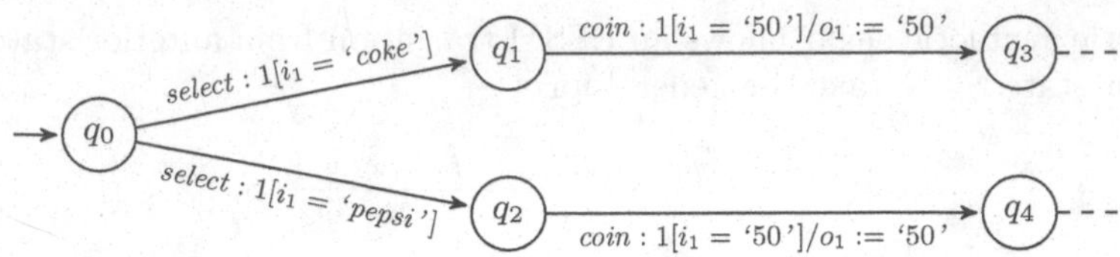

(a) A fragment of the PTA built from the traces in Figure 1

q_0 $\xrightarrow{select : 1/[r_1 := i_1]}$ $q_{\{1,2\}}$ $\xrightarrow{coin : 1[i_1 = \text{‘50’}]/o_1 := \text{‘50’}}$ $q_{\{3,4\}}$

(b) After merging state q_1 with q_2. The resulting nondeterminism is resolved by merging q_3 with q_4 and then merging the *coin* transitions.

Fig. 4. An EFSM model fragment before and after merging states and transitions

roughly described as follows. Firstly, the transitions must have the same label and arity, otherwise they represent different behaviours and cannot be merged. Next, the guard of one transition should be implied by that of the other. In this way, one transition accepts a subset of inputs of the other. In cases where both transitions may be taken, their output should be identical otherwise there is an observable difference between the transitions and they cannot be merged. Additionally, the data updates performed by the two transitions should be consistent with each other such that the output of subsequent transitions is not affected by the merge. If these conditions are met, the transition with the more specific guard is said to be an *instance* of the one with the more general guard. It can therefore be trivially deleted without affecting the observable behaviour of the model.

To implement this method, we need to define a way to determine when transitions are merged. Subsumption allows us to do this but it is necessary to introduce the idea of contexts to relate the internal data state of the system to observable output values of transitions.

3.2 Contexts

One may be tempted to use observational equivalence when merging transitions since two transitions exhibiting the same observable behaviour can be thought of as equivalent. Two transitions are *observationally equivalent* if, when presented with the same input, they produce the same output. The transitions may make different updates to the data state but register values are not directly observable so the difference is hidden. Since registers may be used as part of the output of subsequent transitions, the use of observational equivalence on a per-transition basis is likely to cause an observable difference at a later point in model execution. While observational equivalence must certainly be maintained, it is not a strong enough criterion for transition merging.

A stronger test would be *trace equivalence.* Trace equivalence extends observational equivalence to a sequence of inputs. If two EFSMs produce identical output sequences for all given sequences of inputs, they are trace equivalent. Since more than one transition is considered, differences in update functions may manifest themselves if affected register values are used in subsequent output. The problem is that trace equivalence is only in terms of concrete traces so is not conducive to the *generalisation* of transitions.

What needs to be used is *contextual equivalence.* This relates possible register values to observable output and is a generalisation of trace equivalence. Consider the transitions $vend : 0/o_1 := \text{'coke'}$ and $vend : 0/o_1 := r_1$. At first glance, the two transitions look quite different, but there is a circumstance where they are observationally equivalent: when r_1 holds the value *'coke'*. In this *context*, there is no observable difference between the two transitions.

In our EFSM inference method, transitions have three contexts during their evaluation. The exact values of registers may not always be known but guard and update expressions allow certain constraints to be inferred. If a transition is taken then its guard must have been satisfied. A transition with guard $i_1 = 50$ may only be taken when i_1 holds the value fifty. If an update expression then assigns the value of i_1 to a register, it is now known that the value of that register is fifty. Similarly, if the value of a register is known to be greater than five before a transition is taken and an update function increments it by five then it is now known that the value of that register must be greater than ten.

Definition 2. *A* context *is a mapping from expressions in terms of inputs and registers to constraints on their values.*

The exact typing is dependent on the types of the inputs and registers. For integers, a context is a mapping from operations on integers (addition, multiplication, etc.) to constraints such as less than, greater than, and equality. When working with lists, contexts map operations such as concatenation, length, and folding to appropriate constraints.

Contexts are written as maps enclosed in double square brackets and use "curried" notation to record constraints on the values of expressions. For example $[\![r_1 + i_1 \mapsto = 6]\!]$ represents the context where the value of $r_1 + i_1$ is equal to six. The key is "$r_1 + i_1$" and the constraint is "$= 6$". This corresponds to the guard $r_1 + i_1 = 6$. Most constraints can be viewed as guards, the exceptions being the literals *true* and *false* which represent unrestrictedness and inconsistency respectively.

Uninitialised register values map to a special "undefined" constraint. This constraint is not satisfiable as it is impossible to access a register without a value, but cannot lead to inconsistent reasoning, since unassigned registers cannot be used in computation. This is not the same as having an explicitly unrestricted register which has been assigned a value about which nothing is known. Inputs which are not explicitly constrained map to literal *true* since nothing about their value is known but if presented, they are known to have a value.

A transition t will have three contexts during its evaluation. The *anterior context*, $A(t)$, is the set of constraints which is known before the transition is taken. This context contains only expressions concerned with registers since the transition has not yet received any input. The *medial context*, $M(t)$, is the set of constraints immediately after the guard has been applied. This includes constraints on input values as these are currently in scope. The *posterior context*, $P(t)$, is the set of constraints after the update function has been executed. This does not include constraints on inputs since they do not persist. This context forms the anterior context for the next transition. In this way, contexts flow through an EFSM tracing constraints on register values.

Constraints do not relate variables. The reason for this is best illustrated with an example. If r_1 is known to be greater than i_1 for a particular transition, but nothing is known about the value of i_1 then nothing meaningful is known about r_1 either. To say that it is greater than an unknown value is meaningless since there is always a possible valuation of the pair such that the property holds. Only when something more concrete about one of the two variables is known can this constraint be of use.

3.3 Computing Contexts

Algorithm 1 describes how to compute the posterior context of a transition. Line 2 applies the guards of the transition to the anterior context to form the medial context. If the medial context is consistent, the update functions can be applied, looking up constraints from the medial context as necessary. Any constraints on expressions involving input values are then removed. To say that a context is consistent is to say that all of the constraints are satisfiable simultaneously. An inconsistent medial context means that the guard was not satisfied and the transition cannot be taken with the given anterior context.

Algorithm 1. Computing the posterior context

```
1: function POSTERIOR(Transition t, AnteriorContext c)
2:     c' ← MEDIAL(c, t.guards)
3:     if CONSISTENT(c') then
4:         return APPLYUPDATES(c', t.updates)
5:     else
6:         return FALSE
7:     end if
8: end function
```

A key step when building the medial context is the rearrangement of expressions. If a guard states that r_1 must be greater than i_1 then it is also the case that i_1 is less than r_1. Both must be added to the context at this stage as the constraint affects both variables. Similarly, if it is known that $r_1 = i_1 + r_2$ then it is also known that $i_1 = r_1 - r_2$ and that $r_2 = r_1 - i_1$. If constraints on two of the variables are known then constraints on the third can be calculated.

4 Subsumption and Generalisation

In this section we use contexts to solve the problem of merging transitions in EFSMs. The inference process begins by observing the outputs of a system when presented with particular inputs. An initial PTA is constructed to reflect this behaviour and states are iteratively merged to create a more concise and general model of the system.

States with similar outgoing transitions, such as q_1 and q_2 in Fig. 4a, are good candidates for merging but the resulting model is often nondeterministic. This can be resolved by merging subsequent states and transitions, however this requires some notion of transition equality and generalisation. The idea of subsumption presented in [15] deals nicely with guards but does not consider data update functions. With the help of a running example, this section uses contexts to extend the idea of subsumption to output and update functions, ensuring that observational equivalence is maintained when transitions are merged.

Observe the EFSM in Fig. 5 and note transitions $q_1 \rightarrow q_2$ and $q_2 \rightarrow q_2$ labelled with *coin* which will be referred to as c_1 and c_2 respectively. The merging process now merges state q_1 with state q_2 into a new state, $q_{\{1,2\}}$, which introduces nondeterminism to the model since there are two outgoing *coin* transitions, c_1 and c_2, from $q_{\{1,2\}}$ either of which may be taken when i_1 is 50. This can be resolved by merging the two transitions into one.

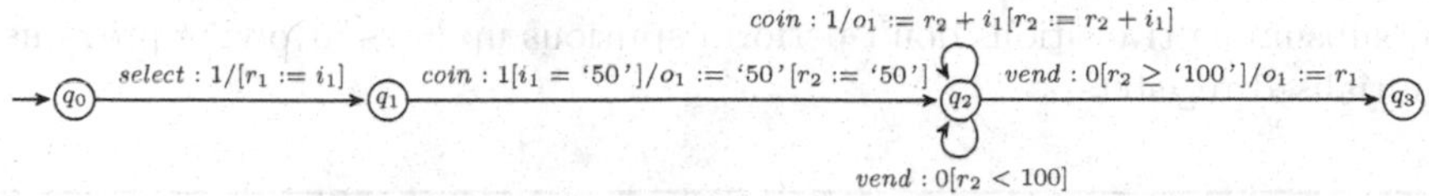

Fig. 5. An EFSM with a transition to be merged

Transitions may not always be compatible for merging so how exactly do we know if two transitions *are* compatible? Firstly they must have the same label and arity, otherwise they represent different behaviour. Lorenzoli *et al.* [15] discuss the idea of subsumption of guards, where one transition *subsumes* another if its guard is *more general*. Applying this principle to the example has the transition with no guard (corresponding to the literal guard *true*) subsuming the transition with guard $i_1 = `50'$. This looks promising but the outputs and updates need to be considered too. The principle of subsumption must therefore be extended to take these into account.

Definition 3. *Transition* t_2 *can be said to* subsume *transition* t_1 *if*

1. *The guard of* t_1 *implies that of* t_2
2. *In the cases where it is possible to take* t_1*, the output of* t_2 *is identical*
3. *The posterior data state of* t_2 *is consistent with that of* t_1*.*

The general idea is similar to refinement [6], the aim being to widen the precondition and reduce nondeterminism. Subsuming transitions are allowed to accept *more* inputs but under circumstances where either transition may be taken, it is important that the output of both is identical. If this is not the case, the two transitions are observably different and cannot be merged. Even though data registers are not directly observable – it is not possible to ask "what is the value of register r?" – they may be used as part of output functions so have the potential to affect observable behaviour of future transitions. It is therefore important that any register updates performed by the subsuming transition are consistent with those performed by the one being subsumed.

Contexts are used in our inference method when determining if one transition subsumes another because they help to place restrictions on the values of expressions. Algorithm 2 describes the conditions which must be satisfied for transition t_2 to subsume t_1. Line 2 checks to see if each condition in the medial context of t_2 is implied by that of t_1. In other words, that each condition in $M(t_2)$ is more general than its counterpart in $M(t_1)$. The second conjunct, on line 3, ensures that the output of both transitions is equal in every case where it is possible to take t_1. This is the check for observational equivalence. The conjunct on line 4 ensures that the posterior context of t_2 is more specific than that of t_1 in the cases where t_1 may be taken. This means that the restrictions on the values of expressions in $P(t_2)$ are at least as tight as those in $P(t_1)$. The final conjunct, on line 5, enforces that the posterior context of the subsuming transition is consistent whenever that of the subsumed transition is. This ensures that subsuming transitions don't perform spurious updates involving previously uninitialised registers.

Algorithm 2. Transition subsumption in context

1: **function** SUBSUMES(Transition t_2, t_1, AnteriorContext c)
2: **return** $\forall x.\ \text{MEDIAL}(t_1, c)[x] \implies \text{MEDIAL}(t_2, c)[x] \wedge$
3: $\forall i\ r.\ \text{CANTAKE}(t_1, i, r) \implies \text{OUTPUTS}(t_1, i, r) = \text{OUTPUTS}(t_2, i, r) \wedge$
4: $\forall x.\ \text{POSTERIOR}(t_2, \text{MEDIAL}(t_1, c))[x] \implies \text{POSTERIOR}(t_1, c)[x] \wedge$
5: $\text{CONSISTENT}(\text{POSTERIOR}(t_1, c)) \implies \text{CONSISTENT}(\text{POSTERIOR}(t_2, c))$
6: **end function**

The concept of subsumption is used in our method when merging transitions since, in a given pair of nondeterministic transitions, one will often subsume the other. Algorithm 3 describes the process in detail. Lines 1–4 describe the simplest merging case. If one transition subsumes the other directly, the subsumed transition can be trivially deleted without causing a contextual difference.

Lines 5–10 describe the case where one transition subsumes the other in a different context, for example if a register held a particular value. The OBTAINANTERIOR function tries to modify update functions of incoming transitions to accommodate this. Usually this involves assigning a value to a previously undefined register. If this is achieved, one transition then subsumes the other and we are back to the simple case.

Algorithm 3. Merging two transitions

Input: Transition t_1, t_2, AnteriorContext c, EFSM e, State s
if SUBSUMES(t_1, t_2, c) **then**
    t_2 can simply be deleted, leaving t_1 as the result of the merge
else if SUBSUMES(t_2, t_1, c) **then**
    t_1 can be deleted, leaving t_2 as the result of the merge
else if $\exists c'$. SUBSUMES$(t_2, t_1, c') \vee$ SUBSUMES(t_1, t_2, c') **then**
    if OBTAINANTERIOR(c', e, s) **then**
        Delete either t_1 or t_2 as appropriate
    else
        The transitions cannot be merged
    end if
else
    The transitions cannot be merged
end if

If it is not possible to modify update functions of incoming transitions, for example if a relevant register value is already set by an update function, then no subsumption exists and the merge fails. This is also the case if no anterior context exists in which one transition may subsume the other directly.

Example 1. Let us now apply our method to the running drinks machine example from Fig. 5 and carry out the process with the nondeterministic *coin* transitions from state $q_{\{1,2\}}$. Intuitively, c_2 should subsume c_1 because it has no guard. Running Algorithm 3 should verify this.

The anterior context of both transitions is $[\![r_1 \mapsto \mathit{true}]\!]$ since the only way to reach state $q_{\{1,2\}}$ from the initial state is to take the *select* transition which assigns a value to r_1 but places no restriction on it. The guard of c_1 gives $M(c_1) = [\![r_1 \mapsto \mathit{true}, i_1 \mapsto = 50]\!]$. Since there is only one guard expression which restricts a single variable, i_1, to a literal value, there is no rearranging step here.

The medial context of c_2 is equal to the anterior context since c_2 has no guard. There is no explicit restriction on i_1 in this context so, as discussed in Sect. 3, it's constraint is literal *true*. In this case, since $\mathit{true} \implies \mathit{true}$ and $= 50 \implies \mathit{true}$ condition one of Algorithm 2 has been met.

Now to investigate condition two. The only case where it is possible to take c_1 is when $i_1 = 50$. In this case the output of c_1 is literal 50. Transition c_2 cannot produce an output since r_2 has not been initialised, hence condition two fails. This means that c_2 does not subsume c_1 directly.

If, in the anterior context, r_2 was equal to zero then the outputs of the two transitions would be identical in the case where $i_1 = 50$. The posterior contexts of the two transitions would also be identical and consistent, satisfying conditions three and four of Algorithm 2. In this case, the addition of the update $r_2 :=$ '0' to the *select* transition produces the desired anterior context, allowing transition c_2 to subsume c_1. This may take place without breaking contextual equivalence since r_2 was previously undefined in the posterior context of *select*. With the new anterior context, c_2 subsumes c_1 directly meaning that c_1 may be trivially deleted, resulting in the EFSM in Fig. 3. □

When faced with two transitions to merge, it may be the case that neither subsumes the other directly but there exists a transition which subsumes both. Consider the transitions $coin : 1[i_1 = \text{'20'}]/o_1 := \text{'20'}[r_2 := \text{'20'}]$ and c_1. Clearly they are instances of the same behaviour but neither subsumes the other. If presented with a candidate for a subsuming transition, contexts may be applied in the same way to establish the validity of the candidate. How such candidates are obtained is outside the scope of this paper and is the intended subject of future work but the method presented here can be used to validate such candidates.

5 Analysing System Properties

Another benefit of introducing contexts is the following. Having created an EFSM model of a system, it is possible to use it to prove properties of that model. With the drinks machine example, it is desired that a user will always receive the drink they originally selected. Another desirable property, for the proprietors at least, is that customers only receive their drinks if they have inserted enough money. Contexts allow us to prove properties like these.

Example 2. Consider the drinks machine model in Fig. 3. Looking only at the labels, as would be provided by a classical FSM model, it appears to be possible to go straight from q_1 to q_2 without inserting any coins. The trace $select(coke) \rightarrow vend()/[coke]$ seems like a valid option, meaning that a user could get their drink for free. Contexts help to show that this is not the case.

The *vend* transition can only be triggered from state q_1. The only way to reach this state from the initial state is to do a *select* transition. This transition produces a posterior context of $[\![r_1 \mapsto true, r_2 \mapsto = 0]\!]$. Triggering *vend* with this anterior context will only allow the one which dispenses nothing to fire, since r_2 holds value zero which is less than 100. The only way to obtain a drink from *vend* is if r_2 holds a value greater than or equal to 100. The only transition from q_1 with an update function which increases r_2 is the *coin* transition. This means that the customer must insert at least one coin to receive their drink. □

The exact proof strategy varies depending on the property being proven but the general idea is to use the constraints of a particular context to prove that a transition may or may not be taken. In the case of Example 2, the guard of the *vend* transition with the desired output cannot be satisfied with an anterior context in which the value of r_2 is less than 100.

Another technique is to analyse update functions to see if any have the potential to affect variables of interest in the desired way. In Example 2, the variable of interest is r_2 and needs to be increased. The *coin* transition has no guard so may be taken with any anterior context and produces a posterior context with r_2 incremented by the value of the input. Assuming that coins have a positive value, this increases the value of r_2. The destination state is equal to the origin, so the transition may be taken again if the input value was insufficient.

Contexts can also help prove observable equivalence of EFSM models. Consider the EFSM shown in Fig. 6, an alternative model of the drinks machine in Fig. 3. Contexts can be used to prove equivalence of the two models.

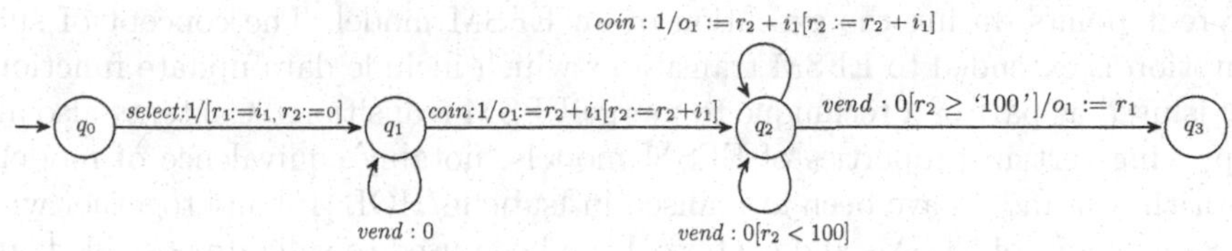

Fig. 6. A model which is observationally equivalent to the one in Fig. 3

The idea here is similar to bisimulation with the aim being to form a relation between the states of two machines such that for all inputs, if one machine in a given state can accept an input, the other machine accepts the same input and produces the same output. The models must not only be trace equivalent but also contextually equivalent since register values may be used as part of output functions, potentially exposing differences in the data state. The model in Fig. 6, M_1, can be proven to be contextually equivalent to the model in Fig. 3, M_2, as follows.

Example 3. Starting both machines off in their respective initial states, it is only possible to do a *select* transition. Both machines are now in their respective q_1 states from which it is possible to do a *coin* or a *vend* transition. The context of M_1 at this point is $[\![r_1 \mapsto \mathit{true}, r_2 \mapsto = 0]\!]$ and the context of M_2 is $[\![r_1 \mapsto \mathit{true}, r_2 \mapsto = 0]\!]$. Both machines can do an unguarded *coin* transition to produce the context $[\![r_1 \mapsto \mathit{true}, r_2 \mapsto \mathit{true}]\!]$. Both may do a *vend* transition which outputs nothing and leaves the context and state unchanged. M_2 also has a second outgoing *vend* transition but this may not be taken as r_2 is less than 100.

After having done a *coin* transition, M_1 is in state q_2 and M_2 is in state q_1. Subsequent *coin* transitions leave the state and context unchanged but allow a choice of either *vend* transition since nothing is known about the value of r_2. The guards on the two transitions are mutually exclusive so determinism is maintained. If r_2 is greater than or equal to 100 then adding further coins is futile but continues to be observationally equivalent. Alternatively, the *vend* transition which outputs the selected drink may be taken. This is the value of r_1 in both machines, set as the input of the *select* transition and not changed so identical inputs produce identical outputs. If r_2 is less than 100 then the *vend* transition in both cases leaves the state unchanged but produces a posterior context of $[\![r_1 \mapsto \mathit{true}, r_2 \mapsto < 100]\!]$. Subsequently, the same *vend* transition may be repeated indefinitely or another *coin* transition may be taken. □

These are just some of the ways context can be used to prove properties of systems. A full methodological breakdown is left for future work.

6 Conclusions

This paper presents contexts, a way of recording constraints on data values at different points during the execution of an EFSM model. The concept of subsumption is extended to EFSM transitions which include data update functions and is used as part of a technique to merge EFSM transitions. Contexts also aid in proving certain properties of EFSM models, notably equivalence of models. Algorithms 1 and 2 have been formalised in Isabelle/HOL [16] and together with representations of EFSMs and contexts have been used to validate possible transition merges and prove the properties of the drinks machine example discussed in Sect. 5. It is the intention of the authors to submit these theory files to the AFP (https://www.isa-afp.org/).

The task of inferring a model from a set of software execution traces has been an active area of research since the 1960s [11]. Most inference algorithms fit into one of two categories: active and passive. Active techniques such as [1, 7, 12] allow the user to guide the inference process by categorising possible actions as possible or impossible from the current state. Most modern techniques (including the one presented in this work) tend to be more passive, inferring a generalised system model from observed system traces without reference to the user.

Classical FSM inference techniques produce models with atomic labels which struggle with systems exhibiting value-dependent behaviour. EFSM models feature parametrised inputs and a separate data state which solves this problem. EFSM inference techniques such as [14, 19] build on classical techniques to infer EFSMs from program execution traces by state and transition merging. These approaches do not attempt to infer register update functions so do not have to consider the merging of transitions which feature them. The inference of register update functions is a key challenge in EFSM inference, so a technique to merge such transitions is required. This work presents such a technique.

Future work includes the identification and prioritisation of potential EFSM state and transition merges as well as the provision of candidate transitions as discussed in Sect. 4. The inference of register and input types from traces is also an area of interest.

References

1. Angluin, D.: Learning regular sets from queries and counterexamples. Inf. Comput. **75**, 87–106 (1987). https://doi.org/10.1016/0890-5401(87)90052-6
2. Biermann, A.W., Feldman, J.A.: On the synthesis of finite-state machines from samples of their behavior. IEEE Trans. Comput. **C-21**(6), 592–597 (1972). https://doi.org/10.1109/TC.1972.5009015
3. Börger, E., Stärk, R.: Abstract State Machines. Springer, Heidelberg (2003). https://doi.org/10.1007/978-3-642-18216-7

4. Cheng, K.T., Krishnakumar, A.S.: Automatic functional test generation using the extended finite state machine model. In: International Design Automation Conference (DAC), pp. 86–91. ACM Press, New York (1993). https://doi.org/10.1145/157485.164585
5. Damas, C., Lambeau, B., Dupont, P., Van Lamsweerde, A.: Generating annotated behavior models from end-user scenarios. IEEE Trans. Softw. Eng. **31**(12), 1056–1073 (2005). https://doi.org/10.1109/TSE.2005.138
6. Derrick, J., Boiten, E.A.: Refinement in Z and Object-Z, 2nd edn. Springer, London (2014). https://doi.org/10.1007/978-1-4471-5355-9
7. Dupont, P., Lambeau, B., Damas, C., Van Lamsweerde, A.: The QSM algorithm and its application to software behavior model induction. Appl. Artif. Intell. **22**(1–2), 77–115 (2008). https://doi.org/10.1080/08839510701853200
8. Eilenberg, S.: Automata, Languages, and Machines. Academic Press Inc., Orlando (1974)
9. Ernst, M.D., Cockrell, J., Griswold, W.G., Notkin, D.: Dynamically discovering likely program invariants to support program evolution. IEEE Trans. Softw. Eng. **27**(2), 99–123 (2001). https://doi.org/10.1109/32.908957
10. Fraser, G., Walkinshaw, N.: Behaviourally adequate software testing. In: International Conference on Software Testing, Verification and Validation, pp. 300–309, April 2012. https://doi.org/10.1109/ICST.2012.110
11. Gold, E.M.: Language identification in the limit. Inf. Control **10**(5), 447–474 (1967)
12. Isberner, M., Howar, F., Steffen, B.: The TTT algorithm: a redundancy-free approach to active automata learning. In: Bonakdarpour, B., Smolka, S.A. (eds.) RV 2014. LNCS, vol. 8734, pp. 307–322. Springer, Cham (2014). https://doi.org/10.1007/978-3-319-11164-3_26
13. Lang, K.J., Pearlmutter, B.A., Price, R.A.: Results of the Abbadingo one DFA learning competition and a new evidence-driven state merging algorithm. In: Honavar, V., Slutzki, G. (eds.) ICGI 1998. LNCS, vol. 1433, pp. 1–12. Springer, Heidelberg (1998). https://doi.org/10.1007/BFb0054059
14. Lorenzoli, D., Mariani, L., Pezzè, M.: Inferring state-based behavior models. In: International Workshop on Dynamic Systems Analysis (WODA), p. 25. ACM Press, New York (2006). https://doi.org/10.1145/1138912.1138919
15. Lorenzoli, D., Mariani, L., Pezzè, M.: Automatic generation of software behavioral models. In: International Conference on Software Engineering (ICSE), p. 501. ACM Press, New York (2008). https://doi.org/10.1145/1368088.1368157
16. Nipkow, T., Wenzel, M., Paulson, L.C. (eds.): Isabelle/HOL. LNCS, vol. 2283. Springer, Heidelberg (2002). https://doi.org/10.1007/3-540-45949-9
17. Petrenko, A., Boroday, S., Groz, R.: Confirming configurations in EFSM testing. IEEE Trans. Softw. Eng. **30**(1), 29–42 (2004). https://doi.org/10.1109/TSE.2004.1265734
18. Walkinshaw, N., Lambeau, B., Damas, C., Bogdanov, K., Dupont, P.: STAMINA: a competition to encourage the development and assessment of software model inference techniques. Empir. Softw. Eng. **18**(4), 791–824 (2013). https://doi.org/10.1007/s10664-012-9210-3
19. Walkinshaw, N., Taylor, R., Derrick, J.: Inferring extended finite state machine models from software executions. Empir. Softw. Eng. **21**(3), 811–853 (2016). https://doi.org/10.1007/s10664-015-9367-7
20. Weyuker, E.J.: Assessing test data adequacy through program inference. ACM Trans. Program. Lang. Syst. **5**(4), 641–655 (1983)

Checking Activity Transition Systems with Back Transitions Against Assertions

Cunjing Ge[1,3], Jiwei Yan[2(✉)], Jun Yan[1,2,3], and Jian Zhang[1,3(✉)]

[1] State Key Laboratory of Computer Science, Institute of Software, Chinese Academy of Sciences, Beijing, China
{gecj,yanjun,zj}@ios.ac.cn

[2] Technology Center of Software Engineering, Institute of Software, Chinese Academy of Sciences, Beijing, China
yanjw@ios.ac.cn

[3] University of Chinese Academy of Sciences, Beijing, China

Abstract. The Android system is in widespread use currently, and Android apps play an important role in our daily life. How to specify and verify apps is a challenging problem. In this paper, we study a formalism for abstracting the behaviour of Android apps, called Activity Transition Systems (ATS), which includes back transitions, value assignments and assertions. Given such a transition system with a corresponding Activity Transition Graph (ATG), it is interesting to know whether it violates some value assertions. We first prove some theoretical properties of transitions and propose a state-merging strategy. Then we further introduce a post-reachability graph technique. Based on this technique, we design an algorithm to traverse an ATG that avoids path cycles. Lastly, we also extend our model and our algorithm to handle more complicated problems.

1 Introduction

The Android system, which provides rich and flexible features to ease the development of applications (apps), is one of the most popular mobile operating systems currently. Various Android apps are developed and released to the app market, which attracts high downloads due to the convenient interaction, user-friendly windows, and event-driven nature.

In Android system, the major component, **activity**, is a container which consists of various GUI widgets (e.g., button). Users can interact with widgets on an activity and trigger transitions between activities to perform a certain job. Thus activity transition model for event-driven callbacks is a fundamental model for analysis of Android apps. This serves as a cornerstone for many clients, such as vulnerability detection [6,9,12–15,19,20], malware detection and mitigation [10,11,19], GUI model generation [22,23], and GUI testing [3–5,16,17].

This work is partially supported by the National Key Basic Research (973) Program of China (Grant No.2014CB340701), the National Natural Science Foundation of China (Grant No. 61672505), and the Key Research Program of Frontier Sciences, CAS (Grant No. QYZDJ-SSW-JSC036).

J. Sun and M. Sun (Eds.): ICFEM 2018, LNCS 11232, pp. 388–403, 2018.
https://doi.org/10.1007/978-3-030-02450-5_23

All launched activities are arranged in the back stack in the order in which each activity is opened. Take a short message (SMS) manager app as an example, which may have an activity to show the list of contacts. When the user selects a contact person, a new activity is opened to view all the messages from or to the person. At the same time, the system will add the new activity to the back stack. Then if the user presses the back button on the bottom of the screen, that new activity is finished and popped off the stack. By default, activities in the stack can only be rearranged by push and pop operations. This back-stack mechanism is so flexible that a developer has to carefully inspect the status of the back stack when developing the transitions between activities. An activity with different back stacks may lead to different program behaviors, which brings the difficulty to the modeling of apps. When the launch-mode of activity is involved, the task will be more complicated.

Recent works [3,21,23,24] construct transition models of apps and traverse models to generate transition paths or even sequences to guide the GUI testing, some of them discuss the influences brought by the stack mechanism. These works adopt the same assumption that when the back operation is triggered, the model will roll back to the previous state. However, the assignments of global variables will not roll back. For example, the operations in the setting activity are also impossible to be rollback. As shown in Fig. 1, when the app `TippyTipper` are transited in the order of main $\xrightarrow{OpenSetting}$ setting1 $\xrightarrow{ClickCheckbox}$ setting2 $\xrightarrow{Back}$ main, the global variables that are changed in setting2 will not roll back by simply pressing the back button.

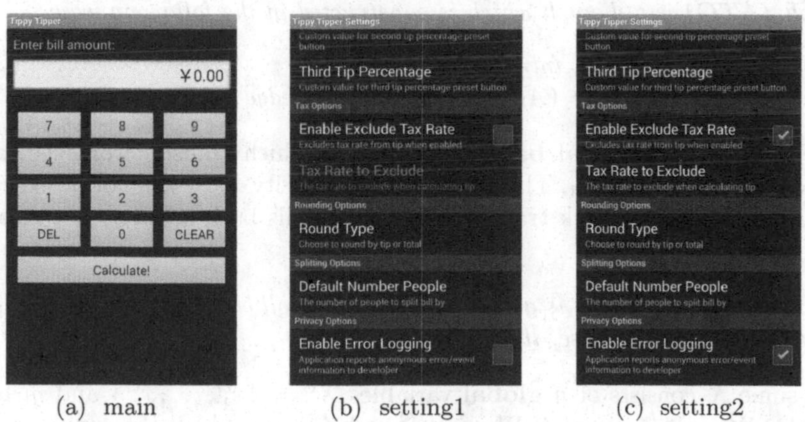

(a) main (b) setting1 (c) setting2

Fig. 1. Tippy tipper application

Because the back transition will lead to state change, in this paper, we consider a problem of determining if there exists a path that violates one of the assertions in the ATG with back transitions.

The main contributions of this work are summarized as follows:

- We propose an Activity Transition Graph (ATG) model with back transitions, value assignments and assertions, to describe the activity relations of Android apps in detail.
- We introduce a post-reachability graph and an algorithm to traverse an ATG that avoids path cycles.
- We extend our model and our algorithm to handle more complicated and also more interesting tasks.

The rest of this paper is organized as follows. Background and preliminary material is in Sect. 2, the algorithm in Sect. 3, several extensions of our model and approach in Sect. 4, related works in Sect. 5, and finally, concluding remarks in Sect. 6.

2 Background

Definition 1. *An **Activity Transition System (ATS)** $(X, \mathcal{V}, V_0, \mathcal{A}, A_0, \mathcal{T})$ consists of a set X of Boolean-valued variables, a set $\mathcal{V}$ of domains of variables in X, an initial assignment V_0, a set $\mathcal{A}$ of activities, an initial activity $A_0 \in \mathcal{A}$ and a set $\mathcal{T}$ of transitions.*

Each transition $\tau \in \mathcal{T}$ is a tuple (A, A') where A and A' are activities. Each activity or transition corresponds to a set of statements such as assignment statements like $x := 0$ and assertions like $x = 1 \rightarrow y = 0$.

Definition 2. *Given an ATS $(X, \mathcal{V}, V_0, \mathcal{A}, A_0, \mathcal{T})$, the **Activity Transition Graph (ATG)** is a digraph which is constructed in the following way:*

1. *For each activity in $\mathcal{A}$, introduce a vertex A_i.*
2. *For each transition $\tau = (A_i, A_j)$, introduce an edge from A_i to A_j.*

We introduce a special **back** transition τ_b which transits from the latest visited activity A_k to A_{k-1}. The statements of activity A_{k-1} will not be executed after back transition. Back transition not only rolls back activity, but also the part of assignments.

Definition 3. *A variable is **global** if it does not roll back its assignment during back transitions. Otherwise, it is a **local** variable.*

Assume X consists of n **global** variables $X^G = \{x_1^G, \ldots, x_n^G\}$ and m **local** variables $X^L = \{x_1^L, \ldots, x_m^L\}$. We use V^G and V^L to represent the assignments of X^G and X^L respectively. So back transition generates the $k+1$ step $\langle A_{k+1}, V_{k+1} \rangle$ that $V_{k+1}^G = V_k^G$, $V_{k+1}^L = V_{k-1}^L$ and $A_{k+1} = A_{k-1}$. We extend the ATS and ATG with such back transitions.

In this paper, we consider a problem of determining if there exists a path that violates one of the assertions in the ATG with back transitions.

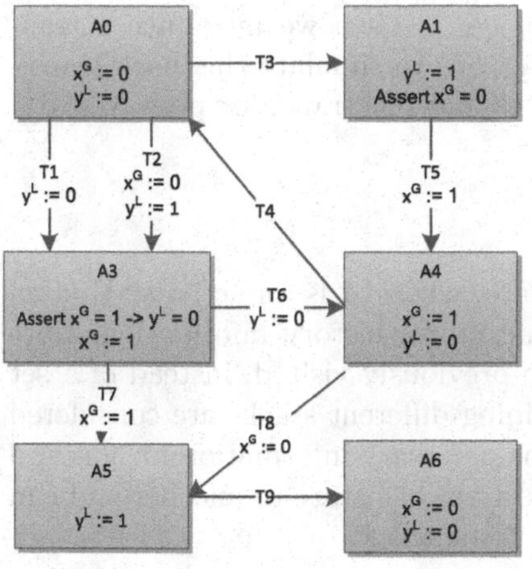

Fig. 2. An example of an ATG

Path:
$\langle A0,(0,0)\rangle \xrightarrow{T1} \langle A3,(1,0)\rangle \xrightarrow{back}$
$\langle A0,(1,0)\rangle \xrightarrow{T3} \langle A1,(1,1)\rangle$

Statements:

```
A0    x := 0
A0    y := 0
T1    y := 0
A3    Assert x = 1 -> y = 0
A3    x := 1
BACK  y roll back 0
A1    y := 1
A1    Assert x = 0
```

Fig. 3. Statements of a path

Example. Figure 2 presents an example of the ATG with back transitions. It has 6 activities, 9 forward transitions and 2 boolean variables (one of them is global and another one is local). The initial values for variable x and y are both zero. Activity $A1$ and $A3$ contain assertions. The ATG starts from $A0$. There exists a path that violates the assertion in $A1$: $\langle A0,(0,0)\rangle \xrightarrow{T1} \langle A3,(1,0)\rangle \xrightarrow{back} \langle A0,(1,0)\rangle \xrightarrow{T3} \langle A1,(1,1)\rangle$. Concatenating the blocks of statements in transitions and activities, this path can be represented as Fig. 3. So a path can be considered as a sequence of statements. Since the initial assignment is determined, the assignment of variables on each statement is determined.

Relation with Pushdown Automata. There is a straightforward way to transform the assertion violation problem of an ATG with back transitions into a reachability problem of a pushdown automata:

- Let Q denote the set of states and Γ denote the stack alphabet. Since the assignments at an activity are finite, Q and Γ are also finite. We introduce an input symbol I_τ for the forward transition τ and an additional symbol $BACK$ to represent back transitions.
- Consider a pair (A,V) where A is an activity and V is an assignment. For (A,V), we introduce a state $q_{(A,V)} \in Q$ and a symbol $S_{(A,V)}$.
- We introduce a transition from $q_{(A_1,V_1)}$ to $q_{(A_2,V_2)}$ for a transition τ from activity A_1 to A_2 in the original ATG, where V_2 is the assignment result after executing statements of τ and A_2 with input V_1. This transition can be simulated by $(q_{(A_1,V_1)}, I_\tau, S^*, q_{(A_2,V_2)}, S_{(A_1,V_1)}S^*)$, where S^* represents an arbitrary stack symbol in Γ and $S_{(A_1,V_1)}S^*$ indicates that this transition pushes symbol $S_{(A_1,V_1)}$ into stack.
- Consider a back transition from (A_2,V_2) to the previous state (A_1,V_1) in the stack. Let V_0 represent the assignment after the back transition. We

first introduce two states $q_{(A_2,V_2)}$ and $q_{(A_1,V_0)}$. Then we introduce a transition $(q_{(A_2,V_2)}, BACK, S_{(A_1,V_1)}S^*, q_{(A_1,V_0)}, S^*)$ to simulate this back transition, where $S^* \in \Gamma$ and $S_{(A_1,V_1)}S^*$ indicates that this transition pops $S_{(A_1,V_1)}$.

3 Approach

We use a 3-tuple (A, V, S) to represent a state, where A is an activity, V is an assignment of variables and S is a stack that stores history information. Note that the stack S is a set of states which are previously visited, instead of a set of pairs like (A, V). Therefore, states containing different stacks are considered to be different in our model. A state contains necessary information for forward and back transitions. We can transit forward from one state to another and can also transit back to the previous state with the stack S.

3.1 A Straightforward Method

Algorithm 1 is the basic framework of breadth-first-search over the given ATG. It employs a queue Q to store states in this BFS algorithm. At the beginning, it adds the initial state (A_0, V_0, Φ) into Q. Then it visits every state in Q. For an unvisited element $q = (A, V, S)$ in Q, it enumerates each forward transition $\tau = (A, A_{next})$ from A. After that it executes statements and checks assertions on τ and the next activity A_{next} to obtain the new assignment V_{next}. After copy stack S to S_{next} and push state q into stack S_{next}, the algorithm adds the new state $(A_{next}, V_{next}, S_{next})$ into Q. After forward transitions, we consider the back transition at the state q. The algorithm pops the stack S to obtain the previous state $(A_{back}, V_{back}, S_{back})$. Since the assignment of global variables remains, we assign V^G to V^G_{back}. Then the algorithm adds the new state $(A_{back}, V_{back}, S_{back})$ into Q. At last, it visits another unvisited state in Q.

3.2 Post-reachability Graphs

The straightforward method may not terminate since it cannot handle cycle. Consider the example in Fig. 2, assume that we have already obtained a sequence of states: $7 : (A_0, (1, 0), \Phi) \xrightarrow{T1} 15 : (A_3, (1, 0), \{7\}) \xrightarrow{T6} S1 : (A_1, (1, 0), \{7, 15\}) \xrightarrow{T4} S2 : (A_0, (0, 0), \{7, 15, S1\})$. It is a sequence starting from state 7 to state $S2$ (states 7 and 15 are obtained in real execution of our algorithm while $S1$ and $S2$ are not, for details, see Fig. 6). Since the assignments of state 7 and state $S2$ are different, the sequence is not a cycle. However, if we start from state $S2$ through transition $T2$ and a back transition, we obtain a new state $S4 : (A_0, (1, 0), \{7, 15, S1\})$. Then we find a cycle from state 7 to $S4$. The straightforward method will keep visiting activities starting from state $S4$, since $S4$ is different with state 7 in the perspective of stacks. In this example, it is also not sufficient to avoid cycles by only checking the existence of the pair $(A_0, (1, 0))$, since it lacks path information. So, in this section, we introduce a

Algorithm 1: Straightforward Version

function
  $Q \leftarrow \{(A_0, V_0, \Phi)\}$;
  while Q *not all visited* **do**
    pick an unvisited element $q = (A, V, S)$ in Q;
    for each $\tau = (A, A_{next})$ *start from* A **do**
      execute statements on τ and A_{next} and obtain V_{next};
      if assertions on τ or A_{next} violated **then return** false;
      $S_{next} \leftarrow S$, S_{next}.push(q);
      $Q \leftarrow Q \cup \{(A_{next}, V_{next}, S_{next})\}$;
    if $S \neq \Phi$ **then**
      $(A_{back}, V_{back}, S_{back}) \leftarrow S$.pop();
      $V^G_{back} \leftarrow V^G$;
      $Q \leftarrow Q \cup \{(A_{back}, V_{back}, S_{back})\}$;
    set q visited;

post-reachability graph for each activity to store sufficient history information for cycle avoidance.

Consider two states (A, V, S) and (A, V, S') on same activity A. They contain same variable assignment V, but different stacks S and S'. Intuitively, the forward transitions starting from these two states will lead to similar results, since in this case, stacks of history states only affect back transitions. So we could merge these two states into a virtual state with variable assignment V for the exploration of forward transitions. In other words, given a new state (A, V, S''), it is unnecessary to explore forward transitions starting from it. However, we have to store S, S' and S'' as they represent different path traces which are useful for the exploration of back transitions. To precisely describe the previous strategy, we introduce following lemmas and Theorem 1.

Lemma 1. *Given two states* (A, V, S) *and* (A, U, R) *on the same activity* A. *Consider a transition* $\tau = (A, A_{next})$, *let* $(A_{next}, V_{next}, S_{next})$ *and* $(A_{next}, U_{next}, R_{next})$ *denote the states after transition* τ. *Then* $V = U \Rightarrow V_{next} = U_{next}$.

Lemma 2. *Given two states* (A, V, S) *and* (A, U, R) *on the same activity* A. *Let* $(A_{last}, V_{last}, S_{last})$ *and* $(A_{last}, U_{last}, R_{last})$ *denote the last element of* S *and* R *respectively. Consider two states* $(A_{last}, V_{back}, S_{last})$ *and* $(A_{last}, U_{back}, R_{last})$ *after a back transition. Then* $V = U, V_{last} = U_{last} \Rightarrow V_{back} = U_{back}$.

Proof. Recall the definition of roll back operation on variable assignments, we know that $V^G_{back} = V^G$, $V^L_{back} = V^L_{last}$, $U^G_{back} = U^G$ and $U^L_{back} = U^L_{last}$. Since $V = U$ and $V_{last} = U_{last}$, it is obvious that $V^G = U^G$ and $V^L_{last} = U^L_{last}$. As a result, $V_{back} = U_{back}$. □

Theorem 1. *Given two states* (A_0, V_0, S_0) *and* (A_0, U_0, R_0) *on the same activity* A_0 *and a sequence of normal and back transitions* $\tau_1 \dots \tau_k$. *There are two sequences of states* $(A_0, V_0, S_0) \dots (A_k, V_k, S_k)$ *and* $(A_0, U_0, R_0) \dots (A_k, U_k, R_k)$. *Then* $\forall i \in \{1, \dots, k\}, V_0 = U_0, S_0 \subset S_i, R_0 \subset R_i \Rightarrow V_k = U_k$.

Proof. (Mathematical Induction)

Basis: τ_1 should be a forward transition as $S_0 \subset S_1$ and $R_0 \subset R_1$. From Lemma 1, we obtain $V_1 = U_1$ as $V_0 = U_0$.

Inductive Step: Show that $V_n = U_n$ if $V_0 = U_0, V_1 = U_1, \dots, V_{n-1} = U_{n-1}$.

Assume τ_n is a forward transition. From Lemma 1, we obtain $V_n = U_n$ as $V_{n-1} = U_{n-1}$. Assume τ_n is a back transition. We observe that stacks S_{n-1} and R_{n-1} are parts of sequences $(A_0, V_0, S_0) \dots (A_{n-2}, V_{n-2}, S_{n-2})$ and $(A_0, U_0, R_0) \dots (A_{n-2}, U_{n-2}, R_{n-2})$. So the last elements of S_{n-1} and R_{n-1} should be a pair of states $\big((A_l, V_l, S_l), (A_l, U_l, R_l)\big)$ from two sequences, where $0 \leq l \leq n-2$. From induction hypothesis, we know that $V_l = U_l$. From Lemma 2, we obtain $V_n = U_n$ as $V_{n-1} = U_{n-1}$ and $V_l = U_l$. □

Theorem 1 shows that two states with same variable assignments are always equivalent after a sequence of transitions (the number of forward transitions is not less than back transitions) in perspective of variable assignments. When the number of back transitions is more than forward transitions, we only have to consider the stacks of two states respectively. To apply such strategy in algorithm, we introduce the following concepts of post-reachable state and post-reachability graph.

Definition 4. *Given a state* (A_0, V_0, S_0). *After a sequence of normal and back transitions* $\tau_1 \dots \tau_k$, *we obtain a sequence of states* $(A_0, V_0, S_0) \dots (A_k, V_k, S_k)$ *that* $\forall i \in \{1, \dots, k\}, S \subset S_i$. *If* $A_k = A_0$ *and* $S_k = S_0$, *the state* (A_k, V_k, S_k) *is called a* ***post-reachable state*** *of* (A_0, V_0, S_0).

Definition 5. *Given a set of states* $\mathcal{S} = \{(A, V_1, S_1), \dots, (A, V_n, S_n)\}$ *on an activity* A. *Then the* ***Post-Reachabilitiy Graph (PRG)*** *over* $\mathcal{S}$ *is a digraph which is constructed in the following steps:*

1. *For each different variable assignment* V_i *in* $\mathcal{S}$, *introduce a vertex* v_i.
2. *For each vertex* v_i, *introduce the set of stacks* $\bigcup_{V_i = V_j} \{S_j\}$ *as its vertex value.*
3. *If* (A, V_j, S_j) *is a post-reachable state of* (A, V_i, S_i), *where* $V_j \neq V_i$, *introduce an edge from* v_i *to* v_j.

In general, the PRG merges states with same variable assignment, and also stores different stacks for the exploration of back transitions. Figure 4 shows an example of a PRG over 8 states

$$\begin{aligned}\mathcal{S} = \{&(A, (1,0,0), \{1\}), (A, (1,0,0), \{3\}), (A, (1,0,1), \{3\}), (A, (0,1,1), \{1,2\}),\\ &(A, (0,1,1), \{3\}), (A, (1,1,1), \{7\}), (A, (0,0,0), \{1,2\}), (A, (0,0,0), \{7\})\}.\end{aligned}$$

There are 5 different value assignments in $\mathcal{S}$, so there are 5 vertices in this PRG. Each vertex corresponds to a set of stacks, e.g., vertex $(0, 1, 1)$ corresponds to stacks $\Sigma_{(0,1,1)} = \{\{1,2\},\{3\}\}$. The edges present the post-reachability between vertices. Besides the state-merging feature, the PRG also has a propagation property. We present this property in the following theorem.

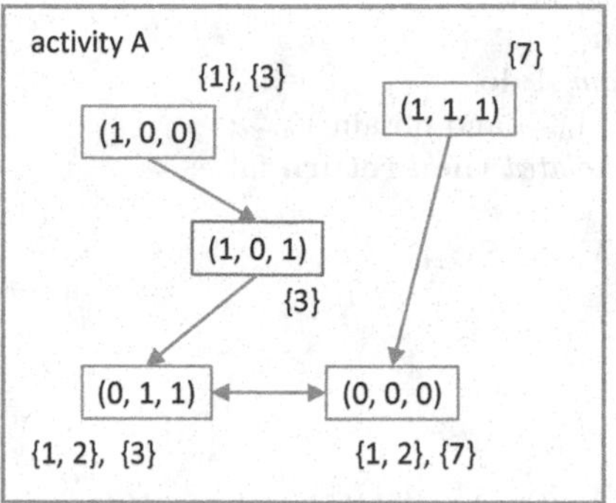

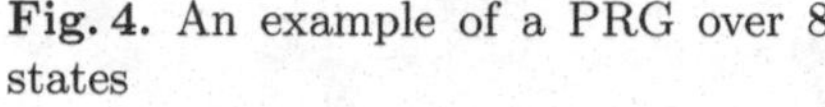

Fig. 4. An example of a PRG over 8 states

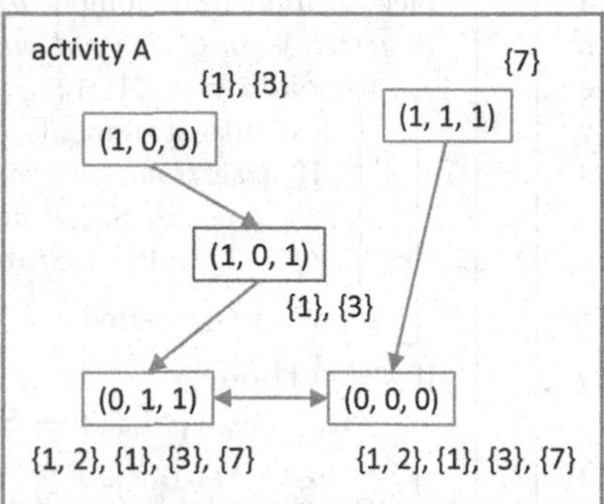

Fig. 5. Propagate values of vertices on the left PRG

Theorem 2. *Consider two vertices in a PRG of an activity A, e.g., v_1 and v_2. Let Σ_1 and Σ_2 denote the values of v_1 and v_2 (i.e., two sets of stacks), respectively. If there exists an edge from v_1 to v_2 in this PRG, we have $\Sigma_1 \subset \Sigma_2$.*

Proof. Since there exists an edge from v_1 to v_2, from the property of the post-reachable state, we could find a sequence of transitions that will transit (A, V_1, S) into (A, V_2, S), $\forall S \in \Sigma_1$. Then each stack in Σ_1 also belongs to Σ_2. □

Theorem 2 indicates that we could propagate values of vertices on an PRG. In the example of Fig. 4, we find that the stacks in $\Sigma_{(1,0,0)}$ should also belong to $\Sigma_{(1,0,1)}$, i.e., $\Sigma_{(1,0,1)} = \{\{1\},\{3\}\}$, from Theorem 2. As a result, we obtain the new PRG presented in Fig. 5 by such value propagation, which contains 5 more states.

3.3 The Algorithm with PRGs

Based on the PRG technique, we introduce our improved algorithm, which is also a BFS procedure. The pseudo-code is presented in Algorithm 2. It maintains a PRG G_A for each activity A. The value of the vertex V in G_A is denoted as $\Sigma_{G_A,V}$. Similar to the straightforward method, the improved BFS exploration also contains two parts: the exploration of forward transitions from line 5 to 11 and back transitions from line 12 to 15. Q is the queue of states to explore.

Algorithm 2 contains two sub-functions `InsertState()` and `AddEdge()`. In the function `InsertState(`A, V, S`)`, we introduce a new vertex if V is different

Algorithm 2: Improved Version with PRGs

1 **function**
2 $Q \leftarrow$ InsertState(A_0, V_0, Φ);
3 **while** *Q not all visited* **do**
4 pick an unvisited element $q = (A, V, S)$ in Q;
5 **if** *vertex V in G_A is not visited* **then**
6 **for each** $\tau = (A, A_{next})$ *start from A* **do**
7 execute statements on τ and A_{next} and obtain V_{next};
8 **if** *assertions on τ or A_{next} violated* **then return** false;
9 $S_{next} \leftarrow S$, S_{next}.push(q);
10 $Q \leftarrow Q \cup$ InsertState(A_{next}, V_{next}, S_{next});
11 set V in G_a visited;
12 **if** $s \neq \Phi$ **then**
13 $(A_{back}, V_{last}, S_{back}) \leftarrow S$.pop();
14 $V_{back}^L \leftarrow V_{last}^L$, $V_{back}^G \leftarrow V^G$;
15 $Q \leftarrow Q \cup$ InsertState(A_{back}, V_{back}, S_{back}) $\cup$ AddEdge(A_{back}, V_{last}, V_{back});
16 set q in Q visited;
17 **function** *InsertState(A, V, S)*
18 **if** *V is not yet a vertex in G_A* **then**
19 add vertex V into G_A and set $\Sigma_{G_A,V} \leftarrow \{S\}$;
20 **else**
21 $\Sigma_{G_A,V} \leftarrow \Sigma_{G_A,V} \cup \{S\}$;
22 propagate on G_A and obtain new states $\mathcal{S}$;
23 **return** $\{(A, V, S)\} \cup \mathcal{S}$;
24 **function** *AddEdge(A, U, V)*
25 add an edge $\langle U, V \rangle$ into G_A;
26 propagate on G_A and obtain new states $\mathcal{S}$;
27 **return** $\mathcal{S}$;

with the existing vertices in G_A, otherwise, we only have to update $\Sigma_{G_A,V}$ with the new stack S. Then we apply propagation procedure on G_A and return new states which are obtained in `InsertState()`. In the function `AddEdge(`A, U, V`)`, we add a new edge from vertex U to vertex V ($U \neq V$) in G_A. Then it also propagates values on G_A and returns these new states.

The algorithm starts from the initial state (A_0, V_0, Φ). It invokes the function `InsertState()` to build the PRG with the initial state and generates the initial queue Q. Then the algorithm repeatedly enumerates unvisited states in Q.

For an unvisited state $q = (A, V, S)$, we first explore forward transitions starting from q. Recall the state-merging strategy over PRGs, we only have to explore the forward transition once for each variable assignment. So at line 5, the algorithm checks whether vertex V in G_A is already considered. Then it explores each forward transition $\tau = (A, A_{next})$. After that it executes statements and checks assertions on τ and the next activity A_{next} to obtain the new assignment V_{next}. Then it copies stack S to S_{next} and pushes the state q into the stack S_{next}. At last, it obtains the new state $(A_{next}, V_{next}, S_{next})$ and invokes `InsertState()` for it.

After the forward transitions, we consider the back transition at state q. Note that different with the forward transitions, the back transition is always explored. At first, our approach pops S to obtain the previous state $(A_{back}, V_{last}, S_{back})$. From the definition of back transitions, we know that V^L_{back} is equal to V^L_{last} and V^G_{back} is equal to V^G. Thus our approach obtains the new state $(A_{back}, V_{back}, S_{back})$. Then it invokes `InsertState()` and `AddEdge()` to update G_A and Q. Recall the definition of post-reachable state that stacks of two states should be same, so there is no new edge during the exploration of forward transitions. However, since the algorithm has already explored a path from $(A_{back}, V_{last}, S_{back})$ to $(A_{back}, V_{back}, S_{back})$, the new state with V_{back} is the post-reachable state of the last state V_{last} when $V_{back} \neq V_{last}$. Thus `AddEdge()` is invoked at line 15. At last, the algorithm visits another unvisited state in Q.

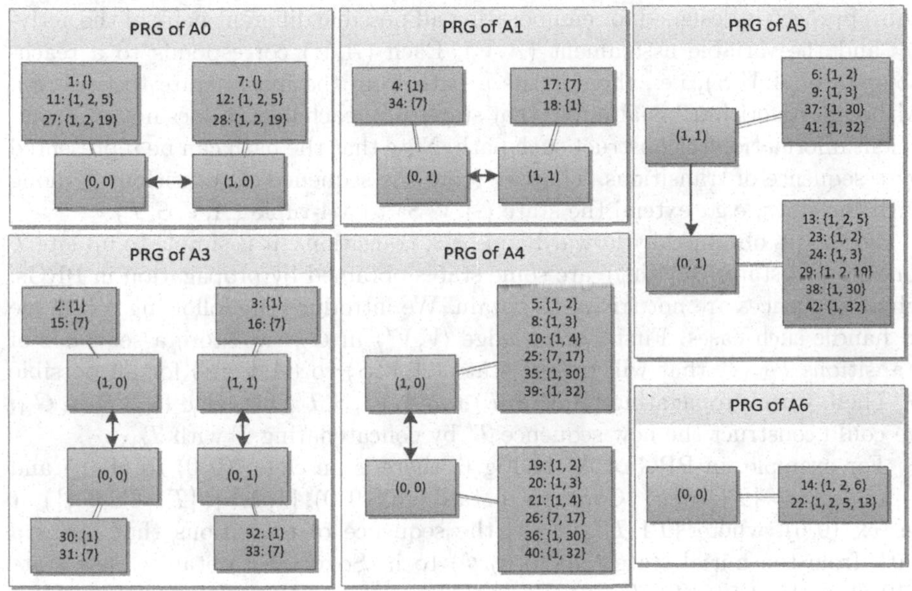

Fig. 6. All PRGs for activities in the example in Fig. 2 (Color figure online)

Example. Consider the cycle mentioned in Sect. 3.2: $7 : (A_0, (1,0), \Phi) \xrightarrow{T1} 15 : (A_3, (1,0), \{7\}) \xrightarrow{T6} S1 : (A_4, (1,0), \{7, 15\}) \xrightarrow{T4} S2 : (A_0, (0,0), \{7, 15, S1\}) \xrightarrow{T2} S3 : (A_3, (1,1), \{7, 15, S1, S2\}) \xrightarrow{back} S4 : (A_0, (1,0), \{7, 15, S1\})$. It is a cycle from A_0 to A_0. Since the vertex $(1,0)$ in G_{A_0} has already been visited at state

7, it is easy to see that our algorithm will not explore forward transitions from $S4$. In practice, the algorithm stops exploration of forward transitions earlier at $S2$, as the vertex $(0,0)$ in G_{A_0} has already been visited at the initial state $(A_0,(0,0),\Phi)$. Figure 6 presents the PRGs for all activities in the example in Fig. 2, which are generated by Algorithm 2. There are 42 states in total. Note that 12 of them (states in red) are generated by value propagation in PRGs.

4 Extensions

The model of ATG with back transitions is sometimes not sufficient for practical analysis over Android apps. However, our approach is flexible to extend to handle more complicated problems. In this section, we present several extensions to the ATG model and also our algorithm. Some extensions are orthogonal to each other, i.e., they could be employed at the same time.

4.1 Construct Paths for States

Our approach is designed for enumerating all possible different pairs of the activity and the variable assignment (A,V). Each (A,V) corresponds to a reachable state (A,V,S), i.e., there exists a path from the initial state to (A,V,S). Although Algorithm 2 guarantees that states are reachable, it does not store sufficient information to construct such path. Note that the path can be represented by a sequence of transitions. Thus we store the sequence of transitions T along with the stack, e.g., extend the state (A,V,S) to a 4-tuple (A,V,S,T).

For states obtained by forward and back transitions, it is simple to update T for this new state. But there are some states obtained by propagation in PRGs, whose sequences are not trivial to obtain. We introduce the following technique to handle such cases. First, for an edge $\langle V,V'\rangle$ in G_A, we store a sequence of transitions $T_{\langle V,V'\rangle}$ that will transit state (A,V,S) to (A,V',S) for all possible S. Then, when propagating (A,V,S,T) to (A,V',S,T') via edge $\langle V,V'\rangle$ in G_A, we could construct the new sequence T' by concatenating T with $T_{\langle V,V'\rangle}$.

For example, in PRG of A0 in Fig. 6, there is an edge $\langle(0,0)$ to $(1,0)\rangle$ and $T_{\langle(0,0),(1,0)\rangle}=\{T1,\mathit{back}\}$. Consider a state $(A0,(0,0),\{1,2,5\},\{T1,T6,T4\})$ at vertex $(0,0)$, where $\{T1,T6,T4\}$ is the sequence of transitions that forms a path from the initial state $(A0,(0,0),\Phi)$ to it. So we can obtain a new state $(A0,(1,0),\{1,2,5\},\{T1,T6,T4,T1,\mathit{back}\})$ by propagation.

4.2 Enumerated Variables and Arithmetic Expressions

We only consider Boolean-valued variables so far. However, it is easy to extend our approach to handle enumerated variables. For enumerated variables, our approach will still terminate in finite steps. Moreover, the results and techniques presented in previous sections will still work with this modification.

Since our approach only relies on sequential executions over statements instead of the satisfiability checking over constraints, it is easy to extend our approach to support statements with complex expressions, such as, arithmetic expressions, comparison between variables, etc. In general, it supports extensions to expressions that return definite values after substituting values of variables. For example, $x := x + y$, assert $x > y$, $x := (y > 0)$.

4.3 Conditional Transitions

Transitions in the ATG do not contain any conditions. However, it is common that transitions between activities contain conditions in practical Android apps, e.g., transit from a Log-in activity to another unless users fill in correct passwords. For problems with such conditional transitions, it is sufficient to modify our approach by checking conditions before exploring transitions.

4.4 Self Loops

The self transition is a forward transition $\tau = (A, A)$. It also contains statements, but the statements of activity A will not be executed after τ. Note that the roll back operation is also enabled after τ. Self loops are generated by such self transitions. In practice, there are Android apps contain self loops. For example, in a video play activity, switching between the horizontal screen and the vertical screen is a self loop. Exploring a self transition is just like exploring a normal forward transition, except that the algorithm may have to introduce a new edge in a PRG during the exploration of a self transition. Based on this observation, we could extend our approach for self loops.

4.5 Overloading and Disabling Back Transitions

Overloading roll back function is common in practical Android apps, e.g., overload a back transition as a program exit. Moreover, overloading is so flexible that the overloaded transition may be very complicated. It may contain multiple functions. However, after some modifications, our approach still works. For example, in Fig. 7, the back transition on $A3$ is overloaded by a transition from $A3$ to $EXIT$. In this case, we have to disable the roll back operation at activity $A3$. Then we introduce a forward transition from $A3$ to $EXIT$ to simulate this overloading back transition.

Obviously, disabling a back transition can be viewed as a special case of overloading a back transition which does not introduce a new transition.

4.6 Activity Launch Modes

In Android, a parent activity can start a child activity by invoking, e.g., `startActivity()` as a form of an inter-component communication (ICC) call, passing it an intent that describes the child activity to be launched. In addition, an instance of an activity class A can be launched in one of the four launch modes, `standard`, `singleTask`, `singleTop` and `singleInstance`, either configured in

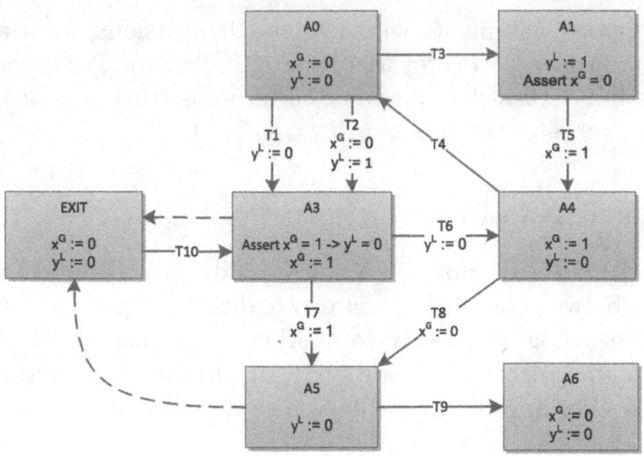

Fig. 7. An example of overloading back transitions

AndroidManifest.xml or specified in the intent passed to startActivity(). The first one is the default while the other three are known as special launch modes. These launch modes affect which activity instances are launched and their transitions.

standard. For the default launch mode, standard always creates a new activity instance of A and pushes the new instance into the back-stack. In our model, the default mechanism of forward transitions is exactly same as standard. Thus our algorithm naturally supports this mode.

singleTop. If the activity to be started has the same type as the top activity, then the top activity is reused. Otherwise, we handle it identically as in the case of standard. It is trivial to prove Theorem 1 for problems with singleTop. It shows that the state-merging strategy still works. However, the PRG technique is no longer working since forward transitions may pop element from stack. As a result, problems with this mode can be handled by Algorithm 1 with state-merging strategy, which also has termination guarantee.

singleTask. This mode is similar to singleTop, except that the activity instance closest to the top of the back-stack will be reused if it has the same type as the new activity to be started. Otherwise, we fall back to the case where standard is handled. For example, consider a forward transition $\tau = (A, A_{next})$ with singleTask and a state (A, V, S). Then we tries to find a state on activity A_{next} in S. If a state $(A_{next}, V_{old}, S_{old}) \in S$ is found, we adopt it as the next state and pops all state above it in S. Otherwise, we obtain the state $(A_{next}, V_{next}, S_{next})$ like standard. Similar to singleTop, the state-merging strategy still works, but the PRG technique is no longer working. Intuitively, transitions with singleTask will always generate states no more than standard. Therefore, Algorithm 1 with state-merging strategy also has termination guarantee.

singleInstance. This mode is similar to `singleTask`, except that only one instance of its activity class resides in its task. To simulate `singleInstance`, we have to maintain more than one stack for each state. Thus it is not trivial to extend our algorithm to this mode.

5 Related Work

An existing work [18] defines operational semantics for a fragment of Android that includes its Dalvik bytecode and intercommunication mechanism of the activities. It considers the Android specific activity stack and back operation. However, this work does not define GUI static models or give any analysis algorithms. Another work [7] proposes a formal model, Android Stack Machine (ASM), to capture key mechanisms of Android multi-tasking such as activities, back stacks, launch modes, as well as task affinities.

Aiming to describe real-world apps precisely, some static models are designed by researchers. Azim et al. [3] extract the Static activity Transfer Graph (SATG) for a given app, and use dynamic GUI exploration to handle dynamic activities layouts to complement the SATG. They also implement a tool A^3E which can explore real-world Android apps and construct models for them. S. Yang et al. [23] design a model called Window Transition Graph (WTG), with comprehensive behavior analysis for the key aspects of GUI behavior: widgets, event handlers, callback sequences, and especially the window stack changes. Based on the modeling of window stack, they develop analysis algorithms for WTG construction and traversal. And a recent work [24] constructs more precise activity Transition Graph with consideration of the launch-mode of each activity, which is more precise in capturing activity transitions. With help of the statically constructed activity Transition Model (ATM), Mirzaei et al. [17] give an approach to reduce the number of test cases by extracting the dependencies of GUI elements, which achieves a comparable coverage under exhaustive GUI testing using significantly fewer test cases.

Some researchers leverage dynamic techniques to construct transition model for Android apps. Amalfitano et al. [1,2] implemented a tool called *AnroidRipper* which builds model using a depth-first search over the user interface. When visiting a new state, it keeps a list of events belongs to the current state and systematically triggers them. And it restarts the exploration from the entry state when no new state can be detected in the current exploration. SwiftHand [8] builds an approximate model for the application under test, which could guide the test execution into unexplored parts of the state space while maximizing the code coverage and fault revelation. These works do not take into consideration the Android specific back stack. Yan et al. [21] make use of dynamic techniques to construct a labeled transition model (LATTE), which considers the information of activity back stack. They also implement a tool *LAND* to systematically explore real-world Android apps and construct the widget-sensitive and back-stack-aware models.

6 Conclusion

In this paper, an ATG with back transitions, value assignments and assertions, is introduced. It is a formalism for abstracting the behaviour of Android apps. Based on the PRG technique, we propose an algorithm for assertion checking over our formalism model, which has termination guarantee. Lastly, we study interesting extensions of our model and our algorithm. In the future, we would like to apply our algorithm to analyze Android apps with more activities and more states. On the other hand, automated modeling technique is also an interesting and challenging direction of our future works.

Acknowledgements. The authors are grateful to the reviewers for helpful comments and suggestions, and to Ping Wang for reading a preliminary version of this paper carefully.

References

1. Amalfitano, D., Fasolino, A.R., Tramontana, P., De Carmine, S., Memon, A.M.: Using GUI ripping for automated testing of Android applications. In: Proceedings of of ASE, pp. 258–261 (2012)
2. Amalfitano, D., Fasolino, A.R., Tramontana, P., Ta, B.D., Memon, A.M.: Mobiguitar: automated model-based testing of mobile apps. IEEE Softw. **32**(5), 53–59 (2015)
3. Azim, T., Neamtiu, I.: Targeted and depth-first exploration for systematic testing of Android apps. In: Proceedings of of OOPSLA, pp. 641–660 (2013)
4. Baek, Y.M., Bae, D.: Automated model-based android GUI testing using multi-level GUI comparison criteria. In: Proceedings of of ASE, pp. 238–249 (2016)
5. Bhoraskar, R., et al.: Brahmastra: driving apps to test the security of third-party components. In: Proceedings of USENIX, pp. 1021–1036 (2014)
6. Chen, Q.A., Qian, Z., Mao, Z.M.: Peeking into your app without actually seeing it: UI state inference and novel android attacks. In: Proceedings of USENIX, pp. 1037–1052 (2014)
7. Chen, T., He, J., Song, F., Wang, G., Wu, Z., Yan, J.: Android stack machine. In: Chockler, H., Weissenbacher, G. (eds.) CAV 2018. LNCS, vol. 10982, pp. 487–504. Springer, Cham (2018). https://doi.org/10.1007/978-3-319-96142-2_29
8. Choi, W., Necula, G.C., Sen, K.: Guided GUI testing of android apps with minimal restart and approximate learning. In: Proceedigns of OOPSLA, pp. 623–640 (2013)
9. Do, L.N.Q., Ali, K., Livshits, B., Bodden, E., Smith, J., Murphy-Hill, E.R.: Just-in-time static analysis. In: Proceedings of SIGSOFT, pp. 307–317 (2017)
10. Feng, Y., Anand, S., Dillig, I., Aiken, A.: Apposcopy: semantics-based detection of android malware through static analysis. In: Proceedings of FSE, pp. 576–587 (2014)
11. Feng, Y., Bastani, O., Martins, R., Dillig, I., Anand, S.: Automated synthesis of semantic malware signatures using maximum satisfiability. In: Proceedings of NDSS (2017)
12. Gordon, M.I., Kim, D., Perkins, J.H., Gilham, L., Nguyen, N., Rinard, M.C.: Information flow analysis of android applications in DroidSafe. In: Proceedings of NDSS (2015)

13. Huang, W., Dong, Y., Milanova, A., Dolby, J.: Scalable and precise taint analysis for android. In: Proceedings of ISSTA, pp. 106–117 (2015)
14. Li, L., et al.: IccTA: detecting inter-component privacy leaks in android apps. In: Proceedings of ICSE, pp. 280–291 (2015)
15. Lu, L., Li, Z., Wu, Z., Lee, W., Jiang, G.: CHEX: statically vetting android apps for component hijacking vulnerabilities. In: Proceedings of CCS, pp. 229–240 (2012)
16. Mahmood, R., Mirzaei, N., Malek, S.: Evodroid: segmented evolutionary testing of android apps. In: Proceedings of FSE, pp. 599–609 (2014)
17. Mirzaei, N., Garcia, J., Bagheri, H., Sadeghi, A., Malek, S.: Reducing combinatorics in GUI testing of Android applications. In: Proceedings of ICSE, pp. 559–570 (2016)
18. Payet, E., Spoto, F.: An operational semantics for android activities. In: Proceedings of PEPM, pp. 121–132 (2014)
19. Shao, Y., Luo, X., Qian, C., Zhu, P., Zhang, L.: Towards a scalable resource-driven approach for detecting repackaged android applications. In: Proceedings of ACSAC, pp. 56–65 (2014)
20. Wei, F., Roy, S., Ou, X., Robby: Amandroid: a precise and general inter-component data flow analysis framework for security vetting of android apps. In: Proceedings of SIGSAC, pp. 1329–1341 (2014)
21. Yan, J., Wu, T., Yan, J., Zhang, J.: Widget-sensitive and back-stack-aware GUI exploration for testing android apps. In: Proceedings of QRS, pp. 42–53 (2017)
22. Yang, S., Yan, D., Wu, H., Wang, Y., Rountev, A.: Static control-flow analysis of user-driven callbacks in android applications. In: Proceedings of ICSE, pp. 89–99 (2015)
23. Yang, S., Zhang, H., Wu, H., Wang, Y., Yan, D., Rountev, A.: Static window transition graphs for Android(T). In: Proceedings of ASE, pp. 658–668 (2015)
24. Zhang, Y., Sui, Y., Xue, J.: Launch-mode-aware context-sensitive activity transition analysis. In: ICSE (2018, accepted)

Emerging Applications of Formal Methods

Towards Trustworthy AI for Autonomous Systems

Hadrien Bride[2], Jin Song Dong[1,2], Zhé Hóu[2(✉)], Brendan Mahony[3], and Martin Oxenham[3]

[1] School of Computing, National University of Singapore, Singapore, Singapore
[2] Institute for Integrated and Intelligent Systems, Griffith University, Brisbane, Australia
z.hou@griffith.edu.au
[3] Defence Science and Technology Group, Edinburgh, Australia

Abstract. Trust remains a major challenge in the development, implementation and deployment of artificial intelligence and autonomous systems in defence and law enforcement industries. To address the issue, we follow the verification as planning paradigm based on model checking techniques to solve planning and goal reasoning problems for autonomous systems. Specifically, we present a novel framework named Goal Reasoning And Verification for Independent Trusted Autonomous Systems (GRAVITAS) and discuss how it helps provide trustworthy plans in uncertain and dynamic environment.

1 Introduction

Planning is a central and hard computer science problem that is essential in the development of autonomous systems. Many existing solutions require a controlled environment in order to function correctly and reliably. However, there are situations where adaptive autonomous systems are required to run for a long period of time and cope with uncertain events during the deployment. Our work is motivated by the requirements of next generation autonomous underwater vehicles (AUV) in law enforcement and defence industries. Particularly, we are currently developing a decision making system suitable for an AUV designed to stay underwater for up to 6 months with very limited communication with the outside world. The AUV is expected to carry out survey missions on its own and report details of its surveillance at semi-regular intervals. During the mission, the AUV may encounter underwater currents, deep ocean terrain, fishing boats, objects and places of interest, hostile vehicles etc., each of which may affect its ability to achieve its goals. The AUV must be able to decide which goals to pursue when such uncertain events occur and plan tasks to achieve the goals in an agile manner.

In the face of uncertain events in execution, planning becomes an even harder problem. In this case, the agent's goal may be affected and thus both selecting a new goal and re-planning are necessary. This generally follows a *note-assess-guide* procedure, where *note* detects discrepancies, *assess* hypothesises causes for

J. Sun and M. Sun (Eds.): ICFEM 2018, LNCS 11232, pp. 407–411, 2018.
https://doi.org/10.1007/978-3-030-02450-5_24

discrepancies, and *guide* performs a suitable response. Differing from classical planning where the goal is fixed, when a discrepancy is detected, it is often necessary to change the current goal. Goal reasoning is about selecting a suitable goal for the planning process. There have been various formalisms that attempt to solve planning problems in a dynamic environment, including hierarchical planning methods, such as hierarchical task networks (HTN) [3] and hierarchical goal networks (HGN) [8], and goal reasoning systems such as the Metacognitive Integrated Dual-Cycle Architecture (MIDCA) [2].

Although some of the above formalisms have been successfully applied to solve real life problems, the verification aspect of the problem remains to be addressed. Usually planning is solved by heuristic search, but this approach does not confer a sufficient level of trust. The correctness, safety, and security issues of autonomous systems are particularly important in mission-critical use cases such as our AUV example. To tackle this problem, we turn to formal methods, which have been used to solve planning problems in the literature. For example, Giunchiglia et al. proposed to solve planning problems using model checking [4] and Kress-Gazit et al.'s framework translates high-level tasks defined in linear temporal logic (LTL) to hybrid controllers [5].

Following the above ideas, in this short paper we introduce a new system called Goal Reasoning And Verification for Independent Trusted Autonomous Systems (GRAVITAS). This novel planning and goal reasoning framework has the ability to produce verifiable and explainable plans for autonomous systems. It is build upon the model checker Process Analysis Toolkit (PAT) [9], which is a self-contained tool that supports composing, simulating and reasoning about concurrent, probabilistic and timed systems with non-deterministic behaviours. The benefits of the proposed approach notably include the capacity to formulate inconsistency and incompatibility of plans as reachability/LTL properties and the ability to verify them on the fly. For instance, when a new goal is generated during execution, we can check whether the new goal conflicts with existing goals, and select the subset of goals that are compatible with each other. Finally, we can also verify the planning model itself, such that a given planning model does not output plans that may lead to undesired events.

2 Planning and Goal Reasoning via PAT

The plan and goal reasoning problems to be solved are expressed and formally defined as Goal task networks (GTNs) – an extension and unification of hierarchical task networks and hierarchical goal networks [8]. GTNs explicitly models the hierarchy among tasks and goals in ways that generally mirrors well the hierarchical structure of many real-world planning applications. This hierarchy can then be used during the planning phase following the well know *divide and conquer* scheme. Due to this, GTNs planners are much more scalable and performant than classical planners in practice.

In GRAVITAS, the verification and resolution of plan and goal reasoning problems expressed as GTNs is based on their translation to CSP# – one of the input language of PAT. This translation is fully automated and notably considers the autonomous system capabilities as well as its environments. The translated CSP# code models all the elementary actions that the autonomous system can perform together with their effects on its environment. Furthers, it also considers resource constraints and goal reasoning (e.g., prioritization of goals). To do so, it assigns economic values to both its resources and its goals in order to leverage economic reasoning. By doing so, we leverage PAT optimisation features to formulate plans that incentivises the completion of goals providing the most rewards while compromising with the resources they require to be completed. These economic notions therefore lead to the formulation of highly cost-effective plan. Additionally, when multi-agents missions are considered, they provide further benefits as market-based mechanisms [1] can be leveraged to obtain greater collaboration among agents as well as to optimise resources and tasks allocation.

Since tasks and goals are both translated into processes in CSP#, it is straightforward to check properties for tasks and goals using PAT. For instance, using we can verify that the proposed plans respect predefined safety and liveness properties (e.g., the autonomous system does not collide with obstacles, the autonomous system has the ability to join the recovery area).

3 A Trustworthy Framework for Planning and Goal Reasoning

Compared with traditional AI techniques, the planning and goal reasoning methods in our work are realised by model checking, which is an automated reasoning technique that has been successfully applied in formal verification tasks. Hence an advantage of our approach is that we can use model checking to verify correctness, safety, and security properties of the underlying model.

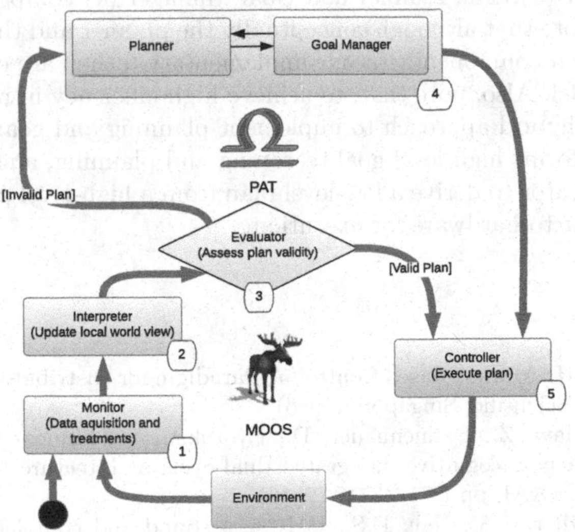

Fig. 1. Overall workflow of GRAVITAS.

To demonstrate the strengths of such approach we are developing *Goal Reasoning And Verification for Independent Trusted Autonomous Systems* (GRAVITAS) – a fully automated system enabling unmanned agents such as AUVs to autonomously operate with a high level of trust in a dynamic environment.

GRAVITAS follows a cyclic pattern composed of four main phases: Monitor, Interpret, Evaluate and Control. Figure 1 is a UML activity diagram of the overall control flow of GRAVITAS.

The main operative cycle of GRAVITAS begins with the Monitor (1). This component perceives the environment through the signal processing and fusion of the raw outputs of available sensors. It is also in charge of processing this data in order to provide information such as the estimated position and speed of the agent to the Interpreter (2). Once the Interpreter (2) receives the required information, it updates the agent's local model of the system and its environment. This formally defined local model is then forwarded to the Evaluator (3) – a component in charge of assessing the validity of the previously established plan with respect to pre-defined specifications. If the Evaluator assesses the plan to be valid, the Controller (5) is tasked with executing the plan. Alternatively, if the Evaluator (3) finds the plan invalid e.g. an uncertain event creates inconsistencies in the previously established plan and the mission requirements, a new plan needs to be formulated. The formulation of a new plan is accomplished by the joint operation of the Planner and Goals Manager components (4). After a new plan is formulated, the Controller (5) is tasked with executing this plan. This step involves processing based on control theory [6] which we do not discuss here.

In the developed framework, the components in the lower loop in Fig. 1 are orchestrated via the Mission Oriented Operating Suite [7] (MOOS) – a middleware mainly in charge of the communication. The main computational workload of the Evaluator (3), The Planner and Goal Manager (4) components are powered by PAT. Note that although conceptually the planner and the goal manager are two separated components, in our implementation they are concretized as a single PAT model. Also, note that, to achieve high efficiency in real-life applications, we use a hybrid approach to implement planning and goal reasoning: the PAT model performs high-level goal reasoning and planning, and we implement an external actuator to derive a low-level plan from a high-level plan, the former will then be sent to hardware for execution.

References

1. Clearwater, S.H.: Market-Based Control: A Paradigm for Distributed Resource Allocation. World Scientific, Singapore (1996)
2. Cox, M.T., Alavi, Z., Dannenhauer, D., Eyorokon, V., Munoz-Avila, H., Perlis, D.: MIDCA: a metacognitive, integrated dual-cycle architecture for self-regulated autonomy. In: AAAI, pp. 3712–3718 (2016)
3. Erol, K., Hendler, J.A., Nau, D.S.: UMCP: a sound and complete procedure for hierarchical task-network planning. In: AIPS, vol. 94, pp. 249–254 (1994)

4. Giunchiglia, F., Traverso, P.: Planning as model checking. In: Biundo, S., Fox, M. (eds.) ECP 1999. LNCS (LNAI), vol. 1809, pp. 1–20. Springer, Heidelberg (2000). https://doi.org/10.1007/10720246_1
5. Kress-Gazit, H., Fainekos, G.E., Pappas, G.J.: Temporal-logic-based reactive mission and motion planning. IEEE Trans. Robot. **25**(6), 1370–1381 (2009)
6. Lee, E.B., Markus, L.: Foundations of optimal control theory. Technical report, Minnesota University Minneapolis Center for Control Sciences (1967)
7. Newman, P.M.: MOOS-mission orientated operating suite (2008)
8. Shivishankar, V.: Hierarchical goal network planning: formalisms and algorithms for planning and acting. Ph.D. thesis, Department of Computer Science, University of Maryland College Park (2015)
9. Sun, J., Liu, Y., Dong, J.S., Pang, J.: PAT: towards flexible verification under fairness. In: Bouajjani, A., Maler, O. (eds.) CAV 2009. LNCS, vol. 5643, pp. 709–714. Springer, Heidelberg (2009). https://doi.org/10.1007/978-3-642-02658-4_59

Towards Dependable and Explainable Machine Learning Using Automated Reasoning

Hadrien Bride[2], Jie Dong[3], Jin Song Dong[1,2], and Zhé Hóu[2(✉)]

[1] School of Computing, National University of Singapore, Singapore, Singapore
[2] Institute for Integrated and Intelligent Systems, Griffith University, Brisbane, Australia
z.hou@griffith.edu.au
[3] Dependable Intelligence, Brisbane, Australia
jacob@depintel.com

Abstract. The ability to learn from past experience and improve in the future, as well as the ability to reason about the context of problems and extrapolate information from what is known, are two important aspects of Artificial Intelligence. In this paper, we introduce a novel automated reasoning based approach that can extract valuable insights from classification and prediction models obtained via machine learning. A major benefit of the proposed approach is that the user can understand the reason behind the decision-making of machine learning models. This is often as important as good performance. Our technique can also be used to reinforce user-specified requirements in the model as well as to improve the classification and prediction.

1 Introduction

Philip Wadler once wrote that "powerful insights arise from linking two fields of study previously thought separate" [6]. This paper, although does not provide a similar correspondence relation between two fields such as logic and computation, aims at finding an interesting application that combines machine learning and automated reasoning. There have been various attempts at applying machine learning in automated reasoning. For instance, the automated reasoning tool Sledgehammer, which is a subsystem of the proof assistant Isabelle/HOL, has a module named MaSh [3] which uses machine learning to rank the relevance of known facts in the proof context based on previous successful proofs and select a subset of facts that is estimated most helpful in proving the existing goals. The other direction, i.e., applying automated reasoning in machine learning, has not seen an application as far as we are aware of.

Recently, eXplainable Artificial Intelligence (XAI) has been gaining attention. The prestigious International Joint Conference on Artificial Intelligence (IJCAI) has notably been running a workshop specialised in this topic. From the automated reasoning community, Bonacina recently envisaged that automated

J. Sun and M. Sun (Eds.): ICFEM 2018, LNCS 11232, pp. 412–416, 2018.
https://doi.org/10.1007/978-3-030-02450-5_25

reasoning could be the key to the advances of XAI and machine learning [1]. To this end, she posed several questions and challenges in this direction. Specifically,

> "How can we bridge the gap between the statistical inferences of machine learning and the logical inferences of reasoning, applying the latter to extract, build, or speculate and test, explanations of the former?" [1]

This paper addresses the above challenge by proposing a novel framework which enables the application of automated reasoning in machine learning. First, we study a range of machine learning techniques and identify that models produced by (ensemble) decision trees based techniques are suitable for formal analysis and automated reasoning. We then propose to use satisfiability modulo theories (SMT) solvers to perform analysis on classification and prediction models given by machine learning. We discuss some preliminary results using a new machine learning tool called Silas [4].

2 Machine Learning Techniques Reviewed

To solve a problem one has to choose the right tool. In our context, to fully support the integration of automated reasoning techniques and to build towards a machine learning approach that is explainable and dependable, we require efficient machine learning techniques (in term of both memory and time) that produce interpretable models.

Linear regressions (LR), while being easily interpretable, often fall short in performance compared to other approaches [7].

Support vector machines (SVM) are popular and efficient tools, which, thanks to a large number of kernels, can be applied to a variety of classification problems. However, interpreting the models produced by SVM is far from trivial, especially when non-linear kernels are used. Hence, SVM is often used as black-boxes.

Neural networks (NN) and deep learning (DL) techniques have been exceptionally successful in analysing both structured and unstructured data, but the models they produce are intricate, hence NN and DL are often used as black-boxes, too. Also, NN and DL are often computationally expensive.

In contrast to SVMs and NNs, decision trees (DT) based techniques such as random forests (RF) and gradient boosting machines (GBM) are capable of producing interpretable and explainable models due to the formal semantics associated with there underlying tree structures. Moreover, when analysing structured data, RF and GBM often outperform other approaches including DL [5,7].

Given all the above observations, we conclude that a decision tree based machine learning approach fits our needs. The formal semantics of decision trees offers an ideal support for the application of formal methods.

3 Model Analysis and Engineering Using SMT

This sections briefly presents some of the ideas we are actively developing. They provide the basic building blocks for the application of automated reasoning tools such as SMT solvers to perform the analysis of decision tree based models.

Obtaining Model Predicates: Given a classification or a prediction model that consists of a set of decision trees, we first need to extract logical formulae from the trees. A decision tree in this context is a data structure in which every non-leaf node is associated with a logical formula that splits the data entries into two subsets. Assuming that $A, B, \cdots$ are the classes to be classified or predicted in a data set. Each leaf node contains a subset of data entries labelled by the classes. An algorithm such as majority voting is then needed to obtain the final decision. There are multiple ways to obtain logical formulae for model analysis. One can collect all the formulae from the root of a tree to a leaf node with decision A, and the *conjunction* of these formulae, called the *branch formula*, gives the reason why the subset of data entries in the leaf node are classified/predicted as A. There could be multiple leaf nodes whose decisions are all class A. The *disjunction* of all branch formulae which lead to class A represents the overall decision-making of the tree with respect to class A. We refer to this disjunction as the *decision formula* for class A. The decision formula for a class can then be used in the analysis to check inconsistencies and extract the core reason behind the decision-making. For a set of decision trees, we can extract the decision formula for class A on each tree and perform analysis on the conjunction of multiple decision formulae.

Model Anlaysis and Engineering: Once the logical formulae are extracted, we can perform a number of analyses on the formulae using automated reasoning techniques. We list some of the specific techniques we have been successfully using so far.

Maximum Satisfiable Subset (MSS): To obtain the MSS, we assign a weight to each sub-formula, and try to maximise the accumulated weight in the MAX-SMT optimisation problem. This can be achieved by certain SMT solvers such as Z3 and MathSAT 5. The weight assigned to each formula can be optimised to reflect the predictive performance of the decision node or the decision tree. For instance, a decision node with more information gain may have more weight, and a decision tree with higher predictive accuracy may have more weight. The resulting MSS can give an indication of the core attributes and the range of the attributes that lead to the decision-making of the classification and prediction model. Note that a similar analysis is to extract *maximal satisfiable subsets*, which is computationally cheaper, but we prefer the maximum subset because it may give more insight about the decision-making.

Minimal Unsatisfiable Core (MUC): Solvers such as Z3 provide a straightforward way to compute the MUC of a set of formulae. We can use this functionality to obtain the inconsistencies in the model and use this information to fine-turn the model by trimming the decision tree. This can form a recursive procedure in which we repeatedly find the MUCs in a decision tree and trim the tree accordingly until the tree becomes a consistent model. Another application is to use the MUC in boosting. A boosting algorithm usually consists of iterative learning steps in which weak classifiers are introduced to compensate the shortcomings of existing weak learners. The MUC can be effectively used as the shortcomings of multiple learners, because it represents the disagreements of multiple decision trees. We can then build weak classifiers around the MUC to boost the model performance.

Model Verification: In certain applications, the user may specify some requirements that a decision making procedure must satisfy. For instance, if machine learning is applied to classify whether a node in a network cluster is secure, our method may produce a logical condition for deciding network security. If the user has other security requirements that must be satisfied, we can use SMT solving and model checking to verify that the requirements hold in the learned model. If this is not true, then the MUC analysis can pinpoint the reason why the learned condition fails and we can use the MUC to tweak the model by inserting decision nodes that reinforce the user requirements and obtain machine learning results that conform the user's specifications.

4 Discussion

The model analysis and engineering component for machine learning can provide several benefits to users at different levels: (1) The analysis can pinpoint the reason behind the classification and prediction. This will help the user (e.g., decision maker) understand what the key attributes are and how they lead to the result. Therefore, the user can use the analytical information provided by this approach to make the final decision based on their discretion. Moreover, the analytical information can help transform the machine learning algorithm into a transparent process in which every decision can be inspected and verified. (2) The analysis can also provide the reason why some models have good performance while others have bad performance. Data scientists can use this information to improve the learning process and perform hyperparameter tuning. (3) Machine learners can use the MUC to fine-tune the models and improve classification and prediction results. They can also use the MSC to build new and consistent models that potentially have better results. (4) Model verification helps obtain machine learning results that conform with user-specified requirements. This is vital in providing a machine learning technique that can be trusted.

We have implemented and experimented with the approach introduced in this paper. We have produced a module for the machine learning tool Silas [4]. As an example, on a diabetes data set [2], we are able to analyse a random forest model and obtain a set of "core reasons" behind each class (negative/positive diabetes). By comparing the core reasons, we derive that $30 \leq age \leq 34$ and $0 < number\ of\ times\ pregnant \leq 2$ are among the key indicators for classifying positive diabetes, whereas $21 \leq age \leq 22$ and $number\ of\ times\ pregnant \leq 0$ strongly indicate negative diabetes. On the other hand, we were able to deduce that *2-hour serum insulin* is not a strong indicator for either classes, which implies that data scientists can perform certain feature engineering on the data set to improve the results. Note that the data set only contains 768 data entries (patients), so the analysis may not be representative for a large population.

Nonetheless, our implementation demonstrates the feasibility of the proposed method and shows that the combination of machine learning and automated reasoning has the potential to provide a new explainable and dependable data analysis technology.

References

1. Bonacina, M.P.: Automated reasoning for explainable artificial intelligence. In: ARCADE Workshop (in association with CADE-26), Gothenburg, Sweden (2017)
2. Dheeru, D., Taniskidou, E.K.: UCI machine learning repository (2017)
3. Kühlwein, D., Blanchette, J.C., Kaliszyk, C., Urban, J.: MaSh: machine learning for Sledgehammer. In: Blazy, S., Paulin-Mohring, C., Pichardie, D. (eds.) ITP 2013. LNCS, vol. 7998, pp. 35–50. Springer, Heidelberg (2013). https://doi.org/10.1007/978-3-642-39634-2_6
4. Dependable Intelligence Pty Ltd., Silas (2018). https://depintel.com/silas/
5. Pafka, S.: A minimal benchmark for scalability, speed and accuracy of commonly used open source implementations of the top machine learning algorithms for binary classification (2018). https://github.com/szilard/benchm-ml
6. Wadler, P.: Propositions as types. Commun. ACM **58**(12), 75–84 (2015)
7. Zhang, C., Liu, C., Zhang, X., Almpanidis, G.: An up-to-date comparison of state-of-the-art classification algorithms. Expert Syst. Appl. **82**, 128–150 (2017)

Doctoral Symposium

Modeling and Verification of Component Connectors

Xiyue Zhang(✉)

Department of Informatics and LMAM, School of Mathematical Sciences, Peking University, Beijing, China
zhangxiyue@pku.edu.cn

Abstract. Connectors have shown their great potential for coordination of different components in the large-scale distributed systems. Formal modeling and verification of connectors becomes more critical due to the rapid growth of the size of connectors. In this paper, we present a novel modeling and verification approach of Reo connectors in Coq, including the timed and probabilistic extensions of Reo. When failing to prove whether a property is satisfiable or not with Coq, Z3 solver can be used to generate counterexamples automatically. To promote automated theorem proving in Coq, we proposed an approach based on recurrent neural networks (RNNs) to predict tactics in the proving process.

Keywords: Connector · Verification · Coq

1 Introduction

Most modern software systems are distributed over large networks of components. The coordination of interactions among these components should be carefully dealt with to avoid safety problems. Coordination models introduce a formalization of connectors that integrate a number of heterogeneous components together and organize the mutual interactions among them. Reo [1,3], as a coordination model, provides a powerful mechanism for the implementation of such coordinating connectors. It is a channel-based coordination model where complex connectors are constructed from channels via composition operators.

The reliability of component-based systems highly depends on the correctness of connectors, which makes formal modeling and verification of connectors much more significant. This report presents part of the work in my PhD focusing on a modeling and verification framework for Reo and its two extensions based on the interactive theorem prover Coq [7].

Firstly, we developed a modeling and verification framework in Coq for primitive Reo, which is different from [11] in modeling method and expressive power. When failing to prove the satisfiability of connector properties in Coq, we resort to Z3 [5] to generate counterexamples automatically. Then we extended the modeling framework to cover timed channels and timed connectors as those provided in [2]. We also developed an approach based on RNNs for tactic prediction to

J. Sun and M. Sun (Eds.): ICFEM 2018, LNCS 11232, pp. 419–422, 2018.
https://doi.org/10.1007/978-3-030-02450-5_26

promote automated theorem proving, and proposed the concept *timed data distribution streams* (TDDS) to facilitate the representation of probabilistic behavior of connectors in Coq. Based on this concept, we implemented the model of probabilistic connectors and further demonstrated refinement and equivalence checking between probabilistic connectors in Coq.

2 Related Work

The coordination model Reo has been widely studied in the last decade. A comparison of various formal semantics for Reo can be found in [8].

An operational semantics for Reo using Constraint Automata (CA) was provided by Baier et al. [3] and different extensions of the CA model have been investigated in the past years. Another approach is to take advantage of existing verification tools by translating Reo to other formal models such as mCRL2 [10] and UTP [13]. In recent years, the increasing growth in the complexity of coordination connectors has made the verification of connector properties more challenging. All the automata-based or state-based modeling approaches are faced with an inherent problem: *state space explosion*. But this is not a problem in our framework. The formalization of Reo encoded in Coq can support specification of infinite behavior co-inductively and the properties can be verified through constructive proofs based on high-order logic.

Recently, machine learning has been applied to theorem proving. A comparison between the performance of a set of machine learning methods (e.g. support vector machines (SVM), gaussian processes (GP), etc.) towards automation of first-order logic proofs was provided in [4]. It has been demonstrated that deep learning based guidance in the proof search of theorem provers can gain a better performance in [12]. Kaliszyk et al. launched the first experiments with learning proof dependencies and compared various machine learning methods on a dataset from the CoRN repository [9]. Our work presented an approach of tactic-level automation for Coq based on RNN, which can guide the selection of appropriate tactics instead of manual intervention.

3 Modeling and Verification of Reo Connectors in Coq

The unified modeling and verification framework in Coq for Reo and its timed and probabilistic extensions looks like this: Basic channels, i.e. the simplest connectors, and the composition operators are specified as the basis of the modeling architecture. Complex connectors can be further constructed by channels and composition operators according to the topological structures. Connector properties under analysis are specified as lemmas or theorems in Coq as the verification goals. We then use different tactics and strategies provided in Coq to construct the proofs of the goals. Once the proof is completed, we will obtain a machine-checked proof for the properties.

The behaviors of Reo connectors (including the two extensions) are all characterized by observations on their source nodes and sink nodes. But the observations are specified through different models in different extensions. For primitive

Reo and the timed extension of Reo, the observations are captured by the notion of timed data streams. In the works of primitive Reo [15] and the timed extension [6], a set of basic channels and timed channels are specified by means of logical predicates which illustrate the relation between the timed data streams for input and output, respectively. Three types of composition operators are modeled with different methods according to their function. Some examples are provided to demonstrate how to reason about connector properties especially time-related ones and prove refinement/equivalence relations between connectors in Coq. The main difficulty of modeling probabilistic Reo lies in the representation of probability in Coq. We proposed the concept of TDDS capturing the observations of probability connectors to meet the challenge in [14]. A family of probabilistic channels were specified based on the relation characterization by means of TDDS. Compared with the formalization for non-probabilistic Reo connectors, the probabilistic properties connected closely with the uncertainty in real life coordination scenarios can be captured in this probabilistic extension and further verified in Coq [16].

4 Counterexample Generation and Tactic Prediction

Verification in Coq is capable of proving the satisfaction of properties. However, when failing to construct a proof for some property, Coq cannot automatically provide a counterexample. In such cases, we resorted to Z3, an SMT solver, to search for counterexamples automatically as a complement of property verification in Coq. Especially, we developed an algorithm for refinement relation checking. Some experiments were conducted to evaluate the performance of the approach for counterexample generation.

Property proving in Coq requires a lot of human interaction. We designed a RNN-based network architecture for tactic prediction to promote automated theorem proving in Coq. We performed experiments using two kinds of hidden units in recurrent layers and defined an evaluation standard. The comparison results between the two hidden units were collected and the network using LSTM (Long Short Term Memory) units demonstrated a better performance.

5 Conclusion and Future Work

In this paper, we summarized the main results of our research on modeling and verification of Reo and its two extensions in Coq, together with counterexample generation in Z3 solver and tactic-level automation based on RNN. Up to now, our research on this topic has led to three publications, one accepted paper and two journal submissions under the second round review.

In the future, we plan to investigate more applications of Reo to real life scenarios, such as blockchain, IoT, and deal with more properties users care about in these applications. We also want to investigate the hybrid extension of Reo which captures both discrete and continuous behavior of cyber-physical systems as well.

Acknowledgement. The work was partially supported by the National Natural Science Foundation of China under grant no. 61772038, 61532019, 61202069 and 61272160.

References

1. Arbab, F.: Reo: a channel-based coordination model for component composition. Math. Struct. Comput. Sci. **14**(3), 329–366 (2004)
2. Arbab, F., Baier, C., de Boer, F., Rutten, J.: Models and temporal logics for timed component connectors. In: Cuellar, J.R., Liu, Z. (eds.) Proceedings of SEFM 2004, pp. 198–207. IEEE Computer Society (2004)
3. Baier, C., Sirjani, M., Arbab, F., Rutten, J.: Modeling component connectors in Reo by constraint automata. Sci. Comput. Program. **61**, 75–113 (2006)
4. Bridge, J.P., Holden, S.B., Paulson, L.C.: Machine learning for first-order theorem proving - learning to select a good heuristic. J. Autom. Reason. **53**(2), 141–172 (2014)
5. de Moura, L., Bjørner, N.: Z3: an efficient SMT solver. In: Ramakrishnan, C.R., Rehof, J. (eds.) TACAS 2008. LNCS, vol. 4963, pp. 337–340. Springer, Heidelberg (2008). https://doi.org/10.1007/978-3-540-78800-3_24
6. Hong, W., Nawaz, M.S., Zhang, X., Li, Y., Sun, M.: Using Coq for formal modeling and verification of timed connectors. In: Cerone, A., Roveri, M. (eds.) SEFM 2017. LNCS, vol. 10729, pp. 558–573. Springer, Cham (2018). https://doi.org/10.1007/978-3-319-74781-1_37
7. Huet, G., Kahn, G., Paulin-Mohring, C.: The Coq proof assistant a tutorial. Rapport Technique, vol. 178 (1997)
8. Jongmans, S.T.Q., Arbab, F.: Overview of thirty semantic formalisms for Reo. Sci. Ann. Comput. Sci. **22**(1), 201–251 (2012)
9. Kaliszyk, C., Mamane, L., Urban, J.: Machine learning of coq proof guidance: first experiments. In: Proceedings of SCSS 2014. EPiC Series in Computing, vol. 30, pp. 27–34. EasyChair (2014)
10. Kokash, N., Krause, C., de Vink, E.: Reo+mCRL2: a framework for model-checking dataflow in service compositions. Form. Asp. Comput. **24**, 187–216 (2012)
11. Li, Y., Sun, M.: Modeling and verification of component connectors in Coq. Sci. Comput. Program. **113**(3), 285–301 (2015)
12. Loos, S.M., Irving, G., Szegedy, C., Kaliszyk, C.: Deep network guided proof search. In: Proceedings of LPAR 2017. EPiC Series in Computing, vol. 46, pp. 85–105. EasyChair (2017)
13. Sun, M., Arbab, F., Aichernig, B.K., Astefanoaei, L., de Boer, F.S., Rutten, J.: Connectors as designs: modeling, refinement and test case generation. Sci. Comput. Program. **77**(7–8), 799–822 (2012)
14. Sun, M., Zhang, X.: A relational model for probabilistic connectors based on timed data distribution streams. In: Jansen, D.N., Prabhakar, P. (eds.) FORMATS 2018. LNCS, vol. 11022, pp. 125–141. Springer, Cham (2018). https://doi.org/10.1007/978-3-030-00151-3_8
15. Zhang, X., Hong, W., Li, Y., Sun, M.: Reasoning about connectors in Coq. In: Kouchnarenko, O., Khosravi, R. (eds.) FACS 2016. LNCS, vol. 10231, pp. 172–190. Springer, Cham (2017). https://doi.org/10.1007/978-3-319-57666-4_11
16. Zhang, X., Sun, M.: Towards formal modeling and verification of probabilistic connectors in Coq. In: Proceedings of SEKE 2018, pp. 385–390. KSI Research Inc. and Knowledge Systems Institute Graduate School (2018)

Model Based Testing of Cyber-Physical Systems

Teck Ping Khoo(✉)

Singapore University of Technology and Design, Singapore, Singapore
teckping_khoo@mymail.sutd.edu.sg
https://sutd.edu.sg/

Abstract. Testing, inspection, and certification (TIC) are essential activities on consumer and industrial systems. The conformance to system specifications and standards can then provide assurances on system safety, security, reliability, and interoperability. TIC needs to evolve in tandem with growing system size and complexity. Common modern systems such as autonomous vehicles and smart health-care systems take the form of Cyber Physical Systems (CPSs). Model Based Testing (MBT) is one promising approach to test CPSs. An MBT framework for testing CPSs will be useful to systems testers and can raise the standard of systems testing as a whole.

Keywords: Model Based Testing · Cyber-Physical Systems
Testing framework

1 Introduction

Testing is classically done manually - A system expert will determine the right properties to be tested, derive the test cases, and carry out the tests. This well accepted approach has served the industry well. For large systems, test cases can be set up for automatic execution - this provides repeatability and productivity.

This classical approach breaks down as systems grow in scale and complexity. A Cyber-Physical System (CPS) straddles both the physical and cyber space and its output can become smarter with more inputs over time. To test CPSs, the industry needs to evolve to *automatically create* test cases, and not just *automatically execute* them. Model Based Testing (MBT) has been identified as an ideal approach for such systems. The research goal is the development of a testing framework for CPS based on MBT.

The rest of this paper is organized as follows. Section 2 provides the problem statement and motivations of the research. Section 3 provides the current development and related work. Section 4 provides the proposed solutions, approaches, methodology and their significance. Section 5 provides some current results and assessment. Section 6 provides directions for future work.

Supported by TÜV SÜD Asia Pacific Pte Ltd.

J. Sun and M. Sun (Eds.): ICFEM 2018, LNCS 11232, pp. 423–426, 2018.
https://doi.org/10.1007/978-3-030-02450-5_27

2 Problem Statement and Motivations

CPSs are systems which harness closed loop feedback from physical processes via a communication network to computational resources running smart algorithms. Such systems are integrated with the real environment, via digital control and sensing. Examples of CPSs include autonomous vehicles, smart medical services, smart manufacturing, and robotics systems. Conventional testing breaks down for such systems. Software Based Testing and virtual testing approaches have been proposed to test CPSs.

A good example of such an approach is MBT, which tests the system implementation against a model of the system specification. A system model serves as input to MBT. This model abstracts the system input and defines the expected output. A test case generator then uses the model to automatically create test cases. Should the system requirement change (and this happens often in the industry), the model can be readily updated and new test cases created.

MBT has not achieved widespread industry adoption despite its obvious value to the testing process, as well as the availability of tools. This is due to the challenging system modeling process. A clear and easy-to-use testing framework, which defines clearly how systems should be modeled, can make MBT a viable approach to testing CPSs for industry practitioners.

3 Current Development and Related Work

Related work exists which applies formal techniques to CPS. In [1], the authors developed a methodology for formally verifying a CPS. Measurements were compared against a formal description of required CPS behavior, in an attempt to discover bugs. In [2], predictive maintenance of a railroad network was done using voluminous sensor data. These sensors include temperature, strain, vision, infrared, weight and impact. This was combined with failure information, servicing records and information about the types of trains using the network. In [3], the authors used a multi-classifier machine learning approach for predictive maintenance, and applied it to semiconductor manufacturing. The authors opined that in predictive maintenance, maintenance is carried out using a gauge of the health of machinery. These works either model the system manually and then apply formal methods on the model, or build a model of the system using sensor data and use the model for prediction. A testing framework based on MBT can support the TIC activities for CPSs in these cases and is the goal of this research.

4 Proposed Approach and Significance

Our approach has three main steps. Firstly, we determine the level of system abstraction, which is essential for model building. The right level of abstraction is derived based on the analysis objective with the help from domain experts and the related standards. Secondly, once important features and variables are

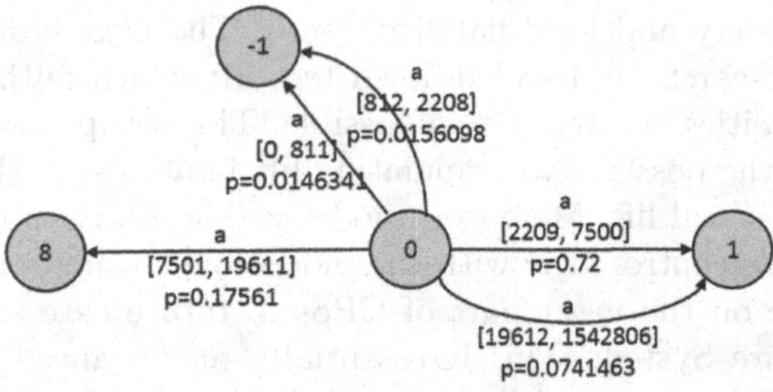

Fig. 1. Part of the PDRTA. Each transition is labeled with the event name, a timing guard, and the transition probability

identified in the first step, we develop data-driven approaches of obtaining values of features and variables from the actual system, based on sensing techniques. We remark that sensors provide only low-level system information (like instant acceleration or air pressure). To derive high-level features and variables, often domain expertise is required. Lastly, we validate the model so as to have certain confidence that the model reflects the actual system.

5 Current Results and Assessment

Applying the above-mentioned approach, we were able to model a passenger lift system in a commercial building. Sensors were installed in the lift to measure air pressure and magnetic field. The lift motion and door states were derived from these sensor readings using purpose-built inference algorithms. These data are time-stamped and becomes system events. Therefore the system is abstracted to just the lift motion and door activity. Model validation is conducted by checking that the events collected as described co-relate to reality as far as possible. Video of the door state was captured and compared to the event timings. Adjustments to event timings were made for each of the four door states of "fully closed", "opening", "fully opened" and "closing".

The processed data was fed into the Real Time Identification from Positive Samples (RTI+) algorithm [4]. The resulting model is a Probabilistic Deterministic Real Time Automata (PDRTA). Figure 1 shows part of the PDRTA. This PDRTA was subjected to model checking by the Process Analysis Toolkit (PAT) [5]. The properties to be checked are determined by lift safety standards. The model checking results fall within expectations, and variances were properly accounted for. We believe that our experience is useful for modeling other systems and our approach is applicable across a variety of systems.

6 Future Work

The current case study on lift modeling is heavily focused on a very *physical* CPS, as the lift's controller, which is the *cyber* part of the system, cannot be accessed due to safety and legal liability issues. The next best arrangement is to continue the research on a scaled-down test lift which faithfully reproduces as many functionalities of a real lift as possible. This setup allows control of the lift, and provides the possibility of emulating lift faults - something that cannot be easily done on a real lift. Moreover, model validation is straightforward - by comparing the lift's control logic with the model built using sensor data.

To cover more on the *cyber* part of CPSs, a future case study can involve a Smart Healthcare System. This is essentially an advanced web application which supports safe healthcare delivery among distributed healthcare consumers, providers and medical devices. In this case, manual modeling of the system using accepted languages, such as UML, can be done. The completed model provides a detailed specification of the system, from which test cases can be automatically generated using commercially-available tools. System logs collected at various parts of the system can be consolidated and used to model the system. These models can then be compared to the manually-derived models for accuracy. Iteration of this *model, run and compare* process will improve the testing framework and may lead to unexpected research insights into MBT or CPSs.

Additionally, there is no need to mount sensors into this system to collect data and convert them to system events - such a system should be able to create and store system logs readily. This makes the model-building process easier and less prone to errors. Finally, inputs to such a system can be more readily sent as compared to a real lift. The ability to iterate through a variety of inputs should make model validation more straightforward.

References

1. Woehrle, M., Lampka, K., Thiele, L.: Conformance testing for cyber-physical systems. ACM Trans. Embed. Comput. Syst. **11**(4), 1–23 (2012). Article 84. https://doi.org/10.1145/2362336.2362351
2. Li, H., et al.: Improving rail network velocity: a machine learning approach to predictive maintenance. Transp. Res. Part C: Emerg. Technol. **50**(1), 1726 (2014). https://doi.org/10.1145/1188913.1188915
3. Susto, G.A., Schirru, A., Pampuri, S., McLoone, S., Beghi, A.: Machine learning for predictive maintenance: a multiple classifier approach. IEEE Trans. Ind. Inform. **11**(3), 812–820 (2015)
4. Verwer, S.: Efficient identification of timed automata: theory and practice. Ph.D. dissertation. TU Delft, Delft University of Technology, July 2010. https://repository.tudelft.nl/islandora/object/uuid:61d9f199-7b01-45be.../download. Accessed 14 May 2018
5. National University of Singapore. PAT: Process Analysis Toolkit (2014). http://pat.comp.nus.edu.sg/. Accessed 17 May 2018

Service-Oriented Design and Verification of Hybrid Control Systems

Timm Liebrenz(✉)

Software and Embedded Systems Engineering, Technische Universität Berlin, Berlin, Germany
timm.liebrenz@tu-berlin.de

1 Introduction

Hybrid control systems combine discrete and continuous behavior. They switch between discrete control states and influence continuous values that evolve according to differential equations. Such systems often contain multiple interacting components that fulfill specific subtasks. To cope with the increasing complexity of the resulting systems, they are increasingly designed with model-driven development and tools like Matlab Simulink [1]. At the same time, application of these systems in safety-critical areas, like in the automotive industry or medical context, require high safety standards. Simulink is widely used in the system design in these areas and allows the design and simulation of hybrid systems. While simulation and testing can be used to validate the system for selected inputs, formal verification can ensure the correct behavior for all possible inputs.

However, the means of Simulink to use and reuse verified components in the design process is limited. While subsystems and blocks enable component-based and structural modeling in Simulink, the variability that can be modeled is limited to parameters and choosing simple functionality (e.g., whether an arithmetic block performs addition or subtraction). Furthermore, Simulink only provides limited means to verify properties for hybrid control systems. The semantics of Simulink is only informally defined, and most existing formal verification techniques are limited to a discrete subset. Additionally, most existing approaches for the formal verification of Simulink suffer from scalability issues.

In this thesis, we propose a formally well-founded, service-oriented design and verification approach for Simulink. Our approach enables flexible and reusable modeling, and compositional formal verification of hybrid control systems.

2 Related Work

Approaches that model variability in Simulink introduce elements that capture the differences between variants of the model. These differences can be captured by different representations, e.g. variability operators [2] or deltas [3]. However, these approaches are limited by the provided operators and they provide no means to describe how the changes influence the interface behavior.

J. Sun and M. Sun (Eds.): ICFEM 2018, LNCS 11232, pp. 427–431, 2018.
https://doi.org/10.1007/978-3-030-02450-5_28

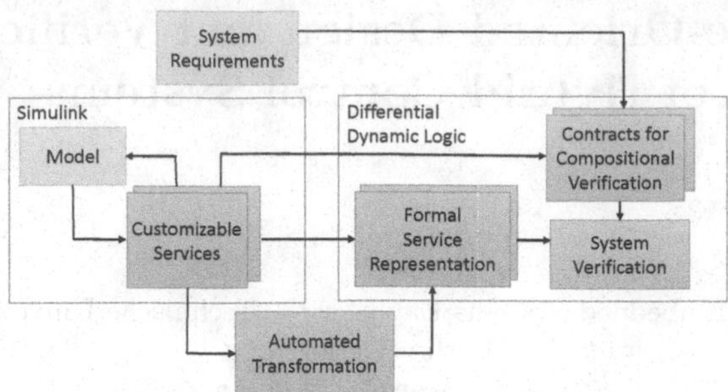

Fig. 1. Service oriented modeling and verification

The semantics of Simulink is only informally defined and this impedes the verification. Some approaches provide a formal foundation for Simulink [4], but do not provide a verification of transformed systems. Other approaches that aim for the verification of Simulink models also transform the model into a formal representation. A limitation is that they only consider a subset of blocks that can be transformed. In most approaches [5–7], only a discrete subset is considered. An extension by continuous blocks is not easily possible. Other approaches [8,9] support hybrid behavior, but only for a very special class of hybrid systems.

There also exists a few approaches that use the concept of contracts in the context of Simulink to describe the interface behavior of blocks or components. The authors of [10] present a type contract system for Simulink, which is applicable to hybrid systems. However, they only provide checks for the signal types for block outputs and inputs, and no further verification of other properties is possible. In [11], a more general approach for contracts for Simulink is presented. However, this approach only considers time-discrete components.

3 Proposed Solution

In this thesis, we propose a formally founded approach for service-orientation in Simulink to cope with the previously stated problems. The general approach is depicted in Fig. 1. We have introduced a concept of *services* for Simulink in [12], which extends components by structural variability, abstract functionality, and an abstract behavioral interface. Services can be customized with means of feature modeling, by adding, removing, and changing functionality, and applying structural changes. To provide a formal foundation for the verification of services and general Simulink models, we provide an automatic transformation into differential dynamic logic $d\mathcal{L}$ [13]. Our transformation, which is presented in [14], enables us to transform Simulink models that have hybrid behavior into a $d\mathcal{L}$ representation and allows us to use the interactive theorem prover KeYmaera X [15] for semi-automated formal verification. In [12], we have sketched a preliminary idea for *hybrid contracts*, which provide a formal foundation for the description of the interface behavior of services. They capture both the discrete and the continuous dynamic behavior of services. A contract provides guarantees for the behavior of outgoing signals if assumptions for incoming signals hold. The major advantage of contracts is that we can use them for compositional verification. The idea is that we replace subsystems (i.e. services) in a given complex Simulink model by their contracts and thus reduce the complexity of the model and the verification effort. To achieve this, we plan to extend our transformation from Simulink to d$\mathcal{L}$ [14] to use hybrid contracts instead of the inner block structure for services. There are some challenges in the introduction of contracts into the transformation. First, the contract behavior needs to be integrated into the data-flow oriented behavior of Simulink. Second, the parallel execution of different services in the contract composition must be considered, since hybrid programs in d$\mathcal{L}$ are combined with a sequential operator. Third, it is necessary to capture different behavior in the assumptions and guarantees of a contract, e.g., value bounds, discrete values, or continuous behavior.

Overall, we propose a service-oriented design and verification methodology for Simulink and a framework for efficient design and formal analysis of Simulink services. This enables compositional verification of hybrid systems that are constructed from various services. To demonstrate the applicability of our approach, we aim to apply the compositional verification approach to larger case studies with interacting components. So far, we applied our transformation to a component of a distance warner system, which was provided by an industrial partner, and were able to prove crucial properties. Previously, properties could only be verified for an adapted discrete version of this model [6]. In 21 min with interactive verification, we could show that no overflows occur in the hybrid version of the system and in 7 h we could show that according to the continuous input signal a correct time-discrete value for the distance difference is calculated. We aim to reuse these verification results in our next steps for the compositional verification of the whole distance warner system. This means that the verification of components is only done once and verification results can be reused in a compositional verification of systems that contain the respective component.

4 Conclusion and Future Work

With this thesis, we aim at providing a formally well-founded, service-oriented design and verification approach for Simulink. The key ideas of our approach are threefold: First, we have presented a service-oriented design approach for Simulink in [12], where we introduce services for Simulink, hybrid contracts to cleanly define these services, and feature models to model their variability. Second, to enable formal verification, we have presented a transformation of Simulink models in d$\mathcal{L}$ and means to verify properties for simple models in [14]. Third, to overcome scalability issues, we intend to enable compositional verification, in which the block structure of services is abstracted by their contracts. We have demonstrated the applicability of our service-oriented design approach and of our transformation from Simulink to d$\mathcal{L}$ with small and industrial case studies. In future work, we plan to integrate our service-oriented approach with our transformation into d$\mathcal{L}$ to enable compositional verification. Therefore, we intend to develop a formal representation of hybrid contracts and plan to integrate them into our transformation from Simulink to d$\mathcal{L}$. Furthermore, we aim to extend our contracts to consider the different variabilities provided by the feature models of services. We intend to investigate combined Simulink and Stateflow models to extend the set of supported systems.

References

1. MathWorks: MATLAB Simulink. www.mathworks.com/products/simulink.html
2. Alalfi, M.H., Rapos, E.J., Stevenson, A., Stephan, M., Dean, T.R., Cordy, J.R.: Semi-automatic identification and representation of subsystem variability in simulink models. In: 2014 IEEE International Conference on Software Maintenance and Evolution (ICSME), pp. 486–490. IEEE (2014)
3. Haber, A., Kolassa, C., Manhart, P., Nazari, P.M.S., Rumpe, B., Schaefer, I.: First-class variability modeling in Matlab/Simulink. In: Proceedings of the Seventh International Workshop on Variability Modelling of Software-intensive Systems, p. 4. ACM (2013)
4. Bourke, T., Carcenac, F., Colaço, J.L., Pagano, B., Pasteur, C., Pouzet, M.: A synchronous look at the simulink standard library. ACM Trans. Embed. Comput. Syst. (TECS) **16**, 176 (2017)
5. Araiza-Illan, D., Eder, K., Richards, A.: Verification of control systems implemented in simulink with assertion checks and theorem proving: a case study. In: 2015 European Control Conference (ECC), pp. 2670–2675. IEEE (2015)
6. Herber, P., Reicherdt, R., Bittner, P.: Bit-precise formal verification of discrete-time MATLAB/Simulink models using SMT solving. In: 2013 Proceedings of the International Conference on Embedded Software (EMSOFT), pp. 1–10. IEEE (2013)
7. Reicherdt, R., Glesner, S.: Formal verification of discrete-time MATLAB/Simulink models using boogie. In: Giannakopoulou, D., Salaün, G. (eds.) SEFM 2014. LNCS, vol. 8702, pp. 190–204. Springer, Cham (2014). https://doi.org/10.1007/978-3-319-10431-7_14
8. Sanfelice, R., Copp, D., Nanez, P.: A toolbox for simulation of hybrid systems in Matlab/Simulink: hybrid equations (HyEQ) toolbox. In: Proceedings of the 16th International Conference on Hybrid Systems: Computation and Control, pp. 101–106. ACM (2013)
9. Chutinan, A., Krogh, B.H.: Computational techniques for hybrid system verification. IEEE Trans. Autom. Control. **48**, 64–75 (2003)
10. Roy, P., Shankar, N.: SimCheck: a contract type system for Simulink. Innov. Syst. Softw. Eng. **7**, 73–83 (2011)
11. Boström, P., Wiik, J.: Contract-based verification of discrete-time multi-rate Simulink models. Softw. Syst. Model. **15**, 1141–1161 (2016)
12. Liebrenz, T., Herber, P., Göthel, T., Glesner, S.: Towards service-oriented design of hybrid systems modeled in simulink. In: 2017 IEEE 41st Annual Computer Software and Applications Conference (COMPSAC), vol. 2, pp. 469–474. IEEE (2017)
13. Platzer, A.: Differential dynamic logic for hybrid systems. J. Autom. Reason. **41**, 143–189 (2008)

14. Liebrenz, T., Herber, P., Glesner, S.: Deductive verification of hybrid control systems modeled in simulink with KeYmaera X. In: 20th International Conference on Formal Engineering Methods (ICFEM) (to appear)
15. Fulton, N., Mitsch, S., Quesel, J.-D., Völp, M., Platzer, A.: KeYmaera X: an axiomatic tactical theorem prover for hybrid systems. In: Felty, A.P., Middeldorp, A. (eds.) CADE 2015. LNCS (LNAI), vol. 9195, pp. 527–538. Springer, Cham (2015). https://doi.org/10.1007/978-3-319-21401-6_36

Developing Reliable Component-Based Software in *Mediator*

Yi Li(✉)

LMAM and Department of Informatics, School of Mathematical Sciences, Peking University, Beijing, China
liyi_math@pku.edu.cn

Abstract. Component-based development is widely used to reduce the development cost of complex systems. In this pattern, software features are organized, encapsulated and reused as components. In this report, we present a component-based modeling framework based on the modeling language *Mediator* that aims to build formally verified software, both on model-level and code-level. This work is the core part of a Ph.D. thesis.

Keywords: Component-based · Modeling language · *Mediator*

1 Introduction

Modern software systems are becoming more and more complex. To simplify the development phase, software developers encapsulate the features in smaller components that are easier to be developed and tested. The correctness of components are important since they are often reused by other software, hence any small vulnerabilities may lead to dozens of potential bugs. In this report, we present a formal modeling and code-generation framework based on *Mediator* where *Mediator* is a new modeling language proposed in [12]. With this framework, we can easily design high-level models and specify their properties, automatically generate runnable codes and verify both of them.

Part of this work has been published, including the modeling language *Mediator* and its formal semantics [12], and a code generator to C language [13]. We have also built a model checking integration with help of NuSMV [5] and another code generator to System C. These two works have been developed but still unpublished.

2 Related Work

Component-based software engineering has been prospering for decades. Currently, there are various tools, both formal and informal, that supports component-based modeling. For example, NI LabVIEW [16], MATLAB Simulink [7] and Ptolemy [9] provide powerful modeling platforms and a large number of built-in component libraries to support commonly-used platforms.

J. Sun and M. Sun (Eds.): ICFEM 2018, LNCS 11232, pp. 432–435, 2018.
https://doi.org/10.1007/978-3-030-02450-5_29

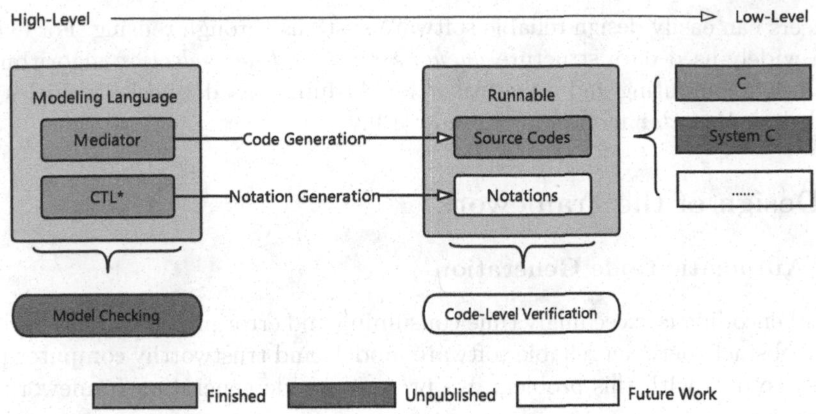

Fig. 1. The reliable development framework based on *Mediator*

However, due to the complexity of models, such tools mainly focus on synthesis and simulation, instead of formal verification. There is also a set of formal tools that prefer simple but verifiable model, e.g. Esterel SCADE [1] and rCOS [14] (Fig. 1).

In the recent years, formal method has shown its power in industrial use [8,10,15]. These works proved that formal verification techniques are capable of handling large-scale component-based embedded systems. However, the unfamiliarity of formal specifications is still one of the main obstacles hampering programmers from using formal tools. For example, even in the most famous formal modeling tools with perfect graphical user interfaces (like UPPAAL [2] and PRISM [11]), sufficient knowledge about automata theory is necessary to properly encode the models.

Importance of code generation has also been uncovered for a long time. A large number of formal and industrial code generation tools have been built for different target platforms. For example, Rodin for Event-B [4] and SCADE [3] are very popular formal tools that can generate executable codes from abstract models.

3 *Mediator*

Mediator is a component-based modeling language [12], which provides proper formalism for both high-level *system* layouts and low-level *automata*-based behavior units. Both automata and systems are encapsulated with *a set of input or output ports* (which we call an *interface*) and *a set of template parameters* so that they can be easily reused in multiple applications.

Mediator is designed to serve both software engineers and formal researchers. On the one hand, the behavior of automata is captured by guarded transitions, whose semantics is clear and self-contained. On the other hand, interfaces of automata and systems are precisely defined by ports and their types, where engineers can easily design reliable software systems through reusing. For example, a widely-used data structure *queue*, a popular *leader election* algorithm in distributed computing and a controller for Arduino-based wheeled vehicles are encoded as *Mediator* models in [12] and [13].

4 Design of the Framework

4.1 Automatic Code Generation

Manual encoding is exceedingly time consuming and error prone, and has become a huge obstacle between reliable software models and trustworthy computer programs. To deal with this problem, we present a code generation framework for *Mediator*.

The first code generator in this framework aims to generate *Arduino* C programs that can be directly downloaded to the hardware without any manual adaption [13]. As an open-sourced embedded hardware platform, various Arduino motherboards are applied in different domains, robots and quad-copters, for example. Another code generator for System C is already developed by not published yet. The framework is designed to be extensible so that users can easily develop code generators themselves.

4.2 Verification

The presented framework plans to support multi-level verification on both high-level models and low-level codes. For high-level models, we can specify properties as CTL* formulae to both *automata* and *systems*. *Mediator* models and these properties are exported into NuSMV and checked. For low-level source codes, we plan to transform the property formulae to code notations that are supported by many code-level verifiers, such as Frama-C [6], etc.

5 Conclusion and Future Work

In this report, we summarize the current status of our research on *Mediator* and its corresponding component-based modeling and verification framework which forms the core part of the presented Ph.D. thesis. Driven by this topic, we have two publications [12,13] and another two submitted. At least three more publications on this topic are planned.

In the remaining years, we will complete this framework, mainly the code-level verification part and work on more practical case studies. We are investigating the notation language of Frama-C [6], and plan to generate these notations directly from our models and CTL* properties.

Acknowledgements. The work is supervised by Prof. Meng Sun, and partially supported by the National Natural Science Foundation of China under grant no. 61532019, 61202069, 61272160 and 61772038.

References

1. Abdulla, P.A., Deneux, J., Stålmarck, G., Ågren, H., Åkerlund, O.: Designing safe, reliable systems using scade. In: Margaria, T., Steffen, B. (eds.) ISoLA 2004. LNCS, vol. 4313, pp. 115–129. Springer, Heidelberg (2006). https://doi.org/10.1007/11925040_8
2. Amnell, T., et al.: UPPAAL - now, next, and future. In: Cassez, F., Jard, C., Rozoy, B., Ryan, M.D. (eds.) MOVEP 2000. LNCS, vol. 2067, pp. 99–124. Springer, Heidelberg (2001). https://doi.org/10.1007/3-540-45510-8_4
3. Berry, G., Gonthier, G.: The Esterel synchronous programming language: design, semantics, implementation. Sci. Comput. Program. **19**(2), 87–152 (1992)
4. Cataño, N., Rivera, V.: EventB2Java: a code generator for Event-B. In: Rayadurgam, S., Tkachuk, O. (eds.) NFM 2016. LNCS, vol. 9690, pp. 166–171. Springer, Cham (2016). https://doi.org/10.1007/978-3-319-40648-0_13
5. Cavada, R., et al.: The NUXMV symbolic model checker. In: Biere, A., Bloem, R. (eds.) CAV 2014. LNCS, vol. 8559, pp. 334–342. Springer, Cham (2014). https://doi.org/10.1007/978-3-319-08867-9_22
6. Cuoq, P., Kirchner, F., Kosmatov, N., Prevosto, V., Signoles, J., Yakobowski, B.: Frama-C. In: Eleftherakis, G., Hinchey, M., Holcombe, M. (eds.) SEFM 2012. LNCS, vol. 7504, pp. 233–247. Springer, Heidelberg (2012). https://doi.org/10.1007/978-3-642-33826-7_16
7. Hahn, B., Valentine, D.T.: SIMULINK toolbox. In: Essential MATLAB for Engineers and Scientists, pp. 341–356. Academic Press (2016)
8. Jeannin, J., et al.: Formal verification of ACAS X, an industrial airborne collision avoidance system. In: Proceedings of EMSOFT 2015, pp. 127–136. IEEE (2015)
9. Kim, H., Lee, E.A., Broman, D.: A toolkit for construction of authorization service infrastructure for the internet of things. In: Proceedings of IoTDI 2017, pp. 147–158. ACM (2017)
10. Klein, G., et al.: seL4: formal verification of an OS kernel. In: Proceedings of SOSP 2009, pp. 207–220. ACM (2009)
11. Kwiatkowska, M., Norman, G., Parker, D.: PRISM 4.0: verification of probabilistic real-time systems. In: Gopalakrishnan, G., Qadeer, S. (eds.) CAV 2011. LNCS, vol. 6806, pp. 585–591. Springer, Heidelberg (2011). https://doi.org/10.1007/978-3-642-22110-1_47
12. Li, Y., Sun, M.: Component-based modeling in mediator. In: Proença, J., Lumpe, M. (eds.) FACS 2017. LNCS, vol. 10487, pp. 1–19. Springer, Cham (2017). https://doi.org/10.1007/978-3-319-68034-7_1
13. Li, Y., Sun, M.: Generating arduino C codes from *mediator*. In: de Boer, F., Bonsangue, M., Rutten, J. (eds.) It's All About Coordination. LNCS, vol. 10865, pp. 174–188. Springer, Cham (2018). https://doi.org/10.1007/978-3-319-90089-6_12
14. Liu, Z., Morisset, C., Stolz, V.: rCOS: theory and tool for component-based model driven development. In: Arbab, F., Sirjani, M. (eds.) FSEN 2009. LNCS, vol. 5961, pp. 62–80. Springer, Heidelberg (2010). https://doi.org/10.1007/978-3-642-11623-0_3
15. Miller, S.P., Whalen, M.W., Cofer, D.D.: Software model checking takes off. Commun. ACM **53**(2), 58–64 (2010)
16. National Instruments: Labview. http://www.ni.com/zh-cn/shop/labview.html

Model Checking Nash-Equilibrium - Automatic Verification of Robustness in Distributed Systems

Dileepa Fernando(✉)

National University of Singapore, Computing 1, 13 Computing Drive, Singapore 117417, Singapore
fdileepa@comp.nus.edu.sg

Abstract. Verifying whether rational participants in a BAR system (a distributed system including *Byzantine*, *Altruistic* and *Rational* participants) would deviate from the specified behaviour is important but challenging. Existing works consider this as Nash-equilibrium verification in a multi-player game. There is no automatic verification algorithm to address it in probabilistic settings. In this work, we introduce PBAR system and propose model checking algorithms to verify Nash-equilibrium. We perform case studies to validate the algorithms.

1 Introduction

In general, most real-world systems involve collaboration of many distributed parties, e.g., Internet routing [15], peer-to-peer file sharing [4], cooperative backup [12], etc. In these distributed systems, agents are assumed to follow the rules or specifications in the system designs to achieve system correctness. However, even if distributed systems are designed correctly, errors can be introduced in implementation and real operation. Hence, a system is not only expected to be correct but also to be robust in the sense that system should be able to withstand and recover the implementation and operation errors. Verification of robustness has become necessary but challenging with the increasing complexity of systems and the uncertainty of the errors e.g. Incompatibility with new systems.

Verification of robustness has been explored in physical systems and software systems. Simulation and software testing are conventional methods used to verify robustness in both physical and software systems respectively. With the increasing criticality, researchers are interested on more rigorous verification methodologies. As a result, model checking based verification algorithms have been developed [1].

Currently, profit motivated design has been popular in distributed systems, which reward agents based on their contribution towards system goals (i.e. block chain [8]). In this setting, rational agents may deviate from the system rules to improve their profit. Hence, a new source of error is added to a system which is named as rational fault. Another source of error is the adversarial agents

J. Sun and M. Sun (Eds.): ICFEM 2018, LNCS 11232, pp. 436–440, 2018.
https://doi.org/10.1007/978-3-030-02450-5_30

aiming more at the failures of other agents than the maximisation of their own profits which is named as Byzantine fault. This fault can also be introduced from misconfigured agents. Agents who follow the system rules are called 'Altruistic'. This model was introduced in [3] and called BAR system. In a BAR system, it is important that system goals are achieved irrespective of the existence of rational and Byzantine agents. The above property is named as BAR-tolerance and it is an important sub area of ensuring system robustness.

Rigorous verification of BAR-tolerance is studied in [2,5,11] where game theoretic property Nash-equilibrium is used to formalise BAR-tolerance property in most approaches. However, all of the above work used manual proof for property verification which is infeasible in complex BAR system analysis. Mari et. al. proposes automatic verification algorithms for BAR-tolerance in [13]. These automatic BAR-tolerance verification algorithms are limited to non probabilistic BAR systems. We observe that automatic verification of probabilistic BAR (PBAR) tolerance has not yet been studied and is of high importance.

Problem Statement. Therefore, we aim to develop a framework to automatically verify PBAR-tolerance.

The above aim can be achieved by the following objectives.

1. Formalize PBAR system.
2. Formalize PBAR-tolerance property as Nash-equilibrium.
3. Develop verification algorithm to automatically verify Nash-equilibrium of PBAR system.
4. Validate the algorithm using case studies.

2 Nash Equilibrium Verification of PBAR [6]

In order to meet our objectives we first formalize the PBAR system as a probabilistic finite state machine where operations are defined as probabilistic state transitions. We assume a set of agents with Byzantine faults named as the set of Byzantine agents Z. For each non-Byzantine agent, we analyse whether the agent would deviate from the specification. That is, given a non-Byzantine agent i, we consider i as rational, having the choice of following or deviating from the specification, while considering other non-Byzantine agents as altruistic-following specification. We consider the important class of PBAR systems in which the protocol termination with probability 1 is necessary (e.g.: Randomized secret sharing [2]). To verify the PBAR-tolerance property we calculate non Byzantine agent i's maximum rational reward from initial state in k-steps $V_i^k(\mathit{init})$ and his altruistic reward from initial state in k-steps $U_i^k(\mathit{init})$. If $U_i^k(\mathit{init}) \geq V_i^k(\mathit{init})$ remains true after $k \geq m$ for some $m \geq 0$ then we say that the protocol is PBAR-tolerant. This exactly captures Nash-equilibrium in game-theory that given a Byzantine set, a rational and remaining set of altruistic agents there is no better choice for the rational agent. i.e. following the specification is Nash-equilibrium strategy.

We propose an efficient verification algorithm to verify Nash-equilibrium of the PBAR system. Finally, we apply the algorithm in two case studies, Rock-paper-scissors and Shamir's secret sharing. For the best of our knowledge, this is the first attempt of verifying Nash-equilibrium of PBAR systems.

In this work we only consider games terminating with probability 1. However, there is a class of PBAR systems in which the protocols never end (i.e.blockchain [8]). In addition, we verify PBAR tolerance by considering individual deviations. This is not sufficient for PBAR systems as agents may not be profitable by individual deviation but may be profitable by forming a group. We introduce in our second work, an extended PBAR model and a new formalization of PBAR-tolerance which addresses the coalition of rational agents in non-terminating game.

3 ϵ-Strong Nash Equilibrium Verification of PBAR [7]

The extended PBAR system in this work represents non-terminating protocol and its reward is discounted with discount factor β for convergence in long-run. In the extended PBAR system, the non-termination is addressed by discounting the reward with factor β for convergence in the long-run.

Since we consider group deviations, the rational strategy is defined for infinite length for a group of agents (Σ_C^∞). We also define regret value (ϵ) to specify the minimum significant reward gain of rational reward over altruistic reward. For any non Byzantine group C, If agents in C has no strategy Σ_C^∞ from initial state s which gives rational reward ($v_{i',Z}(s, \Sigma_C^\infty)$) that is significantly (ϵ) larger than altruistic reward ($U_{i',Z}^\infty(s)$), we say that the protocol is PBAR-tolerant with ϵ. The above PBAR-tolerance property follows the concept of strong Nash-equilibrium [14].

We propose an approximate verification algorithm by allowing a precision value δ (to approximate the reward value for infinite steps) verify strong Nash-equilibrium of the extended PBAR system. We also performed three case studies job scheduling [13], apple picking game [10] and secret sharing [2] to validate the algorithm. Our algorithm worked more efficiently compared to the state-of-art optimal strategy computing tools [9]. The apple picking game case study revealed that there is need for improving the scalability of the algorithm.

Currently developed automatic PBAR-tolerance verification algorithms can be efficiently applied to real systems such as shamir's secret sharing. However, when finer details are considered, system can be complex (e.g. blockchain [8]). In this scenario current verification algorithm is not scalable. In the next work, we consider improving the scalability of algorithms.

4 Nash Equilibrium Verification for Large PBAR Systems

As highlighted in the previous section, we propose methods to improve scalability of the verification algorithms in this work. Since the algorithms perform a state space exploration in the finite state machine, the efficiency is highly dependant on the size of state space. We plan to apply statistical model checking to neglect the states which provide minor rewards. In order to choose such states we plan to introduce heuristic functions that can provide estimations of long-run rewards in short steps.

5 Future Directions

As future work, we plan to aggregate all our algorithms in a tool and integrate to Process Analysis Toolkit (PAT) model checker [16]. We will also design a specification language for more intuitive specification of PBAR systems. In addition, we only considered PBAR-tolerance aspect which is a sub area of ensuring system robustness as mentioned in Sect. 1. In order to ensure the robustness, error recoverability should also be considered. Formalizing PBAR-recoverability as Nash-equilibrium stability (i.e. ensuring that small deviation of one rational agent is not profitable and do not encourage another rational agent to deviate), opens an interesting research direction.

References

1. Abdulla, P.A., Jonsson, B., Nilsson, M., Saksena, M.: A survey of regular model checking. In: Gardner, P., Yoshida, N. (eds.) CONCUR 2004. LNCS, vol. 3170, pp. 35–48. Springer, Heidelberg (2004). https://doi.org/10.1007/978-3-540-28644-8_3
2. Abraham, I., Alvisi, L., Halpern, J.Y.: Distributed computing meets game theory: combining insights from two fields. SIGACT News **42**(2), 69–76 (2011)
3. Aiyer, A., Alvisi, L., Clement, A., Dahlin, M., Martin, J.P., Porth, C.: BAR fault tolerance for cooperative services. In: Proceedings of 20th ACM Symposium on Operating Systems Principles 2005, pp. 45–58 (2005)
4. Backes, M., Ciobotaru, O., Krohmer, A.: RatFish: a file sharing protocol provably secure against rational users. In: Gritzalis, D., Preneel, B., Theoharidou, M. (eds.) ESORICS 2010. LNCS, vol. 6345, pp. 607–625. Springer, Heidelberg (2010). https://doi.org/10.1007/978-3-642-15497-3_37
5. Clement, A., Li, H.C., Napper, J., Martin, J.P., Alvisi, L., Dahlin, M.: Bar primer. In: International Conference on Dependable Systems and Networks, vol. 8, pp. 287–296. Citeseer (2008)
6. Fernando, D., Dong, N., Jegourel, C., Dong, J.: Verification of Nash-equilibrium for probabilistic bar systems. In: International Conference on Engineering of Complex Computer Systems, pp. 53–62. IEEE (2016)
7. Fernando, D., Dong, N., Jegourel, C., Dong, J.: Verification of strong Nash-equilibrium for probabilistic bar systems. In: International Conference on Formal Engineering Methods (2018, to appear)
8. Kiayias, A., Koutsoupias, E., Kyropoulou, M., Tselekounis, Y.: Blockchain mining games. In: Proceedings of 2016 ACM Conference on Economics and Computation, pp. 365–382. ACM (2016)
9. Kwiatkowska, M., Parker, D., Wiltsche, C.: PRISM-games 2.0: a tool for multi-objective strategy synthesis for stochastic games. In: Chechik, M., Raskin, J.-F. (eds.) TACAS 2016. LNCS, vol. 9636, pp. 560–566. Springer, Heidelberg (2016). https://doi.org/10.1007/978-3-662-49674-9_35

10. Leibo, J., Zambaldi, V., Lanctot, M., Marecki, J., Graepel, T.: Multi-agent reinforcement learning in sequential social dilemmas. In: Proceedings of 16th Conference on Autonomous Agents and MultiAgent Systems, pp. 464–473. ACM (2017)
11. Li, H., et al.: BAR gossip. In: 7th Symposium on Operating Systems Design and Implementation, pp. 191–204 (2006)
12. Lillibridge, M., Elnikety, S., Birrell, A., Burrows, M., Isard, M.: A cooperative internet backup scheme. In: Proceedings of the General Track: 2003 USENIX Annual Technical Conference, pp. 29–41. USENIX (2003)
13. Mari, F.: Verification and synthesis for discrete time linear hybrid systems. Ph.D. thesis, Universita di Roma (2009)
14. Shinohara, R.: Coalition-proof equilibria in a voluntary participation game. Int. J. Game Theory **39**(4), 603–615 (2010)
15. Shneidman, J., Parkes, D.C.: Specification faithfulness in networks with rational nodes. In: Proceedings of 23rd Annual ACM Symposium on Principles of Distributed Computing, pp. 88–97. ACM (2004)
16. Sun, J., Liu, Y., Dong, J.S., Pang, J.: PAT: towards flexible verification under fairness. In: Bouajjani, A., Maler, O. (eds.) CAV 2009. LNCS, vol. 5643, pp. 709–714. Springer, Heidelberg (2009). https://doi.org/10.1007/978-3-642-02658-4_59

Analyzing Security and Privacy in Design and Implementation of Web Authentication Protocols

Kailong Wang(✉)

National University of Singapore, Singapore, Singapore
dcswaka@nus.edu.sg

Abstract. Web authentication protocols have become the basis in safeguarding the users' sensitive data managed by the web services. Provided the critical role of web authentication protocols, their security and privacy properties deserve rigorous analysis. In this work, the target is to formally analyze both security and privacy properties of web authentication protocol designs and implementations.

1 Introduction

Web authentication protocols (e.g. Single Sign-on protocol) serve as a crucial safe-guard of the sensitive data (such as private communication contents, photos, browsing history, banking information, etc.) from millions of individuals and organizations against the malicious activities (such as data modification, identity spoofing) over the Internet.

However, previous research has continually revealed that the web authentication is vulnerable and prone to security attacks [1,5,15]. The commonly used informal techniques such as program analysis is efficient to identify security flaws in the web authentication protocols yet impossible to prove the correctness of the security property. Moreover, privacy has become a critical concern for the web users who are easily exposed to the malicious activities over the Internet. The recent notorious privacy leakage from Facebook has affected as many as 87 million people [9]. Nonetheless, few of the prior work has focused on the privacy property of web authentication protocols. Given the important role of the web authentication protocols, it is imperative to rigorously analyze and formally verify the security and privacy properties before they are practically deployed.

The challenge for rigorously assessing and formally verifying web authentication protocols is at least three fold. First, an accurate formal model of the complex web infrastructure utilized by web authentication protocols is required. The web infrastructure includes at least web servers, web browsers and various communication channels. Second, web authentication protocols are exposed to a large attack surface (i.e. attacks from malicious communicating entities, network, etc.), therefore, a comprehensive set of security and privacy attacker behaviors should be formalized. Third, abstraction or reduction techniques need

J. Sun and M. Sun (Eds.): ICFEM 2018, LNCS 11232, pp. 441–445, 2018.
https://doi.org/10.1007/978-3-030-02450-5_31

to be applied to the complex designs and implementations of web authentication protocols, before the state-of-the-art formal analysis tools can be used.

In order to address the challenges, this work consists of three following steps. First, at the protocol design level, cryptographic protocol design is notoriously known as error prone. Additionally, some web authentication protocols are designed without privacy in mind. Therefore, it is desirable to develop a framework to facilitate the formal analysis of the security and privacy properties of the web authentication protocol design. Second, at the implementation level, security and privacy vulnerabilities can still be introduced even with a correct protocol design. Therefore, it is desirable to propose a framework to formally analyze the security and privacy properties of the web authentication protocol implementation. Last, I aim to propose and implement a more powerful web authentication protocol (e.g. a new single sign-on protocol) that is both security- and privacy-preserving. At the same time, the proposed protocol design and implementation should be verified utilizing the previously proposed two frameworks.

2 Related Work

Security Property Analysis. Many prior work facilitates the security analysis of web authentication protocols using program analysis (including static program analysis and dynamic program analysis such as whitebox and blackbox testing) directly on the web authentication protocol implementations [10,13]. In addition to program analysis presented earlier, some formal analysis approaches have been applied on the analysis of security properties of web authentication protocol designs [1,14]. Bansal et al. [4] analyzed the OAuth2.0 protocol using the applied pi-calculus and the WebSpi library which facilitates the modeling of web applications and web-based attackers.

Privacy Property Analysis. Few work has focused on the privacy of web authentication protocols. Fett et al. [5,6] manually analyzed the privacy property of BrowserID using trace indistinguishability. They construct a comprehensive BrowserID protocol model and the web infrastructure model but they are too complex to be analyzed using the state-of-the-art formal verification tools.

Web Infrastructure Modeling. Prior work [11] considers a very limited web model. TrustFound [2,8] has included a model for network attacker. Bansal et al. [3,4] have proposed a more comprehensive web infrastructure model in the applied pi calculus named WebSpi. Fett et al. [5–7] have constructed a complete web infrastructure model following the published standards and specifications for the web.

3 Preliminary Work

The following work I have completed [12] is to formally analyze the security and privacy properties on the design level of single sign-on (SSO) protocols which are the well-known and widely-deployed web authentication protocols. We have proposed a framework facilitating formal modeling of SSO protocols and analysis of their security and privacy properties. Our framework incorporates a formal model of the web infrastructure that is relevant to SSO protocols (network channels including HTTP and HTTPS channels, client browser and web servers), a set of attacker models (three types of malicious IDPs (identity providers): honest-but-curious IDP which can sniff traffic and infer user activity information, malicious IDP server which can send fake responses and malicious IDP client which resides in the client's browser and is able to invoke browser APIs) and formalizations of the security and privacy properties with respect to SSO protocols. The modeling language used in this work is the applied pi calculus which can be automatically verified by the tool ProVerif. The authentication (the security property considered in this work) of SSO protocol is formalized as correspondence and privacy property is formalized as observational equivalence.

I formally analyzed four well-known SSO protocols: SPRESSO, BrowserID, OAuth1.0a and OAuth2.0. Each of the analysis requires an SSO model consisting of sub models of the IDP, the RPs (relying parties which are the third party websites the user logs in to), the web browser, the web infrastructure and the attackers. I first manually modeled the RPs, IDPs and web browser as paralleled processes according to the SSO protocol specifications. The web infrastructure is provided by the framework. Then, I transformed the honest IDP into the malicious IDP according to the attacker model in the framework. Last, the security and privacy properties were queried against the SSO model in ProVerif. A new type of privacy attack has been identified that allows malicious participants to learn which websites the victim users have logged in to. This type of attacks occur even for the declared privacy-respecting SSO protocols such as SPRESSO and BrowserID.

4 Future Work

Analyzing Security and Privacy Properties on Web Authentication Protocol Implementations. For the next step, I target at the formal analysis of the web authentication protocol implementations on the source code which is assumed to be available to the web service providers. Software model checking can be used to directly check the security and privacy properties against certain attack models on the protocol implementation. Similar to the traditional model checking, software model checking performs exhaustive search on the protocol implementation state space for the property violations. One prominent challenge is the state-explosion problem in software model checking especially when analyzing large-scale and complicated programs. This can possibly be mitigated using reduction and program abstraction techniques.

Design and Implementation of a Secure and Privacy-Respecting Web Authentication Protocol. The aim is to provide a solution towards a secure and privacy-respecting web authentication protocol. A possible solution is to introduce a proxy server in the original three-participant architecture. The proxy server is acting as the "sorting and delivery center" that accepts the user login requests and delivers the requests to the corresponding relying parties or the identity providers, and vice versa. Further, the traffic through the proxy adds a randomized but acceptable delay to eliminate the corresponding timestamps of the incoming and outgoing network packets to form anonymous communication. I plan to design the protocol following this idea and then implement the protocol. I will apply the formal analysis on the security and privacy properties of the proposed protocol at both design level and implementation level utilizing the framework proposed previously.

References

1. Bai, G., et al.: AuthScan: automatic extraction of web authentication protocols from implementations. In: NDSS (2013)
2. Bai, G., Hao, J., Wu, J., Liu, Y., Liang, Z., Martin, A.: Trustfound: towards a formal foundation for model checking trusted computing platforms. In: FM, pp. 110–126 (2014)
3. Bansal, C., Bhargavan, K., Delignat-Lavaud, A., Maffeis, S.: Keys to the cloud: formal analysis and concrete attacks on encrypted web storage. In: Basin, D., Mitchell, J.C. (eds.) POST 2013. LNCS, vol. 7796, pp. 126–146. Springer, Heidelberg (2013). https://doi.org/10.1007/978-3-642-36830-1_7
4. Bansal, C., Bhargavan, K., Maffeis, S.: Discovering concrete attacks on website authorization by formal analysis. In: CSF, pp. 247–262 (2012)
5. Fett, D., Küsters, R., Schmitz, G.: An expressive model for the web infrastructure: definition and application to the BrowserID SSO system. In: IEEE S&P (2014)
6. Fett, D., Küsters, R., Schmitz, G.: Analyzing the BrowserID SSO system with primary identity providers using an expressive model of the web. In: Pernul, G., Ryan, P.Y.A., Weippl, E. (eds.) ESORICS 2015. LNCS, vol. 9326, pp. 43–65. Springer, Cham (2015). https://doi.org/10.1007/978-3-319-24174-6_3
7. Fett, D., Küsters, R., Schmitz, G.: SPRESSO: a secure, privacy-respecting single sign-on system for the web. In: CCS, pp. 1358–1369 (2015)
8. Hao, J., Liu, Y., Cai, W., Bai, G., Sun, J.: vTRUST: a formal modeling and verification framework for virtualization systems. In: ICFEM, pp. 329–346 (2013)
9. Reuters: Facebook says data leak hits 87 million users, widening privacy scandal. https://www.reuters.com/article/us-facebook-privacy/facebook-says-data-leak-hits-87-million-users-widening-privacy-scandal-idUSKCN1HB2CM
10. Sciarretta, G., Carbone, R., Ranise, S., Armando, A.: Anatomy of the Facebook solution for mobile single sign-on: security assessment and improvements (2017)
11. Sun, S.T., Hawkey, K., Beznosov, K.: Systematically breaking and fixing openID security: formal analysis, semi-automated empirical evaluation, and practical countermeasures. Comput. Secur. **31**(4), 465–483 (2012)
12. Wang, K., Bai, G., Dong, N., Dong, J.S.: A framework for formal analysis of privacy on SSO protocols. In: Lin, X., Ghorbani, A., Ren, K., Zhu, S., Zhang, A. (eds.) SecureComm 2017. LNICST, vol. 238, pp. 763–777. Springer, Cham (2018). https://doi.org/10.1007/978-3-319-78813-5_41
13. Wang, R., Chen, S., Wang, X.: Signing me onto your accounts through Facebook and Google: a traffic-guided security study of commercially deployed single-sign-on web services. In: IEEE S&P (2012)

14. Wang, R., Zhou, Y., Chen, S., Qadeer, S., Evans, D., Gurevich, Y.: Explicating SDKs: uncovering assumptions underlying secure authentication and authorization. In: USENIX Security, pp. 399–414 (2013)
15. Ye, Q., Bai, G., Wang, K., Dong, J.S.: Formal analysis of a single sign-on protocol implementation for Android. In: ICECCS, pp. 90–99 (2015)

Combining Deep Learning and Probabilistic Model Checking in Sports Analytics

Kan Jiang(✉)

School of Computing, National University of Singapore, Singapore, Singapore
jiangkan@comp.nus.edu.sg

Abstract. Deep Learning (DL) is good at finding the patterns hidden in big data, while Markov Decision Process (MDP) is good at modeling the dynamics in a complex system for formal analysis, e.g. Probabilistic Model Checking (PMC). The two models complement each other. Unlike the black box DL-Only model, the combined model is interpretable. Unlike the MDP-Only model, the combined model is able to draw deep insights from the data. Both interpretability and capability of finding deep insights are desirable in many applications, including sports analytics. In this paper, we propose to combine DL and PMC, and apply it in sports analytics to find an accurate and interpretable winning strategy.

Keywords: Machine learning · Model checking
Markov Decision Process · Sports strategy analytics

1 Background, Motivation and Our Approach

The recent development in Artificial Intelligence (AI) has been considered as the fourth industrial revolution [1]. Much of this development is due to the rapid progress of Deep Learning (DL). DL is a class of algorithms designed to discover the patterns hidden in big data by using many layers of computing units, also known as Deep Neural Network (DNN). DNN has already exceeded the human experts performance in specific fields. For example, in the task of detecting pneumonia using chest X-Rays, a Deep Neural Network which achieved higher accuracy than human radiologists was reported by [2]. However, such high performance DNNs are often too complex to be interpretable, because they consist of many neurons, and many more connections between the neurons [3]. The lack of interpretability restricts the usage of DNN in many domains, for example, in sports analytics, where the goal is to find an interpretable strategy to improve the winning chance.

Traditionally, sports analytics uses the approach in Fig. 1(a), i.e. DL-Only model. For example, in this approach, a tennis game is modelled as a black box with several input features such as player rankings, court surface, ace rates, double fault rates, etc. and with winning chance as the output. Although this

J. Sun and M. Sun (Eds.): ICFEM 2018, LNCS 11232, pp. 446–449, 2018.
https://doi.org/10.1007/978-3-030-02450-5_32

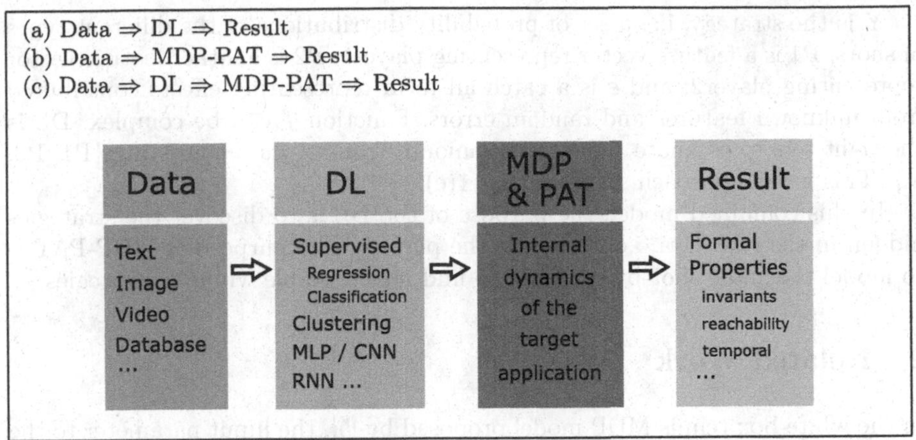

Fig. 1. (a), (b) and (c) represent the 3 ways of using DL and MDP. A diagram shows the many options of Data, DL, MDP and Results applicable in the (c) approach. PAT is a software for probabilistic model checking.

model can predict the winning chance quite well [4], it cannot suggest interpretable strategy to improve the winning chance. For example, suggestion such as "improve your ranking will improve your winning chance" is correct, but does not really help the players.

To overcome the interpretability issue, we look beyond DL. Traditionally, Markov Decision Process (MDP) is used in formal analysis for software, computer system, and protocols. In 2015, the authors in [5] proposed an innovative idea of modeling the tennis game using MDP. The goal is to model every shot in the tennis game and to find interpretable strategies to improve the winning chance. Essentially, each shot moves the game into the next state. The choice made by the player, such as forehand or backhand, and the direction of the shot, such as cross court or downline, represent the player's strategy. The strategy, in the form of a set of probability distributions, is the input to the MDP model. Using probabilistic model checker, e.g. PAT [6,7], one can calculate the winning chance associated with the input.

One challenge of this model is how to find the input parameters from the raw data for all pairs of players. If we assume the strategy between a pair of players remains the same, and if we have enough historical matches between this exact pair, we can count the frequencies of the different types of shots, and use that as the strategy between these 2 players. However, it is difficult to find enough matches with sufficient details for every pair of players.

We plan to solve this problem based on a reasonable assumption that the strategy is related to both players in the pair, although the relation can be complex.

$$Y = f(P1, P2) + \varepsilon \tag{1}$$

Y is the strategy, i.e. a set of probability distributions of the different types of shots; P1 is a feature vector representing player1; P2 is another feature vector representing player2; and ε is a catch all term representing effects contributed from unknown features and random errors. Function f can be complex. DL is the right tool to estimate f by a large amount training data consisting {P1, P2, Y}. This is the approach shown in Fig. 1(c).

In this combined model, the purpose of the DL is to discover the strategies hidden in the raw data, i.e. to profile the players. The purpose of MDP-PAT is to model the game shot-by-shot and to find interpretable winning strategies.

2 Related Work

In the white-box tennis MDP model proposed by [5], the input parameter to the model, i.e. a set of distributions, was calculated using simple average based on the historical matches. It followed the approach shown in Fig. 1(b). In our work, we applied deep learning to calculate these distributions.

Like the traditional approach, The work in [4] models a tennis game as a black-box. Players or coaches cannot use this kind of model to find an interpretable strategy. In our work, we use white-box MDP model, hence are able to find an interpretable winning strategy.

In [8], the authors focused on predicting 1st serve pattern using Hawk-Eye data. Hawk-Eye is a high speed camera system, which constantly captures the tennis ball and player positions and movements. Their paper used un-supervised machine learning technique to cluster the large amount of Hawk-Eye data to find the patterns. In our work, we use supervised learning based on a smaller amount of labelled data, without relying on Hawk-Eye data.

3 Challenges and Research Plan

Since the goal is to find an interpretable winning strategy, we should start by constructing a suitable MDP model for the intended game. Once the MDP model is available, we then know what input parameters, i.e. a set of probability distributions, are needed, consequently, we can build DNN to discover these parameters. If the required training data for the DL is readily available, we can start the DL right away. However, in case the required data is missing, we will apply computer vision and multimedia analysis techniques to source for the data.

We have already conducted several experiments following the above mentioned steps in the tennis analytics. The tennis MDP model was proposed by [5]. Having experimented with several DNNs, we are able to discover a set of probability distributions for every pair of players. However, the accuracy of the predicted final match result is not good enough. We need to re-design the DNN in order to achieve better result.

In summary, our plan is:

- We will apply PMC to a wider range of sports analytics. For example, we are building MDP models to model cricket, which is a team-based sport requiring many decisions to be made. In particular, we aim to identify best practices to balance the MDP model complexity, interpretability and its accuracy.
- We will further experiment how to best design DNNs to discover the parameters for the MDP model. In particular, we aim to achieve high accuracy with limited data.
- We will apply video and audio recognition techniques to acquire the missing data or to improve the quality of existing data.

References

1. The Fourth Industrial Revolution: what it means and how to respond. World Economic Forum. http://www.weforum.org/agenda/2016/01/the-fourth-industrial-revolution-what-it-means-and-how-to-respond/. Accessed 16 May 2018
2. Rajpurkar, P., et al.: CheXNet: radiologist-level pneumonia detection on chest x-rays with deep learning. arXiv preprint arXiv:1711.05225 (2017)
3. Doshi-Velez, F., Kim, B.: Towards a rigorous science of interpretable machine learning. arXiv preprint arXiv:1702.08608 (2017)
4. Sipko, M.: Machine learning for the prediction of professional tennis matches. MEng Computing - Final Year Project, Imperial College London (2015)
5. Dong, J.S., Shi, L., Chuong, L.V.N., Jiang, K., Sun, J.: Sports strategy analytics using probabilistic reasoning. In: Proceedings of the 2015 20th International Conference on Engineering of Complex Computer Systems (ICECCS) (ICECCS 2015), pp. 182–185. IEEE Computer Society, Washington, DC (2015)
6. Sun, J., Liu, Y., Dong, J.S., Pang, J.: PAT: towards flexible verification under fairness. In: Bouajjani, A., Maler, O. (eds.) CAV 2009. LNCS, vol. 5643, pp. 709–714. Springer, Heidelberg (2009). https://doi.org/10.1007/978-3-642-02658-4_59
7. Song, S., Sun, J., Liu, Y., Dong, J.S.: A model checker for hierarchical probabilistic real-time systems. In: Madhusudan, P., Seshia, S.A. (eds.) CAV 2012. LNCS, vol. 7358, pp. 705–711. Springer, Heidelberg (2012). https://doi.org/10.1007/978-3-642-31424-7_53
8. Wei, X., Lucey, P., Morgan, S., Carr, P., Reid, M., Sridharan, S.: Predicting serves in tennis using style priors. In: Proceedings of the 21th ACM SIGKDD International Conference on Knowledge Discovery and Data Mining, pp. 2207–2215. (2015)

Security Analysis of Smart Home Implementations

Kulani Mahadewa(✉)

National University of Singapore, Singapore, Singapore
kulani41@comp.nus.edu.sg

Abstract. A key feature of the emerging smart home is the integration of heterogeneous technologies, including multiple standards, protocols, and platforms. However, the integration may introduce critical security vulnerabilities, due to the customizations, unsatisfied assumptions and incompatibilities of the technologies. Hence, it is necessary to address the security problems in smart home systems from an integration perspective, as a complement to existing studies that focus on the analysis of individual system components or technologies. As part of an ongoing Ph.D. research project, this paper presents the author's current work which is a framework for security analysis of implementation of smart home integrations, and future work which is a standalone tool automating the framework and applying it on smart home systems for elderly healthcare and wellbeing. Applying on three real-world smart home systems, the proposed framework identifies twelve security vulnerabilities.

1 Introduction

Internet of Things (IoT) is rapidly evolving and applied extensively in smart home systems to realize a low-cost and convenient solution. With the help of heterogeneous technologies, smart home systems connect nearly all devices and appliances at home environment, and allow remote control over Local Area Network (LAN) or Internet. As reported by Deloitte, more than half (52%) of consumers own connected household devices [2]. The statistics also show that the worldwide market size of smart home has reached $27.5 billion, and will grow to $53.45 billion by 2022 [1].

Researchers have made efforts to address security issues in smart home systems. In previous work, several aspects of security in smart home systems have been studied, i.e., smart devices [3,10], protocols [8,9], platforms and application frameworks [4–6]. In the literature, the author observes that the security research only considers the security of individual components or technologies of a smart home system. However, the integration of them may introduce new security implications. Hence, there exists a gap in the literature on the security analysis of the smart home systems.

In a typical smart home system, the controls are initiated from hand-held trigger devices such as smart phones, tablets, and voice sensors, forwarded by

J. Sun and M. Sun (Eds.): ICFEM 2018, LNCS 11232, pp. 450–454, 2018.
https://doi.org/10.1007/978-3-030-02450-5_33

intermediate relays such as wireless routers, gateways, Sensor Interface Units (SIU) and hubs, and finally executed by the end devices such as bulbs, cameras, and locks. These subsystems communicate with each other over wired or wireless standards such as Bluetooth, Z-Wave, ZigBee, and Wi-Fi. Due to the involvement of such heterogeneous technologies and smart devices manufactured by diverse vendors, the integration of them in to a secure system is challenging. The challenges may be the incompatibilities, unsatisfied assumptions, or customizations of the technologies used by the smart home system.

The motivation for this research project is that, despite the challenges, it is essential to integrate multiple technologies ensuring security of a smart home system. In this paper, the author presents the results of the investigation on security of smart home systems from an integration perspective.

2 Approach

In this section, the author first presents background of a smart home system, then an overview of the methodology and finally the results of applying the methodology on real-world smart home systems.

2.1 Background

A smart home system consists of three subsystems, i.e., a control point (denoted by *CP*) which interacts with the end users and issues the controls, several smart devices (denoted by *SD*) which are operable electronic end devices, and several relays (denoted by *hub*) which bridge the communications. Covering from configuration to control, the working procedure of the smart home is divided into three stages, i.e., discovery, authentication and control. Figure 1 is an example of a smart home, which comprises of four subsystems, i.e., a *CP*, a *SD*, and a *hub* with an HTTP server (denoted by *HS*) and a ZigBee Front End (denoted by *ZFE*). The CP and the HS communicates over Wi-Fi, and the SD and the ZFE communicates over ZigBee. The arrows in the Fig. 1 shows the information exchanged between the subsystems in each stage.

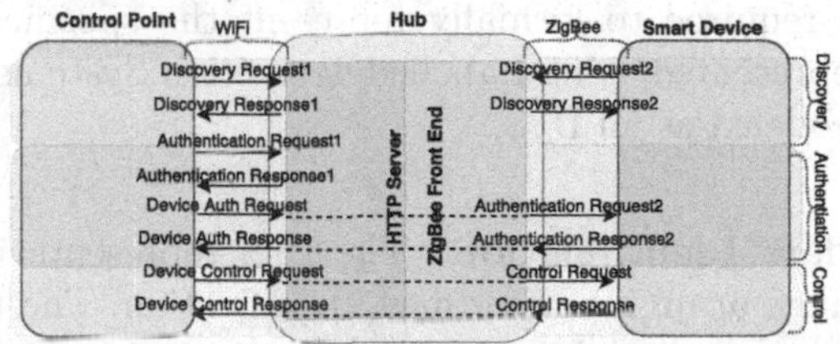

Fig. 1. An example of a smart home system containing a control point, hub and a smart device

2.2 Methodology

In order to analyze the security of a smart home from the integration perspective, it is required to extract the end-to-end application-layer specification from the input smart home. Next, the extracted specification is formally verified to identify security flaws of the system. We propose a framework which includes three steps, i.e., pre-processing, specification extraction, and flaw identification, to address the security problem.

Pre-processing. This step takes the smart home implementation as input, and runs the system to generate traffic traces of communication between the subsystems. The objective is to extract a preliminary abstraction of the information exchanged between the subsystems of the smart home. For each message exchanged between the subsystems, the extracted information includes the sender, receiver, communication channel, and message components. The message components are represented as a set of values.

Specification Extraction. The input to this step is the abstract information extracted by the pre-processing. The objective is to infer the semantics of the extracted set of values and security-relevant internal behaviors of each subsystem. However, challenges stem from the incomplete availability of the implementations. First, unavailability of the source code, while only the executables and/or libraries are provided by the vendors. Second, the communication is not apparent, due to the use of cryptographic protocols. To overcome the challenges, the framework uses a hybrid analysis including whitebox analysis and trace analysis. In particular, the whitebox analysis analyzes the available source code to identify semantics, and the trace analysis infers the semantics of a value by the association relation between that value and an already identified semantics, a participant, or a session. In order to formally verify the specification, it is required to formally represent the specification. Hence, the specification is represented using Labelled Transition Systems (LTS)s, where each subsystem is modeled as an LTS.

Flaw Identification. The LTS representation of the smart home system is taken as an input for flaw identification. The framework uses an inference algorithm to check IoT-specific security properties against predefined attack models. The framework uses two types of attack models i.e. malicious participant and network attacker. The malicious participant violates access security properties (i.e., authentication and authorization) by pretending to be a honest participant to collect sensitive information or send control commands. The network attacker violates data security (i.e., confidentiality and integrity) and association security properties by eavesdropping, intercepting, and modifying messages on the network.

2.3 Results

The effectiveness of the framework was evaluated by applying it to three real-world smart home systems i.e., Philips Hue, LIFX, and Chromecast. The framework identifies twelve security flaws from the three systems, i.e., 5 from Philips Hue, 4 from LIFX, and 3 from Chromecast. In the following, the author describes the impacts of several flaws.

First, in the Philips Hue system, misuse of ZigBee Light Link (ZLL) protocol allows a malicious *hub* to hijack a victim SD, and lack of control to administration commands result in uncontrolled CP authentication, and denial-of-service at HS and SD. Second, in the LIFX system, unprotected SD's Wi-Fi hotspot allows a malicious SD with a fake hotspot to steal the password of the victim's home Wi-Fi. Finally, in the Chromecast system, lack of device or user authentication allows a malicious CP to obtain the identity of a private YouTube video of the victim, and misresponse to discovery request allows a malicious CP to obtain the identity of the TV screen and casting a video to the TV.

3 Future Work

Currently, the framework is implemented as a semi-automatic approach and applied on smart home systems. As future work, the author plans to fully automate the framework as a standalone tool and apply the tool on smart home for elderly healthcare systems.

3.1 Automatic Tool

This tool takes the pre-processed data which was extracted from traffic traces, and additionally, available programs and attack models as input, and returns whether this system has any vulnerabilities as output.

Specification Extraction. The author plans to develop an algorithm to automatically infer the semantics of the input pre-processed data and internal behaviors of the subsystems, and generate the LTS representation of the end-to-end system.

Flaw Identification. This component takes two inputs, i.e., the LTS model of the system and the attacker's LTS model. This component uses a model checker called (PAT) [11] as the inference engine. However, the author plans to extend the PAT tool to support verification of the extracted specification, since the current LTS module of PAT tool does not allow verification of a set of LTS having internal communication.

3.2 Smart Home for Elderly Healthcare (SHEH)

Smart Home for Elderly Healthcare (SHEH) is an emerging research area. In contrast to typical smart homes, SHEH [7] allows remote monitoring of physiological signs (e.g., heart rate, body temperature, blood pressure and blood oxygen level) and activities of the occupants, and communication with remote healthcare facilities and caregivers. Hence, the SHEH is a complex smart home system with additional attributes and functionalities than a typical smart home system. The author plans to apply the proposed tool on SHEH and extend (e.g., adding new attack models) it to find new security problems.

References

1. Forecast market size of the global smart home market from 2016 to 2022. https://www.statista.com/statistics/682204/global-smart-home-market-size/
2. Deloitte: Switch on to the connected home: the Deloitte consumer review. https://www2.deloitte.com/content/dam/Deloitte/uk/Documents/consumer-business/deloitte-uk-consumer-review-16.pdf
3. Fawaz, K., Kim, K.H., Shin, K.G.: Protecting privacy of BLE device users. In: USENIX Security, pp. 1205–1221 (2016)
4. Fernandes, E., Paupore, J., Rahmati, A., Simionato, D., Conti, M., Prakash, A.: Flowfence: practical data protection for emerging IoT application frameworks. In: USENIX Security, pp. 531–548 (2016)
5. Fernandes, E., Rahmati, A., Jung, J., Prakash, A.: Security implications of permission models in smart-home application frameworks. IEEE S&P **15**, 24–30 (2017)
6. Jia, Y.J., Chen, Q.A.W.S., Rahmati, A., Fernandes, E., Mao, Z.M., Prakash, A.: ContexIoT: towards providing contextual integrity to appified IoT platforms. In: NDSS (2017)
7. Majumder, S.: Smart homes for elderly healthcare recent advances and research challenges. Sensors **7**(11), 2496 (2017)
8. Michalevsky, Y., Nath, S., Liu, J.: MASHaBLE: mobile applications of secret handshakes over bluetooth LE. In: MobiCom, pp. 387–400 (2016)
9. Ronen, E., Shamir, A., Weingarten, A.O., O'Flynn, C.: IoT goes nuclear: creating a ZigBee chain reaction. In: IEEE S&P, pp. 195–212 (2017)
10. Simpson, A.K., Roesner, F., Kohno, T.: Securing vulnerable home IoT devices with an in-hub security manager. In: IEEE PerCom Workshop, pp. 551–556 (2017)
11. Sun, J., Liu, Y., Dong, J.S., Pang, J.: PAT: towards flexible verification under fairness. In: Bouajjani, A., Maler, O. (eds.) CAV 2009. LNCS, vol. 5643, pp. 709–714. Springer, Heidelberg (2009). https://doi.org/10.1007/978-3-642-02658-4_59

Principled Greybox Fuzzing

Yuekang Li(✉)

Nanyang Technological University, Singapore, Singapore
yli044@e.ntu.edu.sg

Abstract. Greybox fuzzing has become one of the most effective approaches for detecting software vulnerabilities. Various new techniques have been continuously emerging to enhance the effectiveness and/or efficiency by incorporating novel ideas into different components of a greybox fuzzer. However, there lacks a modularized fuzzing framework that can easily plugin new techniques and hence facilitate the reuse and integration of different techniques.

To address this problem, we propose a fuzzing framework, namely Fuzzing Orchestration Toolkit (FOT). FOT is designed to be *versatile*, *configurable* and *extensible*. With FOT and its extensions, we have found 111 new bugs from 11 projects. Among these bugs, 18 CVEs were assigned.

Keywords: Fuzzing · Software testing · Software vulnerability

1 Problem Statement and Motivation

Greybox fuzzing is recognized as one of the most effective approaches to detecting vulnerabilities in a program under test (PUT). Compared with whitebox and blackbox fuzzing, greybox fuzzing strikes a balance between execution speed and effectiveness. In recent years, a number of greybox fuzzers have been proposed, e.g., *AFL* [7], libFuzzer [5], and honggfuzz [3], followed by their various extensions [4,6] to enhance their effectiveness and/or efficiency. Notably, most of the variants are based on *AFL*.

However, there lacks a modularized fuzzing framework to easily reuse, integrate and compare different fuzzing techniques and experiment with new ideas. Taking *AFL* as an example, the fuzzer is implemented all in one file with around 8K LOC, which contains around 100 global variables. Hence, the implementation of one feature often involves modifications in many places. In short, *AFL* is compact and concrete but also highly coupled because *AFL* is designed for *requiring essentially no configuration* [7]. In fact, like *AFL*, most of the existing fuzzers are designed for easy deployment and usage, but not easy extension. Therefore, it is desirable to have a fuzzing framework that can allow the easy plugin-and-play of a variety of features, easy configuration of them and easy extension for new features.

J. Sun and M. Sun (Eds.): ICFEM 2018, LNCS 11232, pp. 455–458, 2018.
https://doi.org/10.1007/978-3-030-02450-5_34

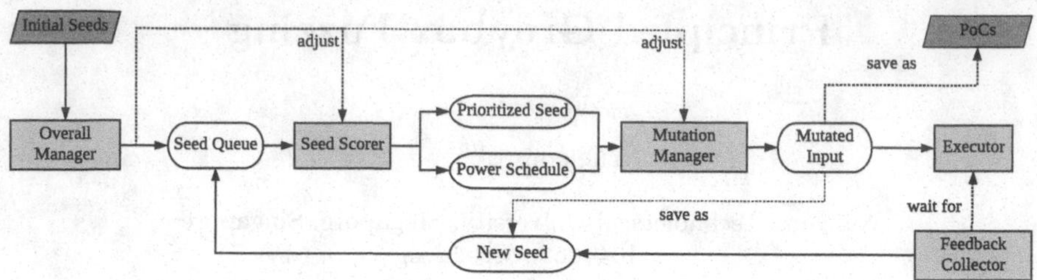

Fig. 1. Overview of the fuzzer in FOT. (Color figure online)

2 Approach

To tackle the aforementioned problems, we developed a configurable, extensible and versatile fuzzing framework, namely *Fuzzing Orchestration Toolkit (FOT)*. Figure 1 shows the overall structure of the fuzzer. The blue rectangles are the main components of the fuzzer, which are configurable and extensible.

Overall Manager. As FOT is designed to support multi-threaded parallel fuzzing, it contains an overall manager in the fuzzer. This overall manager is in charge of managing the workload of each worker thread. Specifically, it can listen to a special directory to actively import seed inputs from external sources such as symbolic executors like KLEE [1]. This part is *configurable* as the user can choose different strategies for the overall management. It is *extensible* as it can inter-operate with other seed generation tools.

Seed Scorer. The seed scorer is in charge of selecting a seed from the queue for mutation (seed prioritization) and determining how many new inputs should be generated based on the selected seed (power scheduling). This part is *configurable* as the users can select from several built-in scoring strategies to evaluate seeds. It is *extensible* as the users can implement their own strategies with the provided modules in FOT.

Mutation Manager. The mutation manager is in charge of incorporating different mutation operators. It can mutate the seeds in a pure random manner or according to some predefined grammar. This part is *configurable* as FOT provides various mutation operators for the users to choose from. This part is *extensible* as the users can implement their own mutation operators with the provided library.

Executor. The executor takes charge of executing the PUT. This part is *configurable* as the default executor in FOT allows the user to choose to enable or disable the usage of forkserver [7]. This part is *extensible* as the users can extend the executor for different scenarios. For example, they may add a secondary executor to execute a secondary PUT to perform differential testing.

Table 1. Selected trophies and the projects

Project name	0-day bugs	Time since release	GitHub stars	KLOC
mjs	21	1y7m	787	16.5
liblnk	20	8y9m	42	56.9
GNU bc	18	26y8m	–	31.4
radare2	10	9y4m	7645	857.1
Espruino	10	4y9m	1395	1392.6
libsass	10	6y5m	3813	43.8
libpff	7	3y8m	85	137.7
Oniguruma	6	5y8m	556	119.1
apcalc	4	19y	–	98.7
FLIF	3	2y9m	2989	43.6
diffutils	2	29y7m	–	147.4

Feedback Collector. The feedback collector collects the feedback emitted by the instrumented PUT. The exact feedback often corresponds to the instrumented information. This part is *configurable* as the users are allowed to select from the default feedback options provided by FOT. The default feedbacks currently include basic-block level feedback (like *AFL*) and function level feedback. It is *extensible* as the users can specify their customized types of feedbacks for collection.

3 Assessment

Till now, FOT has been used to fuzz more than 100 projects. Table 1 lists some of the 0-day vulnerabilities we found with FOT. Among them, 6 CVEs have been assigned to Oniguruma, 9 CVEs have been assigned to Espruino and 3 CVEs have been assigned to radare2.

4 Related Work

Table 2 shows a comparison of supported features between FOT and existing popular greybox fuzzers. We can clearly see that FOT supports the most features. Specifically, FOT is highly modularized, making it easy to add new features and extensions.

Table 2. Comparisons between different fuzzers (○: not supported; ◐: partially supported; ●: fully supported)

Features \ Framework	AFL	libFuzzer	honggfuzz	FOT
Binary-Fuzzing Support	●	○	●	●
Multi-threading Mode	○	●	●	●
In-memory Fuzzing	●	●	●	●
Advanced Configuration	○	◐	○	●
Modularized Functionality	○	◐	○	●
Structure-aware Mutation	○	○	○	◐
Interoperability	○	○	○	◐
Toolchain Support	●	○	○	●
Precise Crash Analysis	○	○	●	●
Runtime Visualization	◐	○	○	●

5 Future Work

In the future, we plan to embed several extensions into FOT. For example, we can integrate static analysis with fuzzing. With various vulnerability metrics (e.g., calls to unsafe functions and cyclomatic complexity), we can calculate a vulnerability score for each function. Then we can modify the seed scorer in Fig. 1 so that it can utilize the static analysis results for seed evaluation and eventually guide the fuzzer towards more vulnerable code. Another possible extension is directed fuzzing like Hawkeye [2]. Directed fuzzer will try to execute towards user defined targets. An ideal directed fuzzer requires modifications in the seed scorer as well as mutation manager shown in Fig. 1.

To summarize, we present a configurable, extensible and versatile fuzzing framework named FOT. With FOT as the basic framework, we can design various extensions and embed novel techniques. Finally, with FOT and all its extensions, we can uncover numerous real-world vulnerabilities.

References

1. Cadar, C., Dunbar, D., Engler, D.: Klee: unassisted and automatic generation of high-coverage tests for complex systems programs. In: OSDI 2008, pp. 209–224 (2008)
2. Chen, H., et al.: Hawkeye: towards a desired directed grey-box fuzzer. In: CCS (2018)
3. Google: honggfuzz (2018). https://github.com/google/honggfuzz
4. Li, Y., Chen, B., Chandramohan, M., Lin, S.W., Liu, Y., Tiu, A.: Steelix: program-state based binary fuzzing. In: ESEC/FSE 2017, pp. 627–637. ACM (2017)
5. LLVM: libfuzzer (2018). https://llvm.org/docs/LibFuzzer.html
6. Wang, J., Chen, B., Wei, L., Liu, Y.: Skyfire: data-driven seed generation for fuzzing, pp. 579–594, May 2017. https://doi.org/10.1109/SP.2017.23
7. Zalewski, M.: American fuzzy lop (2014). http://lcamtuf.coredump.cx/afl/. Accessed 01 Apr 2018

Engineering Software for Modular Formalisation and Verification of STV Algorithms

Milad K. Ghale(✉)

Research School of Computer Science, ANU, Canberra, Australia
milad.ketabghale@anu.edu.au

Abstract. We introduce new software for provably correct computation with Single Transferable Voting (STV) algorithms. The software is engineered as a framework for modular formalisation, verification, extraction of executable certifying programmes, and verified certificate checking for various STV algorithms. We demonstrate functionality and effectiveness of our approach by evaluating the software on some real-size elections.

1 Introduction

STV is a family of vote counting algorithms, where voters express their preferences by ranking candidates, widely used in various elections in several countries such as Ireland, New Zealand, and Australia.

There are many subtleties hidden in details of particular STV schemes. Due to such complexities, mistakes have happened in both hand counting methods and computerised counting [2], where the election was re-run or a wrong candidate was declared a winner. Moreover, these programmes merely output winners of the election without providing any detail as through what computational steps the end result is obtained. Also, the source code of the programmes are kept secret with excuses of commercial and intellectual property protection, so that outsiders cannot analyse or test them. Consequently, voters have no choice but to lay huge trust in authorities that tallying is processed correctly.

The above mistakes adversely effect trust in authorities and elections which are cornerstones of democratic processes. Methods currently employed for vote counting stand in sharp contrast with universal verifiability [13], which requires an election result to be verifiable by any member of the public.

Our approach frames electronic vote counting as certified computation [5–7]. Here each execution of the counting algorithms on a given input, produces an output and a trace of computation, called *certificate*, preformed by the execution to obtain the output. Such a certificate consists of all of the necessary information to understand how the counting has progressed from the input value to terminate at the corresponding output. Any voter can independently check a certificate for correctness to ascertain that the execution computes the final result correctly. Certificates, along with a component of our software explained shortly afterwards, contribute to satisfaction of the universal verifiability property.

J. Sun and M. Sun (Eds.): ICFEM 2018, LNCS 11232, pp. 459–463, 2018.
https://doi.org/10.1007/978-3-030-02450-5_35

We use formal engineering tools and techniques of certifying algorithms for producing verified software that provably correctly computes winners of elections, outputs a certificate for independent verification by scrutineers and offers a verified certificate checker to provide the voter with means of verifying correctness of tallying. Our software[1] is a framework where variety of STV algorithms can be formally specified and then verified with respect to some desired properties in the theorem prover Coq [3]. It facilitates extraction of provably correct Haskell programmes for actual computations. Each of these programmes outputs a run-time certificate for each execution. The software also has a second standalone component, formalised in HOL [9] and synthesised by CakeML [1], for checking certificates independent of means used in producing them.

2 Extraction of Verified Programmes for STV Algorithms

Variants of STV share a large set of data structure. For example, the counting progresses in a finite sequence of discrete states. These states encapsulate all essential information needed to know in order to realise how the counting has proceeded up to that stage of the computation. We abstract this underlying common data to specify a data type in Coq whose values formally represent states of the computation.

Additionally, STV schemes have a common mechanism to advance the counting by using transitions whose names are invariably called *count*, *elect*, *transfer*, *eliminate*, and a step for finishing the counting by *declaring the winners*. We formalise the transitions as parameters to be instantiated later. Furthermore, there are repeated patterns of when those transitions may apply and in what order. We distil the recurring algorithmic patterns into a minimal set of rules for specifying when a transition is legitimately applicable.

The abstracted data type and parametric transitions respectively form the states and transition labels for a generic formalisation of STV as an abstract machine. The minimal applicability criteria above operate as a small-step semantics for the machine. We demonstrate that the generic machine satisfies some properties such as termination. Moreover, we prove that for any input to the machine, a sequence of machine states and transitions taken to terminate exists. This trace, which is the *certificate*, is output upon each execution of extracted Haskell programmes on an input.

We formalise the generic STV in a parent module, developed once and for all, consisting of about 2500 lines of code. Concrete cases of STV are formalised in separate modules (each about 500 lines) by instantiation of the parametric transitions and discharging applicability criteria above. These modules have zero level of coupling among themselves and only depend on the parent.

3 Synthesis of Verified Checkers for Various STV

There can be several implementations for an algorithm. To check which ones are correct realisations of the algorithm, it is sufficient and efficient to require those

[1] Source codes are at https://github.com/MiladKetabGhale.

programmes to output a certificate. Then examine their correctness by synthesising a verified certificate checker, instead of verifying each single programme.

We use the theorem prover HOL to formalise the STV vote counting scheme, and obtain a fully verified certificate checker inside HOL. By the trustworthy mechanisms of connecting HOL with the verified compiler CakeML, we then extract an executable checker that is guaranteed to behave correctly with respect to the formal specification of the STV down to machine code.

Synthesis of executable checker happens in four steps. We first formally specify in HOL what a certificate and certificate checker are. Second, we define boolean-valued functions in HOL that are expected to be the computational counterpart of the declarative assertions in the previous step. Third, we prove inside HOL that indeed the specification and boolean-value functions match. Fourth and last, by using the verified CakeML translator, we translate the HOL computational definitions of step two into equivalent CakeML functions. Therefore we lift all of the proofs established in HOL to CakeML level. Then by using the verified proof-synthesis mechanism of CakeML, we obtain an executable checker that is guaranteed to behave as the specification of the first step expects.

Evaluations. We have already formalised some STV algorithms used in senate, parliamentary, and union elections in Australia. Formalised modules are automatically extractable into the Haskell language for provably correct computations. Figure 1 illustrates evaluation of the extracted module for the STV employed in the ACT state of Australia for the lower house elections. The certification column demonstrates the amount of time taken for the Haskell programme to terminate with a certificate output. On the other hand, the checking column depicts how much time the checker consumes to verify the certificates.

4 Future and Related Work

Future Work. There are some possibilities for further engineering and research on STV which interest us. We need to perform code refactoring to modularise the certificate checker. We would create a base of the formalisation containing common features of checkers for different STV and encode distinctive aspects of each scheme into separate modules.

Our framework accommodates a large class of various STV algorithms. However, one may wish to extend it further to include radically divergent instances such as Meek STV. Also current development does not support versions of STV which use randomness in determining which set of surplus ballots to transfer.

electoral	ballots	seats	candidates	certificate size(mb)	certification time	checking time
Brindabella	63562	5	20	94.3	205	75
Ginninderra	66076	5	28	126.1	289	191
Molonglo	91534	7	27	126.1	664	286

Fig. 1. ACT legislative assembly 2012 (time in seconds)

Another dimension is analysis of STV algorithms for computing margin of victory to determine what is the smallest set of votes that if changed results in divergence of election winners. Moreover, one can study STV algorithms from the social choice theory perspective to mathematically measure how fair they are compared to each other and different multi-seated voting schemes.

Related Work. Employing heavy weight formal methods for vote counting is fairly recent and there is much work to come. DeYoung and Schurmann [4] use Linear Logic [8] to formally specify a STV scheme and then discharge proofs inside the logical framework of Celf. Technical knowledge of linear logic is required to understand how the textual description of the protocol matches with the formal one. Pattinson and Shurmann [10], and Verity and Pattinson [12] formalise a simple version of STV and First-past-The-Post elections in Coq. They prove properties such as existence of winners in every formal execution. Then they extract certifying executable in Haskell which can compute large size elections. Pattinson and Tiwari [11] tackle verification of Schultz method by the similar approach of specifying the algorithm in Coq, discharging proofs and extracting executables in Haskell and OCaml. Their extracted executable performs effectively and outputs run-time certificates. They implement a certificate checker in the Haskell language. However as the implementation is unverified, it does not add to reliability of the computation.

References

1. CakeML: A Verified Implementation of ML. https://cakeml.org/
2. Conway, A., Blom, M., Naish, L., Teague, V.: An analysis of New South Wales electronic vote counting. In: Proceeding of ACSW 2017, pp. 24:1–24:5 (2017)
3. The Coq Theorem Prover. https://coq.inria.fr/
4. DeYoung, H., Schürmann, C.: Linear logical voting protocols. In: Kiayias, A., Lipmaa, H. (eds.) Vote-ID 2011. LNCS, vol. 7187, pp. 53–70. Springer, Heidelberg (2012). https://doi.org/10.1007/978-3-642-32747-6_4
5. Ghale, M.K., Goré, R., Pattinson, D.: A formally verified single transferable voting scheme with fractional values. In: Krimmer, R., Volkamer, M., Braun Binder, N., Kersting, N., Pereira, O., Schürmann, C. (eds.) E-Vote-ID 2017. LNCS, vol. 10615, pp. 163–182. Springer, Cham (2017). https://doi.org/10.1007/978-3-319-68687-5_10
6. Ghale, M.K., Gore, R., Pattinson, D., Tiwari, M.: Modular formalisation and verification of STV algorithms. In: Forthcoming E-Vote-ID 2018. LNCS. Springer, Heidelberg (2018)
7. Ghale, M.K., Pattinson, D., Kummar, R., Norrish, M.: Verified certificate checking for counting votes. In: Forthcoming VSTTE 2018. LNCS. Springer, Heidelberg (2018)
8. Girard, J.Y.: Linear logic. Theor. Comput. Sci. **50**, 1–102 (1987)
9. HOL Interactive Theorem Prover. https://hol-theorem-prover.org/
10. Pattinson, D., Schürmann, C.: Vote counting as mathematical proof. In: Australasian Conference on Artificial Intelligence, pp. 464–475 (2015)
11. Pattinson, D., Tiwari, M.: Schulze voting as evidence carrying computation. In.: Proceedings of ITP, pp. 410–426 (2017)

12. Verity, F., Pattinson, D.: Formally verified invariants of vote counting schemes. In: ACSW, pp. 31:1–31:10 (2017)
13. Cortier, V., Galindo, D., Küsters, R., Müller, J., Truderung, T.: Verifiability notions for E-Voting protocols. IACR Cryptology ePrint Archive 2016: 287 (2016)

Towards Building a Generic Vulnerability Detection Platform by Combining Scalable Attacking Surface Analysis and Directed Fuzzing

Xiaoning Du(✉)

Nanyang Technological University, Singapore, Singapore
duxi0002@ntu.edu.sg

1 Introduction

Vulnerabilities are one of the major threats to software security. Usually, they are hunted by security experts via manual code audits, or with some automated tools like fuzzers (e.g., [1,5,12]) and symbolic execution (e.g., [4,7,10,13]), which can provide concrete inputs to trigger and validate the vulnerabilities. As fuzzy static scanners usually flag a list of potential vulnerable codes or functions with high rate of false positive, we deem them in the spectrum of attack surface identification approaches. The scalability of symbolic execution is extremely restricted by the path exploration problem and solver capability, which makes it not a preferable choice for large scale vulnerability detection. Coverage-based undirected fuzzing is hardly scalable and effective in general due to the large size of the program and the lack of good seeds to trigger various behaviors or executions. Faced with the fact that all existing static and dynamic detection tools are concerned with the trade-off problem between scalability and precision, a generic and scalable vulnerability detection platform is desirable.

As only a few vulnerabilities are scattered across a large amount of code, vulnerability hunting is a challenging task that requires intensive knowledge and skills and is comparable to finding "a needle in a haystack" [17]. Identifying potentially vulnerable locations in a code base is critical as a pre-step for effective vulnerability assessment. Metric-based techniques, inspired by bug prediction [11], leverage machine learning to predict vulnerable code at the granularity level of a source file. It cannot work well due to the severe imbalance between non-vulnerable and vulnerable code as well as the lack of features to reflect characteristics of vulnerabilities. Pattern-based use patterns of known vulnerabilities to identify potentially vulnerable code through static analysis. The patterns are formulated by security experts using their domain knowledge, e.g., missing security checks on security-critical objects [16], security properties [14], and vulnerability specifications [15]. Due to the requirement on prior knowledge of known vulnerabilities, it can only identify similar but not new types of vulnerabilities.

Among the automated assessment tools, directed fuzzing [5,8] stands out for its ability to reach a target program location efficiently and fuzz it effectively.

J. Sun and M. Sun (Eds.): ICFEM 2018, LNCS 11232, pp. 464–468, 2018.
https://doi.org/10.1007/978-3-030-02450-5_36

Experimentally fed with a limited portion of heuristically selected attack surface, AFLGo [5] is reported to outperform directed symbolic-execution-based whitebox fuzzing and undirected fuzzing. We believe its vulnerability-hunting power can be further boosted with wisely identified attack surface. Currently, the guiding in AFLGo is achieved just via power scheduling, which can be obtuse and insensitive. Much improvement can be done to make the guiding strategy more swift and intelligent.

In this study, we aim at combining attack surface identification and directed fuzzing for building a generic and scalable vulnerability detection platform.

2 Our Approach

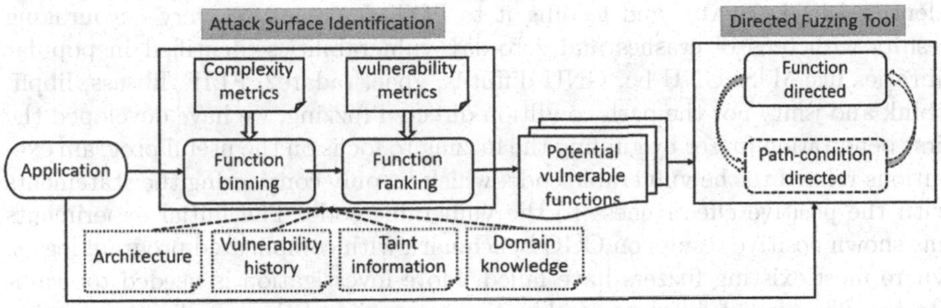

Fig. 1. An overview of the proposed framework

An overview of our proposed framework is shown in Fig. 1. Given an application's source code, the attack surface identification component is used to generate a list of potential vulnerable functions based on the complexity and vulnerability metrics of the application. These functions can be directly fed to the directed fuzzing tool as targets to confirm the vulnerability with concrete triggering input. Within the fuzzing tool, we use the function-directed fuzzing to reach the target function, and combine with path-directed method to penetrate the target function to trigger the vulnerability. Note that finished components of the framework are drawn with solid lines and explained below, and unfinished ones are drawn with dashed lines as explained in next section.

We have proposed and implemented a *generic*, *lightweight* and *extensible* framework, named LEOPARD, to identify attack surfaces at the function level through program metrics. LEOPARD does not require any prior knowledge about known vulnerabilities. It works in two steps by combining two sets of systematically derived metrics. Complexity metrics capture the complexity of a function in two dimensions: the control structures in the function, and the loop structures in the function. Vulnerability metrics reflect the characteristics of vulnerabilities in three dimensions: the constants, pointers, and coupling level of predicates in a function. Details about the metrics and some supplementary experimental results are available at our website [2]. First, it uses complexity metrics to group the functions in a target application into a set of bins. Then, it leverages vulnerability metrics to rank the functions in each bin and identifies the top ones as potentially vulnerable. Experimental results on nine real-life projects have demonstrated that LEOPARD can cover 74% of vulnerable functions by identifying 25% of functions as vulnerable; and LEOPARD can outperform machine learning-based techniques. Based on the identified vulnerable functions in the current stable release of PHP, a security expert discovered six zero-day vulnerabilities.

For the directed fuzzing, we have integrated the attack surface identification framework with some off-the-shell directed fuzzing tools. We choose FOT [3], which is a versatile, configurable and extensible fuzzing framework. It provides a basic function-level directed fuzzing interface, requiring only a list of target functions. The initial evaluation of the combined approach of using attack surface identified by LEOPARD and feeding it to FOT demonstrates very encouraging results with tens of crashes and zero-day vulnerabilities identified in popular libraries like MJS, GNU bc, GNU diffutils, gpac, radare2, FLIF, libsass, libpff, liblnk and jsmn. For the path-condition directed fuzzing, we have developed the first penetration fuzzer by guiding the fuzzing to focus on the useful program executions related to the vulnerable code, which by only considering the statements with the positive effectiveness to the vulnerable code. The initial experiments has shown positive results on CGC benchmark with complicated program logics, where most existing fuzzers have failed. More investigation is needed to evaluate the efficiency of different combination strategies of the two directed fuzzing techniques, which have been further discussed in next section.

3 Future Work and Conclusion

3.1 Metrics Extension

The set of complexity and vulnerability metrics can be refined and extended, by adjusting scores of existing metrics or incorporating new metrics, to highlight interesting functions via capturing different perspectives. To this end, we have identified the following information to be vital to further improve our findings.

Taint Information. Leveraging taint information will help an analyst to identify the functions that process the external (i.e., taint) input.

Vulnerability History. In general, recently patched functions are straightforward attack surface due to the verified reachability, with considerable risks of incomplete patch or introducing new issues, but functions that are patched long before the release of the current version tend to involve no vulnerabilities.

Domain Knowledge. Domain knowledge can play a vital role in prioritizing the interesting functions for further assessment. Information such as the modules that are currently fuzzed by others can be used to refine the ranking. It is also interesting to explore what information can be mined from mailing list, twitters and security blogs.

Architecture. Strong correlations between bug/vulnerability-prone files and architecture design flaws [6,9] can also be considered in to light up attack surface identification with some high level information.

3.2 Directed Fuzzing

To enhance the directed fuzzing for the effective usage of the potential vulnerable functions, we are looking at two directions. Firstly, we want to investigate how to combine the two directed fuzzing techniques into one holistic approach. Function-level directed fuzzing is good at reaching target vulnerable functions, however to trigger the vulnerability in the vulnerable function requires further penetration. Therefore we can conduct the directed fuzzing in two steps by invoking the two directed techniques sequentially. However, function-level directed fuzzing may stuck in some code to reach the target function due to the lack of low-level penetration in local path conditions. To address this, we need to invoke the path-condition directed fuzzing together with the function-level directed fuzzing. These phenomenons require a better interplay between the two techniques and dynamic scheduling of them based on the progress. We are planning to propose a runtime scheduler to orchestrate the two techniques dynamically.

Secondly, the metrics used to generated during the attack surface identification step is statically calculated, which may not be precise. Hence the ranking of vulnerable functions is less ideal. To address this, we can combine the fuzzer deeper with the metrics calculation and vulnerable function ranking so that we use the runtime information generated by fuzzer and adjust ranking of the vulnerable function dynamically. For example, this approach can directly remove the easily reachable functions with high vulnerability metrics hence improving the effectiveness of the approach.

3.3 Conclusion

This paper presented a generic framework for effectively finding vulnerabilities in source code level. The key idea is to combine the scalable static analysis and directed fuzzing to balance the trade off between scalability and accuracy.

References

1. American fuzzy lop. http://lcamtuf.coredump.cx/afl/ (2017)
2. Leopard. https://sites.google.com/site/leopardsite2017/ (2017)
3. FOT. https://sites.google.com/view/fot-the-fuzzer (2018)
4. Babić, D., Martignoni, L., McCamant, S., Song, D.: Statically-directed dynamic automated test generation. In: ISSTA, pp. 12–22 (2011)
5. Böhme, M., Pham, V.T., Nguyen, M.D., Roychoudhury, A.: Directed greybox fuzzing. In: CCS, pp. 2329–2344 (2017)

6. Cai, Y., Xiao, L., Kazman, R., Mo, R., Feng, Q.: Design rule spaces: a new model for representing and analyzing software architecture. TSE (2018)
7. Cha, S.K., Woo, M., Brumley, D.: Program-adaptive mutational fuzzing. In: SP, pp. 725–741 (2015)
8. Chen, H., et al.: Hawkeye: towards a desired directed grey-box fuzzer. In: CCS (2018)
9. Feng, Q., Kazman, R., Cai, Y., Mo, R., Xiao, L.: Towards an architecture-centric approach to security analysis. In: WICSA, pp. 221–230 (2016)
10. Godefroid, P., Levin, M.Y., Molnar, D.A.: Automated whitebox fuzz testing. In: NDSS (2008)
11. Malhotra, R.: A systematic review of machine learning techniques for software fault prediction. Appl. Soft Comput. **27**(C), 504–518 (2015)
12. Rawat, S., Jain, V., Kumar, A., Cojocar, L., Giuffrida, C., Bos, H.: Vuzzer: application-aware evolutionary fuzzing. In: NDSS (2017)
13. Stephens, N., et al.: Driller: augmenting fuzzing through selective symbolic execution. In: NDSS (2016)
14. Vanegue, J., Lahiri, S.K.: Towards practical reactive security audit using extended static checkers. In: SP, pp. 33–47 (2013)
15. Yamaguchi, F., Golde, N., Arp, D., Rieck, K.: Modeling and discovering vulnerabilities with code property graphs. In: SP, pp. 590–604 (2014)
16. Yamaguchi, F., Wressnegger, C., Gascon, H., Rieck, K.: Chucky: exposing missing checks in source code for vulnerability discovery. In: CCS, pp. 499–510 (2013)
17. Zimmermann, T., Nagappan, N., Williams, L.: Searching for a needle in a haystack: predicting security vulnerabilities for windows vista. In: ICST, pp. 421–428 (2010)

Formalising Performance Guarantees in Meta-Reinforcement Learning

Amanda Mahony(✉)

Institute for Integrated Intelligent Systems, Griffith University, Brisbane, Australia
amanda.mahony3@griffithuni.edu.au

Abstract. Reinforcement learning has had great empirical success in different domains, which has left theoretical foundations, such as performance guarantees, lagging behind. The usual asymptotic convergence to an optimal policy is not strong enough for applications in the real world. Meta learning algorithms aim to use experience from multiple tasks to increase performance on all tasks individually and decrease time taken to reach an acceptable policy. This paper proposes to study the provable properties of meta-reinforcement learning.

1 Introduction

Some of the most popular recent successes in machine learning have come from reinforcement learning, including human level results in playing Go [7] and Atari games [6]. Reinforcement learning considers an agent that learns primarily through direct interaction with the environment [8]. In this setting, an agent must learn to perform a task without explicit guidance from a user or expert on the correct action to take at any given time or state. They simply receive a reward signal indicating how well they performed. Recent successes in complex domains make use of deep neural networks. While one-hidden-layer nets are universal approximators, performance guarantees in terms of convergence rate are not well formalised.

The focus of maximising the final performance leads to ignoring other important factors. Practices such as low number of empirical tests due to time considerations or cherry picking the top few runs that performed well do not adequately display the general performance of deep reinforcement learning algorithms, or the hidden difficulties in reproducing an algorithm's reported performance. For some applications, time spent learning, variability in performance, and safety are just as important as maximising final performance.

For Reinforcement Learning to be accepted and used in critical applications, such as health care, it's performance must be consistent and predictable. Bounds on regret can help users measure the cost of learning a policy by reinforcement learning. Explicitly including safety considerations in the reward signal is a common method of inducing safety in an agent. This project aims to formalise the performance of meta-learning. This can provide insights to guide design of future algorithms, as well as provide criteria to aid in the choice of algorithm for certain problems.

J. Sun and M. Sun (Eds.): ICFEM 2018, LNCS 11232, pp. 469–472, 2018.
https://doi.org/10.1007/978-3-030-02450-5_37

2 Background

2.1 Reinforcement Learning

The environment of a learning agent is modelled by a Markov Decision Process. In an episodic setting, the agent interacts with the environment for a fixed horizon of H steps, which is repeated over T episodes. The agents' actions are guided by a policy π that determines the action choice in each state. The current policy is evaluated, $J(\pi)$, commonly using the expected total or average return. The agent uses the history of explored trajectories and J to improve their policy.

Temporal difference is a simple method of policy improvement that makes a prediction about the average return of a state then continually bootstrap updates this prediction based on how unexpected the experienced reward is. Q-learning is such a method that updates state-action pair value predictions, commonly referred to as Q-values, to find an optimal policy. For each state-action pair, the Q-value details the expected future reward when taking an action in a given state. This induces a policy by choosing an action greedily at every state.

Tabular Q-learning (i.e. a finite table of updated Q-values) works well for simple problems with small state and action spaces. The majority of interesting problems have state and action spaces large enough that tabular methods are infeasible. Function approximation is used in these cases. Deep reinforcement learning uses deep neural networks as universal function approximators. The success of deep neural networks is poorly understood and occurs despite the lack of theoretical foundations and guarantees on their performance. The performance of various learning algorithms can vary greatly across different architectures and environments, with high levels of parameter tuning being the greatest cause of performance gains.

2.2 Meta-Learning

Meta-learning uses data to learn a better method for learning a policy. A useful meta-task is learning over a distribution of tasks. For tasks which are conceptually similar to a human observer, such as walking and running, it is reasonable that experience with one task may help with other tasks. There are a few approaches to learning in a setting of a distribution of task MDPs. Transfer learning, Multi-task, learning to learn and life-long learning all attempt to solve learning over multiple tasks.

Temporal difference methods in reinforcement learning behave similarly to the role of dopamine for learning in the brain. A form of meta-learning takes inspiration from learning in the pre-frontal cortex [9], modelled using recurrent neural networks such as long short-term memory. Meta-reinforcement learning has also lead to methods for dealing with acting in a dynamic system that changes over time in a dependent manner [1]. In N-shot learning, experience from a distribution of tasks is used to increase performance in unseen tasks after a small number of episodes worth of learning [4].

2.3 Performance Guarantees

The common frameworks for performance measures on reinforcement learning algorithms are comparisons of performance to an optimal policy. First is Probably Approximately Correct (PAC) learning. Given small (ϵ, δ), an algorithm is PAC if it gives a policy with expected returns ϵ-close to the optimal return, with probability $1 - \delta$, with a polynomial bound on the sample complexity. Second is the total regret over the whole learning process. The regret of a learning algorithm is the loss in returns compared with having acting according to the optimal policy from the start.

These two settings are not directly comparable without weakening their bounds and each has limitations. PAC learning algorithms often stop improvements once ϵ-close to optimal policy, while regret bounds provide no knowledge about the distribution of errors. There can be many small errors or a few large errors, which may require different responses in applications such as healthcare.

The setting of performance guarantees for life-long learning has been studied under the framework of transfer learning for multiple tasks [3]. Meta-learning is usually used in environments with large state and action spaces, typically using function approximation methods. Currently function approximation methods only have PAC analysis for MDPs and function classes of low Bellman Rank [5].

3 Approach

To study the performance of meta-reinforcement learning, we first examine a set of tasks over finite state and action spaces, with tabular Q-learning as the within task algorithm and the meta-agent learning how to initialise the Q-values for the within task learning.

Optimistic exploration of the space is induced by optimistic initialisations of the Q-values. For goals in a common space, this shared structure could provide knowledge to leverage a better Q-value initialisation for all goals. The meta-agent learning such an initialisation can be viewed as an extension of infinite armed bandits [2] to a multidimensional action space.

The meta-agent initialises the Q-values and the learner performs N episodes of Q-learning receiving an average reward $\frac{1}{N}\sum_n^N \sum_h^H r_{n,h}$. This is the reward received by the meta-learner for their choice of initialisation. These actions are explored until confidence bounds on the reward have tightened sufficiently. This will result in a sample complexity bound dependant on the within task algorithm. The sample complexity of the meta-agent is in terms of number of tasks sampled. As each episode for the meta-agent on a task is of fixed N episodes, this gives a bound on the total number of within task actions required to learn a good initialisation. This will then be compared with the total sample complexity of learning all tasks individually.

In N-shot learning, the agent continuously learns in a single environment for at most N episodes. The meta-agent uses this experience to create a new agent that will have better performance on future unseen tasks. We begin by considering task distributions of different reward in a fixed environment. For example a set of navigation tasks in a finite grid world with fixed obstacles, requiring navigating to different end states. Other distributions of tasks that are of interest are tasks with different transition probabilities, for example navigation under different conditions like winds of varying strengths or differing obstacles, or sequences of tasks that represent an environment changing over time.

This only studies Q-learning for episodic finite MDP tasks. Further work includes higher dimensional, continuous MDPs, as well as function approximation reinforcement learning. This meta architecture and sample complexity bound will be formalised in the theorem prover Isabelle, as well as previous results for performance guarantees in the single task settings.

References

1. Al-Shedivat, M., Bansal, T., Burda, Y., Sutskever, I., Mordatch, I., Abbeel, P.: Continuous adaptation via meta-learning in nonstationary and competitive environments, pp. 1–21, March 2017
2. Aziz, M., Anderton, J., Kaufmann, E., Aslam, J.: Pure exploration in infinitely-armed bandit models with fixed-confidence, pp. 1–22 (2018)
3. Brunskill, E.: PAC continuous state online multitask reinforcement learning with identification. In: AAMAS 2016, pp. 438–446 (2016)
4. Finn, C., Abbeel, P., Levine, S.: Model-agnostic meta-learning for fast adaptation of deep networks (2017)
5. Jiang, N., Krishnamurthy, A., Agarwal, A., Langford, J., Schapire, R.E.: Contextual decision processes with low Bellman rank are PAC-learnable, pp. 1–42 (2016)
6. Mnih, V., et al.: Human-level control through deep reinforcement learning. Nature **518**, 529 (2015)
7. Silver, D., et al.: Mastering the game of Go with deep neural networks and tree search. Nature **529**, 484 (2016)
8. Sutton, R.S., Barto, A.G.: Reinforcement learning: an introduction. UCL, Computer Science Department, Reinforcement Learning Lectures, p. 1054 (2017)
9. Wang, J.X., et al.: Prefrontal cortex as a meta-reinforcement learning system. Nat. Neurosci. **21**(6), 860–868 (2018)

Author Index

Printed in the United States
By Bookmasters